Data Structures Using C++

Data Structures Using C++

D. S. Malik

THOMSON
™
COURSE TECHNOLOGY

Australia • Canada • Mexico • Singapore • Spain • United Kingdom • United States

THOMSON

COURSE TECHNOLOGY

Data Structures Using C++

by D. S. Malik

Senior Editor:
Jennifer Muroff

Managing Editor:
Jennifer Locke

Development Editor:
Susan Gilbert, Edex

Associate Product Manager:
Janet Aras

Editorial Assistant:
Christy Urban

Production Editor:
Aimee Poirier

Associate Product Marketing Manager:
Angie Laughlin

Cover Designer:
Steve Deschene

Compositor:
Gex Publishing Services

Manufacturing Coordinator:
Laura Burns

TO

My Parents

BRIEF
Contents

TABLE OF
Contents

4. Standard Template Library (STL)   217

5. Linked Lists   273

APPENDIX I Answers to Selected Exercises   **905**

Preface

Welcome to *Data Structures Using C++*. Designed for a second Computer Science (CS2) C++ course, this text will provide a breath of fresh air to you and your students. A CS2 course typically completes the programming requirements of the Computer Science curriculum. This text is a culmination and development of my classroom notes throughout more than fifty semesters of successfully teaching programming and data structures to computer science students.

This book is a continuation of the work started in the CS1 book, *C++ Programming: From Problem Analysis to Program Design*, published by Course Technology. The approach taken in this book, similar to the one used in the CS1 book, is to present material that was driven by the students' demand for clarity and readability. The material was written and rewritten until students felt comfortable with it. Most of the examples in this book resulted from student interaction in the classroom.

This book assumes that the reader is familiar with the basic elements of C++ such as data types, control structures, functions and parameters, and arrays. However, if you need to review these concepts, or have taken Java as a first programming language, you will find the relevant material in Appendix G quite helpful. If you need to review CS1 topics in more detail than given in Appendix G, refer to the C++ programming book by the author mentioned in the preceding paragraph, as well as the resources listed in Appendix H. In addition, some adequate mathematics background such as college algebra is required.

APPROACH

Intended as a second course in computer programming, this book focuses on data structures as well as object-oriented design (OOD). The programming examples given in this book effectively use OOD techniques to solve and program a particular problem.

Chapter 1 introduces the software engineering principles. After describing the software life cycle, this chapter discusses why algorithm analysis is important and introduces the Big-O notation used in algorithm analysis. OOD has three basic principles—encapsulation, inheritance, and polymorphism. Encapsulation in C++ is achieved via the use of classes. The second half of Chapter 1 discusses user-defined classes. If you are familiar with how to create and use your own classes, you can skip this section. This chapter also discusses a basic OOD technique to solve a particular problem.

Chapter 2 continues with the principles of OOD, and discusses inheritance as well as two types of polymorphism. (The third type of polymorphism is discussed in Appendix F). If the reader is familiar with how inheritance, operator overloading, and templates work in C++, then the user can skip this chapter.

C++ has three basic data types: simple, structured, and pointers. This book assumes that the reader is familiar with the simple data types, as well as arrays (a structured data type.) The structured data type classes are introduced in Chapter 1; Chapter 3 discusses how the pointer data type works in C++. Chapter 3 also describes the relationship between pointers and classes. Using pointers and templates, this chapter explains and develops a generic code to implement lists using dynamic arrays.

C++ is equipped with the Standard Template Library (STL). Among other things, the STL provides code to process lists (contiguous or linked), stacks, and queues. Chapter 4 discusses some of the STL's important features, and shows how to use certain STL tools in a program. In particular, this chapter discusses the sequence containers `vector` and `deque`. The ensuing chapters explain how to develop your own code to implement and manipulate data, as well as how to use professionally written code.

Chapter 5 discusses linked lists. This chapter first explains the basic properties of linked lists such as item insertion and deletion, and how to construct a linked list. This chapter then develops a generic code to process data in a single linked list. Chapter 5 also discusses doubly linked lists, linked lists with header and trailer nodes, and circular linked lists. Moreover, this chapter discusses the STL class `list`.

Chapter 6 introduces recursion and gives various examples to show how to use recursion to solve a problem, as well as to think in terms of recursion.

Chapters 7 and 8 discuss stacks and queues. In addition to showing how to develop your own generic codes to implement stacks and queues, these chapters explain how the STL classes `stack` and `queue` work. The programming code developed in these chapters is generic.

Chapter 9 describes the searching algorithms. After analyzing the sequential search algorithm, it discusses the binary search algorithm and provides a brief analysis of this algorithm. After giving the lower bound on comparison-based search algorithms, this chapter discusses hashing.

Sorting algorithms such as the selection sort, insertion sort, quick sort, merge sort, and heap sort are introduced in Chapter 10. Chapter 11 discusses binary trees. Chapter 12 introduces graphs and discusses graph algorithms such as the shortest path, minimal spanning tree, and topological sorting.

Chapter 13 continues the discussion of the STL started in Chapter 4. In particular, it introduces the STL associative containers and algorithms.

Appendix A lists the reserved words in C++. Appendix B shows the precedence and associativity of the C++ operators. Appendix C lists the ASCII (American Standard Code for Information Interchange) and EBCDIC (Extended Binary Code Decimal Interchange) character sets. Appendix D lists the C++ operators that can be overloaded. Appendix E describes some of the most widely used library routines. Appendix F discusses additional C++ topics—virtual functions, and the address of operator and classes. Appendix G reviews the basic elements of C++ and compares the basic concepts of the languages C++ and Java, such as data types, control structures, functions and parameters, and arrays. Therefore, if you have taken Java as a first programming language, Appendix G helps familiarize you with these basic elements of C++. Appendix H provides a list of references for further study and how to find additional C++ topics not reviewed in Appendix G. Appendix I gives the answers to selected exercises in the text.

How to Use This Book

The main objective of this book is to teach data structure topics using C++ and OOD to solve a particular problem. To do so, the book discusses data structures such as linked lists, stacks, queues, and binary trees. C++'s STL also provides the necessary code to implement these data structures. However, our emphasis is to teach you how to develop your own code. At the same time, we also want you to learn how to use professionally written code.

Chapter 4 introduces the STL. In the subsequent chapters, after explaining how to develop your own code, we also illustrate how to use the existing STL code. This book can therefore be used in various ways. If you are not interested in the STL, say in the first reading, then you can skip Chapter 4 and in the subsequent chapters, sections where we discuss a particular STL component.

Chapter 6 discusses recursion. However, Chapter 6 is not a prerequisite for Chapters 7 and 8. If you read Chapter 6 after these chapters, then you can skip the section "Removing Recursion" in Chapter 7, and read this section after reading Chapter 6. Even though Chapter 6 is not required to understand Chapter 9, Chapters 9 and 10 should, ideally, be studied in sequence. Therefore, we recommend that you study Chapter 6 before Chapter 9. The following diagram illustrates the dependency of the chapters.

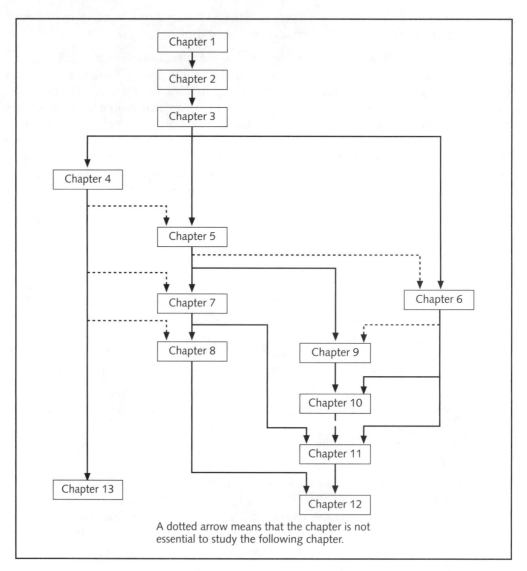

Figure 1 Chapter dependency diagram

Features

This book includes the following features in every chapter. These features are both conducive to learning and make it possible for readers to learn the material at their own pace.

- *Objectives* offer an outline of the C++ programming concepts that are discussed in the chapter.

- *Notes* highlight important facts regarding the concepts introduced in the chapter.

- Visual diagrams, both extensive and exhaustive, illustrate difficult concepts. The book contains over 350 figures.

- Numbered *Examples* within each chapter are small programs that explain the key concepts with relevant code. Each line of the programming code in these examples is numbered. Each program, illustrated through a sample run, is then explained line-by-line. The rationale behind each line is discussed in detail.

- *Programming Examples* are programs featured at the end of each chapter. These examples contain the accurate, concrete stages of Input, Output, Problem Analysis and Algorithm Design, and a Program Listing. Moreover, the problems in these programming examples are solved and programmed using OOD. These Programming Examples form the backbone of the book and are highlighted with an icon in the margin. The programs are designed to be methodical and user-friendly. Beginning with the Problem Analysis, the Programming Example is then followed by the Algorithm Design. Every step of the algorithm is then coded in C++. In addition to teaching problem-solving techniques, these detailed programs show the user how to implement concepts in an actual C++ program. I strongly recommend that students study the Programming Examples very carefully in order to learn C++ effectively.

- *Quick Review* sections at the end of each chapter reinforce learning by summarizing the concepts covered within the chapter. After reading the chapter, readers can quickly walk through the chapter's highlights and then test themselves using the ensuing Exercises. Many readers refer to the Quick Review as a way to quickly review the chapter before an exam.

- *Exercises* further reinforce learning and ensure that students have, in fact, learned the material.

- *Programming Exercises* challenge students to write C++ programs with a specified outcome.

From beginning to end, the concepts are introduced at a pace that is conducive to learning. The writing style of this book is simple and straightforward. Before introducing a key concept, we explain why certain elements are necessary. The concepts introduced are then explained using examples and small programs.

All the source code and solutions have been written, compiled, and quality assurance tested. Programs can be compiled with Microsoft Visual C++ .NET or Metrowerks CodeWarrior.

Teaching Tools

The following supplemental materials are available when this book is used in a classroom setting. All of the teaching tools available with this book are provided to the instructor on a single CD-ROM.

Electronic Instructor's Manual. The Instructor's Manual that accompanies this textbook includes:

- Additional instructional material to assist in class preparation, including suggestions for lecture topics.

- Solutions to all the end-of-chapter materials, including the Programming Exercises.

ExamView®. This textbook is accompanied by ExamView, a powerful testing software package that allows instructors to create and administer printed, computer (LAN-based), and Internet exams. ExamView includes hundreds of questions that correspond to the topics covered in this text, enabling students to generate detailed study guides that include page references for further review. The computer-based and Internet testing components allow students to take exams at their computers, and also save the instructor time by grading each exam automatically.

PowerPoint Presentations. This book comes with Microsoft PowerPoint slides for each chapter. These are included as a teaching aid for classroom presentations, either to make available to students on the network for chapter review, or to be printed for classroom distribution. Instructors can add their own slides for additional topics that they introduce to the class.

Distance Learning. Course Technology is proud to present online courses in WebCT and Blackboard, as well as at MyCourse.com, Course Technology's own course enhancement tool, to provide the most complete and dynamic learning experience possible. When you add online content to one of your courses, you're adding a lot: self tests, links, glossaries, and—most of all—a gateway to the 21st century's most important information resource. We hope you will make the most of your course, both online and offline. For more information on how to bring distance learning to your course, contact your local Course Technology sales representative.

Source Code. The source code is available at www.course.com, and also on the Teaching Tools CD-ROM. The input files needed to run some of the programs are also included with the source code. However, the input files should first be stored on a floppy disk in drive A:.

Solution files. The source code for all the programming exercises is available at www.course.com, and on the Teaching Tools CD-ROM. The input files needed to run some of the programming exercises are also included with the source code. However, the input files should first be stored on a floppy disk in drive A:.

ACKNOWLEDGEMENTS

I owe a great deal to the following reviewers who patiently read each page of every chapter of the current version and made critical comments to improve on the book: Richard Albright, University of Delaware; Steve Armstrong, LeTourneau University; John DaPonte, Southern Connecticut State University; Charles Dowling, Community College of Baltimore County, Catonsville; Marguerite Nedreberg, Youngstown State University. The reviewers will recognize that their suggestions have not been overlooked and, in fact, made this a better book. Thanks to Development Editor Susan Gilbert for carefully editing each chapter. All this would not have been possible without the planning of Senior Editor Jennifer Muroff. My sincere thanks to Jennifer, as well as to Production Editor Aimee Poirier, and also to the QA department of Course Technology for carefully testing the code.

I am thankful to my parents, to whom this book is dedicated, for their blessings. I also want to thank my brothers for their encouragement and support.

Finally, I am thankful for the support of my wife, Sadhana, and especially my daughter Shelly Malik. She cheered me up whenever I was overwhelmed during the writing of this book. Shelly always draws special joy whenever I undertake such projects.

I welcome any comments concerning the text. Comments may be forwarded to the following e-mail address: `malik@creighton.edu`.

D. S. Malik

SOFTWARE ENGINEERING PRINCIPLES AND C++ CLASSES

> ### In this chapter, you will:
>
> - Learn about software engineering principles
> - Discover what an algorithm is and explore problem-solving techniques
> - Become aware of structured design and object-oriented design programming methodologies
> - Learn about classes
> - Learn about `private`, `protected`, and `public` members of a class
> - Explore how classes are implemented
> - Become aware of Unified Modeling Language (UML) notation
> - Examine constructors and destructors
> - Learn about the abstract data type (ADT)
> - Explore how classes are used to implement ADT
> - Learn about information hiding
> - Explore how information hiding is implemented in C++

Most everyone working with computers is familiar with the term "software." Software are computer programs designed to accomplish a specific task. For example, word-processing software is a program that enables you to write term papers, create impressive looking résumés, and even write a book. This book, for example, was created with the help of a word processor. Students no longer type their papers on typewriters or write them by hand. Instead, they use word-processing software to complete their term papers. Many people maintain and balance their checkbooks on computers.

Powerful, yet easy-to-use software has drastically changed the way we live and communicate. Terms such as "the Internet," which were unfamiliar just a few years ago, are very common today. With the help of computers and the software running on them, you can send letters to, and receive letters from, loved ones within seconds. You no longer need to send a résumé by mail to apply for a job; in many cases, you can simply submit your job application via the Internet. You can watch how stocks perform in real time, and instantly buy and sell them. Kids in elementary school regularly "surf" the Internet and use computers to design their classroom projects.

Without software a computer is of no use. It is the software that enables you to do things that were, perhaps, fiction a few years ago. However, software is not created overnight. From the time a software program is conceived until it is delivered, it goes through several phases. There is a branch of computer science, called software engineering, that specializes in this area. Most colleges and universities offer a course in software engineering. This book is not concerned with the teaching of software engineering principles. However, this chapter briefly describes some of the basic software engineering principles that can simplify program design.

SOFTWARE LIFE CYCLE

A program goes through many phases from the time it is first conceived until the time it is retired, called the **life cycle** of the program. The three fundamental stages a program goes through are: **development**, **use**, and **maintenance**. Usually a program is initially conceived by a software developer because a customer has some problem that needs to be solved and the customer is willing to pay money to have it solved. The new program is created in the **software development** stage. The next section describes this stage in some detail.

Once the program is considered complete, it is released for the user to use. Once users start using the program, they most certainly discover problems or have suggestions to improve it. The problems and/or ideas for improvements are conveyed to the software developer, and the program goes through the maintenance phase.

In the **software maintenance** process, the program is modified to fix the (identified) problems or to enhance it. If there are serious or numerous changes, typically a new version of the program is created and released for use.

When a program is considered too expensive to maintain, the developer might decide to *retire* the program and no new version of the program is released.

The software development phase is the first and perhaps most important phase of the software life cycle. A program that is well developed is easy and less expensive to maintain. The next section describes this phase.

Software Development Phase

1

Software engineers typically break the software development process into the following four phases:

- Analysis
- Design
- Implementation
- Testing and debugging

The next few sections describe these four phases in some detail.

Analysis

Analyzing the problem is the first and most important step. This step requires you to do the following:

- Thoroughly understand the problem.
- **Requirement analysis:** Understand the problem requirements. Requirements can include whether the program requires interaction with the user, whether it manipulates data, whether it produces output, and what the output looks like.

  For example, suppose that you need to develop a program to make an automated teller machine (ATM) operational. In the analysis phase, you determine the functionality of the machine. Here you determine the necessary operations performed by the machine, such as allow withdrawals, deposits, and transfers; provide account balances; and so on. During this phase, you also talk to potential customers who will use the machine. To make it user-friendly, you must understand their requirements and add any necessary operations.

- If the program manipulates data, the programmer must know what the data is and how it is represented. That is, you need to look at sample data. If the program produces output, you should know how the results should be generated and formatted.
- If the problem is complex, divide the problem into subproblems, analyze each subproblem, and understand each subproblem's requirements.

Design

After you carefully analyze the problem, the next step is to design an algorithm to solve the problem. If you broke the problem into subproblems, you need to design an algorithm for each subproblem.

Algorithm: A step-by-step problem-solving process in which a solution is arrived at in a finite amount of time.

Structured Design

Dividing a problem into smaller subproblems is called **structured design**. The structured design approach is also known as **top-down design**, **stepwise refinement**, and **modular programming**. In structured design, the problem is divided into smaller subproblems. Each subproblem is then analyzed, and a solution is obtained to solve the subproblem. The solutions of all the subproblems are then combined to solve the overall problem. This process of implementing a structured design is called **structured programming**.

Object-Oriented Design

In object-oriented design (OOD), the first step in the problem-solving process is to identify the components called "objects," which form the basis of the solution, and determine how these objects interact with one another. For example, suppose you want to write a program that automates the video rental process for a local video store. The two main objects in this problem are the video and the customer.

After identifying the objects, the next step is to specify for each object the relevant data and possible operations to be performed on that data. For example, for a video object, the data might include the movie name, starring actors, producer, production company, number of copies in stock, and so on. Some of the operations on a video object might include checking the name of the movie, reducing the number of copies in stock by one after a copy is rented, and incrementing the number of copies in stock by one after a customer returns a particular video.

This illustrates that each object consists of data and operations on those data. An object combines data and operations on the data into a single unit. In OOD, the final program is a collection of interacting objects. A programming language that implements OOD is called an **object-oriented programming (OOP)** language. You will learn about the many advantages of OOD in later chapters.

OOD has the three basic principles:

- Encapsulation—The ability to combine data and operations in a single unit.

- Inheritance—The ability to create new data types from existing data types.

- Polymorphism—The ability to use the same expression to denote different operations.

In C++, encapsulation is accomplished via the use of the data types called "classes." How classes are implemented in C++ is described later in this chapter. Chapter 2 discusses inheritance and polymorphism.

In object-oriented design, you decide what classes you need and what are their relevant data members and member functions. You then describe how classes interact with each other.

Implementation

In the *implementation* phase, you write and compile programming code to implement the classes and functions that were discovered in the design phase.

This book uses the OOD technique (in conjunction with structured programming) to solve a particular problem. It contains many case studies—called Programming Examples—to solve a real-world problem.

In its final form, a program consists of several functions, each accomplishing a specific goal. Some functions are part of the main program, others are used to implement various operations on objects. Clearly, functions interact with each other, taking advantage of each other's capabilities. In order to use a function, the user needs to know only how to use the function and what the function does. The user should not be concerned with the details of the function, that is, how the function is written. The following example illustrates this concept.

Suppose that you want to write a function that converts a measurement given in inches into centimeters. The conversion formula is 1 inch = 2.54 centimeters. The following function accomplishes the job.

```
double inchesToCentimeters(double inches)
{
    if(inches < 0)
    {
        cerr<<"The given measurement must be nonnegative"<<endl;
        return -1.0;
    }
    else
        return 2.54 * inches;
}
```

 The object `cerr` corresponds to the unbuffered standard error stream. Unlike the object `cout` (the output of which first goes to the buffer), the output of `cerr` is immediately sent to the standard error stream, which is usually the screen.

If you look at the body of the function, you can recognize that if the value of inches is less than 0, that is, negative, the function returns −1.0; otherwise, the function returns the equivalent length in centimeters. The user of this function does not need to know the specific details of how the algorithm that finds the equivalent length in centimeters is implemented. However, the user must know that in order to get the valid answer, the input must be a nonnegative number. If the input to this function is a negative number, the program returns −1.0. This information can be provided as part of the documentation of this function using specific statements, called preconditions and postconditions.

Precondition: A statement specifying the condition(s) that must be true before the function is called.

Postcondition: A statement specifying what is true after the function call is completed.

The precondition and postcondition for the function `inchesToCentimeters` can be specified as follows:

```
//Precondition: The value of inches must be nonnegative.
//Postcondition: If the value of inches is < 0, the
//               function returns -1.0; otherwise, the
//               function returns the equivalent length in
//               centimeters.
double inchesToCentimeters(double inches)
{
    if(inches < 0)
    {
        cerr<<"The given measurement must be nonnegative"<<endl;
        return -1.0;
    }
    else
        return 2.54 * inches;
}
```

In certain situations, you could use C++'s `assert` statement to validate the input. For example, the preceding function can be written as follows:

```
//Precondition: The value of inches must be nonnegative.
//Postcondition: If the value of inches is < 0, the
//               function terminates; otherwise, the
//               function returns the equivalent length in
//               centimeters.
double inchesToCentimeters(double inches)
{
    assert(inches >= 0);
    return 2.54 * inches;
}
```

If the `assert` statement fails, the entire program terminates, which might be appropriate if the remainder of the program depends on the execution of the function. On the other hand, the user can check the value returned by the function, determine if the returned value is appropriate, and proceed accordingly. To use the `assert` function, you need to include the header file `cassert` in your program.

 To turn off the `assert` statements in a program, use the preprocessor directive `#define NDEBUG`. This directive must be placed before the statement `#include <cassert>`

As you can see, the same function can be implemented differently by different programmers. Because the user of a function need not be concerned with the details of the function, the preconditions and postconditions are specified with the function prototype. That is, the user is given the following information:

```
double inchesToCentimeters(double inches);
   //Precondition: The value of inches must be nonnegative.
   //Postcondition: If the value of inches is < 0, the
   //               function returns -1.0; otherwise, the
   //               function returns the equivalent length in
   //               centimeters.
```

As another example, to use a function that searches a list for a specific item, the list must exist before the function is called. After the search is complete, the function returns `true` or `false` depending on whether the search was successful.

```
bool search(int list[], int listLength, int searchItem);
   //Precondition: list must exist.
   //Postcondition: The function returns true if searchItem
   //               is in the list; otherwise, the function returns
   //               false.
```

Testing and Debugging

The term "testing" refers to testing the correctness of the program, that is, making sure that the program does what it is supposed to do. The term "debugging" refers to finding and fixing the errors, if they exist.

Once a function or an algorithm is written, the next step is to verify that it works properly. However, in a large and complex program, errors almost certainly exist. Therefore, to increase the reliability of the program, errors must be discovered and fixed before the program is released to the user.

You can certainly prove the correctness of a program by using some (perhaps mathematical) analysis of the program. However, for large and complex programs, this technique alone might not be enough because errors can be made in the proof. Therefore, we also rely on testing to determine the quality of the program. The program is run through a series of specific tests, called **test cases**, in an attempt to find any problems.

A test case consists of a set of inputs, user actions, or other initial conditions, and the expected output. Because a test case can be repeated several times, it must be properly documented. Typically, a program manipulates a large set of data. It is therefore impractical (although possible) to create test cases for all possible inputs. For example, suppose that a program manipulates integers. Clearly, it is not possible to create a test case for each integer. You can categorize test cases into separate categories, called equivalence categories. An equivalence category is a set of input values that are likely to produce the same output. For example, suppose that you have a function that takes an integer as input and returns `true` if the integer is nonnegative, and `false` otherwise. In this case, you can form two equivalence categories, one consisting of negative numbers and the other consisting of nonnegative numbers.

There are two types of testing—**black-box** testing and **white-box** testing. In black-box testing, you do not know the internal working of the algorithm or function. You know only what the function does. Black-box testing is based on inputs and outputs. The test cases for black-box testing are usually selected by creating equivalence categories. If a function works for one input in the equivalence category, it is expected to work for other inputs in the same category.

Suppose that the function `isWithinRange` returns a value `true` if an integer is greater than or equal to 0 and less than or equal to 100. In black-box testing, the function is tested on values that surround and fall on the boundaries, called **boundary values**, as well as general values from the equivalence categories. For the function `isWithinRange`, in black-box testing, the boundary values might be: -1, 0, 1, 99, 100, and 101; therefore, the test values might be -500, -1, 0, 1, 50, 99, 100, 101, and 500.

White-box testing relies on the internal structure and implementation of a function or algorithm. The objective is to ensure that every part of the function or algorithm is executed at least once. Suppose that you want to ensure whether an `if` statement works properly. The test cases must consist of at least one input for which the `if` statement evaluates to `true` and at least one case for which it evaluates to `false`. Loops and other structures can be tested similarly.

ALGORITHM ANALYSIS: THE BIG-O NOTATION

Just as a problem is analyzed before writing the algorithm and the computer program, after an algorithm is designed it should also be analyzed. Usually, there are various ways to design a particular algorithm. Certain algorithms take very little computer time to execute, while others take a considerable amount of time.

Consider the following problem. The holiday season is approaching and a gift shop expects sales to be double or even triple the regular amount. The shop has hired extra delivery people to deliver the packages on time. The company calculates the shortest distance from the shop to a particular destination and hands the route to the driver. Suppose that 50 packages are to be delivered to 50 different houses. The shop, while determining the route, finds that the 50 houses are one mile apart and are in the same area. The first house is also one mile from the shop (see Figure 1-1).

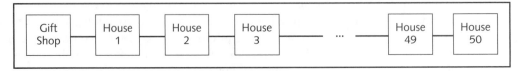

Figure 1-1   Gift shop and the 50 houses

To simplify this figure, we use Figure 1-2.

Each dot represents a house and the distance between houses is 1 mile, as shown in Figure 1-2.

Figure 1-2   Gift shop; each dot represents a house

To deliver 50 packages to their destinations, one of the drivers picks up all 50 packages, drives one mile to the first house and delivers the first package. Then the driver drives another mile and delivers the second package, and another mile to deliver the third package, and so on. Figure 1-3 illustrates this delivery scheme.

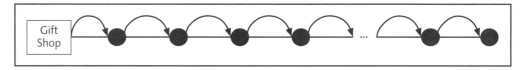

Figure 1-3   Package delivering scheme

It now follows that using this scheme, the distance driven by the driver to deliver the packages is:

$1 + 1 + 1 + ... + 1 = 50$ miles

Therefore, the total distance traveled by the driver to deliver the packages and then get back to the shop is:

$50 + 50 = 100$ miles

Another driver has a similar route to deliver another set of 50 packages. The driver looks at the route and delivers the packages as follows: The driver picks up the first package, drives one mile to the first house, delivers the package, and then comes back to the shop. Next, the driver picks up the second package, drives 2 miles, delivers the second package, and then returns to the shop. The driver then picks up the third package, drives 3 miles, delivers the package, and comes back to the shop. Figure 1-4 illustrates this delivery scheme.

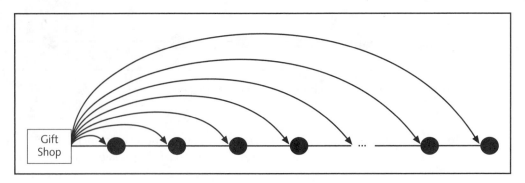

Figure 1-4   Another package delivery scheme

This driver delivers only one package at a time. After delivering a package, the driver comes back to the shop to pick up and deliver the next package. Using this scheme, the total distance traveled by this driver to deliver the packages and then get back to the store is

2 * (1 + 2 + 3 + ... + 50) = 2550 miles

Now suppose that there are n packages to be delivered to n houses, and each house is one mile apart from each other as shown in Figure 1-4. If the packages are delivered using the first scheme, the following equation gives the total distance traveled:

$$\underbrace{1+1+1+...+1}_{n \text{ times}}+ n = 2n \qquad\qquad (1\text{-}1)$$

If the packages are delivered using the second method, the distance traveled is:

$$2 * (1 + 2 + 3 + ... + n) = 2 *(\frac{n(n+1)}{2}) = n^2 + n \quad (1\text{-}2)$$

In Equation (1-1), we say that the distance traveled is a function of n. Let us consider Equation (1-2). In this equation, for large values of n, we will find that the term consisting of n^2 becomes the dominant term and the term containing n becomes negligible. In this case, we say that the distance traveled is a function of n^2. Table 1-1 evaluates Equations (1-1) and (1-2) for certain values of n. (The table also shows the value of n^2.)

Table 1-1   The Values of n, $2n$, n^2, and $n^2 + n$

n	$2n$	n^2	$n^2 + n$
1	2	1	2
10	20	100	110
100	200	10,000	10,100
1,000	2,000	1,000,000	1,001,000
10,000	20,000	100,000,000	100,010,000

While analyzing a particular algorithm, we usually count the number of operations the algorithm executes. We focus on the number of operations, not the actual computer time to execute the algorithm. This is due to the fact that a particular algorithm can be implemented on a variety of computers and the speed of the computer can affect the execution time. However, the number of operations performed by the algorithm would be the same on each computer. Let us consider the following examples.

Example 1-1

Consider the following algorithm. (Assume that all variables are properly declared.)

```
cout<<"Enter two numbers";                    //Line 1
cout<<flush;                                  //Line 2

cin>>num1>>num2;                              //Line 3

if(num1 >= num2)                             //Line 4
    max = num1;                              //Line 5
else                                          //Line 6
    max = num2;                              //Line 7

cout<<"The maximum number is: "<<max<<endl;   //Line 8
```

Line 1 has one operation, <<; Line 2 has one operation, <<; Line 3 has two, >>, operations; Line 4 has one operation, >=; Line 5 has one operation, =; Line 7 has one operation, =; and Line 8 has three, <<, operations. Either Line 5 or Line 7 executes. Therefore, the total number of operations executed in the preceding code is 1 + 1 + 2 + 1 + 1 + 3 = 9. In this algorithm, the number of operations executed is fixed.

Example 1-2

Consider the following algorithm:

```
cout<<"Enter positive integers ending with -1"<<endl;  //Line 1

count = 0                                     //Line 2
sum = 0;                                      //Line 3

cin>>num;                                     //Line 4

while(num != -1)                             //Line 5
{
    sum = sum + num;                         //Line 6
    count++;                                 //Line 7
    cin>>num;                                //Line 8
}
```

```
cout<<"The sum of the numbers is: "<<sum<<endl;          //Line 9

if(count != 0)                                            //Line 10
    average = sum / count;                                //Line 11
else                                                      //Line 12
    average = 0;                                          //Line 13

cout<<"The average is: "<<average<<endl;                  //Line 14
```

This algorithm has 5 operations (Lines 1 through 4) before the `while` loop. Similarly, there are 9 or 8 operations after the `while` loop, depending on whether Line 11 or Line 13 executes.

Line 5 has one operation, and 4 operations within the `while` loop (Line 6 through 8). Thus, Lines 5 through 8 have 5 operations. If the `while` loop executes 10 times, these 5 operations execute 10 times. One extra operation is also executed at Line 5 to terminate the loop. Therefore, the number of operations executed is 51 from Lines 5 through 8.

If the `while` loop executes 10 times, the total number of operations executed is

10 * 5 + 1 + 5 + 9 or 10 * 5 + 1 + 5 + 8

that is,

10 * 5 + 15 or 10 * 5 + 14

We can generalize it to the case when the `while` loop executes n times. If the `while` loop executes n times, the number of operations executed is

$5n$ + 15 or $5n$ + 14

In these expressions, for very large values of n, the term $5n$ becomes the dominating term and the terms 15 and 14 become negligible.

Usually, in an algorithm, certain operations are dominant. For example, in the preceding algorithm, to add numbers, the dominant operation is in Line 6. Similarly, in a search algorithm, because the search item is compared with the items in the list, the dominant operation would be comparison, that is, the relational operation. Therefore, in the case of a search algorithm we count the number of comparisons. For another example, suppose that we write a program to multiply matrices. The multiplication of matrices involves addition and multiplication. Because multiplication takes more computer time to execute, to analyze a matrix multiplication algorithm, we count the number of multiplications.

This book not only develops algorithms, but also provides a reasonable analysis of each algorithm. In fact, if there are various algorithms to accomplish a particular task, the algorithm analysis allows the programmer to choose between various options.

Suppose that an algorithm performs $f(n)$ basic operations to accomplish a task, where n is the size of the problem. Suppose that you want to determine whether an item is in a list. Moreover, suppose that the size of the list is n. To determine whether or not the item is in the list, there are various algorithms, as you will see in Chapter 9. However, the basic method is to compare the item with the items in the list. Therefore, the performance of the algorithm depends on the number of comparisons.

In the case of a search, n is the size of the list and $f(n)$ becomes the count function, that is, $f(n)$ gives the number of comparisons done by the search algorithm. Suppose that, on a particular computer, it takes c units of computer time to execute one operation. Thus, the computer time it would take to execute $f(n)$ operations is $cf(n)$. Clearly, the constant c depends on the speed of the computer, and therefore varies from computer to computer. However, $f(n)$, the number of basic operations, is the same on each computer. If we know how the function $f(n)$ grows as the size of the problem grows, we can determine the efficiency of the algorithm. Consider Table 1-2.

Table 1-2   Growth Rate of Various Functions

n	$\log_2 n$	$n\log_2 n$	n^2	2^n
1	0	0	1	2
2	1	2	2	4
4	2	8	16	16
8	3	24	64	256
16	4	64	256	65,536
32	5	160	1,024	4,294,967,296

Table 1-2 shows how certain functions grow as the parameter n, that is, the problem size, grows. Suppose that the problem size is doubled. From Table 1-2, it follows that if the number of basic operations is a function of $f(n) = n^2$, the number of basic operations is quadrupled. If the number of basic operations is a function of $f(n) = 2^n$, then the number of basic operations is squared. However, if the number of operations is a function of $f(n) = \log_2 n$, the change in the number of basic operations is insignificant.

Suppose that a computer can execute 1 billion steps per second. Table 1-3 shows the time that a computer takes to execute $f(n)$ steps.

Table 1-3   Time for $f(n)$ Instructions on a Computer that Executes 1 Billion Instructions per Second

n	$f(n)=n$	$f(n)=\log_2 n$	$f(n)=n\log_2 n$	$f(n)=n^2$	$f(n)=2^n$
10	0.01µs	0.003µs	0.033µs	0.1µs	1µs
20	0.02µs	0.004µs	0.086µs	0.4µs	1ms
30	0.03µs	0.005µs	0.147µs	0.9µs	1s

In this table, 1µs = 10^{-6} seconds and 1ms = 10^{-3} seconds

Table 1-3 Time for $f(n)$ Instructions on a Computer that Executes 1 Billion Instructions per Second (continued)

n	$f(n)=n$	$f(n)=\log_2 n$	$f(n)=n\log_2 n$	$f(n)=n^2$	$f(n)=2^n$
40	0.04µs	0.005µs	0.213µs	1.6µs	18.3 min
50	0.05µs	0.006µs	0.282µs	2.5µs	13 days
100	0.10ms	0.007µs	0.664µs	10µs	4×10^{13} years
1,000	1.00µs	0.010µs	9.966µs	1ms	
10,000	10µs	0.013µs	130µs	100ms	
100,000	0.10ms	0.017µs	1.67ms	10s	
1,000,000	0.01s	0.020µs	19.93ms	16.7m	
10,000,000	0.10s	0.023µs	0.23s	1.16 days	
100,000,000	1.00s	0.027µs	2.66s	115.7 days	

In this table, $1µs = 10^{-6}$ seconds and $1ms = 10^{-3}$ seconds

The remainder of this section develops a notation that shows how a function $f(n)$ grows as n increases without bound. That is, the section develops a notation that is useful in describing the behavior of the algorithm and gives us the most useful information about the algorithm. First, we define the term "asymptotic."

Definition: Let f be a function of n. The term "**asymptotic**" means the study of the function f as n becomes larger and larger without bound.

Consider the functions $g(n) = n^2$ and $f(n) = n^2+4n+20$. Clearly, the function g does not contain any linear term, that is, the coefficient of n in g is zero. Consider Table 1-4.

Table 1-4 Growth Rate of n^2 and $n^2 + 4n + 20$

n	$g(n)=n^2$	$f(n)=n^2+4n+20$
10	300	360
50	2500	2720
100	10,000	10,420
1,000	1,000,000	1,004,020
10,000	100,000,000	100,040,020

From Table 1-4, it follows that as n becomes larger and larger the term $4n+20$ in $f(n)$ becomes insignificant, and the term n^2 becomes the dominant term. For large values of n, we can predict the behavior of $f(n)$ by looking at the behavior of $g(n)$. In the algorithm analysis, if the complexity of a function can be described by the complexity of a quadratic function without the linear term, we say that the function is of $O(n^2)$, called "Big-O of n^2."

Let f and g be real-valued functions. Assume that f and g are nonnegative.

Definition: We say that $f(n)$ is **Big-O** of $g(n)$ written $f(n) = O(g(n))$ if there exists positive constants c and n_0 such that

$f(n) \leq cg(n)$ for all $n \geq n_0$

Table 1-5 shows some common Big-O functions that appear in the algorithm analysis. Let $f(n) = O(g(n))$, where n is the problem size.

Table 1-5 Some Big-O Functions that Appear in Algorithm Analysis

Function $g(n)$	Growth rate of $f(n)$
$g(n) = 1$	The growth rate is constant and so does not depend on n, the size of the problem.
$g(n) = \log_2 n$	The growth rate is a function of $\log_2 n$. Because a logarithm function grows slowly, the growth rate of the function f is also slow.
$g(n) = n$	The growth rate is linear. The growth rate of f is directly proportional to the size of the problem.
$g(n) = n * \log_2 n$	The growth rate is faster than the linear algorithm.
$g(n) = n^2$	The growth rate of such functions increases rapidly with the size of the problem. The growth rate is quadrupled when the problem size is doubled.
$g(n) = 2^n$	The growth rate is exponential. The growth rate is squared when the problem size is doubled.

Using the preceding notations, we can conclude that Equation (1–1) is of $O(n)$, and Equation (1–2) is of $O(n^2)$. Moreover, the algorithm in Example 1–1 is of $O(1)$, and the algorithm in Example 1–2 is of $O(n)$.

$O(1) < O(\log_2 n) < O(n) < O(n) < O(n*\log_2 n) < O(n^2) < O(2^n)$

CLASSES

The reader can skip this section, if the reader is familiar with how classes are implemented in C++.

Recall that in OOD, the first step is to identify the components called objects; an object encapsulates or combines data and the operations on that data in a single unit. In C++, the mechanism that allows you to combine data and the operations on that data in a single unit is called a "class." This section describes how to use classes in C++.

A **class** is a collection of a fixed number of components. The components of a class are called the **members** of the class.

The general syntax for defining a class is

```
class classIdentifier
{
    classMemberList
};
```

where `classMemberList` consists of variable declarations and/or functions. That is, a member of a class can be either a variable (to store data) or a function.

- If a member of a class is a variable, you declare it just like any other variable. Moreover, in the definition of the class, you cannot initialize a variable when you declare it.

- If a member of a class is a function, you typically use the function prototype to define that member.

- If a member of a class is a function, it can (directly) access any member of the class—data members and function members. That is, when you write the definition of the member function, you can directly access any data member of the class without passing it as a parameter. The only obvious condition is that you must declare an identifier before you can use it.

In C++, `class` is a reserved word, and it defines only a data type; no memory is allocated. It announces the declaration of a class. Moreover, note the semicolon (`;`) after the right brace. The semicolon is part of the syntax. A missing semicolon, therefore, results in a syntax error.

The members of a `class` are classified into three categories: `private`, `public`, and `protected`, called **member access specifiers**. This chapter mainly discusses the first two types—`private` and `public`.

Following are some facts about `private` and `public` members of a class:

- By default, all members of a class are `private`.

- If a member of a class is `private`, you cannot access it outside the class.

- A `public` member is accessible outside the class.

- To make a member of a class `public`, you use the member access specifier `public` with a colon.

In C++, `private`, `protected`, and `public` are reserved words.

Example 1-3

Suppose that we want to define the **class clockType**, to implement the time of day in a program. Furthermore, suppose that the time is represented as a set of three integers: one to represent the hours, one to represent the minutes, and one to represent the seconds. We also want to perform the following operations on the time:

1. Set the time.

2. Return the time.

3. Print the time.

4. Increment the time by one second.

5. Increment the time by one minute.

6. Increment the time by one hour.

7. Compare the two times for equality.

From this discussion, it is clear that the **class clockType** has 10 members: three data members and seven function members.

Some members of the **class clockType** are `private`, others are `public`. Deciding which members to make `private` and which to make `public` depends on the nature of the member. The general rule is that any member that needs to be accessed outside the class is declared `public`; any member that should not be accessed directly by the user should be declared `private`. For example, the user should be able to set the time and print the time. Therefore, the members that set the time and print the time should be declared `public`.

Similarly, the members to increment the time, and compare the time for equality, should be declared `public`. On the other hand, to control the *direct* manipulation of the data members `hr`, `min`, and `sec`, we will declare these data members `private`. Furthermore, note that if the user has direct access to the data members, member functions such as `setTime` are not needed.

The following statements define the **class clockType**:

```
class clockType
{
public:
    void setTime(int hours, int minutes, int seconds);
      //Function to set the time.
      //The time is set according to the parameters.
      //Postcondition: hr = hours; min = minutes;
      //                sec = seconds
      //  The function checks whether the values of hours,
```

```
      //  minutes, and seconds are valid. If a value is
      //  invalid, the default value 0 is assigned.

   void getTime(int& hours, int& minutes, int& seconds);
     //Function to return the time.
     //Postcondition: hours = hr; minutes = min;
     //                  seconds = sec

   void printTime() const;
     //Function to print the time.
     //Postcondition: The time is printed in the form
     //                  hh:mm:ss.

   void incrementSeconds();
     //Function to increment the time by one second.
     //Postcondition: The time is incremented by one
     //              second.
     //  If the before-increment time is 23:59:59, the
     //  time is reset to 00:00:00.

   void incrementMinutes();
     //Function to increment the time by one minute.
     //Postcondition: The time is incremented by one
     //              minute.
     //  If the before-increment time is 23:59:53, the
     //  time is reset to 00:00:53.

   void incrementHours();
     //Function to increment the time by one hour.
     //Postcondition: The time is incremented by one
     //              hour.
     //  If the before-increment time is 23:45:53,
     //  the time is reset to 00:45:53.

   bool equalTime(const clockType& otherClock) const;
     //Function to compare the two times.
     //Postcondition: Returns true if this time is
     //                  equal to otherClock; otherwise,
     //                  returns false.

private:
    int hr;  //store the hours
    int min; //store the minutes
    int sec; //store the seconds
};
```

Note the following in the definition of the **class clockType**:

- The **class clockType** has seven function members: **setTime, getTime, printTime, incrementSeconds, incrementMinutes, incrementHours,** and **equalTime**. It has three data members: **hr, min,** and **sec**.

- The three data members—**hr, min,** and **sec**—are **private** to the class and cannot be accessed outside the class.

- The seven function members—**setTime, getTime, printTime, incrementSeconds, incrementMinutes, incrementHours,** and **equalTime**—can directly access the data members (**hr, min,** and **sec**). In other words, we do not pass data members as parameters to member functions.

- In the function **equalTime**, the parameter **otherClock** is a constant reference parameter. That is, in a call to the function **equalTime**, the parameter **otherClock** receives the address of the actual parameter, but **otherClock** cannot modify the value of the actual parameter. You could have declared **otherClock** as a value parameter, but that would require **otherClock** to copy the value of the actual parameter, which could result in poor performance. (For an explanation, see the section "Reference Parameters and Class Objects (Variables)" located later in this chapter.)

- The word **const** at the end of the member functions **printTime** and **equalTime** specifies that these functions cannot modify the data members of a variable of the type **clockType**.

 (Order of public and private members of a class) C++ has no fixed order in which you declare **public** and **private** members; you can declare them in any order. The only thing you need to remember is that, by default, all members of a class are **private**. You must use the member access specifier **public** to make a member available for **public** access. If you decide to declare the **private** members after the **public** members (as is done in the case of **clockType**), you must use the member access specifier **private** to begin the declaration of the **private** members.

 In the definition of the **class clockType**, all data members are **private** and all function members are **public**. However, a function member can also be **private**. For example, if a member function is used only to implement other member functions of the class, and the user does not need to access this function, you make it **private**. Similarly, a data member of a class can also be **public**.

Note that we have not yet written the definitions of the function members of the **class clockType**. You will learn how to write them shortly.

The function **setTime** sets the three data members—**hr, min,** and **sec**—to given values. The given values are passed as parameters to the function **setTime**. The function **printTime** prints the time, that is, the values of **hr, min,** and **sec**. The function **incrementSeconds** increments the time by one second, the function **incrementMinutes** increments the time by one minute, the function `incrementHours` increments the time by one hour, and the function `equalTime` compares the two times for equality.

Unified Modeling Language Diagrams

A class and its members can be described graphically using a notation known as **Unified Modeling Language** (UML) notation. For example, Figure 1-5 shows the UML diagram of the `class clockType`.

```
                    clockType

        -hr: int
        -min: int
        -sec: int

        +setTime (int, int, int): void
        +getTime (int&, int&, int&): void
        +printTime (): void
        +incrementSeconds (): int
        +incrementMinutes (): int
        +incrementHours (): int
        +equalTime (const clockType&): bool
```

Figure 1-5   UML diagram of the `class clockType`

The top box contains the name of the class. The middle box contains the data members and their data types. The last box contains the member function name, parameter list, and the return type of the function. A plus (+) sign in front of a member indicates that this member is a `public` member; a minus (-) sign indicates that this is a `private` member. The symbol (#) before the member name indicates that the member is a `protected` member.

Variable (Object) Declaration

Once a class is defined, you can declare variables of that type. In C++ terminology, a class variable is called a **class object** or **class instance**. To help you become familiar with this terminology, from now on we will use the term **class object**, or simply **object**, for a class variable.

The syntax for declaring a class object is the same as that for declaring any other variable. The following statements declare two objects of the type `clockType`:

```
clockType     myClock;
clockType     yourClock;
```

Each object has 10 members: seven function members and three data members. Each object has separate memory allocated for hr, min, and sec. At any particular time, for example, myClock's hr, min, and sec might contain 5, 12, and 30, respectively, and yourClock's hr, min, and sec might contain 12, 35, and 45, respectively.

In actuality, memory is allocated only for the data members of each class object. The C++ compiler generates only one physical copy of a function member of a class, and each class object executes the same copy of the member function.

Accessing Class Members

Once an object is declared, it can access the public members of a class. The general syntax to access the members of a class is

```
classVariableName.memberName
```

Recall that in C++, the dot, . (period), is an operator called the **member access operator**.

Example 1-4 illustrates how to access the members of a class.

Example 1-4

Consider the following statements:

```
myClock.setTime(5,2,30);
myClock.printTime();
yourClock.setTime(x,y,z);      //Assume x, y, and z are
                               //variables of the type int

if(myClock.equalTime(yourClock))
.
.
.
```

These statements are legal; that is, they are syntactically correct.

In the first statement, myClock.setTime(5,2,30);, the function member setTime is executed. The values 5, 2, and 30 are passed as parameters to the function setTime, and the function uses these values to set the values of the three data members hr, min, and sec of myClock to 5. 2, and 30, respectively. Similarly, the second statement executes the member function printTime and outputs the contents of the three data members of myClock. In the third statement, the values of the variables x, y, and z are used to set the values of the three data members of yourClock.

In the fourth statement, the member function equalTime executes and compares the three data members of myClock with the corresponding data members of yourClock.

Because in this statement `equalTime` is a member of the object `myClock`, it has direct access to the three data members of `myClock`. So it needs one more object, which in this case is `yourClock`, with which to compare. This explains why the function `equalTime` has only one parameter.

A class object can access only `public` members of the class. Therefore, the following statements are illegal, because `hr` and `min` are `private` members of the `class clockType` and, therefore, cannot be accessed by the object `myClock`:

```
myClock.hr = 10;                   //illegal
myClock.min = yourClock.min;       //illegal
```

Built-In Operations on Classes

Most of C++'s built-in operations do not apply to classes. You cannot use arithmetic operators to perform arithmetic operations on class objects (unless they are overloaded; see Chapter 2). For example, you cannot use the operator (+) to add two class objects of, say, the type `clockType`. Also, you cannot use relational operators to compare two class objects for equality (unless they are overloaded; see Chapter 2).

The two built-in operations that are valid for class objects are member access (.) and assignment (=). You have seen how to access an individual member of a class by using the name of the class object, then a dot, and then the member name.

The following section shows how an assignment statement works with the help of an example.

Assignment Operator and Classes

Suppose that `myClock` and `yourClock` are variables of the type `clockType` as previously defined. Furthermore, suppose that the values of `myClock` and `yourClock` are as shown in Figure 1-6.

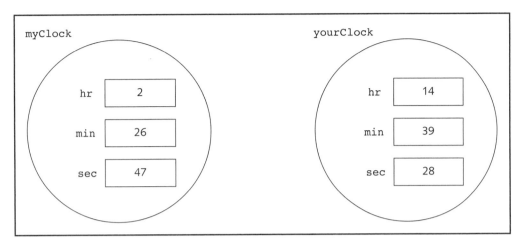

Figure 1-6   Objects myClock and yourClock

The statement

myClock = yourClock;   //Line 1

copies the value of **yourClock** into **myClock**. That is,

    1. The value of **yourClock.hr** is copied into **myClock.hr**.

    2. The value of **yourClock.min** is copied into **myClock.min**.

    3. The value of **yourClock.sec** is copied into **myClock.sec**.

In other words, the values of the three data members of **yourClock** are copied into the corresponding data members of **myClock**. Therefore, an assignment statement performs a member-wise copy. After the statement in Line 1 executes, the values of **myClock** and **yourClock** are as shown in Figure 1-7.

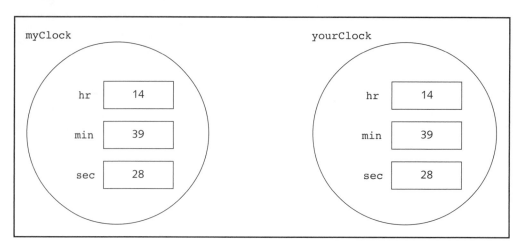

Figure 1-7   Objects `myClock` and `yourClock` after the assignment statement `myClock = yourClock;` executes

Class Scope

As with variables of simple types, a class object can be either automatic (that is, created each time the control reaches its declaration and destroyed when the control exits the surrounding block) or static (created once when the control reaches its declaration and destroyed when the program terminates). You can also declare an array of class objects. A class object has the same scope as other variables. A member of a class is local to the class. You access a `public` class member outside the class by using the class object name and the member access operator (`.`).

Functions and Classes

The following rules describe the relationship between functions and classes:

- Class objects can be passed as parameters to functions and returned as function values.

- As parameters to functions, classes can be passed either by value or by reference.

- If a class object is passed by value, the contents of the data members of the actual parameter are copied into the corresponding data members of the formal parameter.

Reference Parameters and Class Objects (Variables)

Recall that when a variable is passed by value, the formal parameter copies the value of the actual parameter. That is, memory is allocated to copy the value of the actual parameter for the formal parameter. As a parameter, a class object can be passed by value.

Suppose that a class has several data members requiring a large amount of memory to store the data, and you need to pass a variable by value. The corresponding formal parameter then receives a copy of the data of the variable. That is, the compiler must allocate memory for the formal parameter so as to copy the value of the data members of the actual parameter. This operation might require, in addition to a large amount of storage space, a considerable amount of computer time to copy the value of the actual parameter into the formal parameter.

On the other hand, if a variable is passed by reference, the formal parameter receives only the address of the actual parameter. Therefore, an efficient way to pass a variable as a parameter is by reference. If a variable is passed by reference, then when the formal parameter changes, the actual parameter also changes. Sometimes, however, you do not want the function to be able to change the values of the data members. In C++, you can pass a variable by reference and still prevent the function from changing its value by using the keyword `const` in the formal parameter declaration. As an example, consider the following function definition:

```
void testTime(const clockType& otherTime)
{
    clockType dTime;
    ...
}
```

The function `testTime` contains a reference parameter, `otherTime`. The parameter `otherTime` is declared using the keyword `const`. Therefore, in a call to the function `testTime`, the formal parameter `otherTime` receives the address of the actual parameter, but `otherTime` cannot modify the contents of the actual parameter. For example, after the following statement executes, the value of `myClock` is not altered:

```
testTime(myClock);
```

Generally, if you want to declare a class object as a value parameter, you declare it as a reference parameter using the keyword `const` as previously described.

Recall that if a formal parameter is a value parameter, then within the function definition you can change the value of the formal parameter. That is, you can use an assignment statement to change the value of the formal parameter (which, of course, would have no effect on the actual parameter). However, if a formal parameter is a constant reference parameter, you cannot use an assignment statement to change its value within the function, nor can you use any other function to change its value. Therefore, within the definition of the function `testTime`, you cannot alter the value of `otherTime`. For example, the following would be illegal in the definition of the function `testTime`:

```
otherTime.setTime(5, 34, 56);    //illegal
otherTime = dTime;               //illegal
```

Implementation of Member Functions

When the `class clockType` was defined for the function members, only the function prototypes were included. For these functions to work properly, we must write the related algorithms. One way to implement these functions is to provide the function definition rather than the function prototype in the class itself. Unfortunately, the class definition would then be very long and difficult to comprehend. Another reason for providing function proto-types instead of function definitions relates to **information hiding**; that is, we want to hide the details of the operations on the data.

Next, let us write the definitions of the function members of the **class clockType**. That is, we will write the definitions of the functions **setTime**, **getTime**, **printTime**, **incrementSeconds**, **equalTime**, and so on. Because the identifiers **setTime**, **printTime**, and so forth are local to the class, we cannot reference them (directly) out-side the class. In order to reference these identifiers, we use the **scope resolution operator**, a double colon (**::**). In the function definition's heading, the name of the function is the name of the class, followed by the scope resolution operator, followed by the function name. For example, the definition of the function **setTime** is as follows:

```
void clockType::setTime(int hours, int minutes, int seconds)
{
        if(0 <= hours && hours < 24)
           hr = hours;
        else
           hr = 0;

        if(0 <= minutes && minutes < 60)
           min = minutes;
        else
           min = 0;

        if(0 <= seconds && seconds < 60)
           sec = seconds;
        else
           sec = 0;
}
```

Note that the definition of the function **setTime** checks for the valid values of **hours**, **minutes**, and **seconds**. If the value of a parameter is out of range, the corresponding data member is initialized to 0. For example, if the value of **hours** is out of range, then the data member **hr** is initialized to 0.

Suppose that **myClock** is an object of the type **clockType** (as previously declared). Con-sider the following statement:

```
myClock.setTime(3,48,52);
```

After this statement executes, the object **myClock** is as shown in Figure 1-8.

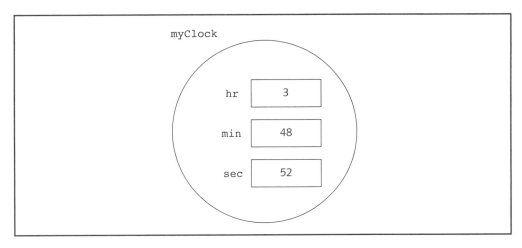

Figure 1-8   Object `myClock` after the statement `myClock.setTime (3,48,52);` executes

Next, we give the definitions of the other function members of the **class clockType**. The definitions of these functions are simple and easy to follow.

```
void clockType::getTime(int& hours, int& minutes, int& seconds)
{
      hours = hr;
      minutes = min;
      seconds = sec;
}

void clockType::printTime() const
{
      if(hr < 10)
         cout<<"0";
      cout<<hr<<":";

      if(min < 10)
         cout<<"0";
      cout<<min<<":";

      if(sec < 10)
         cout<<"0";
      cout<<sec;
}
```

```
void clockType::incrementHours()
{
      hr++;
      if(hr > 23)
          hr = 0;
}

void clockType::incrementMinutes()
{
      min++;
      if(min > 59)
      {
        min = 0;
        incrementHours(); //increment the hours
      }
}

void clockType::incrementSeconds()
{
      sec++;
      if(sec > 59)
      {
          sec = 0;
          incrementMinutes(); //increment the minutes
      }
}
```

From the definitions of the functions `incrementMinutes` and `incrementSeconds`, it is clear that a member function can call other member functions.

The function `equalTime` has the following definition:

```
bool clockType::equalTime(const clockType& otherClock) const
{
    return(hr == otherClock.hr
           && min == otherClock.min
           && sec == otherClock.sec);
}
```

Let us see how the member function `equalTime` works.

Suppose that `myClock` and `yourClock` are objects of the type `clockType`, as previously declared. Further suppose that we have `myClock` and `yourClock` as shown in Figure 1-9.

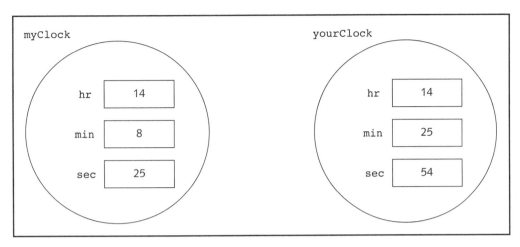

Figure 1-9   Objects `myClock` and `yourClock`

Consider the following statement:

```
if(myClock.equalTime(yourClock))
   .
   .
   .
```

In the expression

```
myClock.equalTime(yourClock)
```

the object **myClock** accesses the member function **equalTime**. The address of the parameter **yourClock** is passed to the formal parameter **otherClock**, as shown in Figure 1-10.

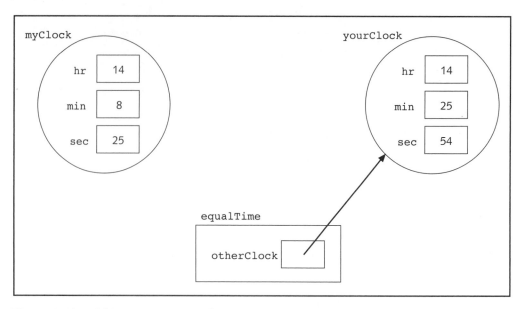

Figure 1-10   Object `myClock` and parameter `otherClock`

The data members `hr`, `min`, and `sec` of `otherClock` have the values `14`, `25`, and `54`, respectively. In other words, when the body of the function `equalTime` executes, the value of `otherClock.hr` is `14`, the value of `otherClock.min` is `25`, and the value of `otherClock.sec` is `54`. The function `equalTime` is a member of the function `myClock`. When the function `equalTime` executes, the variables `hr`, `min`, and `sec` in the body of the function `equalTime` are the data members of the variable `myClock`. Therefore, the member `hr` of `myClock` is compared with `otherClock.hr`, the member `min` of `myClock` is compared with `otherClock.min`, and the member `sec` of `myClock` is compared with `otherClock.sec`.

Once again, from the definition of the function `equalTime`, it is clear why it has only one parameter.

Constructors

Consider the following statements:

```
clockType myClock;               //Line 1

myClock.setTime(6,27,46);        //Line 2
myClock.printTime();             //Line 3
```

The statement in Line 2 sets the values of the data members `hr`, `min`, and `sec` of `myClock` to `6`, `27`, and `46`, respectively. The statement in Line 3 causes the following output:

```
06:27:46
```

However, if a program executes the statement in Line 3 without properly setting the time, the program can output some strange numbers. This is due to the fact that C++ does not automatically initialize the variables. Because the **private** members of a class cannot be accessed outside the class (in our case, the data members), if the user forgets to initialize these variables by calling the function **setTime**, the program produces erroneous results.

To guarantee that the data members of a class are initialized, you use constructors. There are two types of constructors: with parameters and without parameters. The constructor without parameters is called the **default constructor**.

Constructors have the following properties:

- The name of a constructor is the same as the name of the class.

- A constructor, even though it is a function, has no type. That is, it is neither a value-returning function nor a **void** function.

- A class can have more than one constructor. However, all constructors of a class have the same name.

- If a class has more than one constructor, either they have a different number of formal parameters or, if the number of formal parameters is the same, then the data types of the formal parameters, in the order you list, must differ in at least one position.

- Which constructor executes depends on the type of values passed to the class object when the class object is declared.

- Constructors are automatically executed when a class object enters its scope. Because they have no types, they cannot be called like other functions.

Let us extend the definition of the **class clockType** by including two constructors.

```
class clockType
{
public:
    void setTime(int hours, int minutes, int seconds);
      //Function to set the time.
      //The time is set according to the parameters.
      //Postcondition: hr = hours; min = minutes;
      //               sec =  seconds
      //  The function checks whether the values of
      //  hours, minutes, and seconds are valid. If a
      //  value is invalid, the default value 0 is
      //  assigned.

    void getTime(int& hours, int& minutes, int& seconds);
      //Function to return the time.
      //Postcondition: hours = hr; minutes = min;
      //               seconds = sec
```

```
void printTime() const;
   //Function to print the time.
   //Postcondition: The time is printed in the form
   //                 hh:mm:ss.

void incrementSeconds();
   //Function to increment the time by one second.
   //Postcondition: Time is incremented by one
   //                 second.
   //  If the before-increment time is 23:59:59,
   //  the time is reset to 00:00:00.

void incrementMinutes();
   //Function to increment the time by one minute.
   //Postcondition: The time is incremented by one
   //                 minute.
   //  If the before-increment time is 23:59:53,
   //  the time is reset to 00:00:53.

void incrementHours();
   //Function to increment the time by one hour.
   //Postcondition: The time is incremented by one
   //                 hour.
   //  If the before-increment time is 23:45:53,
   //  the time is reset to 00:45:53.

bool equalTime(const clockType& otherClock) const;
   //Function to compare the two times.
   //Postcondition: Returns true if this time is equal
   //                 to otherClock; otherwise, returns
   //                 false.

clockType(int hours, int minutes, int seconds);
   //constructor with parameters
   //The time is set according to the parameters.
   //Postcondition: hr = hours; min = minutes;
   //                 sec = seconds
   //  The constructor checks whether the values of
   //  hours, minutes, and seconds are valid. If a
   //  value is invalid, the default value 0 is
   //  assigned.

clockType();
   //default constructor
   //The time is set to the default values.
   //Postcondition: hr = 0; min = 0; sec = 0
```

```
private:
    int hr;      //store the hours
    int min;     //store the minutes
    int sec;     //store the seconds
};
```

This definition of the **class clockType** includes two constructors: one with three parameters and one with no parameters. Let us now write the definitions of these constructors.

```
clockType::clockType(int hours, int minutes, int seconds)
{
    if(0 <= hours && hours < 24)
        hr = hours;
    else
        hr = 0;

    if(0 <= minutes && minutes < 60)
        min = minutes;
    else
        min = 0;

    if(0 <= seconds && seconds < 60)
        sec = seconds;
    else
        sec = 0;
}

clockType::clockType()   //default constructor
{
    hr = 0;
    min = 0;
    sec = 0;
}
```

From the definitions of these constructors, it follows that the default constructor sets the three data members—hr, min, and sec—to 0. Also, the constructor with parameters sets the data members to whatever values are assigned to the formal parameters. Moreover, you can write the definitions of these constructors by calling the function **setTime**, as follows:

```
clockType::clockType(int hours, int minutes, int seconds)
{
    setTime(hours, minutes, seconds);
}

clockType::clockType()
{
    setTime(0, 0, 0);
}
```

These definitions of the constructors make debugging easier because only one code, for the function **setTime**, must be checked.

Invoking a Constructor

Recall that when a class object is declared, a constructor is automatically executed. Because a class might have more than one constructor, including the default constructor, the next section discusses how to invoke a specific constructor.

Invoking the Default Constructor Suppose that a class contains the default constructor. The syntax to invoke the default constructor is

```
className  classVariableName;
```

For example, the statement

```
clockType yourClock;
```

declares `yourClock` to be an object of the type `clockType`. In this case, the default constructor is executed and the data members of `yourClock` are initialized to 0.

If you declare an object and want the default constructor to be executed, the empty parentheses after the object name are not required in the object declaration statement. In fact, if you accidentally include the parentheses, the compiler generates a syntax error message. For example, the following statement is illegal:

```
clockType yourClock();   //illegal
```

Invoking a Constructor with Parameters Suppose a class contains constructors with parameters. The syntax to invoke a constructor with a parameter is

```
className  classVariableName(argument1, argument2, ...);
```

where `argument1`, `argument2`, and so on, is either a variable or an expression.

Note the following:

- The number of arguments and their type should match the formal parameters (in the order given) of one of the constructors.
- If the type of the arguments does not match the formal parameters of any constructor (in the order given), C++ uses type conversion and looks for the best match. For example, an integer value might be converted to a floating-point value with a zero decimal part. Any ambiguity results in a compile-time error.

Consider the statement

```
clockType myClock(5,12,40);
```

This statement declares the object `myClock` of the type `clockType`. Here we are passing three values of the type `int`, which matches the type of the formal parameters of the constructor with the parameters. Therefore, the constructor with parameters of the **class clockType** executes and the three data members—**hr, min,** and **sec**—of the object **myClock** are set to **5, 12,** and **40,** respectively.

Constructors and Default Parameters

A constructor can also have default parameters. In such a case, the rules for declaring formal parameters are the same as those for declaring default formal parameters in a function. Moreover, actual parameters to a constructor with default parameters are passed according to the rules for functions with default parameters. Using the rules for defining default parameters, in the definition of the **class clockType,** you can replace both constructors using the following statement. (Notice that in the function prototype, the name of a formal parameter is optional.)

```
clockType clockType(int = 0, int = 0, int = 0); //Line 1
```

In the implementation file, the definition of this constructor is the same as the definition of the constructor with parameters.

If you replace the constructors of the **class clockType** with the constructor in Line 1 (the constructor with the default parameters), then you can declare **clockType** objects with 0, 1, 2, or 3 arguments as follows:

```
clockType clock1;                    //Line 2
clockType clock2(5);                 //Line 3
clockType clock3(12, 30);            //Line 4
clockType clock4(7, 34, 18);         //Line 5
```

The data members of **clock1** are initialized to 0. The data member **hr** of **clock2** is initialized to 5, and the data members **min** and **sec** of **clock2** are initialized to 0. The data member **hr** of **clock3** is initialized to 12, the data member **min** of **clock3** is initialized to 30, and the data member **sec** of **clock3** is initialized to 0. The data member **hr** of **clock4** is initialized to 7, the data member **min** of **clock4** is initialized to 34, and the data member **sec** of **clock4** is initialized to 18.

Using these conventions, we can say that a constructor that has no parameters, or has all default parameters, is called the **default constructor**.

Destructors

Like constructors, destructors are also functions. Moreover, like constructors, a destructor does not have a type; that is, it is neither a value-returning function nor a **void** function. However, a class can have only one destructor, and the destructor can have no parameters. The name of a destructor is the (~) character followed by the name of the class. (The character (~) is called a tilde.) For example, the name of the destructor for the **class clockType** is

```
~clockType();
```

The destructor automatically executes when the class object goes out of scope. Therefore, just like constructors, a destructor *cannot* be called explicitly.

Structs

Structs are a special type of classes. By default, all members of a class are `private`, while by default all members of a struct are `public`. In C++, you define structs by using the reserved word `struct`. If all members of a class are `public`, C++ programmers prefer to use a struct to group the members, as you will do in this book. A struct is defined just like a class.

DATA ABSTRACTION, CLASSES, AND ABSTRACT DATA TYPES

 The reader can skip this section, if the reader is familiar with these topics.

Have you ever wondered how the engine of your car works? Most people want to know only how to start a car and drive it, and are not concerned with the complexity of how the engine works. By separating the design details of a car's engine from its use, the manufacturer helps the driver to focus on how to drive the car. Our daily life has other similar examples. For the most part, people are concerned with only how to use certain items, rather than how they work.

Separating the implementation details (that is, how the car's engine works) from an item's use is called **abstraction**. In other words, abstraction focuses on what the engine does and not on how it works. Therefore, abstraction is the process of separating the logical properties from the implementation details. Driving the car is a logical property; the construction of the engine constitutes the implementation details. You have an abstract view of what the engine does, but are not interested in the engine's actual implementation.

Abstraction can also be applied to data. Earlier sections of this chapter defined the data type `clockType`. The data type `clockType` has three data members and the following basic operations:

1. Set the time.

2. Return the time.

3. Print the time.

4. Increment the time by one second.

5. Increment the time by one minute.

6. Increment the time by one hour.

7. Compare the two times to see whether they are equal.

The actual implementation of the operations on `clockType` was postponed. Data abstraction is defined as a process of separating the logical properties of the data from its implementation. The definition of `clockType` and its basic operations are the logical properties; the storing of `clockType` in the computer, and the algorithms to perform these operations, are the implementation details of `clockType`.

Abstract data type (ADT): A data type that specifies the logical properties without the implementation details.

The ADT is concerned with the specification details (what), not the implementation details (how).

Like any other data type, an ADT has three things associated with it: the name of the ADT, called the **type name**; the set of values belonging to the ADT, called the **domain**; and the set of **operations** on the data. Following these conventions, we can define the `clockType` ADT as follows:

```
typeName
    clockType
domain
    Each clockType value is a time of day in the form of
    hours, minutes, and seconds.
operations
    Set the time.
    Return the time.
    Print the time.
    Increment the time by one second.
    Increment the time by one minute.
    Increment the time by one hour.
    Test the two times to see whether they are equal.
```

Example 1-5

A list is defined as a set of values of the same type. Because all values in a list are of the same type, a convenient way to represent and process a list is to use an array. You can define a list as an ADT as follows:

```
typeName
    listType
domain
    Every element of the type listType is a set
    of, say, 1000 numbers.
operations
    Check to see whether the list is empty.
    Check to see whether the list is full.
    Search the list for a given item.
    Delete an item from the list.
    Insert an item in the list.
    Sort the list.
```

```
Destroy the list.
Print the list.
```

The next obvious question is how to implement an ADT in a program. To implement an ADT, you must represent the data and write algorithms to perform the necessary operations.

The previous section used classes to group data and functions together. Furthermore, our definition of a class consisted only of the specifications of the operations; functions to implement the operations were written separately. Therefore, you see that classes are a convenient way to implement an ADT. In fact, in C++ classes were specifically designed to handle an ADT.

The following class defines the list as an ADT. (See also Figure 1-11.) To be specific, suppose that the list is a set of elements of the type int.

```
class intListType
{
public:
    bool isEmpty();
        //Function to determine whether the list is empty.
        //Precondition: The list must exist.
        //Postcondition: Returns true if the list is empty,
        //               false otherwise.

    bool isFull();
        //Function to determine whether the list is full.
        //Precondition: The list must exist.
        //Postcondition: Returns true if the list is full,
        //               false otherwise.

    int search(int searchItem);
        //Function to determine whether searchItem is
        //in the list.
        //Postcondition: If searchItem is in the list,
        //               returns its index, that is,
        //               its position in the list;
        //               otherwise, it returns -1.

    void insert(int newItem);
        //Function to insert newItem in the list.
        //Precondition: The list must exist and must not be
        //              full.
        //Postcondition: newItem is inserted in the list and
        //               the length is incremented by one.

    void remove(int removeItem);
        //Function to delete removeItem from the list.
        //Precondition: The list must exist and must not be
        //              empty.
```

```
    //Postcondition: If found, removeItem is deleted
    //                from the list and the length is
    //                decremented by one; otherwise,
    //                an appropriate message is printed.

void destroy();
    //Function to remove all the elements of the list.
    //Precondition: The list must exist.
    //Postcondition: The length is set to 0.

void printList();
    //Function to output the elements of the list.
    //Precondition: The list must exist.
    //Postcondition: The elements of the list are
    //                printed on the standard output
    //                device.

intListType();
    //default constructor
    //Postcondition: length = 0

private:
    int list[1000];
    int length;
};
```

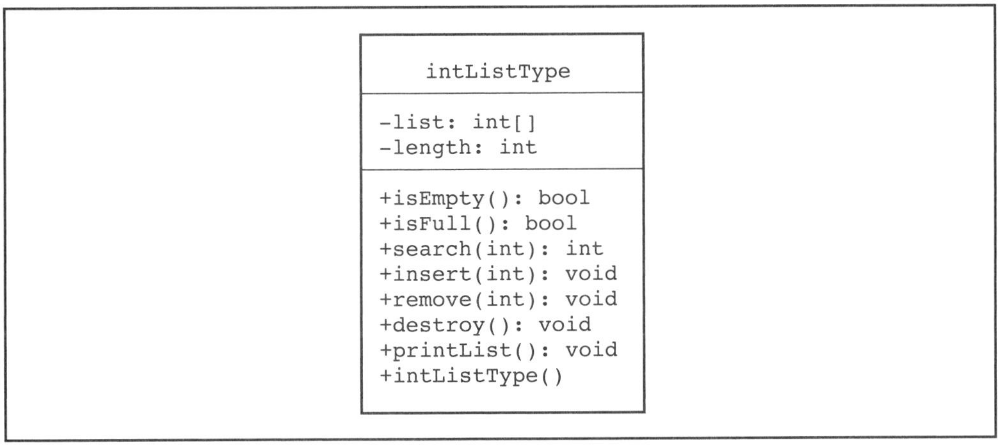

Figure 1-11   UML diagram of the class `intListType`

Information Hiding

The previous section defined the **class clockType** to implement the time of day in a program. Note that the data members are declared **private**. Moreover, to use the **class clockType** in a program, the user should be concerned only with what each function does; not how it does it. That is, we must hide the implementation details of each function. In C++, information hiding is achieved by declaring the data members **private** and also hiding the implementation details of the member functions.

The definition of the **class clockType** contains only the data members, function prototypes, and a description of what each function does. To implement information hiding, we must separate the definition of the class from the definitions of the member functions and provide the user *only* the definition of the class. To be able to use the functions, the user is provided with the compiled code of the functions.

This section discusses how to implement information hiding. For illustration purposes, we will use the **class clockType**.

To implement **clockType** in a program, the user must declare objects of the type **clockType**, and know which operations are allowed and what the operations do. So the user must have access to the specification details. Because the user is not concerned with the implementation details, you must put those details in a separate file, called an **implementation file**. Also, because the specification details can be too long, you must free the user from having to include them directly in the program. However, the user must be able to look at the specification details so that he or she can correctly call the functions, and so forth. You must therefore put the specification details in a separate file. The file that contains the specification details is called the **header file** (or **interface file**).

The implementation file contains the definitions of the functions to implement the operations of an object. This file contains, among other things (such as the preprocessor directives), the C++ statements. Because a C++ program can have only one function, **main**, the implementation file does not contain the function **main**. Only the user program contains the function **main**. Because the implementation file does not contain the function **main**, you cannot produce the executable code from this file. In fact, you produce what is called the object code from the implementation file. The user then links the object code produced by the implementation file with the object code of the program that uses the class to create the final executable code.

Finally, the header file has the extension **h**, whereas the implementation file has the extension **cpp**. Suppose the specification details of the **class clockType** are in a file called **clockType**. The complete name of the header file should then be **clockType.h**. If the implementation details of the **class clockType** are in a file—say, **clockTypeImp**—the name of this file must be **clockTypeImp.cpp**.

The file **clockTypeImp.cpp** contains only the definitions of the functions, not the definition of the class. Therefore, to resolve the problem of an undeclared identifier (such as the function names and variables names), you include the header file **clockType.h** in the file clockTypeImp.cpp with the help of the include statement. The following include statement is required by any program that uses the **class clockType**, as well as by the implementation file that defines the operations for the **class clockType**:

```
#include "clockType.h"
```

Note that the header file clockType.h is enclosed in double quotation marks, not angular brackets. The header file clockType.h is called the **user–defined header file**. All user-defined header files are enclosed in double quotation marks, whereas the system-provided header files (such as iostream) are enclosed between angular brackets.

Following are the specification and implementation files for the **class clockType**:

```
//clockType.h, the specification file for the class clockType

class clockType
{
public:
    void setTime(int hours, int minutes, int seconds);
        //Function to set the time.
        //The time is set according to the parameters.
        //Postcondition: hr = hours; min = minutes;
        //                sec = seconds
        //    The function checks whether the values of
        //    hours, minutes, and seconds are valid. If a
        //    value is invalid, the default value 0 is
        //    assigned.

    void getTime(int& hours, int& minutes, int& seconds)
        //Function to return the time.
        //Postcondition: hours = hr; minutes = min;
        //                seconds = sec

    void printTime() const;
        //Function to print the time.
        //Postcondition: The time is printed in the form
        //                hh:mm:ss.

    void incrementSeconds();
        //Function to increment the time by one second.
        //Postcondition: The time is incremented by one
        //                second.
        //    If the before-increment time is 23:59:59, the
        //    time is reset to 00:00:00.

    void incrementMinutes();
        //Function to increment the time by one minute.
        //Postcondition: The time is incremented by one
        //                minute.
```

```
        //    If the before-increment time is 23:59:53,
        //    the time is reset to 00:00:53.

    void incrementHours();
        //Function to increment the time by one hour.
        //Postcondition: The time is incremented by one
        //               hour.
        //    If the before-increment time is 23:45:53, the
        //    time is reset to 00:45:53.

    bool equalTime(const clockType& otherClock) const;
        //Function to compare the two times.
        //Postcondition: Returns true if this time is
        //               equal to otherClock; otherwise,
        //               returns false.

    clockType(int hours, int minutes, int seconds);
        //constructor with parameters
        //The time is set according to the parameters.
        //Postcondition: hr = hours; min = minutes;
        //               sec = seconds
        //    The constructor checks whether the values of
        //    hours, minutes, and seconds are valid. If a
        //    value is invalid, the default value 0 is
        //    assigned.

    clockType();
        //default constructor
        //The time is set to the default values.
        //Postcondition: hr = 0; min = 0; sec = 0

private:
    int hr;  //store the hours
    int min; //store the minutes
    int sec; //store the seconds
};


//clockTypeImp.cpp, the implementation file
#include <iostream>
#include "clockType.h"

using namespace std;
  .
  .
  .
//The definitions of the member functions of clockType go here.
  .
  .
  .
```

Next, we describe the user file containing the program that uses the **class clockType**.

```
//testClock.cpp

//The user program that uses the class clockType

#include <iostream>
#include "clockType.h"
using namespace std;
    .
    .
    .
//Place the definitions of the function main and the other
//user-defined functions here.
    .
    .
    .
```

Example 1-6 further illustrates how classes are designed and implemented. The **class personType**, designed in Example 1-6, is very useful; we will use this class in subsequent chapters.

Example 1-6

The most common attributes of a person are the person's first name and last name. The typical operations on a person's name are to set the name and print the name. The following statements define the **class personType** with these properties. (See also Figure 1-12.)

```
class personType
{
public:
    void print() const;
        //Function to output the first name and last name
        //in the form firstName lastName.

    void setName(string first, string last);
        //Function to set firstName and lastName according
        //to the parameters.
        //Postcondition: firstName = first; lastName = last

    void getName(string& first, string& last);
        //Function to return firstName and lastName via the
        //parameters.
        //Postcondition: first = firstName; last = lastName

    personType(string first = "", string last = "");
        //constructor
        //Sets firstName and lastName according to the
        //parameters.
        //The default values of the parameters are empty
        //strings.
        //Postcondition: firstName = first; lastName = last
```

```
private:
    string firstName; //stores the first name
    string lastName;  //stores the last name
};
```

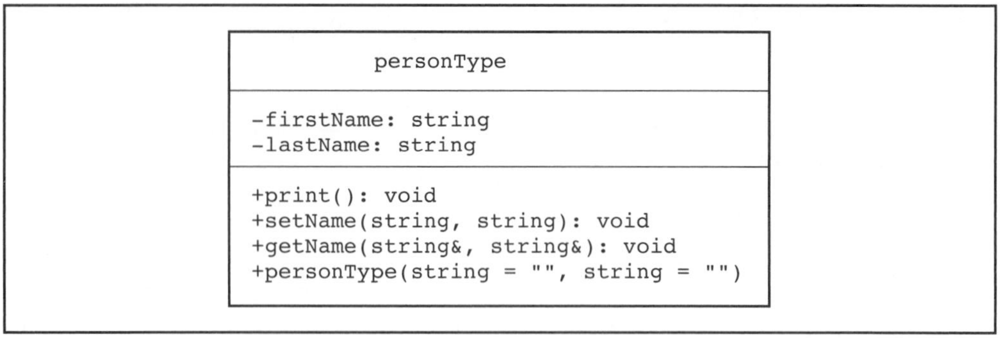

```
                    personType
        -firstName: string
        -lastName: string

        +print(): void
        +setName(string, string): void
        +getName(string&, string&): void
        +personType(string = "", string = "")
```

Figure 1-12   UML diagram of the `class personType`

We now give the definitions of the function members of the **class personType**.

```
void personType::print() const
{
      cout<<firstName<<" "<<lastName;
}

void personType::setName(string first, string last)
{
      firstName = first;
      lastName = last;
}

void personType::getName(string& first, string& last)
{
      first = firstName;
      last = lastName;
}

//constructor
personType::personType(string first, string last)

{
      firstName = first;
      lastName = last;
}
```

PROGRAMMING EXAMPLE: CANDY MACHINE

A common place to buy candy is from a candy machine. A new candy machine is bought for the gym, but it is not working properly. The machine sells candies, chips, gum, and cookies. You have been asked to write a program for this candy machine so that it can be put into operation.

The program should do the following:

1. Show the customer the different products sold by the candy machine.
2. Let the customer make the selection.
3. Show the customer the cost of the item selected.
4. Accept money from the customer.
5. Release the item.

Input The item selection and the cost of the item.

Output The selected item.

Problem Analysis and Algorithm Design

A candy machine has two main components: a built-in cash register, and several dispensers to hold and release the products.

Cash Register

Let us first discuss the properties of a cash register. The register has some cash in it, and it accepts the amount from the customer. If the amount entered is more than the cost of the item, then—if possible—it returns the change. For simplicity, assume that the user enters the exact amount for the product. The cash register should also be able to show to the candy machine's owner the amount of money in the register at any given time. The following class defines the properties of a cash register. (See also Figure 1-13.)

```
class cashRegister
{
public:
    int currentBalance();
        //Function to show the current amount in the cash
        //register.
        //Postcondition: The value of cashOnHand is returned.

    void acceptAmount(int amountIn);
        //Function to receive the amount deposited by
        //the customer and update the amount in the register.
        //Postcondition: cashOnHand = cashOnHand + amountIn
```

```
        cashRegister(int cashIn = 500);
            //Constructor to set the cash in the register to a
            //specific amount.
            //Postcondition: cashOnHand = cashIn
            //  If no value is specified when the object is
            //  declared, the default value assigned to cashOnHand
            //  is 500.

private:
        int cashOnHand;         //variable to store the cash
                                //in the register
};
```

cashRegister
–cashOnHand: int
+currentBalance(): int +acceptAmount(int): void +cashRegister(int = 500)

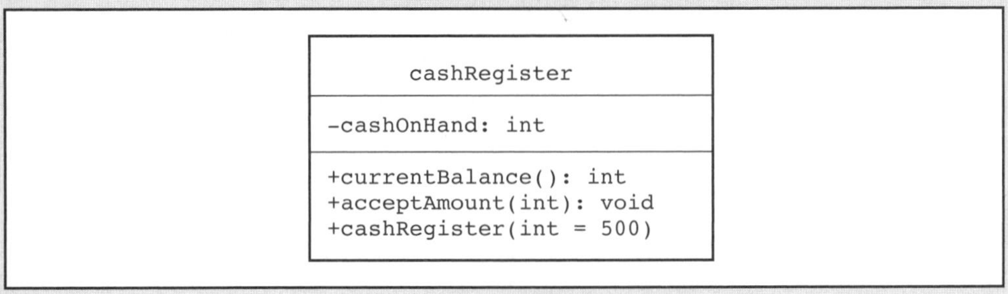

Figure 1-13   UML diagram of the class `cashRegister`

Next, we give the definitions of the functions to implement the operations of the **class cashRegister**. The definitions of these functions are very simple and easy to follow.

The function **currentBalance** shows the current amount in the cash register. It returns the value of the **private** data member **cashOnHand**. So its definition is

```
int cashRegister::currentBalance()
{
        return cashOnHand;
}
```

The function **acceptAmount** accepts the amount entered by the customer. It updates the cash in the register by adding the amount entered by the customer to the previous amount in the cash register. Essentially, the definition of this function is

```
void cashRegister::acceptAmount(int amountIn)
{
        cashOnHand += amountIn;
}
```

In the definition of the **class cashRegister**, the constructor is declared with a default value. Therefore, if the user does not specify a value when the object is declared, the default value is used to initialize the data member `cashOnHand`. Because we have specified the default value for the constructor parameter in the definition of the class, in the definition of the constructor we do not specify the default value in the heading. The definition of the constructor is as follows:

```
cashRegister::cashRegister(int cashIn)
{
      if(cashIn >= 0)
         cashOnHand = cashIn;
      else
         cashOnHand = 500;
}
```

Note that the definition of the constructor checks for valid values of the parameter `cashIn`. If the value of `cashIn` is less than 0, the value assigned to the data member `cashOnHand` is 500.

Dispenser

The dispenser releases the selected item if it is not empty. It should also show the number of items in the dispenser and the cost of the item. The following class defines the properties of a dispenser. Let us call it the **class dispenserType**. (See also Figure 1-14.)

```
class dispenserType
{
public:
    int count();
       //Function to show the number of items in the machine.
       //Postcondition: The value of the data member
       //                 numberOfItems is returned.

    int productCost();
       //Function to show the cost of the item.
       //The value of the data member cost is returned.
       //Postcondition: The value of cost is returned.

    void makeSale();
       //Function to reduce the number of items by 1.
       //Postcondition: numberOfItems--

    dispenserType(int setNoOfItems = 50, int setCost = 50);
       //Constructor to set the cost and number of items in the
       //dispenser specified by the user.
       //Postcondition: numberOfItems = setNoOfItems;
       //                 cost = setCost
       //   If no value is specified for a parameter, then its
       //   default value is assigned to the corresponding
       //   data member.
```

```
private:
    int numberOfItems;      //variable to store the number of
                            //items in the dispenser
    int cost;   //variable to store the cost of an item
};
```

```
                        dispenserType

        -numberOfItems: int
        -cost: int

        +count(): int
        +productCost(): int
        +makeSale(): void
        +dispenserType(int = 50, int = 50)
```

Figure 1-14   14 UML diagram of the `class dispenserType`

Because the candy machine sells four types of items, you declare four objects of the type
`dispenserType`. For example, the statement

`dispenserType chips(100,65);`

declares `chips` to be an object of the type `dispenserType`, and sets the number of chip
bags in the dispenser to 100 and the cost of each chip bag to 65 cents. (See Figure 1-15.)

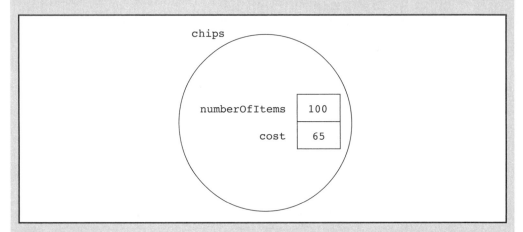

Figure 1-15   Object `chips`

Next, we discuss the definitions of the functions to implement the operations of the `class dispenserType`.

The function `count` returns the number of items of a particular product. Because the number of items currently in the dispenser is stored in the `private` data member `numberOfItems`, it returns the value of the `private` data member `numberOfItems`. The definition of this function is

```
int dispenserType::count()
{
    return numberOfItems;
}
```

The function `productCost` returns the cost of a product. Because the cost of a product is stored in the `private` data member `cost`, it returns the value of the `private` data member `cost`. The definition of this function is

```
int dispenserType::productCost()
{
    return cost;
}
```

When a product is sold, the number of items in that dispenser is reduced by 1. Therefore, the function `makeSale` reduces the number of items in the dispenser by 1. That is, it decrements the value of the `private` data member `numberOfItems` by 1. The definition of this function is

```
void dispenserType::makeSale()
{
    numberOfItems--;
}
```

The definition of the constructor checks for the valid values of the parameters. If these values are less than 0, the default values are assigned to the data members. The definition of the constructor is

```
    //constructor
dispenserType::dispenserType(int setNoOfItems, int setCost)
{
    if(setNoOfItems >= 0)
       numberOfItems = setNoOfItems;
    else
       numberOfItems = 50;

    if(setCost >= 0)
       cost = setCost;
    else
       cost = 50;
}
```

Main Program

When the program executes, it must do the following:

1. Show the different products sold by the candy machine.
2. Show how to select a particular product.
3. Show how to terminate the program.

Furthermore, these instructions must be displayed after processing each selection (except exiting the program), so that the user need not remember what to do if he or she wants to buy two or more items. Once the user makes the appropriate selection, the candy machine must act accordingly. If the user opts to buy a product and if that product is available, the candy machine should show the cost of the product and ask the user to deposit the money. If the money deposited is at least the cost of the item, the candy machine should sell the item and display an appropriate message.

This discussion translates into the following algorithm:

1. Show the selection to the customer.
2. Get the selection.
3. If the selection is valid and the dispenser corresponding to the selection is not empty, sell the product.

We divide this program into three functions—showSelection, sellProduct, and main.

Function showSelection   This function displays the necessary information to help the user select and buy a product. Essentially, it contains the following output statements. (We assume that the candy machine sells four types of products.)

```
*** Welcome to Shelly's Candy Shop ***"
To select an item, enter
1 for Candy
2 for Chips
3 for Gum
4 for Cookies
9 to exit
```

The definition of the function showSelection is

```
void showSelection()
{
    cout<<"*** Welcome to Shelly's Candy Shop ***"<<endl;
    cout<<"To select an item, enter"<<endl;
    cout<<"1 for Candy"<<endl;
    cout<<"2 for Chips"<<endl;
    cout<<"3 for Gum"<<endl;
    cout<<"4 for Cookies"<<endl;
    cout<<"9 to exit"<<endl;
}//end showSelection
```

Function sellProduct This function attempts to sell the product selected by the customer. Therefore, it must have access to the dispenser holding the product. The first thing that this function does is check whether the dispenser holding the product is empty. If the dispenser is empty, the function informs the customer that this product is sold out. If the dispenser is nonempty, it tells the user to deposit the necessary amount to buy the product.

If the user does not deposit enough money to buy the product, **sellProduct** tells the user how much additional money must be deposited. If the user fails to deposit enough money, in two tries (see Programming Exercise 9), to buy the product, the function simply returns the money. If the money deposited by the user is sufficient, it accepts the money and sells the product. Selling the product means to decrement the number of items in the dispenser by 1, and update the money in the cash register by adding the cost of the product. (Because this program does not return the extra money deposited by the customer, the cash register is updated by adding the money entered by the user.)

From this discussion, it is clear that the **sellProduct** function must have access to both the dispenser holding the product (to decrement the number of items in the dispenser by 1 and to show the cost of the item) and the cash register (to update the cash). Therefore, this function has two parameters: one corresponding to the dispenser, and the other corresponding to the cash register. Furthermore, both parameters must be referenced.

In pseudocode, the algorithm for this function is:

    a. If the dispenser is nonempty:

        i.   Show and prompt the customer to enter the cost of the item.

        ii. Get the amount entered by the customer.

        iii. If the amount entered by the customer is less than the cost of the product:

             1. Show and prompt the customer to enter the additional amount.

             2. Calculate the total amount entered by the customer.

        iv. If the amount entered by the customer is at least the cost of the product:

             1. Update the amount in the cash register.

             2. Sell the product—that is, decrement the number of items in the dispenser by 1.

             3. Display an appropriate message.

        v. If the amount entered by the user is less than the cost of the item, return the amount.

    b. If the dispenser is empty, tell the user that this product is sold out.

This definition of the function **sellProduct** is

```
void sellProduct(dispenserType& product, cashRegister& pCounter)
{
    int amount;  //variable to hold the amount entered
    int amount2; //variable to hold the extra amount needed
```

```
if(product.count() > 0)                              //Step a
{
  cout<<"Please deposit "<<product.productCost()
      <<" cents"<<endl;                              //Step a.i
  cin>>amount;                                       //Step a.ii

  if(amount < product.productCost())                 //Step a.iii
  {
    cout<<"Please deposit another "
        <<product.productCost() - amount             //Step a.iii.1
        <<" cents"<<endl;
    cin>>amount2;                                     //Step a.iii.2
    amount = amount + amount2;                        //Step a.iii.3
  }

  if(amount >= product.productCost())                //Step a.iv
  {
      pCounter.acceptAmount(amount);                 //Step a.iv.1
      product.makeSale();                            //Step a.iv.2
      cout<<"Collect your item at the bottom"
          <<" and enjoy."<<endl;                     //Step a.iv.3
  }
  else
    cout<<"The amount is not enough. "
        <<"Collect what you deposited."<<endl; //Step a.v
    cout<<"*-*-*-*-*-*-*-*-*-*-*-*-*-*-*-*-*-*"
        <<endl<<endl;
}
else
  cout<<"Sorry this item is sold out."<<endl;     //Step b
}//end sellProduct
```

Now that the functions `showSelection` and `sellProduct` have been described, the function `main` is described next.

Function `main` The algorithm for the function `main` is as follows:

1. Create the cash register—that is, declare a variable of the type `cashRegister`.
2. Create four dispensers—that is, declare four objects of the type `dispenserType` and initialize these objects. For example, the statement

   ```
   dispenserType candy(100, 50);
   ```

   creates a dispenser object, `candy`, to hold the candies. The number of items in the dispenser is 100, and the cost of an item is 50 cents.
3. Declare additional variables as necessary.
4. Show the selection; call the function `showSelection`.
5. Get the selection.

6. While not done (a selection of 9 exits the program):

   a. Sell the product; call the function sellProduct.

   b. Show the selection; call the function showSelection.

   c. Get the selection.

The definition of the function main is as follows:

```cpp
int main()
{
    cashRegister counter;                       //Step 1
    dispenserType candy(100,50);                //Step 2
    dispenserType chips(100,65);                //Step 2
    dispenserType gum(75,45);                   //Step 2
    dispenserType cookies(100,85);              //Step 2

    int choice;                                 //Step 3

    showSelection();                            //Step 4
    cin>>choice;                                //Step 5

    while(choice != 9)                          //Step 6
    {
        switch(choice)                          //Step 6a
        {
        case 1: sellProduct(candy, counter);
                break;
        case 2: sellProduct(chips, counter);
                break;
        case 3: sellProduct(gum, counter);
                break;
        case 4: sellProduct(cookies, counter);
                break;
        default: cout<<"Bad Selection"<<endl;
        }//end switch

        showSelection();                        //Step 6b
        cin>>choice;                            //Step 6c
    }//end while

    return 0;
}//end main
```

Program Listing

```cpp
//Main Program
#include <iostream>
```

```
#include "cashRegister.h"

#include "dispenserType.h"

using namespace std;

void showSelection();
void sellProduct(dispenserType& product, cashRegister& pCounter);


//Place the definition of the function main here.

//Place the definition of the function showSelection here.

//Place the definition of the function sellProduct here.
```

Sample Run: In this sample run, the user input is shaded.

```
*** Welcome to Shelly's Candy Shop ***
To select an item, enter
1 for Candy
2 for Chips
3 for Gum
4 for Cookies
9 to exit
1
Please deposit 50 cents
50
Collect your item at the bottom and enjoy
*-*-*-*-*-*-*-*-*-*-*-*-*-*-*-*-*-*-*

*** Welcome to Shelly's Candy Shop ***
To select an item, enter
1 for Candy
2 for Chips
3 for Gum
4 for Cookies
9 to exit
3
Please deposit 45 cents
45
Collect your item at the bottom and enjoy
*-*-*-*-*-*-*-*-*-*-*-*-*-*-*-*-*-*-*

*** Welcome to Shelly's Candy Shop ***
To select an item, enter
1 for Candy
2 for Chips
3 for Gum
```

```
4 for Cookies
9 to exit
9
```

IDENTIFYING CLASSES, OBJECTS, AND OPERATIONS

The hardest part of OOD is to identify the classes and objects. This section describes a common and simple technique to identify classes and objects.

Begin with a description of the problem and then identify all of the nouns and verbs. From the list of nouns you choose your classes, and from the list of verbs you choose your operations.

For example, suppose that you want to write a program that calculates and prints the volume and surface area of a cylinder. You can state this problem as follows:

Write a **program** to *input* the **dimensions** of a **cylinder** and *calculate* and *print* the **surface area** and **volume**.

In this statement, the nouns are bold and the verbs are italic. From the list of nouns—**program**, **dimensions**, **cylinder**, **surface area**, and **volume**—you can easily visualize **cylinder** to be a class—say, `cylinderType`—from which you can create many cylinder objects of various dimensions. The nouns **dimensions**, **surface area**, and **volume** are characteristics of a **cylinder**, and therefore can hardly be considered classes.

After you identify a class, the next step is to determine three pieces of information:

- Operations that an object of that class type can perform
- Operations that can be performed on an object of that class type
- Information that an object of that class type must maintain

From the list of verbs identified in the problem description, choose a list of possible operations that an object of that class can perform, or has performed, on itself. For example, from the list of verbs for the cylinder problem description—*write*, *input*, *calculate*, and *print*—the possible operations for a cylinder object are *input*, *calculate*, and *print*.

For the **class** `cylinderType`, the dimensions represent the data. The **center** of the base, **radius** of the base, and **height** of the cylinder are the characteristics of the dimensions. You can input data to the object either by a constructor or by a function.

The verb *calculate* applies to determining the volume and the surface area. From this you can deduce the operations: `cylinderVolume` and `cylinderSurfaceArea`. Similarly, the verb *print* applies to the display of the volume and the surface area on an output device.

Identifying classes via the nouns and verbs from the descriptions of the problem is not the only technique possible. There are several other OOD techniques used in the literature. However, this technique is sufficient for the programming exercises in this book.

QUICK REVIEW

1. Software are programs run by the computer.
2. A program goes through many phases from the time it is first conceived until the time it is retired; this is called the life cycle of the program.
3. The three fundamental stages a program goes through are development, use, and maintenance.
4. The new program is created in the software development stage.
5. In the software maintenance process, the program is modified to fix the (identified) problems and/or to enhance it.
6. A program is retired if no new version of the program will be released.
7. The software development phases are: analysis, design, implementation, and testing and debugging.
8. During the design phase, algorithm(s) are designed to solve the problem.
9. An algorithm is a step-by-step problem-solving process in which a solution is arrived at in a finite amount of time.
10. Two well-known design techniques are structured design and object-oriented design.
11. In structured design, a problem is divided into smaller subproblems. Each subproblem is solved, and the solutions of all the subproblems are then combined to solve the problem.
12. In object-oriented design (OOD), a program is a collection of interacting objects.
13. An object consists of data and operations on the data.
14. The three basic principles of OOD are encapsulation, inheritance, and polymorphism.
15. In the implementation phase, you write and compile programming code to implement the classes and functions that were discovered in the design phase.
16. A precondition is a statement specifying the condition(s) that must be true before the function is called.
17. A postcondition is a statement specifying what is true after the function call is completed.
18. During the testing phase, the program is tested for its correctness, that is, making sure that the program does what it is supposed to do.
19. Debugging is the process of finding and fixing any errors, if they exist.
20. To find any problems in a program, it is run through a series of test cases.
21. A test case consists of a set of inputs, user actions, or other initial conditions, and the expected output.

22. There are two types of testing—black-box testing and white-box testing.

23. While analyzing a particular algorithm, you usually count the number of operations performed by the algorithm.

24. Let f be a function of n. The term "asymptotic" refers to the study of the function f as n becomes larger and larger without bound.

25. A class is a collection of a fixed number of components.

26. Components of a class are called the members of the class.

27. Members of a class are accessed by name.

28. In C++, `class` is a reserved word.

29. Members of a class are classified into one of three categories: `private`, `protected`, and `public`.

30. The `private` members of a class are not accessible outside the class.

31. The `public` members of a class are accessible outside the class.

32. By default, all members of a class are `private`.

33. The `private` members are declared using the member access specifier `private`.

34. The `public` members are declared using the member access specifier `public`.

35. A member of a class can be a function or a variable (that is, data).

36. If any member of a class is a function, you usually use the function prototype to declare it.

37. If any member of a class is a variable, it is declared like any other variable.

38. In the definition of the class, you cannot initialize a variable when you declare it.

39. In the Unified Modeling language (UML) diagram of a class, the top box contains the name of the class. The middle box contains the data members and their data types. The last box contains the member function name, parameter list, and the return type of the function. A plus (+) sign in front of a member indicates that this member is a `public` member; a minus (–) sign indicates that this is a `private` member. The symbol (#) before the member name indicates that the member is a `protected` member.

40. In C++, a class is a definition. No memory is allocated; memory is allocated for the class variables when you declare them.

41. In C++, class variables are called class objects or simply objects.

42. A class member is accessed using the class variable name, followed by the dot operator (`.`), followed by the member name.

43. The only built-in operations on classes are the assignment and member selection.

44. As parameters to functions, classes can be passed either by value or by reference.

45. A function can return a value of the type `class`.

46. Constructors guarantee that the data members are initialized when an object is declared.

47. The name of a constructor is the same as the name of the class.

48. A class can have more than one constructor.

49. A constructor without parameters is called the default constructor.

50. A constructor automatically executes when a class object enters its scope.

51. Destructors automatically execute when a class object goes out of scope.

52. A class can have only one destructor and the destructor has no parameters.

53. The name of a destructor is a tilde (~), followed by the class name (no spaces in between).

54. Constructors and destructors are functions without any type; they are neither value-returning nor **void**. As a result, they cannot be called like other functions.

55. A data type that specifies the logical properties without the implementation details is called an abstract data type (ADT).

56. To implement an ADT, you must represent the data and write related algorithms to implement the operations.

57. An easy way to identify classes, objects, and operations is to describe the problem in English and then identify all of the nouns and verbs. Choose your classes (objects) from the list of nouns and operations from the list of verbs.

EXERCISES

1. Mark the following statements as true or false.

   a. The life cycle of software refers to the phases from the point the software was conceived until it is retired.

   b. The three fundamental stages of software are development, use, and discard.

   c. The expression $4n + 2n^2 + 5$ is $O(n)$.

   d. The data members of a class must be of the same type.

   e. The function members of a class must be `public`.

   f. A class can have more than one constructor.

   g. A class can have more than one destructor.

   h. Both constructors and destructors can have parameters.

2. Consider the following function prototype, which returns the square root of a real number:

   ```
   double sqrt(double x);
   ```

   What should be the preconditions and postconditions for this function?

3. Each of the following expressions represents the number of operations for certain algorithms. What is the order of each of these expressions?

   a. $n^2 + 6n + 4$

   b. $5n^3 + 2n + 8$

   c. $(n^2 + 1)(3n + 5)$

   d. $5(6n + 4)$

4. Consider the following function:

```cpp
void funcExercise4(int x, int y)
{
    int z;

    z = x + y;
    x = y;
    y = z;
    z = x;
    cout<<"x = "<<x<<", y = "<<y<<", z = "<<z<<endl;
}
```

   Find the exact number of operations executed by the function `funcExercise4`.

5. Consider the following function:

```cpp
int funcExercise5(int list[], int size)
{
    int sum = 0;

    for(int index = 0; index < size; index++)
        sum = sum + list[index];

    return sum;
}
```

   a. Find the number of operations executed by the function `funcExercise5` if the value of `size` is 10.

   b. Find the number of operations executed by the function `funcExercise5` if the value of `size` is n.

   c. What is the order of the function `funcExercise5`?

6. Consider the following function prototype:

```cpp
int funcExercise6(int x);
```

   The function `funcExercise6` returns the value as follows: if $0 <= x <= 50$, it returns `2x`; if $-50 <= x < 0$, it returns `x`^{2}; otherwise, it returns -999. What are the reasonable boundary values for the function `funcExercise6`?

7. What statement turns off all the `assert` statements in a program?

8. Write a function that uses a loop to find the sum of the squares of all integers between 1 and n. What is the order of your function?

9. What is black-box testing?

10. What is white-box testing?

11. Find the syntax errors in the definitions of the following classes:

a.

```
class AA
{
public:
        void print();
        int sum();
        AA();
        int AA(int, int);
private:
        int x ;
        int y ;
};
```

b.

```
class BB
{
        int one ;
        int two;
public:
        bool equal();
        print();
        BB(int, int);
}
```

c.

```
class CC
{
public:
        void set(int, int);
        void print();
        CC();
        CC(int, int);
        bool CC(int, int);
private:
        int u;
        int v;
};
```

12. Consider the following declarations:

```
class xClass
{
public:
        void func();
        void print() const;
```

```
        xClass ();
        xClass (int, double);
private:
        int u;
        double w;
};
```

```
xClass x;
```

a. How many members does **class xClass** have?

b. How many **private** members does **class xClass** have?

c. How many constructors does **class xClass** have?

d. Write the definition of the member function **func** so that u is set to **10** and w is set to **15.3**.

e. Write the definition of the member function **print** that prints the contents of u and w.

f. Write the definition of the default constructor of the **class xClass** so that the **private** data members are initialized to 0.

g. Write a C++ statement that prints the values of the data members of the object x.

h. Write a C++ statement that declares an object t of the type **xClass**, and initializes the data members of t to **20** and **35.0**, respectively.

13. Consider the definition of the following class:

```
class CC
{
public:
        CC();                   //Line 1
        CC(int);                //Line 2
        CC(int, int)            //Line 3
        CC(double, int)         //Line 4
private:
        int u;
        double v;
};
```

a. Give the line number containing the constructor that is executed in each of the following declarations:

  (i) **CC one;**

  (ii) **CC two(5, 6);**

  (iii) **CC three(3.5, 8);**

b. Write the definition of the constructor in Line 1 so that the **private** data members are initialized to 0.

c. Write the definition of the constructor in Line 2 so that the **private** data member u is initialized according to the value of the parameter, and the **private** data member **v** is initialized to 0.

d. Write the definition of the constructors in Lines 3 and 4 so that the **private** data members are initialized according to the values of the parameters.

14. Consider the definition of the following class:

```
class testClass
{
public:
   int sum();
      //Postcondition: Returns the sum of the
      //                private data members.
   void print() const;
      //Prints the values of the private data
      //members.
   testClass();
      //default constructor
      //Postcondition: x = 0; y = 0
   testClass(int a, int b);
      //constructor with parameters
      //Initializes the private data members to the
      //values specified by the parameters.
      //Postcondition: x = a; y = b
private:
   int x;
   int y;
};
```

a. Write the definitions of the member functions as described in the definition of the class testClass.

b. Write a test program to test the various operations of the class testClass.

PROGRAMMING EXERCISES

1. Write a program to test the various operations of the **class clockType**.

2. Write a program that converts a number entered in Roman numerals to decimal. Your program should consist of a class, say **romanType**. An object of the type **romanType** should do the following:

   a. Store the number as a Roman numeral.

   b. Convert and store the number into decimal.

c. Print the number as a Roman numeral or decimal number as requested by the user. The decimal values of the Roman numerals are:

```
M    1000
D     500
C     100
L      50
X      10
V       5
I       1
```

d. Test your program using the following Roman numerals: MCXIV, CCCLIX, MDCLXVI.

3. Design and implement a **class dayType** that implements the day of the week in a program. The **class dayType** should store the day, such as **Sun** for Sunday. The program should be able to perform the following operations on an object of the type **dayType**:

a. Set the day.

b. Print the day.

c. Return the day.

d. Return the next day.

e. Return the previous day.

f. Update the day, stored in a **dayType** object, by adding certain days to it. For example, if the day is Monday and you add 4 days, the updated day is Friday. Similarly, if the day is Tuesday and you add 13 days, the updated day is Monday.

g. Add the appropriate constructors.

4. Write the definitions of the functions to implement the operations for the **class dayType** as defined in Programming Exercise 3. Also, write a program to test the various operations of the **class dayType**.

5. Example 1-6 defined a **class personType** to store the name of a person. The member functions that you included merely print and set a person's name. Redefine the **class personType** so that you can also:

a. Set the last name only.

b. Set the first name only.

c. Store and set the middle name.

d. Check whether a given last name is the same as the last name of this person.

e. Check whether a given first name is the same as the first name of this person.

f. Write the definitions of the member functions to implement the operations for this class.

6.

a. Some of the characteristics of a book are the title, author(s), publisher, ISBN, price, and year of publication. Design the **class bookType** that defines the book as an ADT.

Each object of the **class bookType** can hold the following information about a book: title, up to four authors, publisher, ISBN, price, and number of copies in stock. To keep track of the number of authors, add another data member.

Include the member functions to perform the various operations on the objects of **bookType**. For example, the typical operations that can be performed on the title are to show the title, set the title, and check whether a title is the same as the actual title of the book. Similarly, the typical operations that can be performed on the number of copies in stock are to show the number of copies in stock, set the number of copies in stock, update the number of copies in stock, and return the number of copies in stock. Add similar operations for the publisher, ISBN, book price, and authors. Add the appropriate constructors and a destructor (if one is needed).

b. Write the definitions of the member functions of the **class bookType**.

c. Write a program that uses the **class bookType** and tests the various operations on the objects of **class bookType**. Declare an array of 100 components of the type **bookType**. Some of the operations that you should perform are to search for a book by its title, search by ISBN, and update the number of copies in stock.

7. In this exercise, you will design a **class memberType**.

a. Each object of **memberType** can hold the name of a person, member ID, number of books bought, and amount spent.

b. Include the member functions to perform the various operations on the objects of **memberType**—for example, modify, set, and show a person's name. Similarly, update, modify, and show the number of books bought and the amount spent.

c. Add the appropriate constructors and a destructor (if one is needed).

d. Write the definitions of the member functions of **memberType**.

8. Using the classes designed in Programming Exercises 6 and 7, write a program to simulate a bookstore. The bookstore has two types of customers: those who are members of the bookstore and those who buy books from the bookstore only occasionally. Each member has to pay a $10 annual membership fee and receives a 5% discount on each book bought.

For each member, the bookstore keeps track of the number of books bought and the total amount spent. For every eleventh book that a member buys, the bookstore takes the average of the total amount of the last 10 books bought, applies this amount as a discount, and then resets the total amount spent to 0.

Write a program that can process up to 1000 book titles and 500 members. Your program should contain a menu that gives the user different choices to effectively run the program; in other words, your program should be menu-driven.

9. The function **sellProduct** of the Programming Example: Candy Machine gives only two chances to the user to enter enough money to buy the product. Rewrite the definition of the function **sellProduct** so that it keeps prompting the user to enter the money as long as the user has not entered enough money to buy the product. Also, write a program to test your function.

2

OBJECT-ORIENTED DESIGN (OOD) AND C++

In this chapter, you will:

♦ Learn about inheritance

♦ Learn about derived and base classes

♦ Explore how to redefine the member functions of a base class

♦ Examine how the constructors of base and derived classes work

♦ Learn how to construct the header file of a derived class

♦ Explore three types of inheritance: `public`, `protected`, and `private`

♦ Learn about composition

♦ Become familiar with the three basic principles of object-oriented design

♦ Learn about overloading

♦ Become aware of the restrictions on operator overloading

♦ Examine the pointer `this`

♦ Learn about `friend` functions

♦ Explore the members and nonmembers of a class

♦ Discover how to overload various operators

♦ Learn about templates

♦ Explore how to construct function templates and class templates

---

Chapter 1 introduced classes, abstract data types (ADT), and ways to implement ADT in C++. By using classes, you can combine data and operations in a single unit. An object therefore becomes a self-contained entity. Operations can directly access the data, but the internal state of an object cannot be manipulated directly.

In addition to implementing ADT, classes have other features. For instance, you can create new classes from existing classes. This important feature encourages code reuse.

INHERITANCE

Suppose that you want to design a `class`, `partTimeEmployee`, to implement and process the characteristics of a part-time employee. The main features associated with a part-time employee are the name, pay rate, and number of hours worked. In Example 1-6 (in Chapter 1), we designed a class to implement a person's name. Every part-time employee is a person. Therefore, rather than design the `class partTimeEmployee` from scratch, we want to be able to extend the definition of the `class personType` (from Example 1-6) by adding additional members (data and/or functions).

Of course, we do not want to make the necessary changes directly to the `class personType`—that is, edit the `class personType` by adding or deleting members. In fact, we want to create the `class partTimeEmployee` without making any physical changes to the `class personType` by adding only the members that are necessary. For example, because the `class personType` already has data members to store the first name and last name, we will not include any such members in the `class partTimeEmployee`. In fact, these data members will be inherited from the `class personType`. (We will design such a `class` in Example 2-2.)

In Chapter 1, we extensively studied and designed the `class clockType` to implement the time of day in a program. The `class clockType` has three data members to store the hours, minutes, and seconds. In addition to hours, minutes, and seconds, certain applications might also require us to store the time zone. In this case, we would like to extend the definition of the `class clockType` and create a `class`, `extClockType`, to accommodate this new information. That is, we want to derive the `class extClockType` by adding a data member—say, `timeZone`—and the necessary function members to `clockType` to manipulate the time. In C++, the mechanism that allows us to accomplish this task is the principle of **inheritance**. Inheritance is an "is-a" relationship; for instance, "every employee is a person."

Inheritance lets us create new classes from existing classes. An existing class is called a **base class**; the new class that we create from an existing class is called the **derived class**. The derived class inherits the properties of the base class. Rather than create completely new classes from scratch, we can take advantage of inheritance and reduce software complexity.

Each derived class, in turn, becomes a base class for a future derived class. Inheritance can be either a single inheritance or a multiple inheritance. In a **single inheritance**, the derived class is derived from a single base class; in a **multiple inheritance**, the derived class is derived from more than one base class. This chapter concentrates on single inheritance.

Inheritance can be viewed as a treelike, or hierarchical, structure wherein a base class is shown with its derived classes. Consider the tree diagram in Figure 2-1, which shows the relationship between various types of shapes.

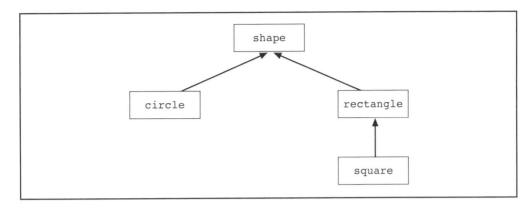

Figure 2-1   Inheritance hierarchy

In this diagram, `shape` is the base class. The `classes circle` and `rectangle` are derived from `shape`, and the `class square` is derived from `rectangle`. Every `circle` and every `rectangle` is a `shape`. Every `square` is a `rectangle`.

The general syntax to define a derived class is

```
class className: memberAccessSpecifier baseClassName
{
      member list
};
```

where `memberAccessSpecifier` is `public`, `protected`, or `private`. When no `memberAccessSpecifier` is specified, it is assumed to be a `private` inheritance. (We discuss `protected` inheritance later in this chapter.)

Keep in mind the following facts about the base and derived classes:

- The `private` members of the base class are `private` to the base class; hence, the members of the derived class cannot directly access them. When you write the definitions of the member functions of the derived class, you cannot directly access the `private` members of the base class.

- The `public` members of a base class can be inherited either as `public` members or as `private` members by the derived class. That is, the `public` members of the base class can become either `public` or `private` members of the derived class.

- The derived class can include additional data and/or function members.

- The derived class can redefine the `public` member functions of the base class. That is, in the derived class, you can have a function member with the same name, number, and types of parameters as a function in the base class. However, this redefinition applies only to the objects of the derived class, not to the objects of the base class.

- All data members of the base class are also data members of the derived class. Similarly, the member functions of the base class (unless redefined) are also the member functions of the derived class. (Remember the first bulleted item when accessing a member of the base class in the derived class.)

Example 2-1

Suppose that we have the **class shape**.

(a) The following statements specify that the **class circle** is derived from **shape**, and it is a **public** inheritance:

```
class circle: public shape
{
      .
      .
      .
};
```

(b) Consider the following definition of the **class circle**:

```
class circle: private shape
{
      .
      .
      .
};
```

These statements specify that the **class circle** is derived from the **class shape** and that it is a **private** inheritance. The **public** members of **shape** become **private** members of the **class circle**. So any object of the type **circle** cannot directly access these members. The preceding definition of **circle** is equivalent to

```
class circle: shape
{
      .
      .
      .
};
```

The next two sections describe two important issues related to inheritance. The first issue is the redefinition of the member functions of the base class in the derived class. While discussing this issue, we will also address how to access the **private** (data) members of the base class in the derived class. The second key inheritance issue is related to the constructor. The constructor of a derived class cannot *directly* access the **private** data members of the base class. Therefore, we need to ensure that the **private** data members that are inherited from the base class are initialized when a constructor of the derived class executes.

Redefining Member Functions of the Base Class

Suppose that a `class derivedClass` is derived from a `class baseClass`. Further assume that both `derivedClass` and `baseClass` have some data members. It then follows that the data members of the `class derivedClass` are its own data members, together with the data members of `baseClass`. Suppose that `baseClass` contains a function, `print`, that prints the values of the data members of `baseClass`. Now, `derivedClass` contains other data members in addition to the data members inherited from `baseClass`. Suppose that you want to include a function that prints the data members of `derivedClass`. You can give any name to this function. However, in the `class derivedClass`, you can also name this function as `print` (the same name used by `baseClass`). This is called **redefining** (also called **overriding**) the member function of the base class. Next, we illustrate how to redefine **(override)** the `public` member functions of a base class.

> To redefine (**override**) a `public` member function of the base class in the derived class, the corresponding function in the derived class must have the same name, number, and types of parameters. In other words, the name of the function being redefined in the derived class must have the same formal parameter list. If the corresponding functions in the base class and the derived class have the same name but a different formal parameter list, then this is function overloading in the derived class, which is also allowed.

Consider the definition of the following class:

```
class baseClass
{
public:
    void print() const;

private:
    int u;
    int v;
    char ch;
};
```

The `class baseClass` has four members. Suppose that the definition of the member function `print` of `baseClass` is

```
void baseClass::print() const
{
    cout<<"Base Class: u = "<<u<<", v = "<<v
        <<", ch = "<<ch<<endl;
}
```

Now consider the definition of the following class:

```
class derivedClass: public baseClass
{
public:
    void print() const;

private:
    int first;
    double second;
};
```

From the definition of the class derivedClass, it is clear that the class derivedClass is derived from the class baseClass and it is a public inheritance. Therefore, all public members of baseClass are inherited as public members of derivedClass. The class derivedClass also overwrites the print function.

Next, let us write the definition of the member function print of derivedClass.

The class derivedClass has five data members: u, v, ch, first, and second. The print function of derivedClass prints the values of these data members. To write the definition of the member function print of derivedClass, keep the following in mind:

- The data members u, v, and ch are private members of the class baseClass and so cannot be directly accessed in the derivedClass. Therefore, when writing the definition of the function print of derivedClass, we cannot access u, v, and ch directly.

- The data members u, v, and ch of the class baseClass are accessible in derivedClass through the public members of baseClass.

Therefore, when writing the definition of the function print of derivedClass, we first call the member function print of baseClass to print the values of u, v, and ch. After printing the values of u, v, and ch, we output the values of first and second.

To call the function print of baseClass in the definition of the function print of derivedClass, we must use the following statement:

```
baseClass::print();
```

This statement ensures that we call the member function print of baseClass, not of derivedClass.

The definition of the member function print of derivedClass is

```
void derivedClass::print() const
{
    baseClass::print();
    cout<<"Derived Class: first = "<<first
        <<", second = "<<second<<endl;
    cout<<"_____"
        <<"_____"<<endl;
}
```

Constructors of Derived and Base Classes

A derived class can have its own `private` data members; therefore, a derived class can have its own constructors. A constructor typically serves to initialize the data members. When we declare a derived class object, this object inherits the members of the base class; however, the derived class object *cannot* directly access the `private` (data) members of the base class. The same is true for the member functions of a derived class. That is, the member functions of the derived class cannot directly access the `private` members of the base class.

Consequently, the constructors of the derived class can (directly) initialize only the `private` data members of the derived class. Therefore, when a derived class object is declared, it must also automatically execute one of the constructors of the base class. Because constructors cannot be called like other functions, the execution of a derived class's constructor must trigger the execution of one of the base class's constructors. This is, in fact, what happens. Furthermore, a call to the base class's constructor is specified in the heading part of the derived class constructor's definition.

Let us illustrate this concept with the help of an example. We first define a base class and then a derived class. Both classes have their own constructors.

Consider the definition of the following class (see also Figure 2-2):

```cpp
class baseClass
{
public:
    void print();                       //baseClass Line 1

    baseClass();                        //baseClass Line 2
    baseClass(int x, int y);            //baseClass Line 3
    baseClass(int x, int y, char w);    //baseClass Line 4

private:
    int u;
    int v;
    char ch;
};
```

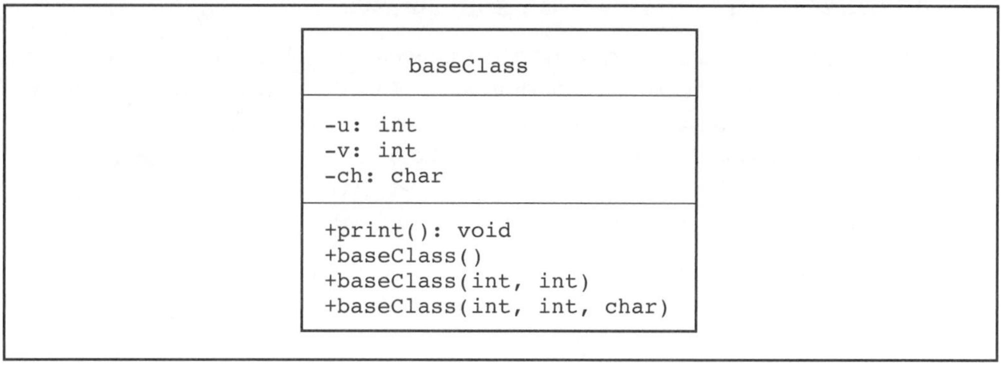

```
                        baseClass

            -u: int
            -v: int
            -ch: char

            +print(): void
            +baseClass()
            +baseClass(int, int)
            +baseClass(int, int, char)
```

Figure 2-2   UML diagram of the class baseClass

The class baseClass has three constructors, a member function print, and three data members. Suppose that the definitions of the member function and the constructors of baseClass are as follows:

```cpp
void baseClass::print()
{
    cout<<"Base Class: u = "<<u<<", v = "<<v
        <<", ch = "<<ch<<endl;
}

    //default constructor; baseClass Line 2
baseClass::baseClass()
{
    u = 0;
    v = 0;
    ch = '*';
}

    //constructor; baseClass Line 3
baseClass::baseClass(int x, int y)
{
    u = x;
    v = y;
    ch = '*';
}

    //constructor; baseClass Line 4
baseClass::baseClass(int x, int y, char w)
{
    u = x;
    v = y;
    ch = w;
}
```

Now consider the definition of the following class (see also Figure 2-3):

```
class derivedClass: public baseClass
{
public:
    void print();                               //derivedClass Line 1

    derivedClass();                             //derivedClass Line 2
    derivedClass(int x, int y,
                int one, double two); //derivedClass Line 3
    derivedClass(int x, int y, char w,
                int one, double two); //derivedClass Line 4

private:
    int first;
    double second;
};
```

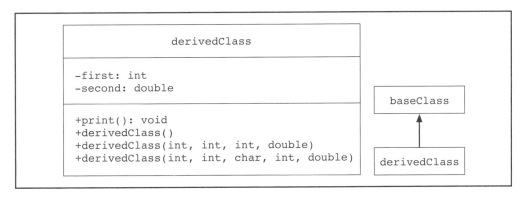

Figure 2-3   UML diagram of the class derivedClass and inheritance hierarchy

The class derivedClass is derived from the class baseClass, and it is a public inheritance. The class derivedClass has five data members: u, v, ch, first, and second. The data members u, v, and ch are inherited from the class baseClass.

Let us first write the definition of the member function print of derivedClass.

```
void derivedClass::print()
{
    baseClass::print();
    cout<<"Derived Class: first = "<<first
        <<", second = "<<second<<endl;
    cout<<"_____"
        <<"_____"<<endl;
}
```

We will now write the definitions of the constructors of derivedClass. Recall that a call to a base class's constructor is specified in the heading of the definition of the derived class's constructor.

First, let us write the definition of the default constructor of derivedClass. Recall that, if a class contains the default constructor and no values are specified during object declaration, the default constructor executes and initializes the object. Because the class baseClass contains the default constructor, when writing the definition of the default constructor of derivedClass, we do not specify any constructor of the base class.

```
derivedClass::derivedClass()     //default constructor
{
        first = 0;
        second = 0;
}
```

Next, we discuss how to write the definitions of constructors with parameters. To trigger the execution of a constructor (with parameters) of the base class, you specify the name of the constructor of the base class with the parameters in the heading of the definition of a constructor of the derived class.

Consider the following definition of the constructor of derivedClass (declared in the line derivedClass, Line 3):

```
derivedClass::derivedClass(int x, int y, int one, double two)
        : baseClass(x,y)
{
        first = one;
        second = two;
}
```

In this definition, we specify the constructor of baseClass with two parameters (declared in the line baseClass, Line 3). When this constructor of derivedClass executes, it triggers the execution of the constructor with two int parameters (declared in the line baseClass, Line 3).

Next, consider the following definition of the constructor of derivedClass (declared in the line derivedClass, Line 4):

```
derivedClass::derivedClass(int x, int y, char w,
                              int one, double two)
        :baseClass(x,y,w)
{
        first = one;
        second = two;
}
```

This definition specifies the constructor of `baseClass` with three parameters (declared in the line `baseClass`, Line 4). When this constructor of `derivedClass` executes, it triggers the execution of the constructor with three parameters in the order `int`, `int`, `char` (declared in the line `baseClass`, Line 4).

Example 2-2

Suppose that you want to define a class to group the attributes of an employee. There are both full-time employees and part-time employees. Part-time employees are paid based on the number of hours worked and an hourly rate. Suppose that you want to define a class to keep track of a part-time employee's information such as `name`, `pay rate`, and `hours worked`. You can then print the employee's name together with his or her wages. Because every employee is a person, and Example 1-6 (Chapter 1) defined the `class personType` to store a first name and a last name together with the necessary operations on `name`, we can define a `class partTimeEmployee` based on the `class personType`. (See Figure 2-4.) You can also redefine the `print` function to print the appropriate information.

```
class partTimeEmployee: public personType
{
public:
    void print();
      //Function to output the first name, last name,
      //and the wages.
      //Postcondition: Outputs:
      //          firstName lastName wages are $$$$.$$

    double calculatePay();
      //Function to calculate and return the wages.
      //Postcondition: The pay is calculated and returned.

    void setNameRateHours(string first, string last,
                          double rate, double hours);
      //Function to set the first name, last name,
      //payRate, and hoursWorked according to the
      //parameters.
      //Postcondition: firstName = first; lastName = last;
      //                payRate = rate; hoursWorked = hours

    partTimeEmployee(string first = "", string last = "",
                    double rate = 0, double hours = 0);
      //constructor with parameters
      //Sets the first name, last name, pay rate, and
      //hours worked according to the parameters. If
      //no value is specified, the default values are
      //assumed.
      //Postcondition: firstName = first;
      //                lastName = last; payRate = rate;
      //                hoursWorked = hours
```

```
private:
    double payRate;     //stores the pay rate
    double hoursWorked; //stores the hours worked
};
```

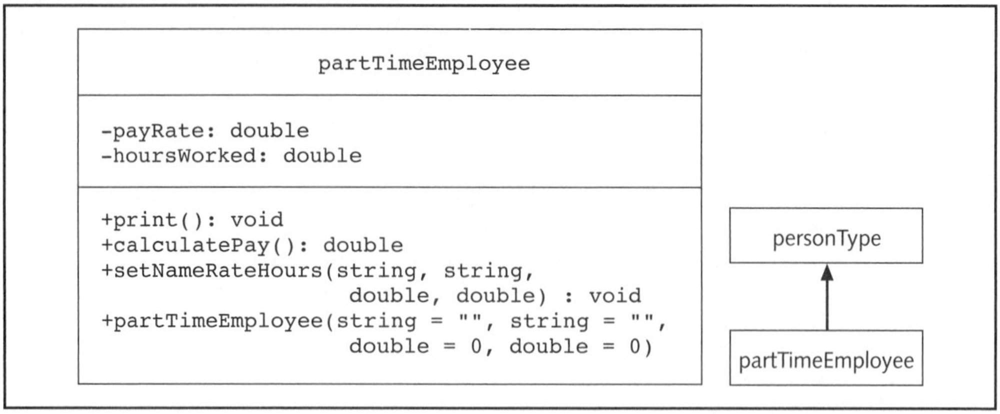

partTimeEmployee
-payRate: double -hoursWorked: double

+print(): void
+calculatePay(): double
+setNameRateHours(string, string,
                  double, double) : void
+partTimeEmployee(string = "", string = "",
                  double = 0, double = 0)

Figure 2-4   UML diagram of the class partTimeEmployee and inheritance hierarchy

The definitions of the member functions of the **class partTimeEmployee** are as follows:

```
void partTimeEmployee::print()
{
      personType::print();//print the name of the
                          //employee
      cout<<" wages are: "<<calculatePay()<<endl;
}

double partTimeEmployee::calculatePay()
{
      return (payRate * hoursWorked);
}

void partTimeEmployee::setNameRateHours(string first, string last,
                                        double rate, double hours)
{
      personType::setName(first, last);
      payRate = rate;
      hoursWorked = hours;
}
```

```
partTimeEmployee::partTimeEmployee(string first, string last,
                                   double rate, double hours)
          : personType(first, last) //constructor
{
    payRate = rate;
    hoursWorked = hours;
}
```

Header File of a Derived Class

The previous section explained how to derive new classes from previously defined classes. To define new classes, you create new header files. The base classes are already defined, and their definitions are contained in header files. To create new classes based on the previously defined classes, the header files of the new classes contain commands that tell the computer where to look for the definitions of the base classes.

Suppose that the definition of the class personType is placed in the header file personType.h. To create the definition of the class partTimeEmployee, the header file—say, ptEmployee.h—must contain the preprocessor directive

```
#include "personType.h"
```

before the definition of the class partTimeEmployee. To be specific, the header file ptEmployee.h is

```
//Header file ptEmployee.h
#include "personType.h"

class partTimeEmployee: public personType
{
public:
    void print() const;
    double calculatePay();
    void setNameRateHours(string first, string last,
                          double rate, double hours)
    partTimeEmployee(string first = "", string last = "",
                     double rate = 0, double hours = 0);

private:
    double payRate;
    double hoursWorked;
};
```

The definitions of the member functions can be placed in a separate file. Recall that to include a system-provided header file, such as **iostream**, in a user program, you enclose the header file between angular brackets; to include a user-defined header file in a program, you enclose the header file between double quotation marks.

Multiple Inclusions of a Header File

The previous section discussed how to create the header file of a derived class. To include a header file in a program, you use the preprocessor command. Recall that before a program is compiled, the preprocessor first processes the program. Consider the following header file:

```
//Header file test.h
const int ONE = 1;
const int TWO = 2;
```

Suppose that the header file `testA.h` includes the file `test.h` in order to use the identifiers `ONE` and `TWO`. To be specific, suppose that the header file `testA.h` looks like this:

```
//Header file testA.h
#include "test.h"
  .
  .
  .
```

Now consider the following program code:

```
//Program headerTest.cpp
#include "test.h"
#include "testA.h"
  .
  .
  .
```

When the program `headerTest.cpp` is compiled, it is first processed by the preprocessor. The preprocessor includes first the header file `test.h` and then the header file `testA.h`. When the header file `testA.h` is included, because it contains the preprocessor directive `#include "test.h"`, the header file `test.h` is included twice in the program. The second inclusion of the header file `test.h` results in compile-time errors, such as the identifier `ONE` already declared. This problem occurs because the first inclusion of the header file `test.h` has already defined the variables `ONE` and `TWO`. To avoid multiple inclusions of a file in a program, we use certain preprocessor commands in the header file. Let us first rewrite the header file `test.h` using these preprocessor commands and then explain the meaning of these commands.

```
//Header file test.h

#ifndef H_test
#define H_test
const int ONE = 1;
const int TWO = 2;
#endif
```

- `#ifndef H_test` means "if not defined `H_test`"

- `#define H_test` means "define `H_test`"

- `#endif` means "end if"

Here `H_test` is a preprocessor identifier.

The effect of these commands is as follows: If the identifier `H_test` is not defined, define the identifier `H_test` and let the remaining statements between `#define` and `#endif` pass through the compiler. If the header file `test.h` is included the second time in the program, the statement `#ifndef` fails and all statements until `#endif` are skipped. In fact, all header files are written using similar preprocessor commands.

Protected Members of a Class

The `private` members of a class are `private` to the class and cannot be directly accessed outside the class. Only member functions of that class can access the `private` members. As discussed previously, a derived class cannot directly access the `private` members of a base class. However, it is sometimes necessary for a derived class to access a `private` member of a base class. If you make a `private` member become `public`, then anyone can access that member. Recall that the members of a class are classified into three categories: `public`, `private`, and `protected`. So, for a base class to give access to a member to its derived class and still prevent its direct access outside the class, you must declare that member under the member access specifier `protected`. Therefore, the accessibility of a `protected` member of a class is in between `public` and `private`. A derived class can directly access the `protected` member of a base class.

To summarize, if a derived class needs to access a member of a base class, and to prevent the direct access of the member outside the base class, that member of the base class is declared under the member access specifier `protected`.

Inheritance as `public`, `protected`, or `private`

Suppose `class B` is derived from `class A`. Then B cannot directly access the `private` members of A. What about the `public` and `protected` members of A? This section gives the rules that generally apply when accessing the members of a base class.

Consider the following statement:

```
class B: memberAccessSpecifier A
{
    .
    .
    .
};
```

In this statement, `memberAccessSpecifier` is either `public`, `protected`, or `private`.

1. If `memberAccessSpecifier` is `public`—that is, the inheritance is `public`—then

   a. The `public` members of A are `public` members of B. They can be directly accessed in `class B`.

    b. The `protected` members of A are `protected` members of B. They can be directly accessed by the member functions (and `friend` functions) of B.

    c. The `private` members of A cannot be directly accessed in B. They can be accessed by the member functions (and `friend` functions) of B only through the `public` or `protected` members of A.

2. If `memberAccessSpecifier` is `protected`—that is, the inheritance is `protected`—then

    a. The `public` members of A are `protected` members of B. They can be directly accessed by the member functions (and `friend` functions) of B.

    b. The `protected` members of A are `protected` members of B. They can be directly accessed by the member functions (and `friend` functions) of B.

    c. The `private` members of A cannot be directly accessed in B. They can be accessed by the member functions (and `friend` functions) of B only through the `public` or `protected` members of A.

3. If `memberAccessSpecifier` is `private`—that is, the inheritance is `private`—then

    a. The `public` members of A are `private` members of B. They can be accessed by the member functions (and `friend` functions) of B.

    b. The `protected` members of A are `private` members of B. They can be accessed by the member functions (and `friend` functions) of B.

    c. The `private` members of A cannot be directly accessed in B. They can be accessed by the member functions (and `friend` functions) of B only through the `public` or `protected` members of A.

 The section "`friend` Functions of Classes" (located later in this chapter) describes the `friend` functions.

COMPOSITION

Composition is another way to relate two classes. In composition, one or more members of a class are objects of another class type. Composition is a "has-a" relation; for example, "every person has a date of birth."

Example 1-6, in Chapter 1, defined a class called `personType`. The `class personType` stores a person's first name and last name. Suppose we want to keep track of additional information for a person, such as a personal ID (for example, a Social Security number) and a date of birth. Because every person has a personal ID and a date of birth, we can define a new class, called personalInfo, in which one of the members is an object of the type personType. We can declare additional members to store the personal ID and date of birth for the class personalInfo.

First we define another class, dateType, to store only a person's date of birth, and then construct the class personalInfo from the classes personType and dateType. This way, we can demonstrate how to define a new class using two classes.

To define the class dateType, we need three data members to store the month, day number, and year. Some of the operations that need to be performed on a date are to set the date and to print the date. The following statements define the class dateType (see also Figure 2-5):

```
class dateType
{
public:
    void setDate(int month, int day, int year);
      //Function to set the date.
      //Data members dMonth, dDay, and dYear are set
      //according to the parameters.
      //Postcondition: dMonth = month; dDay = day;
      //               dYear = year

    void getDate(int& month, int& day, int& year);
      //Function to return the date.
      //Postcondition: month = dMonth; day = dDay;
      //               year = dYear

    void printDate() const;
      //Function to output the date in the form
      //mm-dd-yyyy.

    dateType(int month = 1, int day = 1, int year = 1900);
      //constructor to set the date
      //Data members dMonth, dDay, and dYear are set
      //according to the parameters.
      //Postcondition: dMonth = month; dDay = day;
      //               dYear = year
      //If no values are specified, the default values are
      //used to initialize the data members.

private:
    int dMonth;            //variable to store the month
    int dDay;              //variable to store the day
    int dYear;             //variable to store the year
};
```

```
                        ┌─────────────────────────────────────────┐
                        │              dateType                   │
                        ├─────────────────────────────────────────┤
                        │ -dMonth: int                            │
                        │ -dDay: int                              │
                        │ -dYear: int                             │
                        ├─────────────────────────────────────────┤
                        │ +setDate(int, int, int): void           │
                        │ +getDate(int&, int&, int&): void        │
                        │ +printDate() const: void                │
                        │ +dateType(int = 1, int = 1, int = 1900) │
                        └─────────────────────────────────────────┘
```

Figure 2-5   UML diagram of the `class dateType`

The definitions of the member functions of the **`class dateType`** are as follows:

```
void dateType::setDate(int month, int day, int year)
{
      dMonth = month;
      dDay = day;
      dYear = year;
}
```

The definition of the function **`setDate`**, before storing the date into the data members, does not check whether the date is valid. That is, it does not confirm whether **`month`** is between 1 and 12, **`year`** is greater than 0, and **`day`** is valid (for example, for January, **`day`** should be between 1 and 31). In Programming Exercise 2 at the end of this chapter, you are asked to rewrite the definition of the function **`setDate`** so that the date is validated before storing it in the data members.

The definitions of the remaining member functions are as follows:

```
void dateType::getDate(int& month, int& day, int& year)
{
      month = dMonth;
      day = dDay;
      year = dYear;
}

void dateType::printDate() const
{
      cout<<dMonth<<"-"<<dDay<<"-"<<dYear;
}

      //constructor
```

```
dateType:: dateType(int month, int day, int year)
{
     setDate(month, day, year);
}
```

Because the constructor uses the function **setDate** before storing the date into the data members, the constructor also does not check whether the date is valid. In Programming Exercise 2 at the end of this chapter, when you rewrite the definition of the function **setDate** to validate the date, and the constructor uses the function **setDate**, the date set by the constructor will also be validated.

Next, we give the definition of the **class personalInfoType** (see also Figure 2-6):

```
class personalInfoType
{
public:
    void setpersonalInfo(string first, string last,
                         int month, int day,
                         int year, int ID);
      //Function to set the personal information.
      //Data members are set according to the
      //parameters.
      //Postcondition: firstName = first;
      //     lastName = last; dMonth = month;
      //     dDay = day; dYear = year; personID = ID;

    void printpersonalInfo() const;
      //Function to print the personal information.

    personalInfoType(string first = "", string last = "",
                     int month = 1, int day = 1,
                     int year = 1900, int ID = 0);
      //constructor
      //Data members are set according to the
      //parameters.
      //Postcondition: firstName = first;
      //     lastName = last; dMonth = month;
      //     dDay = day; dYear = year; personID = ID

private:
    personType name;
    dateType bDay;
    int personID;
};
```

```
                        personalInfoType

           -name: personType
           -bDay: dateType
           -personID: int

           setpersonalInfo(string, string, int, int,
                           int, int): void
           printpersonalInfo() const: void
           personalInfoType(string = "", string = "",
                           int = 1, int = 1,
                           int = 1900, int = 0)
```

Figure 2-6 UML diagram of the `class personalInfoType`

Before we give the definition of the member functions of the `class personalInfoType`, let us discuss how the constructors of the objects `bDay` and `name` are invoked.

Recall that a class constructor automatically executes when a class object enters its scope. Suppose that we have the following statement:

`personalInfoType student;`

When the object `student` enters its scope, the objects `bDay` and `name`, which are members of `student`, also enter their scopes; as a result, one of their constructors is executed. We therefore need to know how to pass arguments to the constructors of the member objects (that is, `bDay` and `name`). Recall that constructors do not have a type and so cannot be called like other functions. The arguments to the constructor of a member object (such as `bDay`) are specified in the heading part of the definition of the class's constructor. The following statements illustrate how to pass arguments to the constructors of the member objects:

```
personalInfoType::personalInfoType(string first, string last,
                int month, int day, int year, int ID)
        : name(first,last), bDay(month,day,year)
{
    .
    .
    .
}
```

Member objects of a class are constructed (that is, initialized) in the order they are declared (not in the order they are listed in the constructor's member initialization list), and before the enclosing class objects are constructed. Therefore, in this case, the object `name` is initialized first, then `bDay`, and finally `student`.

Following are the definitions of the member functions of the `class personalInfo`:

```
void personalInfoType::setpersonalInfo(string first, string last,
                                       int month, int day,
                                       int year, int ID)
{
    name.setName(first, last);
    bDay.setDate(month, day, year);
    personID = ID;
}

void personalInfoType::printpersonalInfo () const
{
    name.print();
    cout<<"'s date of birth is ";
    bDay.printDate();
    cout<<endl;
    cout<<"and personal ID is "<<personID;
}

personalInfoType::personalInfoType(string first, string last,
                                   int month, int day,
                                   int year, int ID)
        :name(first, last), bDay(month, day, year)
{
    personID = ID;
}
```

In the case of inheritance, use the class name to invoke the base class's constructor. In the case of composition, use the member object name to invoke its own constructor.

POLYMORPHISM: OPERATOR AND FUNCTION OVERLOADING

In Chapter 1, you learned how classes in C++ are used to combine data, and operations on that data, in a single entity. The ability to combine data and operations on that data is called **encapsulation**. It is the first principle of object-oriented design (OOD). Chapter 1 defined the abstract data type (ADT) and described how classes in C++ implement ADT. The first section of this chapter discussed how new classes can be derived from existing classes through the mechanism of inheritance. Inheritance, the second principle of OOD, encourages code reuse.

The remainder of this chapter discusses the third principle of OOD—polymorphism. First we discuss polymorphism via **operator overloading**, and then via **templates**. Templates enable the programmer to write generic codes for related functions and classes. We will simplify function overloading through the use of templates, called **function templates**. The third type of polymorphism via virtual functions is discussed in Appendix F.

OPERATOR OVERLOADING

This section describes how operators are overloaded in C++. But, first let us see why you would want to overload operators.

Why Operator Overloading Is Needed

Chapter 1 defined and implemented the **class clockType**. It also showed how you can use the **class clockType** to represent the time of day in a program. Let us review some of the characteristics of the **class clockType**.

Consider the following statements:

```
clockType myClock(8,23,34);
clockType yourClock(4,5,30);
```

The first statement declares **myClock** to be an object of the type **clockType** and initializes the data members **hr, min**, and **sec** of **myClock** to 8, 23, and 34, respectively. The second statement declares **yourClock** to be an object of the type **clockType** and initializes the data members **hr, min**, and **sec** of **yourClock** to 4, 5, and 30, respectively.

Now consider the following statements:

```
myClock.printTime();
myClock.incrementSeconds();
if(myClock.equalTime(yourClock))
    .
    .
    .
```

The first statement prints the value of **myClock** in the form **hr:min:sec**. The second statement increments the value of **myClock** by one second. The third statement checks whether the value of **myClock** is the same as the value of **yourClock**.

These statements do their job. However, if we can use the insertion operator, **<<**, to output the value of **myClock**, the increment operator, **++**, to increment the value of **myClock** by one second, and relational operators for comparison, we can enhance the flexibility of C++ considerably. More specifically, we prefer to use the following statements instead of the previous statements:

```
cout<<myClock;
myClock++;
if(myClock == yourClock)
    .
    .
    .
```

Recall that the only built-in operations on classes are the assignment operator and the member selection operator. Therefore, other operators cannot be directly applied to class objects. However, C++ allows the programmer to extend the definitions of most of the operators so that operators—such as relational operators, arithmetic operators, insertion operators for data output, and extraction operators for data input—can be applied to classes. In C++ terminology, this is called **operator overloading**. In addition to operator overloading, this chapter discusses function overloading.

Operator Overloading

Recall how the arithmetic operator / works. If both operands of / are integers, the result is an integer; otherwise, the result is a floating-point number. Similarly, the stream insertion operator, <<, and the stream extraction operator, >>, are overloaded. The operator << is used as both a stream insertion operator and a left shift operator. The operator >> is used as both a stream extraction operator and a right shift operator. These are examples of operator overloading.

Other examples of overloaded operators are + and −. The results of + and − are different for integer arithmetic and floating-point arithmetic.

C++ allows the user to overload most of the operators so that the operators can work effectively in a specific application. It does not allow the user to create new operators. Most of the existing operators can be overloaded to manipulate class objects.

In order to overload an operator, you must write a function definition (that is, the header and body). The name of the function that overloads an operator is the reserved word `operator` followed by the operator to be overloaded. For example, the name of the function to overload the operator >= is

```
operator>=
```

Operator function: The function that overloads an operator.

Syntax for Operator Functions

The result of an operation is a value; therefore, the operator function is a value-returning function.

The syntax of the heading for an operator function is

```
returnType   operator operatorSymbol(arguments)
```

In C++, `operator` is a reserved word.

Recall that the only built-in operations on classes are assignment (=) and member selection. To use other operators on class objects, they must be explicitly overloaded. Operator overloading provides the same concise expressions for user-defined data types as it does for built-in data types.

To overload an operator for a class:

1. Include the statement to declare the function to overload the operator (that is, the operator function) in the definition of the class.

2. Write the definition of the operator function.

Certain rules must be followed when you include an operator function in a class definition. These rules are described later in this chapter in the section, "Operator Functions as Member Functions and Nonmember Functions."

Overloading an Operator: Some Restrictions

When overloading an operator, keep the following in mind:

- You cannot change the precedence of an operator.

- The associativity cannot be changed. (For example, the associativity of the arithmetic operator + is from left to right and it cannot be changed.)

- You cannot use default arguments with an overloaded operator.

- You cannot change the number of arguments that an operator takes.

- You cannot create new operators. Only existing operators can be overloaded. The operators that cannot be overloaded are

  .   .*   ::   ?:   sizeof

- The meaning of how an operator works with built-in types, such as int, remains the same.

- Operators can be overloaded either for objects of the user-defined type, or for a combination of objects of the user-defined type and objects of the built-in type.

Pointer this

A member function of a class can (directly) access the data members of that class for a given object. Sometimes it is necessary for a function member to refer to the object as a whole, rather than the object's individual data members. How do you refer to the object as a whole (that is, as a single unit) in the definition of the member function, especially when the object is not passed as a parameter? Every object of a class maintains a (hidden) pointer to itself, and the name of this pointer is this. In C++, this is a reserved word. The pointer this is available for you to use. When an object invokes a member function, the member function references the pointer this of the object. For example, suppose that test is a class and has a member function called funcOne. Further suppose that the definition of funcOne looks like the following:

```
test test::funcOne()
{
    .
    .
    .
    return *this;
}
```

If x and y are objects of the type test, then the statement

```
y = x.funcOne();
```

copies the value of the object x into the object y; that is, the data members of x are copied into the corresponding data members of y. When the object x invokes the function funcOne, the pointer this in the definition of the member function funcOne refers to the object x, and so this means the address of x and *this means the value of x.

The following example illustrates how the pointer this works.

Example 2-3

In Example 1-6 (in Chapter 1), we designed a class to implement a person's name in a program. Here, we extend the definition of the class personType to set a person's first name and last name individually, and then return the entire object. The extended definition of the class personType is

```
class personType
{
public:
    void print() const;
        //Function to output the first name and last name.
        //Postcondition: The name is printed in the form
        //                  firstName lastName

    void setName(string first, string last);
        //Function to set firstName and lastName according
        //to the parameters.
        //Postcondition: firstName = first; lastName = last

    personType& setFirstName(string first);
        //Function to set the first name.
        //Postcondition: firstName = first
        //       After setting the first name, a reference
        //       to the object, that is, the address of the
        //       object, is returned.

    personType& setLastName(string last);
        //Function to set the last name.
        //Postcondition: lastName = last
        //       After setting the last name, a reference
        //       to the object, that is, the address of the
        //       object, is returned.
```

```
    void getName(string& first, string& last);
        //Function to return firstName and lastName via
        //the parameters.
        //Postcondition: first = firstName; last = lastName

    personType(string first = "", string last = "");
        //constructor
        //Sets firstName and lastName according to the
        //parameters.
        //Postcondition: firstName = first; lastName = last

private:
    string firstName; //stores the first name
    string lastName;  //stores the last name
};
```

The definitions of the functions `print`, `setTime`, `getName`, and the constructor are the same as before (see Example 1-6). The definitions of the functions `setFirstName` and `setLastName` are as follows:

```
personType& personType::setLastName(string last)
{
        lastName = last;

        return *this;
}

personType& personType::setFirstName(string first)
{
        firstName = first;

        return *this;
}
```

Consider the following function `main`:

```
int main()
{
    personType student1("Angela", "Clodfelter");          //Line 1

    personType student2;                                  //Line 2

    personType student3;                                  //Line 3

    cout<<"Line 4 -- Student 1: ";                        //Line 4
    student1.print();                                     //Line 5
    cout<<endl;                                           //Line 6

    student2.setFirstName("Shelly").setLastName("Malik"); //Line 7
```

```
    cout<<"Line 8 -- Student 2: ";                    //Line 8
    student2.print();                                 //Line 9
    cout<<endl;                                        //Line 10

    student3.setFirstName("Chelsea");                 //Line 11

    cout<<"Line 12 -- Student 3: ";                   //Line 12
    student3.print();                                 //Line 13
    cout<<endl;                                        //Line 14

    student3.setLastName("Tomek");                    //Line 15

    cout<<"Line 16 -- Student 3: ";                   //Line 16
    student3.print();                                 //Line 17
    cout<<endl;                                        //Line 18

    return 0;
}
```

Output

```
Line 4 -- Student 1: Angela Clodfelter
Line 8 -- Student 2: Shelly Malik
Line 12 -- Student 3: Chelsea
Line 16 -- Student 3: Chelsea Tomek
```

The statements in Lines 1, 2, and 3 declare and initialize the objects student1, student2, and student3, respectively. The objects student2 and student3 are initialized to empty strings. The statement in Line 5 outputs the value of student1 (see Line 4 in the output, which contains the output of Lines 4, 5, and 6). The statement in Line 7 works as follows. In the statement

```
student2.setFirstName("Shelly").setLastName("Malik");
```

first the expression

```
student2.setFirstName("Shelly")
```

is executed because the associativity of the dot operator is from left to right. This expression sets the first name to "Shelly" and returns a reference to the object, which is student2. Therefore, the next expression executed is

```
student2.setLastName("Malik")
```

which sets the last name of student2 to "Malik". The statement in Line 9 outputs the value of student2. The statement in Line 11 sets the first name of the object student3 to "Chelsea", and the statement in Line 13 outputs the value of student3. Notice the output in Line 12. The output shows only the first name, not the last name, because we have not yet set the last name of student3. The last name of student3 is still empty, which was set by the statement in Line 3 when student3 was declared. Next, the statement in Line 15 sets the last name of student3, and the statement in Line 16 outputs the value of student3.

`friend` Functions of Classes

A function that is defined outside the scope of a class is called a `friend` function of the class. A `friend` function is a **nonmember function** of the class, but has access to the class's `private` data members. To make a function be a friend to a class, the reserved word `friend` precedes the function prototype (in the class definition). (The word `friend` appears only in the function prototype in the class definition, not in the definition of the `friend` function.)

Consider the following statements:

```
class classIllusFriend
{
    friend void friendFunc(...);
        .
        .
        .
};
```

In the definition of the `class classIllusFriend`, `friendFunc` is declared as a `friend` of the `class classIllusFriend`; that is, it is a nonmember function of the `class classIllusFriend`. When you write the definition of the function `friendFunc`, any object of the type `classIllusFriend`—which is either a local variable of `friendFunc` or a formal parameter of `friendFunc`—can access its `private` members within the definition of the function `friendFunc`. (Example 2-4 illustrates this concept.) Moreover, because a `friend` function is not a member of a class, its declaration can be placed within the `private`, `protected`, or `public` part of the class.

Definition of a `friend` Function

When writing the definition of a `friend` function, the name of the class and the scope resolution operator do not precede the name of the `friend` function in the function heading. Also, recall that the word `friend` does not appear in the heading of the `friend` function's definition. Therefore, the definition of the function `friendFunc` in the previous `class classIllusFriend` is

```
void friendFunc(...)
{
    .
    .
    .
}
```

Of course, we will place the definition of the `friend` function in the implementation file.

The next section illustrates the difference between a member function and a nonmember function (`friend` function), when we overload some of the operators for a specific class.

Example 2-4 illustrates how a `friend` function accesses the `private` members of a class.

Example 2-4

Consider the following class:

```
class classIllusFriend
{
    friend void friendFunc(classIllusFriend cIFObject);

public:
    void print();
    void setx(int a);

private:
    int x;
};
```

In the definition of the `class classIllusFriend`, `friendFunc` is declared as a `friend` function. Suppose that the definitions of the member functions of the `class classIllusFriend` are as follows:

```
void classIllusFriend::print()
{
    cout<<"In class classIllusFriend: x = "<<x<<endl;
}

void classIllusFriend::setx(int a)
{
    x = a;
}
```

Now consider the following definition of the function `friendFunc`:

```
#include <iostream>
#include "classIllusFriend.h"

using namespace std;

void classIllusFriend::print()
{
    cout<<"In class classIllusFriend: x = "<<x<<endl;
}

void classIllusFriend::setx(int a)
{
    x = a;
}

void friendFunc(classIllusFriend cIFObject)   //Line 1
{
    classIllusFriend localObject;             //Line 2
```

```
    localObject.x = 45;                       //Line 3

    localObject.print();                      //Line 4
    cout<<endl;                               //Line 5
    cout<<"Line 6: In friendFunc accessing "
        <<"the private data member x "
        <<localObject.x<<endl;                //Line 6

    cIFObject.x = 88;                         //Line 7

    cIFObject.print();                        //Line 8
    cout<<endl;                               //Line 9
    cout<<"Line 10: In friendFunc accessing "
        <<"the private data member x "
        <<cIFObject.x<<endl;                  //Line 10
}
```

The function `friendFunc` contains a formal parameter `cIFObject` and a local variable `localObject`, both of the type `classIllusFriend`. In the statement in Line 3, the object `localObject` accesses its `private` data member `x` and sets its value to `45`. If `friendFunc` is not declared as a `friend` function of the `class classIllusFriend`, this statement would result in a syntax error because an object cannot directly access its `private` members. Similarly, in the statement in Line 7, the formal parameter `cIFObject` accesses its `private` data member `x` and sets its value to `88`. Once again, this statement would result in a syntax error if `friendFunc` is not declared as a `friend` function of the `class classIllusFriend`. The statement in Line 6 outputs the value of the `private` data member `x` of `localObject` by directly accessing `x`. Similarly, the statement in Line 10 outputs the value of `x` of `cIFObject` by directly accessing it. The function `friendFunc` also prints the value of `x` by using the function `print` (see the statements in Lines 4 and 8).

Now consider the definition of the following function `main`:

```
//Friend Function Illustration

#include <iostream>
#include "classIllusFriend.h"

using namespace std;

int main()
{
    classIllusFriend aObject;                 //Line 11

    aObject.setx(32);                         //Line 12

    cout<<"Line 13: aObject.x: ";             //Line 13
    aObject.print();                          //Line 14
```

```
    cout<<endl;                                //Line 15
    cout<<"*~*~*~*~*~* Testing friendFunc "
        <<"*~*~*~*~*~*"<<endl<<endl;            //Line 16

    friendFunc(aObject);                       //Line 17

    return 0;
}
```

Output

```
Line 13: aObject.x: In class classIllusFriend: x = 32

*~*~*~*~*~* Testing friendFunc *~*~*~*~*~*

In class classIllusFriend: x = 45

Line 6: In friendFunc accessing the private data member x 45
In class classIllusFriend: x = 88

Line 10: In friendFunc accessing the private data member x 88
```

For the most part, the output is self-explanatory. The statement in Line 17 calls the function friendFunc (a friend function of the class classIllusFriend) and passes the object aObject as an actual parameter. Notice that the function friendFunc generates the last six lines of the output, including the two blank lines.

Operator Functions as Member Functions and Nonmember Functions

The beginning of this section stated that certain rules must be followed when you include an operator function in the definition of a class. This section describes these rules.

Most operator functions can be either member functions or nonmember functions—that is, friend functions of a class. To make an operator function be a member or nonmember of a class, keep the following in mind:

- The function that overloads any of the operators ( ), [ ], ->, or = for a class must be declared as a member of the class.

- Suppose that an operator op is overloaded for a class—say, opOverClass.

  - If the leftmost operand of op is an object of a different type (that is, not of the type opOverClass), the function that overloads the operator op for opOverClass must be a nonmember—that is, a friend of the class opOverClass.

  - If the operator function that overloads the operator op for the class opOverClass is a member of the class opOverClass, then when applying op on objects of the type opOverClass, the leftmost operand of op must be of the type opOverClass.

You must follow these rules when including an operator function in a class definition.

You will see later in this chapter that functions that overload the insertion operator, <<, and the extraction operator, >>, for a class must be nonmembers—that is, **friend** functions of the class.

Except for certain operators as noted previously, operators can be overloaded either as member functions or as nonmember functions. The ensuing sections shows the difference between these two types of functions.

To facilitate this discussion, we use the following class to illustrate operator overloading:

```
class opOverClass
{
    .
    .
    .
private:
    int a;
    int b;
};
```

The **class opOverClass** has two **private** data members, **a** and **b**, of the type **int**. We add operator functions to the **class opOverClass** as we overload the operators.

Also, suppose that you have the following statements:

```
opOverClass x;
opOverClass y;
opOverClass z;
```

These statements declare **x**, **y**, and **z** to be objects of the type **opOverClass**.

OVERLOADING BINARY OPERATORS

C++ consists of both binary and unary operators. It also has a ternary operator, which *cannot* be overloaded. This section and the next few sections discuss how to overload various binary and unary operators. We begin by describing how to overload binary operators.

Suppose that # represents a binary operator (arithmetic or relational) that is to be overloaded for the **class opOverClass**. This operator can be overloaded as either a member function of the class or a **friend** function. We will describe both ways to overload this operator.

Overloading Binary Operators (Arithmetic or Relational) as Member Functions

Suppose that # is overloaded as a member function of the **class opOverClass**. The name of the function to overload # for the **class opOverClass** is

```
operator#
```

Because **x** and **y** are objects of the type `opOverClass`, you can perform the operation

```
x # y
```

The compiler translates this expression into the following expression:

```
x.operator#(y)
```

In this expression, you can see that the function `operator#` has only one argument, which is **y**.

Because `operator#` is a member of the **class opOverClass** and x is an object of the type `opOverClass`, in the previous statement, `operator#` has direct access to the `private` members of object **x**. Therefore, the first argument to `operator#` is the object that is invoking the function `operator#`, and the second argument is passed as a parameter to this function.

General Syntax to Overload Binary Operators (Arithmetic or Relational) as Member Functions

This section describes the general form of the functions to overload binary operators as member functions of a class.

Function Prototype (to be included in the definition of the class):

```
returnType operator op(const className&) const;
```

where **op** stands for the binary operator, arithmetic or relational, to be overloaded; `returnType` is the type of value returned by the function; and `className` is the name of the class for which the operator is being overloaded.

Function Definition:

```
returnType className::operator op
                    (const className& otherObject) const
{
    //algorithm to perform the operation

    return (value);
}
```

Example 2-5

Let us overload + and == for the **class opOverClass**. These operators are overloaded as member functions.

```
class opOverClass
{
public:
    void print() const;

    opOverClass operator+(const opOverClass&) const;
```

```
                  //Overloads the operator +

          bool operator==(const opOverClass&) const;
                  //Overloads the operator ==

          opOverClass(int i = 0, int j = 0);

     private:
          int a;
          int b;
     };
```

The definitions of the functions print, operator+, operator==, and the constructor are

```
void opOverClass::print() const
{
     cout<<"("<<a<<", "<<b<<")";
}

opOverClass::opOverClass(int i, int j)
{
     a = i;
     b = j;
}

opOverClass opOverClass::operator+
                         (const opOverClass& right) const
{
     opOverClass temp;

     temp.a = a + right.a;
     temp.b = b + right.b;

     return temp;
}

bool opOverClass::operator==(const opOverClass& right) const
{
     return(a == right.a && b == right.b);
}
```

Overloading Binary Operators (Arithmetic or Relational) as Nonmember Functions

Suppose that # represents the binary operator (arithmetic or relational) that is to be over-loaded as a nonmember function of the **class opOverClass**.

Further suppose that the following operation is to be performed:

```
x # y
```

In this case, the expression is compiled as

```
operator#(x,y)
```

Here we see that the function `operator#` has two arguments. It is also clear that in this expression, the function `operator#` is neither a member of the object `x` nor a member of the object `y`. The objects to be added are passed as arguments to the function `operator#`.

To include the operator function `operator#` as a nonmember of the class in the definition of the class, the reserved word `friend` must appear before the function heading. Also, the function `operator#` must have two arguments.

General Syntax to Overload Binary Operators (Arithmetic or Relational) as Nonmember Functions

This section describes the general form of the functions to overload binary operators as nonmember functions of a class.

Function Prototype (to be included in the definition of the class):

```
friend returnType operator op(const className&,
                              const className&);
```

where `op` stands for the binary operator to be overloaded, `returnType` is the type of value returned by the function, and `className` is the name of the class for which the operator is being overloaded.

Function Definition:

```
returnType operator op(const className& firstObject,
                       const className& secondObject)
{
      //algorithm to perform the operation
      return (value);
}
```

Overloading Stream Insertion (<<) and Extraction (>>) Operators

The operator function that overloads the insertion operator, `<<`, or the extraction operator, `>>`, for a class must be a nonmember of that class for the following reason.

Consider the following expression:

```
cout<<x;
```

In this expression, the leftmost operand of `<<` (that is, `cout`) is an object of the type `ostream`, not an object of the type `opOverClass`. Because the leftmost operand of `<<` is not an object of the type `opOverClass`, the operator function that overloads the insertion operator for `opOverClass` must be a nonmember of the `class opOverClass`.

Similarly, the operator function that overloads the stream extraction operator for opOverClass must be a nonmember function of opOverClass.

Overloading the Stream Insertion Operator (<<)

This section describes the general syntax to overload the stream insertion operator, <<, for a class.

Function Prototype (to be included in the definition of the class):

```
friend ostream& operator<<(ostream&, const className&);
```

Function Definition:

```
ostream& operator<<(ostream& osObject, const className& object)
{
        //local declaration if any
        //Output the members of the object
        //osObject<<. . .

        //Return the ostream object
        return osObject;
}
```

In the preceding function definition:

- Both parameters are reference parameters.

- The first parameter—that is, osObject—is a reference to an **ostream** object.

- The second parameter is usually a **const** reference to a particular class, because (recall from Chapter 1) the most effective way to pass an object as a parameter to a class is by reference. In this case, the formal parameter does not need to copy the data members of the actual parameter. In the previous definition, the word "const" appears before the class name because we want only to print the data members of the object. That is, the function should not modify the data members of the object.

- The return type of the function is a reference to an **ostream** object.

Notice that the return type of the function to overload the stream insertion operator, <<, is a reference. This is so that statements such as

```
cout<<x<<y;
```

can be executed; that is, the stream insertion operator can be used in a cascaded form.

Overloading the Stream Extraction Operator (>>)

This section describes the general syntax to overload the stream extraction operator, >>, for a class.

Function Prototype (to be included in the definition of the class):

```
friend istream& operator>>(istream&, className&);
```

Function Definition:

```
istream& operator>>(istream& isObject, className& object)
{
        //local declaration if any
        //Read the data into the object
        //isObject>>. . .

        //Return the istream object
        return isObject;
}
```

In the preceding function definition:

- Both parameters are reference parameters.

- The first parameter—that is, **isObject**—is a reference to an **istream** object.

- The second parameter is usually a reference to a particular class. The data read will be stored in the object.

- The return type of the function is a reference to an **istream** object.

Notice that the return type of the function to overload the stream extraction operator, >>, is a reference. This is so that statements such as

```
cin>>x>>y;
```

can be executed; that is, the stream extraction operator can be used in a cascaded form.

Example 2-6

Consider the following definition of the **class opOverClass** and the definitions of the operator functions:

```
class opOverClass
{
        //Overload the stream insertion and
        //extraction operators.
    friend ostream& operator<<(ostream&, const opOverClass&);
    friend istream& operator>>(istream&, opOverClass&);

public:
        //Overload + and ==
    opOverClass operator+(const opOverClass&) const;
    bool operator==(const opOverClass&) const;

    opOverClass(int i = 0, int j = 0);
```

```
private:
    int a;
    int b;
};
        //The definitions of the functions operator+,
        //operator==, and the constructor are the same
        //as in Example 2-5.

ostream& operator<<(ostream& osObject, const opOverClass& right)
{
        osObject<<"("<<right.a<<", "<<right.b<<")";

        return osObject;
}

istream& operator>>(istream& isObject, opOverClass& right)
{
        isObject>>right.a>>right.b;

        return isObject;
}
```

Consider the following function `main`:

```
int main()
{
    opOverClass u(23, 45);                      //Line 1
    opOverClass v;                              //Line 2

    cout<<"Line 3: u : "<<u<<endl;              //Line 3

    cout<<"Line 4: Enter two integers: ";       //Line 4
    cin>>v;                                     //Line 5
    cout<<endl;                                 //Line 6
    cout<<"Line 7: v : "<<v<<endl;              //Line 7

    cout<<"Line 8: u + v : "<<u + v<<endl;      //Line 8

    return 0;
}
```

Sample Run: In this sample run, the user input is shaded.

```
Line 3: u = (23, 45)
Line 4: Enter two integers: 5 6

Line 7: v = (5, 6)
Line 8: u + v = (28, 51)
```

The statements in Lines 1 and 2 declare and initialize u and v to be objects of the type opOverClass. The statement in Line 3 outputs the value of u using cout and the insertion operator. The statement in Line 5 inputs data into **v** using **cin** and the extraction operator. The statement in Line 7 outputs the value of **v** using **cout** and the insertion operator. The **cout** statement in Line 8 adds **u** and **v** and outputs the result. The output shows that both the stream insertion and stream extraction operators were overloaded successfully.

Overloading Unary Operators

The process of overloading unary operators is similar to the process of overloading binary operators. The only difference is that in the case of a unary operator, the operator has only one operand; in the case of a binary operator, the operator has two operands. Therefore, to overload a unary operator for a class:

- If the operator function is a member of the class, it has no parameters.

- If the operator function is a nonmember—that is, a **friend** function of the class—it has one parameter.

OPERATOR OVERLOADING: MEMBER VERSUS NONMEMBER

The preceding sections discussed and illustrated how to overload operators. Certain operators must be overloaded as member functions of the class, and some must be overloaded as nonmember (**friend**) functions. What about the ones that can be overloaded as either member functions or nonmember functions? For example, the binary arithmetic operator **+** can be overloaded as a member function or a nonmember function. If you overload **+** as a member function, the operator **+** has direct access to the data members of one of the objects, and you need to pass only one object as a parameter. On the other hand, if you overload **+** as a nonmember function, you must pass both objects as parameters. Therefore, overloading **+** as a nonmember could require additional memory and computer time to make a local copy of the data. Therefore, for efficiency purposes, wherever possible you should overload operators as member functions.

PROGRAMMING EXAMPLE: COMPLEX NUMBERS

A number of the form $a + ib$, where $i^2 = -1$, and a and b are real numbers, is called a complex number. We call a the real part and b the imaginary part of $a + ib$. Complex numbers can also be represented as ordered pairs (a, b). The addition and multiplication of complex numbers is defined by the following rules:

$$(a + ib) + (c + id) = (a + c) + i(b + d)$$

$$(a + ib) * (c + id) = (ac - bd) + i(ad + bc)$$

Using the ordered pair notation, these rules are written as

$$(a, b) + (c, d) = ((a + c), (b + d))$$

$$(a, b) * (c, d) = ((ac - bd), (ad + bc))$$

In this example, we construct a data type, `complexNumber`, that can be used to process complex numbers. We overload the stream insertion and stream extraction operators for easy input and output. We also overload the operators + and * to perform addition and multiplication of complex numbers. If x and y are complex numbers, we can evaluate expressions such as $x + y$ and $x * y$. Overloading the operators − and / are left as an exercise for you; see Programming Exercise 12 at the end of this chapter.

Consider the following definition of the `class complexType` (see also Figure 2-7):

```
//Specification file complexType.h
#ifndef H_complexNumber
#define H_complexNumber

#include <iostream>
using namespace std;

class complexType
{
        //Overload the stream insertion and extraction operators.
    friend ostream& operator<< (ostream&, const complexType&);
    friend istream& operator>> (istream&, complexType&);

public:
    void setComplex(const double& real, const double& imag);
    //Function to set the complex numbers according to
    //the parameters.
    //Postcondition: realPart = real; imaginaryPart = imag

    complexType(double real = 0, double imag = 0);
    //constructor
    //Initializes the complex numbers according to
    //the parameters.
    //Postcondition: realPart = real; imaginaryPart = imag

    complexType operator+(const complexType& otherComplex) const;
    //Overload the operator +

    complexType operator*(const complexType& otherComplex) const;
    //Overload the operator *

    bool operator==(const complexType& otherComplex) const;
    //Overload the operator ==

private:
    double realPart;        //variable to store the real part
    double imaginaryPart;   //variable to store the imaginary part
```

```
};
#endif
```

```
                              complexType

           -realPart: double
           -imaginaryPart: double

           +operator<<(ostream&, const complexType&): ostream&
           +operator>>(istream&, complexType&): istream&
           +setComplex(const double&, const double&): void
           +complexType(double = 0, double = 0)
           +operator+(const complexType&) const: complexType
           +operator*(const complexType&) const: complexType
           +operator==(const complexType&) const: bool
```

Figure 2-7 UML diagram of the `class complexType`

We now write the definitions of the functions to implement the various operations of the `class complexType`.

The definitions of most functions are quite simple and straightforward. We discuss only the definitions of the functions to overload the stream insertion operator, **<<**, and the stream extraction operator, **>>**.

To output a complex number in the form

`(a, b)`

where **a** is the real part and **b** is the imaginary part, the algorithm is

    a. Output the left parenthesis, (.

    b. Output the real part.

    c. Output the comma.

    d. Output the imaginary part.

    e. Output the right parenthesis,).

Therefore, the definition of the function **operator<<** is

```
ostream& operator<<(ostream& osObject, const complexType& complex)

{
     osObject<<"(";                                  //Step a
     osObject<<complex.realPart;                     //Step b
```

```
        osObject<<", ";                          //Step c
        osObject<<complex.imaginaryPart;          //Step d
        osObject<<")";                            //Step e

        return osObject;
}
```

Next, we discuss the definition of the function to overload the stream extraction operator, >>.

The input is of the form

`(3, 5)`

In this input, the real part of the complex number is 3 and the imaginary part is 5. The algorithm to read a complex number is

    a. Read and discard the left parenthesis.
    b. Read and store the real part.
    c. Read and discard the comma.
    d. Read and store the imaginary part.
    e. Read and discard the right parenthesis.

Following these steps, the definition of the function `operator>>` is

```
istream& operator>> (istream& isObject, complexType& complex)
{
        char ch;

        isObject>>ch;                     //Step a
        isObject>>complex.realPart;       //Step b
        isObject>>ch;                     //Step c
        isObject>>complex.imaginaryPart;  //Step d
        isObject>>ch;                     //Step e

        return isObject;
}
```

The definitions of the other functions are as follows:

```
bool complexType::operator==(const complexType& otherComplex) const
{
    return(realPart == otherComplex.realPart &&
           imaginaryPart == otherComplex.imaginaryPart);
}

void complexType::setComplex(const double& real,
                             const double& imag)
{
        realPart = real;
        imaginaryPart = imag;
```

```
}

      //constructor
complexType::complexType(double real, double imag)
{
    setComplex(real, imag);

}

      //Overload the operator +
complexType complexType::operator+
                        (const complexType& otherComplex) const
{
    complexType temp;

    temp.realPart = realPart + otherComplex.realPart;
    temp.imaginaryPart = imaginaryPart
                        + otherComplex.imaginaryPart;

    return temp;
}

      //Overload the operator *
complexType complexType::operator*
                        (const complexType& otherComplex) const
{
   complexType temp;

   temp.realPart = (realPart * otherComplex.realPart) -
                  (imaginaryPart * otherComplex.imaginaryPart);
   temp.imaginaryPart = (realPart * otherComplex.imaginaryPart)
                  + (imaginaryPart * otherComplex.realPart);
   return temp;
}
```

The following program illustrates the use of the class complexType:

```
//Program that uses the class complexType

#include <iostream>
#include "complexType.h"

using namespace std;

int main()
{
        complexType num1(23,34);                        //Line 1
        complexType num2;                               //Line 2
        complexType num3;                               //Line 3

        cout<<"Line 4: Num1 = "<<num1<<endl;            //Line 4
        cout<<"Line 5: Num2 = "<<num2<<endl;            //Line 5

        cout<<"Line 6: Enter the complex number "
            <<"in the form (a,b) ";                     //Line 6
        cin>>num2;                                      //Line 7
        cout<<endl;                                     //Line 8

        cout<<"Line 9: New value of num2 = "
            <<num2<<endl;                               //Line 9

        num3 = num1 + num2;                             //Line 10

        cout<<"Line 11: Num3 = "<<num3<<endl;           //Line 11
        cout<<"Line 12: "<<num1<<" + "<<num2
            <<" = "<<num1 + num2<<endl;                 //Line 12
        cout<<"Line 13: "<<num1<<" * "<<num2
            <<" = "<<num1 * num2<<endl;                 //Line 13

        return 0;
}
```

Sample Run: In this sample run, the user input is shaded.

```
Line 4: Num1 = (23, 34)
Line 5: Num2 = (0, 0)
Line 6: Enter the complex number in the form (a,b) (3,4)
Line 9: New value of num2 = (3, 4)
Line 11: Num3 = (26, 38)
Line 12: (23, 34) + (3, 4) = (26, 38)
Line 13: (23, 34) * (3, 4) = (-67, 194)
```

FUNCTION OVERLOADING

The previous section discussed operator overloading. Operator overloading provides the programmer with the same concise notation for user-defined data types as the operator has with built-in types. The types of arguments used with an operator determine the action to take.

Similar to operator overloading, C++ allows the programmer to overload a function name. Recall that a class can have more than one constructor, but all constructors of a class have the same name, which is the name of the class. This case is an example of overloading a function.

Overloading a function refers to the creation of several functions with the same name. However, if several functions have the same name, every function must have a different formal parameter list. The types of parameters determine which function to execute.

Suppose you need to write a function that determines the larger of two items. Both items can be integers, floating-point numbers, characters, or strings. You could write several functions as follows:

```
int largerInt(int x, int y);
char largerChar(char first, char second);
double largerDouble(double u, double v);
string largerString(string first, string second);
```

The function `largerInt` determines the larger of the two integers, the function `largerChar` determines the larger of the two characters, and so on. These functions all perform similar operations. Instead of giving different names to these functions, you can use the same name—say, `larger`—for each function; that is, you can overload the function `larger`. Therefore, you can write the previous function prototypes simply as

```
int larger(int x, int y);
char larger(char first, char second);
double larger(double u, double v);
string larger(string first, string second);
```

If the call is `larger(5,3)`, for example, the first function executes. If the call is `larger('A', '9')`, the second function executes, and so on.

For function overloading to work, we must give the definition of each function. The next section teaches you how to overload functions with a single code segment and leave the job of generating code for separate functions to the compiler.

TEMPLATES

Templates are very powerful features of C++. By using templates, you can write a single code segment for a set of related functions, called a **function template**, and for related classes, called a **class template**. The syntax we use for templates is

```
template<class Type>
declaration;
```

where `Type` is the type of data, and `declaration` is either a function declaration or a class declaration. In C++, `template` is a reserved word. The word `class` in the heading refers to any user-defined type or built-in type. `Type` is referred to as a formal parameter to the template.

Just as variables are parameters to functions, types (that is, data types) are parameters to templates.

Function Templates

In the section "Function Overloading" (located earlier in this chapter), when function overloading was introduced, the function `larger` was overloaded to find the larger of two integers, characters, floating-point numbers, or strings. To implement the function `larger`, we need to write four function definitions for the data type: one for `int`, one for `char`, one for `double`, and one for `string`. However, the body of each function is similar. C++ simplifies the process of overloading functions by providing function templates.

The syntax of the function template is

```
template<class Type>
function definition;
```

where `Type` is referred to as a formal parameter of the template. It is used to specify the type of parameters of the function and the return type of the function, and to declare variables within the function.

The statements

```
template<class Type>
Type larger(Type x, Type y)
{
    if(x >= y)
        return x;
    else
        return y;
}
```

define a function template `larger`, which returns the larger of two items. In the function heading, the type of the formal parameters `x` and `y` is `Type`, which will be specified by the type of the actual parameters when the function is called. For example, the statement

```
cout<<larger(5,6)<<endl;
```

is a call to the function template `larger`. Because 5 and 6 are of the type `int`, the data type `int` is substituted for `Type` and the compiler generates the appropriate code.

If you omit the body of the function in the function template definition, the function template, as usual, is the prototype.

The following example illustrates the use of function templates.

Example 2-7

This example uses the function template `larger` to determine the larger of two items.

```cpp
#include <iostream>
#include <string>

using namespace std;

template<class Type>
Type larger(Type x, Type y);

int main()
{
    cout<<"Line 1: Larger of 5 and 6 = "
        <<larger(5, 6)<<endl;                        //Line 1

    cout<<"Line 2: Larger of A and B = "
        <<larger('A', 'B')<<endl;                    //Line 2

    cout<<"Line 3: Larger of 5.6 and 3.2 = "
        <<larger(5.6, 3.2)<<endl;                    //Line 3

    string str1 = "Hello";                           //Line 4
    string str2 = "Happy";                           //Line 5

    cout<<"Line 6: Larger of "<<str1<<" and "
        <<str2<<" = "<<larger(str1, str2)
        <<endl;                                      //Line 6

    return 0;
}

template<class Type>
Type larger(Type x, Type y)
{
    if(x >= y)
        return x;
    else
        return y;
}
```

Output

```
Line 1: Larger of 5 and 6 = 6
Line 2: Larger of A and B = B
Line 3: Larger of 5.6 and 3.2 = 5.6
Line 6: Larger of Hello and Happy = Hello
```

Class Templates

Like function templates, class templates are used to write a single code segment for a set of related classes. For example, in Chapter 1, we defined a list as an ADT; our list element type there was int. If the list element type changes from int to, say, char, double, or string, you need to write separate classes for each element type. For the most part, the operations on the list and the algorithms to implement those operations remain the same. Using class templates, you can create a generic class listType, and the compiler can generate the appropriate source code for a specific implementation.

The syntax we use for a class template is

```
template< class Type>
class declaration
```

Class templates are called **parameterized types** because, based on the parameter type, a specific class is generated. For example, if the template parameter type is int, you can generate a list to process integers; if the parameter type is string, you can generate a list to process strings.

A class template for the ADT listType is defined as follows:

```
template<class elemType>
class listType
{
public:
    bool isEmpty();
        //Function to determine whether the list is empty.
        //Postcondition: Returns true if the list is empty;
        //               otherwise, returns false.

    bool isFull();
        //Function to determine whether the list is full.
        //Postcondition: Returns true if the list is full;
        //               otherwise, returns false.

    void search(const elemType& searchItem, bool& found);
        //Funtion to search the list for searchItem.
        //Postcondition: found is set to true if the
        //    searchItem is found in the list; otherwise,
        //    found is set to false.
```

```
    void insert(const elemType& newElement);
        //Funtion to insert newElement in the list.
        //Precondition: Prior to insertion, the list must
        //    not be full.
        //Postcondition: The list is the old list plus the
        //    newElement.

    void remove(const elemType& removeElement);
        //Funtion to remove an element from the list.
        //Postcondition: If the list is empty, it outputs
        //    the message, "Cannot delete from the empty
        //    list".
        //    If the list is nonempty, then if
        //    removeElement is found, the list is the
        //    old list minus removeElement; otherwise,
        //    the list is the same as the old list.

    void destroyList();
        //Funtion to destroy the list.
        //Postcondition: length = 0
    void printList();
        //Funtion to output the elements of the list.

    listType();
        //default constructor
        //Sets the length of the list to 0.
        //Postcondition: length = 0
private:
    elemType list[100];   //array to hold the list elements
    int length;           //variable to store the number
                          //of elements in the list
};
```

This definition of the class template `listType` is a generic definition and includes only the basic operations on a list. To derive a specific list from this list and to add or rewrite the operations, we declare the array containing the list elements and the length of the list as `protected`.

Next, we describe a specific list. Suppose that you want to create a list to process integer data. The statement

```
listType<int> intList;          //Line 1
```

declares `intList` to be a list of 100 components, with each component being of the type `int`. Similarly, the statement

```
listType<string> stringList;    //Line 2
```

declares `stringList` to be a list of 100 components, with each component being of the type `string`.

In the statements in Lines 1 and 2, `listType<int>` and `listType<string>` are referred to as **template instantiations** or **instantiations** of the class template `listType<elemType>`, where `elemType` is the class parameter in the template header. A template instantiation can be created with either a built-in or user-defined type.

The function members of a class template are considered function templates. Therefore, when giving the definitions of function members of a class template, you must follow the definition of the function template. For example, the definition of the member `insert` of the `class listType` is

```
template<class elemType>
void listType<elemType>::insert(const elemType& newElement)
{
    .
    .
    .
}
```

In the heading of the member function's definition, `elemType` specifies the data type of the list elements.

Header File and Implementation File of a Class Template

Until now, we have placed the definition of the class (in the specification file) and the definitions of the member functions (in the implementation file) in separate files. The object code was generated from the implementation file (independently of any client code) and linked with the client code. This strategy does not work with class templates. Passing parameters to a function has an effect at run time, whereas passing a parameter to a class template has an effect at compile time. Because the actual parameter to a class is specified in the client code, and because the compiler cannot instantiate a function template without the actual parameter to the template, we can no longer compile the implementation file independently of the client code.

This problem has several possible solutions. We could put the class definition and the definitions of the function templates directly in the client code, or we could put the class definition and the definitions of the function templates together in the same header file. Another alternative is to put the class definition and the definitions of the functions in separate files (as usual), but include a directive to the implementation file at the end of the header file (that is, the specification file). In either case, the function definitions and the client code are compiled together. For illustrative purposes, you will put the class definition and the function definitions in the same header file.

QUICK REVIEW

1. Inheritance and composition are meaningful ways to relate two or more classes.
2. Inheritance is an "is-a" relationship.
3. Composition is a "has-a" relationship.
4. In a single inheritance, the derived class is derived from only one existing class, called the base class.
5. In a multiple inheritance, a derived class is derived from more than one base class.
6. The `private` members of a base class are `private` to the base class. The derived class cannot directly access them.
7. The `public` members of a base class can be inherited either as `public`, `protected`, or `private` by the derived class.
8. A derived class can redefine the function members of a base class, but this redefinition applies only to the objects of the derived class.
9. A call to a base class's constructor is specified in the heading of the definition of the derived class's constructor.
10. When initializing the object of a derived class, the constructor of the base class is executed first.
11. Review the inheritance rules given in this chapter.
12. In composition, a member of a class is an object of another class.
13. In composition, a call to the constructor of the member objects is specified in the heading of the definition of the class's constructor.
14. The three basic principles of OOD are encapsulation, inheritance, and polymorphism.
15. An operator that has different meanings with different data types is said to be overloaded.
16. In C++, `<<` is used as a stream insertion operator and as a left shift operator. Similarly, `>>` is used as a stream extraction operator and as a right shift operator. Both are examples of operator overloading.
17. The function that overloads an operator is called an operator function.
18. The syntax of the heading of the operator function is

```
returnType operator operatorSymbol(parameters)
```

19. In C++, `operator` is a reserved word.
20. Operator functions are value-returning functions.
21. Except for the assignment operator and the member selection operator, to use an operator on class objects, that operator must be overloaded. The assignment operator performs a default memberwise copy.
22. Operator overloading provides the same concise notation for user-defined data types as is available with built-in data types.

23. When an operator is overloaded, its precedence cannot be changed, its associativity cannot be changed, default arguments cannot be used, the number of arguments that the operator takes cannot be changed, and the meaning of how an operator works with built-in data types remains the same.

24. It is not possible to create new operators. Only existing operators can be overloaded.

25. Most C++ operators can be overloaded.

26. The operators that cannot be overloaded are ., .*, ::, ?:, and `sizeof`.

27. The pointer `this` refers to the object as a whole.

28. The operator function that overloads the operators ( ), [ ], ->, or = must be a member of a class.

29. A `friend` function is a nonmember of a class.

30. The heading of a `friend` function is preceded by the word `friend`.

31. In C++, `friend` is a reserved word.

32. If an operator function is a member of a class, the leftmost operand of the operator must be a class object (or a reference to a class object) of that operator's class.

33. When the binary operator function is a member of a class, it has only one parameter; when it is a nonmember of a class, it has two parameters.

34. The operator functions that overload the stream insertion operator, <<, and the stream extraction operator, >>, for a class must be `friend` functions of that class.

35. In C++, a function name can be overloaded.

36. Every instance of an overloaded function has a different formal parameter list.

37. In C++, `template` is a reserved word.

38. Using templates, you can write a single code segment for a set of related functions called the function template.

39. Using templates, you can write a single code segment for a set of related classes called the class template.

40. The syntax of a template is

```
template<class elemType>
declaration;
```

where `elemType` is a user-defined identifier that is used to pass types (that is, data types) as parameters, and `declaration` is either a function or a class. The word `class` in the heading refers to any user-defined data type or built-in data type.

41. Class templates are called parameterized types.

42. In a class template, the parameter `elemType` specifies how a generic class template is to be customized to form a specific class.

43. The parameter `elemType` is mentioned in every class header and member function definition.

2

44. Suppose **cType** is a class template and **func** is a member function of **cType**. The heading of the function definition of **func** is

```
template<class elemType>
funcType cType<elemType>::func(formal parameters)
```

where **funcType** is the type of the function, such as **void**.

45. Suppose **cType** is a class template, which can take **int** as a parameter. The statement

```
cType<int> x;
```

declares **x** to be an object of the type **cType**, and the type passed to the **class cType** is **int**.

EXERCISES

1. Mark the following statements as true or false.

   a. The constructor of a derived class specifies a call to the constructor of the base class in the heading of the function definition.

   b. The constructor of a derived class specifies a call to the constructor of the base class using the name of the class.

   c. Suppose that **x** and **y** are classes, one of the data members of **x** is an object of the type **y**, and both classes have constructors. The constructor of **x** specifies a call to the constructor of **y** by using the object name of the type **y**.

   d. A derived class must have a constructor.

   e. In C++, all operators can be overloaded for user-defined data types.

   f. In C++, operators cannot be redefined for built-in types.

   g. The function that overloads an operator is called the **operator** function.

   h. C++ allows users to create their own operators.

   i. The precedence of an operator cannot be changed, but its associativity can be changed.

   j. Every instance of an overloaded function has the same number of parameters.

   k. It is not necessary to overload relational operators for classes that have only **int** data members.

   l. The member function of a **class** template is a function template.

   m. When writing the definition of a **friend** function, the keyword **friend** must appear in the function heading.

   n. The function heading of the operator function to overload the preincrement operator (**++**) and the postincrement operator (**++**) is the same because both operators have the same symbols.

2. Draw a class hierarchy in which several classes are derived from a single base class.

3. Suppose that a **class employeeType** is derived from the **class personType** (see Example 1-6, in Chapter 1). Give examples of data and function members that can be added to the **class employeeType**.

4. Explain the difference between the `private` and `protected` members of a class.

5. Consider the following class definition:

```
class aClass
{
public:
    void print() const;
    void set(int, int);
    aClass();
    aClass(int, int);

private:
    int u;
    int v;
};
```

What is wrong with the following `class` definitions?

a.

```
class bClass public aClass
{
public:
        void print()
        void set(int, int, int);
private:
        int z;
}
```

b.

```
class cClass: public aClass
{
public:
    void print();
    int sum();
    cClass();
    cClass(int)
}
```

6. Consider the following statements:

```
class yClass
{
 public:
    void one();
    void two(int, int);
    yClass();
 private:
    int a;
    int b;
};
```

2

```
class xClass: public yClass
{
public:
    void one();
    xClass();
private:
    int z;
};

yClass y;
xClass x;
```

a. The **private** members of **yClass** are **public** members of **xClass**. True or False?

b. Mark the following statements as valid or invalid. If a statement is invalid, explain why.

   (i)

```
void yClass::one()
{
    cout<<a+b<<endl;
}
```

   (ii)

```
y.a = 15;
x.b = 30;
```

   (iii)

```
void xClass::one()
{
    a = 10;
    b = 15;
    z = 30;
    cout<<a+b+z<<endl;

}
```

   (iv)

```
cout<<y.a<<" "<<y.b<<" "<<x.z<<endl;
```

7. Assume the declaration of Exercise 6.

   a. Write the definition of the default constructor of **yClass** so that the **private** data members of **yClass** are initialized to 0.

   b. Write the definition of the default constructor of **xClass** so that the **private** data members of **xClass** are initialized to 0.

   c. Write the definition of the member function **two** of **yClass** so that the **private** data member **a** is initialized to the value of the first parameter of **two**, and the **private** data member **b** is initialized to the value of the second parameter of **two**.

8. What is wrong with the following code?

```
class classA
{
protected:
    void setX(int a);                    //Line 1
        //Postcondition: x = a           //Line 2
private:                                 //Line 3
    int x;                               //Line 4
};
    .
    .
    .
int main()
{
    classA aObject;                      //Line 5

    aObject.setX(4);                     //Line 6
    return 0;                            //Line 7
}
```

9. Consider the following code:

```
class one
{
public:
    void print() const;
        //Outputs the values of x and y.
protected:
    void setData(int u, int v);
        //Postcondition: x = u; y = v
private:
    int x;
    int y;
};

class two: public one
{
public:
    void setData(int a, int b, int c);
        //Postcondition: x = a; y = b; z = c
    void print() const;
        //Outputs the values of x, y, and z.
private:
        int z;
};
```

a. Write the definition of the function `setData` of the `class two`.

b. Write the definition of the function `print` of the `class two`.

10. What is the output of the following C++ program?

```cpp
#include <iostream>
#include <string>

using namespace std;

class baseClass
{
public:
   void print()const;

   baseClass(string s =" ", int a = 0);
      //Postcondition: str = s; x = a
protected:
   int x;

private:
   string str;
};

class derivedClass: public baseClass
{
public:
   void print()const;

   derivedClass(string s = "", int a = 0, int b = 0);
      //Postcondition: str = s; x = a; y = b

private:
   int y;
};

int main()
{
   baseClass baseObject("This is base class", 2);
   derivedClass derivedObject("DDDDDD", 3, 7);

   baseObject.print();
   derivedObject.print();

   return 0;
}

void baseClass::print() const
{
      cout<<x<<" "<<str<<endl;
}
```

```cpp
baseClass::baseClass(string s, int a)
{
    str = s;
    x = a;
}

void derivedClass::print()const
{
    cout<<"Derived class: "<<y<<endl;
    baseClass::print();
}

derivedClass::derivedClass(string s, int a,
                                int b)
                :baseClass("Hello Base", a + b)
{
    y = b;
}
```

11. What is the output of the following program?

```cpp
#include <iostream>

using namespace std;

class baseClass
{
public:
    void print()const;

    int getX();

    baseClass(int a = 0);

protected:
    int x;
};

class derivedClass: public baseClass
{
public:
    void print()const;

    int getResult();

    derivedClass(int a = 0, int b = 0);

private:
    int y;
```

2

```
};

int main()
{
    baseClass baseObject(7);
    derivedClass derivedObject(3,8);

    baseObject.print();
    derivedObject.print();

    cout<<"**** "<<baseObject.getX()<<endl;
    cout<<"#### "<<derivedObject.getResult()<<endl;

    return 0;
}
void baseClass::print()const
{
        cout<<"In base: x = "<<x<<endl;
}

baseClass::baseClass(int a)
{
    x = a;
}

int baseClass::getX()
{
    return x;
}

void derivedClass::print()const
{
    cout<<"In derived: x = "<<x<<", y = "<<y
        <<", x + y = "<<x + y<<endl;
}

int derivedClass::getResult()
{
    return x + y;
}

derivedClass::derivedClass(int a, int b)
            :baseClass(a)
{
    y = b;
}
```

12. What is a `friend` function?

13. Suppose that the operator `<<` is to be overloaded for a user-defined `class mystery`. Why must `<<` be overloaded as a `friend` function?

14. Suppose that the binary operator `+` is overloaded as a member function for a `class strange`. How many parameters does the function `operator+` have?

15. Consider the following statement:

```
class strange
{
    .
    .
    .
};
```

a. Write a statement that shows the declaration in the `class strange` to overload the operator `>>`.

b. Write a statement that shows the declaration in the `class strange` to overload the binary operator `+` as a member function.

c. Write a statement that shows the declaration in the `class strange` to overload the operator `==` as a member function.

d. Write a statement that shows the declaration in the `class strange` to overload the postincrement operator `++` as a member function.

16. Assume the declaration of Exercise 15.

a. Write a statement that shows the declaration in the `class strange` to overload the binary operator `+` as a `friend` function.

b. Write a statement that shows the declaration in the `class strange` to overload the operator `==` as a `friend` function.

c. Write a statement that shows the declaration in the `class strange` to overload the postincrement operator `++` as a `friend` function.

17. Find the error(s) in the following code:

```
class mystery                      //Line 1
{
    ...
    bool operator <= (mystery);    //Line 2
    ...
};

bool mystery::<=(mystery rightObj)  //Line 3
{
    ...
}
```

2

18. Find the error(s) in the following code:

```
class mystery                              //Line 1
{
   ...
   bool operator <= (mystery, mystery); //Line 2
   ...
};
```

19. Find the error(s) in the following code:

```
class mystery                              //Line 1
{
   ...
   friend operator+ (mystery);            //Line 2
     //Overload the binary operator +
   ...
};
```

20. How many parameters are required to overload the preincrement operator for a class as a member function?

21. How many parameters are required to overload the preincrement operator for a class as a **friend** function?

22. How many parameters are required to overload the postincrement operator for a class as a member function?

23. How many parameters are required to overload the postincrement operator for a class as a **friend** function

24. Find the error(s) in the following code:

```
template<class type>                    //Line 1
class strange                           //Line 2
{
   ...
};

strange<int> s1;                        //Line 3
strange<type> s2;                       //Line 4
```

25. Consider the following declaration:

```
template<class Type>
class strange
{
    ...
private:
    Type a;
    Type b;
};
```

a. Write a statement that declares sObj to be an object of the type strange such that the private data members a and b are of the type int.

b. Write a statement that shows the declaration in the class strange to overload the operator == as a member function.

c. Assume that two objects of the type strange are equal if their corresponding data members are equal. Write the definition of the function operator== for the class strange, which is overloaded as a member function.

26. Consider the definition of the following function template:

```
template<class Type>
Type surprise(Type x, Type y)
{
    return x + y ;
}
```

What is the output of the following statements?

a. cout<<surprise(5, 7)<<endl;

b. string str1 = "Sunny";
   string str2 = " Day";
   cout<<surprise(str1, str2)<<endl;

27. Consider the definition of the following function template:

```
template<class Type>
Type funcExp(Type list[], int size)
{
    int j;
    Type x = list[0];
    Type y = list[size - 1];

    for(j = 1; j < (size - 1)/2; j++)
    {
            if(x < list[j])
                x = list[j];
            if(y > list[size - 1 -j])
                y = list[size - 1 -j];
    }
```

```
        return x + y;
}
```

Further suppose that you have the following declarations:

```
int list[10] = {5, 3, 2, 10, 4, 19, 45, 13, 61, 11};
string strList[] = {"One", "Hello", "Four", "Three", "How",
                    "Six"};
```

What is the output of the following statements?

a. `cout<<funExp(list, 10);`

b. `cout<<funExp(strList, 6)<<endl;`

28. Write the definition of the function template that swaps the contents of two variables.

PROGRAMMING EXERCISES

1. In Chapter 1, the **class clockType** was designed to implement the time of day in a program. Certain applications, in addition to hours, minutes, and seconds, might require you to store the time zone. Derive the **class extClockType** from the **class clockType** by adding a data member to store the time zone. Add the necessary member functions and constructors to make the class functional. Also, write the definitions of the member functions and the constructors. Finally, write a test program to test your **class**.

2. In this chapter, the **class dateType** was designed to implement the date in a program, but the member function **setDate** and the constructor do not check whether the date is valid before storing the date in the data members. Rewrite the definitions of the function **setDate** and the constructor so that the values for the month, day, and year are checked before storing the date into the data members. Add a function member, **isLeapYear**, to check whether a year is a leap year. Moreover, write a test program to test your **class**.

3. A point in the x-y plane is represented by its x-coordinate and y-coordinate. Design a **class, pointType**, that can store and process a point in the x-y plane. You should then perform operations on the point, such as showing the point, setting the coordinates of the point, printing the coordinates of the point, returning the x-coordinate, and returning the y-coordinate. Also, write a test program to test various operations on the point.

4. Every circle has a center and a radius. Given the radius, you can determine the circle's area and circumference. Given the center, you can determine its position in the x-y plane. The center of a circle is a point in the x-y plane. Design a **class, circleType**, that can store the radius and center of the circle. Because the center is a point in the x-y plane and you designed a class to capture the properties of a point in Programming Exercise 3, you must derive the **class circleType** from the **class pointType**. You should be able to perform the usual operations on a circle, such as setting the radius, printing the radius, calculating and printing the area and circumference, and carrying out the usual operations on the center.

5. Every cylinder has a base and height, where the base is a circle. Design a **class**, **cylinderType**, that can capture the properties of a cylinder and perform the usual operations on a cylinder. Derive this class from the **class circleType** designed in Programming Exercise 4. Some of the operations that can be performed on a cylinder are as follows: calculate and print the volume, calculate and print the surface area, set the height, set the radius of the base, and set the center of the base.

6. In Programming Exercise 2, the **class dateType** was designed and implemented to keep track of a date, but it has very limited operations. Redefine the **class dateType** so that it can perform the following operations on a date in addition to the operations already defined:

   a. Set the month.

   b. Set the day.

   c. Set the year.

   d. Return the month.

   e. Return the day.

   f. Return the year.

   g. Test whether the year is a leap year.

   h. Return the number of days in the month. For example, if the date is 3-12-2003, the number of days to be returned is 31 because there are 31 days in March.

   i. Return the number of days passed in the year. For example, if the date is 3-18-2003, the number of days passed in the year is 77. Note that the number of days returned also includes the current day.

   j. Return the number of days remaining in the year. For example, if the date is 3-18-2003, the number of days remaining in the year is 288.

   k. Calculate the new date by adding a fixed number of days to the date. For example, if the date is 3-18-2003 and the days to be added are 25, the new date is 4-12-2003.

7. Write the definitions of the functions to implement the operations defined for the **class dateType** in Programming Exercise 6.

8. The **class dateType** defined in Programming Exercise 6 prints the date in numerical form. Some applications might require the date to be printed in another form, such as March 24, 2003. Derive the **class extDateType** so that the date can be printed in either form.

   Add a data member to the **class extDateType** so that the month can also be stored in string form. Add a function member to output the month in the string format followed by the year—for example, in the form March 2003.

   Write the definitions of the functions to implement the operations for the **class extDateType**.

9. Using the **classes extDateType** (Programming Exercise 8) and **dayType** (Chapter 1, Programming Exercise 3), design the **class calendarType** so that, given the month

and the year, you can print the calendar for that month. To print a monthly calendar, you must know the first day of the month and the number of days in that month. Therefore, you must store the first day of the month, which is of the form `dayType`, and the month and the year of the calendar. The month and the year can be stored in an object of the form `extDateType` by setting the day component of the date to 1, and the month and year as specified by the user. Therefore, the `class calendarType` has two data members: an object of the type `dayType`, and an object of the type `extDateType`.

Design the `class calendarType` so that the program can print a calendar for any month starting January 1, 1500. Note that the day for January 1 of the year 1500 is a Monday. To calculate the first day of a month, you can add the appropriate days to Monday of January 1, 1500.

For the `class calendarType`, include the following operations:

a. Determine the first day of the month for which the calendar will be printed. Call this operation `firstDayOfMonth`.

b. Set the month.

c. Set the year.

d. Return the month.

e. Return the year.

f. Print the calendar for the particular month.

g. Add the appropriate constructors to initialize the data members.

10. a. Write the definitions of the member functions of the `class calendarType` (designed in Programming Exercise 9) to implement the operations of the `class calendarType`.

b. Write a test program to print the calendar for either a particular month or a particular year. For example, the calendar for September 2003 is

```
                  September 2003
   Sun    Mon    Tue    Wed    Thu    Fri    Sat
           1      2      3      4      5      6
    7      8      9     10     11     12     13
   14     15     16     17     18     19     20
   21     22     23     24     25     26     27
   28     29     30
```

11. In Chapter 1, the `class clockTime` was designed to implement the time of day in a program. This chapter discussed how to overload various operators. Redesign the `class clockTime` by overloading the following operators: the stream insertion `<<` and stream extraction `>>` operators for input and output, the preincrement and postincrement operators to increment the time by one second, and the relational operators to compare the two times. Also, write a test program to test various operations of the `class clockTime`.

12. a. Extend the definition of the **class complexType** (from the Programming Example Complex Numbers) so that it performs the subtraction and division operations. Overload the operators subtraction and division for this class as member functions.

If (a, b) and (c, d) are complex numbers, then

$(a, b) - (c, d) = (a - c, b - d)$

If (c, d) is nonzero, $(a, b) / (c, d) = ((ac + bd) / (c^2 + d^2), (-ad + bc) / (c^2 + d^2))$

b. Write the definitions of the functions to overload the operators $-$ and $/$ as defined in part a.

c. Write a test program that tests various operations on the **class complexType**. Format your answer with two decimal places.

13. a. Rewrite the definition of the **class complexType** so that the arithmetic and relational operators are overloaded as nonmember functions.

b. Write the definitions of the member functions of the **class complexType** as designed in part a.

c. Write a test program that tests various operations on the **class complexType** as designed in parts a and b. Format your answer with two decimal places.

14. Let $a + ib$ be a complex number. The conjugate of $a + ib$ is $a - ib$ and the absolute value of $a + ib$ is $\sqrt{a^2 + b^2}$. Extend the definition of the **class complexType** of the Programming Example Complex Numbers by overloading the operators $\sim$ and **!** as member functions so that $\sim$ returns the conjugate of a complex number and **!** returns the absolute value. Write the definitions of these operator functions.

15. Redo Programming Exercise 14 so that the operators $\sim$ and **!** are overloaded as nonmember functions.

16. Rational fractions are of the form a / b, where a and b are integers and $b \neq 0$. In this exercise, fractions mean rational fractions. Suppose a / b and c / d are fractions. Arithmetic operations on fractions are defined by the following rules:

$a / b + c / d = (ad + bc) / bd$

$a / b - c / d = (ad - bc) / bd$

$a / b \times c / d = ac / bd$

$(a / b) / (c / d) = ad / bc$, where $c / d \neq 0$.

Fractions are compared as follows: a / b op c / d if ad op bc, where op is any of the relational operations. For example, $a / b < c / d$ if $ad < bc$.

a. Design a **class**—say, **fractionType**—that performs the arithmetic and relational operations on fractions. Overload the arithmetic and relational operators so that the appropriate symbols can be used to perform these operations. Also, overload the stream insertion and stream extraction operators for easy input and output.

b. Write a C++ program that, using the **class fractionType**, performs operations on fractions.

c. Among other things, test the following: Suppose x, y, and z are objects of the type fraction. If the input is 2/3, the statement

```
cin>>x;
```

should store 2/3 in x. The statement

```
cout<<x+y<<endl;
```

should output the value of x + y in fraction form. The statement

```
z = x + y;
```

should store the sum of x and y in z in fraction form. Your answer need not be in the lowest terms.

17. a. In Programming Exercise 2 in Chapter 1, you defined a class romanType to implement Roman numerals in a program. In that exercise, you also implemented a function, romanToDecimal, to convert a Roman numeral into its equivalent decimal number.

Modify the definition of the class romanType so that the data members are declared as protected. Use the class string to manipulate the strings. Furthermore, overload the stream insertion and stream extraction operators for easy input and output. The stream insertion operator outputs the Roman numeral in the Roman format.

Also, include a member function, decimalToRoman, that converts the decimal number (the decimal number must be a positive integer) to an equivalent Roman numeral format. Write the definition of the member function decimalToRoman.

For simplicity, assume that only the letter I can appear in front of another letter and that it appears only in front of the letters V and X. For example, 4 is represented as IV, 9 is represented as IX, 39 is represented as XXXIX, and 49 is represented as XXXXIX. Also, 40 is represented as XXXX, 190 is represented as CLXXXX, and so on.

b. Derive a class extRomanType from the class romanType to do the following. In the class extRomanType, overload the arithmetic operators +, −, *, and / so that arithmetic operations can be performed on Roman numerals. Also, overload the preincrement, postincrement, decrement operators as member functions of the class extRomanType.

To add (subtract, multiply, or divide) Roman numerals, add (subtract, multiply, or divide, respectively) their decimal representations and then convert the result to the Roman numeral format. For subtraction, if the first number is smaller than the second number, output a message stating that, "Because the first number is smaller than the second, the numbers cannot be subtracted." Similarly, for division, the numerator must be larger than the denominator. Use similar conventions for the increment and decrement operators.

c. Write the definitions of the functions to overload the operators described in part b.

d. Test your **class extRomanType** on the following program. (Include the appropriate header files.)

```cpp
int main()
{
    extRomanType num1("XXXIV");
    extRomanType num2("XV");
    extRomanType num3;

    cout<<"Num1 = "<<num1<<endl;
    cout<<"Num2 = "<<num2<<endl;
    cout<<"Num1 + Num2 = "<<num1+num2<<endl;
    cout<<"Num1 * Num2 = "<<num1*num2<<endl;

    cout<<"Enter two numbers in Roman format: ";
    cin>>num1>>num2;
    cout<<endl;

    cout<<"Num1 = "<<num1<<endl;
    cout<<"Num2 = "<<num2<<endl;

    num3 = num2 * num1;
    cout<<"Num3 = "<<num3<<endl;

    return 0;
}
```

3

POINTERS AND
ARRAY-BASED LISTS

In this chapter, you will:

♦ Learn about the pointer data type and pointer variables

♦ Explore how to declare and manipulate the pointer variables

♦ Learn about the address of operator and dereferencing operator

♦ Discover dynamic variables

♦ Examine how to use the `new` and `delete` operators to manipulate dynamic variables

♦ Learn about pointer arithmetic

♦ Discover dynamic arrays

♦ Become aware of the shallow and deep copies of data

♦ Discover the peculiarities of classes with pointer data members

♦ Explore how dynamic arrays are used to process lists

The data types in C++ are classified into three categories: simple, structured, and pointers. Until now, you have worked with only the first two data types. This chapter discusses the third data type: the pointer data type. You will first learn how to declare pointer variables (or pointers, for short) and manipulate the data to which they point. Later, you will use these concepts when you study dynamic arrays and linked lists. Linked lists are discussed in Chapter 5.

POINTER DATA TYPES AND POINTER VARIABLES

The values belonging to pointer data types are the memory addresses of your computer. As in many other languages, no name is associated with the pointer data type in C++. Because the domain—that is, the values of a pointer data type—are the addresses (memory locations), a pointer variable is a variable whose content is an address, that is, a memory location.

Pointer variable: A variable whose content is an address (a memory address).

Declaring Pointer Variables

Because no name is associated with pointer data types, pointer variables are not declared like other variables. When you declare a pointer variable, you also specify the data type of the value to be stored in the memory location pointed to by the pointer variable. In C++, you declare a pointer variable by using the asterisk symbol (*) between the data type and the variable name. The general syntax to declare a pointer variable is

```
dataType *identifier;
```

As an example, consider the following statements:

```
int    *p;
char   *ch;
```

In these statements, both **p** and **ch** are pointer variables. The content of **p** (when properly assigned) points to a memory location of the type **int**; the content of **ch** points to a memory location of the type **char**. Usually **p** is called a pointer variable of the type **int**, and **ch** is called a pointer variable of the type **char**.

Before discussing how pointers work, let us make the following observations. The statement

```
int    *p;
```

is equivalent to the statement

```
int*   p;
```

which is equivalent to the statement

```
int  *  p;
```

Therefore, the character * can appear anywhere between the data type name and the variable name.

Now consider the following statement:

```
int*    p, q;
```

In this statement, only p is the pointer variable, not q. Here q is an int variable. To avoid confusion, we prefer to attach the character * to the variable name. So the preceding statement is written as

```
int    *p, q;
```

Of course, the statement

```
int    *p, *q;
```

declares both p and q to be pointer variables of the type int.

Now that you know how to declare pointers, next we discuss how to make a pointer point to a memory space and how to manipulate the data stored in these memory locations.

Because the value of a pointer is a memory address, a pointer can store the address of a memory space of the designated type. For example, if p is a pointer of the type int, p can store the address of any memory space of the type int. C++ provides two operators—the address of operator (&) and the dereferencing operator (*)—to work with pointers. The next two sections describe these operators.

Address of Operator (&)

In C++, the ampersand, &, called the **address of operator**, is a unary operator that returns the address of its operand. For example, given the statements

```
int   x;
int *p;
```

the statement

```
p = &x;
```

assigns the address of x to p. That is, x and the value of p refer to the same memory location.

Dereferencing Operator (*)

Until now, you have used the asterisk character, *, as the binary multiplication operator. C++ also uses * as a unary operator. When used as a unary operator, *, commonly referred to as the **dereferencing operator** or **indirection operator**, refers to the object to which its operand (that is, a pointer) points. For example, given the statements

```
int x = 25;
int *p;
p = &x;    //store the address of x in p
```

the statement

```
cout<<*p<<endl;
```

prints the value stored in the memory space pointed to by p, which is the value of x. Also, the statement

```
*p = 55;
```

stores **55** in the memory location pointed to by **p**—that is, in **x**.

Let us consider the following statements:

```
int *p;
int  num;
```

In these statements, **p** is a pointer variable of the type `int` and `num` is a variable of the type `int`. See Figure 3-1.

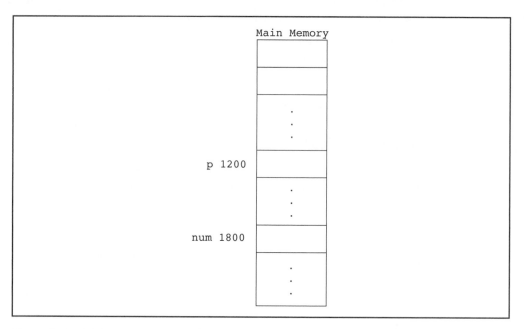

Figure 3-1   Main memory, p, and num

Let us assume that memory location **1200** is allocated for **p** and memory location **1800** is allocated for **num**. The statement

```
num = 78;
```

stores **78** in **num**—that is, in memory location **1800**. See Figure 3-2.

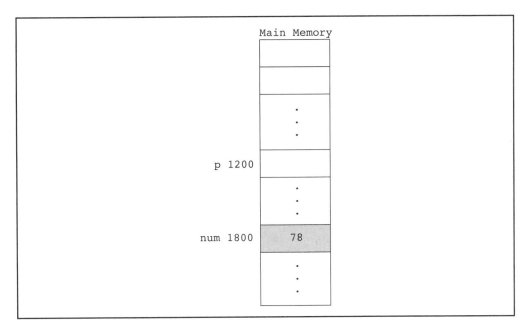

Figure 3-2   num after the statement num = 78; executes

The statement

p = #

stores the address of **num**—that is, 1800—into **p**. After this statement executes, both *p and **num** refer to the content of memory location 1800—that is, **num**. See Figure 3-3.

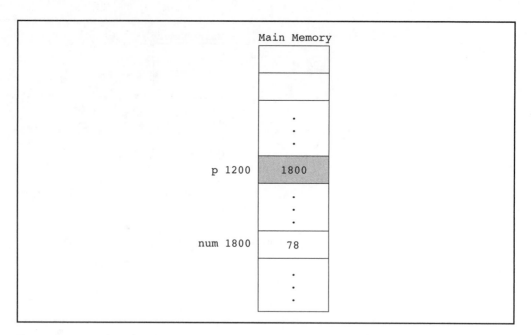

Figure 3-3 p after the statement p = # executes

The assignment statement

```
*p = 24;
```

changes the content of memory location 1800 and therefore also changes the content of num. See Figure 3–4.

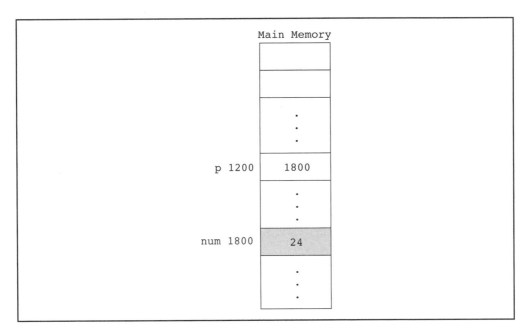

Figure 3-4   *p and num after the statement *p = 24; executes

Let us summarize the preceding discussion:

- &p, p, and *p all have different meanings:
- &p means the address of p—that is, 1200 (in Figure 3-4).
- p means the content of p (1800 in Figure 3-4).
- *p means the content (24 in Figure 3-4) of the memory location (1800 in Figure 3-4) pointed to by p (that is, pointed to by the content of memory location 1200).

Example 3-1

Consider the following statements:

```
int *p;
int  x;
```

Suppose that we have the memory allocation for p and x as shown in Figure 3-5.

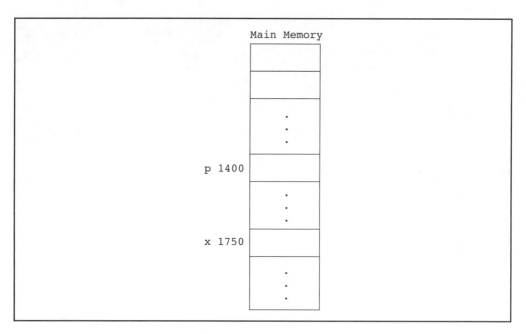

Figure 3-5   Main memory, p, and x

The values of &p, p, *p, &x, and x are as follows:

	Value
&p	1400
p	??? (unknown)
*p	Does not exist (undefined)
&x	1750
x	??? (unknown)

Suppose that the following statements are executed in the order given:

```
x = 50;
p = &x;
*p = 38;
```

The values of &p, p, *p, &x, and x are shown after each of these statements executes. After the statement

```
x = 50;
```

executes, the values of &p, p, *p, &x, and x are as follows:

	Value
&p	1400
p	??? (unknown)
*p	does not exist (undefined)
&x	1750
x	50

After the statement

```
p = &x;
```

executes, the values of &p, p, *p, &x, and x are as follows:

	Value
&p	1400
p	1750
*p	50
&x	1750
x	50

Note that after the statement p = &x; executes, p contains the address of x, and so *p and x refer to the same memory space, which is x. Therefore, the value of *p is 50.

After the statement

```
*p = 38;
```

executes, the values of &p, p, *p, &x, and x are as follows. (Because *p and x refer to the same memory space, the value of x also changes to 38.)

	Value
&p	1400
p	1750
*p	38
&x	1750
x	38

Let us note the following from Example 3-1:

1. A declaration such as

   ```
   int *p;
   ```

   allocates memory for **p** only, not for ***p**. Later, you will learn how to allocate memory for ***p** and what it means to allocate memory for ***p**.

2. Assume the following:

   ```
   int *p;
   int x;
   ```

   Then,

   a. **p** is a pointer variable.

   b. The content of **p** points only to a memory location of the type **int**.

   c. Memory location **x** exists and is of the type **int**. Therefore, the assignment statement

      ```
      p = &x;
      ```

      is legal. After this assignment statement executes, ***p** is valid and meaningful.

Example 3-2

The following program illustrates how pointer variables work.

```
//Chapter 3: Example 3-2
#include <iostream>

using namespace std;

int main()
{
    int *p;
    int x = 37;
```

```
    cout<<"Line 1: x = "<<x<<endl;                        //Line 1

    p = &x;                                               //Line 2

    cout<<"Line 3: *p = "<<*p
        <<", x = "<<x<<endl;                              //Line 3

    *p = 58;                                              //Line 4

    cout<<"Line 5: *p = "<<*p
        <<", x = "<<x<<endl;                              //Line 5

    cout<<"Line 6: Address of p = "<<&p<<endl;            //Line 6

    cout<<"Line 7: Value of p = "<<p<<endl;               //Line 7

    cout<<"Line 8: Value of the memory location "
        <<"pointed to by *p = "<<*p<<endl;                //Line 8
    cout<<"Line 9: Address of x = "<<&x<<endl;            //Line 9
    cout<<"Line 10: Value of x = "<<x<<endl;              //Line 10

    return 0;
}
```

Sample Run

```
Line 1: x = 37
Line 3: *p = 37, x = 37
Line 5: *p = 58, x = 58
Line 6: Address of p = 006BFDF4
Line 7: Value of p = 006BFDF0
Line 8: Value of the memory location pointed to by *p = 58
Line 9: Address of x = 006BFDF0
Line 10: Value of x = 58
```

The preceding program works as follows. The statement in Line 1 outputs the value of x; the statement in Line 2 stores the address of x into p. The statement in Line 3 outputs the values of *p and x. Because p contains the address of x, the values of *p and x are the same, as shown by the output of Line 3. The statement in Line 4 changes the value of *p to 58; the statement in Line 5 outputs the values of *p and x, which are again the same. The statements between Lines 6 and 10 output the address of p, the value of p, the value of *p, the address of x, and the value of x. Note that the value of p and the address of x are the same because the address of x is stored in p by the statement in Line 2. (Note that the address of p, the value of p, and the address of x, as shown by the outputs of Lines 6, 7, and 9, respectively, are machine dependent. Moreover, these values are in hexadecimal form. When you run this program on your computer, you are likely to get different values.)

Classes, `structs`, and Pointer Variables

In the previous section, you learned how to declare and manipulate pointers to simple data types such as `int` and `char`. You can also declare pointers to other data types, such as classes. You will now learn how to declare and manipulate pointers to classes and `structs`. (Recall that both classes and `structs` have the same capabilities; the only difference is that, by default, all members of a class are `private` and all members of a `struct` are `public`. Therefore, the following discussion applies to both.)

Consider the following declaration of a `struct`:

```
struct studentType
{
    char name[27];
    double gpa;
    int sID;
    char grade;
};
```

```
studentType     student;
studentType*    studentPtr;
```

In this declaration, `student` is an object of the type `studentType`, and `studentPtr` is a pointer variable of the type `studentType`. The following statement stores the address of `student` in `studentPtr`:

```
studentPtr = &student;
```

The following statement stores `3.9` in the component `gpa` of the object `student`:

```
(*studentPtr).gpa = 3.9;
```

The expression `(*studentPtr).gpa` is a mixture of pointer dereferencing and the class component selection. In C++, the dot operator has a higher precedence than the dereferencing operator. Because of this fact, the parentheses are important. To simplify the accessing of class components via a pointer, C++ provides another operator, called the **member access operator arrow**, `->`. The operator `->` consists of two consecutive symbols: a hyphen and the "greater than" symbol.

The syntax for accessing a `class` (`struct`) member using the operator `->` is

```
pointerVariableName->classMemberName
```

Therefore, the statement

```
(*studentPtr).gpa = 3.9;
```

is equivalent to the statement

```
studentPtr->gpa = 3.9;
```

Accessing `class` (`struct`) components via pointers using the operator `->` therefore eliminates the use of both parentheses and the dereferencing operator. Because typos are unavoidable and missing parentheses can result in either abnormal program termination or erroneous results, when accessing `class` (`struct`) components via pointers, this book uses the arrow notation.

Example 3-3 illustrates how pointers work with `class` member functions.

3

Example 3-3

Consider the following class:

```
class classExample
{
public:
    void setX(int a);
        //Function to set the value of the data member x.
        //Postcondition: x = a
    void print() const;
        //Function to output the value of x.

private:
    int x;
};
```

The definition of the member function is as follows:

```
void classExample::setX(int a)
{
    x = a;
}

void classExample::print() const
{
    cout<<"x = "<<x<<endl;
}
```

Consider the following function `main`:

```
int main()
{
        classExample *cExpPtr;              //Line 1
        classExample cExpObject;            //Line 2

        cExpPtr = &cExpObject;              //Line 3

        cExpPtr->setX(5);                   //Line 4
        cExpPtr->print();                   //Line 5

        return 0;
}
```

Output

```
x = 5
```

In the function `main`, the statement in Line 1 declares `cExpPtr` to be a pointer of the type `classExample`; the statement in Line 2 declares `cExpObject` to be an object of the type `classExample`. The statement in Line 3 stores the address of `cExpObject` into `cExpPtr`. See Figure 3-6.

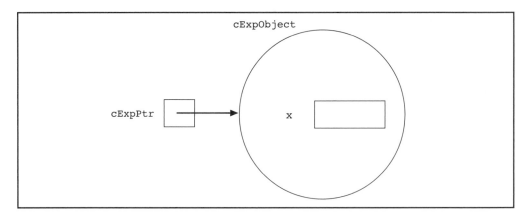

Figure 3-6   `cExpObject` and `cExpPtr` after the statement `cExpPtr = &cExpObject;` executes

In the statement in Line 4, the pointer `cExpPtr` accesses the member function `setX` to set the value of the data member `x`. See Figure 3-7.

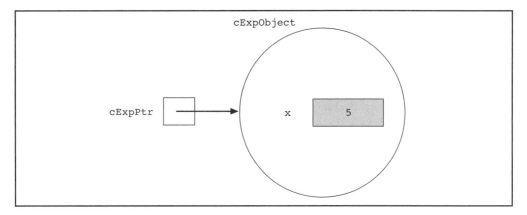

Figure 3-7   `cExpObject` and `cExpPtr` after the statement `cExpPtr ->setX(5);`
executes

In the statement in Line 5, the pointer **cExpPtr** accesses the member function **print** to
print the value of **x**, as shown in the output.

Initializing Pointer Variables

Because C++ does not automatically initialize variables, pointer variables must be initialized
if you do not want them to point to anything. Pointer variables are initialized using the constant value 0, called the **null pointer**. Therefore, the statement p = 0; stores the null pointer
in p; that is, p points to nothing. Some programmers use the named constant NULL to initialize pointer variables. The following two statements are equivalent:

```
p = NULL;
p = 0;
```

 The number 0 is the only number that can be directly assigned to a pointer variable.

Dynamic Variables

In the previous sections, you learned how to declare pointer variables, how to store the address
of a variable into a pointer variable of the same type as the variable, and how to manipulate
data using pointers. However, you learned how to use pointers to manipulate data only into
memory spaces that were created using other variables. In other words, the pointers manipulated data into existing memory spaces. So what is the big deal about using pointers? You can
access these memory spaces by working with the variables that were used to create them. In

this section, you learn about the power behind pointers. In particular, you learn how to allocate and deallocate memory during program execution using pointers.

Variables that are created during program execution are called **dynamic variables**. With the help of pointers, C++ creates dynamic variables. C++ provides two operators—**new** and **delete**—to create and destroy, respectively, dynamic variables. When a program requires a new dynamic variable, the operator **new** is used; when a program no longer needs a dynamic variable, the operator **delete** is used.

In C++, **new** and **delete** are reserved words.

The operator **new** has two forms: one to allocate a single variable, and another to allocate an array of variables. The syntax to use the operator **new** is

```
new dataType;            //to allocate a single variable
new dataType[intExp];   //to allocate an array of variables
```

where **intExp** is any expression that evaluates to a positive integer. The operator **new** allocates memory (a variable) of the designated type and returns a pointer to it—that is, the address of this allocated memory. Moreover, the allocated memory is uninitialized.

Consider the following declaration:

```
int  *p;
char *q;
int  x;
```

The statement

```
p = &x;
```

stores the address of **x** in **p**. However, no new memory is allocated. On the other hand, consider the following statement:

```
p = new int;
```

This statement allocates memory space of the type **int** during program execution, somewhere in memory, and stores the address of the allocated memory in **p**. The allocated memory is accessed via pointer dereferencing—namely, ***p**. Similarly, the statement

```
q = new char[16];
```

creates an array of **16** components of the type **char** and stores the base address of the array in **q**.

Because a dynamic variable is unnamed, it cannot be accessed directly. It is accessed indirectly by the pointer returned by **new**. The following statements illustrate this concept:

```
int  *p;               //p is a pointer of the type int

char *name;            //name is a pointer of the type char
```

```
string *str;              //str is a pointer of the type
                          //string

p = new int;              //Allocates memory of the type
                          //int and stores the address of
                          //the allocated memory in p.
*p = 28;                  //Stores 28 in the allocated
                          //memory.

name = new char[5];       //Allocates memory for an array
                          //of five components of the type
                          //char and stores the base
                          //address of the array in name.
strcpy(name, "John");     //Stores John in name.

str = new string;         //Allocates memory of the type
                          //string and stores the address
                          //of the allocated memory in
                          //str.
*str = "Sunny Day";       //Stores the string "Sunny Day"
                          //in the memory pointed to by
                          //str.
```

3

When a dynamic variable is no longer needed, it can be destroyed; that is, its memory can be deallocated. The C++ operator `delete` is used to destroy dynamic variables. The syntax to use the operator `delete` has two forms:

```
delete pointer;           //to destroy a single dynamic variable
delete [] pointer;        //to destroy a dynamically created array
```

Therefore, the statements

```
delete p;
delete [] name;
```

deallocate the memory referenced by the pointers `p` and `name`.

Operations on Pointer Variables

The operations that are allowed on pointer variables are the assignment and relational operations as well as some limited arithmetic operations. The value of one pointer variable can be assigned to another pointer variable of the same type. Two pointer variables of the same type can be compared for equality, and so on. Integer values can be added and subtracted from a pointer variable. The value of one pointer variable can be subtracted from another pointer variable.

For example, suppose that we have the following statements:

```
int *p, *q;
```

The statement

```
p = q;
```

copies the value of q into p. After this statement executes, both p and q point to the same memory location. Any changes made to *p automatically change the value of *q, and vice versa.

The expression

```
p == q
```

evaluates to **true** if p and q have the same value—that is, if they point to the same memory location. Similarly, the expression

```
p != q
```

evaluates to **true** if p and q point to different memory locations.

The arithmetic operations that are allowed differ from the arithmetic operations on numbers. First, let us use the following statements to explain the increment and decrement operations on pointer variables:

```
int *p;
double *q;
char *chPtr;
studentType *stdPtr;   //studentType is as defined before
```

Usually, the size of the memory allocated for an **int** variable is 4 bytes, a **double** variable is 8 bytes, and a **char** variable is 1 byte. The memory allocated for a variable of the type **studentType** is then 40 bytes.

The statement

```
p++;      or      p = p + 1;
```

increments the value of p by 4 bytes because p is a pointer of the type **int**. Similarly, the statements

```
q++;
chPtr++;
```

increment the value of q by 8 bytes and the value of chPtr by 1 byte. The statement

```
stdPtr++;
```

increments the value of **stdPtr** by 40 bytes.

The increment operator increments the value of a pointer variable by the size of the memory to which it is pointing. Similarly, the decrement operator decrements the value of a pointer variable by the size of the memory to which it is pointing.

Moreover, the statement

```
p = p + 2;
```

increments the value of p by 8 bytes.

Therefore, when an integer is added to a pointer variable, the value of the pointer variable is incremented by the integer times the size of the memory to which the pointer is pointing. Similarly, when an integer is subtracted from a pointer variable, the value of the pointer variable is decremented by the integer times the size of the memory to which the pointer is pointing.

 If you are not careful, pointer arithmetic can be very dangerous. Using pointer arithmetic, the program can accidentally access the memory locations of other variables and change their content without warning, leaving the programmer in a state of disbelief and trying to find out what went wrong. If a pointer variable tries to access either the memory spaces of other variables or an illegal memory space, some systems might terminate the program with an appropriate error message. Always exercise extra care when doing pointer arithmetic.

DYNAMIC ARRAYS

The arrays that we have used until now are called static arrays because their size was fixed at compile time. One of the limitations of a static array is that every time you execute the program, the size of the array is fixed, so it might not be possible to use the same array to process different data sets of the same type. One way to handle this limitation is to declare an array that is large enough to process a variety of data sets. However, if the array is very big and the data set is small, such a declaration would result in memory waste. On the other hand, it would be extremely helpful if, during program execution, you could prompt the user to enter the size of the array and then create an array of the appropriate size. This approach is especially helpful if you cannot even guess the array size while writing the program. In this section, you learn how to create arrays during program execution and process such arrays.

An array created during the execution of a program is called a **dynamic array**. To create a dynamic array, we use the second form of the `new` operator—the one to allocate an array of variables.

The statement

```
int *p;
```

declares `p` to be a pointer variable of the type `int`. The statement

```
p = new int[10];
```

allocates 10 contiguous memory locations, each of the type `int`, and stores the address of the first memory location into `p`. In other words, the operator `new` creates an array of 10 components of the type `int`, it returns the base address of the array, and the assignment operator stores the base address of the array into `p`. Therefore, the statement

```
*p = 25;
```

stores 25 into the first memory location, and the statements

```
p++;                    //p points to the next array component
*p = 35;
```

store 35 into the second memory location. Therefore, by using the increment and decrement operations, you can access the components of the array. Of course, after performing a few increment operations, it is possible to lose track of the first array component. C++ allows us to use the array notation to access these memory locations. For example, the statements

```
p[0] = 25;
p[1] = 35;
```

store 25 and 35 into the first and second array components, respectively. That is, p[0] refers to the first array component, p[1] refers to the second array component, and so on. In general, p[i] refers to the (i + 1)th array component. After the preceding statements execute, p still points to the first array component. Similarly, the following **for** loop initializes each array component to 0:

```
for(j = 0; j < 10; j++)
    p[j] = 0;
```

where j is an **int** variable.

When the array notation is used to process the array pointed to by p, p stays fixed at the first memory location. Moreover, p is an array created during program execution, called a **dynamic array**.

 The statement

```
int list[10];
```

declares list to be an array of 10 components. There is a memory space named list, and the value stored in that memory space is the base address of the array, which is the address of the first array component. Because the memory space named list contains an address, list is a pointer. However, the increment and decrement operations cannot be applied to list because we want list always to point to the first array component. Any attempt to use the increment or decrement operations on list results in a compile-time error. Furthermore, if p is a pointer variable of the type int, then the statement

```
p = list;
```

copies the value of list, which is the base address of the array, into p. We are allowed to perform increment and decrement operations on p.

An array name, such as list, is a constant pointer; it always points to the first component of the array. Moreover, when you declare an array, such as list, then list always points to the same array.

Example 3-4

The following program illustrates how to obtain a user's response to get the array size and create a dynamic array during program execution. Consider the following statements:

```
int *intList;                          //Line 1
int arraySize;                         //Line 2

cout<<"Enter the array size: ";        //Line 3
cin>>arraySize;                        //Line 4
cout<<endl;                            //Line 5

intList = new int[arraySize];          //Line 6
```

The statement in Line 1 declares intList to be a pointer of the type int; the statement in Line 2 declares arraySize to be an int variable. The statement in Line 3 prompts the user to enter the size of the array; the statement in Line 4 inputs the array size into the variable arraySize. The statement in Line 6 creates an array of the size specified by arraySize, and the base address of the array is stored in intList. From this point on, you can treat intList just like any other array. For example, you can use the array notation to process the elements of intList and pass intList as a parameter to a function.

Functions and Pointers

A pointer variable can be passed as a parameter to a function either by value or by reference. To declare a pointer as a value parameter in a function heading, you use the same mechanism as you do to declare a variable. To make a formal parameter a reference parameter, you use an ampersand (&) when you declare the formal parameter in the function heading. Therefore, to declare a formal parameter as a reference parameter, you must use the &. Between the data type name and the identifier name, you must include both an asterisk (*) to make the identifier a pointer and an ampersand (&) to make it a reference parameter. The obvious question is: in what order should the & and * appear between the data type name and the identifier to declare a pointer as a reference parameter? In C++, to make a pointer a reference parameter in a function heading, the * appears before the & between the data type name and the identifier. The following example illustrates this concept:

```
void example(int* &p, double *q)
{
    .
    .
    .
}
```

In this example, both p and q are pointers. The parameter p is a reference parameter; the parameter q is a value parameter.

Pointers and Function Return Values

In C++, a function can return a value of the type pointer. For example, the return type of the function

```
int* testExp(...)
{
    .
    .
    .
}
```

is a pointer of the type `int`.

SHALLOW VERSUS DEEP COPY AND POINTERS

The section "Operations on Pointer Variables," located earlier in this chapter, discussed pointer arithmetic and explained that if we are not careful, one pointer might access the data of another (completely unrelated) pointer. This might result in unsuspected or erroneous results. Here, we discuss another peculiarity of pointers. To facilitate this discussion, we will use pictorial diagrams to show the pointers and their related memory.

Consider the following statements:

```
int *p;

p = new int;
```

The first statement declares `p` to be a pointer variable of the type `int`. The second statement allocates memory of the type `int`, and the address of the allocated memory is stored in `p`. Figure 3-8 illustrates this situation.

Figure 3-8 Pointer p and the memory to which it points

The box indicates the allocated memory (in this case, of the type `int`). p, together with the arrow, indicates that p points to the allocated memory. Now consider the following statement:

```
*p = 87;
```

This statement stores 87 in the memory pointed to by p. Figure 3-9 illustrates this situation.

Figure 3-9   Pointer p with 87 in the memory to which it points

Consider the following statements:

```
int *first;
int *second;

first = new int[10];
```

The first two statements declare **first** and **second** to be pointer variables of the type **int**. The third statement creates an array of **10** components, and the base address of the array is stored into **first**. See Figure 3-10.

Figure 3-10   Pointer **first** and the array to which it points

Suppose that some meaningful data is stored in the array pointed to by **first**. To be specific, suppose that this array is as shown in Figure 3-11.

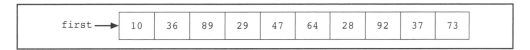

Figure 3-11   Pointer **first** and the array to which it points

Next, consider the following statement:

```
second = first;                 //Line A
```

This statement copies the value of **first** into **second**. After this statement executes, both **first** and **second** point to the same array, as shown in Figure 3-12.

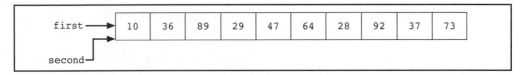

Figure 3-12 `first` and `second` after the statement `second = first;` executes

Notice that the statement in Line A is allowed, even though `first` points to an array. This is because both `first` and `second` are pointer variables of the same type. On the other hand if, say, `list1` and `list2` are arrays of the same type, then `list1` and `list2` are constant pointers and so the statement `list1 = list2;` is not allowed. In such a case, we also say that there is no aggregate assignment operation for arrays. An aggregate operation on an array is one that manipulates the entire array as a single unit.

Let us next execute the following statement:

`delete [] second;`

After this statement executes, the array pointed to by **second** is deleted. This action results in Figure 3-13.

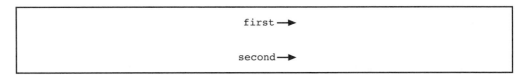

Figure 3-13 `first` and `second` after the statement `delete [] second;` executes

Because `first` and `second` pointed to the same array, after the statement

`delete [] second;`

executes, `first` becomes invalid. Therefore, if the program later tries to access the memory pointed to by `first`, either the program might access the wrong memory or it might terminate in an error. This case is an example of a **shallow copy**. In a shallow copy, two or more pointers of the same type point to the same memory; that is, they point to the same data as shown in Figure 3-12.

On the other hand, suppose that we have the following statements instead of the earlier statement, `second = first;` (in Line A):

```
second = new int[10];

for(int j = 0; j < 10; j++)
    second[j] = first[j];
```

The first statement creates an array of 10 components of the type int, and the base address of the array is stored in **second**. The second statement copies the array pointed to by **first** into the array pointed to by **second**. See Figure 3-14.

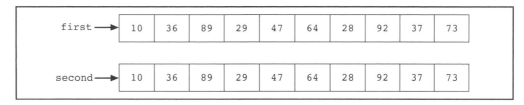

Figure 3-14   first and second both pointing to their own data

Both **first** and **second** now point to their own data. If **second** deletes its memory, there is no effect on **first**. This case is an example of a **deep copy**. In a deep copy, each pointer refers to its own data, as shown in Figure 3-14, *not* the same data as in Figure 3-12.

From the preceding discussion, it follows that you must know when to use a shallow copy and when to use a deep copy.

CLASSES AND POINTERS: SOME PECULIARITIES

If a pointer variable is of a class type, we discussed, in the previous section, how to access class members via the pointer by using the arrow notation. Because a class can have pointer data members, this section describes some peculiarities of such classes. To facilitate the discussion, we use the following class:

```
class pointerDataClass
{
public:
    ...

private:
    int x;
    int lenP;
    int *p;
};
```

Also consider the following statements (see Figure 3-15):

```
pointerDataClass objectOne;
pointerDataClass objectTwo;
```

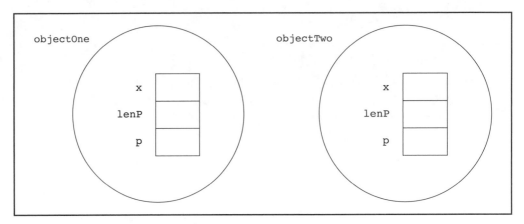

Figure 3-15 Objects `objectOne` and `objectTwo`

Destructor

The object `objectOne` has a pointer data member `p`. Suppose that during program execution the pointer `p` creates a dynamic array. When `objectOne` goes out of scope, all data members of `objectOne` are destroyed. However, `p` created a dynamic array, and dynamic memory must be deallocated using the operator `delete`. Therefore, if the pointer `p` does not use the `delete` operator to deallocate the dynamic array, the memory space of the dynamic array would stay marked as allocated, even though no one can access it. This is known as a "memory leak." How do we ensure that when `p` is destroyed, the dynamic memory created by `p` is also destroyed? Suppose that `objectOne` is as shown in Figure 3-16.

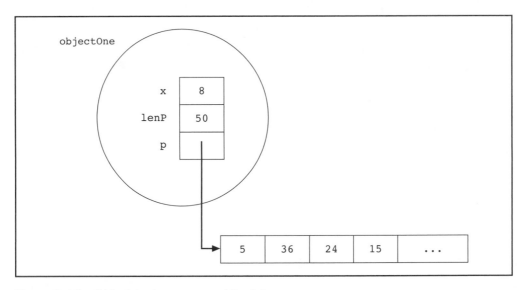

Figure 3-16 Object `objectOne` and its data

Recall that if a class has a destructor, the destructor automatically executes whenever a class object goes out of scope (see Chapter 1). Therefore, we can put the necessary code in the destructor to ensure that when **objectOne** goes out of scope, the memory created by the pointer **p** is deallocated. This is one of the main purposes of including a destructor. For example, the definition of the destructor for the **class pointerDataClass** is

```
pointerDataClass::~pointerDataClass()
{
      delete [] p;
}
```

Of course, you must include the destructor as a member of the class in its definition. Let us extend the definition of the **class pointerDataClass** by including the destructor. Moreover, the remainder of this section assumes that the definition of the destructor is as given previously—that is, the destructor deallocates the memory space pointed to by **p**.

```
class pointerDataClass
{
public:
    ~pointerDataClass();
...

private:
    int x;
    int lenP;
    int *p;
};
```

 For the destructor to work properly, the pointer p must have a valid value. If p is not properly initialized (that is, if the value of p is garbage) and the destructor executes, either the program terminates with an error message or the destructor deallocates an unrelated memory space. For this reason, you should exercise extra caution while working with pointers.

Assignment Operator

This section describes the limitations of the built-in assignment operators for classes with pointer data members. Suppose that **objectOne** and **objectTwo** are as shown in Figure 3-17.

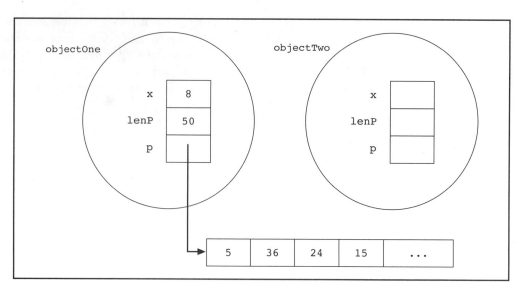

Figure 3-17   Objects `objectOne` and `objectTwo`

Recall that one of the built-in operations on classes is the assignment operator. For example, the statement

`objectTwo = objectOne;`

copies the data members of `objectOne` into `objectTwo`. That is, the value of `objectOne.x` is copied into `objectTwo.x`, the value of `objectOne.lenP` is copied into `objectTwo.lenP`, and the value of `objectOne.p` is copied into `objectTwo.p`. Because `p` is a pointer, this member-wise copying of data would lead to a shallow copying of the data. That is, both `objectTwo.p` and `objectOne.p` would point to the same memory space, as shown in Figure 3-18.

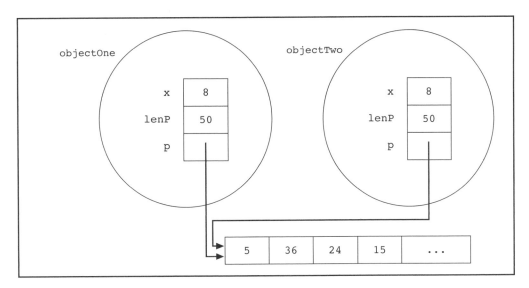

Figure 3-18   Objects `objectOne` and `objectTwo` after the statement `objectTwo = objectOne;` executes

Now if `objectTwo.p` deallocates the memory space to which it points, `objectOne.p` would become invalid. This situation could very well happen, if the **class pointerDataClass** has a destructor that deallocates the memory space pointed to by p when an object of the type **pointerDataClass** goes out of scope. It suggests that there must be a way to avoid this pitfall. To avoid this shallow copying of data for classes with a pointer data member, C++ allows the programmer to extend the definition of the assignment operator. This process is called overloading the assignment operator. Once the assignment operator is properly overloaded, both the objects `objectOne` and `objectTwo` have their own data, as shown in Figure 3-19.

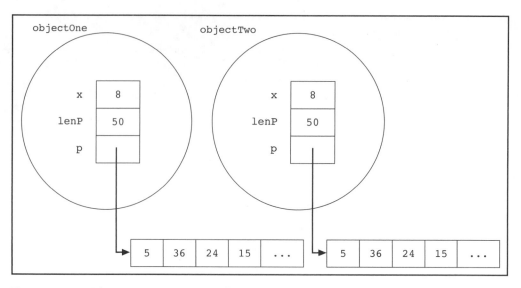

Figure 3-19 Objects `objectOne` and `objectTwo`

Overloading the Assignment Operator

Next we describe how to overload the assignment operator.

General Syntax to Overload the Assignment Operator (=) for a Class

Function Prototype (to be included in the definition of the class):

```
const className& operator=(const className&);
```

Function Definition:

```
const className& className::operator=(const className& rightObject)
{
        //local declaration, if any

        if(this != &rightObject)  //avoid self-assignment
        {
          //algorithm to copy rightObject into this object
        }

        //return the object assigned
        return *this;
}
```

In the definition of the function `operator=`:

- There is only one formal parameter.
- The formal parameter is generally a **const** reference to a particular class.
- The return type of the function is a reference to a particular class.

Consider the statement

```
x = x;
```

Here we are trying to copy the value of **x** into **x**; that is, this statement is a self-assignment. We must prevent such statements because they waste computer time.

The body of the function `operator=` *does* prevent such assignments. Let us see how.

Consider the **if** statement in the body of the operator function `operator=`:

```
if(this != &rightObject)   //avoid self-assignment
{
        //algorithm to copy rightObject into this object
}
```

Now the statement

```
x = x;
```

is compiled into the statement

```
x.operator=(x);
```

Because the function `operator=` is invoked by the object **x**, the pointer **this** in the body of the function `operator=` refers to the object **x**. Furthermore, because **x** is also a parameter to the function `operator=`, the formal parameter **rightObject** also refers to the object **x**. Therefore, in the expression

```
this != &rightObject
```

this means the address of **x**, and **&rightObject** also means the address of **x**. Therefore, this expression will evaluate to **false** and, therefore, the body of the **if** statement will be skipped.

Notice that the return type of the function to overload the assignment operator is a reference. This is so that the statements such as x = y = z; can be executed, that is, the assignment operator can be used in a cascaded form.

The following example illustrates how to overload the assignment operator.

Example 3-5

Consider the following class:

```
class cAssignmentOprOverload
{
public:
    const cAssignmentOprOverload& operator=
                    (const cAssignmentOprOverload& otherList);
        //Overload the assignment operator.

    void print() const;
        //Function to print the list.

    void insertEnd(int item);
        //Function to insert an item at the end of the list.
        //Postcondition: If the list is not full, length++;
        //               list[length] = item
        //               If the list is full, outputs an
        //               appropriate message.

    void destroyList();
        //Function to destroy the list.
        //Postcondition: length = 0; maxSize = 0;
        //               list = NULL

    cAssignmentOprOverload(int size = 10);
        //constructor
        //Postcondition: length = 0; maxSize = size;
        //               list is an array of size maxSize

private:
    int maxSize;
    int length;
    int *list;
};
```

The definitions of the member functions of the **class cAssignmentOprOverload** are

```
void cAssignmentOprOverload::print() const
{
        if(length == 0)
           cout<<"List is empty."<<endl;
        else
        {
           for(int i = 0; i < length; i++)
               cout<<list[i]<<" ";
           cout<<endl;
        }
}
```

```
void cAssignmentOprOverload::insertEnd(int item)
{
      if(length == maxSize)
         cout<<"List is full."<<endl;
      else
         list[length++] = item;
}

void cAssignmentOprOverload::destroyList()
{
      delete [] list;
      list = NULL;
      length = 0;
      maxSize = 0;
}

cAssignmentOprOverload::cAssignmentOprOverload(int size)
{
      length = 0;

      if(size <= 0)
         maxSize = 10;
      else
         maxSize = size;

      list = new int[maxSize];
      assert(list != NULL);
}


const cAssignmentOprOverload& cAssignmentOprOverload::operator=
                    (const cAssignmentOprOverload& otherList)
{
      if(this != &otherList) //avoid self-assignment;   //Line 1
      {
         if(list != NULL)                               //Line 2
            destroyList();                              //Line 3
         maxSize = otherList.maxSize;                   //Line 4
         length = otherList.length;                     //Line 5

         if(maxSize != 0)                               //Line 6
         {
            list = new int[maxSize];                    //Line 7
            assert(list != NULL);                       //Line 8

            for(int i = 0; i < length; i++)             //Line 9
                list[i] = otherList.list[i];            //Line 10
         }
         else                                           //Line 11
```

3

```
        list = NULL;                            //Line 12
    }

    return *this;                               //Line 13
}
```

The function to overload the assignment operator works as follows. The statement in Line 1 checks whether an object is copying itself. The statement in Line 2 checks whether `list` is nonempty. If it is nonempty, then `list` is destroyed by deallocating the memory occupied by `list`. The statements in Lines 4 and 5 copy the values of the data members `maxSize` and `length` of `otherList` into `maxSize` and `length` of `list`, respectively. If `otherList` is not `NULL` and not empty, the statements between Lines 6 and 10 create the array `list` and copy `otherList` into `list`. If `otherList` is `NULL`, `list` is initialized to `NULL`. Notice that if the program is not able to allocate memory for the array, the statement in Line 8 terminates the program.

The statement in Line 13 returns the address of this list because the return type of the function `operator=` is a reference type.

We leave it as an exercise for you to write a program to test the assignment operator for the `class cAssignmentOprOverload`.

The Copy Constructor

When declaring a class object, you can initialize it by using the value of an existing object of the same type. For example, consider the following statement:

```
pointerDataClass objectThree(objectOne);
```

The object `objectThree` is being declared and also being initialized by using the value of `objectOne`. That is, the values of the data members of `objectOne` are copied into the corresponding data members of `objectThree`. This initialization is called the **default member-wise initialization**. The default member-wise initialization is due to the constructor, called the **copy constructor** (provided by the compiler). Just as in the case of the assignment operator, because the **class pointerDataClass** has pointer data members, this default initialization would lead to a shallow copying of the data as shown in Figure 3-20. (Assume that `objectOne` is given as before.)

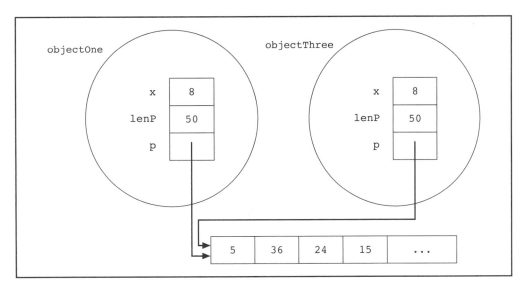

Figure 3-20   Objects `objectOne` and `objectThree`

Before describing how to overcome this deficiency, let us describe another situation, which could also lead to a shallow copying of data. The solution to both these problems is the same.

Recall that, as parameters to a function, class objects can be passed either by reference or by value. Remember that the **class pointerDataClass** has the destructor, which deallocates the memory space pointed to by **p**. Suppose that **objectOne** is as shown in Figure 3-21.

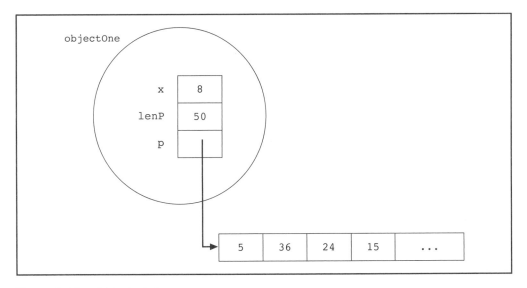

Figure 3-21   Object `objectOne`

Let us consider the following function prototype:

```
void destroyList(pointerDataClass paramObject);
```

The function `destroyList` has a formal value parameter, `paramObject`. Now consider the following statement:

```
destroyList(objectOne);
```

In this statement, `objectOne` is passed as a parameter to the function `destroyList`. Because `paramObject` is a value parameter, the copy constructor copies the members of `objectOne` into the corresponding data members of `paramObject`. Just as in the previous case, `paramObject.p` and `objectOne.p` would point to the same memory space, as shown in Figure 3-22.

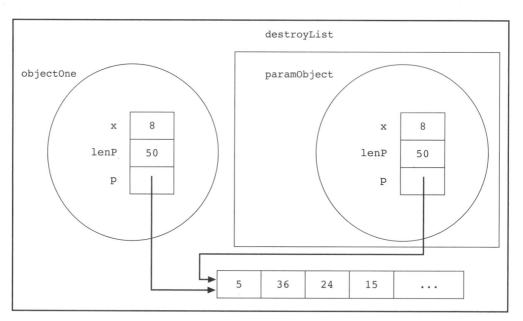

Figure 3-22 Pointer data members of the objects `objectOne` and `paramObject` pointing to the same array

Because `objectOne` is passed by value, the data members of `paramObject` should have their own copy of the data. In particular, `paramObject.p` should have its own memory space to store data. How do we ensure that this is, in fact, the case?

If a class has pointer data members:

- During object declaration, the initialization of one object using the value of another object would lead to a shallow copying of the data if the default member-wise copying of data is allowed.
- If, as a parameter, an object is passed by value and the default member-wise copying of data is allowed, it would lead to a shallow copying of the data.

In these cases, to force each object to have its own copy of the data, we must override the definition of the copy constructor provided by the compiler; that is, we must provide our own definition of the copy constructor. This is usually done by putting a statement that includes the copy constructor in the definition of the class, and then writing the definition of the copy constructor. Then, whenever the copy constructor needs to be executed, the system executes the definition of the copy constructor that we provide, not the one provided by the compiler. Therefore, for the `class pointerDataClass`, we can overcome this shallow copying of data problem by including the copy constructor in the `class pointerDataClass`. Example 3-6 illustrates this.

The copy constructor automatically executes in the following situations (the first two were previously described):

- When an object is declared and initialized by using the value of another object

- When, as a parameter, an object is passed by value

- When the return value of a function is an object

Therefore, once the copy constructor is properly defined for the `class pointerDataClass`, both `objectOne.p` and `objectThree.p` will have their own copies of the data. Similarly, `objectOne.p` and `paramObject.p` will have their own copies of the data, as shown in Figure 3-23.

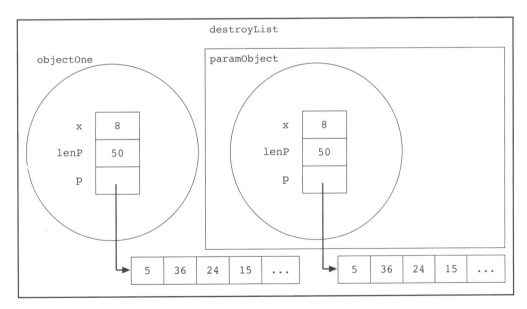

Figure 3-23 Pointer data members of the objects `objectOne` and `paramObject` with their own data

When the function `destroyList` exits, the formal parameter `paramObject` goes out of scope, and the destructor for the object `paramObject` deallocates the memory space pointed to by `paramObject.p`. However, this deallocation has no effect on `objectOne`.

The general syntax to include the copy constructor in the definition of a class is

```
className(const className& otherObject);
```

Example 3-6 illustrates how to include the copy constructor in a class and how it works.

Example 3-6

Consider the following class:

```
class pointerDataClass
{
public:
    void print() const;
        //Function to output the value of x and
        //the value of the array p.
    void setData();
        //Function to input data into x and
        //into the array p.
    void destroyP();
        //Function to deallocate the memory space
        //occupied by the array p.

    pointerDataClass(int sizeP = 10);
        //constructor
        //Create an array of the size specified by the
        //parameter sizeP; the default array size is 10.

    ~pointerDataClass();
        //destructor
        //Deallocate the memory space occupied by the
        //array p.

    pointerDataClass (const pointerDataClass& otherObject);
        //copy constructor

private:
    int x;
    int lenP;
    int *p;         //pointer to an int array
};
```

Suppose that the definitions of the member functions of the **class pointerDataClass** are as follows:

```
void pointerDataClass::print() const
{
      cout<<"x = "<<x<<endl;

      cout<<"p = ";

      for(int i = 0; i < lenP; i++)
          cout<<p[i]<<" ";
      cout<<endl;
}

void pointerDataClass::setData()
{
      cout<<"Enter an integer for x: ";
      cin>>x;
      cout<<endl;

      cout<<"Enter "<<lenP<<" numbers: ";

      for(int i = 0; i < lenP; i++)
          cin>>p[i];

      cout<<endl;
}

void pointerDataClass::destroyP()
{
       lenP = 0;
       delete [] p;
       p = NULL;
}

pointerDataClass::pointerDataClass(int sizeP)
{
      x = 0;

      if(sizeP <= 0)
      {
         cout<<"Array size must be positive."<<endl;
         cout<<"Creating an array of size 10."<<endl;

         lenP = 10;
      }
      else
         lenP = sizeP;

      p = new int[lenP];
      assert(p != NULL);
}
```

```
pointerDataClass::~pointerDataClass()
{
        delete [] p;
}

        //copy constructor
pointerDataClass::pointerDataClass
                (const pointerDataClass& otherObject)
{
        x = otherObject.x;

        lenP = otherObject.lenP;
        p = new int[lenP];
        assert(p != NULL);

        for(int i = 0; i < lenP; i++)
            p[i] = otherObject.p[i];

}
```

We leave it as an exercise for you to write a program to test the copy constructor of the class pointerDataClass.

For classes with pointer data members, we normally do three things:

1. Include the destructor in the class.
2. Overload the assignment operator for the class.
3. Include the copy constructor.

Next, we define a class, called newString, and overload the assignment and relational operators. This is so that when we declare a variable of the type newString, we will be able to use the assignment operator to copy one string into another, and be able to use relational operators to compare the two strings.

Before discussing the class newString, however, we examine the overloading of the operator [ ]. Recall that we have used the operator [ ] to access the components of an array. To access individual characters in a string of the type newString, we have to overload the operator [ ] for the class newString.

OVERLOADING THE ARRAY INDEX (SUBSCRIPT) OPERATOR ([ ])

Recall that the function to overload the operator [ ] for a class must be a member of the class. Furthermore, because an array can be declared as constant or nonconstant, we need to overload the operator [ ] to handle both these cases.

The syntax to declare the operator function operator[ ] as a member of a class for non-constant arrays is

```
Type& operator[](int index);
```

The syntax to declare the operator function `operator[ ]` as a member of a class for constant arrays is

```
const Type& operator[](int index) const;
```

where **Type** is the data type of the array elements.

Suppose that `classTest` is a class that has an array data member. The definition of `classTest` to overload the operator [ ] is

```
class classTest
{
public:
    Type& operator[](int index);
        //Overload the operator for nonconstant arrays.
         const Type& operator[](int index) const;
        //Overload the operator for constant arrays.
    .
    .
    .
private:
    Type *list;   //pointer to the array
    int arraySize;
};
```

where **Type** is the data type of the array elements.

The definitions of the functions to overload the operator [ ] for `classTest` are

```
    //Overload the operator [] for nonconstant arrays.
Type& classTest::operator[](int index)
{
    assert(0 <= index && index < arraySize);
    return(list[index]);    //Return a pointer to the
                            //array component.
}


      //Overload the operator [] for constant arrays.
const Type& classTest::operator[](int index) const
{
    assert(0 <= index && index < arraySize);
    return(list[index]);    //Return a pointer to the
                            //array component.
}
```

PROGRAMMING EXAMPLE: `newString`

In C++:

- A C-string is a sequence of one or more characters.
- C-strings are enclosed in double quotation marks.
- C-strings are null terminated.
- C-strings are stored in character arrays.

In this example, by a string we mean a C-string.

The only aggregate operations allowed on strings are input and output. To use other operations, the programmer needs to include the header file `cstring`, which contains the specification of many functions for string manipulation.

Initially, C++ did not provide any built-in data types to handle strings. More recent versions of C++, however, provide a string class to handle strings and operations on strings.

Our objective in this example is to define our own class for string manipulation and, at the same time, further illustrate operator overloading. More specifically, we overload the assignment operator, the relational operators, and the stream insertion and extraction operators for easy input and output. Let us call this `class newString`. First we give the definition of the `class newString`. See Figure 3-24 for the UML diagram.

```
//Header file newString.h
#ifndef H_newString
#define H_newString
#include <iostream>
using namespace std;

class newString
{
        //Overload the stream insertion and extraction operators.
    friend ostream& operator<<(ostream&, const newString&);
    friend istream& operator>>(istream&, newString&);

public:
    const newString& operator=(const newString&);
      //Overload the assignment operator.
    newString(const char *);
      //constructor; conversion from the char string
    newString();
      //default constructor to initialize the string to null
    newString(const newString&);
      //copy constructor
    ~newString();
      //destructor

    char& operator[] (int);
    const char& operator[] (int) const;
          //Overload the relational operators.
```

```
    bool operator==(const newString&) const;
    bool operator!=(const newString&) const;
    bool operator<=(const newString&) const;
    bool operator<(const newString&)  const;
    bool operator>=(const newString&) const;
    bool operator>(const newString&)  const;
private:
    char *strPtr;     //pointer to the char array
                      //that holds the string
    int strLength;    //data member to store the length
                      //of the string
};
#endif
```

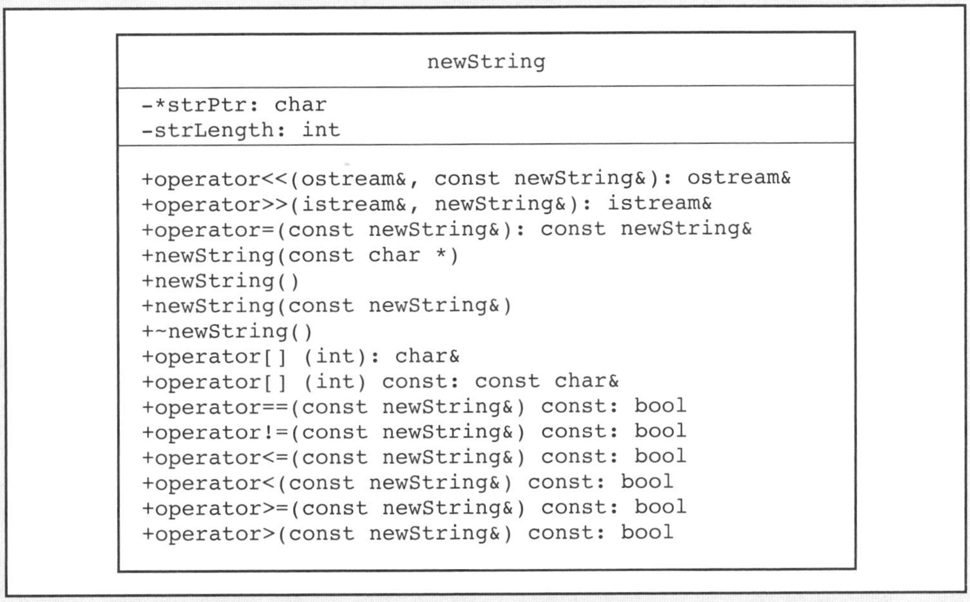

```
                         newString

-*strPtr: char
-strLength: int

+operator<<(ostream&, const newString&): ostream&
+operator>>(istream&, newString&): istream&
+operator=(const newString&): const newString&
+newString(const char *)
+newString()
+newString(const newString&)
+~newString()
+operator[] (int): char&
+operator[] (int) const: const char&
+operator==(const newString&) const: bool
+operator!=(const newString&) const: bool
+operator<=(const newString&) const: bool
+operator<(const newString&) const: bool
+operator>=(const newString&) const: bool
+operator>(const newString&) const: bool
```

Figure 3-24   UML diagram of the class newString

The class newString has two private data members: one to store the string, and one to store the length of the string.

Next, we give the definitions of the functions to implement the newString operations. The implementation file includes the header file cassert because we are using the function assert. For an explanation of the function assert, see the header file cassert in Appendix E.

```cpp
//Implementation file newString.cpp
#include <iostream>
#include <iomanip>
#include <cstring>
#include <cassert>
#include "newString.h"

using namespace std;


    //constructor; conversion from the char string to newString
newString::newString(const char *str)
{
   strLength = strlen(str);
   strPtr = new char[strLength + 1];  //allocate memory to store
                                      //the char string
   assert(strPtr != NULL);
   strcpy(strPtr,str);                //copy the string into strPtr
}

    //default constructor to store the null string
newString::newString()
{
    strLength = 0;
    strPtr = new char[1];
    assert(strPtr != NULL);
    strcpy(strPtr,"");
}

    //copy constructor
newString::newString(const newString& rightStr)
{
    strLength = rightStr.strLength;
    strPtr = new char[strLength + 1];
    assert(strPtr != NULL);
    strcpy(strPtr, rightStr.strPtr);
}

newString::~newString()  //destructor
{
    delete [] strPtr;
}

    //Overload the assignment operator.
const newString& newString::operator=(const newString& rightStr)
{
    if(this != &rightStr) //avoid self-copy
    {
```

```cpp
            delete [] strPtr;
            strLength = rightStr.strLength;
            strPtr = new char[strLength + 1];
            assert(strPtr != NULL);
            strcpy(strPtr, rightStr.strPtr);
        }
        return *this;
}

char& newString::operator[] (int index)
{
        assert(0 <= index && index < strLength);
        return strPtr[index];
}

const char& newString::operator[] (int index) const
{
        assert(0 <= index && index < strLength);
        return strPtr[index];
}

        //Overload the relational operators.
bool newString::operator==(const newString& rightStr) const
{
        return(strcmp(strPtr, rightStr.strPtr) == 0);
}

bool newString::operator<(const newString& rightStr) const
{
        return(strcmp(strPtr, rightStr.strPtr) < 0);
}

bool newString::operator<=(const newString& rightStr) const
{
        return(strcmp(strPtr, rightStr.strPtr) <= 0);
}

bool newString::operator>(const newString& rightStr) const
{
        return(strcmp(strPtr, rightStr.strPtr) > 0);
}

bool newString::operator>=(const newString& rightStr) const
{
        return(strcmp(strPtr, rightStr.strPtr) >= 0);
}

bool newString::operator!=(const newString& rightStr) const
```

```
{
      return(strcmp(strPtr, rightStr.strPtr) != 0);
}


      //Overload the stream insertion operator <<
ostream& operator<<(ostream& osObject, const newString& str)
{
      osObject<<str.strPtr;
      return osObject;
}


      //Overload the stream extraction operator >>
istream& operator>>(istream& isObject, newString& str)
{
      char temp[81];

      isObject>>setw(81)>>temp;
      str = temp;
      return isObject;
}
```

Consider the statement

```
isObject>>setw(81)>>temp;
```

in the definition of the function `operator>>`. Because `temp` is declared to be an array of size 81, the largest string that can be stored into `temp` is of length 80. The manipulator `setw` in this statement (that is, in the input statement) ensures that no more than 80 characters are read into `temp`.

The **conversion constructor** is a single-parameter function that converts its argument to the object of the constructor's class. In our case, the conversion constructor converts a string to an object of the `newString` type.

Note that the **assignment operator** is explicitly overloaded only for objects of the `newString` type. However, the overloaded assignment operator also works if we want to store a character string into a `newString` object. Consider the declaration

```
newString str;
```

and the statement

```
str = "Hello there";
```

The compiler translates this statement into

```
str.operator=("Hello there");
```

First, the compiler automatically invokes the conversion constructor to create an object of the `newString` type to temporarily store the string `"Hello there"`.

Second, the compiler invokes the overloaded assignment operator to assign the temporary `newString` object to the object `str`.

Hence, it is not necessary to explicitly overload the assignment operator to store a character string into an object of the newString type.

Next, we write a C++ program that tests some of the operations of the class newString.

```cpp
//Test Program
#include <iostream>
#include <cstring>
#include "newString.h"

using namespace std;

int main()
{
  newString s1 = "Sunny";        //Initialize s1 using
                                 //the assignment operator
  const newString s2("Warm");    //Initialize s2 using
                                 //the conversion constructor
  newString s3;                  //Initialize s3 to null
  newString s4;                  //Initialize s4 to null

  cout<<"Line 1: "<<s1<<"     "<<s2<<"   ***"
     <<s3<<"###."<<endl;                                    //Line 1

  if(s1 <= s2)                             //Compare s1 and s2; Line 2
    cout<<"Line 3: "<<s1<<" is less than or equal to "<<s2
       <<endl;                                              //Line 3
  else                                                      //Line 4
    cout<<"Line 5: "<<s2<<" is less than "<<s1
       <<endl;                                              //Line 5

  cout<<"Line 6: Enter a string that has "
     <<"at least 7 characters --> ";                        //Line 6
  cin>>s1;                                     //input s1; Line 7
  cout<<endl<<"Line 8: New value of s1 = "<<s1
     <<endl;                                                //Line 8

  s4 = s3 = "Birth Day";                                    //Line 9
  cout<<"Line 10: s3 = "<<s3<<", s4 = "<<s4<<endl;          //Line 10

  s3 = s1;                                                  //Line 11
  cout<<"Line 12: The new value of s3 = "<<s3<<endl;        //Line 12

  s1 = "Bright Sky";                                        //Line 13

  s3[1] = s1[5];                                            //Line 14
  cout<<"Line 15: After replacing the second character, s3 = "
     <<s3<<endl;                                            //Line 15
```

```
    s3[2] = s2[3];                                              //Line 16
    cout<<"Line 17: After replacing the third character, s3 = "
       <<s3<<endl;                                              //Line 17

    s3[5] = 'g';                                                //Line 18
    cout<<"Line 19: After replacing the sixth character, s3 = "
       <<s3<<endl;                                              //Line 19

    return 0;
}
```

Sample Run: In this sample run, the user input is shaded.

```
Line 1: Sunny    Warm  ***###.
Line 3: Sunny is less than or equal to Warm
Line 6: Enter a string that has at least 7 characters --> 123456789

Line 8: New value of s1 = 123456789
Line 10: s3 = Birth Day, s4 = Birth Day
Line 12: The new value of s3 = 123456789
Line 15: After replacing the second character, s3 = 1t3456789
Line 17: After replacing the third character, s3 = 1tW456789
Line 19: After replacing the sixth character, s3 = 1tW45g789
```

Notice that in the statement (Line 9)

```
s4 = s3 = "Birth Day";
```

because the associativity of the assignment operator is from right to left, first the statement **s3 = "Birth Day";** executes and then the statement **s4 = s3;** executes. The statement in Line 11 copies **s1** into **s3** by using the assignment operator. The statements in Lines 14 through 19 illustrate that by using the array subscripting operator **[ ]**, you can manipulate the individual characters of a string.

ARRAY-BASED LISTS

Everyone is familiar with the term "list." You might have a list consisting of employee data, student data, sales data, or a list of rental properties. One thing common to all lists is that all the elements of a list are of the same type. More formally, we can define a list as follows:

List: A collection of elements of the same type.

The **length** of a list is the number of elements in the list.

Following are some of the operations performed on a list:

      1. Create the list. The list is initialized to an empty state.

      2. Determine whether the list is empty.

3. Determine whether the list is full.

4. Find the size of the list.

5. Destroy, or clear, the list.

6. Determine whether an item is the same as a given list element.

7. Insert an item in the list at the specified location.

8. Remove an item from the list at the specified location.

9. Replace an item at the specified location with another item.

10. Retrieve an item from the list at the specified location.

11. Search the list for a given item.

Before discussing how to implement these operations, we must first decide how to store the list in the computer's memory. Because all the elements of a list are of the same type, an effective and convenient way to process a list is to store it in an array. Initially, the size of the array holding the list elements is usually larger than the number of elements in the list so that, at a later stage, the list can grow to a specific size. Therefore, we must know how full the array is; that is, we must keep track of the number of list elements stored in the array. C++ allows the programmer to create dynamic arrays. Therefore, we will leave it for the user to specify the size of the array. The size of the array can be specified when a list object is declared. It follows that, in order to maintain and process the list in an array, we need the following three variables:

- The array holding the list elements

- A variable to store the length of the list (that is, the number of list elements currently in the array)

- A variable to store the size of the array (that is, the maximum number of elements that can be stored in the array)

Suppose that the variable `length` indicates the number of elements in the list and the variable `maxSize` indicates the maximum number of elements that can be stored in the list. Then `length` and `maxSize` are nonnegative integers and therefore we can declare them to be of the type `int`. What about the type of the array, that is, the data type of the array elements? If we have a list of numbers, then the array elements could either be of the type `int` or `double`. If we a have a list of names, then the array elements are of the type `string`. Similarly, if we have a list of students, then the array elements are of the type `studentType`, (a data type you can define). We, therefore, see that there are various types of lists.

A list of sales data or a list of students' data is empty if its length is zero. To insert an item at the end of a list of any type would require us to add the element after the current last element, and then increment the length by one. Similarly, it can be seen that for the most part, the algorithms to implement the operations on a list of names, a list of sales data, or a list of students' data are the same. We do not want to spend time and effort to develop separate code for each type of list we encounter. Instead, we would like to develop a generic code that can be used to implement any type of list in a program. In other words, while designing the algorithms, we do not want to be concerned with whether we are processing a list of numbers, a list of names, or a list of students' data. However, while illustrating a particular algorithm, we will consider a specific type of list. To develop generic algorithms to implement list operations, we use class templates.

Now that you know the operations to be performed on a list and how to store the list in the computer's memory, next we define the class implementing the list as an abstract data type (ADT). The following `class`, `arrayListType`, defines the list as an ADT:

```
template<class elemType>
class arrayListType
{
public:
    const arrayListType<elemType>&
                  operator=(const arrayListType<elemType>&);
        //Overload the assignment operator.

    bool isEmpty();
        //Function to determine whether the list is empty.
        //Postcondition: Returns true if the list is empty;
        //               otherwise, returns false.
    bool isFull();
        //Function to determine whether the list is full.
        //Postcondition: Returns true if the list is full;
        //               otherwise, returns false.
    int listSize();
        //Function to determine the number of elements in
        //the list.
        //Postcondition: Returns the value of length.
    int maxListSize();
        //Function to determine the size of the list.
        //Postcondition: Returns the value of maxSize.
    void print() const;
        //Function to output the elements of the list.
        //Postcondition: The elements of the list are output
        //               on the standard output device.
    bool isItemAtEqual(int location, const elemType& item);
        //Function to determine whether the item is the
        //same as the item in the list at the position
        //specified by location.
        //Postcondition: Returns true if the
        //               list[location] is the same as
        //               the item; otherwise, returns
        //               false.
    void insertAt(int location, const elemType& insertItem);
        //Function to insert an item in the list at the
        //position specified by location. The item to be
        //inserted is passed as a parameter to the
```

3

```
        //function.
        //Postcondition: Starting at location, the
        //                elements of the list are
        //                shifted down,
        //                list[location] = insertItem;,
        //                and length++;
        //    If the list is full or location is out of
        //    range, an appropriate message is displayed.
    void insertEnd(const elemType& insertItem);
        //Function to insert an item at the end of the
        //list.
        //The parameter insertItem specifies the item to
        //be inserted.
        //Postcondition: list[length] = insertItem; and
        //                length++;
        //    If the list is full, an appropriate message
        //    is displayed.
    void removeAt(int location);
        //Function to remove the item from the list at
        //the position specified by location.
        //Postcondition: The list element at
        //                list[location] is removed
        //                and length is decremented by 1.
        //    If location is out of range, an appropriate
        //    message is displayed.
    void retrieveAt(int location, elemType& retItem);
        //Function to retrieve the element from the list at
        //the position specified by location.
        //Postcondition: retItem = list[location]
        //    If location is out of range, an appropriate
        //    message is displayed.
    void replaceAt(int location, const elemType& repItem);
        //Function to replace the element in the list at
        //the position specified by location. The item to be
        //replaced is specified by the parameter repItem.
        //Postcondition: list[location] = repItem
        //    If location is out of range, an appropriate
        //    message is displayed.
    void clearList();
        //Function to remove all the elements from the list.
        //After this operation, the size of the list is
        //zero.
        //Postcondition: length = 0
    int seqSearch(const elemType& item);
        //Function to search the list for a given item.
        //Postcondition: If the item is found, returns the
        //                location in the array where the
        //                item is found; otherwise,
        //                returns -1.
```

```
    void insert(const elemType& insertItem);
        //Function to insert the item specified by the
        //parameter insertItem at the end of the list.
        //However, first the list is searched to see whether
        //the item to be inserted is already in the list.
        //Postcondition: list[length] = insertItem; and
        //                length++
        //   If the item is already in the list or the
        //   list is full, an appropriate message is
        //   displayed.
    void remove(const elemType& removeItem);
        //Function to remove an item from the list. The
        //parameter removeItem specifies the item to be
        //removed.
        //Postcondition: If removeItem is found in the
        //                list, it is removed from the list
        //                and length is decremented by one.

    arrayListType(int size = 100);
        //constructor
        //Creates an array of the size specified by the
        //parameter size. The default array size is 100.
        //Postcondition: The list points to the array;
        //                length = 0; and maxSize = size

    arrayListType(const arrayListType<elemType>& otherList);
        //copy constructor

    ~arrayListType();
        //destructor
        //Deallocates the memory occupied by the array.

protected:
    elemType *list;     //array to hold the list
                        //elements
    int length;         //variable to store the length of the
                        //list
    int maxSize;        //variable to store the maximum size of
                        //the list
};
```

Figure 3-25 shows the UML diagram of the class `arrayListType`.

arrayListType
#*list: elemType #length: int #maxSize: int
+isEmpty(): bool +isFull(): bool +listSize(): int +maxListSize(): int +print() const: void +isItemAtEqual(int, const elemType&): bool +insertAt(int, const elemType&): void +insertEnd(const elemType&): void +removeAt(int): void +retrieveAt(int, elemType&): void +replaceAt(int, const elemType&): void +clearList(): void +seqSearch(const elemType&): int +insert(const elemType&): void +remove(const elemType&): void +arrayListType(int = 100) +arrayListType(const arrayListType\<elemType\>&) +~arrayListType() +operator=(const arrayListType\<elemType\>&):   const arrayListType\<elemType\>&

Figure 3-25 UML diagram of the class arrayListType

Notice that the data members of the **class arrayListType** are declared as **protected**. This is because we would like to derive classes from this class to implement special lists such as an ordered list. Next, we write the definitions of these functions.

The list is empty if **length** is **zero**; it is full if **length** is equal to **maxSize**. Therefore, the definitions of the functions **isEmpty** and **isFull** are

```
template<class elemType>
bool arrayListType<elemType>::isEmpty()
{
      return (length == 0);
}

template<class elemType>
bool arrayListType<elemType>::isFull()
{
      return (length == maxSize);
}
```

The data member `length` of the class stores the number of elements currently in the list. Similarly, because the size of the array holding the list elements is stored in the data member `maxSize`, `maxSize` specifies the maximum size of the list. Therefore, the definitions of the functions `listSize` and `maxListSize` are

```
template<class elemType>
int arrayListType<elemType>::listSize()
{
        return length;
}

template<class elemType>
int arrayListType<elemType>::maxListSize()
{
        return maxSize;
}
```

Each of the functions `isEmpty`, `isFull`, `listSize`, and `maxListSize` contain only one statement, which is either a comparison statement or a statement returning a value. It follows that each of these functions is of $O(1)$.

The member function `print` outputs the elements of the list. We assume that the output is sent to the standard output device.

```
template<class elemType>
void arrayListType<elemType>::print() const
{
   for(int i = 0; i < length; i++)
      cout<<list[i]<<" ";

   cout<<endl;
}
```

The function `print` uses a loop to output the elements of the list. The number of times the `for` loop executes depends on the number of list elements. If the list has 100 elements, the `for` loop executes 100 times. In general, suppose that the number of elements in the list is n. Then the function `print` is of $O(n)$.

The definition of the function `isItemAt` is given next.

```
template<class elemType>
bool arrayListType<elemType>::isItemAtEqual
                              (int location, const elemType& item)
{
        return(list[location] == item);
}
```

The body of the function `isItemAtEqual` has only one statement, which is a comparison statement. It is easy to see that this function is of $O(1)$.

The function `insertAt` inserts an item at a specific location in the list. The item to be inserted, and the insert location in the array, are passed as parameters to this function. In order to insert the item somewhere in the middle of the list, we must first make room for the new item. That is, we need to move certain elements down one array slot. Figure 3-26 illustrates this concept.

3

	[0]	[1]	[2]	[3]	[4]	[5]	[6]	[7]	[8]	[9]
list	35	24	45	17	26	78				

Figure 3-26 Array list

The number of elements currently in the list is 6 and so length is 6. Therefore, after inserting a new element, the length of the list is 7. If the item is to be inserted at, say, location 6, we can easily do this by copying the item into list[6]. On the other hand, if the item is to be inserted at, say, location 3, we first need to move elements list[3], list[4], and list[5] one array slot to the right to make room for the new item. Therefore, we must first copy list[5] into list[6], list[4] into list[5], and list[3] into list[4], in this order. Then we can copy the new item into list[3].

Of course, special cases such as trying to insert in a full list must be handled separately. Other member functions can handle some of these cases.

The definition of the function insertAt is as follows:

```cpp
template<class elemType>
void arrayListType<elemType>::insertAt
                    (int location, const elemType& insertItem)
{
    if(location < 0 || location >= maxSize)
        cerr<<"The position of the item to be inserted "
            <<"is out of range."<<endl;
    else
        if(length >= maxSize)  //list is full
            cout<<"Cannot insert in a full list."<<endl;
    else
    {
        for(int i = length; i > location; i--)
            list[i] = list[i - 1];        //move the elements
                                          //down

        list[location] = insertItem;     //insert the item
                                         //at the specified
                                         //position

        length++;   //increment the length
    }
}//end insertAt
```

The function `insertAt` uses a `for` loop to shift the elements of the list. The number of times the `for` loop executes depends on where in the list the item is to be inserted. If the item is to be inserted at the first position, then all the elements of the list are shifted. It can be easily shown that this function is of $O(n)$.

The function `insertEnd` can be implemented by using the function `insertAt`. However, the function `insertEnd` does not require the shifting of elements. Therefore, we give its definition directly:

```
template<class elemType>
void arrayListType<elemType>::insertEnd(const elemType& insertItem)
{

    if(length >= maxSize)  //the list is full
        cerr<<"Cannot insert in a full list."<<endl;
    else
    {
        list[length] = insertItem; //insert the item at the
                                   //end
        length++;                  //increment the length
    }
}//end insertEnd
```

The number of statements, and hence the number of operations, executed in the body of the function `insertEnd` are fixed. Therefore, this function is of $O(1)$.

The function `removeAt` is the opposite of the function `insertAt`. The function `removeAt` removes an item from a specific location in the list. The location of the item to be removed is passed as a parameter to this function. After removing the item from the list, the length of the list is reduced by 1. If the item to be removed is somewhere in the middle of the list, after removing the item we must move certain elements one array slot to the left because we cannot leave holes in the portion of the array containing the list. Consider the list in Figure 3-27.

	[0]	[1]	[2]	[3]	[4]	[5]	[6]	[7]	[8]	[9]
list	35	24	45	17	26	78				

Figure 3-27   Array `list`

The number of elements currently in the list is **6**, and so `length` is **6**. Therefore, after removing an element, the `length` of the list is **5**. Suppose that the item to be removed is at, say, location 3. Clearly, we must move `list[4]` into `list[3]` and `list[5]` into `list[4]`, in this order.

The definition of the function **removeAt** is

```
template<class elemType>
void arrayListType<elemType>::removeAt(int location)
{
    if(location < 0 || location >= length)
        cerr<<"The location of the item to be removed "
            <<"is out of range."<<endl;
    else
    {
        for(int i = location; i < length - 1; i++)
            list[i] = list[i+1];

        length--;
    }
}//end removeAt
```

Similar to the function **insertAt**, it is easily seen that the function **removeAt** is of $O(n)$.

The definition of the function **retrieveAt** is given next. The index of the item to be retrieved, and the location from where to retrieve the item, are passed as parameters to this function.

```
template<class elemType>
void arrayListType<elemType>::retrieveAt
                                (int location, elemType& retItem)
{
    if(location < 0 || location >= length)
        cerr<<"The location of the item to be retrieved is "
            <<"out of range."<<endl;
    else
        retItem = list[location];
} //end retrieveAt
```

The definition of the function **replaceAt** is as follows:

```
template<class elemType>
void arrayListType<elemType>::replaceAt
                                (int location, const elemType& repItem)
{
    if(location < 0 || location >= length)
        cerr<<"The location of the item to be replaced is "
            <<"out of range."<<endl;
    else
        list[location] = repItem;

}//end replaceAt
```

The function `clearList` removes the elements from the list, leaving it empty. Because the data member `length` indicates the number of elements in the list, the elements are removed by simply setting `length` to `zero`. Therefore, the definition of this function is

```
template<class elemType>
void arrayListType<elemType>::clearList()
{
        length = 0;
}//end clearList
```

We now discuss the definition of the constructor and the destructor. The constructor creates an array of the size specified by the user, and initializes the `length` of the list to `zero` and `maxSize` to the size of the array specified by the user. The size of the array is passed as a parameter to the constructor. The default array size is `100`. The destructor deallocates the memory occupied by the array holding the list elements. The definition of the constructor and the destructor are as follows:

```
template<class elemType>
arrayListType<elemType>::arrayListType(int size)
{
        if(size < 0)
        {
            cerr<<"The array size must be positive. Creating "
                <<"an array of size 100."<<endl;

            maxSize = 100;
        }
        else
            maxSize = size;

        length = 0;

        list = new elemType[maxSize];
        assert(list != NULL);
}

template<class elemType>
arrayListType<elemType>::~arrayListType()
{
        delete [] list;
}
```

As before, it is easy to see that each of the functions `retrieveAt`, `replaceAt`, and `clearList`, as well as the constructor and destructor, is of $O(1)$.

Copy Constructor

Recall that the copy constructor is called when an object is passed as a (value) parameter to a function, and when an object is declared and initialized using the value of another object of the same type. It copies the data members of the actual object into the corresponding data members of the formal parameter and the object being created. Its definition is

```cpp
template<class elemType>
arrayListType<elemType>::arrayListType
                    (const arrayListType<elemType>& otherList)
{
   maxSize = otherList.maxSize;
   length = otherList.length;
   list = new elemType[maxSize];      //create the array
   assert(list != NULL);              //terminate if unable to
                                      //allocate memory space

   for(int j = 0; j < length; j++)   //copy otherList
       list [j] = otherList.list[j];
}//end copy constructor
```

Overloading the Assignment Operator

Next, because we are overloading the assignment operator for the `class arrayListType`, we give the definition of the function template to overload the assignment operator:

```cpp
template<class elemType>
const arrayListType<elemType>&
                   arrayListType<elemType>::operator=
                   (const arrayListType<elemType>& otherList)
{
     if(this != &otherList)               //avoid self-assignment
     {
        delete [] list;
        maxSize = otherList.maxSize;
        length = otherList.length;

        list = new elemType[maxSize];    //create the array
        assert(list != NULL);            //if unable to allocate
                                         //memory space, terminate
                                         //the program
        for(int i = 0; i < length; i++)
            list[i] = otherList.list[i];
     }

     return *this;
}
```

Similar to the function `print`, it is easy to see that both the copy constructor and the function to overload the assignment operator are of $O(n)$.

Search

The search algorithm described next is called a **sequential**, or **linear**, search.

Consider the list of seven elements shown in Figure 3-28.

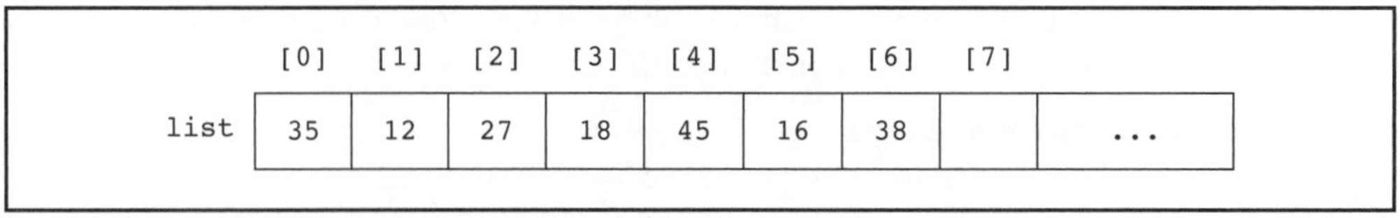

	[0]	[1]	[2]	[3]	[4]	[5]	[6]	[7]	
list	35	12	27	18	45	16	38		...

Figure 3-28 List of seven elements

Suppose that you want to determine whether 27 is in the list. The sequential search works as follows: First, you compare 27 with list[0]—that is, compare 27 with 35. Because list[0] ≠ 27, you then compare 27 with list[1] (that is, with 12, the second item in the list). Because list[1] ≠ 27, you compare 27 with the next element in the list—that is, compare 27 with list[2]. Because list[2] is equal to 27, the search stops. This is a successful search.

Let us now search for 10. As before, the search starts with the first element in the list—that is, at list[0]. This time the search item, which is 10, is compared with every item in the list. Eventually, no more data is left in the list to compare with the search item. This is an unsuccessful search.

It now follows that, as soon as you find an element in the list that is equal to the search item, you must stop the search and report "success." (In this case, you usually also tell the location in the list where the search item was found.) Otherwise, after the search item is compared with every element in the list, you must stop the search and report "failure."

Suppose that the name of the array containing the list elements is list. The previous discussion translates into the following algorithm for the sequential search:

```
found is set to false;

for(loc = 0; loc < length; loc++)
    if(list[loc] is equal to searchItem)
    {
        found is set to true
        exit loop
    }

if(found)
    return loc;
else

    return -1;
```

The following function performs a sequential search on a list:

```
template<class elemType>
int arrayListType<elemType>::seqSearch(const elemType& item)
{
     int loc;
     bool found = false;

     for(loc = 0; loc < length; loc++)
         if(list[loc] == item)
         {
             found = true;
             break;
         }

     if(found)
         return loc;
     else
         return -1;
} //end seqSearch
```

Now that we know how to implement the (sequential) search algorithm, we can give the definitions of the functions **insert** and **remove**. Recall that the function **insert** inserts a new item at the end of the list if this item does not exist in the list and the list is not full. The function **remove** removes an item from the list if the list is not empty and the item to be removed is in the list.

Chapter 9 will explicitly show that the function **seqSearch** is of $O(n)$.

Insert

The function **insert** inserts a new item in the list. Because duplicates are not allowed, this function first searches the list to determine whether the item to be inserted is already in the list. To determine whether or not the item to be inserted is already in the list, this function calls the member function **seqSearch**, as previously described. If the item to be inserted is not in the list, the new item is inserted at the end of the list and the **length** of the list is increased by 1. Also, the item to be inserted is passed as a parameter to this function. The definition of this function is

```
template<class elemType>
void arrayListType<elemType>::insert(const elemType& insertItem)
{
   int loc;

   if(length == 0)                      //the list is empty
      list[length++] = insertItem;      //insert the item and
                                        //increment the length
   else
      if(length == maxSize)
         cerr<<"Cannot insert in a full list."<<endl;
      else
```

```
        {
            loc = seqSearch(insertItem);

            if(loc == -1)                   //the item to be inserted
                                            //does not exist in the list
                list[length++] = insertItem;
            else
                cerr<<"The item to be inserted is already in "
                    <<"the list. No duplicates are allowed."<<endl;
        }
}//end insert
```

The function **insert** uses the function **seqSearch** to determine whether **insertItem** is already in the list. Because the function **seqSearch** is of $O(n)$, it follows that the function **insert** is of $O(n)$.

Remove

The function **remove** removes an item from the list. The item to be removed is passed as a parameter to this function. In order to remove the item, the function calls the member function **seqSearch** to determine whether or not the item to be removed is in the list. If the item to be removed is found in the list, the item is removed from the list and the length of the list is decremented by 1. If the item to be removed is found in the list, the function **seqSearch** returns the **index** of the item in the list to be removed. We can now use the index returned by the function **seqSearch**, and use the function **removeAt** to remove the item from the list. Therefore, the definition of the function **remove** is

```
template<class elemType>
void arrayListType<elemType>::remove(const elemType& removeItem)
{
        int loc;

        if(length == 0)
            cerr<<"Cannot delete from an empty list."<<endl;
        else
        {
            loc = seqSearch(removeItem);

            if(loc != -1)
                removeAt(loc);
            else
                cout<<"The item to be deleted is not in the list."
                    <<endl;
        }

}//end remove
```

The function **remove** uses the functions **seqSearch** and **removeAt** to remove an item from the list. Because each of these functions is of $O(n)$ and is called in sequence, it follows that the function **remove** is of $O(n)$.

Time Complexity of List Operations

The following table summarizes the time complexity of list operations.

Function	Time complexity
isEmpty	$O(1)$
isFull	$O(1)$
listSize	$O(1)$
maxListSize	$O(1)$
print	$O(n)$
isItemAtEqual	$O(1)$
insertAt	$O(n)$
insertEnd	$O(1)$
removeAt	$O(n)$
retrieveAt	$O(1)$
replaceAt	$O(1)$
clearList	$O(1)$
constructor	$O(1)$
destructor	$O(1)$
copy constructor	$O(n)$
overloading the assignment operator	$O(n)$
seqSearch	$O(n)$
insert	$O(n)$
remove	$O(n)$

 If you use the class arrayListType to process a list, you must ensure that the relational and assignment operators are defined for the data you are processing.

The following program tests various operations on array-based lists.

```
#include <iostream>

#include "newString.h"
#include "arrayListType.h"

using namespace std;
```

```
int main()
{
    arrayListType<int> intList(100);                       //Line 1
    arrayListType<newString> stringList;                   //Line 2

    int counter;                                           //Line 3
    int number;                                            //Line 4

    cout<<"Line 5: Processing the integer list"
        <<endl;                                            //Line 5
    cout<<"Line 6: Enter 5 integers: ";                    //Line 6

    for(counter = 0; counter < 5; counter++)               //Line 7
    {
        cin>>number;                                       //Line 8
        intList.insertAt(counter, number);                 //Line 9
    }

    cout<<endl;                                            //Line 10
    cout<<"Line 11: The list you entered is: ";            //Line 11
    intList.print();                                       //Line 12
    cout<<endl;                                            //Line 13

    cout<<"Line 14: Enter the item to be deleted: ";       //Line 14
    cin>>number;                                           //Line 15
    intList.remove(number);                                //Line 16
    cout<<"Line 17: After removing "<<number
        <<", the list is:"<<endl;                          //Line 17
    intList.print();                                       //Line 18
    cout<<endl;                                            //Line 19

    newString str;                                         //Line 20

    cout<<"Line 21: Processing the string list"
        <<endl;                                            //Line 21

    cout<<"Line 22: Enter 5 strings: ";                    //Line 22

    for(counter = 0; counter < 5; counter++)               //Line 23
    {
        cin>>str;                                          //Line 24
        stringList.insertAt(counter, str);                 //Line 25
    }

    cout<<endl;                                            //Line 26
    cout<<"Line 27: The list you entered is: "
        <<endl;                                            //Line 27
    stringList.print();                                    //Line 28
    cout<<endl;                                            //Line 29
```

```
cout<<"Line 30: Enter the string to be deleted: ";    //Line 30

cin>>str;                                             //Line 31
stringList.remove(str);                               //Line 32
cout<<"Line 33: After removing "<<str
    <<", the list is:"<<endl;                         //Line 33
stringList.print();                                   //Line 34
cout<<endl;                                            //Line 35

int intListSize;                                      //Line 36

cout<<"Line 37: Enter the size of the integer "
    <<"list: ";                                       //Line 37
cin>>intListSize;                                     //Line 38

arrayListType<int> intList2(intListSize);             //Line 39

cout<<"Line 40: Processing the integer list"
    <<endl;                                           //Line 40
cout<<"Line 41: Enter "<<intListSize
    <<" integers: ";                                  //Line 41

for(counter = 0; counter < intListSize; counter++)    //Line 42
{
    cin>>number;                                      //Line 43
    intList2.insertAt(counter, number);               //Line 44
}

cout<<endl;                                            //Line 45
cout<<"Line 46: The list you entered is: "<<endl;     //Line 46
intList2.print();                                     //Line 47
cout<<endl;                                            //Line 48

    return 0;
}
```

Sample Run: In this sample run, the user input is shaded.

```
Line 5: Processing the integer list
Line 6: Enter 5 integers: 23 78 56 12 79

Line 11: The list you entered is: 23 78 56 12 79

Line 14: Enter the item to be deleted: 56
Line 17: After removing 56, the list is:
23 78 12 79

Line 21: Processing the string list
Line 22: Enter 5 strings: hello sunny warm winter summer
```

```
Line 27: The list you entered is:
hello sunny warm winter summer

Line 30: Enter the string to be deleted: hello
Line 33: After removing hello, the list is:
sunny warm winter summer

Line 37: Enter the size of the integer list: 7
Line 40: Processing the integer list
Line 41: Enter 7 integers: 23 67 77 10 12 89 34

Line 46: The list you entered is:
23 67 77 10 12 89 34
```

The preceding program works as follows. The statement in Line 1 declares `intList` to be an object of the type `arrayListType`. The data member `list` of `intList` is an array of 100 components and the component type is `int`. The statement in Line 2 declares `stringList` to be an object of the type `arrayListType`. The data member list of `stringList` is an array of 100 components (the default size) and the component type is `newString`. The statement in Line 6 prompts the user to enter 5 integers. The statement in Line 8 gets the next number from the input stream. The statement in Line 9 uses the member function `insertAt` of `intList` to store the number into `intList`. The statement in Line 12 uses the member function `print` of `intList` to output the elements of `intList`. The statement in Line 14 prompts the user to enter the number to be deleted from `intList`; the statement in Line 15 gets the number to be deleted from the input stream. The statement in Line 16 uses the member function `remove` of `intList` to remove the number from `intList`.

The statements in Lines 21 through 35 work the same way as the statements in Lines 5 through 19. These statements process a list of strings.

The statement in Line 37 prompts the user to input the size of a list of integers; the statement in Line 38 stores this size into the variable `intListSize`. The statement in Line 39 declares `intList2` to be an object of the type `arrayListType` such that the data member `list` of `intList2` is an array in which the number of components is `intListSize`. This shows that you can specify the size of the array to store the data during program execution. The meaning of the remaining statements is straightforward.

PROGRAMMING EXAMPLE: POLYNOMIAL OPERATIONS

You learned in a college algebra or calculus course that a polynomial, $p(x)$, in one variable, x, is an expression of the form:

$$p(x) = a_0 + a_1x + \ldots + a_{n-1}x^{n-1} + a_nx^n,$$

where a_i's are real (or complex) numbers and n is a nonnegative integer. If $p(x) = a_0$, then $p(x)$ is called a **constant** polynomial. If $p(x)$ is a nonzero constant polynomial, then the degree of $p(x)$ is defined to be 0. Even though, in mathematics, the degree of the zero polynomial is undefined, for the purpose of this program, we will consider the degree of such polynomials to be zero. If $p(x)$ is not a constant and $a_n \neq 0$, then n is called the degree of $p(x)$; that is, the degree of a nonconstant polynomial is defined to be the exponent of the highest power of x.

The basic operations performed on polynomials are add, subtract, multiply, and divide. You can also evaluate a polynomial at any given point. For example, suppose that

$$p(x) = 1 + 2x + 3x^2,$$

and

$$q(x) = 4 + x.$$

The degree of $p(x)$ is 2 and the degree of $q(x)$ is 1. Moreover,

$$p(2) = 1 + 2 \cdot 2 + 3 \cdot 2^2 = 17$$
$$p(x) + q(x) = 5 + 3x + 3x^2$$
$$p(x) - q(x) = -3 + x + 3x^2$$
$$p(x) * q(x) = 4 + 9x + 14x^2 + 3x^3$$

The purpose of this programming example is to design and implement the **class polynomialType** to perform the various polynomial operations in a program.

To be specific, in this program, we implement the following operations on polynomials:

1. Evaluate a polynomial at a given value.
2. Add polynomials.
3. Subtract polynomials.
4. Multiply polynomials.

Moreover, we assume that the coefficients of polynomials are real numbers. You will be asked in Programming Exercise 12 to generalize it so that the coefficients can also be complex numbers.

To store a polynomial, we use a dynamic array as follows: Suppose $p(x)$ is a polynomial of degree $n \geq 0$. Let **list** be an array of size $n + 1$. The coefficient a_i of x^i is stored in **list[i]**. See Figure 3-29.

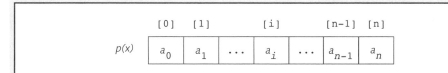

Figure 3-29   Polynomial $p(x)$

Figure 3-29 shows that if $p(x)$ is a polynomial of degree n, then we need an array of size $n + 1$ to store the coefficients of $p(x)$. Suppose that

$$p(x) = 1 + 8x - 3x^2 + 5x^4 + 7x^8$$

then the array storing the coefficients of $p(x)$ is as given in Figure 3-30.

	[0]	[1]	[2]	[3]	[4]	[5]	[6]	[7]	[8]
$p(x)$	1	8	-3	0	5	0	0	0	7

Figure 3-30 Polynomial $p(x)$ of degree 8 and its coefficients

Similarly, if

$$q(x) = -5x^2 + 16x^5,$$

then the array storing the coefficients of $q(x)$ is as given in Figure 3-31.

	[0]	[1]	[2]	[3]	[4]	[5]
$q(x)$	0	0	-5	0	0	16

Figure 3-31 Polynomial $q(x)$ of degree 5 and its coefficients

Next, we define the operations $+, -,$ and $*$. Suppose that

$$p(x) = a_0 + a_1x + \ldots + a_{n-1}x^{n-1} + a_nx^n,$$

and

$$q(x) = b_0 + b_1x + \ldots + b_{m-1}x^{m-1} + b_mx^m.$$

Let $t = max(n, m)$. Then

$$p(x) + q(x) = c_0 + c_1x + \ldots + c_{t-1}x^{t-1} + c_tx^t,$$

where for $i = 0, 1, 2, \ldots, t$

$$c_i = \begin{cases} a_i + b_i & \text{if } i \leq min(n, m) \\ a_i & \text{if } i > m \\ b_i & \text{if } i > n \end{cases}$$

The difference, $p(x) - q(x)$, of $p(x)$ and $q(x)$ can be defined similarly. It follows that the degrees of the polynomials $p(x) + q(x)$ and $p(x) - q(x)$ are $\leq max(n, m)$.

The product, $p(x) * q(x)$, of $p(x)$ and $q(x)$ is defined as follows:

$$p(x) * q(x) = d_0 + d_1 x + \ldots + d_{n+m} x^{n+m}.$$

The coefficient d_k, for $k = 0, 1, 2, \ldots, n + m$, is given by the formula

$$d_k = a_0 * b_k + a_1 * b_{k-1} + \ldots + a_k * b_0,$$

where if either a_i or b_i does not exist, it is assumed to be zero. For example,

$$d_0 = a_0 b_0$$
$$d_1 = a_0 b_1 + a_1 b_0$$

...

$$d_{n+m} = a_n b_m$$

In Chapter 2, you learned how to overload various operators. This program overloads the operators +, −, and * to perform polynomial addition, subtraction, and multiplication. Moreover, we can also overload the function call operator, ( ), to evaluate a polynomial at a given value. To simplify the input and output of polynomials, the operators << and >> are also overloaded.

Because the coefficients of a polynomial are stored in a dynamic array, we use the class arrayListType to store and manipulate the coefficients of a polynomial. In fact, we derive the class polynomialType to implement polynomial operations from the class arrayListType, which requires us to implement only the operations needed to manipulate polynomials.

The following class defines polynomials as an ADT.

```
class polynomialType: public arrayListType<double>
{
    friend ostream& operator<<(ostream&, const polynomialType&);
        //Overload the stream insertion operator.
    friend istream& operator>>(istream&, polynomialType&);
        //Overload the stream extraction operator.
public:
    polynomialType operator+(const polynomialType&);
        //Overload the operator +
    polynomialType operator-(const polynomialType&);
        //Overload the operator -
    polynomialType operator*(const polynomialType&);
        //Overload the operator *

    double operator() (double x);
        //Overload the operator () to evaluate the
        //polynomial at a given point.
        //Postcondition: The value of the polynomial at x
```

```
    //                           is calculated and returned.

polynomialType(int size = 100);
    //constructor

int min(int x, int y);
    //Function to return the smaller of x and y.
int max(int x, int y);
    //Function to return the larger of x and y.
};
```

In Exercise 19 (at the end of this chapter), you are asked to draw the UML diagram of the **class polynomialType**.

If $p(x)$ is a polynomial of degree 3, we can create an object, say, p, of the type **polynomialType** and set the size of the array **list** to 4. The following statement declares such an object p:

```
polynomialType p(4);
```

The degree of the polynomial is stored in the data member **length**, which is inherited from the **class arrayListType**.

Next we discuss the definitions of the functions.

The constructor sets the value of **length** to the size of the array and initializes the array **list** to 0.

```
polynomialType::polynomialType(int size)
        : arrayListType<double>(size)
{
    length = size;
    for(int i = 0; i < size; i++)
        list[i] = 0;
}
```

The definition of the function to overload the operator **( )** is given next.

```
double polynomialType::operator() (double x)
{
    double value = 0.0;

    for(int i = 0; i < length; i++)
    {
        if(list[i] != 0.0)
            value = value + list[i] * pow(x,i);
    }

    return value;

}
```

Suppose $p(x)$ is a polynomial of degree n and $q(x)$ is a polynomial of degree m. If $n = m$, then the operator + adds the corresponding coefficients of $p(x)$ and $q(x)$. If $n > m$, then the first m coefficients of $p(x)$ are added with the corresponding coefficients of $q(x)$. The remaining coefficients of $p(x)$ are then copied into the polynomial containing the sum of $p(x)$ and $q(x)$. Similarly, if $n < m$, the first n coefficients of $q(x)$ are added with the corresponding coefficients of $p(x)$. The remaining coefficients of $q(x)$ are then copied into the polynomial containing the sum. The definition of the operator − is similar to the definition of the operator +. The definitions of these two operator functions are as follows:

```
polynomialType polynomialType::operator+
                            (const polynomialType& right)
{
   int size = max(length, right.length);
   int i;

   polynomialType temp(size); //polynomial to store the sum

   for(i = 0; i < min(length, right.length); i++)
      temp.list[i] = list[i] + right.list[i];

   if(size == length)
      for(i = min(length, right.length); i < length; i++)
         temp.list[i] = list[i];
   else
      for(i = min(length, right.length); i < right.length; i++)
         temp.list[i] = right.list[i];

   return temp;
}

polynomialType polynomialType::operator-
                            (const polynomialType& right)
{
   int size = max(length, right.length);
   int i;

   polynomialType temp(size); //polynomial to store the
                              //difference

   for(i = 0; i < min(length, right.length); i++)
      temp.list[i] = list[i] - right.list[i];

   if(size == length)
      for(i = min(length, right.length); i < length; i++)
         temp.list[i] = list[i];
```

```
        else
          for(i = min(length, right.length); i < right.length; i++)
             temp.list[i] = -right.list[i];

    return temp;
}
```

The definition of the function to overload the operator * to multiply two polynomials is left as an exercise for you. See Programming Exercise 10 at the end of this chapter. The definitions of the remaining functions of the **class polynomialType** are:

```
int polynomialType::min(int x, int y)
{
    if(x <= y)
       return x;
    else
       return y;
}

int polynomialType::max(int x, int y)
{
    if(x >= y)
       return x;
    else
       return y;
}

ostream& operator<<(ostream& os, const polynomialType& p)
{
    int i;
    int indexFirstNonzeroCoeff = 0;

    for(i = 0; i < p.length; i++)    //determine the index of
                                     //the first nonzero
                                     //coefficient
        if(p.list[i] != 0.0)
        {
           indexFirstNonzeroCoeff = i;
           break;
        }

    if(indexFirstNonzeroCoeff < p.length)
    {
        if(indexFirstNonzeroCoeff == 0)
           os<<p.list[indexFirstNonzeroCoeff]<<" ";
        else
           os<<p.list[indexFirstNonzeroCoeff]<<"x^"
             <<indexFirstNonzeroCoeff<<" ";
```

```
        for(i = indexFirstNonzeroCoeff + 1; i < p.length; i++)
        {
            if(p.list[i] != 0.0)
                if(p.list[i] >= 0.0)
                    os<<"+ "<<p.list[i]
                        <<"x^"<<i<<" ";
                else
                    os<<"- "<<-p.list[i]
                        <<"x^"<<i<<" ";
        }
    }
    else
        os<<"0";

    return os;
}

istream& operator>>(istream& is, polynomialType& p)
{
    cout<<"The degree of this polynomial is: "
        <<p.length - 1<<endl;
    for(int i = 0; i < p.length; i++)
    {
        cout<<"Enter the coefficient of x^"<<i<<": ";
        is>>p.list[i];
    }

    return is;
}

//Test program: Polynomial Operations

#include <iostream>

#include "polynomialType.h"

using namespace std;

int main()
{
    polynomialType p(8);                              //Line 1
    polynomialType q(4);                              //Line 2
    polynomialType t;                                 //Line 3

    cin>>p;                                           //Line 4
    cout<<endl<<"Line 5: p(x): "<<p
        <<endl;                                       //Line 5
```

```
        cout<<"Line 6: p(5): "<<p(5)
            <<endl<<endl;                                    //Line 6

        cin>>q;                                              //Line 7
        cout<<endl<<"Line 8: q(x): "<<q
            <<endl<<endl;                                    //Line 8

        t = p + q;                                           //Line 9

        cout<<"Line 10: p(x) + q(x): "
            <<t<<endl;                                       //Line 10

        cout<<"Line 11: p(x) - q(x): "
            <<p - q<<endl;                                   //Line 11

        return 0;
}
```

Sample Run:

```
The degree of this polynomial is: 7
Enter the coefficient of x^0: 0
Enter the coefficient of x^1: 1
Enter the coefficient of x^2: 4
Enter the coefficient of x^3: 0
Enter the coefficient of x^4: 0
Enter the coefficient of x^5: 0
Enter the coefficient of x^6: 0
Enter the coefficient of x^7: 6

Line 5: p(x): 1x^1 + 4x^2 + 6x^7
Line 6: p(5): 468855

The degree of this polynomial is: 3
Enter the coefficient of x^0: 1
Enter the coefficient of x^1: 2
Enter the coefficient of x^2: 0
Enter the coefficient of x^3: 3

Line 8: q(x): 1 + 2x^1 + 3x^3

Line 10: p(x) + q(x): 1 + 3x^1 + 4x^2 + 3x^3 + 6x^7
Line 11: p(x) - q(x): -1 - 1x^1 + 4x^2 - 3x^3 + 6x^7
```

QUICK REVIEW

3

1. Pointer variables contain the addresses of other variables as their values.

2. In C++, no name is associated with the pointer data type.

3. A pointer variable is declared using an asterisk (*) between the data type and the variable. For example, the statements

```
int *p;
char *ch;
```

declare p and ch to be pointer variables. The value of p points to a memory space of the type int; the value of ch points to a memory space of the type char. Typically, p is called a pointer variable of the type int, and ch is called a pointer variable of the type char.

4. In C++, & is called the address of operator.

5. The address of operator returns the address of its operand. For example, if p is a pointer variable of the type int and num is an int variable, the statement

```
p = &num;
```

sets the value of p to the address of num.

6. When used as a unary operator, * is called the dereferencing operator.

7. The memory location indicated by the value of a pointer variable is accessed by using the dereferencing operator, *. For example, if p is a pointer variable of the type int, the statement

```
*p = 25;
```

sets the value of the memory location indicated by the value of p to 25.

8. You can use the member access operator arrow, ->, to access the component of an object pointed to by a pointer.

9. Pointer variables are initialized using 0 (the integer zero), NULL, or the address of a pointer variable of the same type.

10. The only integer value that can be directly assigned to a pointer variable is 0.

11. The only arithmetic operations allowed on pointer variables are increment (++), decrement (--), addition of an integer to a pointer variable, subtraction of an integer from a pointer variable, and subtraction of a pointer from another pointer.

12. Pointer arithmetic is different from ordinary arithmetic. When an integer is added to a pointer, the value added to the value of the pointer variable is the integer times the size of the object to which the pointer is pointing. Similarly, when an integer is subtracted from a pointer, the value subtracted from the value of the pointer variable is the integer times the size of the object to which the pointer is pointing.

13. Pointer variables can be compared using relational operators. (It makes sense to compare pointers of the same type.)

14. The value of one pointer variable can be assigned to another pointer variable of the same type.

15. A variable created during program execution is called a dynamic variable.

16. The operator `new` is used to create a dynamic variable.

17. The operator `delete` is used to deallocate the memory occupied by a dynamic variable.

18. In C++, both `new` and `delete` are reserved words.

19. The operator `new` has two forms: one to create a single dynamic variable, and another to create an array of dynamic variables.

20. If `p` is a pointer of the type `int`, then the statement

    ```
    p = new int;
    ```

    allocates storage of the type `int` somewhere in memory and stores the address of the allocated storage in `p`.

21. The operator `delete` has two forms: one to deallocate the memory occupied by a single dynamic variable, and another to deallocate the memory occupied by an array of dynamic variables.

22. If `p` is a pointer of the type `int`, then the statement

    ```
    delete p;
    ```

    deallocates the memory pointed to by `p`.

23. The array name is a constant pointer. It always points to the same memory location, which is the location of the first array component.

24. To create a dynamic array, the form of the `new` operator that creates an array of dynamic variables is used. For example, if `p` is a pointer of the type `int`, the statement

    ```
    p = new int[10];
    ```

    creates an array of `10` components of the type `int`. The base address of the array is stored in `p`. We call `p` a dynamic array.

25. Array notation can be used to access the components of a dynamic array. For example, suppose `p` is a dynamic array of 10 components. Then `p[0]` refers to the first array component, `p[1]` refers to the second array component, and so on. In particular, `p[i]` refers to the `(i + 1)`th component of the array.

26. An array created during program execution is called a dynamic array.

27. If `p` is a dynamic array, then the statement

    ```
    delete [] p;
    ```

    deallocates the memory occupied by `p`—that is, the components of `p`.

28. In a shallow copy, two or more pointers of the same type point to the same memory space, i.e., they point to the same data. (See the section "Shallow versus Deep Copy and Pointers.")

29. In a deep copy, each pointer of the same type has its own copy of the data. (See the section "Shallow versus Deep Copy and Pointers.")

30. If a class has a destructor, the destructor automatically executes whenever a class object goes out of scope.

31. If a class has pointer data members, the built-in assignment operators provide a shallow copy of the data.

32. A copy constructor executes when an object is declared and initialized by using the value of another object, and when an object is passed by value as a parameter.

33. A list is a collection of elements of the same type.

34. The commonly performed operations on a list are: create the list, determine whether the list is empty, determine whether the list is full, find the size of the list, destroy or clear the list, determine whether an item is the same as a given list element, insert an item in the list at a specified location, remove an item from the list at a specified location, replace an item at a specified location with another item, retrieve an item from the list from a specified location, and search the list for a given item.

EXERCISES

1. Mark the following statements as true or false.

   a. In C++, `pointer` is a reserved word.

   b. In C++, pointer variables are declared using the reserved word `pointer`.

   c. The statement `delete p;` deallocates the variable pointer `p`.

   d. The statement `delete p;` deallocates the dynamic variable that is pointed to by `p`.

   e. Given the declaration

      ```
      int list[10];
      int *p;
      ```

      the statement

      ```
      p = list;
      ```

      is valid in C++.

   f. Given the declaration

      ```
      int *p;
      ```

      the statement

      ```
      p = new int[50];
      ```

      dynamically allocates an array of 50 components of the type `int`, and `p` contains the base address of the array.

   g. The address of operator returns the address and value of its operand.

   h. If `p` is a pointer variable, then the statement `p = p * 2;` is valid in C++.

2. Given the declaration

```
int x;
int *p;
int *q;
```

mark the following statements as valid or invalid. If a statement is invalid, explain why.

a. `p = q;`

b. `*p = 56;`

c. `p = x;`

d. `*p = *q;`

e. `q = &x;`

f. `*p = q;`

3. What is the output of the following C++ code?

```
int x;
int y;
int *p = &x;
int *q = &y;
*p = 35;
*q = 98;
*p = *q;
cout<<x<<"   "<<y<<endl;
cout<<*p<<"   "<<*q<<endl;
```

4. What is the output of the following C++ code?

```
int x;
int y;
int *p = &x;
int *q = &y;
x = 35;   y = 46;
p = q;
*p = 78;
cout<<x<<"   "<<y<<endl;
cout<<*p<<"   "<<*q<<endl;
```

5. Given the declaration

```
int num = 6;
int *p = &num;
```

which of the following statements increment the value of num?

a. `p++;`

b. `(*p)++;`

c. `num++`

d. `(*num)++;`

3

6. What is the output of the following code?

```
int *p;
int *q;
p = new int;
q = p;
*p = 46;
*q = 39;
cout<<*p<<" "<<*q<<endl;
```

7. What is the output of the following code?

```
int *p;
int *q;
p = new int;
*p = 43;
q = p;
*q = 52;
p = new int;
*p = 78;
q = new int;
*q = *p;
cout<<*p<<" "<<*q<<endl;
```

8. What is wrong with the following code ?

```
int *p;                    //Line 1
int *q;                    //Line 2

p = new int;               //Line 3
*p = 43;                   //Line 4

q = p;                     //Line 5
*q = 52;                   //Line 6

delete q;                  //Line 7

cout<<*p<<" "<<*q<<endl;   //Line 8
```

9. What is the output of the following code?

```
int x;
int *p;
int *q;
p = new int[10];
q = p;
*p = 4;

for(int j = 0; j < 10; j++)
{
    x = *p ;
    p++;
```

```
        *p = x + j ;
    }

    for(int k = 0; k < 10; k++)
    {
        cout<<*q<<" ";
        q++;
    }
    cout<<endl;
```

10. What is the output of the following code?

```
int *secret;
int j;

secret = new int[10];
secret[0] = 10;
for(j = 1; j < 10; j++)
    secret[j] = secret[j - 1] + 5;
for(j = 0; j < 10; j++)
    cout<<secret[j]<<" ";
cout<<endl;
```

11. Explain the difference between a shallow copy and a deep copy of data.

12. What is wrong with the following code?

```
int *p;                            //Line 1
int *q;                            //Line 2

p = new int[5];                    //Line 3
*p = 2;                            //Line 4

for(int i = 1; i < 5; i++)         //Line 5
    p[i] = p[i - 1] + i;           //Line 6

q = p;                             //Line 7

delete [] p;                       //Line 8

for(int j = 0; j < 5; j++)         //Line 9
    cout<<q[j]<<" ";               //Line 10

cout<<endl;                        //Line 11
```

13. What is the output of the following code?

```
int *p;
int *q;
int i;

p = new int[5];
```

```
p[0] = 5;

for(i = 1; i < 5; i++)
    p[i] = p[i - 1] + 2 * i;

cout<<"Array p: ";
for(i = 0; i < 5; i++)
    cout<<p[i]<<" ";
cout<<endl;

q = new int[5];

for(i = 0; i < 5; i++)
    q[i] = p[4 - i];

cout<<"Array q: ";
for(i = 0; i < 5; i++)
    cout<<q[i]<<" ";

cout<<endl;
```

14. What is the purpose of the copy constructor?

15. Name two situations when a copy constructor executes.

16. Name three things that you should do for classes with pointer data members.

17. a. Overload the operator + for the **class newString** to perform string concatenation. For example, if **s1** is **"Hello "** and **s2** is **"there"**, the statement

```
s3 = s1 + s2;
```

should assign **"Hello there"** to **s3**, where **s1**, **s2**, and **s3** are **newString** objects.

  b. Overload the operator += for the **class newString** to perform the following string concatenation: suppose that **s1** is **"Hello "** and **s2** is **"there"**. Then the statement

```
s1 += s2;
```

should assign **"Hello there"** to **s1**, where **s1** and **s2** are **newString** objects.

18. What is the effect of the following statements?

  a. **arrayListType<int> intList(100);**

  b. **arrayListType<string> stringList(1000);**

  c. **arrayListType<double> salesList(-10);**

19. Draw the UML diagram of the **class polynomialType**. Also show the inheritance hierarchy.

PROGRAMMING EXERCISES

1. Write a program to test the assignment operator for the **class cAssignmentOprOverload** of Example 3-5.

2. Write a program to test the copy constructor of the **class pointerDataClass** of Example 3-6.

3. Extend the definition of the **class newString** as follows:

   a. Overload the operators + and += to perform the string concatenation operations.

   b. Add the function **length** to return the length of the string.

   c. Write the definition of the function to implement the operations defined in part a.

   d. Write a test program to test various operations on the **newString** objects.

4. a. Rewrite the definition of the **class newString** as defined and extended in Programming Exercise 3, so that the relational operators are overloaded as nonmember functions.

   b. Write the definition of the **class newString** as designed in part a.

   c. Write a test program that tests various operations on the **class newString**.

5. The function **removeAt** of the **class arrayListType** removes an element from the list by shifting the elements of the list. However, if the element to be removed is at the beginning of the list and the list is fairly large, it could take a lot of computer time. Because the list elements are in no particular order, you could simply remove the element by swapping the last element of the list with the item to be removed and reducing the length of the list. Rewrite the definition of the function **removeAt** using this technique.

6. The function **remove** of the **class arrayListType** removes only the first occurrence of an element. Add the function **removeAll** to the **class arrayListType** that would remove all occurrences of a given element. Also, write the definition of the function **removeAll** and a program to test this function.

7. Add the function **min** to the **class arrayListType** to return the smallest element of the list. Also, write the definition of the function **min** and a program to test this function.

8. Add the function **max** to the **class arrayListType** to return the largest element of the list. Also, write the definition of the function **max** and a program to test this function.

9. The operators + and – are overloaded as member functions for the **class polynomialType**. Redo Programming Example, Polynomial Operations so that these operators are overloaded as nonmember functions. Also, write a test program to test these operators.

10. Write the definition of the function to overload the operator * (as a member function) for the **class polynomialType** to multiply two polynomials. Also, write a test program to test the operator *.

11. Let the polynomial $p(x) = a_0 + a_1x + \ldots + a_{n-1}x^{n-1} + a_nx^n$ be a polynomial of degree n, where a_i is any real (or complex) number and n is a nonnegative integer. The derivative

of $p(x)$, written $p'(x)$, is defined to be $p'(x) = a_1 + 2a_2x + \ldots + na_nx^{n-1}$. If $p(x)$ is constant, then $p'(x) = 0$. Overload the operator ~ as a member function for the **class polynomialType** so that ~ returns the derivative of a polynomial.

12. The **class polynomialType** as given in the Programming Example, Polynomial Operations processes polynomials with coefficients that are real numbers. Design and implement a similar class that can be used to process polynomials with coefficients as complex numbers. Your class must overload the operators **+**, **-**, and ***** to perform addition, subtraction, and multiplication, as well as the operator **()** to evaluate a polynomial at a given complex number. Also, write a program to test various operations.

13. Using classes, design an online address book to keep track of the names, addresses, phone numbers, and dates of birth of family members, close friends, and certain business associates. Your program should be able to handle a maximum of 500 entries.

   a. Define the **class addressType** that can store a street address, city, state, and ZIP code. Use the appropriate functions to print and store the address. Also, use constructors to automatically initialize the data members.

   b. Define a **class extPersonType** using the **class personType** (as defined in Example 1-6, Chapter 1), the **class dateType** (as designed in Programming Exercise 2 of Chapter 2), and the **class addressType**. Add a data member to this class to classify the person as a family member, friend, or business associate. Also, add a data member to store the phone number. Add (or override) the functions to print and store the appropriate information. Use constructors to automatically initialize the data members.

   c. Derive the **class addressBookType** from the **class arrayListType**, as defined in this chapter, so that an object of the type **addressBookType** can store objects of the type **extPersonType**. An object of the type **addressBookType** should be able to process a maximum of 500 entries. Add any necessary operations to the **class addressBookType** so that the program can perform the following operations:

   (i)   Load the data into the address book from a disk.

   (ii) Search for a person by last name.

   (iii) Print the address, phone number, and date of birth (if it exists) of a given person.

   (iv) Print the names of the people whose birthdays are in a given month or between two given dates.

   (v)   Print the names of all the people having the same status, such as family, friend, or business.

   (vi) Print the names of all the people between two last names.

14. **(Safe Arrays)** In C++, there is no check to determine whether the array index is out of bounds. During program execution, an out-of-bound array index can cause serious problems. Also, recall that in C++ the array index starts at 0.

   Design a **class safeArray** that solves the out-of-bound array index problem and allows the user to begin the array index starting at any integer, positive or negative. Every object of the type **safeArray** should be an array of the type **int**. During execution, when accessing an array component, if the index is out of bounds, the program must terminate with an appropriate error message. For example,

```
safeArray list(2, 13);
safeArray yourList(-5, 9);
```

In this example, `list` is an array of `11` components, the component type is `int`, and the components are `list[2]`, `list[3]`, ..., `list[12]`. Also, `yourList` is an array of `15` components, the component type is `int`, and the components are `yourList[-5]`, `yourlist[-4]`, ..., `yourList[0]`, ..., `yourList[8]`.

15. Programming Exercise 14 processes only `int` arrays. Redesign the `class safeArray` using class templates so that the class can be used in any application that requires arrays to process data.

16. Design a class to perform various matrix operations. A matrix is a set of numbers arranged in rows and columns. Therefore, every element of a matrix has a row position and a column position. If A is a matrix of 5 rows and 6 columns, we say that matrix A is of the size 5 $\times$ 6 and sometimes denote it as $A_{5 \times 6}$. Clearly, a convenient place to store a matrix is in a two-dimensional array. Two matrices can be added and subtracted if they have the same size. Suppose that $A = [a_{ij}]$ and $B = [b_{ij}]$ are two matrices of the size $m \times n$, where a_{ij} denotes the element of A in the ith row and the jth column, and so on. The sum and difference of A and B are given by

$$A + B = [a_{ij} + b_{ij}]$$
$$A - B = [a_{ij} - b_{ij}]$$

The multiplication of A and B, $A * B$, is defined only if the number of columns of A is the same as the number of rows of B. If A is of the size $m \times n$ and B is of the size $n \times t$, then $A * B = [c_{ik}]$ is of the size $m \times t$ and the element c_{ik} is given by the formula

$$c_{ik} = a_{i1}b_{1k} + a_{i2}b_{2k} + ... + a_{in}b_{nk}$$

Design and implement a `class matrixType` that can store a matrix of size 100 $\times$ 100. Overload the operators +, -, and * to perform the addition, subtraction, and multiplication operations, respectively, and overload the operator << to output a matrix. Also, write a test program to test various operations on matrices.

4

STANDARD TEMPLATE LIBRARY (STL)

In this chapter, you will:

♦ Learn about the Standard Template Library (STL)

♦ Become familiar with the three basic components of the STL: containers, iterators, and algorithms

♦ Explore how `vector` and `deque` containers are used to manipulate data in a program

♦ Discover the use of iterators

Chapter 2 introduced and examined templates. With the help of class templates, we developed (and used) a generic code to process lists. For example, in Chapter 3, we used the `class arrayListType` to process a list of integers and a list of strings. In Chapters 5, 7, and 8, we will study the three most important data structures: linked lists, stacks, and queues. In Chapter 5, using class templates, we will develop a generic code to process linked lists. In addition, using the second principle of object-oriented programming (OOP), we will develop a generic code to process ordered lists. Then, in Chapters 7 and 8, we will use class templates to develop a generic code to implement stacks and queues. Along the way, you will see that a template is a powerful tool that promotes code reuse.

ANSI/ISO Standard C++ is equipped with a Standard Template Library (STL). Among other things, the STL provides class templates to process lists (contiguous or linked), stacks, and queues. This chapter discusses some of the important features of the STL, and shows how to use certain tools provided by the STL in a program. Chapter 13 describes some of the features of the STL not described in this chapter.

In ensuing chapters, you will learn how to develop your own code to implement and manipulate data, as well as how to use professionally written code.

COMPONENTS OF THE STL

The main objective of a program is to manipulate data and generate results. Achieving this goal requires the ability to store data into computer memory, access a particular piece of data, and write algorithms to manipulate the data.

For example, if all the data items are of the same type and we have some idea of the number of data items, we could use an array to store the data. We can then use an index to access a particular component of the array. Using a loop and the array index, we can step through the elements of the array. Algorithms, such as those for initializing the array, sorting, and searching, are used to manipulate the data stored in an array. On the other hand, if we do not want to be concerned with the size of the data, we can use a linked list, as will be described in Chapter 5, to process the data. If the data needs to be processed in a Last In First Out (LIFO) manner, we can use a stack (Chapter 7). Similarly, if the data needs to be processed in a First In First Out (FIFO) manner, we can use a queue (Chapter 8).

The STL is equipped with these features to manipulate data effectively. More formally, the STL has three main components:

- Containers
- Iterators
- Algorithms

Containers and iterators are class templates. Iterators are used to step through the elements of a container. Algorithms are used to manipulate data. This chapter discusses some of the containers and iterators. Algorithms are discussed in Chapter 13.

Container Types

Containers are used to manage objects of a given type. The STL containers are classified into three categories:

- Sequence containers (also called sequential containers)
- Associative containers
- Container adapters

Moreover, containers are implemented using class templates. The following sections describe some of the sequence containers. Associative containers are described in Chapter 13; container adapters are described in Chapters 7 and 8.

Sequence Containers

Every object in a sequence container has a specific position. The three predefined sequence containers are:

- `vector`

- `deque`

- `list`

Before discussing sequence container types in general, let us first briefly describe the sequence container **vector**. We do so because vector containers are logically the same as arrays and, therefore, can be processed like arrays. Also, with the help of vector containers, we can describe several properties that are common to all containers. In fact, all containers use the same names for the common operations. Of course, there are operations that are specific to a container, which are discussed when describing a particular container. This chapter discusses **vector** and **deque** containers. Chapter 5 discusses **list** containers.

SEQUENCE CONTAINER: `vector`

A vector container stores and manages its objects in a dynamic array. Because an array is a random access data structure, the elements of a vector can be accessed randomly. Item insertion in the middle or beginning of an array is time consuming, especially if the array is large. However, inserting an item at the end is quite fast.

The name of the class that implements the vector container is **vector**. (Recall that containers are class templates.) The name of the header file containing the **class vector** is **vector**. Therefore, to use a vector container in a program, the program must include the following statement:

`#include <vector>`

Furthermore, to define an object of the type **vector**, we must specify the type of the object because the **class vector** is a class template. For example, the statement

`vector<int> intList;`

declares **intList** to be a vector container and the component type to be **int**. Similarly, the statement

`vector<string> stringList;`

declares **stringList** to be a vector container and the component type to be **string**.

Declaring `vector` Objects

The **class vector** contains several constructors, including the default constructor. Therefore, a vector container can be declared and initialized in several ways. Table 4-1 describes how a vector container of a specific type can be declared and initialized.

Table 4-1 Various Ways to Declare and Initialize a Vector Container

Statement	Effect
`vector<elementType> vecList;`	Creates an empty vector, `vecList`, without any elements. (The default constructor is invoked.)
`vector<elementType> vecList(otherVecList);`	Creates a vector, `vecList`, and initializes `vecList` to the elements of the vector `otherVecList`. `vecList` and `otherVecList` are of the same type.
`vector<elementType> vecList(size);`	Creates a vector, `vecList`, of size `size`. `vecList` is initialized using the default constructor.
`vector<elementType> vecList(n, elem);`	Creates a vector, `vecList`, of size n. `vecList` is initialized using n copies of the element `elem`.
`vector<elementType> vecList(begin, end);`	Creates a vector, `vecList`. `vecList` is initialized to the elements in the range (begin, end), that is, all elements in the range begin...end-1.

Example 4-1

a. The following statement declares `intList` to be an empty vector container and the element type is `int`:

```
vector<int> intList;
```

b. The following statement declares `intList` to be a vector container of size 10 and the element type is `int`. The elements of `intList` are initialized to 0:

```
vector<int> intList(10);
```

c. The following statement declares `intList` to be a vector container of size 5 and the element type is `int`. The container `intList` is initialized using the elements of the array:

```
int intArray[5] = {2, 4, 6, 8, 10};
vector<int> intList(intArray, intArray + 5);
```

The container `intList` is initialized using the elements of the array `intArray`. That is, `intList = {2, 4, 6, 8, 10}`.

Now that we know how to declare a vector container, let us discuss how to manipulate the data stored in a vector container. To do so, we must know the following basic operations:

- Item insertion

- Item deletion

- Stepping through the elements of a vector container

The elements in a vector container can be accessed directly by using the operations given in Table 4-2.

4

Table 4-2 Operations to Access the Elements of a Vector Container

Expression	Effect
vecList.at(index)	Returns the element at the position specified by index.
vecList[index]	Returns the element at the position specified by index.
vecList.front()	Returns the first element. (Does not check whether the container is empty.)
vecList.back()	Returns the last element. (Does not check whether the container is empty.)

From Table 4-2, it follows that the elements in a vector can be processed just as they can in an array. (Recall that in C++, an array index starts at location 0. Similarly, the first element in a vector container is at location 0.)

Example 4-2

Consider the following statement, which declares intList to be a vector container of size 5 and the element type is int:

```
vector<int> intList(5);
```

You can use a loop, such as the following, to the store the elements into intList:

```
for(int j = 0; j < 5; j++)
    intList[j] = j;
```

Similarly, you can use a for loop to output the elements of intList.

The class vector provides various operations to process the elements of a vector container. Suppose that vecList is a container of the type vector. Item insertion and deletion into vecList can be accomplished using the operations given in Table 4-3. These operations are implemented as member functions of the class vector and are shown in bold. Table 4-3 also shows how these operations are used.

Table 4-3 Various Operations on a Vector Container

Statement	Effect
`vecList.clear()`	Deletes all the elements from the container.
`vecList.erase(position)`	Deletes the element at the position specified by `position`.
`vecList.erase(beg, end)`	Deletes all elements in the range starting at beg until end-1.
`vecList.insert(position, elem)`	A copy of `elem` is inserted at the position specified by `position`. The position of the new element is returned.
`vecList.insert(position, n, elem)`	n copies of `elem` are inserted at the position specified by `position`.
`vecList.insert(position, beg, end)`	A copy of the elements, in the range starting at beg until end-1, is inserted into `vecList` at the position specified by `position`.
`vecList.push_back(elem)`	A copy of `elem` is inserted into `vecList` at the end.
`vecList.pop_back()`	Deletes the last element.
`vecList.resize(num)`	Changes the number of elements to num. If `size()` increases, the default constructor creates the new elements.
`vecList.resize(num, elem)`	Changes the number of elements to num. If `size()` increases, the default constructor creates the new elements.

 In Table 4-3, the argument `position` in STL terminology is called an **iterator**. An iterator works just like a pointer. In general, iterators are used to step through the elements of a container. In other words, with the help of an iterator we can walk through the elements of a container and process them one at a time. The next section describes how to declare an iterator into a vector container and how to manipulate the data stored in a container. Because iterators are an integral part of the STL, they are discussed in detail in the section "Iterators," located later in this chapter.

The function `push_back` is quite useful. This function is used to add an element into a container at the end of the container. Example 4-2 declared the container `intList` of size 5. You might think that you can add only 5 elements into the container `intList`. However, this is not the case. If you need to add more than 5 elements, you can use the function `push_back`. You cannot use the array subscripting operator, as in Example 4-2, to add elements past position 4 unless you increase the size of the container.

If you do not know the number of elements you need to store into a vector container, when you declare the vector container you do not need to specify its size. See Example 4-3. In this case, you can use the function **push_back**, as shown in Examples 4-3 and 4-5, to add elements into a vector container.

Example 4-3

The following statement declares **intList** to be a vector container of size 0:

```
vector<int> intList;
```

To add elements to **intList**, we can use the function **push_back** as follows:

```
intList.push_back(34);
intList.push_back(55);
```

After these statements execute, the size of **intList** is 2 and **intList** = {34, 55}. Of course, you could have used the **resize** function to first increase the size of **intList** and then used the array subscripting operator. However, at times, the **push_back** function is more convenient because it does not need to know the size of the container; it simply adds the elements at the end.

Declaring an Iterator into a Vector Container

Even though we can process a vector container just like an array using the array subscripting operator, there are situations where we would like to process the elements of a vector container using an iterator. (Recall that an iterator is similar to a pointer.) For example, suppose that we want to insert an element at a specific position in a vector container. Because the element is to be inserted at a specific position, this requires shifting the elements of the container (unless the element is added at the end). Of course, we must also think about the size of the container. To make element insertion convenient, the **class vector** provides the function **insert** to insert the elements at a specific position in a vector container. However, to use the function **insert**, the position where to insert the element must be specified by an iterator. Similarly, the function **erase**, to remove an element, also requires the use of an iterator. This section describes how to declare and use an iterator into a vector container.

The **class vector** contains a **typedef iterator**, which is declared as a **public** member. An iterator to a vector container is declared using the **typedef iterator**. For example, the statement

```
vector<int>::iterator intVecIter;
```

declares **intVecIter** to be an iterator into a vector container of the type **int**.

Because **iterator** is a **typedef** defined inside the **class vector**, we must use the container name (**vector**), container element type, and scope resolution operator to use the **typedef iterator**.

Suppose that the iterator **intVecIter** points to an element of a vector container with elements of the type **int**. The expression

```
++intVecIter
```

advances the iterator `intVecIter` to the next element in the container. The expression

`*intVecIter`

returns the element at the current iterator position.

Note that these operations are the same as the operations on pointers, discussed in Chapter 3. Recall that when used as a unary operator, `*` is called the dereferencing operator.

We now discuss how to use an iterator into a vector container to manipulate the data stored in a vector container. Suppose that we have the following statements:

```
vector<int> intList;                     //Line 1
vector<int>::iterator  intVecIter;       //Line 2
```

The statement in Line 1 declares `intList` to be a **vector** container and the element type is `int`. The statement in Line 2 declares `intVecIter` to be an iterator into a **vector** container whose element type is `int`.

Containers and the Functions `begin` and `end`

Every container has the member functions `begin` and `end`. The function `begin` returns the position of the first element in the container; the function `end` returns the position of the last element in the container. These functions have no parameters.

After the following statement executes:

`intVecIter = intList.begin();`

the iterator `intVecIter` points to the first element in the container `intList`.

The following `for` loop uses an iterator to output the elements of `intList` onto the standard output device:

```
for(intVecIter = intList.begin(); intVecIter != intList.end();
                                   ++intVecIter)
    cout<<*intVecIter<<" ";
```

Example 4-4

Consider the following statements:

```
int intArray[7] = {1, 3, 5, 7, 9, 11, 13};     //Line 1
vector<int> vecList(intArray, intArray + 7);   //Line 2
vector<int>::iterator  intVecIter;             //Line 3
```

The statement in Line 2 declares and initializes the vector container `vecList`. Now consider the following statements:

```
intVecIter = vecList.begin();            //Line 4
++intVecIter;                            //Line 5
vecList.insert(intVecIter, 22);          //Line 6
```

The statement in Line 4 initializes the iterator `intVecIter` to the first element of `vecList`. The statement in Line 5 advances `intVecIter` to the second element of `vecList`. The statement in Line 6 inserts `22` at the position specified by `intVecIter`.

After the statement in Line 6 executes, `vecList = {1, 22, 3, 5, 7, 9, 11, 13}`. Notice that the size of the container also increases.

___

The **class vector** also contains member functions that can be used to find the number of elements currently in a container, the maximum number of elements that can be inserted in a container, and so on. Table 4-4 describes some of these operations. (Suppose that `vecCont` is a vector container.)

Table 4-4 Functions to Determine the Size of a Vector Container

Expression	Effect
`vecCont.capacity()`	Returns the maximum number of elements that can be inserted into the container `vecCont` without reallocation.
`vecCont.empty()`	Returns `true` if the container `vecCont` is empty, and `false` otherwise.
`vecCont.size()`	Returns the number of elements currently in the container `vecCont`.
`vecCont.max_size()`	Returns the maximum number of elements that can be inserted into the container `vecCont`.

Example 4-5 illustrates how to use a vector container in a program and how to process the elements in a vector container.

Example 4-5

```cpp
#include <iostream>

#include <vector>

using namespace std;

int main()
{
    vector<int> intList;                    //Line 1
    int i;                                  //Line 2

    intList.push_back(13);                  //Line 3
    intList.push_back(75);                  //Line 4
    intList.push_back(28);                  //Line 5
    intList.push_back(35);                  //Line 6

    cout<<"Line 7: List Elements: ";        //Line 7
    for(i = 0; i < 4; i++)                   //Line 8
        cout<<intList[i]<<" ";              //Line 9
    cout<<endl;                             //Line 10
```

```
for(i = 0; i < 4; i++)                      //Line 11
    intList[i] *= 2;                        //Line 12

cout<<"Line 13: List Elements: ";          //Line 13
for(i = 0; i < 4; i++)                      //Line 14
    cout<<intList[i]<<" ";                  //Line 15
cout<<endl;                                 //Line 16

vector<int>::iterator listIt;              //Line 17

cout<<"Line 18: List Elements: ";          //Line 18
for(listIt = intList.begin(); listIt != intList.end();
                              ++listIt)     //Line 19
    cout<<*listIt<<" ";                     //Line 20
cout<<endl;                                 //Line 21
listIt = intList.begin();                   //Line 22
++listIt;                                   //Line 23
++listIt;                                   //Line 24
intList.insert(listIt,88);   //Insert 88 at the
                    //position specified
                    //by listIt.            //Line 25

cout<<"Line 26: List Elements: ";          //Line 26
for(listIt = intList.begin(); listIt != intList.end();
                              ++listIt)
                                            //Line 27
    cout<<*listIt<<" ";                     //Line 28
cout<<endl;                                 //Line 29

return 0;
}
```

Output

```
Line 7: List Elements: 13 75 28 35
Line 13: List Elements: 26 150 56 70
Line 18: List Elements: 26 150 56 70
Line 26: List Elements: 26 150 88 56 70
```

The statement in Line 1 declares a vector container (or vector for short), `intList`, of the type `int`. The statement in Line 2 declares `i` to be an `int` variable. The statements in Lines 3 through 6 use the function `push_back` to insert four numbers—13, 75, 28, and 35—into `intList`. The statements in Lines 8 and 9 use the `for` loop and the array subscripting operator `[ ]` to output the elements of `intList`. In the output, see the line marked Line 7, which contains the output of Lines 7 through 10 of the program. The statements in Lines 11 and 12 use a `for` loop to double the value of each element of `intList`; the statements in Lines 14 and 15 output the elements of `intList`. In the output, see the line marked Line 13, which contains the output of Lines 13 through 16 of the program.

The statement in Line 17 declares `listIt` to be a vector iterator that processes any vector container whose elements are of the type `int`. Using the iterator `listIt`, the statements in Lines 19 and 20 output the elements of `intList`. After the statement in Line 22 executes, `listIt` points to the first element of `intList`. The statements in Lines 23 and 24 advance `listIt` twice; after these statements execute, `listIt` points to the third element of `intList`. The statement in Line 25 inserts 88 into `intList` at the position specified by the iterator `listIt`. Because `listIt` points to the component at position 2 (the third element of `intList`), 88 is inserted at position 2 in `intList`; that is, 88 becomes the third element of `intList`. The statements in Lines 27 and 28 output the modified `intList`.

4

Member Functions Common to All Containers

The previous section discussed vector containers. We now look at operations that are common to all containers. For example, every container class has a default constructor, several constructors with parameters, a destructor, a function to insert an element into a container, and so on.

Recall that a class encapsulates data, and operations on that data, into a single unit. Because every container is a class, several operations are directly defined for a container and are provided as part of the class's definition. Also, recall that the operations to manipulate the data are implemented with the help of functions and are called member functions of the class. Table 4-5 describes some of the member functions that are common to all containers; that is, these functions are included as members of the class template implementing the container.

Suppose that `ct`, `ct1`, and `ct2` are containers of the same type. Table 4-5 shows the name of the function in bold, and shows how a function is called.

Table 4-5 Some Member Functions Common to All Containers

Member Function	Effect
Default constructor	Initializes the object to an empty state.
Constructor with parameters	In addition to the default constructor, every container has constructors with parameters. We will describe these constructors when we discuss a specific container.
Copy constructor	Executes when an object is passed as a parameter by value, when an object is declared and initialized using another object of the same type, and when a function returns its value as an object.
Destructor	Executes when the object goes out of scope.
`ct.empty()`	Returns `true` if container `ct` is empty, and `false` otherwise.
`ct.size()`	Returns the number of elements, as an `unsigned int`, currently in container `ct`.
`ct.max_size()`	Returns the maximum number of elements that can be inserted into container `ct`.

Table 4-5 Some Member Functions Common to All Containers (continued)

Member Function	Effect
ct1.swap(ct2)	Swaps the elements of containers ct1 and ct2.
ct.begin()	Returns an iterator to the first element in container ct.
ct.end()	Returns an iterator to the last element in container ct.
ct.rbegin()	Reverse begin. Returns a pointer to the last element in container ct. This function is used to process the elements of ct in reverse.
ct.rend()	Reverse end. Returns a pointer to the first element in container ct.
ct.insert(position, elem)	Inserts elem into the container ct at the position specified by the argument position. Note that here position is an iterator.
ct.erase(begin, end)	Deletes all elements between begin and end-1 from container ct.
ct.clear()	Deletes all elements from the container. After a call to this function, container ct is empty.
Operator Functions	
ct1 = ct2;	Copies the elements of ct2 into ct1. After this operation, the elements in both containers are the same.
ct1 == ct2	Returns true if containers ct1 and ct2 are equal, and false otherwise.
ct1 != ct2	Returns true if containers ct1 and ct2 are not equal, and false otherwise.

 Because these operations are common to all containers, when discussing a specific container, to save space, these operations will not be listed again.

Member Functions Common to Sequence Containers

The previous section described the member functions that are common to all containers. In addition to these member functions, Table 4-6 describes the member functions that are common to all sequence containers—that is, containers of the type **vector**, **deque**, and **list**. (Suppose that **seqCont** is a sequence container.)

Table 4-6 Member Functions Common to All Sequence Containers

Expression	Effect
seqCont.**insert**(position, elem)	A copy of elem is inserted into seqCont at the position specified by position. The position of the new element is returned.
seqCont.**insert**(position, n, elem)	n copies of elem are inserted into seqCont at the position specified by position.
seqCont.**insert**(position, beg, end)	A copy of the elements, starting at beg until end-1, are inserted into seqCont at the position specified by position.
seqCont.**push_back**(elem)	A copy of elem is inserted into seqCont at the end.
seqCont.**pop_back**()	Deletes the last element.
seqCont.**erase**(position)	Deletes the element at the position specified by position.
seqCont.**erase**(beg, end)	Deletes all elements starting at beg until end-1.
seqCont.**clear**()	Deletes all elements from the container.
seqCont.**resize**(num)	Changes the number of elements to num. If size() grows, the new elements are created by their default constructor.
seqCont.**resize**(num, elem)	Changes the number of elements to num. If size() grows, the new elements are copies of elem.

copy Algorithm

Example 4-5 used a **for** loop to output the elements of a vector container. The STL provides a convenient way to output the elements of a container with the help of the function **copy**. The function **copy** is provided as a part of the generic algorithm and can be used with any container type as well as arrays. Because we frequently need to output the elements of a container, before continuing with our discussion of containers, let us describe this function.

 Like the function copy, the STL contains many functions as part of the generic algorithms, which are described in Chapter 13.

The function **copy** does more than output the elements of a container. In general, it allows us to copy the elements from one place to another. For example, to output the elements of a vector or to copy the elements of a vector into another vector, we can use the function copy. The prototype of the function template **copy** is

```
template<class inputIterator, class outputIterator>
outputItr copy(inputIterator first1, inputIterator last,
          outputIterator first2);
```

The parameter `first1` specifies the position from which to begin copying the elements; the parameter `last` specifies the end position. The parameter `first2` specifies where to copy the elements. Therefore, the parameters `first1` and `last` specify the source, and the parameter `first2` specifies the destination. Note that the elements within the range `first1...last-1` are copied.

The definition of the function template `copy` is contained in the header file `algorithm`. Therefore, to use the function `copy`, the program must include the statement:

```
#include <algorithm>
```

The function `copy` works as follows. Consider the following statements:

```
int intArray[] = {5, 6, 8, 3, 40, 36, 98, 29, 75};   //Line 1
vector<int> vecList(9);                                //Line 2
```

The statement in Line 1 creates the array `intArray` of nine components:

```
intArray = {5, 6, 8, 3, 40, 36, 98, 29, 75}
```

Here `intArray[0]` = 5, `intArray[1]` = 6, and so on.

The statement in Line 2 creates an empty vector container of nine components and the element type is `int`.

Recall that the array name, `intArray`, is actually a pointer and contains the base address of the array. Therefore, `intArray` points to the first component of the array, `intArray + 1` points to the second component of the array, and so on.

Now consider the statement

```
copy(intArray, intArray + 9, vecList.begin());       //Line 3
```

This statement copies the elements starting at the location `intArray`, which is the first component of the array `intArray`, until `intArray + 9 - 1` (that is, `intArray + 8`), which is the last element of the array `intArray`, into the container `vecList`. (Note that here `first1` is `intArray`, `last` is `intArray + 9`, and `first2` is `vecList.begin()`.) After the statement in Line 3 executes,

```
vecList = {5, 6, 8, 3, 40, 36, 98, 29, 75}           //Line 4
```

Next, consider the statement

```
copy(intArray + 1, intArray + 9, intArray);          //Line 5
```

Here `first1` is `intArray + 1`; that is, `first1` points to the location of the second element of the array `intArray`, and `last` is `intArray + 9`. Also, `first2` is `intArray`; that is, `first2` points to the location of the first element of the array `intArray`. Therefore, the second array element is copied into the first array component, the third array element into the second array component, and so on. After the statement in Line 5 executes,

```
intArray[] = {6, 8, 3, 40, 36, 98, 29, 75, 75}       //Line 6
```

Notice that the elements of the array `intArray` are shifted to the left by one position.

Suppose that **vecList** is as given in Line 4. Consider the statement

```
copy(vecList.rbegin() + 2, vecList.rend(),
                    vecList.rbegin());     //Line 7
```

Recall that the function **rbegin** (reverse begin) returns a pointer to the last element in a container; it is used to process the elements of a container in reverse. Therefore, **vecList.rbegin() + 2** returns a pointer to the third-to-last element in the container **vecList**. Similarly, the function **rend** (reverse end) returns a pointer to the first element in a container. The previous statement shifts the elements of the container **vecList** to the right by two positions. After the statement in Line 7 executes, the container **vecList** is:

```
vecList = {5, 6, 5, 6, 8, 3, 40, 36, 98}
```

Example 4-6 shows the effect of the preceding statements using a C++ program. Before discussing Example 4-6, let us describe a special type of iterators, called **ostream iterators**, which work well with the function **copy** to copy the elements of a container to an output device.

ostream Iterator and Function copy

One way to output the contents of a container is to use a **for** loop and the function **begin** to initialize the **for** loop control variable, and to use the function **end** to set the limit. Alternatively, the function **copy** can be used to output the elements of a container. In this case, an iterator of the type **ostream** specifies the destination (**ostream** iterators are discussed in detail later in this chapter). When we create an iterator of the type **ostream**, we also specify the type of element the iterator will output.

The following statement illustrates how to create an **ostream** iterator of the type **int**:

```
ostream_iterator<int> screen(cout, " "); //Line A
```

This statement creates **screen** to be an **ostream** iterator with the element type **int**. The iterator **screen** has two arguments: the object **cout** and a space. Therefore, the iterator **screen** is initialized by using the object **cout**, and when this iterator outputs the elements they are separated by a space.

The statement

```
copy(intArray, intArray + 9, screen);
```

outputs the elements of **intArray** on the screen.

Similarly, the statement

```
copy(vecList.begin(), vecList.end(), screen);
```

outputs the elements of the container **vecList** on the screen.

We will frequently use the function **copy** to output the elements of a container by using an **ostream** iterator. Also, until we discuss **ostream** iterators in detail, we will use statements similar to the statement in Line A to create an **ostream** iterator.

Of course, we can directly specify an `ostream` iterator in the function `copy`. For example, the statement (shown previously)

```
copy(vecList.begin(), vecList.end(), screen);
```

is equivalent to the statement

```
copy(vecList.begin(), vecList.end(),
                    ostream_iterator<int>(cout, " "));
```

Finally, the statement

```
copy(vecList.begin(), vecList.end(),
                    ostream_iterator<int>(cout, ", "));
```

outputs the elements of `vecList` with a comma and space between them.

Example 4-6 illustrates how to use the function `copy` and an `ostream` iterator in a program.

Example 4-6

```cpp
#include <algorithm>
#include <vector>
#include <iterator>
#include <iostream>

using namespace std;

int main()
{
    int intArray[] = {5, 6, 8, 3, 40, 36, 98, 29, 75};    //Line 1

    vector<int> vecList(9);                               //Line 2

    ostream_iterator<int> screen(cout, " ");              //Line 3

    cout<<"Line 4: intArray: ";                           //Line 4
    copy(intArray, intArray + 9, screen);                 //Line 5
    cout<<endl;                                           //Line 6

    copy(intArray, intArray + 9, vecList.begin());        //Line 7

    cout<<"Line 8: vecList: ";                            //Line 8
    copy(vecList.begin(), vecList.end(), screen);         //Line 9
    cout<<endl;                                           //Line 10

    copy(intArray + 1, intArray + 9, intArray);           //Line 11
    cout<<"Line 12: After shifting the elements one "
        <<"position to the left, intArray: "<<endl;       //Line 12
    copy(intArray, intArray + 9, screen);                 //Line 13
    cout<<endl;                                           //Line 14
```

```
    copy(vecList.rbegin() + 2, vecList.rend(),
                      vecList.rbegin());                    //Line 15
    cout<<"Line 16: After shifting the elements down "
        <<"by two positions, vecList:"<<endl;               //Line 16
    copy(vecList.begin(), vecList.end(), screen);           //Line 17
    cout<<endl;                                             //Line 18

    return 0;
}
```

Output

```
Line 4: intArray: 5 6 8 3 40 36 98 29 75
Line 8: vecList: 5 6 8 3 40 36 98 29 75
Line 12: After shifting the elements one position to the left,
intArray:
6 8 3 40 36 98 29 75 75
Line 16: After shifting the elements down by two positions, vecList:
5 6 5 6 8 3 40 36 98
```

SEQUENCE CONTAINER: deque

This section describes the **deque** sequence containers. The term **deque** stands for double-ended queue. Deque containers are implemented as dynamic arrays in such a way that the elements can be inserted at both ends. Therefore, a **deque** can expand in either direction. Elements can also be inserted in the middle. Inserting elements at the beginning or at the end is fast; inserting elements in the middle, however, is time consuming because the elements in the queue need to be shifted.

The name of the class defining the deque containers is **deque**. The definition of the **class deque**, and the functions to implement the various operations on a **deque** object, are contained in the header file **deque**. Therefore, to use a deque container in a program, the program must include the following statement:

```
#include <deque>
```

The **class deque** contains several constructors. Therefore, a **deque** object can be initialized in various ways when it is declared, as described in Table 4–7.

Table 4-7 Various Ways to Declare a **deque** Object

Statement	Effect
deque<elementType> deq;	Creates an empty deque container without any elements. (The default constructor, deq, is invoked.)
deque<elementType> deq(otherDeq);	Creates a deque container, deq, and initializes deq to the elements of otherDeq; deq and otherDeq are of the same type.

Table 4-7 Various Ways to Declare a deque Object (continued)

Statement	Effect
deque<elementType> deq(size);	Creates a deque container, deq, of size size. deq is initialized using the default constructor.
deque<elementType> deq(n, elem);	Creates a deque container, deq, of size n. deq is initialized using n copies of the element elem.
deque<elementType> deq(begin, end);	Creates a deque container, deq. deq is initialized to the elements in the range (begin, end)—that is, all elements in the range begin...end-1.

In addition to the operations that are common to all containers (see Table 4-6), Table 4-8 describes the operations that can be used to manipulate the elements of a **deque** container. The name of the function implementing the operations is shown in bold. The statement also shows how to use a particular function. Suppose that **deq** is a **deque** container.

Table 4-8 Various Operations that Can Be Performed on a deque Object

Expression	Effect
deq.**assign**(n, elem)	Assigns n copies of elem.
deq.**assign**(beg, end)	Assigns all the elements in the range beg...end-1.
deq.**push_front**(elem)	Inserts elem at the beginning of deq.
deq.**pop_front**()	Removes the first element from deq.
deq.**at**(index)	Returns the element at the position specified by index.
deq[index]	Returns the element at the position specified by index.
deq.**front**()	Returns the first element. (Does not check whether the container is empty.)
deq.**back**()	Returns the last element. (Does not check whether the container is empty.)

Example 4-7 illustrates how to use a **deque** container in a program.

Example 4-7

```
//Deque Example
#include <iostream>
#include <deque>
#include <algorithm>
#include <iterator>
```

```
using namespace std;

int main()
{
    deque<int> intDeq;                                      //Line 1
    ostream_iterator<int> screen(cout, " ");                //Line 2

    intDeq.push_back(13);                                   //Line 3
    intDeq.push_back(75);                                   //Line 4
    intDeq.push_back(28);                                   //Line 5
    intDeq.push_back(35);                                   //Line 6

    cout<<"Line 7: intDeq: ";                               //Line 7
    copy(intDeq.begin(), intDeq.end(), screen);             //Line 8
    cout<<endl;                                             //Line 9
    intDeq.push_front(0);                                   //Line 10
    intDeq.push_back(100);                                  //Line 11

    cout<<"Line 12: After adding two more "
        <<"elements, one at the front "<<endl
        <<"            and one at the back, intDeq: ";       //Line 12
    copy(intDeq.begin(), intDeq.end(), screen);             //Line 13
    cout<<endl;                                             //Line 14

    intDeq.pop_front();                                     //Line 15
    intDeq.pop_front();                                     //Line 16

    cout<<"Line 17: After removing the first "
        <<"two elements, intDeq: ";                         //Line 17
    copy(intDeq.begin(), intDeq.end(), screen);             //Line 18
    cout<<endl;                                             //Line 19

    intDeq.pop_back();                                      //Line 20
    intDeq.pop_back();                                      //Line 21

    cout<<"Line 22: After removing the last "
        <<"two elements, intDeq = ";                        //Line 22
    copy(intDeq.begin(), intDeq.end(), screen);             //Line 23
    cout<<endl;                                             //Line 24

    deque<int>::iterator deqIt;                             //Line 25

    deqIt = intDeq.begin();                                 //Line 26
    ++deqIt;                      //deqIt points to the
                                  //second element          //Line 27
    intDeq.insert(deqIt, 444); //insert 444 at the
                                  //location deqIt           //Line 28
```

4

```
        cout<<"Line 29: After inserting 444, intDeq:   ";   //Line 29

        copy(intDeq.begin(), intDeq.end(), screen);         //Line 30
        cout<<endl;                                          //Line 31

        intDeq.assign(2, 45);                                //Line 32

        cout<<"Line 33: After assigning two "
            <<"copies of 45, intDeq: ";                      //Line 33
        copy(intDeq.begin(), intDeq.end(), screen);          //Line 34
        cout<<endl;                                          //Line 35

        intDeq.push_front(-10);                              //Line 36
        intDeq.push_back(-999);                              //Line 37

        cout<<"Line 38: After inserting two "
            <<"elements, one at the front "<<endl
            <<"            and one at the back, intDeq: ";   //Line 38
        copy(intDeq.begin(), intDeq.end(), screen);          //Line 39
        cout<<endl;                                          //Line 40

        return 0;
}
```

Output

```
Line 7:  intDeq: 13 75 28 35
Line 12: After adding two more elements, one at the front
         and one at the back, intDeq: 0 13 75 28 35 100
Line 17: After removing the first two elements, intDeq: 75 28 35 100
Line 22: After removing the last two elements, intDeq = 75 28
Line 29: After inserting 444, intDeq: 75 444 28
Line 33: After assigning two copies of 45, intDeq: 45 45
Line 38: After inserting two elements, one at the front
         and one at the back, intDeq: -10 45 45 -999
```

The statement in Line 1 declares a **deque** container **intDeq** of the type **int**; that is, all the elements of **intDeq** are of the type **int**. The statement in Line 2 declares **screen** to be an **ostream** iterator initialized to the standard output device. The statements in Lines 3 through 6 use the **push_back** operation to insert four numbers—13, 75, 28, and 35—into **intDeq**. The statement in Line 8 outputs the elements of **intDeq**. In the output, see the line marked Line 7, which contains the output of the statements in Lines 7 through 9 of the program.

The statement in Line 10 inserts 0 at the beginning of **intDeq**; the statement in Line 11 inserts 100 at the end of **intDeq**. The statement in Line 13 outputs the modified **intDeq**.

The statements in Lines 15 and 16 use the operation **pop_front** to remove the first two elements of **intDeq**; the statement in Line 18 outputs the modified **intDeq**. The statements in

Lines 20 and 21 use the operation `pop_back` to remove the last two elements of `intDeq`; the statement in Line 23 outputs the modified `intDeq`.

The statement in Line 25 declares `deqIt` to be a deque iterator that processes all `deque` containers whose elements are of the type `int`. After the statement in Line 26 executes, `deqIt` points to the first element of `intDeq`. The statement in Line 27 advances `deqIt` to the next element of `intDeq`. The statement in Line 28 inserts `444` into `intDeq` at the position specified by `deqIt`. The statement in Line 30 outputs `intDeq`.

The statement in Line 32 assigns two copies of `45` to `intDeq`. After the statement in Line 32 executes, the old elements of `intDeq` are removed and `intDeq` contains only two copies of `45`. The output of the statement in Line 34 illustrates this activity. In the output, see the line marked Line 33, which contains the output of the statements in Lines 33 through 35 of the program.

The meaning of the remaining statements is self-explanatory.

4

ITERATORS

Examples 4-5 through 4-7 clarify that iterators are quite important to efficiently process the elements of a container. Let us discuss iterators in some detail.

Iterators work just like pointers. In general, an iterator points to the elements of a container (sequence or associative). Therefore, with the help of iterators, we can successively access each element of a container.

The two most common operations on iterators are `++` (the increment operator) and `*` (the dereferencing operator). Suppose that `cntItr` is an iterator into a container. The statement

```
++cntItr;
```

advances `cntItr` so that it points to the next element in the container. Similarly, the statement

```
*cntItr;
```

returns the value of the container element pointed to by `cntItr`.

Types of Iterators

There are five types of iterators:

- Input iterators
- Output iterators
- Forward iterators
- Bidirectional iterators
- Random access iterators

The following five sections describe each of these iterators.

Input Iterators

Input iterators, with read access, step forward element by element and so return the values element by element. These iterators are provided for reading data from an input stream.

Suppose `inputIterator` is an input iterator. Table 4-9 describes some of the operations on `inputIterator`.

Table 4-9 Some Operations on an Input Iterator

Expression	Effect
`*inputIterator`	Gives access to the element that `inputIterator` points to.
`inputIterator->member`	Gives access to the member of the element.
`++inputIterator`	Moves forward, returns the new position (preincrement).
`inputIterator++`	Moves forward, returns the old position (postincrement).
`inputIt1 == inputIt2`	Returns `true` if the two iterators are the same, and `false` otherwise.
`inputIt1 != inputIt2`	Returns `true` if the two iterators are not the same, and `false` otherwise.

Output Iterators

Output iterators, with write access, step forward element by element. These iterators are provided for writing data to an output stream. They are also used as inserters.

Suppose `outputIterator` is an output iterator. Table 4-10 describes some of the operations on `outputIterator`.

Table 4-10 Some Operations on an Output Iterator

Expression	Effect
`*outputIterator = value;`	Writes the value at the position specified by `outputIterator`.
`++outputIterator`	Moves forward, returns the new position (preincrement).
`outputIterator++`	Moves forward, returns the old position (postincrement).

 Output iterators cannot be used to iterate over a range twice. Therefore, if we write data at the same position twice, there is no guarantee that the new value will replace the old value.

Forward Iterators

Forward iterators combine all of the functionality of input iterators and almost all of the functionality of output iterators. Suppose `forwardIterator` is a forward iterator. Table 4-11 describes the operations on `forwardIterator`.

Table 4-11 Operations on a Forward Iterator

Expression	Effect
`*forwardIterator`	Gives access to the element that `forwardIterator` points to.
`forwardIterator->member`	Gives access to the member of the element.
`++forwardIterator`	Moves forward, returns the new position (preincrement).
`forwardIterator++`	Moves forward, returns the old position (postincrement).
`forwardIt1 == forwardIt2`	Returns `true` if the two iterators are the same, and `false` otherwise.
`forwardIt1 != forwardIt2`	Returns `true` if the two iterators are not the same, and `false` otherwise.
`forwardIt1 = forwardIt2`	Assignment.

 A forward iterator can refer to the same element in the same collection and process the same element more than once.

Bidirectional Iterators

Bidirectional iterators are forward iterators that can also iterate backwards over the elements. Suppose `biDirectionalIterator` is a bidirectional iterator. The operations defined for forward iterators (Table 4-11) are also applicable to bidirectional iterators. To step backwards, the decrement operations are also defined for `biDirectionalIterator`. Table 4-12 shows additional operations on a bidirectional iterator.

Table 4-12 Additional Operations on a Bidirectional Iterator

Expression	Effect
`--biDirectionalIterator`	Moves backward, returns the new position (predecrement).
`biDirectionalIterator--`	Moves backward, returns the old position (postdecrement).

Bidirectional iterators can be used only with containers of the type `vector`, `deque`, `list`, `set`, `multiset`, `map`, and `multimap`.

Random Access Iterators

Random access iterators are bidirectional iterators that can randomly process the elements of a container. These iterators can be used with containers of the type **vector**, **deque**, **string**, and arrays. The operations defined for bidirectional iterators (for example, Tables 4–11 and 4–12) are also applicable to random access iterators. Table 4–13 describes additional operations that are defined for random access iterators. (Suppose `rAccessIterator` is a random access iterator.)

Table 4-13 Additional Operations on a Random Access Iterator

Expression	Effect
`rAccessIterator[n]`	Accesses the nth element.
`rAccessIterator += n`	Moves `rAccessIterator` forward n elements if n >= 0 and backward if n < 0.
`rAccessIterator -= n`	Moves `rAccessIterator` backward n elements if n >= 0 and forward if n < 0.
`rAccessIterator + n`	Returns the iterator of the next nth element.
`n + rAccessIterator`	Returns the iterator of the next nth element.
`rAccessIterator - n`	Returns the iterator of the previous nth element.
`rAccessIt1 - rAccessIt2`	Returns the distance between the iterators `rAccessIt1` and `rAccessIt2`.
`rAccessIt1 < rAccessIt2`	Returns `true` if `rAccessIt1` is before `rAccessIt2`, and `false` otherwise.
`rAccessIt1 <= rAccessIt2`	Returns `true` if `rAccessIt1` is before or equal to `rAccessIt2`, and `false` otherwise.
`rAccessIt1 > rAccessIt2`	Returns `true` if `rAccessIt1` is after `rAccessIt2`, and `false` otherwise.
`rAccessIt1 >= rAccessIt2`	Returns `true` if `rAccessIt1` is after or equal to `rAccessIt2`, and `false` otherwise.

Figure 4–1 shows the iterator hierarchy.

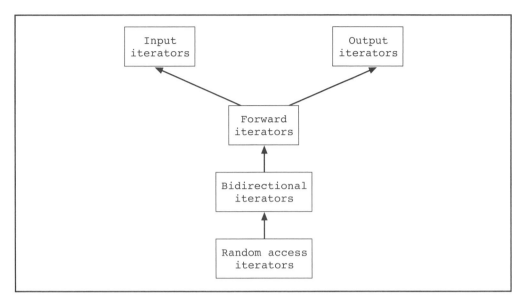

Figure 4-1   Iterator hierarchy

Now that you know the different types of iterators, next we describe how to declare an iterator into a container.

typedef iterator

Every container (sequence or associative) contains a **typedef iterator**. Therefore, an iterator into a container is declared using the **typedef iterator**. For example, the statement

```
vector<int>:: iterator intVecIter;
```

declares **intVecIter** to be an iterator into a **vector** container of the type **int**. Moreover, the iterator **intVecIter** can be used on any **vector<int>**, but not on any other container, such as, for example, **vector<double>**, **vector<string>**, or **deque**.

Because **iterator** is a **typedef** defined inside a container (that is, a class) such as **vector**, we must use the appropriate container name, container element type, and the scope resolution operator to use the **typedef iterator**.

typedef const_iterator

An iterator works like a pointer. Therefore, with the help of an iterator into a container and the dereferencing operator, *****, we can modify the elements of the container. However, if a container is declared as **const**, we must prevent the iterator from modifying the elements of the container, especially accidentally. To handle this situation, every container has another **typedef, const_iterator**. For example, the statement

```
vector<int>::const_iterator intConstVecIt;
```

declares `intConstVecIt` to be an iterator into a **vector** container whose elements are of the type `int`. The iterator `intConstVecIt` is used to process the elements of those vector containers that are declared as constant vector containers of the type **vector<int>**.

An iterator of the type `const_iterator` is a read-only iterator.

typedef reverse_iterator

Every container also contains the `typedef reverse_iterator`. An iterator of this type is used to iterate through the elements of a container in reverse.

typedef const_reverse_iterator

An iterator of this type is a read-only iterator and is used to iterate through the elements of a container in reverse. It is required if the container is declared as **const** and we need to iterate through the elements of the container in reverse.

In addition to the previous four **typedefs**, several other **typedefs** are common to all containers. Table 4–14 describes them.

Table 4-14 Various `typedefs` Common to All Containers

typedef	Effect
difference_type	The type of result from subtracting two iterators referring to the same container.
pointer	A pointer to the type of elements stored in the container.
reference	A reference to the type of elements stored in the container.
const_reference	A constant reference to the type of elements stored in the container. A constant reference is read-only.
size_type	The type used to count the elements in a container. This type is also used to index through sequence containers, except list containers.
value_type	The type of container elements.

Stream Iterators

Another useful set of iterators are stream iterators: `istream` iterators and `ostream` iterators. This section describes both types of iterators.

istream_iterator

The `istream` iterators are used to input data into a program from an input stream. The **class istream_iterator** contains the definition of an input stream iterator. The general syntax to use an `istream` iterator is

```
istream_iterator<Type> isIdentifier(istream&);
```

where `Type` is either a built-in type or a user-defined class type for which an input iterator is defined. The identifier `isIdentifier` is initialized using the constructor whose argument is either an `istream` class object such as `cin`, or any publicly defined `istream` subtype, such as `ifstream`.

ostream_iterator

The `ostream` iterators are used to output data from a program into an output stream. These iterators were defined earlier in this chapter. We review them here for the sake of completeness.

The `class ostream_iterator` contains the definition of an output stream iterator. The general syntax to use an `ostream` iterator is

```
ostream_iterator<Type> osIdentifier(ostream&);
```

or

```
ostream_iterator<Type> osIdentifier(ostream&, char* deLimit);
```

where `Type` is either a built-in type or a user-defined class type for which an output iterator is defined. The identifier `osIdentifier` is initialized using the constructor whose argument is either an `ostream` class object such as `cout`, or any publicly defined `ostream` subtype, such as `ofstream`. In the second form used for declaring an `ostream` iterator, by using the second argument (`deLimit`) of the initializing constructor, we can specify a character separating the output.

PROGRAMMING EXAMPLE: GRADE REPORT

This programming example further illustrates the concepts of inheritance and composition.

The midsemester point at your local university is approaching. The registrar's office wants to prepare the grade reports as soon as the students' grades are recorded. Some of the students enrolled have not yet paid their tuition, however.

If a student has paid the tuition, the grades are shown on the grade report together with the grade-point average (GPA).

If a student has not paid the tuition, the grades are not printed. For these students, the grade report contains a message indicating that the grades have been held for nonpayment of the tuition. The grade report also shows the billing amount.

The registrar's office and the business office want your help in writing a program that can analyze the students' data and print the appropriate grade reports. The data is stored in a file in the following form:

```
tuitionRate
studentName studentID isTuitionPaid numberOfCourses
courseName courseNumber creditHours grade
courseName courseNumber creditHours grade
    .
    .
    .
studentName studentID isTuitionPaid numberOfCourses
courseName courseNumber creditHours grade
courseName courseNumber creditHours grade
    .
    .
    .
```

The first line indicates the tuition rate per credit hour. The students' data is given thereafter.

A sample input file follows:

```
345
Lisa Miller 890238 Y 4
Mathematics MTH345 4 A
Physics PHY357 3 B
ComputerSci CSC478 3 B
History HIS356 3 A
    .
    .
    .
```

The first line indicates that the tuition rate is $345 per credit hour. Next, the course data for student **Lisa Miller** is given: Lisa Miller's ID is **890238**, she has paid the tuition, and is taking **4** courses. The course number for the mathematics class she is taking is **MTH345**, the course has 4 credit hours, her midsemester grade is **A**, and so on.

The desired output for each student is of the following form:

```
Student Name: Lisa Miller
Student ID: 890238
Number of courses enrolled: 4

Course No  Course Name  Credits Grade
CSC478     ComputerSci      3       B
HIS356     History          3       A
MTH345     Mathematics      4       A
PHY357     Physics          3       B
```

```
Total number of credits: 13
Midsemester GPA: 3.54
```

This output shows that the courses must be ordered according to the course number. To calculate the GPA, we assume that the grade A is equivalent to 4 points, B is equivalent to 3 points, C is equivalent to 2 points, D is equivalent to 1 point, and F is equivalent to 0 points.

Input   A file containing the data in the form shown previously. For easy reference in the rest of the discussion, let us assume that the name of the input file is `ch4_GradeData.txt` and this file is on floppy disk A.

Output   A file containing the output in the form shown previously. ·

Problem Analysis and Algorithm Design

We must first identify the main components of the program. The university has students, and every student takes courses. Therefore, the two main components are the student and the course.

Let us first describe the component course.

Course   The main characteristics of a course are the course name, course number, and number of credit hours. Although the grade a student receives is not really a characteristic of a course, to simplify the program this component also includes the student's grade.

Some of the basic operations that need to be performed on an object of the course type are:

1. Set the course information.
2. Print the course information.
3. Show the credit hours.
4. Show the course number.
5. Show the grade.

The following class defines the course as an ADT (see also Figure 4–2):

```
class courseType
{
public:
    void setCourseInfo(string cName, string cNo,
                      char grade, int credits);
        //Function to set the course information.
        //The course information is set according to the
        //incoming parameters.
        //Postcondition: courseName = cName; courseNo = cNo;
        //                courseGrade = grade;
        //                courseCredits = credits;
```

```
void print(bool isGrade);
   //Function to print the course information.
   //This function prints the course information on the
   //screen. Furthermore, if the bool parameter isGrade is
   //true, the grade is shown; otherwise, three stars
   //are printed.

void print(ofstream& outp, bool isGrade);
   //Function to print the course information.
   //This function sends the course information to a file.
   //Furthermore, if the bool parameter isGrade is true,
   //the grade is shown; otherwise, three stars are printed.

int getCredits();
   //Function to return the credit hours.
   //Postcondition: The value of the data member
   //               courseCredits is returned.

void getCourseNumber(string& cNo);
   //Function to return the course number.
   //Postcondition: cNo = courseNo

char getGrade();
   //Function to return the grade for the course.
   //Postcondition: The value of the data member courseGrade
   //               is returned.

   //Overload the relational operators.
bool operator==(const courseType&) const;
bool operator!=(const courseType&) const;
bool operator<=(const courseType&) const;
bool operator<(const courseType&) const;
bool operator>=(const courseType&) const;
bool operator>(const courseType&) const;


courseType(string cName = "", string cNo = "",
        char grade = '*', int credits = 0);
   //constructor
   //The object is initialized according to the
   //parameters.
   //Postcondition: courseName = cName; courseNo = cNo;
   //               courseGrade = grade;
   //               courseCredits = credits;
```

```
private:
    string courseName;     //variable to store the course name
    string courseNo;       //variable to store the course number
    char courseGrade;      //variable to store the grade
    int courseCredits;     //variable to store the number of credits
};
```

```
┌─────────────────────────────────────────────────────────────┐
│   ┌───────────────────────────────────────────────────────┐ │
│   │                      courseType                       │ │
│   ├───────────────────────────────────────────────────────┤ │
│   │ -courseName: string                                   │ │
│   │ -courseNo: string                                     │ │
│   │ -courseGrade: char                                    │ │
│   │ -courseCredits: int                                   │ │
│   ├───────────────────────────────────────────────────────┤ │
│   │ +setCourseInfo(string, string, char, int): void      │ │
│   │ +print(bool): void                                    │ │
│   │ +print(ofstream&, bool): void                         │ │
│   │ +getCredits(): int                                    │ │
│   │ +getCourseNumber(string&): void                       │ │
│   │ +getGrade(): char                                     │ │
│   │ +operator==(const courseType&) const: bool           │ │
│   │ +operator!=(const courseType&) const: bool           │ │
│   │ +operator<=(const courseType&) const: bool           │ │
│   │ +operator<(const courseType&) const: bool            │ │
│   │ +operator>=(const courseType&) const: bool           │ │
│   │ +operator>(const courseType&) const: bool            │ │
│   │ +courseType(string = "", string = "", char = '*', int = 0)│
│   └───────────────────────────────────────────────────────┘ │
└─────────────────────────────────────────────────────────────┘
```

Figure 4-2   UML diagram of the class courseType

Next, we discuss the definitions of the functions to implement the operations of the class courseType.

The function setCourseInfo sets the values of the private data members according to the values of the parameters. Its definition is

```
void courseType::setCourseInfo(string cName, string cNo,
                               char grade, int credits)
{     courseName = cName;
      courseNo = cNo;
      courseGrade = grade;
      courseCredits = credits;
}
```

The function `print` with one parameter prints the course information on the screen. If the `bool` parameter `isGrade` is `true`, the grade is printed on the screen; otherwise, three stars are shown in place of the grade. Also, we print the course name and course number left justified rather than right justified (the default). Therefore, we need to set the `left` manipulator. This manipulator is unset before we print the grade and the credit hours. The following steps describe this function:

1. Set the `left` manipulator.
2. Print the course number.
3. Print the course name.
4. Unset the `left` manipulator.
5. Print the credit hours.
6. If `isGrade` is `true`
      Output the grade
   Else
      Output three stars.

The definition of the function `print` is

```
void courseType::print(bool isGrade)
{
        cout<<left;                              //Step 1
        cout<<setw(8)<<courseNo<<"   ";          //Step 2
        cout<<setw(15)<<courseName;              //Step 3
        cout.unsetf(ios::left);                  //Step 4
        cout<<setw(3)<<courseCredits<<"   ";     //Step 5

        if(isGrade)                              //Step 6
           cout<<setw(4)<<courseGrade<<endl;
        else
           cout<<setw(4)<<"***"<<endl;
}
```

The function `print`, which has two parameters, sends the course information to a file. Other than sending the output to a file, which is passed as a parameter, this function has exactly the same definition as the definition of the previous `print` function. The definition of this function is

```
void courseType::print(ofstream& outp, bool isGrade)
{
        outp<<left;                              //Step 1
        outp<<setw(8)<<courseNo<<"   ";          //Step 2
        outp<<setw(15)<<courseName;              //Step 3
        outp.unsetf(ios::left);                  //Step 4
        outp<<setw(3)<<courseCredits<<"   ";     //Step 5
```

```
            if(isGrade)                                    //Step 6
                outp<<setw(4)<<courseGrade<<endl;
            else
                outp<<setw(4)<<"***"<<endl;
}
```

The constructor is declared with default values. If no values are specified when a **courseType** object is declared, the constructor uses the default values to initialize the object. Using the default values, the object's data members are initialized as follows: **courseNo** to blank, **courseName** to blank, **courseGrade** to *, and **creditHours** to 0. Otherwise, the values specified in the object declaration are used to initialize the object. Its definition is

```
courseType::courseType(string cName, string cNo,
                       char grade, int credits)
{
    setCourseInfo(cName, cNo, grade, credits);
}
```

The definitions of the remaining functions are straightforward.

```
int courseType::getCredits()
{
    return courseCredits;
}

char courseType::getGrade()
{
    return courseGrade;
}

void courseType::getCourseNumber(string& cNo)
{
    cNo = courseNo;
}

bool courseType::operator==(const courseType& right) const
{
    return (courseNo == right.courseNo);
}

bool courseType::operator!=(const courseType& right) const
{
    return (courseNo != right.courseNo);
}
```

```
bool courseType::operator<=(const courseType& right) const
{
    return (courseNo <= right.courseNo);
}

bool courseType::operator<(const courseType& right) const
{
    return (courseNo < right.courseNo);
}

bool courseType::operator>=(const courseType& right) const
{
    return (courseNo >= right.courseNo);
}

bool courseType::operator>(const courseType& right) const
{
    return (courseNo > right.courseNo);
}
```

Next we discuss the component student.

Student The main characteristics of a student are the student name, student ID, number of courses in which enrolled, names of courses in which enrolled, and the grade for each course. Because every student has to pay tuition, we also include a member to indicate whether the student has paid the tuition.

Every student is a person, and every student takes courses. We have already designed a **class personType** to process a person's first name and last name. We have also designed a class to process the information of a course. Therefore, we see that we can derive the **class studentType** to keep track of a student's information from the **class personType**, and one member of this class is of the type **courseType**. We can add more members as needed.

The basic operations to be performed on an object of the type **studentType** are:

1. Set the student information.
2. Print the student information.
3. Calculate the number of credit hours taken.
4. Calculate the GPA.
5. Calculate the billing amount.
6. Because the grade report will print the courses in ascending order, sort the courses according to the course number.

The following class defines **studentType** as an ADT. We assume that a student takes no more than six courses per semester (see also Figure 4-3).

```
class studentType: public personType
{
public:
    void setInfo(string fname, string lName, int ID,
                 bool isTPaid,
                 vector<courseType> courses);
       //Function to set a student's information.
       //Postcondition: The data members are set according
       //               to the parameters.

    void print(double tuitionRate);
       //Function to print a student's grade report.

    void print(ofstream& out, double tuitionRate);
       //Function to print a student's grade report.
       //The output is stored in a file specified by the
       //parameter out.

    studentType();
       //default constructor
       //Postcondition: The data members are initialized to
       //               the default values.

    int getHoursEnrolled();
       //Function to return the credit hours in which a student
       //is enrolled.
       //Postcondition: The number of credit hours in which a
       //               student is enrolled is calculated and
       //               returned.

    double getGpa();
       //Function to return the grade point average.
       //Postcondition: The GPA is calculated and returned.

    double billingAmount(double tuitionRate);
       //Function to return the tuition fees.
       //Postcondition: The tuition fees due are calculated
       //               and returned.


private:
    int sId;                //variable to store the student ID
    int numberOfCourses;    //variable to store the number of
                            //courses
    bool isTuitionPaid;     //variable to indicate whether the
                            //tuition is paid
```

```
       vector<courseType> coursesEnrolled; //vector to store the
                                            //courses
};
```

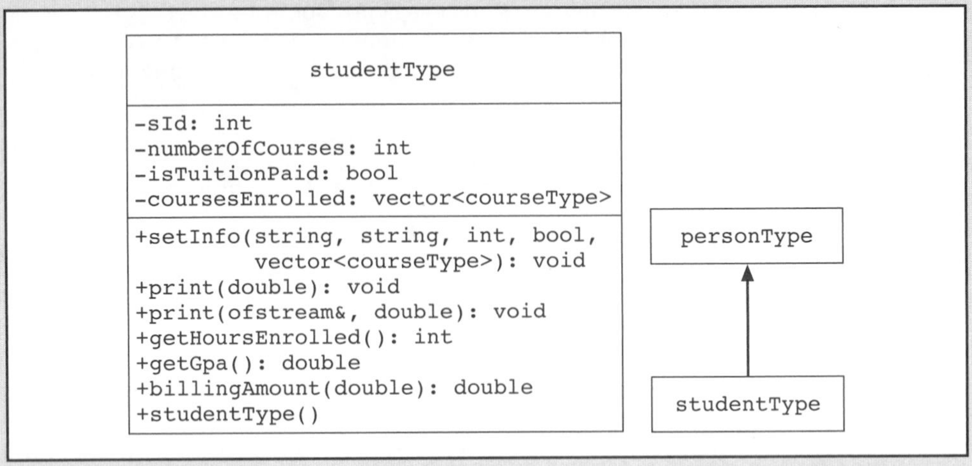

Figure 4-3   UML diagram of the class studentType and the inheritance hierarchy

Next, we discuss the definitions of the functions to implement the operations of the class studentType.

The function setInfo first initializes the private data members according to the incoming parameters. The class studentType is derived from the class personType, and the variables to store the first name and last name are private data members of that class. Therefore, we call the member function setName of the class personType, and we pass the appropriate variables to set the first name and last name. To sort the array coursesEnrolled, in ascending order, we use the algorithm sort provided by the STL.

To use the algorithm sort to sort the vector coursesEnrolled, we need to know the position of the first element and last element in the vector coursesEnrolled. When we declared the vector coursesEnrolled, we did not specify its size. The function begin of the class vector returns the position of the first element in a **vector** container; the function end specifies the position of the last element. Therefore, coursesEnrolled.begin() specifies the position of the first element of the vector coursesEnrolled, and coursesEnrolled.end() specifies the position of the last element. The operator <= is overloaded for the class courseType and it compares the courses by the course number; the sort algorithm uses this criteria to sort the vector coursesEnrolled. The following statement sorts the vector coursesEnrolled:

```
sort(coursesEnrolled.begin(), coursesEnrolled.end());
```

The definition of the function `setInfo` is:

```
void studentType::setInfo(string fName, string lName, int ID,
                          bool isTPaid,
                          vector<courseType> courses)
{
   personType::setName(fName, lName);   //set the name

   sId = ID;                            //set the student ID
   isTuitionPaid = isTPaid;             //set isTuitionPaid
   numberOfCourses = courses.size()     //set the number of courses


   coursesEnrolled = courses;     //set the vector coursesEnrolled

        //sort the array coursesEnrolled
   sort(coursesEnrolled.begin(), coursesEnrolled.end());
}
```

The default constructor initializes the **private** data members to the default values. Note that because the **private** data member `coursesEnrolled` is of the type **vector**, the default constructor of the **class vector** executes automatically and initializes `coursesEnrolled`.

```
studentType::studentType()
{
     numberOfCourses = 0;
     sId = 0;
     isTuitionPaid = false;
}
```

The function **print**, which has one parameter, outputs the grade report on the screen. If the student has paid his or her tuition, the grades and the GPA are shown. Otherwise, three stars are output in place of each grade, the GPA is not shown, a message indicates that the grades are being held for nonpayment of the tuition, and the amount due is shown. This function has the following steps:

1. Output the student's name.
2. Output the student's ID.
3. Output the number of courses in which enrolled.
4. Output heading: `CourseNo CourseName Credits Grade`
5. Print each course's information.
6. Print the total credit hours.
7. To output the GPA and billing amount in a fixed decimal format with the decimal point and trailing zeros, use the manipulators **fixed** and **showpoint**. Also, set the precision to two decimal places.

8. If isTuitionPaid is true

    Output the GPA

Else

    Output the billing amount and a message about withholding the grades.

```cpp
void studentType::print(double tuitionRate)
{
    int i;

    cout<<"Student Name: ";                            //Step 1
    personType::print();                               //Step 1
    cout<<endl;

    cout<<"Student ID: "<<sId<<endl;                   //Step 2

    cout<<"Number of courses enrolled: "
        <<numberOfCourses<<endl;                       //Step 3
    cout<<endl;

    cout<<left;        //set the output left justified
    cout<<"Course No"<<setw(15)<<"  Course Name"
        <<setw(8)<<"Credits"
        <<setw(6)<<"Grade"<<endl;                      //Step 4

    cout.unsetf(ios::left);

    for(i = 0; i < numberOfCourses; i++)               //Step 5
        coursesEnrolled[i].print(isTuitionPaid);
    cout<<endl;

    cout<<"Total number of credit hours: "
        <<getHoursEnrolled()<<endl;                    //Step 6

    cout<<fixed<<showpoint<<setprecision(2);           //Step 7

    if(isTuitionPaid)                                  //Step 8
        cout<<"Midsemester GPA: "<<getGpa()<<endl;
    else
    {
        cout<<"*** Grades are being held for not paying "
            <<"the tuition. ***"<<endl;
        cout<<"Amount Due: $"<<billingAmount(tuitionRate)
            <<endl;
    }

    cout<<"-*-*-*-*-*-*-*-*-*-*-*-*-*-*-*-*"
        <<"-*-*-*-*-*-*-"<<endl<<endl;
}
```

The function print, which has two parameters, sends the output to a file. For the most part, its definition is the same as the other function print, which has one parameter. Because the class personType has no function to send the output to a file, we first use the member function getName of the class personType to retrieve the first and last names. We then print the first and last names. The definition of this function is now the same as the definition of the previous function print. The definition of this function is:

```cpp
void studentType::print(ofstream& outp, double tuitionRate)
{
    int i;
    string first;
    string last;

    personType::getName(first, last);

    outp<<"Student Name: "<<first<<" "<<last<<endl;

    outp<<"Student ID: "<<sId<<endl;

    outp<<"Number of courses enrolled: "
        <<numberOfCourses<<endl;
    outp<<endl;

    outp<<left;
    outp<<"Course No"<<setw(15)<<"  Course Name"
        <<setw(8)<<"Credits"
        <<setw(6)<<"Grade"<<endl;

    outp.unsetf(ios::left);

    for(i = 0; i < numberOfCourses; i++)
        coursesEnrolled[i].print(outp, isTuitionPaid);
    outp<<endl;

    outp<<"Total number of credit hours: "
        <<getHoursEnrolled()<<endl;

    outp<<fixed<<showpoint<<setprecision(2);

    if(isTuitionPaid)
        outp<<"Midsemester GPA: "<<getGpa()<<endl;
    else
    {
        outp<<"*** Grades are being held for not paying "
            <<"the tuition. ***"<<endl;
        outp<<"Amount Due: $"<<billingAmount(tuitionRate)
            <<endl;
    }
```

```
        outp<<"-*-*-*-*-*-*-*-*-*-*-*-*-*-*-*-*-*-*-*-*"
          <<"-*-*-*-*-"<<endl<<endl;
}
```

The function `getHoursEnrolled` calculates and returns the total credit hours that a
student is taking. These credit hours are needed to calculate both the GPA and the billing
amount. The total credit hours are calculated by adding the credit hours of each course in
which the student is enrolled. The credit hours for a course are in the `private` data
member of an object of the type `courseType`. Therefore, we use the member function
`getCredits` of the `class courseType` to retrieve the credit hours. The definition of
this function is:

```
int studentType::getHoursEnrolled()
{
        int totalCredits = 0;
        int i;

        for(i = 0; i < numberOfCourses; i++)
            totalCredits += coursesEnrolled[i].getCredits();

        return totalCredits;
}
```

If a student has not paid the tuition, the function `billingAmount` calculates and
returns the amount due, based on the number of credit hours enrolled. The definition of
this function is:

```
double studentType::billingAmount(double tuitionRate)
{
        return tuitionRate * getHoursEnrolled();
}
```

We now discuss the function `getGpa`. This function calculates a student's GPA. To find
the GPA, we find the equivalent points for each grade, add the points, and then divide
the sum by the total credit hours the student is taking. The definition of this function is:

```
double studentType::getGpa()
{
    int i;
    double sum = 0.0;

    for(i = 0; i < numberOfCourses; i++)
    {
        switch(coursesEnrolled[i].getGrade())
        {
        case 'A': sum += coursesEnrolled[i].getCredits() * 4;
                break;
        case 'B': sum += coursesEnrolled[i].getCredits() * 3;
                break;
```

```
        case 'C': sum += coursesEnrolled[i].getCredits() * 2;
                    break;
        case 'D': sum += coursesEnrolled[i].getCredits() * 1;
                    break;
        case 'F': sum += coursesEnrolled[i].getCredits() * 0;
                    break;
        default: cout<<"Invalid Course Grade"<<endl;
        }
    }

    return sum / getHoursEnrolled();
}
```

Main Program

Now that we have designed the **classes courseType** and **studentType**, we use these classes to complete the program.

Because the function **print** of the **class studentType** does the necessary computations to print the final grade report, the main program has very little work to do. In fact, all that is left for the main program is to declare the objects to hold the students' data, load the data into these objects, and then print the grade reports. Because the input is in a file and the output will be sent to a file, we declare stream variables to access the input and output files. Essentially, the main algorithm for the program is

1. Declare the variables.
2. Open the input file.
3. If the input file does not exist, exit the program.
4. Open the output file.
5. Get the tuition rate.
6. Load the students' data.
7. Print the grade reports.

Variables   To store the students' data we use the vector container, **studentList**, whose elements are of the type **studentType**. We also need to store the tuition rate. Because the data is read from a file, and because the output is sent to a file, we need two stream variables to access the input and output files. Therefore, we need the following variables:

```
vector<studentType> studentList;      //vector to store the
                                      //students' data

double tuitionRate;                   //variable to store the tuition rate

ifstream infile;                      //input stream variable
ofstream outfile;                     //output stream variable
```

To simplify the complexity of the function `main`, we write a function, `getStudentData`, to load the students' data and another function, `printGradeReports`, to print the grade reports. The next two sections describe these functions.

Function `getStudentData` This function has two parameters: a parameter to access the input file, and a parameter to access the vector container `studentList`. In pseudocode, the definition of this function is as follows:

For each student in the university,

1. Get the first name, last name, student ID, and `isPaid`.
2. if `isPaid` is 'Y'

    set `isTuitionPaid` to `true`

    `else`

    set `isTuitionPaid` to `false`
3. Get the number of courses the student is taking.
4. Clear the vector, `courses`, that holds the course information.
5. For each course:
    a. Get the course name, course number, credit hours, and grade.
    b. Load the course information into a `courseType` object.
    c. Insert the object containing the course information into the vector container that stores the course data.
6. Load the data into a `studentType` object.
7. Insert the object containing the student's data into the student's list.

We need to declare several local variables to read and store the data. The definition of the function `getStudentData` is

```
void getStudentData(ifstream& infile,
                    vector<studentType> &studentList)
{
            //local variables
    string fName;       //variable to store the first name
    string lName;       //variable to store the last name
    int ID;             //variable to store the student ID
    int noOfCourses;    //variable to store the number of courses
    char isPaid;        //variable to store Y/N; that is, is the
                        //tuition paid?
    bool isTuitionPaid; //variable to store true/false

    string cName;       //variable to store the course name
    string cNo;         //variable to store the course number
    int credits;        //variable to store the course credit hours
```

```
    char grade;                 //variable to store the course grade
    int i;                      //loop control variable

    vector<courseType> courses;//vector of objects to store
                               //the course information

    courseType cTemp;
    studentType sTemp;

    infile>>fName;                                      //Step 1

    while(infile)
    {
        infile>>lName>>ID>>isPaid;                      //Step 1

        if(isPaid == 'Y')                               //Step 2
            isTuitionPaid = true;
        else
            isTuitionPaid = false;

        infile>>noOfCourses;                            //Step 3

        courses.clear()                                 //Step 4

        for(i = 0; i < noOfCourses; i++)                //Step 5
        {
            infile>>cName>>cNo>>credits>>grade;         //Step 5.a
            cTemp.setCourseInfo(cName, cNo,
                           grade, credits);             //Step 5.b
            courses.push_back(cTemp);                   //Step 5.c
        }

        sTemp.setInfo(fName, lName, ID, isTuitionPaid,
                     courses);                          //Step 6
        studentList.push_back(sTemp);                   //Step 7

        infile>>fName;                                  //Step 1
    }//end while
}
```

Function printGradeReports This function prints the grade reports. For each student, it calls the function print of the **class studentType** to print the grade report.

The definition of the function `printGradeReports` is

```
void printGradeReports(ofstream& outfile,
                       vector<studentType> studentList,
                       double tuitionRate)
{
    unsigned int count;

    for(count = 0; count < studentList.size(); count++)
        studentList[count].print(outfile, tuitionRate);
}
```

Program Listing

```
//Header file courseType.h
#ifndef H_courseType
#define H_courseType

#include <fstream>
#include <string>

using namespace std;

//The definition of the class courseType goes here.
     .
     .
     .
#endif


//Implementation file courseTypeImp.cpp
#include <iostream>
#include <fstream>
#include <string>
#include <iomanip>
#include "courseType.h"

using namespace std;

//The definitions of the member functions of the class
//courseType go here.
     .
     .
     .
```

```
//Header file personType.h
#ifndef personType_H
#define personType_H

#include <string>
//The definition of the class personType goes here.
    .
    .
    .

#endif


//Implementation file personTypeImp.cpp
#include <iostream>
#include <string>
#include "personType.h"

using namespace std;

//The definitions of the member functions of the class
//personType go here.
    .
    .
    .

//Header file studentType.h
#ifndef H_studentType
#define H_studentType

#include <fstream>
#include <string>
#include <vector>

#include "personType.h"
#include "courseType.h"

using namespace std;

//The definition of the class studentType goes here.
    .
    .
    .

#endif
```

```cpp
//Implementation file studentTypeImp.cpp
#include <iostream>
#include <iomanip>
#include <fstream>
#include <string>
#include <algorithm>
#include <vector>
#include <iterator>

#include "personType.h"
#include "courseType.h"
#include "studentType.h"

using namespace std;

//The definitions of the member functions of the class
//studentType go here.
    .
    .
    .

//Main Program
#include <iostream>
#include <fstream>
#include <string>
#include <algorithm>
#include <vector>
#include <iterator>

#include "studentType.h"

using namespace std;

void getStudentData(ifstream& infile,
                    vector<studentType> &studentList);

void printGradeReports(ofstream& outfile,
                       vector<studentType> studentList,
                       double tuitionRate);

int main()
{
    vector<studentType> studentList;

    double tuitionRate;

    ifstream infile;
    ofstream outfile;
```

```
    infile.open("a:\\ch4_GradeData.txt");

    if(!infile)
    {
        cerr<<"Input file does not exist. "
            <<"Program terminates."<<endl;
        return 1;
    }

    outfile.open("a:\\sDataOut.txt");

    infile>>tuitionRate;                    //get the tuition rate

    getStudentData(infile, studentList);
    printGradeReports(outfile, studentList, tuitionRate);

    infile.close();
    outfile.close();

    return 0;
}

//Place the definition of the function getStudentData here.
//Place the definition of the function printGradeReports here.
```

Sample Output

```
Student Name: Lisa Miller
Student ID: 890238
Number of courses enrolled: 4

Course No  Course Name  Credits Grade
CSC478     ComputerSci     3       B
HIS356     History         3       A
MTH345     Mathematics     4       A
PHY357     Physics         3       B

Total number of credit hours: 13
Midsemester GPA: 3.54
_*_*_*_*_*_*_*_*_*_*_*_*_*_*_*_*_*_*_*_*_*_

Student Name: Bill Wilton
Student ID: 798324
Number of courses enrolled: 5

Course No  Course Name  Credits Grade
BIO234     Biology         4      ***
CHM256     Chemistry       4      ***
ENG378     English         3      ***
```

```
MTH346      Mathematics      3      ***
PHL534      Philosophy       3      ***

Total number of credit hours: 17
*** Grades are being held for not paying the tuition. ***
Amount Due: $5865.00
-*-*-*-*-*-*-*-*-*-*-*-*-*-*-*-*-*-*-*-*-*-*-*-*-*-

Student Name: Dandy Goat
Student ID: 746333
Number of courses enrolled: 6

Course No   Course Name  Credits Grade
BUS128      Business         3      C
CHM348      Chemistry        4      B
CSC201      ComputerSci      3      B
ENG328      English          3      B
HIS101      History          3      A
MTH137      Mathematics      3      A

Total number of credit hours: 19
Midsemester GPA: 3.16
-*-*-*-*-*-*-*-*-*-*-*-*-*-*-*-*-*-*-*-*-*-*-*-*-*-
```

Input File

```
345
Lisa Miller 890238 Y 4
Mathematics MTH345 4 A
Physics PHY357 3 B
ComputerSci CSC478 3 B
History HIS356 3 A

Bill Wilton 798324 N 5
English ENG378 3 B
Philosophy PHL534 3 A
Chemistry CHM256 4 C
Biology BIO234 4 A
Mathematics MTH346 3 C

Dandy Goat 746333 Y 6
History HIS101 3 A
English ENG328 3 B
Mathematics MTH137 3 A
Chemistry CHM348 4 B
ComputerSci CSC201 3 B
Business BUS128 3 C
```

QUICK REVIEW

1. The STL provides class templates that process lists, stacks, and queues.
2. The three main components of the STL are containers, iterators, and algorithms.
3. STL containers are class templates.
4. Iterators are used to step through the elements of a container.
5. Algorithms are used to manipulate the elements in a container.
6. The main categories of containers are sequence containers, associative containers, and container adapters.
7. The three predefined sequence containers are `vector`, `deque`, and `list`.
8. A vector container stores and manages its objects in a dynamic array.
9. Because an array is a random access data structure, elements of a vector can be accessed randomly.
10. The name of the class that implements the vector container is `vector`.
11. Item insertion in a vector container is accomplished by using the operations `insert` and `push_back`.
12. Item deletion in a vector container is accomplished by using the operations `pop_back`, `erase`, and `clear`.
13. An iterator to a vector container is declared using the `typedef iterator`, which is declared as a `public` member of the `class vector`.
14. Member functions common to all containers are the default constructor, constructors with parameters, the copy constructor, the destructor, `empty`, `size`, `max_size`, `swap`, `begin`, `end`, `rbegin`, `rend`, `insert`, `erase`, `clear`, and the relational operator functions.
15. The member function `begin` returns an iterator to the first element in the container.
16. The member function `end` returns an iterator to the last element in the container.
17. In addition to the member functions listed in 14, the other member functions common to all sequence containers are `insert`, `push_back`, `pop_back`, `erase`, `clear`, and `resize`.
18. The `copy` algorithm is used to copy the elements in a given range to another place.
19. The function `copy`, using an `ostream` iterator, can also be used to output the elements of a container.
20. When we create an iterator of the type `ostream`, we also specify the type of element that the iterator will output.
21. Deque containers are implemented as dynamic arrays in such a way that the elements can be inserted at both ends of the array.
22. A `deque` can expand in either direction.
23. The name of the class containing the definition of the `class deque` is `deque`.

24. In addition to the operations that are common to all containers, the other operations that can be used to manipulate the elements of a deque are assign, push_front, pop_front, at, the array subscripting operator [ ], front, and back.

25. The five categories of iterators are: input, output, forward, bidirectional, and random access.

26. Input iterators are used to input data from an input stream.

27. Output iterators are used to output data to an output stream.

28. A forward iterator can refer to the same element in the same collection and process the same element more than once.

29. Bidirectional iterators are forward iterators that can also iterate backwards over the elements.

30. Bidirectional iterators can be used with containers of the type list, set, multiset, map, and multimap.

31. Random access iterators are bidirectional iterators that can randomly process the elements of a container.

32. Random access iterators can be used with containers of the type vector, deque, string, and arrays.

EXERCISES

1. What are the three main components of the STL?

2. What is the difference between an STL container and an STL iterator?

3. Write a statement that declares a vector object that can store 50 decimal numbers.

4. Write a statement that declares and stores the elements of the following array into a vector object:

```
char vowels[5] = {'a', 'e', 'i', 'o', 'u'};
```

5. Write a statement to declare screen to be an ostream iterator initialized to the standard output device that outputs the elements of an int vector object.

6. Consider the following statement:

```
vector<int> intVector;
```

Suppose that intVector = {5, 7, 9, 11, 13}. Moreover, suppose that screen is an ostream iterator initialized to the standard output device to output the elements of an int vector object. What is the effect of the following statement?

```
copy(vecList.begin(), vecList.end(), screen);
```

7. What is the output of the following program segment?

```
vector<int> vecList(5);
int j;
```

```
for(j = 0; j < 5; j++)
    vecList[j] = 2 * j;
for(j = 0; j < 5; j++)
    cout<<vecList[j]<<" ";
cout<<endl;
```

8. What is the output of the following program segment? (Assume that **screen** is an **ostream** iterator initialized to the standard output device to output elements of the type **int**.)

```
int list[5] = {2, 4, 6, 8, 10};
vector<int> vecList(5);

copy(list, list + 5, vecList.begin());

copy(vecList.begin(), vecList.end(), screen);
cout<<endl;
```

9. What is the output of the following program segment? (Assume that **screen** is an **ostream** iterator initialized to the standard output device to output elements of the type **int**.)

```
vector<int> vecList;
vector<int>::iterator vecIt;

vecList.push_back(3);
vecList.push_back(5);
vecList.push_back(7);
vecIt = vecList.begin();
++vecIt;
vecList.erase(vecIt);
vecList.push_back(9);

copy(vecList.begin(), vecList.end(), screen);
cout<<endl;
```

10. What is the output of the following program segment? (Assume that **screen** is an **ostream** iterator initialized to the standard output device to output elements of the type **int**.)

```
int list[5] = {2, 4, 6, 8, 10};
vector<int> vecList(7);

copy(list, list + 5, vecList.begin());

vecList.push_back(12);

copy(vecList.begin(), vecList.end(), screen);
cout<<endl;
```

11. What is the output of the following program segment? (Assume that **screen** is an **ostream** iterator initialized to the standard output device to output elements of the type **double**.)

```
vector<double> sales(3);

sales[0] = 50.00;
sales[1] = 75.00;
sales[2] = 100.00;

sales.resize(5);

sales[3] = 200.00;
sales[4] = 95.00;

copy(sales.begin(), sales.end(), screen);
cout<<endl;
```

12. What is the output of the following program segment? (Assume that **screen** is an **ostream** iterator initialized to the standard output device that outputs elements of the type **int**.)

```
vector<int> intVector;
vector<int>::iterator vecIt;

intVector.push_back(15);
intVector.push_back(2);
intVector.push_back(10);
intVector.push_back(7);
vecIt = intVector.begin();
vecIt++;
intVector.erase(vecIt);
intVector.pop_back();

copy(intVector.begin(),intVector.end(), screen);
```

13. Suppose that **vecList** is a **vector** container and

```
vecList = {12, 16, 8, 23, 40, 6, 18, 9, 75}
```

Show **vecList** after the following statement executes:

```
copy(vecList.begin() + 2, vecList.end(), vecList.begin());
```

14. Suppose that **vecList** is a **vector** container and

```
vecList = {12, 16, 8, 23, 40, 6, 18, 9, 75}
```

Show **vecList** after the following statement executes:

```
copy(vecList.rbegin() + 3, vecList.rend(), vecList.rbegin());
```

15. What is the output of the following program segment?

```
deque<int> intDeq;
ostream_iterator<int> screen(cout, " ");
deque<int>::iterator deqIt;

intDeq.push_back(5);
intDeq.push_front(23);
intDeq.push_front(45);
intDeq.push_back(35);
intDeq.push_front(0);
intDeq.push_back(50);
intDeq.push_front(34);

deqIt = intDeq.begin();
intDeq.insert(deqIt,76);
intDeq.pop_back();

++deqIt;
++deqIt;

intDeq.erase(deqIt);
intDeq.push_front(2 * intDeq.back());
intDeq.push_back(3 * intDeq.front());

copy(intDeq.begin(), intDeq.end(), screen);
cout<<endl;
```

PROGRAMMING EXERCISES

1. Write a program that allows the user to enter the last names of five candidates in a local election and the votes received by each candidate. The program should then output each candidate's name, the votes received by that candidate, and the percentage of the total votes received by the candidate. Your program should also output the winner of the election. A sample output is

```
Candidate       Votes Received      % of Total Votes
Johnson             5000                 25.91
Miller              4000                 20.72
Duffy               6000                 31.09
Robinson            2500                 12.95
Anthony             1800                  9.33
Total              19300
The Winner of the Election is Duffy.
```

2. Write a program that allows the user to enter students' names followed by their test scores and outputs the following information (assume that the maximum number of students in the class is 50):

a. Class average

b. Names of all the students whose test scores are below the class average with an appropriate message

c. Highest test score and the names of all students having the highest score.

3. Write a program that uses a vector object to store a set of real numbers. The program outputs the smallest, largest, and average of the numbers. When declaring the vector object, do not specify its size. Use the function `push_back` to insert the elements into the vector object.

4. Write the definition of the function template `reverseVector` to reverse the elements of a vector object. Its prototype is:

```
template<class elemType>
void reverseVector(vector<elemType> &list);
    //Reverses the elements of the vector list.
    //Example: Suppose list = {4, 8, 2, 5}.
    //         After a call to this function, list =
    //         {5, 2, 8, 4}.
```

Also, write a program to test the function `reverseVector`. When declaring the vector object, do not specify its size. Use the function `push_back` to insert the elements in the vector object.

5. Write the definition of the function template `seqSearch` to implement the sequential search on a vector object. Its prototype is:

```
template<class elemType>
int seqSearch(const vector<elemType> &list, const
              elemType& item);
  //If the item is found in the list, returns the
  //position of the item in the list; otherwise,
  //returns -1.
```

Also, write a program to test the function `seqSearch`. Use the function `push_back` to insert the elements in the vector object.

6. Redo Programming Exercise 6 of Chapter 1 so that the list of books is maintained in a vector object.

7. Redo Programming Exercise 13 of Chapter 3 so that the address book is stored in a vector object.

8. **(Stock Market)** Write a program to help a local stock-trading company automate its systems. The company invests only in the stock market. At the end of each trading day, the company would like to generate and post the listing of its stocks so that investors can see how their holdings performed that day. Let's assume that the company invests in, say, 10 different stocks. The desired output is to produce a listing, which is sorted by the stock symbol.

The input data is provided in a file in the following format:

```
symbol openingPrice closingPrice todayHigh todayLow prevClose volume
```

For example, the sample data is

```
MSMT 112.50 115.75 116.50 111.75 113.50 6723823
CBA 67.50 75.50 78.75 67.50 65.75 378233
  .
  .
  .
```

The first line indicates that the stock symbol is MSMT, today's opening price was 112.50, the closing price was 115.75, today's high price was 116.50, today's low price was 111.75, yesterday's closing price was 113.50, and the number of shares currently being held is 6723823.

The listing sorted by stock symbols must be of the following form:

```
*********  First Investor's Heaven  **********
*********      Financial Report      **********
Stock              Today              Previous  Percent
Symbol  Open    Close   High    Low     Close     Gain     Volume
------  -----   -----   -----   -----   --------  -------   ------
  ABC   123.45  130.95  132.00  125.00  120.50      8.67%   10000
  AOLK   80.00   75.00   82.00   74.00   83.00     -9.64%    5000
  CSCO  100.00  102.00  105.00   98.00  101.00      0.99%   25000
  IBD    68.00   71.00   72.00   67.00   75.00     -5.33%   15000
  MSET  120.00  140.00  145.00  140.00  115.00     21.74%   30920
Closing Assets: $9628300.00
_*_*_*_*_*_*_*_*_*_*_*_*_*_*_*_*_*_*_*_*_*
```

Develop this programming exercise in two steps. In the first step (part a), design and implement a stock object. In the second step (part b), design and implement an object to maintain a list of stocks.

a. **(Stock Object)** Design and implement the stock object. Call the class that captures the various characteristics of a stock object stockType.

The main components of a stock are the stock symbol, stock price, and number of shares. Moreover, we need to output the opening price, high price, low price, previous price, and the percent gain/loss for the day. These are also all the characteristics of a stock. Therefore, the stock object should store all this information.

Perform the following operations on each stock object:

i.   Set the stock information.

ii. Print the stock information.

iii. Show the different prices.

iv. Calculate and print the percent gain/loss.

v.   Show the number of shares.

a.1. The natural ordering of the stock list is by stock symbol. Overload the relational operators to compare two stock objects by their symbols.

a.2. Overload the insertion operator, <<, for easy output.

a.3.Because the data is stored in a file, overload the stream extraction operator, >>, for easy input.

For example, suppose `infile` is an `ifstream` object and the input file was opened using the object `infile`. Further suppose that `myStock` is a stock object. Then, the statement

```
infile>>myStock;
```

reads the data from the input file and stores it in the object `myStock`. (Note that this statement reads and stores the data in the relevant components of `myStock`.)

b. Now that you have designed and implemented the **class stockType** to implement a stock object in a program, it is time to create a list of stock objects. Let us call the class to implement the list of stock objects **stockListType**. To store the list of stocks you need to declare a **vector**. The component type of this **vector** is **stockType**.

In skeleton form, the definition of the **class stockListType** is

```
class stockListType
{
public:
    void addToStockList(stockType s);
        //Function to add the stocks to the list.
    ...

private:
    vector<stockType> list; //vector to store the list
                            //of stocks
};
```

c. Write a program that uses these two classes to automate the company's analysis of stock data.

5

LINKED LISTS

In this chapter, you will:

- ♦ Learn about linked lists
- ♦ Become aware of the basic properties of linked lists
- ♦ Explore the insertion and deletion operations on linked lists
- ♦ Discover how to build and manipulate a linked list
- ♦ Learn how to construct a doubly linked list
- ♦ Discover how to use the STL container `list`
- ♦ Learn about linked lists with header and trailer nodes
- ♦ Become aware of circular linked lists

You have already seen how data can be organized and processed sequentially using an array, called a *sequential list*. You have performed several operations on sequential lists, such as sorting, inserting, deleting, and searching. You also found that if data is not sorted, then searching for an item in the list can be very time consuming, especially with large lists. Once the data is sorted, you can use another search algorithm, called the binary search (discussed in Chapter 9), and improve the search algorithm. However, if the list is sorted, insertion and deletion become time consuming, especially with large lists, because these operations require data movement since the resulting list must also be sorted. Moreover, because the array size must be fixed during execution, new items can be added only if there is room. Thus, there are limitations when you organize data in an array.

This chapter helps you to overcome some of these problems. Chapter 3 showed how memory (variables) can be dynamically allocated and deallocated using pointers. This chapter uses pointers to organize and process data in lists, called **linked lists**. Recall that when data is stored in an array, memory for the components of the array is contiguous—that is, blocks are allocated one after the other. On the other hand, as you will see, the dynamically allocated components of a linked list are not necessarily contiguous.

LINKED LISTS

A linked list is a collection of components, called **nodes**. Every node (except the last node) contains the address of the next node. Thus, every node in a linked list has two components: one to store the relevant information (that is, the data); and one to store the address, called the **link**, of the next node in the list. The address of the first node in the list is stored in a separate location, called the **head** or **first**. Figure 5-1 is a pictorial representation of a node.

Figure 5-1   Structure of a node

Linked list: A list of items, called **nodes**, in which the order of the nodes is determined by the address, called the **link**, stored in each node.

The list in Figure 5-2 is an example of a linked list.

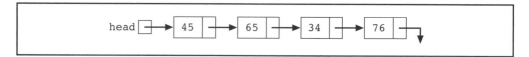

Figure 5-2   Linked list

The down arrow in the last node indicates that this link field is NULL. The arrow in each node indicates that the address of the node to which it is pointing is stored in that node. For a better understanding of this notation, suppose that the first node is at memory location 1200, and the second node is at memory location 1575. We thus have Figure 5-3.

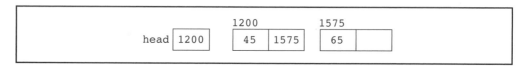

Figure 5-3   Linked list and the values of the links

The value of the head is 1200, the data part of the first node is 45, and the link component of the first node contains 1575, the address of the second node. We use the arrow notation whenever we draw the figure of a linked list.

 In Figures 5-2 and 5-3, for illustration purposes, we assume that the data stored in the node is of the type int. However, the data stored in the node can be of any type including a class or a struct. In fact, after describing in the next few sections the basic properties of linked lists and how to build a linked list, we use class templates to develop a generic code to process linked lists, which can then be used in a variety of applications. Moreover, for simplicity and ease of understanding and clarity, Figures 5-3, 5-4, 5-5, and 5-6 use integers as the values of memory addresses. However, in computer memory, the memory addresses are in binary.

Because each node of a linked list has two components, we need to declare each node as a class or struct. The data type of each node depends on the specific application—that is, what kind of data is being processed; however, the link component of each node is a pointer. The data type of this pointer variable is the node type itself. For the previous linked list, the definition of the node is as follows (suppose that the data type is int):

```
struct nodeType
{
    int info;
    nodeType *link;
};
```

The following statement declares head to be a pointer of the type nodeType.

```
nodeType *head;
```

LINKED LISTS: SOME PROPERTIES

To help you better understand the concept of a linked list and a node, some important properties of linked lists are described next.

Consider the linked list in Figure 5-4.

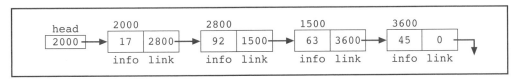

Figure 5-4   Linked list with four nodes

This linked list has four nodes. The address of the first node is stored in the pointer `head`. Each node has two components: `info`, to store the info; and `link`, to store the address of the next node. For simplicity, we assume that `info` is of the type `int`.

Suppose that the first node is at location `2000`, the second node is at location `2800`, the third node is at location `1500`, and the fourth node is at location `3600`. Therefore, the value of `head` is `2000`, the value of the component `link` of the first node is `2800`, the value of the component `link` of the second node is `1500`, and so on. Also, the value `0` in the component link of the last node means that this value is `NULL`, which we indicate by drawing a down arrow. The number at the top of each node is the address of the node.

Table 5-1 shows the values of `head` and some of the nodes of the linked list in Figure 5-4.

Table 5-1 Values of `head` and Some of the Nodes of the Linked List in Figure 5-4

	Value	
head	2000	
head->info	17	Because `head` is `2000` and the `info` of the node at location `2000` is `17`.
head->link	2800	
head->link->info	92	Because `head->link` is `2800` and the `info` of the node at location `2800` is `92`.

Suppose that `current` is a pointer of the same type as the pointer `head`. Then the statement

`current = head;`

copies the value of `head` into `current`. See Figure 5-5.

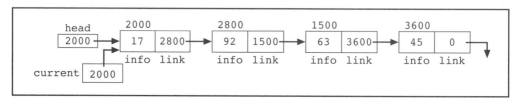

Figure 5-5 Linked list after the statement `current = head;` executes

Table 5-2 shows the values of `current` and some of the nodes of the linked list in Figure 5-5.

Table 5-2 Values of `current` and Some of the Nodes of the Linked List in Figure 5-5

	Value
current	2000
current->info	17
current->link	2800
current->link->info	92

Now consider the statement

`current = current->link;`

This statement copies the value of `current->link`, which is 2800, into `current`. There-fore, after this statement executes, `current` points to the second node in the list. (When working with linked lists, we typically use these types of statements to advance a pointer to the next node in the list, such as when we traverse a linked list.) See Figure 5-6.

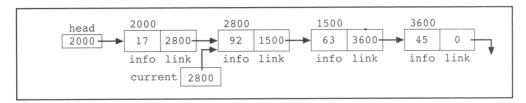

Figure 5-6   Linked list after the statement `current = current->link;` executes

Table 5-3 shows the values of `current` and some of the nodes of the linked list after advancing `current` to the next node.

Table 5-3 Values of `current` and Some of the Nodes of the Linked List in Figure 5-6

	Value
current	2800
current->info	92
current->link	1500
current->link->info	63

Finally, Table 5-4 shows the values of some other pointers and nodes of the linked list in Figure 5-6.

Table 5-4 Values of Various Pointers and Nodes of the Linked List in Figure 5-6

	Value
head->link->link	1500
head->link->link->info	63
head->link->link->link	3600
head->link->link->link->info	45
current->link->link	3600
current->link->link->info	45
current->link->link->link	0 (that is, NULL)
current->link->link->link->info	Does not exist

From now on, when working with linked lists, we use only the arrow notation.

Traversing a Linked List

The basic operations of a linked list are:

- Search the list to determine whether a particular item is in the list.
- Insert an item in the list.
- Delete an item from the list.

These operations require the list to be traversed. That is, given a pointer to the first node of the list, we must step through the nodes of the list.

Suppose that the pointer **head** points to the first node in the list, and the link of the last node is NULL. We cannot use the pointer **head** to traverse the list because if we use **head** to traverse the list we would lose the nodes of the list. This problem occurs because the links go in only one direction. The pointer **head** contains the address of the first node, the first node contains the address of the second node, the second node contains the address of the third node, and so on. If we move **head** to the second node, the first node is lost (unless we save a pointer to this node). If we keep advancing **head** to the next node, we will lose all the nodes of the list (unless we save pointers to each node before advancing **head**, which is impractical because it would require additional computer time and memory space to maintain the list).

Therefore, we always want **head** to point to the first node. It now follows that we must traverse the list using another pointer of the same type. Suppose that **current** is a pointer of the same type as **head**. The following code traverses the list:

```
current = head;
while(current != NULL)
{
    //Process current
    current = current->link;
}
```

For example, suppose that **head** points to a linked list of numbers. The following code outputs the data stored in each node:

```
current = head;
while(current != NULL)
{
    cout<<current->info<<" ";
    current = current->link;
}
```

5

ITEM INSERTION AND DELETION

This section discusses how to insert an item in, and delete an item from, a linked list. Consider the following definition of a node. (For simplicity, we assume that the **info** type is **int**. The section, "Linked List as an ADT," located later in this chapter, which discusses linked lists as an abstract data type (ADT) using templates, uses the generic definition of a node.)

```
struct nodeType
{
    int info;
    nodeType *link;
};
```

We use the following variable declaration:

```
nodeType *head, *p, *q, *newNode;
```

Insertion

Consider the linked list shown in Figure 5-7.

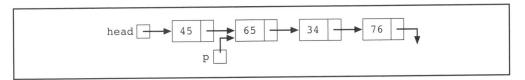

Figure 5-7   Linked list before item insertion

Suppose that **p** points to the node with **info 65**, and a new node with **info 50** is to be created and inserted after **p**. The following statements create and store **50** in the **info** field of a new node:

```
newNode = new nodeType;     //create newNode
assert(newNode != NULL);    //if unable to allocate memory
                            //space, terminate the program
newNode->info = 50;         //store 50 in the new node
```

The first statement (that is, `newNode = new nodeType;`) creates a node somewhere in memory and stores the address of the newly created node in `newNode`. The second statement terminates the program if the system is unable to allocate memory space. The third statement (that is, `newNode->info = 50;`) stores `50` in the `info` field of the new node. See Figure 5-8.

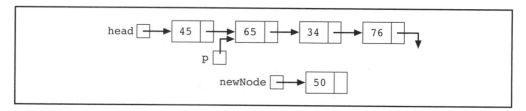

Figure 5-8   Create `newNode` and store `50` in it

The following statements insert the node in the linked list at the required place:

```
newNode->link = p->link;
p->link = newNode;
```

After the first statement (that is, `newNode->link = p->link;`) executes, the resulting list is as shown in Figure 5-9.

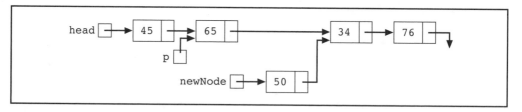

Figure 5-9   Linked list after the statement `newNode->link = p->link;` executes

After the second statement (that is, `p->link = newNode;`) executes, the resulting list is as shown in Figure 5-10.

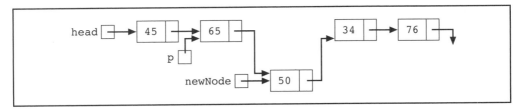

Figure 5-10 Linked list after the statement `p->link = newNode;` executes

Note that the sequence of statements to insert the node is very important because to insert `newNode` in the list we used only one pointer, `p`, to adjust the links of the node of the linked list. If we reverse the sequence of the statements, we do not get the desired result. For example, suppose that we execute the statements in the following order:

```
p->link = newNode;
newNode->link = p->link;
```

Figure 5-11 shows the resulting list after these statements execute.

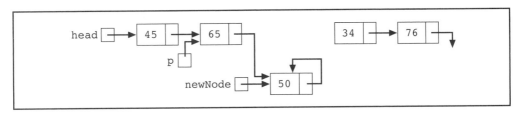

Figure 5-11 Linked list after the statement `p->link = newNode;` executes, followed by the execution of `newNode->link = p->link;`

From Figure 5-11, it is clear that **newNode** points back to itself and the remainder of the list is lost.

Using two pointers, we can simplify the insertion code somewhat. Suppose `q` points to the node with **info 34**. See Figure 5-12.

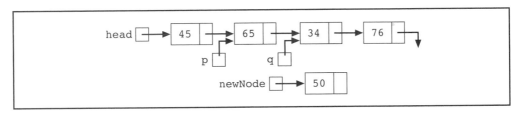

Figure 5-12 Linked list with pointers p and q

The following statements insert `newNode` between p and q:

```
newNode->link = q;
p->link = newNode;
```

The order in which these statements execute does not matter. To illustrate this, suppose that we execute the statements in the following order:

```
p->link = newNode;
newNode->link = q;
```

After the statement `p->link = newNode;` executes, the resulting list is as shown in Figure 5-13.

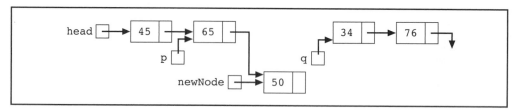

Figure 5-13   Linked list after the statement `p->link = newNode;` executes

Because we have a pointer, q, pointing to the remaining list, the remaining list is not lost. After the statement `newNode->link = q;` executes, the list is as shown in Figure 5-14.

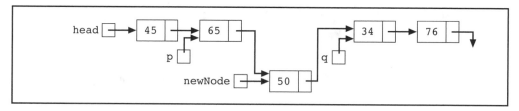

Figure 5-14   Linked list after the statement `newNode->link = q;` executes

Deletion

Consider the linked list shown in Figure 5-15.

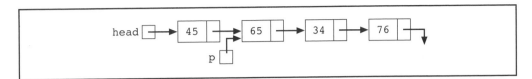

Figure 5-15   Node to be deleted is with `info 34`

Suppose that the node with `info 34` is to be deleted from the list. The following statement removes the node from the list:

```
p->link = p->link->link;
```

Figure 5-16 shows the resulting list after the preceding statement executes.

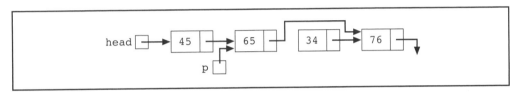

Figure 5-16   Linked list after the statement `p->link = p->link->link;` executes

From Figure 5-16, it clear that the node with `info 34` is removed from the list. However, the memory is still occupied by this node; that is, this node is dangling. To deallocate the memory, we need a pointer to this node. The following statements delete the node from the list and deallocate the memory occupied by this node:

```
q = p->link;
p->link = q->link;
delete q;
```

After the statement `q = p->link;` executes, the list is as shown in Figure 5-17.

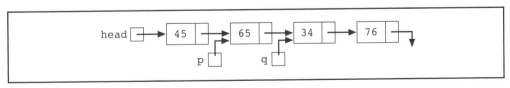

Figure 5-17   Linked list after the statement `q = p->link;` executes

After the statement `p->link = q->link;` executes, the resulting list is as shown in Figure 5-18.

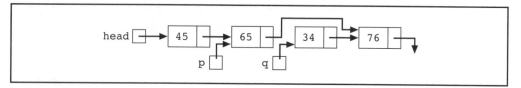

Figure 5-18   Linked list after the statement `p->link = q->link;` executes

After the statement **delete q;** executes, the list is as shown in Figure 5-19.

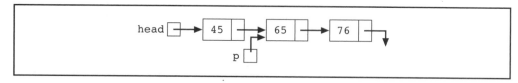

Figure 5-19   Linked list after the statement `delete q;` executes

From the preceding discussion it follows that to delete a node from a linked list, you need two pointers—one to traverse the list, and another to deallocate the memory space of the node to be deleted.

 The statement `delete q;` only marks the memory occupied by the node that q is pointing to as deallocated so that it can be used later on. The pointer q may still contain the address of that memory space. To avoid any side effects, you might like to set q to NULL after the `delete` statement.

BUILDING A LINKED LIST

Now that you know how to insert a node in a linked list, next you learn how to build a linked list. First, we consider a linked list in general. If the data we read is unsorted, the linked list need not be in order. Such a list can be built in two ways: in the forward manner, and in the backward manner. In the forward manner, a new node is always inserted at the end of the linked list; in the backward manner, a new node is always inserted at the beginning of the linked list. We consider both cases.

Building a Linked List Forward

Suppose that the nodes are in the usual `info-link` form and `info` is of the type `int`. Let us assume that we process the following data:

2 15 8 24 34

We need three pointers to build the list: one to point to the first node in the list, which cannot be moved; one to point to the last node in the list; and one to create the new node. Consider the following variable declaration:

```
nodeType *first, *last, *newNode;
int num;
```

Suppose that `first` points to the first node in the list. Initially, the list is empty, so both `first` and `last` are NULL. Thus, we must have the statements

```
first = NULL;
last = NULL;
```

to initialize `first` and `last` to NULL.

Next, consider the following statements:

```
1   cin>>num;                        //read and store a number
                                     //in num
2   newNode = new nodeType;          //allocate memory of the
                                     //type nodeType and store
                                     //the address of the
                                     //allocated memory in
                                     //newNode
3   assert(newNode != NULL)          //if unable to allocate
                                     //memory space,
                                     //terminate the program
4   newNode->info = num;             //copy the value of num
                                     //into the info field
                                     //of newNode
5   newNode->link = NULL;            //initialize the link
                                     //field of newNode to
                                     //NULL
6   if (first == NULL)               //if first is NULL, the
                                     //list is empty; make
                                     //first and last point to
                                     //newNode
    {
      6a        first = newNode;
      6b        last = newNode;
    }
7   else                             //the list is not empty
    {
```

```
7a        last->link = newNode;  //insert newNode at the
                                 //end of the list
7b        last = newNode;        //set last so that it
                                 //points to the actual
                                 //last node in the list
     }
```

Let us now execute these statements. Initially, both `first` and `last` are `NULL`. Therefore, we have the list as shown in Figure 5-20.

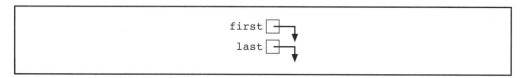

Figure 5-20   Empty linked list

After statement 1 executes, `num` is 2. Statement 2 creates a node and stores the address of that node in `newNode`. Statement 3 terminates the program if the system is unable to allocate memory space. Statement 4 stores 2 in the `info` field of `newNode`; statement 5 stores `NULL` in the link field of `newNode`. See Figure 5-21.

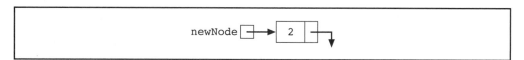

Figure 5-21   `newNode` with `info` 2

Because `first` is `NULL`, we execute statements 6a and 6b. Figure 5-22 shows the resulting list.

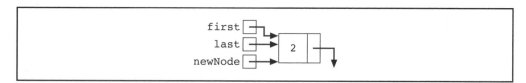

Figure 5-22   Linked list after inserting `newNode` in it

We now repeat statements 1 through 7b. After statement 1 executes, `num` is 15. Statement 2 creates a node and stores the address of the node in `newNode`. Statement 4 stores 15 in the `info` field of `newNode`; statement 5 stores `NULL` in the link field of `newNode`. See Figure 5-23.

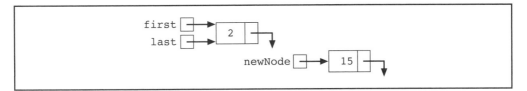

Figure 5-23   Linked list and `newNode` with `info` 15

Because `first` is not `NULL`, we execute statements 7a and 7b. Figure 5-24 shows the resulting list.

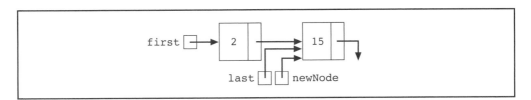

Figure 5-24   Linked list after inserting `newNode` at the end

We now repeat statements 1 through 7b three more times. Figure 5-25 shows the resulting list.

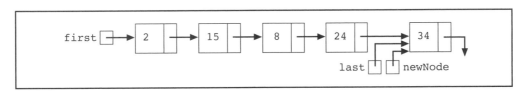

Figure 5-25   Linked list after inserting 8, 24, and 34

We can put the previous statements in a loop, and execute the loop until certain conditions are met to build the linked list. We can, in fact, write a C++ function to build a linked list.

Suppose that we read a list of integers ending with −999. The following function, buildListForward, builds a linked list (in a forward manner) and returns the pointer of the built list:

```
nodeType* buildListForward()
{
    nodeType *first, *newNode, *last;
    int num;

    cout<<"Enter a list of integers ending with -999.\n";
    cin>>num;
    first = NULL;

    while(num != -999)
    {
        newNode = new nodeType;
        assert(newNode != NULL);

        newNode->info = num;
        newNode->link = NULL;

        if(first == NULL)
        {
            first = newNode;
            last = newNode;
        }
        else
        {
            last->link = newNode;
            last = newNode;
        }
        cin>>num;
    }//end while

    return first;
}//end buildListForward
```

Building a Linked List Backwards

We now consider the case of building a linked list backwards. For the previously given data—2, 15, 8, 24, and 34—the linked list is as shown in Figure 5-26.

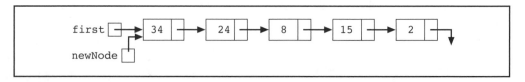

Figure 5-26   Linked list after building it backward

Because the new node is always inserted at the beginning of the list, we do not need to know the end of the list, so the pointer `last` is not needed. Also, after inserting the new node at the beginning, the new node becomes the first node in the list. Thus, we need to update the value of the pointer `first` to point correctly to the first node in the list. We see, then, that we need only two pointers to build the linked list: one to point to the list, and one to create the new node. Because initially the list is empty, the pointer `first` must be initialized to `NULL`. In pseudocode, the algorithm is

1. Initialize `first` to `NULL`.

2. For each item in the list:

    a. Create the new node, `newNode`.

    b. Store the item in `newNode`.

    c. Insert `newNode` before `first`.

    d. Update the value of the pointer `first`.

The following C++ function builds the linked list backwards and returns the pointer of the built list:

```cpp
nodeType* buildListBackward()
{
    nodeType *first, *newNode;
    int num;

    cout<<"Enter a list of integers ending with -999.\n";
    cin>>num;
    first = NULL;

    while(num != -999)
    {
        newNode = new nodeType;      //create a node
        assert(newNode != NULL);     //if unable to allocate
                                     //memory space,
                                     //terminate the program
        newNode->info = num;         //store the data in
                                     //newNode
        newNode->link = first;       //put newNode at the
                                     //beginning of the list
        first = newNode;             //update the head pointer
                                     //of the list
        cin>>num;                    //read the next number
    }

    return first;
}//end buildListBackward
```

LINKED LIST AS AN ADT

The previous sections taught you the basic properties of linked lists and how to construct and manipulate linked lists. Because a linked list is a very important data structure, rather than discuss specific lists such as a list of integers or a list of strings, this section discusses linked lists as an ADT. Using templates, it gives a generic definition of linked lists, which we then use in the next section and later in this book. The programming example at the end of this chapter also uses this generic definition of linked lists.

The basic operations on linked lists are:

1. Initialize the list.

2. Check whether the list is empty.

3. Output the list.

4. Find the length of the list.

5. Destroy the list.

6. Retrieve the `info` contained in the first node.

7. Retrieve the `info` contained in the last node.

8. Search the list for a given item.

9. Insert an item in the list.

10. Delete an item from the list.

11. Make a copy of the linked list.

First, we discuss these operations on arbitrary lists—that is, lists that may be sorted or unsorted. The next section discusses sorted linked lists.

If a list is arbitrary, we can insert a new item at either the end or the beginning. Furthermore, such a list may initially be built in either a forward manner or a backward manner. The function `buildListForward` requires the new item to be inserted at the end; the function `buildListBackward` requires the new item to be inserted at the beginning. To accommodate both operations, we write two functions: `insertFirst`, to insert the new item at the beginning of the list; and `insertLast`, to insert the new item at the end of the list. Also, to make the algorithms somewhat efficient, we maintain two pointers in the list: `first`, which points to the first node in the list; and `last`, which points to the last node in the list. Moreover, we overload the stream insertion operator to output the elements of a list.

The following class defines the linked list as an ADT:

```
//Definition of the node

template<class Type>
struct nodeType
{
   Type info;
   nodeType<Type> *link;
};


template<class Type>
class linkedListType
{
   friend ostream& operator<<(ostream&, const linkedListType<Type>&);
    //Overload the stream insertion operator.

public:
   const linkedListType<Type>& operator=
                       (const linkedListType<Type>&);
     //Overload the assignment operator.
   void initializeList();
     //Function to initialize the list to an empty state.
     //Postcondition: first = NULL; last = NULL;
     //               count = 0
   bool isEmptyList();
     //Function to determine whether the list is empty.
     //Postcondition: Returns true if the list is empty;
     //               otherwise, returns false.

   int length();
     //Function to return the number of nodes in the
     //list.
     //Postcondition: The value of count is returned.
   void destroyList();
     //Function to delete all the nodes from the list.
     //Postcondition: first = NULL; last = NULL;
     //               count = 0
   Type front();
     //Function to return the first element of the list.
     //Precondition: The list must exist and must not
     //   be empty.
     //Postcondition: If the list is empty, then the
     //   program terminates; otherwise, the first
     //   element of the list is returned.
   Type back();
     //Function to return the last element of the
     //list.
     //Precondition: The list must exist and must not
     //   be empty.
```

```
    //Postcondition: If the list is empty, then the
    //   program terminates; otherwise, the last
    //   element of the list is returned.

bool search(const Type& searchItem);
    //Function to determine whether searchItem is in
    //the list.
    //Postcondition: Returns true if searchItem is found
    //   in the list; otherwise, returns false.

void insertFirst(const Type& newItem);
    //Function to insert newItem in the list.
    //Postcondition: first points to the new list,
    //   newItem is inserted at the beginning
    //   of the list, last points to the last node, and
    //   count is incremented by 1.

void insertLast(const Type& newItem);
    //Function to insert newItem at the end of the list.
    //Postcondition: first points to the new list,
    //   newItem is inserted at the end of the list,
    //   last points to the last node in the list, and
    //   count is incremented by 1.

void deleteNode(const Type& deleteItem);
    //Function to delete deleteItem from the list.
    //Postcondition: If found, the node containing
    //   deleteItem is deleted from the list, first points
    //   to the first node, last points to the last
    //   node of the updated list, and count is decremented
    //   by 1.

linkedListType();
    //default constructor
    //Initializes the list to an empty state.
    //Postcondition: first = NULL; last = NULL;
    //                count = 0

linkedListType(const linkedListType<Type>& otherList);
    //copy constructor

~linkedListType();
    //destructor
    //Deletes all the nodes from the list.
    //Postcondition: The list object is destroyed.

protected:
    int count;         //variable to store the number of
                       //elements in the list
```

```
   nodeType<Type> *first; //pointer to the first node of
                          //the list
   nodeType<Type> *last;  //pointer to the last node of
                          //the list
private:
  void copyList(const linkedListType<Type>& otherList);
   //Function to make a copy of otherList.
   //Postcondition: A copy of otherList is created
   //               and assigned to this list.

};
```

Note that the data members of the **class linkedListType** are **protected**, not **private**, because we will derive other classes from this class. This class is referred to in the section "Ordered Linked Lists" located later in this chapter, and in Chapters 9 and 10.

Also notice that the function **copyList** is declared as **private**. This is because we use this function only to implement the copy constructor and the function to overload the assignment operator. To make a copy of another list, you can use the assignment operator after it is overloaded.

The definition of the **class linkedListType** includes a member function to overload the assignment operator. For classes that include pointer data members, the assignment operator must be explicitly overloaded (see Chapters 2 and 3). For the same reason, the definition of the class also includes a copy constructor. Next, we discuss the implementation of the member functions.

The list is empty if **first** is NULL. Therefore, the definition of the function **isEmptyList** to implement this operation is as follows:

```
template<class Type>
bool linkedListType<Type>::isEmptyList()
{
   return(first == NULL);
}
```

Default Constructor

The default constructor initializes the list to an empty state. Recall that when an object of the type **linkedListType** is declared and no value is passed, the default constructor executes automatically. Its definition is

```
template<class Type>
linkedListType<Type>::linkedListType()
{
   first = NULL;
   last = NULL;
   count = 0;
}
```

From the definitions of the function `isEmptyList` and the default constructor, it follows that each of these functions is of $O(1)$.

Destroy List

The function `destroyList` deallocates the memory occupied by each node. We traverse the list starting from the first node and deallocate the memory by calling the operator `delete`. We need a temporary pointer to deallocate the memory. Once the entire list is destroyed, we must set the pointers `first` and `last` to `NULL`, and `count` to 0. Its definition is

```
template<class Type>
void linkedListType<Type>::destroyList()
{
    nodeType<Type> *temp;     //pointer to deallocate
                              //the memory occupied by
                              //the node
    while(first != NULL)      //while there are nodes in
                              //the list
    {
        temp = first;         //set temp to the current
                              //node
        first = first->link;//advance first to the
                              //next node
        delete temp;          //deallocate the memory
                              //occupied by temp
    }

    last = NULL;    //initialize last to NULL; first has
                    //already been set to NULL by the
                    //while loop
    count = 0;
}
```

If the list has n items, the `while` loop executes n times. From this, it follows that the function `destroyList` is of $O(n)$.

Initialize List

The function `initializeList` initializes the list to an empty state. Note that the default constructor or the copy constructor has already initialized the list when the list object was declared. This operation, in fact, reinitializes the list to an empty state, so it must delete the nodes (if any) from the list. This task can be accomplished by using the `destroyList` operation, which also resets the pointers `first` and `last` to `NULL`, and `count` to 0. Its definition is

```
template<class Type>
void linkedListType<Type>::initializeList()
{
    destroyList(); //if the list has any nodes,
                   //delete them
}
```

The function `initializeList` uses the function `destroyList`, which is of $O(n)$. Therefore, the function `initializeList` is of $O(n)$.

Overloading the Stream Insertion Operator

To output the data stored in the nodes of a linked list, we overload the stream insertion operator. Now to output the data contained in each node, we must traverse the list starting at the first node. Because the pointer `first` always points to the first node in the list, we need another pointer to traverse the list. (If we use `first` to traverse the list, the entire list is lost.) The definition of the function to overload the stream insertion operator is:

```
template<class Type>
ostream& operator<<(ostream& osObject,
                    const linkedListType<Type>& list)
{
    nodeType<Type> *current; //pointer to traverse the list

    current = list.first;    //set current so that it points
                             //to the first node
    while(current != NULL)   //while more data to output
    {
        osObject<<current->info<<" ";
        current = current->link;
    }

    return osObject;
}
```

As in the case of the function `destroyList`, the function to overload the stream insertion operator is of $O(n)$.

Length of the List

The length of the linked list (that is, how many nodes are in the list) is stored in the variable `count`. Therefore, this function returns the value of this variable. Its definition is

```
template<class Type>
int linkedListType<Type>::length()
{
    return count;
}//end length
```

Retrieve Data of the First Node

The function `front` returns the `info` contained in the first node and its definition is

```
template<class Type>
Type linkedListType<Type>::front()
{
      assert(last != NULL);
      return first->info; //return the info of the
                          //first node
}//end front
```

Notice that if the list is empty, the **assert** statement terminates the program. Therefore, before calling this function, check to see whether the list is nonempty.

Retrieve Data of the Last Node

The function **back** returns the **info** contained in the last node, and its definition is straightforward.

```
template<class Type>
Type linkedListType<Type>::back()
{
      assert(last != NULL);
      return last->info; //return the info of the
                         //last node
}//end back
```

Notice that if the list is empty, the **assert** statement terminates the program. Therefore, before calling this function, check to see whether the list is nonempty.

From the definitions of the functions **length**, **front**, and **back**, it follows that each of these functions are of $O(1)$.

Search List

The member function **search** searches the list for a given item. If the item is found, it returns **true**. Because a linked list is not a random access data structure, we must sequentially search the list starting from the first node.

The following steps describe this function:

1. Compare the search item with the current node in the list. If the **info** of the current node is the same as the search item, stop the search; otherwise, make the next node the current node.

2. Repeat Step 1 until either the item is found or no more data is left in the list to compare with the search item.

The definition of the function **search** is:

```
template<class Type>
bool linkedListType<Type>::search(const Type& searchItem)
{
    nodeType<Type> *current; //pointer to traverse the list
    bool found;
```

```
    current = first; //set current to point to the
                     //first node in the list
    found = false;   //set found to false

    while(current != NULL && !found)    //search the list
        if(current->info == searchItem) //the item is found
            found = true;
        else
            current = current->link; //make current point
                                     //to the next node

    return found;
}//end search
```

The number of times the while loop executes, in the function **search**, depends on where in the list the search item is located. Suppose the list has *n* items. If the search item is not in the list, the while loop executes *n* times. On the other hand, if the search item is the first item, the while loop executes 1 time. Similarly, if the search item is the *i*th item in the list, the while loop executes *i* times. From these observations, we can show that the function **search** is of $O(n)$. We explicitly analyze a sequential search algorithm in Chapter 9.

Insert First Node

The function **insertFirst** inserts the new item at the beginning of the list—that is, before the node pointed to by **first**. The following steps are needed to implement this function:

1. Create a new node.

2. If unable to create the node, terminate the program.

3. Store the new item in the new node.

4. Insert the node before **first**.

5. Increment **count** by 1.

The definition of the function **insertFirst** is

```
template<class Type>
void linkedListType<Type>::insertFirst(const Type& newItem)
{
    nodeType<Type> *newNode; //pointer to create the new
                             //node

    newNode = new nodeType<Type>; //create the new node

    assert(newNode != NULL);   //if unable to allocate
                               //memory, terminate
                               //the program

    newNode->info = newItem;   //store newItem in
                               //the node
```

```
    newNode->link = first;     //insert newNode before
                               //first
    first = newNode;           //make first point to the
                               //actual first node
    count++;                   //increment count

    if(last == NULL)  //if the list was empty, newNode is
                      //also the last node in the list
        last = newNode;
}
```

Insert Last Node

The definition of the member function insertLast is similar to the definition of the member function insertFirst. Here we insert the new node after last. Essentially, the function insertLast is

```
template<class Type>
void linkedListType<Type>::insertLast(const Type& newItem)
{
    nodeType<Type> *newNode; //pointer to create the new node

    newNode = new nodeType<Type>; //create the new node

    assert(newNode != NULL);  //If unable to allocate memory,
                              //terminate the program

    newNode->info = newItem;   //store the new item in the node
    newNode->link = NULL;      //set the link field of newNode
                               //to NULL

    if(first == NULL)     //if the list is empty, newNode is
                          //both the first and last node
    {
        first = newNode;
        last = newNode;
        count++;          //increment count
    }
    else  //the list is not empty, insert newNode after last
    {
        last->link = newNode; //insert newNode after last
        last = newNode;  //make last point to the actual last node
        count++;    //increment count
    }
}//end insertLast
```

From the definitions of the functions `insertFirst` and `insertLast`, it follows that each of these functions is of O(1).

Delete Node

Next, we discuss the implementation of the function `deleteNode`, which deletes a node from the list with a given `info`. We need to consider several cases:

Case 1: The list is empty.

Case 2: The first node is the node with the given `info`. In this case, we need to adjust the pointer `first`.

Case 3: The node with the given `info` is somewhere in the list. If the node to be deleted is the last node, we must adjust the pointer `last`.

Case 4: The list does not contain the node with the given `info`.

If the list is empty, we can simply print a message indicating that the list is empty. If the list is not empty, we search the list for the node with the given `info` and, if such a node is found, delete this node. After deleting the node, `count` is decremented by 1. In pseudocode, the algorithm is

```
if the list is empty
  Output(cannot delete from an empty list);
else
{
  if the first node is the node with the given info,
    adjust first, last (if necessary),
    count, and deallocate the memory;
  else
  {
    search the list for the node with the given info
    if such a node is found, delete it and adjust the values of
    last (if necessary), and count.
  }
}
```

Let us next illustrate these cases.

Case 1: The list is empty.

If the list is empty, output an error message as shown in the pseudocode.

Case 2: The list is not empty. The node to be deleted is the first node.

This case has two scenarios: `list` has only one node, and `list` has more than one node. Consider the list with one node as shown in Figure 5-27.

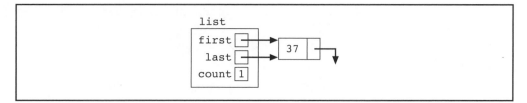

Figure 5-27 list with one node

Suppose that we want to delete 37. After deletion, the list becomes empty. Therefore, after deletion, both first and last are set to NULL and count is set to 0.

Now consider the list of more than one node, as shown in Figure 5-28.

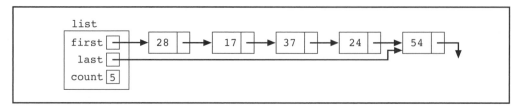

Figure 5-28 list with more than one node

Suppose that the node to be deleted is 28. After deleting this node, the second node becomes the first node. Therefore, after deleting this node the value of the pointer first changes; that is, after deletion, first contains the address of the node with info 17 and count is decremented by 1. Figure 5-29 shows the list after deleting 28.

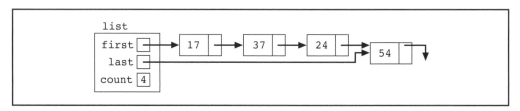

Figure 5-29 list after deleting the node with info 28

Case 3: The node to be deleted is not the first node, but is somewhere in this list.

This case has two subcases: (a) the node to be deleted is not the last node, and (b) the node to be deleted is the last node. Let us illustrate both cases.

Case 3a: The node to be deleted is not the last node.

Consider the list shown in Figure 5-30.

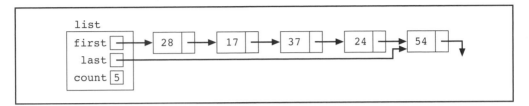

Figure 5-30 `list` before deleting 37

Suppose that the node to be deleted is **37**. After deleting this node, the resulting list is as shown in Figure 5-31. (Notice that the deletion of **37** does not require us to change the values of `first` and `last`. The link field of the previous node—that is, **17**—changes. After deletion, the node with `info` **17** contains the address of the node with **24**.)

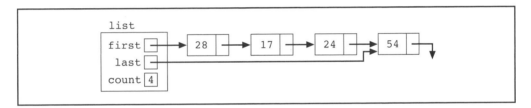

Figure 5-31 `list` after deleting 37

Case 3b: The node to be deleted is the last node.

Consider the list shown in Figure 5-32. Suppose that the node to be deleted is **54**.

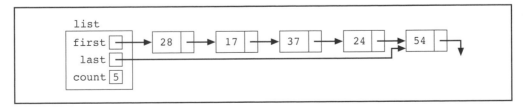

Figure 5-32 `list` before deleting 54

After deleting 54, the node with info 24 becomes the last node. Therefore, the deletion of 54 requires us to change the value of the pointer last. After deleting 54, last contains the address of the node with info 24. Also, count is decremented by 1. Figure 5-33 shows the resulting list.

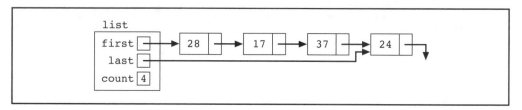

Figure 5-33   list after deleting 54

Case 4: The node to be deleted is not in the list. In this case, the list requires no adjustment. We simply output an error message, indicating that the item to be deleted is not in the list.

From Cases 2, 3, and 4 it follows that the deletion of a node requires us to traverse the list. Because a linked list is not a random access data structure, we must sequentially search the list. (We handle Case 1 separately, because it does not require us to traverse the list.)

We sequentially search the list starting at the second node. If the node to be deleted is in the middle of the list, we need to adjust the link field of the node just before the node to be deleted. Thus, we need a pointer to the previous node. When we search the list for the given info, we use two pointers: one to check the info of the current node, and one to keep track of the node just before the current node. If the node to be deleted is the last node, we must adjust the pointer last.

The definition of the function deleteNode is

```
template<class Type>
void linkedListType<Type>::deleteNode(const Type& deleteItem)
{
    nodeType<Type> *current; //pointer to traverse the list
    nodeType<Type> *trailCurrent; //pointer just before current
    bool found;

    if(first == NULL)      //Case 1; list is empty.
        cerr<<"Cannot delete from an empty list.\n";
    else
    {
        if(first->info == deleteItem) //Case 2
        {
            current = first;
            first = first->link;
            count--;
```

```
         if(first == NULL)      //list has only one node
            last = NULL;
         delete current;
      }
      else  //search the list for the node with the given info
      {
         found = false;
         trailCurrent = first;   //set trailCurrent to point to
                                 //the first node
         current = first->link;  //set current to point to the
                                 //second node

         while(current != NULL && !found)
         {
            if(current->info != deleteItem)
            {
               trailCurrent = current;
               current = current->link;
            }
            else
               found = true;
         } // end while

         if(found) //Case 3; if found, delete the node
         {
            trailCurrent->link = current->link;
            count--;

            if(last == current)      //node to be deleted was
                                     //the last node
               last = trailCurrent;  //update the value of last

            delete current;   //delete the node from the list
         }
         else
            cout<<"Item to be deleted is not in the list."<<endl;
      } //end else
   }//end else
} //end deleteNode
```

From the definition of the function `deleteNode`, it can be shown that this function is of O(*n*).

Copy List

The function `copyList` makes an identical copy of a linked list. Therefore, we traverse the list to be copied starting at the first node. Corresponding to each node in the original list, we:

1. Create a node, and call it `newNode`.

2. Copy the `info` of the node (in the original list) into `newNode`.

3. Insert `newNode` at the end of the list being created.

The definition of the function `copyList` is

```
template<class Type>
void linkedListType<Type>::copyList
                    (const linkedListType<Type>& otherList)
{
    nodeType<Type> *newNode; //pointer to create a node
    nodeType<Type> *current; //pointer to traverse the list

    if(first != NULL)  //if the list is nonempty, make it empty
        destroyList();

    if(otherList.first == NULL) //otherList is empty
    {
        first = NULL;
        last = NULL;
        count = 0;
    }
    else
    {
        current = otherList.first;   //current points to the
                                     //list to be copied
        count = otherList.count;

            //copy the first node
        first = new nodeType<Type>;   //create the node

        assert(first != NULL);

        first->info = current->info;  //copy the info
        first->link = NULL;           //set the link field of
                                      //the node to NULL
        last = first;                 //make last point to the
                                      //first node
        current = current->link;      //make current point to
                                      //the next node
```

```
            //copy the remaining list
        while(current != NULL)
        {
            newNode = new nodeType<Type>;   //create a node

            assert(newNode!= NULL);

            newNode->info = current->info;  //copy the info
            newNode->link = NULL;           //set the link of
                                            //newNode to NULL
            last->link = newNode;      //attach newNode after last
            last = newNode;            //make last point to
                                       //the actual last node
            current = current->link; //make current point to
                                     //the next node
        }//end while
    }//end else
}//end copyList
```

The function `copyList` contains a `while` loop. The number of times the `while` loop executes depends on the number of items in the list. If the list contains n items, the `while` loop executes n times. From this, it can be shown that the function `copyList` is of $O(n)$.

Destructor

The purpose of the destructor is to deallocate the memory occupied by the nodes of a list when the class object goes out of scope. Because memory is allocated dynamically, resetting the pointers `first` and `last` does not deallocate the memory occupied by the nodes in the list. We must traverse the list, starting at the first node, and delete each node in the list. To destroy the list, you can call the function `destroyList`. Therefore, the definition of the destructor is

```
template<class Type>
linkedListType<Type>::~linkedListType() //destructor
{
    destroyList();
}//end destructor
```

Copy Constructor

Because the `class linkedListType` contains pointer data members, the definition of this class contains the copy constructor. Recall that if a formal parameter is a value parameter, the copy constructor provides the formal parameter with its own copy of the data. The copy constructor also executes when an object is declared and initialized using another object. (For more information, see Chapter 3.)

The copy constructor makes an identical copy of the linked list. This can be accomplished by calling the function `copyList`. Now the function `copyList` checks whether the original list is empty by checking the value of `first`. Therefore, we must initialize the pointer `first` to `NULL` before calling the function `copyList`.

The definition of the copy constructor is

```
template<class Type>
linkedListType<Type>::linkedListType
                    (const linkedListType<Type>& otherList)
{
   first = NULL;
   copyList(otherList);
}//end copy constructor
```

Overloading the Assignment Operator

The definition of the function to overload the assignment operator for the **class** `linkedListType` is very similar to the definition of the copy constructor. We give its definition here for the sake of completeness.

```
template<class Type>
const linkedListType<Type>& linkedListType<Type>::operator=
                    (const linkedListType<Type>& otherList)
{
   if(this != &otherList) //avoid self-copy
      copyList(otherList);

   return *this;
}
```

The destructor uses the function `destroyList`, which is of $O(n)$. The copy constructor and the function to overload the assignment operator use the function `copyList`, which is of $O(n)$. Therefore, each of these functions is of $O(n)$.

Table 5-5 summarizes the time-complexity of the operations of the **class** `linkedListType`.

Table 5-5 Time-Complexity of the Operations of the `class linkedListType`

Function	Time-Complexity
`isEmptyList`	$O(1)$
Default constructor	$O(1)$
`destroyList`	$O(n)$
`initializeList`	$O(n)$
Overloading the stream insertion operator	$O(n)$
`length`	$O(1)$
`front`	$O(1)$
`back`	$O(1)$
`search`	$O(n)$
`insertFirst`	$O(1)$
`insertLast`	$O(1)$
`deleteNode`	$O(n)$
`copyList`	$O(n)$
Destructor	$O(n)$
Copy constructor	$O(n)$
Overloading the assignment operator	$O(n)$

 When you create the header file for the `class linkedListType`, you must include the following statements before the definition of the class:

```
#include <iostream>

#include <cassert>

using namespace std;
```

ORDERED LINKED LISTS

Now that you have some idea how pointer variables are used in C++ to dynamically allocate and deallocate memory and how to build and process linked lists, this section discusses how to build ordered linked lists and describes various operations on these lists. The following operations are usually performed on an ordered list:

1. Initialize the list.

2. Check whether the list is empty.

3. Output the list.

4. Output the list in reverse order.

5. Destroy the list.

6. Search the list for a given item.

7. Insert an item in the list.

8. Delete an item from the list.

9. Find the length of the list.

10. Make a copy of the list.

Many of the operations on ordered linked lists are similar to the operations on general lists discussed in the last section. Because the list is ordered, we need to modify only the algorithms to implement the search, insert, and delete operations. Therefore, we derive the class to define the ordered linked list as an ADT from the **class linkedListType**.

To output the data stored in each node in reverse order, the list needs to be traversed in reverse order starting at the last node. Because the links are in only one direction, using the links, we cannot traverse the list backwards. In Chapter 6, we show how to use recursion to traverse a linked list backwards.

The following class defines an ordered linked list as an ADT.

```
template<class Type>
class orderedLinkedListType: public linkedListType<Type>
{
public:
    bool search(const Type& searchItem);
      //Function to determine whether searchItem is in the list.
      //Postcondition: Returns true if searchItem is found in
      //               the list; otherwise, it returns false.

    void insertNode(const Type& newItem);
      //Function to insert newItem in the list.
      //Postcondition: first points to the new list and newItem is
      //               inserted at the proper place in the list, and
      //               count is incremented by 1.

    void deleteNode(const Type& deleteItem);
      //Function to delete deleteItem from the list.
      //Postcondition: If found, the node containing deleteItem
      //               is deleted from the list; first points
      //               to the first node of the new list, and
      //               count is decremented by 1.
      //               If deleteItem is not in the list, an
      //               appropriate message is printed.
};
```

The class `orderedLinkedListType` is derived from the class `linkedListType`. The class `linkedListType` provides the function `insertFirst` to insert an element at the beginning of the list, and the function `insertLast` to insert an element at the end of the list. However, we are now discussing ordered linked lists, in which the elements are ordered according to some criteria. If an element is to be inserted in an ordered list, it must be inserted at the proper place. Even though you can use the functions `insertFirst` and `insertLast` to insert an item at the beginning or the end, there is no guarantee that the resulting list would be ordered. Therefore, we shall not use these functions with ordered linked lists. Moreover, because the elements are to be inserted at the proper place, as described in the upcoming section, "Insert Node," the pointer `last` plays no role in constructing ordered lists. Therefore, we ignore the pointer `last`, which is set to `NULL`, and use only the pointer `first`. Also, the function `back` of the class `linkedListType` uses the pointer `last` to return the last element of the list. Because the pointer `last` is not used for ordered linked lists, we do not use the function `back` to return the last element of an ordered linked list (unless you override the definition of this function for the class `orderedLinkedListType`; see Programming Exercise 8.)

5

Search List

First, we discuss the search operation. The algorithm to implement the search operation is similar to the search algorithm for general lists discussed in the section, "Linked List as an ADT," located earlier in this chapter. Here, because the list is sorted, we can improve the search algorithm somewhat. As before, we start the search at the first node in the list. We stop the search as soon as we either find a node in the list with the `info` greater than or equal to the search item, or we have searched the entire list.

This algorithm has the following steps:

1. Compare the search item with the current node in the list. If the `info` of the current node is greater than or equal to the search item, stop the search; otherwise, make the next node the current node.

2. Repeat Step 1 until either an item in the list that is greater than or equal to the search item is found, or no more data is left in the list to compare with the search item.

Note that the loop does not explicitly check whether the search item is equal to an item in the list. Thus, after the loop executes, we must check whether the search item is equal to the item in the list.

```
template<class Type>
bool orderedLinkedListType<Type>::search(const Type& searchItem)
{
    bool found;
    nodeType<Type> *current; //pointer to traverse the list

    found = false;     //initialize found to false
    current = first;   //start the search at the first node
```

```
    while(current != NULL && !found)
       if(current->info >= searchItem)
           found = true;
       else
           current = current->link;

    if(found)
       found = (current->info == searchItem); //test for equality

    return found;
}//end search
```

Insert Node

To insert an item in an ordered linked list, we first find the place where the new item is supposed to go, and then insert it in the list. To find the place for the new item in the list, as before, we search the list. Here we use two pointers, `current` and `trailCurrent`, to search the list. The pointer `current` points to the node whose `info` is being compared with the item to be inserted; `trailCurrent` points to the node just before `current`. Because the list is in order, the search algorithm is the same as before. The following cases arise:

Case 1: The list is initially empty. The node containing the new item is the only node and thus the first node in the list.

Case 2: The list is not empty, and the new item is smaller than the smallest item in the list. The new item goes at the beginning of the list. In this case, we need to adjust the list's head pointer—that is, `first`. Also, `count` is incremented by 1.

Case 3: The list is not empty, and the item to be inserted is larger than the first item in the list. The item is to be inserted somewhere in the list.

> **Case 3a**: The new item is larger than all the items in the list. In this case, the new item is inserted at the end of the list. Thus, the value of `current` is `NULL` and the new item is inserted after `trailCurrent`. Also, `count` is incremented by 1.

> **Case 3b**: The new item is to be inserted somewhere in the middle of the list. In this case, the new item is inserted between `trailCurrent` and `current`. Also, `count` is incremented by 1.

The following statements can accomplish both Cases 3a and 3b (assume `newNode` points to the new node):

```
trailCurrent->link = newNode;
newNode->link = current;
```

Let us next illustrate these cases.

Case 1: The list is empty.

Consider the list shown in Figure 5-34.

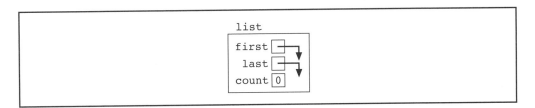

Figure 5-34   Empty list

Suppose that we want to insert 27 in the list. To accomplish this task, we create a node, copy 27 into the node, set the link of the node to NULL, and have first point to the node. Figure 5-35 shows the resulting list.

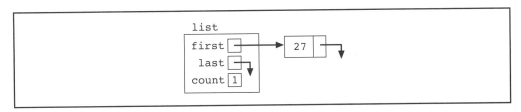

Figure 5-35   list after inserting 27

Notice that, after inserting 27, the values of first and count change.

Case 2: The list is not empty, and the item to be inserted is smaller than the smallest item in the list. Consider the list shown in Figure 5-36.

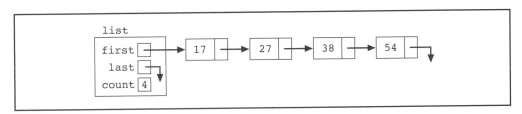

Figure 5-36   Nonempty list before inserting 10

Suppose that 10 is to be inserted. After inserting 10 in the list, the node with info 10 becomes the first node of list. This requires us to change the value of first. Also, count is incremented by 1. Figure 5-37 shows the resulting list.

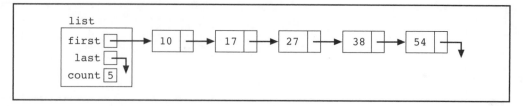

Figure 5-37 list after inserting 10

Case 3: The list is not empty, and the item to be inserted is larger than the first item in the list. As indicated previously, this case has two scenarios.

Case 3a: The item to be inserted is larger than the largest item in the list; that is, it goes at the end of the list. Consider the list shown in Figure 5-38.

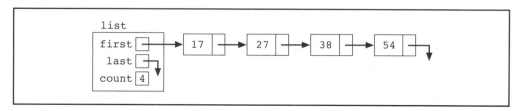

Figure 5-38 list before inserting 65

Suppose that we want to insert **65** in the list. After inserting **65**, the resulting list is as shown in Figure 5-39.

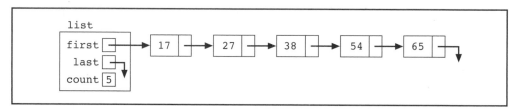

Figure 5-39 list after inserting 65

Case 3b: The item to be inserted goes somewhere in the middle of the list. Consider the list shown in Figure 5-40.

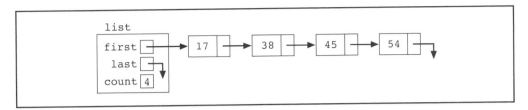

Figure 5-40   `list` before inserting 27

Suppose that we want to insert 27 in this list. Clearly, 27 goes between 17 and 38, which would require the link of the node with `info` 17 to be changed. After inserting 27, the resulting list is as shown in Figure 5-41.

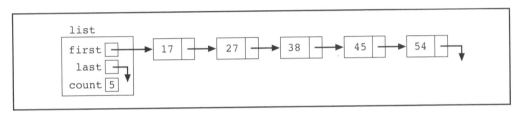

Figure 5-41   `list` after inserting 27

From Case 3, it follows that we must first traverse the list to find the place where the new item is to be inserted. As indicated previously, we must traverse the list with two pointers—say, `current` and `trailCurrent`. The pointer `current` traverses the list and compares the `info` of the node in the list with the item to be inserted. The pointer `trailCurrent` points to the node just before `current`. For example, in Case 3b, when the search stops, `trailCurrent` points to node 17 and `current` points to node 38. The item is inserted after `trailCurrent`. In Case 3a, after searching the list to find the place for 65, `trailCurrent` points to node 54 and `current` is NULL.

Essentially, the function `insertNode` is

```
template<class Type>
void orderedLinkedListType<Type>::insertNode(const Type& newitem)
{
    nodeType<Type> *current;        //pointer to traverse the list
    nodeType<Type> *trailCurrent;   //pointer just before current
    nodeType<Type> *newNode;        //pointer to create a node

    bool  found;
```

```
newNode = new nodeType<Type>; //create the node
assert(newNode != NULL);

newNode->info = newitem;    //store newitem in the node
newNode->link = NULL;       //set the link field of the node
                            //to NULL

if(first == NULL)   //Case 1
{
    first = newNode;
    count++;
}
else
{
    current = first;
    found = false;

    while(current != NULL && !found) //search the list
        if(current->info >= newitem)
            found = true;
        else
        {
            trailCurrent = current;
            current = current->link;
        }

    if(current == first)    //Case 2
    {
        newNode->link = first;
        first = newNode;
        count++;
    }
    else                            //Case 3
    {
        trailCurrent->link = newNode;
        newNode->link = current;
        count++;
    }
}//end else
}//end insertNode
```

 The function `insertNode` does not check whether the item to be inserted is already in the list; that is, it does not check for duplicates. Programming Exercise 7, at the end of this chapter, asks you to revise the definition of the function `insertNode`, so before inserting the item, check whether it is already in the list. If the item to be inserted is already in the list, the function outputs an appropriate error message. In other words, duplicates are not allowed.

Delete Node

To delete a given item from an ordered linked list, first we search the list to see whether the item to be deleted is in the list. The function to implement this operation is the same as the delete operation on general linked lists. Here, because the list is sorted, we can somewhat improve the algorithm for ordered linked lists.

As in the case of `insertNode`, we search the list with two pointers, `current` and `trailCurrent`. Similar to the operation `insertNode`, several cases arise:

Case 1: The list is initially empty. We have an error. We cannot delete from an empty list.

Case 2: The item to be deleted is contained in the first node of the list. We must adjust the head pointer of the list—that is, `first`.

Case 3: The item to be deleted is somewhere in the list. In this case, `current` points to the node containing the item to be deleted, and `trailCurrent` points to the node just before the node pointed to by `current`.

Case 4: The list is not empty, but the item to be deleted is not in the list.

After deleting the node, `count` is decremented by 1. The definition of the function `deleteNode` is

```
template<class Type>
void orderedLinkedListType<Type>::deleteNode
                              (const Type& deleteItem)
{
    nodeType<Type> *current;       //pointer to traverse the list
    nodeType<Type> *trailCurrent; //pointer just before current
    bool found;

    if(first == NULL) //Case 1
        cerr<<"Cannot delete from an empty list."<<endl;
    else
    {
        current = first;
        found = false;

        while(current != NULL && !found)  //search the list
            if(current->info >= deleteItem)
                found = true;
            else
            {
                trailCurrent = current;
                current = current->link;
            }

        if(current == NULL)     //Case 4
            cout<<"The item to be deleted is not in the list."
                <<endl;
```

5

```
            else
               if(current->info == deleteItem) //item to be deleted
                                                     //is in the list
               {
                  if(first == current)       //Case 2
                  {
                     first = first->link;

                     delete current;
                  }
                  else                    //Case 3
                  {
                     trailCurrent->link = current->link;
                     delete current;
                  }
                  count--;
               }
               else                         //Case 4
                  cout<<"The item to be deleted is not in the list."
                        <<endl;
      }
} //end deleteNode
```

Header File of the Ordered Linked List

For the sake of completeness, we now show how to create the header file that defines the class orderedLinkedListType and the operations on such lists. (We assume that the definition of the class linkedListType and the definitions of the functions to implement the operations are in the header file linkedlist.h.)

```
//Ordered linked list derived from general linked list
//Header File: orderedLinkedList.h

#ifndef H_orderedLinkedListType
#define H_orderedLinkedListType

#include <iostream>
#include <cassert>
#include "linkedlist.h"

using namespace std;

template<class Type>
class orderedLinkedListType: public linkedListType<Type>
{
public:
  bool search(const Type& searchItem);
  void insertNode(const Type& newitem);
  void deleteNode(const Type& deleteitem);
};
```

```
//Place the definitions of the functions search,
//insertNode, and deleteNode here.

#endif
```

The following program tests various operations on an ordered linked list:

```
//Program to test various operations on an ordered linked list

#include <iostream>
#include "orderedLinkedList.h"

using namespace std;

int main()
{
    orderedLinkedListType<int> list1, list2;      //Line 1
    int num;                                      //Line 2

    cout<<"Line 3: Enter integers ending with -999"
        <<endl;                                   //Line 3
    cin>>num;                                     //Line 4

    while(num != -999)                            //Line 5
    {
        list1.insertNode(num);                    //Line 6
        cin>>num;                                 //Line 7
    }

    cout<<endl;                                   //Line 8

    cout<<"Line 9: List 1: "<<list1<<endl;        //Line 9

    list2 = list1; //test the assignment operator; Line 10

    cout<<"Line 11: List 2: "<<list2<<endl;       //Line 11

    cout<<"Line 12: Enter the number to be "
        <<"deleted: ";                            //Line 12
    cin>>num;                                     //Line 13
    cout<<endl;                                   //Line 14

    list2.deleteNode(num);                        //Line 15

    cout<<"Line 16: After deleting the node, "
        <<"List 2: "<<endl<<list2
        <<endl;                                   //Line 16

    return 0;
}
```

5

Sample Run: In this sample run, the user input is shaded.

```
Line 3: Enter integers ending with -999
23 65 34 72 12 82 36 55 29 -999

Line 9: List 1: 12 23 29 34 36 55 65 72 82
Line 11: List 2: 12 23 29 34 36 55 65 72 82
Line 12: Enter the number to be deleted: 36

Line 16: After deleting the node, List 2:
12 23 29 34 55 65 72 82
```

DOUBLY LINKED LISTS

A doubly linked list is a linked list in which every node has a **next** pointer and a **back** pointer. In other words, every node (except the last node) contains the address of the next node, and every node (except the first node) contains the address of the previous node. See Figure 5-42.

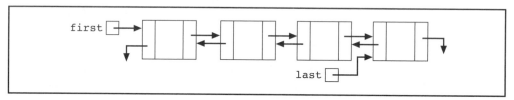

Figure 5-42 Doubly linked list

A doubly linked list can be traversed in either direction. That is, we can traverse the list starting at the first node or, if a pointer to the last node is given, we can traverse the list starting at the last node.

As before, the usual operations on a doubly linked list are:

1. Initialize the list.
2. Destroy the list.
3. Determine whether the list is empty.
4. Search the list for a given item.
5. Retrieve the first element of the list.
6. Retrieve the last element of the list.
7. Insert an item in the list.
8. Delete an item from the list.
9. Find the length of the list.

10. Output the list.

11. Make a copy of the list.

The following class defines a doubly linked list as an ADT:

```cpp
//Definition of the node
template<class Type>
struct nodeType
{
   Type info;
   nodeType<Type> *next;
   nodeType<Type> *back;
};

template <class Type>
class doublyLinkedList
{
    friend ostream& operator<<(ostream&,
                         const doublyLinkedList<Type>&);
       //Overload the stream insertion operator.
public:
    const doublyLinkedList<Type>& operator=
                        (const doublyLinkedList<Type> &);
       //Overload the assignment operator.

    void initializeList();
       //Function to initialize the list to an empty state.
       //Postcondition: first = NULL; last = NULL; count = 0

    bool isEmptyList();
       //Function to determine whether the list is empty.
       //Postcondition: Returns true if the list is empty;
       //               otherwise, returns false.

    void destroy();
       //Function to delete all the nodes from the list.
       //Postcondition: first = NULL; last = NULL; count = 0

    void reversePrint();
       //Function to output the info contained in each node
       //in reverse order.

    int length();
       //Function to return the number of nodes in the list.
       //Postcondition: The value of count is returned.

    Type front();
       //Function to return the first element of the list.
       //Precondition: The list must exist and must not be empty.
```

5

```
                //Postcondition: If the list is empty, the program
                //                terminates; otherwise, the first
                //                element of the list is returned.

        Type back();
          //Function to return the last element of the list.
          //Precondition: The list must exist and must not be empty.
          //Postcondition: If the list is empty, the program
          //                terminates; otherwise, the last
          //                element of the list is returned.

        bool search(const Type& searchItem);
          //Function to determine whether searchItem is in the list.
          //Postcondition: Returns true if searchItem is found
          //                in the list; otherwise, returns false.

        void insertNode(const Type& insertItem);
          //Function to insert newItem in the list.
          //Precondition: If the list is nonempty, it must be in
          //                order.
          //Postcondition: newItem is inserted at the proper place
          //                in the list; first points to the first
          //                node, last points to the last node of the
          //                new list and count is incremented by 1.

        void deleteNode(const Type& deleteItem);
          //Function to delete deleteItem from the list.
          //Postcondition: If found, the node containing
          //   deleteItem is deleted from the list, first points
          //   to the first node of the new list, last points to
          //   the last node of the new list, and count is
          //   decremented by 1; otherwise, an appropriate
          //   message is printed.

        doublyLinkedList();
          //default constructor
          //Initializes the list to an empty state.
          //Postcondition: first = NULL; last = NULL; count = 0

        doublyLinkedList(const doublyLinkedList<Type>& otherList);
          //copy constructor
        ~doublyLinkedList();
          //destructor
          //Postcondition: The list object is destroyed.

    protected:
        int count;
        nodeType<Type> *first; //pointer to the first node
        nodeType<Type> *last;  //pointer to the last node
```

```
private:
    void copyList(const doublyLinkedList<Type>& otherList);
        //Function to make a copy of otherList.
        //Postcondition: A copy of otherList is created and
        //               assigned to this list.
};
```

The functions to implement the operations of a doubly linked list are similar to the ones discussed in the previous two sections. Here, because every node has two pointers, `back` and `next`, some of the operations require the adjustment of two pointers in each node. We give the definition of each function here, with four exceptions. Definitions of the functions `copyList`, the copy constructor, and destructor, and overloading the assignment operator are left as exercises for you. (See Programming Exercise 9 at the end of this chapter.)

Default Constructor

The default constructor initializes the doubly linked list to an empty state. It sets `first` and `last` to NULL, and `count` to 0. Its definition is:

```
template<class Type>
doublyLinkedList<Type>::doublyLinkedList()
{
    first= NULL;
    last = NULL;
    count = 0;
}
```

isEmptyList

This operation returns `true` if the list is empty; otherwise, it returns `false`. The list is empty if the pointer `first` is NULL. Its definition is

```
template<class Type>
bool doublyLinkedList<Type>::isEmptyList()
{
    return(first == NULL);
}
```

Destroy List

This operation deletes all the nodes in the list, leaving the list in an empty state. We traverse the list starting at the first node and then delete each node. Its definition is

```
template<class Type>
void doublyLinkedList<Type>::destroy()
{
    nodeType<Type> *temp; //pointer to delete the node

    while(first != NULL)
    {
        temp = first;
        first = first->next;
        delete temp;
    }
    last = NULL:

    count = 0;
}
```

Initialize List

This operation reinitializes the doubly linked list to an empty state. This task can be accomplished by using the operation `destroy`. The definition of the function `initializeList` is

```
template<class Type>
void doublyLinkedList<Type>::initializeList()
{
    destroy();
}
```

Length of the List

The length of a list is the number of nodes in the list. Its definition is

```
template<class Type>
int doublyLinkedList<Type>::length()
{
    return count;
}
```

Overload the Stream Insertion Operator

To output the data stored in the nodes of a doubly linked list, the stream insertion operator is overloaded. To output the data contained in each node, we must traverse the list starting at the first node. Because the pointer `first` always points to the first node in the list, we use another pointer to traverse the list. The definition of the function to overload the stream insertion operator is

```
template<class Type>
ostream& operator<<(ostream& osObject,
                    const doublyLinkedList<Type>& list)
{
    nodeType<Type> *current;   //pointer to traverse the list

    current = list.first;      //set current to point to
                               //the first node

    while(current != NULL)
    {
        cout<<current->info<<" "; //output the info
        current = current->next;
    }//end while

    return osObject;
}
```

Reverse Print List

This function outputs the info contained in each node in reverse order. We traverse the list in reverse order starting with the last node. Its definition is

```
template<class Type>
void doublyLinkedList<Type>::reversePrint()
{
    nodeType<Type> *current; //pointer to traverse
                             //the list

    current = last; //set current to point to the
                    //last node

    while(current != NULL)
    {
        cout<<current->info<<" ";
        current = current->back;
    }//end while
}//end reversePrint
```

Search List

The function search returns true if the searchItem is in the list; otherwise, it returns false. This search algorithm is exactly the same as the search algorithm for an ordered linked list. Its definition is

```
template<class Type>
bool doublyLinkedList<Type>::search(const Type& searchItem)
{
    bool found;
    nodeType<Type> *current; //pointer to traverse the list

    found = false;
    current = first;

    while(current != NULL && !found)
        if(current->info >= searchItem)
            found = true;
        else
            current = current->next;

    if(found)
        found = (current->info == searchItem); //test for equality

    return found;
}//end search
```

First and Last Element

The function **front** returns the first element of the list; the function **back** returns the last element. If the list is empty, both functions terminate the program. Their definitions are

```
template<class Type>
Type doublyLinkedList<Type>::front()
{
    assert(first != NULL);

    return first->info;
}

template<class Type>
Type doublyLinkedList<Type>::back()
{
    assert(last != NULL);

    return last->info;
}
```

Insert Node

Because we are inserting an item in a doubly linked list, the insertion of a node in the list requires the adjustment of two pointers in certain nodes. As before, we find the place where the new item is supposed to be inserted, create the node, store the new item, and adjust the link fields of the new node and other specific nodes in the list. There are four cases:

Case 1: Insertion in an empty list.

Case 2: Insertion at the beginning of a nonempty list.

Case 3: Insertion at the end of a nonempty list.

Case 4: Insertion somewhere in a nonempty list.

Cases 1 and 2 require us to change the value of the pointer `first`. Cases 3 and 4 are similar. After inserting the item, `count` is incremented by 1. Next, we show Case 4.

Consider the doubly linked list shown in Figure 5-43.

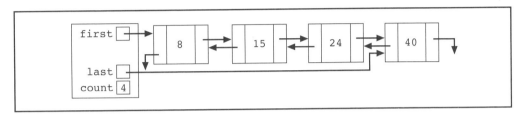

Figure 5-43   Doubly linked list before inserting 20

Suppose that 20 is to be inserted in the list. After inserting 20, Figure 5-44 shows the resulting list.

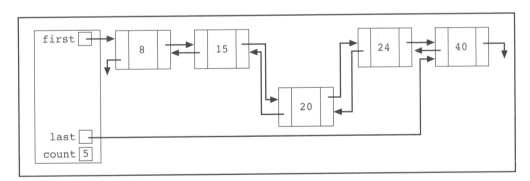

Figure 5-44   Doubly linked list after inserting 20

Figure 5-44 shows that the `next` pointer of node 15, the `back` pointer of node 24, and both the `next` and `back` pointers of node 20 need to be adjusted.

The definition of the function `insertNode` is

```
template<class Type>
void doublyLinkedList<Type>::insertNode(const Type& insertItem)
{
```

```
nodeType<Type> *current;        //pointer to traverse the list
nodeType<Type> *trailCurrent; //pointer just before current
nodeType<Type> *newNode;        //pointer to create a node
bool found;

newNode = new nodeType<Type>; //create the node
assert(newNode != NULL);

newNode->info = insertItem;   //store the new item in the node
newNode->next = NULL;
newNode->back = NULL;

if(first == NULL) //if the list is empty, newNode is
                  //the only node
{
   first = newNode;
   last = newNode;
   count++;
}
else
{
    found = false;
    current = first;

    while(current != NULL && !found) //search the list
        if(current->info >= insertItem)
           found = true;
        else
        {
           trailCurrent = current;
           current = current->next;
        }

    if(current == first) //insert new node before first
    {
       first->back = newNode;
       newNode->next = first;
       first = newNode;
       count++;
    }
    else
    {
           //insert newNode between trailCurrent and current
        if(current != NULL)
        {
           trailCurrent->next = newNode;
           newNode->back = trailCurrent;
           newNode->next = current;
           current->back = newNode;
        }
```

```
        else
        {
            trailCurrent->next = newNode;
            newNode->back = trailCurrent;
            last = newNode;
        }
        count++;
    }//end else
  }//end else
}//end insertNode
```

Delete Node

This operation deletes a given item (if found) from a doubly linked list. As before, we first search the list to see whether the item to be deleted is in the list. The search algorithm is also the same as before. Similar to the `insertNode` operation, this operation (if the item to be deleted is in the list) requires the adjustment of two pointers in certain nodes. The delete operation has several cases:

Case 1: The list is empty.

Case 2: The item to be deleted is in the first node of the list, which would require us to change the value of the pointer `first`.

Case 3: The item to be deleted is somewhere in the list.

Case 4: The item to be deleted is not in the list.

After deleting the node, `count` is decremented by 1. Let us demonstrate Case 3. Consider the list shown in Figure 5-45.

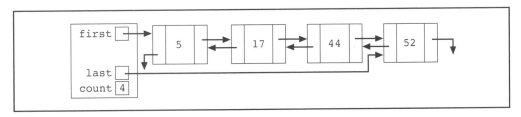

Figure 5-45   Doubly linked list before deleting 17

Suppose that the item to be deleted is 17. We search the list with two pointers and find the node with `info` 17, and then adjust the link fields of the affected nodes. See Figure 5-46.

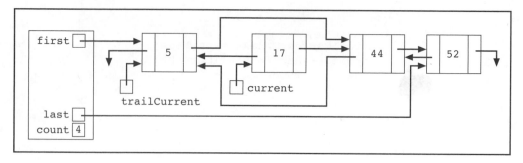

Figure 5-46 List after adjusting the links of the nodes before and after the node with info 17

Next, we decrement **count** by 1 and delete the node pointed to by **current**. See Figure 5-47.

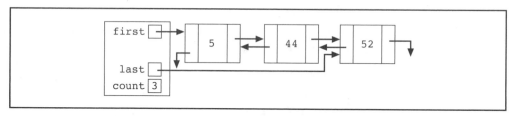

Figure 5-47 List after deleting the node with info 17

The definition of the function **deleteNode** is

```
template<class Type>
void doublyLinkedList<Type>::deleteNode(const Type& deleteItem)
{
    nodeType<Type> *current;       //pointer to traverse the list
    nodeType<Type> *trailCurrent; //pointer just before current

    bool found;

    if(first == NULL)
        cout<<"Cannot delete from an empty list"<<endl;
    else
        if(first->info == deleteItem) //node to be deleted is the
                                      //first node
        {
            current = first;
            first = first->next;
```

```
        if(first != NULL)
            first->back = NULL;
        else
            last = NULL;

        count--;
        delete current;
    }
    else
    {
        found = false;
        current = first;

        while(current != NULL && !found)  //search the list
            if(current->info >= deleteItem)
                found = true;
            else
                current = current->next;

        if(current == NULL)
          cout<<"The item to be deleted is not in the list."
                <<endl;
        else
            if(current->info == deleteItem) //check for equality
            {
                trailCurrent = current->back;
                trailCurrent->next = current->next;

                if(current->next != NULL)
                    current->next->back = trailCurrent;

                if(current == last)
                    last = trailCurrent;

                count--;
                delete current;
            }
            else
                cout<<"The item to be deleted is not in the list."
                        <<endl;
    }//end else
}//end deleteNode
```

The analyses of the functions of the `class doublyLinkedList` are similar to that of the `class linkedListType` and, therefore, are left as exercises for you.

STL SEQUENCE CONTAINER: `list`

Chapter 4 listed three types of sequence containers—`vector`, `deque`, and `list`. The sequence containers `vector` and `deque` are described in Chapter 4. This section describes the STL sequence container `list`. List containers are implemented as doubly linked lists. Thus, every element in a list points to its immediate predecessor and to its immediate successor (except the first and last elements). Recall that a linked list is not a random access data structure such as an array. Therefore, to access, say, the fifth element in the list, we must first traverse the first four elements.

The name of the class containing the definition of the `class list` is `list`. The definition of the `class list`, and the definitions of the functions to implement various operations on a list, are contained in the header file `list`. Therefore, to use `list` in a program, the program must include the following statement:

```
#include <list>
```

Like other container classes, the **class list** contains several constructors. Thus, a `list` object can be initialized in several ways when it is declared, as shown in Table 5-6.

Table 5-6 Various Ways to Declare a `list` Object

Statement	Effect
`list<elementType> listCont;`	Creates the empty list `listCont` without any elements. (The default constructor is invoked.)
`list<elementType> listCont(otherList);`	Creates the list `listCont` and initializes `listCont` to the elements of `otherList`. `listCont` and `otherList` are of the same type.
`list<elementType> listCont(size);`	Creates the list `listCont` of size `size`. `listCont` is initialized using the default constructor.
`list<elementType> listCont(n, elem);`	Creates the list `listCont` of size n. `listCont` is initialized using n copies of the element `elem`.
`list<elementType> listCont(begin, end);`	Creates the list `listCont`. `listCont` is initialized to the elements in the range `(begin, end)`—that is, all the elements in the range `begin...end-1`.

Table 4-5 (in Chapter 4) describes the operations that are common to all containers, and Table 4-6 describes the operations that are common to all sequence containers. In addition to these common operations, Table 5-7 describes the operations that are specific to a `list` container. The name of the function implementing the operation is shown in bold.

Suppose that `listCont` is a container of the type `list`.

Table 5-7 Operations Specific to a `list` Container

Expression	Effect
`listCont.assign(n, elem)`	Assigns `n` copies of `elem`.
`listCont.assign(beg, end)`	Assigns all the elements in the range `beg...end-1`.
`listCont.push_front(elem)`	Inserts `elem` at the beginning of `listCont`.
`listCont.pop_front()`	Removes the last element from `listCont`.
`listCont.front()`	Returns the first element. (Does not check whether the container is empty.)
`listCont.back()`	Returns the last element. (Does not check whether the container is empty.)
`listCont.remove(elem)`	Removes all the elements that are equal to `elem`.
`listCont.remove_if(oper)`	Removes all the elements for which `oper(elem)` is `true`.
`listCont.unique()`	If consecutive elements in `listCont` have the same value, removes the duplicates.
`listCont.unique(oper)`	If consecutive elements in `listCont` have the same value, removes the duplicates for which `oper()` is `true`.
`listCont1.splice(pos, listCont2)`	All the elements of `listCont2` are moved to `listCont1` before the position specified by the iterator `pos`. After this operation, `listCont2` is empty.
`listCont1.splice(pos, listCont2, pos2)`	All the elements starting at `pos2` of `listCont2` are moved to `listCont1` before the position specified by the iterator `pos`.
`listCont1.splice(pos, listCont2, beg, end)`	All the elements in the range `beg...end-1` of `listCont2` are moved to `listCont1` before the position specified by the iterator `pos`.
`listCont.sort()`	The elements of `listCont` are sorted. The sort criterion is `<`.

5

Table 5-7 Operations Specific to a `list` Container (continued)

Expression	Effect
`listCont.`**`sort`**`(oper)`	The elements of `listCont` are sorted. The sort criterion is specified by `oper`.
`listCont1.`**`merge`**`(listCont2)`	Suppose that the elements of `listCont1` and `listCont2` are sorted. This operation moves all the elements of `listCont2` into `listCont1`. After this operation, the elements in `listCont1` are sorted and `listCont2` is empty.
`listCont1.`**`merge`**`(listCont2, oper)`	Suppose that the elements of `listCont1` and `listCont2` are sorted according to the sort criterion `oper`. This operation moves all the elements of `listCont2` into `listCont1`. After this operation, the elements in `listCont1` are sorted according to the sort criterion `oper`.
`listCont.`**`reverse`**`()`	The elements of `listCont` are reversed.

Example 5-1 shows how to use various operations on a list container.

Example 5-1

```
//List Container Example
#include <iostream>
#include <list>
#include <iterator>
#include <algorithm>

using namespace std;

int main()
{
    list<int> intList1, intList2, intList3, intList4;     //Line 1

    ostream_iterator<int> screen(cout," ");               //Line 2

    intList1.push_back(23);                               //Line 3
    intList1.push_back(58);                               //Line 4
    intList1.push_back(58);                               //Line 5
    intList1.push_back(58);                               //Line 6
    intList1.push_back(36);                               //Line 7
    intList1.push_back(15);                               //Line 8
    intList1.push_back(93);                               //Line 9
    intList1.push_back(98);                               //Line 10
    intList1.push_back(58);                               //Line 11
```

```
cout<<"Line 12: intList1: ";                            //Line 12
copy(intList1.begin(), intList1.end(), screen);         //Line 13
cout<<endl;                                              //Line 14

intList2 = intList1;                                    //Line 15

cout<<"Line 16: intList2: ";                            //Line 16
copy(intList2.begin(), intList2.end(), screen);         //Line 17
cout<<endl;                                              //Line 18

intList1.unique();                                      //Line 19

cout<<"Line 20: After removing the consecutive "
    <<"duplicates,"<<endl
    <<"        intList1: ";                             //Line 20
copy(intList1.begin(), intList1.end(), screen);         //Line 21
cout<<endl;                                              //Line 22

intList2.sort();                                        //Line 23

cout<<"Line 24: After sorting, intList2: ";             //Line 24
copy(intList2.begin(), intList2.end(), screen);         //Line 25
cout<<endl;                                              //Line 26

intList3.push_back(13);                                 //Line 27
intList3.push_back(23);                                 //Line 28
intList3.push_back(25);                                 //Line 29
intList3.push_back(136);                                //Line 30
intList3.push_back(198);                                //Line 31

cout<<"Line 32: intList3: ";                            //Line 32
copy(intList3.begin(), intList3.end(), screen);         //Line 33
cout<<endl;                                              //Line 34

intList4.push_back(-2);                                 //Line 35
intList4.push_back(-7);                                 //Line 36
intList4.push_back(-8);                                 //Line 37

cout<<"Line 38: intList4: ";                            //Line 38
copy(intList4.begin(), intList4.end(), screen);         //Line 39
cout<<endl;                                              //Line 40

intList3.splice(intList3.begin(), intList4);            //Line 41

cout<<"Line 42: After moving the elements of "
    <<"intList4 into intList3,"<<endl
    <<"        intList3: ";                             //Line 42
copy(intList3.begin(), intList3.end(), screen);         //Line 43
cout<<endl;                                              //Line 44
```

5

```
    intList3.sort();                                    //Line 45

    cout<<"Line 46: After sorting, intList3: ";         //Line 46
    copy(intList3.begin(), intList3.end(), screen);     //Line 47
    cout<<endl;                                          //Line 48

    intList2.merge(intList3);                           //Line 49

    cout<<"Line 50: After merging intList2 and intList3, "
        <<"intList2: "<<endl<<"    ";                   //Line 50
    copy(intList2.begin(), intList2.end(), screen);     //Line 51
    cout<<endl;                                          //Line 52

    intList2.unique();                                  //Line 53

    cout<<"Line 54: After removing the consecutive "
        <<"duplicates, intList2: "<<endl
        <<"    ";                                        //Line 54
    copy(intList2.begin(), intList2.end(), screen);     //Line 55
    cout<<endl;                                          //Line 56

    return 0;
}
```

Output

```
Line 12: intList1: 23 58 58 58 36 15 93 98 58
Line 16: intList2: 23 58 58 58 36 15 93 98 58
Line 20: After removing the consecutive duplicates,
         intList1: 23 58 36 15 93 98 58
Line 24: After sorting, intList2: 15 23 36 58 58 58 58 93 98
Line 32: intList3: 13 23 25 136 198
Line 38: intList4: -2 -7 -8
Line 42: After moving the elements of intList4 into
         intList3, intList3: -2 -7 -8 13 23 25 136 198
Line 46: After sorting, intList3: -8 -7 -2 13 23 25 136 198
Line 50: After merging intList2 and intList3, intList2:
         -8 -7 -2 13 15 23 23 25 36 58 58 58 58 93 98 136 198
Line 54: After removing the consecutive duplicates, intList2:
         -8 -7 -2 13 15 23 25 36 58 93 98 136 198
```

For the most part, the output of the preceding program is straightforward. The statements in Lines 3 through 11 insert 23, 58, 58, 58, 36, 15, 93, 98, and 58 (in that order) into intList1. The statement in Line 15 copies the elements of intList1 into intList2. After this statement executes, intList1 and intList2 are identical. The statement in Line 19 removes any consecutive occurrences of the same elements. For example, the number 58 appears consecutively three times. The operation unique removes two occurrences of 58. Note that this operation has no effect on the 58 that appears at the end of intList1.

The statement in Line 23 sorts `intList2`. The statements in Lines 27 through 31 insert `13`, `23`, `25`, `136`, and `198` into `intList3`. Similarly, the statements in Lines 35 through 37 insert `-2`, `-7`, and `-8` into `intList4`. The statement in Line 41 uses the operation `splice` to move the elements of `intList4` to the beginning of `intList3`. After the `splice` operation, `intList4` is empty. The statement in Line 45 sorts `intList3`, and the statement in Line 49 merges `intList2` and `intList3` into `intList2`. After the `merge` operation, `intList3` is empty. The meanings of the remaining statements are similar.

LINKED LISTS WITH HEADER AND TRAILER NODES

5

When inserting and deleting items from a linked list (especially an ordered list), we saw that there are special cases, such as inserting (or deleting) either at the beginning (the first node) of the list or in an empty list. These cases needed to be handled separately. As a result, the insertion and deletion algorithms were not as simple and straightforward as we would like. One way to simplify these algorithms is never to insert an item before the first or after the last item and never to delete the first node. Next we discuss how to do this.

Suppose the nodes of a list are in order; that is, they are arranged with respect to a given key. Further suppose that it is possible for us to determine what the smallest and largest keys are in the given data set. In this case, we can set up a node, called the **header**, at the beginning of the list containing a value smaller than the smallest value in the data set. Similarly, we can set up a node, called the **trailer**, at the end of the list containing a value larger than the largest value in the data set. These two nodes, header and trailer, serve merely to simplify the insertion and deletion algorithms and are not part of the actual list. The actual list is between these two nodes.

For example, suppose the data is ordered according to the last name. Further assume that the last name is a string of at most eight characters. The smallest last name is larger than the string `"A"` and the largest last name is smaller than the string `"zzzzzzzz"`. We can set up the header node with the value `"A"` and the trailer node with the value `"zzzzzzzz"`. The list in Figure 5-48 illustrates this concept.

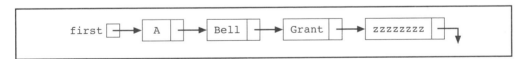

Figure 5-48   Nonempty linked list with header and trailer nodes

An empty linked list with header and trailer nodes has only two nodes, header and trailer. Figure 5-49 shows an empty linked list with header and trailer nodes.

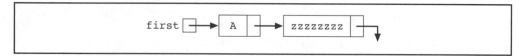

Figure 5-49   Empty linked list with header and trailer nodes

As before, the usual operations on lists with header and trailer nodes are:

1. Initialize the list (to an empty state).
2. Determine whether the list is empty.
3. Destroy the list.
4. Output the list.
5. Find the length of the list.
6. Search the list for a given item.
7. Retrieve the first and the last element of the list.
8. Insert an item in the list.
9. Delete an item from the list.
10. Copy the list.

We leave it as an exercise for you to design a class to implement a linked list with header and trailer nodes. (See Programming Exercise 11 at the end of this chapter.)

CIRCULAR LINKED LISTS

A linked list in which the last node points to the first node is called a **circular linked list**. Figures 5-50 through 5-52 shows various circular linked lists.

Figure 5-50   Empty circular linked list

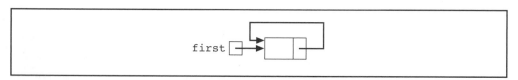

Figure 5-51   Circular linked list with one node

In a circular linked list with more than one node, it is convenient to make the pointer `first` point to the last node of the list. Then, by using the pointer `first` you can access both the first and the last nodes of the list. For example, `first` points to the last node and `first->link` points to the first node. Figure 5-52 shows a circular linked list with more than one node.

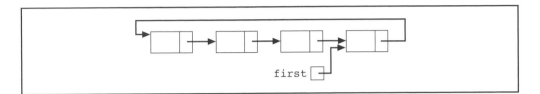

Figure 5-52 Circular linked list with more than one node

As before, the usual operations on a circular linked list are:

1. Initialize the list (to an empty state).
2. Determine whether the list is empty.
3. Destroy the list.
4. Output the list.
5. Find the length of the list.
6. Search the list for a given item.
7. Retrieve the first and the last element of the list.
8. Insert an item in the list.
9. Delete an item from the list.
10. Copy the list.

We leave it as an exercise for you to design a class to implement a sorted circular linked list. (See Programming Exercise 12 at the end of this chapter.)

PROGRAMMING EXAMPLE: VIDEO STORE

For a family or an individual, a favorite place to go on weekends or holidays is to a video store to rent movies. A new video store in your neighborhood is about to open. However, it does not have a program to keep track of its videos and customers. The store managers want someone to write a program for their system so that the video store can function. The program should be able to perform the following operations:

1. Rent a video; that is, check out a video.
2. Return, or check in, a video.
3. Create a list of videos owned by the store.

4. Show the details of a particular video.

5. Print a list of all the videos in the store.

6. Check whether a particular video is in the store.

7. Maintain a customer database.

8. Print a list of all the videos rented by each customer.

Let us write a program for the video store. This example further illustrates the object-oriented design methodology and, in particular, inheritance and overloading.

The programming requirement tells us that the video store has two major components: videos and customers. We describe these two components in detail. We also need to maintain three lists:

- A list of all the videos in the store
- A list of all the store's customers
- A list of the videos currently rented

We will develop the program in two parts. In part 1, we design, implement, and test the video component. In part 2, we design and implement the customer component, which is then added to the video component developed in part 1. After completing parts 1 and 2, we can perform all the operations listed previously.

Part 1: The Video Component

The Video Object   This is the first stage wherein we discuss the components of an object. The common things associated with a video are the:

- Name of the movie
- Names of the stars
- Name of the producer
- Name of the director
- Name of the production company
- Number of copies in the store

From this list, we see that some of the operations to be performed on the video object are:

1. Set the video information: the title, stars, production company, and so on.

2. Show the details of a particular video.

3. Check the number of copies in the store.

4. Check out (that is, rent) the video. In other words, if the number of copies is greater than zero, decrement the number of copies by one.

5. Check in (that is, return) the video. To check in a video, first we must check whether the store owns such a video and, if it does, increment the number of copies by one.

6. Check whether a particular video is available—that is, the number of copies currently in the store is greater than zero.

To delete a video from the video list, the video list must be searched for the video to be deleted. Thus, we need to check the title of a video to find out which video is to be deleted from the list. Two videos are the same if they have the same title.

The following class defines the video object as an ADT:

```cpp
#include <iostream>
#include <string>

using namespace std;

class videoType
{
  friend ostream& operator<<(ostream&, const videoType&);

public:
  void setVideoInfo(string title, string star1,
                    string star2, string producer,
                    string director, string productionCo,
                    int setInStock);
    //Function to set the details of a video.
    //Private data members are set according to the parameters.
    //Postcondition: videoTitle = title; movieStar1 = star1;
    //   movieStar2 = star2; movieProducer = producer;
    //   movieDirector = director;
    //   movieProductionCo = productionCo;
    //   copiesInStock = setInStock

  int getNoOfCopiesInStock() const;
    //Function to check the number of copies in stock.
    //Postcondition: The value of the data member copiesInStock is
    //               returned.
  void checkOut();
    //Function to rent a video.
    //Postcondition: The number of copies in stock is decremented
    //               by one.
  void checkIn();
    //Function to check in a video.
    //Postcondition: The number of copies in stock is incremented
    //               by one.
  void printTitle() const;
    //Function to print the title of a movie.
  void printInfo() const;
    //Function to print the details of a video.
    //Postcondition: The title of the movie, stars, director, and
    //               so on are displayed on the screen.
```

```
bool checkTitle(string title);
    //Function to check whether the title is the same as the title
    //of the video.
    //Postcondition: Returns true if the title is the same as
    //               the title of the video; otherwise, returns
    //               false.
void updateInStock(int num);
    //Function to increment the number of copies in stock by
    //adding the value of the parameter num.
    //Postcondition: copiesInStock = copiesInStock + num
void setCopiesInStock(int num);
    //Function to set the number of copies in stock.
    //Postcondition: copiesInStock = num
string getTitle();
    //Function to return the title of the video.
    //Postcondition: The title of the video is returned.
videoType(string title = "", string star1 = "",
          string star2 = "", string producer = "",
          string director = "", string productionCo = "",
          int setInStock = 0);
    //constructor
    //Private data members are set according to the incoming
    //parameters. If no values are specified, the default
    //values are assigned.
    //Postcondition: videoTitle = title; movieStar1 = star1;
    //   movieStar2 = star2; movieProducer = producer;
    //   movieDirector = director;
    //   movieProductionCo = productionCo;
    //   copiesInStock = setInStock

    //Overload the relational operators.
  bool operator==(const videoType&) const;
  bool operator!=(const videoType) const;

private:
  string videoTitle;          //variable to store the name of the
                              //movie
  string movieStar1;          //variable to store the name of the
                              //star
  string movieStar2;          //variable to store the name of the
                              //star
  string movieProducer;       //variable to store the name of the
                              //producer
  string movieDirector;       //variable to store the name of the
                              //director
```

```
    string movieProductionCo; //variable to store the name of the
                              //production company
    int copiesInStock;        //variable to store the number of
                              //copies in stock
};
```

We leave the UML diagram of the **class videoType** as an exercise for you.

For easy output, we overload the output stream insertion operator, **<<**, for the **class videoType**.

Next, we write the definitions of each function of the **class videoType**.

```
void videoType::setVideoInfo(string title, string star1,
                            string star2, string producer,
                            string director,
                            string productionCo, int setInStock)
{
    videoTitle = title;
    movieStar1 = star1;
    movieStar2 = star2;
    movieProducer = producer;
    movieDirector = director;
    movieProductionCo = productionCo;
    copiesInStock = setInStock;
}

void videoType::checkOut()
{
    if(getNoOfCopiesInStock() > 0)
       copiesInStock--;
    else
       cout<<"Currently out of stock"<<endl;
}

void videoType::checkIn()
{
    copiesInStock++;
}

int videoType::getNoOfCopiesInStock() const
{
    return copiesInStock;
}
```

```cpp
void videoType::printTitle() const
{
    cout<<"Video Title: "<<videoTitle<<endl;
}

void videoType::printInfo() const
{
        cout<<"Video Title: "<<videoTitle<<endl;
        cout<<"Stars: "<<movieStar1<<" and "<<movieStar2<<endl;
        cout<<"Producer: "<<movieProducer<<endl;
        cout<<"Director: "<<movieDirector<<endl;
        cout<<"Production Company: "<<movieProductionCo<<endl;
        cout<<"Copies in stock: "<<copiesInStock<<endl;
}

bool videoType::checkTitle(string title)
{
    return(videoTitle == title);
}

void videoType::updateInStock(int num)
{
    copiesInStock += num;
}

void videoType::setCopiesInStock(int num)
{
    copiesInStock = num;
}

string videoType::getTitle()
{
    return videoTitle;
}

videoType::videoType(string title, string star1,
                     string star2, string producer,
                     string director,
                     string productionCo, int setInStock)
{
   setVideoInfo(title, star1, star2, producer, director,
                productionCo, setInStock);
}

bool videoType::operator==(const videoType& other) const
{
    return (videoTitle == other.videoTitle);
}
```

```
bool videoType::operator!=(const videoType& other) const
{
    return (videoTitle != other.videoTitle);
}

ostream& operator<<(ostream& os, const videoType& video)
{
    os<<endl;
    os<<"Video Title: "<<video.videoTitle<<endl;
    os<<"Stars: "<<video.movieStar1<<" and "
      <<video.movieStar2<<endl;
    os<<"Producer: "<<video.movieProducer<<endl;
    os<<"Director: "<<video.movieDirector<<endl;
    os<<"Production Company: "<<video.movieProductionCo<<endl;
    os<<"Copies in stock: "<<video.copiesInStock<<endl;
    os<<"_____"<<endl;
    return os;
}
```

Video List

This program requires us to maintain a list of all the videos in the store, and we should be able to add a new video to our list. We typically would not know how many videos are in the store, and adding or deleting a video from the store would change the number of videos in the store. Therefore, we use a linked list to create a list of videos. See Figure 5-53. (This figure does not show the variable **count**.)

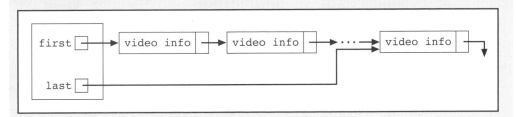

Figure 5-53 `videoList`

Earlier in this chapter, we defined the **class linkedListType** to create a linked list of objects. We also defined the basic operations such as insertion and deletion of a video in the list. However, some operations are very specific to a video list, such as check out a video, check in a video, set the number of copies of a video, and so on. These operations are not available in the **class linkedListType**. We, therefore, derive the **class videoListType** from the **class linkedListType** and add these operations.

The definition of the `class videoListType` is

```
#include <iostream>
#include <string>
#include "linkedList.h"
#include "videoType.h"

using namespace std;

class videoListType: public linkedListType<videoType>
{
public:
  bool videoSearch(string vTitle);
    //Function to search the list to see whether a
    //particular title, specified by the parameter title,
    //is in the store.
    //Postcondition: Returns true if the title is found;
    //               otherwise, returns false.

  bool isVideoAvailable(string vTitle);
    //Function to return true if at least one copy of a
    //particular video is in the store.

  void videoCheckOut(string vTitle);
    //Function to check out a video, that is, rent a video.
    //Postcondition: copiesInStock is decremented by one.

  void videoCheckIn(string vTitle);
    //Function to check in a video returned by a customer.
    //Postcondition: copiesInStock is incremented by one.

  bool videoCheckTitle(string vTitle);
    //Function to determine whether a particular video is in
    //the store.
    //Postcondition: Returns true if the video title is the
    //               same as vTitle; otherwise, returns false.

  void videoUpdateInStock(string vTitle, int num);
    //Function to update the number of copies of a video
    //by adding the value of the parameter num. The
    //parameter vTitle specifies the name of the video for
    //which the number of copies is to be updated.
    //Postcondition: copiesInStock = copiesInStock + num

  void videoSetCopiesInStock(string vTitle, int num);
    //Function to reset the number of copies of a video.
    //The parameter vTitle specifies the name of the video
    //for which the number of copies is to be reset; the
```

```
    //parameter num specifies the number of copies.
    //Postcondition: copiesInStock = num

  void videoPrintTitle();
    //Function to print the titles of all the videos in the store.

private:
  void searchVideoList(string vTitle, bool& found,
            nodeType<videoType>* &current);
    //Function to search the video list for a particular
    //video, specified by the parameter vTitle.
    //Postcondition: If the video is found, the parameter
    //               found is set to true; otherwise,
    //               it is set to false. The parameter current
    //               points to the node containing the video.
};
```

Note that the class videoListType is derived from the class linkedListType via a public inheritance. Furthermore, linkedListType is a class template and we have passed the class videoType as a parameter to this class. That is, the class videoListType is not a template. Because we are now dealing with a very specific data type, the class videoListType no longer needs to be a template. Thus, the info type of each node in the linked list is now videoType. Through the member functions of the class videoType, certain members—such as videoTitle and copiesInStock of an object of the type videoType—can now be accessed.

The definitions of the functions to implement the operations of the class videoListType are given next.

The primary operations on the video list are to check in a video and to check out a video. Both operations require the list to be searched, and the location of the video being checked in or checked out to be found in the video list. Other operations such as checking whether a particular video is in the store, updating the number of copies of a video, and so on also require the video list to be searched. To simplify the search process, we write a function that searches the video list for a particular video. If the video is found, it sets the parameter found to true and returns a pointer to the video so that check-in, check-out, and other operations on the video object can be performed. Note that the function searchVideoList is a private data member of the class videoListType because it is used only for internal manipulation. First, we describe the search procedure.

Consider the node of the video list shown in Figure 5-54.

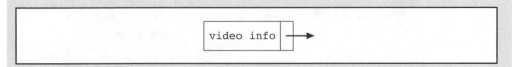

Figure 5-54 Node of a video list

The component `info` is of the type `videoType` and contains the necessary information about a video; specifically, it has seven members: `videoTitle`, `movieStar1`, `movieStar2`, `movieProducer`, `movieDirector`, `movieProductionCo`, and `copiesInStock`. (See the definition of the `class videoType`.) Therefore, the node of a video list has the form shown in Figure 5-55.

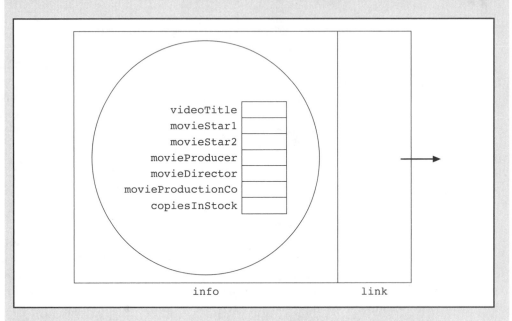

Figure 5-55 Video list node showing the components of `info`

These data members are all `private` and cannot be accessed directly. The member functions of the `class videoType` help us to check and/or set the value of a particular component.

Suppose a pointer—say, `current`—points to a node in the video list. See Figure 5-56.

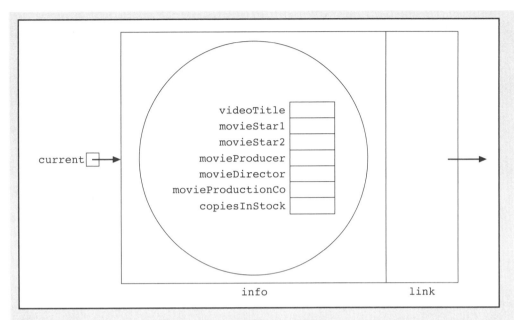

Figure 5-56   Pointer `current` and video list node

Now

```
current->info
```

refers to the `info` part of the node. Suppose that we want to know whether the title of the video stored in this node is the same as the title specified by the variable `title`. The expression

```
current->info.checkTitle(title)
```

is `true` if the title of the video stored in this node is the same as the title specified by the parameter `title`, and `false` otherwise. (Note that the member function `checkTitle` is a value-returning function. See its declaration in the `class videoType`.)

As another example, suppose that we want to set the data member `copiesInStock` of this node to 10. Because `copiesInStock` is a `private` data member, it cannot be accessed directly. Therefore the statement

```
current->info.copiesInStock = 10;  //illegal
```

is incorrect and generates a compile-time error. We have to use the member function `setCopiesInStock` as follows:

```
current->info.setCopiesInStock(10);
```

Now that we know how to access a data member of a video stored in a node, let us describe the algorithm to search the video list.

```
if video list is empty
  Error
else
  while (not found)
    if the title of the current video is the same as the desired
    title, stop the search
  else
    check the next node
```

The following function definition performs the desired search:

```
void videoListType::searchVideoList(string vTitle, bool& found,
                                    nodeType<videoType>* &current)
{
    found = false;    //set found to false

    if(first == NULL)  //list is empty
        cerr<<"Cannot search an empty list. "<<endl;
    else
    {
        current = first;  //set current point to first
                          //node in the list.
        found = false;    // set found to false

        while(!found && current != NULL) //search the list
            if(current->info.checkTitle(vTitle)) //the item is
                                                 //found
                found = true;
            else
                current = current->link; //make current point
                                         //to the next node
    }//end else
}
```

If the search is successful, the parameter **found** is set to **true** and the parameter **current** points to the node containing the video **info**. If it is unsuccessful, **found** is set to **false** and **current** is NULL.

The definitions of the other functions of the **class videoListType** are

```
bool videoListType::isVideoAvailable(string vTitle)
{
        bool found;
        nodeType<videoType> *location;
```

```
        searchVideoList(vTitle, found, location);

        if(found)
            found = (location->info.getNoOfCopiesInStock() > 0);
        else
            found = false;

        return found;
}

void videoListType::videoCheckIn(string vTitle)
{
        bool found = false;
        nodeType<videoType> *location;

        searchVideoList(vTitle, found, location); //search the list

        if(found)
            location->info.checkIn();
        else
            cout<<"The store does not carry this video."<<endl;
}

void videoListType::videoCheckOut(string vTitle)
{
        bool found = false;
        nodeType<videoType> *location;

        searchVideoList(vTitle, found, location); //search the list

        if(found)
            location->info.checkOut();
        else
            cout<<"The store does not carry this video."<<endl;
}

bool videoListType::videoCheckTitle(string vTitle)
{
        bool found = false;
        nodeType<videoType> *location;

        searchVideoList(vTitle, found, location); //search the list

        return found;
}
```

```
void videoListType::videoUpdateInStock(string vTitle, int num)
{
      bool found = false;
      nodeType<videoType> *location;

      searchVideoList(vTitle, found, location); //search the list

      if(found)
         location->info.updateInStock(num);
      else
         cout<<"The store does not carry this video."<<endl;
}

void videoListType::videoSetCopiesInStock(string vTitle, int num)
{
      bool found = false;
      nodeType<videoType> *location;

      searchVideoList(vTitle, found, location);

      if(found)
         location->info.setCopiesInStock(num);
      else
         cout<<"The store does not carry this video."<<endl;
}

bool videoListType::videoSearch(string vTitle)
{
      bool found = false;
      nodeType<videoType> *location;

      searchVideoList(vTitle, found, location);

      return found;
}

void videoListType::videoPrintTitle()
{
      nodeType<videoType>* current;

      current = first;
      while(current != NULL)
      {
          current->info.printTitle();
          current = current->link;
      }
}
```

Part 2: The Customer Component

The Customer Object   The primary characteristics of a customer are:

- The customer's first name
- The customer's last name
- The customer's account number
- The list of rented videos

Suppose that we want to know only the number of videos rented by a customer. Instead of searching the list of rented videos (which could take a long time if the list has many entries), we add a fourth member to our customer object, the number of rentals.

Every customer is a person. We have already designed the `class personType` in Example 1-5 in Chapter 1 and described the necessary operations on the name of a person. Therefore, we can derive the `class customerType` from the `class personType` and add the additional members that we need. First, however, we redefine the `class personType` to take advantage of the new features of object-oriented design that you have learned, such as operator overloading, and then derive the `class customerType`.

The basic operations on an object of the type `personType` are:

1. Set the name.
2. Print the name.
3. Show the first name.
4. Show the last name.

Similarly, the basic operations on an object of the type `customerType` are:

1. Set the name, account number, and number of rentals.
2. Print the name, account number, and number of rentals.
3. Rent a video; that is, add the video to the list of rented videos.
4. Return a video; that is, delete the video from the list of rented videos.
5. Show the account number.

The details of implementing the customer component are left as an exercise for you. (See Programming Exercise 14 at the end of this chapter.)

Main Program

We now write the main program to test the video object. We assume that the necessary data for the videos is stored in a file. We open the file and create the list of videos owned by the video store. The data in the input file is in the following form:

```
video title (the name of the movie)
movie star1
```

```
movie star2
movie producer
movie director
movie production company
number of copies
    .
    .
    .
```

We write a function, `createVideoList`, to read data from the input file and create the list of videos. We also write a function, `displayMenu`, to show the different choices—such as check in a movie or check out a movie—that the user can make. The algorithm of the function `main` is:

1. Open the input file.
2. `if` the input file does not exist, exit the program.
3. Create the list of videos (`createVideoList`).
4. Show the menu (`displayMenu`).
5. `while` not done
   Perform various operations.

Opening the input file is straightforward. Let us describe Steps 2 and 3, which are done by writing two separate functions: `createVideoList` and `displayMenu`.

createVideoList This function reads the data from the input file and creates a linked list of videos. Because the data is read from a file and the input file was opened in the function `main`, we pass the input file pointer to this function. We also pass the video list pointer, declared in the function `main`, to this function. Both parameters are reference parameters. Next, we read the data for each video and then insert the video in the list. The general algorithm is:

a. Read the data and store it in a video object.
b. Insert the video in the list.
c. Repeat steps a and b for each video in the file.

displayMenu This function informs the user what to do. It contains the following output statements.

```
Select one of the following:
1: To check whether a particular title is in stock
2: To check out a video
3: To check in a video
4: To check whether a particular video is in the store
5: To print the titles of all the videos
6: To print a list of all the videos
9: To exit
```

In pseudocode, Step 4 is

```
get choice
while (choice != 9)
{
  switch(choice)
  {
  case 1: a. get the movie name
          b. search the video list
          c. if found, report "success"
             else report "failure"
  case 2: a. get the movie name
          b. search the video list
          c. if found, check out the video
             else report "failure"
  case 3: a. get the movie name
          b. search the video list
          c. if found, check in the video
             else report "failure"
  case 4: a. get the movie name
          b. search the video list
          c. if found
                  if number of copies > 0
                          report "success"
                  else
                          report "currently out of stock"
             else report "failure"
  case 5: print the titles of the videos
  case 6: print all the videos in the store
  default: bad selection
  }//end switch

  displayMenu();
  get choice;
}//end while
```

Main Program Listing

```cpp
#include <iostream>
#include <fstream>
#include <string>
#include "videoType.h"
#include "videoLinkedListType.h"

using namespace std;

void createVideoList(ifstream& infile, videoListType& videoList);
void displayMenu();
```

```
int main()
{
    videoListType  videoList;
    int choice;
    char ch;
    string title;

    ifstream infile;

        //open the input file
    infile.open("a:\\videoDat.txt");
    if(!infile)
    {
       cerr<<"Input file does not exist"<<endl;
       return 1;
    }
        //create the video list
    createVideoList(infile, videoList);
    infile.close();

    displayMenu();                  //show the menu
    cout<<"Enter your choice: ";
    cin>>choice;                    //get the request
    cin.get(ch);
    cout<<endl;

        //process the request
    while(choice != 9)
    {
        switch(choice)
        {
        case 1: cout<<"Enter the title: ";
                getline(cin,title);
                cout<<endl;
                if(videoList.videoSearch(title))
                   cout<<"Title found"<<endl;
                else
                cout<<"The store does not carry this title."
                   <<endl;
                break;
        case 2: cout<<"Enter the title: ";
                getline(cin,title);
                cout<<endl;
                if(videoList.videoSearch(title))
                {
                    if(videoList.isVideoAvailable(title))
                    {
                        videoList.videoCheckOut(title);
```

```
                        cout<<"Enjoy your movie: "<<title<<endl;
                  }
                  else
                     cout<<"The video is currently "
                         <<"out of stock."<<endl;
            }
            else
               cout<<"The video is not in the store."
                   <<endl;
            break;
case 3: cout<<"Enter the title: ";
        getline(cin,title);
        cout<<endl;
        if(videoList.videoSearch(title))
        {
            videoList.videoCheckIn(title);
            cout<<"Thanks for returning "<<title
                <<endl;
        }
        else
           cout<<"This video is not from our store."
               <<endl;

        break;
case 4: cout<<"Enter the title: ";
        getline(cin,title);
        cout<<endl;
        if(videoList.videoSearch(title))
        {
            if(videoList.isVideoAvailable(title))
               cout<<"The video is currently in stock."
                   <<endl;
            else
               cout<<"The video is out of stock."
                   <<endl;
        }
        else
           cout<<"The video is not in the store."
               <<endl;

        break;
case 5: videoList.videoPrintTitle();
        break;
case 6: cout<<videoList<<endl;
        break;
default: cout<<"Bad Selection"<<endl;
}//end switch
```

```
            displayMenu();              //display the menu
            cout<<"Enter your choice: ";
            cin>>choice;                //get the next request
            cin.get(ch);
            cout<<endl;
        }//end while

        return 0;
}
void createVideoList(ifstream& infile, videoListType& videoList)
{
        string Title;
        string Star1;
        string Star2;
        string Producer;
        string Director;
        string ProductionCo;
        char   ch;
        int    InStock;

        videoType newVideo;

        getline(infile, Title);
        while(infile)
        {
            getline(infile, Star1);
            getline(infile, Star2);
            getline(infile, Producer);
            getline(infile, Director);
            getline(infile, ProductionCo);
            infile>>InStock;
            infile.get(ch);
            newVideo.setVideoInfo(Title, Star1, Star2, Producer,
                        Director, ProductionCo, InStock);
              videoList.insertFirst(newVideo);

              getline(infile, Title);
        }//end for
}//end createVideoList
void displayMenu()
{
        cout<<"Select one of the following "<<endl;
        cout<<"1: To check whether a particular video is in the store"
            <<endl;
        cout<<"2: To check out a video"<<endl;
        cout<<"3: To check in a video"<<endl;
        cout<<"4: To check whether a particular title is in stock"
            <<endl;
```

```
      cout<<"5: To print the titles of all the videos"<<endl;
      cout<<"6: To print a list of all the videos"<<endl;
      cout<<"9: To exit"<<endl;
}
```

QUICK REVIEW

1. A linked list is a list of items, called nodes, in which the order of the nodes is determined by the address, called a link, stored in each node.

2. The pointer to a linked list—that is, the pointer to the first node in the list—is stored in a separate location, called the `head` or `first`.

3. A linked list is a dynamic data structure.

4. The length of a linked list is the number of nodes in the list.

5. Item insertion and deletion from a linked list does not require data movement; only the pointers are adjusted.

6. A (single) linked list is traversed in only one direction.

7. The search on a linked list is sequential.

8. The `first` (or `head`) pointer of a linked list is always fixed, pointing to the first node in the list.

9. To traverse a linked list, the program must use a pointer different from the `head` pointer of the list, initialized to the first node in the list.

10. In a doubly linked list, every node has two links: one points to the next node; one points to the previous node.

11. A doubly linked list can be traversed in either direction.

12. In a doubly linked list, item insertion and deletion requires the adjustment of two pointers in a node.

13. List containers are implemented as doubly linked lists. Thus, every element in the list points to its immediate predecessor and its immediate successor (except the first and last elements).

14. The name of the class containing the definition of the `class list` is `list`.

15. In addition to the operations that are common to sequence containers (see Chapter 4), the other operations that can be used to manipulate the elements in a list container are `assign`, `push_front`, `pop_front`, `front`, `back`, `remove`, `remove_if`, `unique`, `splice`, `sort`, `merge`, and `reverse`.

16. A linked list with header and trailer nodes simplifies the insertion and deletion operations.

17. In a linked list with header and trailer nodes, the header and trailer nodes are not part of the actual list. The actual list elements are between the header and trailer nodes.

18. A linked list with header and trailer nodes is empty if the only nodes in the list are the header and the trailer.

19. A circular linked list is a list in which, if the list is nonempty, the last node points to the first node.

EXERCISES

1. Mark the following statements as true or false.

   a. In a linked list, the order of the elements is determined by the order in which the nodes were created to store the elements.

   b. In a linked list, memory allocated for the nodes is sequential.

   c. A single linked list can be traversed in either direction.

   d. In a linked list, the nodes are always inserted either in the beginning or at the end because a linked list is not a random access data structure.

   e. Item insertion (and deletion) in a linked list with header and trailer nodes is simpler than in an ordinary linked list because the former list has no special cases.

   f. The `head` pointer of a linked list should not be used to traverse the list.

   Consider the linked list shown in Figure 5-57. Assume that the nodes are in the usual `info-link` form. Use this list to answer Exercises 2 through 7. If necessary, declare additional variables. (Assume that `list`, `p`, `s`, `A`, and `B` are pointers of the type `nodeType`.)

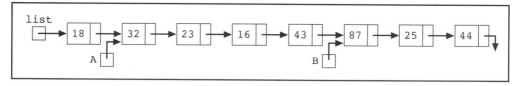

Figure 5-57   Linked list for Exercises 2 through 7

2. What is the output of the following C++ statements?

   a. `cout<<list->info;`

   b. `cout<<A->info;`

   c. `cout<<B->link->info;`

   d. `cout<<list->link->link->info;`

3. What is the value of the following relational expressions?

   a. `list->info >= 18`

   b. `list->link == A`

   c. `A->link->info == 16`

   d. `B->link == NULL`

   e. `list->info == 18`

4. Mark each of the following statements as valid or invalid. If a statement is invalid, explain why.

   a. `A = B;`

   b. `list->link = A->link;`

   c. `list->link->info = 45;`

   d. `*list = B;`

   e. `*A = *B;`

   f. `B = A->link->info;`

   g. `A->info = B->info;`

   h. `list = B->link->link;`

   i. `B = B->link->link->link;`

5. Write C++ statements to do the following:

   a. Make `A` point to the node containing `info 23`.

   b. Make `list` point to the node containing `info 16`.

   c. Make `B` point to the last node in the list.

   d. Make `list` point to an empty list.

   e. Set the value of the node containing `25` to `35`.

   f. Create and insert the node with `info 10` after the node pointed to by `A`.

   g. Delete the node with `info 23`. Also, deallocate the memory occupied by this node.

6. What is the output of the following C++ code?

```
p = List;
while(p != NULL)
    cout<<p->info<<" ";
    p = p->link;
cout<<endl;
```

7. If the following C++ code is valid, show the output. If it is invalid, explain why.

   a.

   ```
   s = A;
   p = B;
   s->info = B;
   p = p->link;
   cout<<s->info<<" "<<p->info<<endl;
   ```

   b.

   ```
   p = A;
   p = p->link;
   s = p;
   p->link = NULL;
   s = s->link;
   cout<<p->info<<" "<<s->info<<endl;
   ```

8. Show what is produced by the following C++ code. Assume that the node is in the usual `info-link` form with `info` of the type `int`. (`list` and `ptr` are pointers of the type `nodeType`.)

   ```
   list = new nodeType;
   list->info = 10;
   ptr = new nodeType;
   ptr->info = 13;
   ptr->link = NULL;
   list->link = ptr;
   ptr = new nodeType;
   ptr->info = 18;
   ptr->link = list->link;
   list->link = ptr;
   cout<<list->info<<" "<<ptr->info<<" ";
   ptr = ptr->link;
   cout<<ptr->info<<endl;
   ```

9. Show what is produced by the following C++ code. Assume that the node is in the usual `info-link` form with `info` of the type `int`. (`list` and `ptr` are pointers of the type `nodeType`.)

   ```
   list = new nodeType;
   list->info = 20;
   ptr = new nodeType;
   ptr->info = 28;
   ptr->link = NULL;
   list->link = ptr;
   ptr = new nodeType;
   ptr->info = 30;
   ptr->link = list;
   list = ptr;
   ptr = new nodeType;
   ptr->info = 42;
   ```

```
ptr->link = list->link;
list->link = ptr;
ptr = list;
while(ptr != NULL)
{
    cout<<ptr->info<<endl;
    ptr = ptr->link;
}
```

10. Consider the following C++ statements. (The class linkedListType is as defined in this chapter.)

```
linkedListType<int> list;

list.insertFirst(15);
list.insertLast(28);
list.insertFirst(30);
list.insertFirst(2);
list.insertLast(45);
list.insertFirst(38);
list.insertLast(25);
list.deleteNode(30);
list.insertFirst(18);
list.deleteNode(28);
list.deleteNode(12);
cout<<list<<endl;
```

What is the output of this program segment?

11. Suppose the input is

```
18 30 4 32 45 36 78 19 48 75 -999
```

What is the output of the following C++ code? (The class linkedListType is as defined in this chapter.)

```
linkedListType<int> list;
linkedListType<int> copyList;
int num;

cin>>num;
while(num != -999)
{
    if(num % 5 == 0 || num % 5 == 3)
        list.insertFirst(num);
    else
        list.insertLast(num);
    cin>>num;
}

cout<<"List :"<<list<<endl;
```

5

```
copyList = list;

copyList.deleteNode(78);
copyList.deleteNode(35);

cout<<"Copy List = "<<copyList<<endl;
```

12. Suppose that `intList` is a `list` container and

    ```
    intList = {3, 23, 23, 43, 56, 11, 11, 23, 25}
    ```

    Show `intList` after the following statement executes:

    ```
    intList.unique();
    ```

13. Suppose that `intList1` and `intList2` are `list` containers and

    ```
    intList1 = {3, 58, 78, 85, 6, 15, 93, 98, 25}
    intList2 = {5, 24, 16, 11, 60, 9}
    ```

    Show `intList1` after the following statement executes:

    ```
    intList1.splice(intList1.begin(),intList2);
    ```

14. What is the output of the following program segment?

    ```
    list<int> intList;
    ostream_iterator<int> screen(cout, " ");
    list<int>::iterator listIt;

    intList.push_back(5);
    intList.push_front(23);
    intList.push_front(45);
    intList.pop_back();
    intList.push_back(35);

    intList.push_front(0);
    intList.push_back(50);
    intList.push_front(34);

    copy(intList.begin(), intList.end(), screen);
    cout<<endl;

    listIt = intList.begin();
    intList.insert(listIt,76);

    ++listIt;
    ++listIt;
    intList.insert(listIt,38);

    intList.pop_back();

    ++listIt;
    ++listIt;
    ```

```
intList.erase(listIt);
intList.push_front(2 * intList.back());
intList.push_back(3 * intList.front());

copy(intList.begin(), intList.end(), screen);
cout<<endl;
```

15. Draw the UML diagram of the **class videoType** of the Programming Example in this chapter.

16. Draw the UML diagram of the **class videoListType** of the Programming Example in this chapter.

5

PROGRAMMING EXERCISES

1. **(Online Address Book Revisited)** Programming Exercise 13 in Chapter 3 could handle a maximum of only 500 entries. Using linked lists, redo the program to handle as many entries as required. Add the following operations to your program:

   a. Add or delete a new entry to the address book.

   b. When the program terminates, write the data in the address book to a disk.

2. Extend the **class linkedListType** by adding the following operations:

   a. Find and delete the node with the smallest **info** in the list. (Delete only the first occurrence. Traverse the list only once.)

   b. Find and delete all the occurrences of a given **info** from the list. (Traverse the list only once.)

3. Extend the **class linkedListType** by adding the following operations:

   a. Write a function that returns the **info** of the kth element of the linked list. If no such element exists, terminate the program.

   b. Write a function that deletes the kth element in the linked list. If no such element exists, output an appropriate message.

4. Add the function **splitMid** to split a linked list into two sublists of (almost) equal size as described here. For example, suppose the given list is 13 72 89 65 34. The two sublists are then 13 72 89 and 65 34. Similarly, if the original list is 12 67 34 65, the two sublists are 12 67 and 34 65.

   a. Add the operation **splitMid** to the **class linkedListType** as follows:

   ```
   void splitMid(linkedListType<Type> &sublist);
     //This operation splits the given list into two
     //sublists of (almost) equal size.
     //Precondition: The list must exist.
     //Postcondition: first points to the first node,
     //  and last points to the last node of the first
     //  sublist. sublist.first points to the first
     //  node, and sublist.last points to the last node
     //  of the second sublist.
   ```

Consider the following statements:

```
linkedListType<int> myList;
linkedListType<int> subList;
```

Suppose `myList` points to a list with the elements 34 65 27 89 12 (in this order). The statement

```
myList.splitMid(subList);
```

splits `myList` into two sublists: `myList` points to the list with the elements 34 65 27, and `subList` points to the sublist with elements 89 12.

b. Write the definition of the function template to implement the operation `splitMid`.

5. Add the function `splitAt` to split a linked list at a node whose `info` is given.

Suppose `oldList` points to a list with the elements

```
10 18 34 6 28 92 56 48
```

and the list is to be split at the node whose `info` is 6. The two sublists are then

```
10 18 34  and  6 28 92 56 48
```

a. Add the following function to the `class linkedListType`:

```
void splitAt(linkedListType<Type> &secondList,
             const Type& item);
    //Splits the list at the node with the info item
    //into two sublists.
    //Precondition: The list must exist.
    //Postcondition: first and last point to the
    //   first and last nodes of the first sublist.
    //   secondList.first and secondList.last
    //   point to the first and last nodes of the
    //   second sublist.
```

Consider the following statements:

```
linkedListType<int> myList;
linkedListType<int> otherList;
```

Suppose `myList` points to a list with the elements 34 65 18 39 27 89 12 (in this order). The statement

```
myList.splitAt(otherList, 18);
```

splits `myList` into two sublists: `myList` points to the list with the elements 34 65, and `otherList` points to the sublist with the elements 18 39 27 89 12.

b. Write the definition of the function template to implement the operation `splitAt`.

6. a. Add the following operation to the `class orderedLinkedListType`:

```
void mergeLists(orderedLinkedListType<Type> &list1,
                orderedLinkedListType<Type> &list2);

//This operation creates a new list by merging the
//elements of list1 and list2.
//Precondition: Both lists, list1 and list2, are
//              ordered.
//Postcondition: first points to the merged list,
//               and list1 and list2 are empty.
```

Example: Consider the following statements:

```
orderedLinkedListType<int> newList;
orderedLinkedListType<int> list1;
orderedLinkedListType<int> list2;
```

Suppose `list1` points to a list with elements 2 6 7, and `list2` points to a list with the elements 3 5 8. The statement

```
newList.mergeLists(list1, list2);
```

creates a new linked list with the elements in the order 2 3 5 6 7 8, and the object `newList` points to this list. Also, after the preceding statement executes, `list1` and `list2` are empty.

   b. Write the definition of the function template `mergeLists` to implement the operation `mergeLists`.

7. The function `insertNode` of the `class orderedLinkedListType` does not check whether the item to be inserted is already in the list; that is, it does not check for duplicates. Rewrite the definition of `insertNode` so that before inserting the item it checks whether the item is already in the list. If the item to be inserted is already in the list, the function outputs an appropriate error message. Also, write a program to test your function.

8. Write the definition of the function template `back` to return the last element of an ordered linked list. Moreover, add this operation to the `class orderedLinkedListType`.

9. Write the definitions of the function `copyList`, the copy constructor, the destructor, and the function to overload the assignment operator for the `class doublyLinkedList`.

10. Write a program to test various operations of the `class doublyLinkedList`.

11. (Linked List with Header and Trailer Nodes) This chapter defined and identified various operations on a linked list with header and trailer nodes.

   a. Write the definition of the class that defines a linked list with header and trailer nodes as an ADT.

   b. Write the definitions of the member functions of the class defined in part a. (You may assume that the elements of the linked list with header and trailer nodes are in ascending order.)

   c. Write a program to test various operations of the class defined in part a.

12. **(Circular Linked Lists)** This chapter defined and identified various operations on a circular linked list.

   a. Write the definition of the class that defines a sorted circular linked list as an ADT.

   b. Write the definitions of the member functions of the class defined in part a. (You may assume that the elements of the circular linked list are in ascending order.)

   c. Write a program to test various operations of the class defined in part a.

13. Write the definition of the function template `seqSearch` to implement a sequential search on a `list` object. Its prototype is

```
template<class elemType>
list<elemType>::iterator seqSearch
               (list<elemType> &searchList,
                 const elemType& item);
    //If the item is found in the list, returns a
    //pointer to the item in the list; otherwise,
    //returns list.end().
```

Also, write a program to test the function `seqSearch`.

14. **(Programming Example, Video Store)**

   a. Complete the design and implementation of the **class customerType** defined in the Programming Example, Video Store.

   b. Design and implement the **class customerListType** to create and maintain a list of customers for the video store.

15. **(Programming Example, Video Store)** Complete the design and implementation of the video store program.

16. Redo the video store program so that the list of videos, list of customers, and the list of videos rented by a customer are kept in a `list` container.

CHAPTER

6

RECURSION

In this chapter, you will:

♦ Learn about recursive definitions

♦ Explore the base case and the general case of a recursive definition

♦ Discover recursive algorithms

♦ Learn about recursive functions

♦ Explore how to use recursive functions to implement recursive algorithms

♦ Learn about recursion and backtracking

Until now, to devise problem solutions we used the most common technique, called iteration. For certain problems, however, using the iterative technique to obtain the solution is quite complicated. This chapter introduces another problem-solving technique, called recursion, and provides several examples to show how recursion works.

RECURSIVE DEFINITIONS

The process of solving a problem by reducing it to smaller versions of itself is called **recursion**. Recursion is a very powerful way to solve certain problems for which the solution would otherwise be very complicated. Let us consider a problem that is familiar to most everyone.

In mathematics, the factorial of an integer is defined as follows:

$$0! = 1 \qquad\qquad\qquad (6\text{-}1)$$

$$n! = n \times (n - 1)! \text{ if } n > 0 \qquad (6\text{-}2)$$

In this definition, 0! is defined to be 1, and if n is an integer greater than 0, we first find $(n - 1)!$ and then multiply it by n. To find $(n - 1)!$, we apply the definition again. If $(n - 1) > 0$, then we use Equation 6-2; otherwise, we use Equation 6-1. Thus, for an integer n greater than 0, $n!$ is obtained by first finding $(n - 1)!$ (that is, $n!$ is reduced to a smaller version of itself), and then multiplying $(n - 1)!$ by n.

Let us apply this definition to find 3!. Here $n = 3$. Because $n > 0$, we use Equation 6-2 to obtain

$$3! = 3 \times 2!$$

Next, we find 2! Here $n = 2$. Because $n > 0$, we use Equation 6-2 to obtain

$$2! = 2 \times 1!$$

Now to find 1!, we again use Equation 6-2 because $n = 1 > 0$. Thus

$$1! = 1 \times 0!$$

Finally, we use Equation 6-1 to find 0!, which is 1. Substituting 0! into 1! gives 1! = 1. This gives 2! = 2 × 1! = 2 × 1 = 2, which in turn gives 3! = 3 × 2! = 3 × 2 = 6.

The solution in Equation 6-1 is direct—that is, the right side of the equation contains no factorial notation. The solution in Equation 6-2 is given in terms of a smaller version of itself. The definition of the factorial as given in Equations 6-1 and 6-2 is called a **recursive definition**. Equation 6-1 is called the **base case** (the case in which the solution is given directly); Equation 6-2 is called the **general case** or **recursive case**.

Recursive definition: A definition in which something is defined in terms of a smaller version of itself.

From the previous example, it is clear that:

- Every recursive definition must have one (or more) base cases.

- The general case must eventually be reduced to a base case.

- The base case stops the recursion.

The concept of recursion in computer science works similarly. Here we talk about recursive algorithms and recursive functions. An algorithm that finds the solution to a given problem by reducing the problem to smaller versions of itself is called a **recursive algorithm**. The recursive algorithm must have one or more base cases, and the general solution must eventually be reduced to a base case.

A function that calls itself is called a **recursive function**. That is, the body of the recursive function contains a statement that causes the same function to execute before completing the current call. Recursive algorithms are implemented using recursive functions.

Next, let us write the recursive function that implements the factorial function.

```
int fact(int num)
{
   if(num == 0)
      return 1;
   else
      return num * fact(num - 1);
}
```

Figure 6-1 traces the execution of the following statement:

```
cout<<fact(4)<<endl;
```

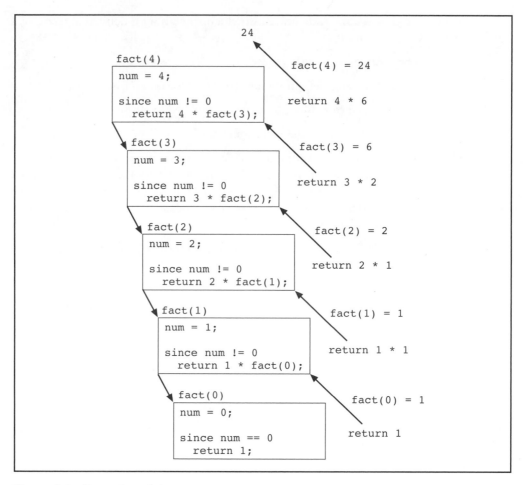

Figure 6-1 Execution of the expression `fact(4)`

The output of the preceding `cout` statement is

24

In Figure 6-1, the downward arrows represent the successive calls to the function `fact`, and the upward arrows represent the values returned to the caller, that is, the calling function.

While tracing through the execution of the recursive function `fact`, let us note the following:

- Logically, you can think of a recursive function as having unlimited copies of itself.

- Every call to a recursive function—that is, every recursive call—has its own code and its own set of parameters and local variables.

- After completing a particular recursive call, the control goes back to the calling environment, which is the previous call. The current (recursive) call must execute completely before the control goes back to the previous call. The execution in the previous call begins from the point immediately following the recursive call.

Direct and Indirect Recursion

A function is called **directly recursive** if it calls itself. A function that calls another function and eventually results in the original function call is said to be **indirectly recursive**. For example, if a function A calls a function B and function B calls function A, then function A is indirectly recursive. Indirect recursion can be several layers deep. For example, suppose that function A calls function B, function B calls function C, function C calls function D, and function D calls function A. Then function A is indirectly recursive.

Indirect recursion requires the same careful analysis as direct recursion. The base cases must be identified and appropriate solutions to them must be provided. However, tracing through indirect recursion can be a tedious process. Therefore, you must exercise extra care when designing indirect recursive functions. For simplicity, the problems in this book involve only direct recursion.

A recursive function in which the last statement executed is the recursive call is called a **tail recursive function**. The function `fact` is an example of a tail recursive function.

Infinite Recursion

Figure 6-1 shows that the sequence of recursive calls eventually reached a call that did not make any further recursive calls. That is, the sequence of recursive calls eventually reached a base case. On the other hand, if every recursive call results in another recursive call, then the recursive function (algorithm) is said to have infinite recursion. In theory, infinite recursion executes forever. Every call to a recursive function requires the system to allocate memory for the local variables and formal parameter. The system also saves the information so that after completing a call, the control can be transferred back to the right caller. Therefore, because computer memory is finite, if you execute an infinite recursive function on a computer, the function executes until the system runs out of memory and results in an abnormal termination of the program.

Recursive functions (algorithms) must be carefully designed and analyzed. You must make sure that every recursive call eventually reduce to a base case. This chapter provides several examples that illustrate how to design and implement recursive algorithms.

To design a recursive function, you must do the following:

    a. Understand the problem requirements.

    b. Determine the limiting condition(s). For example, for a list, the limiting condition is determined by the number of elements in the list.

    c. Identify the base cases and provide a direct solution to each base case.

    d. Identify the general cases and provide a solution to each general case in terms of a smaller version of itself.

PROBLEM SOLVING USING RECURSION

Examples 6-1 through 6-5 show how recursive algorithms are developed and implemented in C++ using recursive functions.

Example 6-1: Largest Element in the Array

This example uses a recursive algorithm to find the largest element in an array. Consider the list given in Figure 6-2.

	[0]	[1]	[2]	[3]	[4]	[5]
list	5	8	2	10	9	4

Figure 6-2   `list` with six elements

The largest element in the list given in Figure 6-2 is 10.

Suppose `list` is the name of the array containing the list elements. Also, suppose that `list[a]...list[b]` stands for the array elements `list[a], list[a + 1], ...,` `list[b]`. For example, `list[0]...list[5]` represents the array elements `list[0],` `list[1], list[2], list[3], list[4],` and `list[5]`. Similarly, `list[1]...list[5]` represents the array elements `list[1], list[2], list[3], list[4],` and `list[5]`. To write a recursive algorithm to find the largest element in `list`, let us think in terms of recursion.

If `list` is of length 1, then `list` has only one element, which is the largest element. Suppose the length of `list` is greater than 1. To find the largest element in `list[a]...list[b]`, we first find the largest element in `list[a + 1]...list[b]` and then compare this largest element with `list[a]`. That is, the largest element in `list[a]...list[b]` is given by

```
maximum(list[a], largest(list[a + 1]...list[b]))
```

Let us apply this formula to find the largest element in the list shown in Figure 6-2. This list has six elements, given by `list[0]...list[5]`. The largest element in `list` is

```
maximum(list[0], largest(list[1]...list[5]))
```

That is, the largest element in `list` is the maximum of `list[0]` and the largest element in `list[1]...list[5]`. To find the largest element in `list[1]...list[5]`, we use the same formula again because the length of this list is greater than 1. The largest element in `list[1]...list[5]` is then

```
maximum(list[1], largest(list[2]...list[5]))
```

and so on. We see that every time we use the preceding formula to find the largest element in a sublist, the length of the sublist in the next call is reduced by one. Eventually, the sublist is of length 1, in which case the sublist contains only one element, which is the largest element in the sublist. From this point onward, we backtrack through the recursive calls. This discussion translates into the following recursive algorithm, which is presented in pseudocode:

```
Base Case: The size of the list is 1
           The only element in the list is the largest element
General Case: The size of the list is greater than 1
           To find the largest element in list[a]...list[b]
   a. Find the largest element in list[a + 1]...list[b] and call it
      max
   b. Compare the elements list[a] and max
      if(list[a] >= max)
           the largest element in list[a]...list[b] is list[a]
      otherwise
           the largest element in list[a]...list[b] is max
```

This algorithm translates into the following C++ function to find the largest element in an array:

```cpp
int largest(const int list[], int lowerIndex, int upperIndex)
{
   int max;

   if(lowerIndex == upperIndex)    //the size of the sublist is 1
      return list[lowerIndex];
   else
   {
      max = largest(list, lowerIndex + 1, upperIndex);
      if(list[lowerIndex] >= max)
         return list[lowerIndex];
      else
         return max;
   }
}
```

Consider the list given in Figure 6-3.

	[0]	[1]	[2]	[3]
list	5	10	12	8

Figure 6-3 list with four elements

Let us trace the execution of the following statement:

```
cout<<largest(list,0,3);
```

Here `upperIndex = 3` and the list has four elements. Figure 6-4 traces the execution of `largest(list,0,3)`.

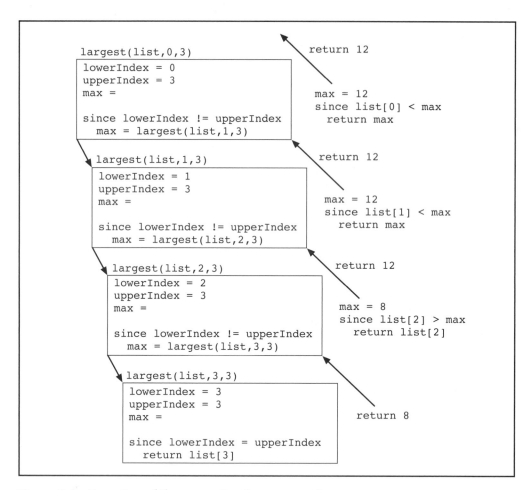

Figure 6-4   Execution of the expression `largest(list,0,3)`

The value returned by the expression `largest(list,0,3)` is 12, which is the largest element in `list`.

The following C++ program uses the function `largest` to determine the largest element in a list:

```
//Largest Element in an Array

#include <iostream>

using namespace std;

int largest(const int list[], int lowerIndex, int upperIndex);

int main()
{
    int intArray[10] = {23, 43, 35, 38, 67, 12, 76, 10, 34, 8};

    cout<<"The largest element in intArray: "
        <<largest(intArray,0,9);
    cout<<endl;
    return 0;
}

int largest(const int list[], int lowerIndex, int upperIndex)
{
   int max;

   if(lowerIndex == upperIndex)    //the size of the sublist is 1
      return list[lowerIndex];
   else
   {
      max = largest(list, lowerIndex + 1, upperIndex);
      if(list[lowerIndex] >= max)
         return list[lowerIndex];
      else
         return max;
   }
}
```

Sample Run:

```
The largest element in intArray: 76
```

Example 6-2: Print a Linked List in Reverse Order

The nodes of an ordered linked list (as constructed in Chapter 5) are in ascending order. Certain applications, however, might require the data to be printed in descending order, which means that we must print the list backwards. We now discuss the function `reversePrint`. Given a pointer to a list, this function prints the elements of the list in reverse order.

Consider the linked list shown in Figure 6-5.

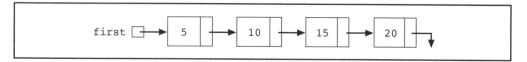

Figure 6-5 Linked list

For the list in Figure 6-5, the output should be in the following form:

```
20 15 10 5
```

Because the links are in only one direction, we cannot traverse the list backwards starting from the last node. Let us see how we can effectively use recursion to print the list in reverse order.

Let us think in terms of recursion. We cannot print the `info` of the first node until we have printed the remainder of the list (that is, the tail of the first node). Similarly, we cannot print the `info` of the second node until we have printed the tail of the second node, and so on. Every time we consider the tail of a node, we reduce the size of the list by 1. Eventually, the size of the list is reduced to zero, in which case the recursion stops.

Base Case: List is empty

        no action

General Case: List is nonempty

        a.   Print the tail

        b.   Print the element

Let us write this algorithm in pseudocode. (Suppose that `current` is a pointer to a linked list.)

```
if(current != NULL)
{
    reversePrint(current->link);  //print the tail
    cout<<current->info<<" ";     //print the node
}
```

Here, we do not see the base case; it is hidden. The list is printed only if the pointer, `current`, to the list is not `NULL`. Also, inside the `if` statement the recursive call is on the tail of the list. Because eventually the tail of a list will be empty, the `if` statement in the next call fails and the recursion stops. Also, note that the statement to print the `info` of the node appears after the recursive call; thus, when the transfer comes back to the calling function, we must execute this statement. Recall that the function exits only after the last statement executes. (By the "last statement" we do not mean the *physical* last statement, but rather the *logical* last statement.)

Let us write a function template to implement the preceding algorithm and then apply it to a list.

```
template<class Type>
void orderedLinkedListType<Type>::reversePrint
                              (nodeType<Type> *current) const
{
    if(current != NULL)
    {
        reversePrint(current->link);  //print the tail
        cout<<current->info<<" ";     //print the node
    }
}
```

Consider the statement

```
reversePrint(first);
```

where `first` is a pointer of the type `nodeType<Type>`.

Let us trace the execution of this statement, which is a function call, for the list shown in Figure 6-5. Because the formal parameter is a value parameter, the value of the actual parameter is passed to the formal parameter. See Figure 6-6.

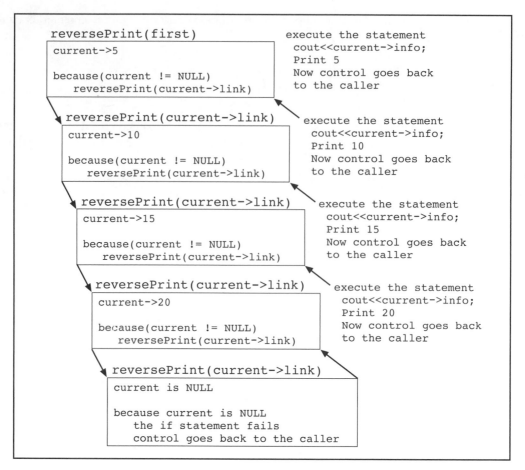

Figure 6-6 Execution of the statement `reversePrint(first);`

Function `printListReverse`

Now that we have written the function `reversePrint`, we can write the definition of the function `printListReverse`, which can be used to print an ordered linked list contained in an object of the type `orderedLinkedListType`. Its definition is:

```
template<class Type>
void orderedLinkedListType<Type>::printListReverse() const
{
    reversePrint(first);
    cout<<endl;
}
```

We can include the function `printListReverse` as a `public` member in the definition of the class and the function `reversePrint` as a `private` member. We include the function

reversePrint as a **private** member because it is used only to implement the function
printListReverse.

Example 6-3: Fibonacci Number

Consider the following sequence of numbers:

1, 1, 2, 3, 5, 8, 13, 21, 34, ...

Given the first two numbers of the sequence (say a_1 and a_2), the nth number a_n, for $n >= 3$,
of this sequence is given by

$$a_n = a_{n-1} + a_{n-2}$$

Thus

$$a_3 = a_2 + a_1$$
$$= 1 + 1$$
$$= 2,$$

$$a_4 = a_3 + a_2$$
$$= 2 + 1$$
$$= 3,$$

and so on.

Such a sequence is called a **Fibonacci sequence**. In the preceding sequence, $a_2 = 1$ and
$a_1 = 1$. However, given any first two numbers, using this process, you can determine the nth
number, a_n, for $n >= 3$. The number determined this way is called the **nth Fibonacci
number**. Suppose $a_2 = 6$ and $a_1 = 3$. Then

$$a_3 = a_2 + a_1 = 6 + 3 = 9$$
$$a_4 = a_3 + a_2 = 9 + 6 = 15$$

In this example, we write a recursive function, rFibNum, to determine the desired
Fibonacci number. The function rFibNum takes as parameters three numbers representing
the first two numbers of the Fibonacci sequence and a number n, the desired nth Fibonacci
number. The function rFibNum returns the nth Fibonacci number in the sequence.

The third Fibonacci number in a Fibonacci sequence is the sum of the first two Fibonacci
numbers. The fourth Fibonacci number in a Fibonacci sequence is the sum of the second
and third Fibonacci numbers. Therefore, to calculate the fourth Fibonacci number, we add
the second Fibonacci number and the third Fibonacci number (which is itself the sum of the
first two Fibonacci numbers). The following recursive algorithm calculates the nth Fibonacci
number, where a denotes the first Fibonacci number, b the second Fibonacci number, and n
the nth Fibonacci number:

$$rFibNum(a,b,n) = \begin{cases} a & \text{if } n = 1 \\ b & \text{if } n = 2 \\ rFibNum(a,b,n-1) + rFibNum(a,b,n-2) & \text{if } n > 2 \end{cases} \quad (6\text{-}3)$$

Suppose that we want to determine

`rFibNum(2,5,4)`

Here $a = 2$, $b = 5$, and $n = 4$. That is, we want to determine the fourth Fibonacci number of the sequence whose first number is 2 and whose second number is 5. Because n is $4 > 2$,

1. `rFibNum(2,5,4)` = `rFibNum(2,5,3)` + `rFibNum(2,5,2)`

Next, we determine `rFibNum(2,5,3)` and `rFibNum(2,5,2)`. Let us first determine `rFibNum(2,5,3)`. Here, $a = 2$, $b = 5$, and n is 3. Since n is 3,

> 1.a `rFibNum(2,5,3)` = `rFibNum(2,5,2)` + `rFibNum(2,5,1)`
>
> This statement requires us to determine `rFibNum(2,5,2)` and `rFibNum(2,5,1)`. In `rFibNum(2,5,2)`, $a = 2$, $b = 5$, and $n = 2$. Therefore, from the definition given in Equation 6-3, it follows that
>
> 1.a.1 `rFibNum(2,5,2)` = 5
>
> To find `rFibNum(2,5,1)`, note that $a = 2$, $b = 5$, and $n = 1$. Therefore, by the definition given in Equation 6-3,
>
> 1.a.2 `rFibNum(2,5,1)` = 2
>
> We substitute the values of `rFibNum(2,5,2)` and `rFibNum(2,5,1)` into (1.a) to get
>
> `rFibNum(2,5,3)` = 5 + 2 = 7

Next, we determine `rFibNum(2,5,2)`. As in (1.a.1), `rFibNum(2,5,2)` = 5. We can substitute the values of `rFibNum(2,5,3)` and `rFibNum(2,5,2)` into (1) to get

> `rFibNum(2,5,4)` = 7 + 5 = 12

The following recursive function implements this algorithm:

```
int rFibNum(int a, int b, int n)
{
   if(n == 1)
      return a;
   else if(n == 2)
         return b;
   else
      return rFibNum(a, b, n - 1) + rFibNum(a, b, n - 2);
}
```

Let us trace the execution of the following statement:

`cout<<rFibNum(2, 3, 5)<<endl;`

In this statement, the first number is 2, the second number is 3, and we want to determine the 5th Fibonacci number of the sequence. Figure 6-7 traces the execution of the expression `rFibNum(2,3,5)`. The value returned is 13, which is the 5th Fibonacci number of the sequence whose first number is 2 and whose second number is 3.

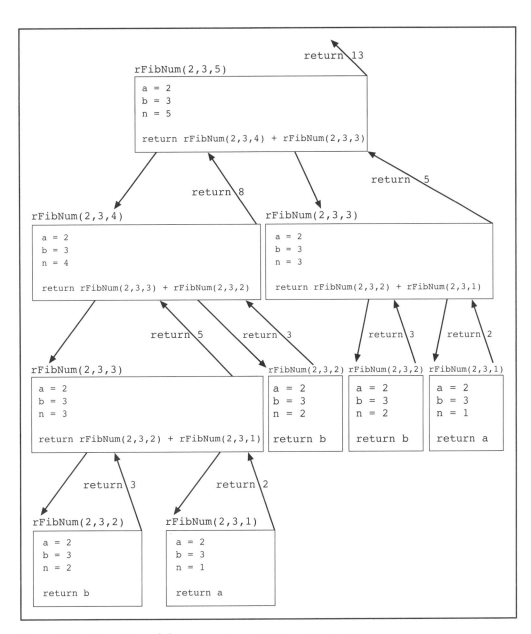

Figure 6-7 Execution of the expression rFibNum(2,3,5)

The following C++ program uses the function rFibNum:

```cpp
//Chapter 6: Fibonacci Number

#include <iostream>

using namespace std;

int rFibNum(int a, int b, int n);

int main()
{
    int firstFibNum;
    int secondFibNum;
    int nth;

    cout<<"Enter the first Fibonacci number: ";
    cin>>firstFibNum;
    cout<<endl;

    cout<<"Enter the second Fibonacci number: ";
    cin>>secondFibNum;
    cout<<endl;

    cout<<"Enter the position of the desired Fibonacci number: ";
    cin>>nth;
    cout<<endl;

    cout<<"The Fibonacci number at position "<<nth<<" is: "
        << rFibNum(firstFibNum, secondFibNum, nth)<<endl;

    return 0;
}

int rFibNum(int a, int b, int n)
{
    if(n == 1)
        return a;
    else if(n == 2)
            return b;
    else
        return rFibNum(a, b, n - 1) + rFibNum(a, b, n - 2);
}
```

Sample Runs: In these sample runs, the user input is shaded.

Sample Run 1

```
Enter the first Fibonacci number: 2

Enter the second Fibonacci number: 5

Enter the position of the desired Fibonacci number: 6

The Fibonacci number at position 6 is: 31
```

Sample Run 2

```
Enter the first Fibonacci number: 3

Enter the second Fibonacci number: 4

Enter the position of the desired Fibonacci number: 6

The Fibonacci number at position 6 is: 29
```

Sample Run 3

```
Enter the first Fibonacci number: 12

Enter the second Fibonacci number: 18

Enter the position of the desired Fibonacci number: 15

The Fibonacci number at position 15 is: 9582
```

Example 6-4: Tower of Hanoi

In the nineteenth century, a game called the Tower of Hanoi became popular in Europe. This game represents work that is under way in the temple of Brahma. At the creation of the universe, priests in the temple of Brahma were supposedly given three diamond needles, with one needle containing 64 golden disks. Each golden disk is slightly smaller than the disk below it. The priests' task is to move all 64 disks from the first needle to the third needle. The rules for moving the disks are as follows:

- Only one disk can be moved at a time.

- The removed disk must be placed on one of the needles.

- A larger disk cannot be placed on top of a smaller disk.

The priests were told that once they had moved all the disks from the first needle to the third needle, the universe would come to an end.

Our objective is to write a program that prints the sequence of moves needed to transfer the disks from the first needle to the third needle. Figure 6-8 shows the Tower of Hanoi problem with three disks.

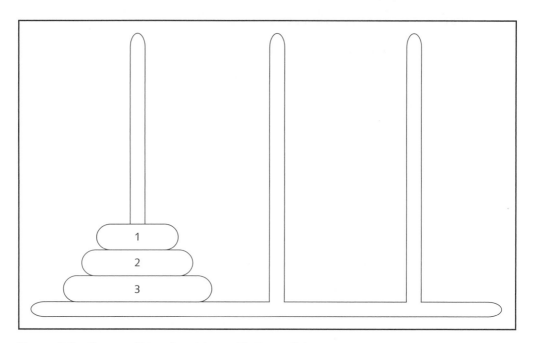

Figure 6-8   Tower of Hanoi problem with three disks

As before, we think in terms of recursion. Let us first consider the case when the first needle contains only one disk. In this case, the disk can be moved directly from needle 1 to needle 3. So let us consider the case when the first needle contains only two disks. In this case, first we move the first disk from needle 1 to needle 2, and then we move the second disk from needle 1 to needle 3. Finally, we move the first disk from needle 2 to needle 3. Next, we consider the case when the first needle contains three disks and then generalize this to the case of 64 disks (in fact, to an arbitrary number of disks).

Suppose that needle 1 contains three disks. To move disk number 3 to needle 3, the top two disks must first be moved to needle 2. Disk number 3 can then be moved from needle 1 to needle 3. To move the top two disks from needle 2 to needle 3, we use the same strategy as before. This time we use needle 1 as the intermediate needle. Figure 6-9 shows a solution to the Tower of Hanoi problem with three disks.

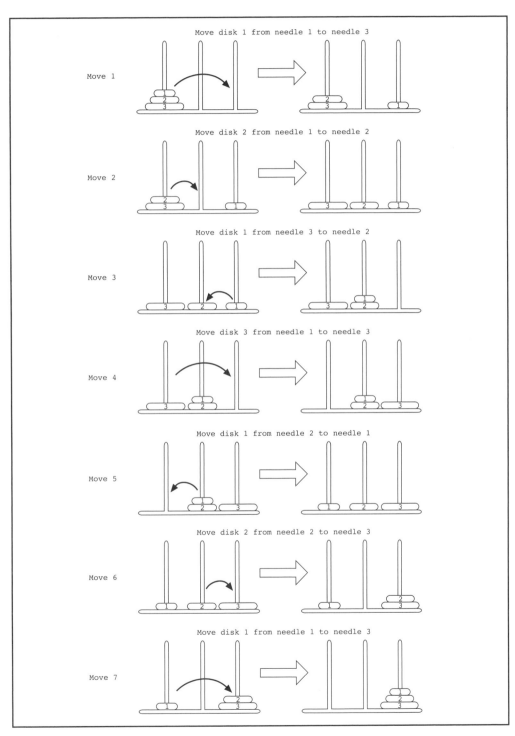

Figure 6-9   Solution to the Tower of Hanoi problem with three disks

Let us now generalize this problem to the case of 64 disks. To begin, the first needle contains all 64 disks. Disk number 64 cannot be moved from needle 1 to needle 3 unless the top 63 disks are on the second needle. So first we move the top 63 disks from needle 1 to needle 2, and then we move disk number 64 from needle 1 to needle 3. Now the top 63 disks are all on needle 2. To move disk number 63 from needle 2 to needle 3, we first move the top 62 disks from needle 2 to needle 1, and then we move disk number 63 from needle 2 to needle 3. To move the remaining 62 disks, we use a similar procedure. This discussion translates into the following recursive algorithm given in pseudocode. Suppose that needle 1 contains n disks, where $n \geq 1$.

1. Move the top $n - 1$ disks from needle 1 to needle 2 using needle 3 as the intermediate needle.

2. Move disk number n from needle 1 to needle 3.

3. Move the top $n - 1$ disks from needle 2 to needle 3 using needle 1 as the intermediate needle.

This recursive algorithm translates into the following C++ function:

```
void moveDisks(int count, int needle1, int needle3, int needle2)
{
    if(count > 0)
    {
        moveDisks(count - 1, needle1, needle2, needle3);
        cout<<"Move disk "<<count<<" from "<<needle1
            <<" to "<<needle3<<"."<<endl;
        moveDisks(count - 1, needle2, needle3, needle1);
    }
}
```

Next, let us determine how long it would take to move all the disks from needle 1 to needle 3.

If needle 1 contains three disks, then the number of moves required to move all 3 disks from needle 1 to needle 3 is $2^3 - 1 = 7$. Similarly, if needle 1 contains 64 disks, then the number of moves required to move all 64 disks from needle 1 to needle 3 is $2^{64} - 1$. Because

$$2^{10} = 1024 \approx 1000 = 10^3,$$

we have

$$2^{64} = 2^4 * 2^{60} \approx 2^4 * 10^{18} = 1.6 * 10^{19}.$$

Here the symbol $\approx$ means approximately equal to. The number of seconds in one year is approximately $3.2 * 10^7$. Suppose the priests move one disk per second and they do not rest. Now

$$1.6 * 10^{19} = 5 * 3.2 * 10^{18} = 5 * (3.2 * 10^7) * 10^{11} = (3.2 * 10^7) * (5 * 10^{11}).$$

The time required to move all 64 disks from needle 1 to needle 3 is roughly $5 * 10^{11}$ years. It is estimated that our universe is about 15 billion ($= 1.5 * 10^{10}$) years old. Also,

$$5 * 10^{11} = 50 * 10^{10} \approx 33 * (1.5 * 10^{10}).$$

This calculation shows that our universe would last about 33 times as long as it already has.

Assume that a computer can generate 1 billion (= 10^9) moves per second. Then the number of moves that the computer can generate in one year is

$(3.2 * 10^7) * 10^9 = 3.2 * 10^{16}$.

So the computer time required to generate 2^{64} moves is

$2^{64} \approx 1.6 * 10^{19} = 1.6 * 10^{16} * 10^3 = (3.2 * 10^{16}) * 500$.

Thus, it would take about 500 years for the computer to generate 2^{64} moves at the rate of 1 billion moves per second.

6

Example 6-5: Converting a Number from Decimal to Binary

This example discusses and designs a program that uses recursion to convert a nonnegative integer in decimal format—that is, base 10—into the equivalent binary number—that is, base 2. First we define some terms.

Let **x** be a non-negative integer. We call the remainder of **x** after division by 2 the **rightmost bit** of **x**.

Thus, the rightmost bit of 33 is 1 because 33 % 2 is 1, and the rightmost bit of 28 is 0 because 28 % 2 is 0.

We first illustrate the algorithm to convert an integer in base 10 to the equivalent number in binary format with the help of an example.

Suppose we want to find the binary representation of 35. First, we divide 35 by 2. The quotient is 17 and the remainder—that is, the rightmost bit of 35—is 1. Next, we divide 17 by 2. The quotient is 8 and the remainder—that is, the rightmost bit of 17—is 1. Next, we divide 8 by 2. The quotient is 4 and the remainder—that is, the rightmost bit of 8—is 0. We continue this process until the quotient becomes 0.

The rightmost bit of 35 cannot be printed until we have printed the rightmost bit of 17. The rightmost bit of 17 cannot be printed until we have printed the rightmost bit of 8, and so on. Thus, the binary representation of 35 is the binary representation of 17 (that is, the quotient of 35 after division by 2), followed by the rightmost bit of 35.

Thus, to convert a non-negative integer **num** in base 10 into the equivalent binary number, we first convert the quotient **num/2** into an equivalent binary number, and then append the rightmost bit of **num** to the binary representation of **num/2**.

This discussion translates into the following recursive algorithm, where `binary(num)` denotes the binary representation of **num**:

1. `binary(num)` = num if num = 0.

2. `binary(num)` = `binary(num/2)` followed by num % 2 if num > 0.

The following recursive function implements this algorithm:

```
void decToBin(int num, int base)
{
   if(num > 0)
   {
      decToBin(num/base, base);
      cout<<num % base;
   }
}
```

Figure 6-10 traces the execution of the following statement:

```
decToBin(13,2);
```

where num is 13 and base is 2.

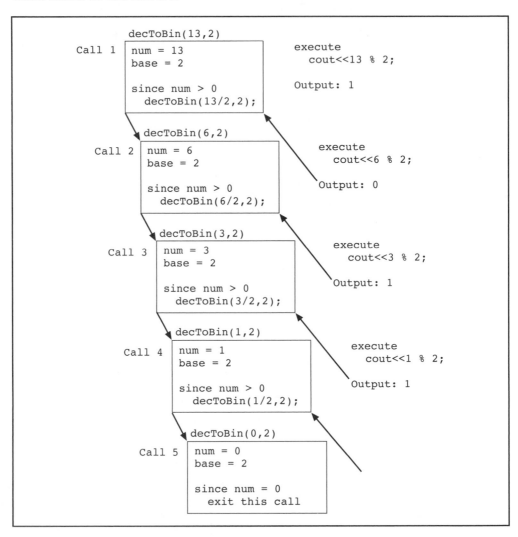

Figure 6-10   Execution of the statement decToBin(13,2);

Because the `if` statement in call 5 fails, this call does not print anything. The first output is produced by call 4, which prints 1; the second output is produced by call 3, which prints 1; the third output is produced by call 2, which prints 0; and the fourth output is produced by call 1, which prints 1. Thus, the output of the statement

```
decToBin(13, 2);
```

is

```
1101
```

The following C++ program uses the function `decToBin`:

```cpp
//Chapter 6: Program - Decimal to Binary

#include <iostream>

using namespace std;

void decToBin(int num, int base);

int main()
{
    int decimalNum;
    int base;

    base = 2;

    cout<<"Enter the number in decimal: ";
    cin>>decimalNum;
    cout<<endl;
    cout<<"Decimal "<<decimalNum<<" = ";
    decToBin(decimalNum, base);
    cout<<" binary"<<endl;

    return 0;
}

void decToBin(int num, int base)
{
   if(num > 0)
   {
       decToBin(num/base, base);
       cout<<num % base;
   }
}
```

Sample Run: In this sample run, the user input is shaded.

```
Enter the number in decimal: 57
Decimal 57 = 111001 binary
```

RECURSION OR ITERATION?

The programs in the preceding chapters used a loop to repeat a set of statements to perform certain calculations. In other words, the programs in the preceding chapters used an iterative control structure to repeat a set of statements. More formally, **iterative control structures** use a looping structure, such as `while`, `for`, or `do...while`, to repeat a set of statements. At the beginning of this chapter, we designed a recursive function to calculate the factorial of a nonnegative integer. From the factorial function, it follows that in recursion a set of statements is repeated by having the function call itself. Moreover, a selection control structure controls the repeated calls in recursion.

In this chapter, we also used recursion to determine the largest element in a list and to determine a Fibonacci number. Using an iterative control structure, we can also write an algorithm to find the largest number in an array. Similarly, an algorithm that uses an iterative control structure can be designed to find the factorial of a nonnegative integer. The only reason to give a recursive solution to these problems is to illustrate how recursion works.

We thus see that there are usually two ways to solve a particular problem—iteration and recursion. The obvious question is which method is better—iteration or recursion? There is no simple answer to this question. In addition to the nature of the problem, the other key factor in determining the best solution method is efficiency.

When a function is called, memory space for its formal parameters and (automatic) local variables is allocated. When the function terminates, that memory space is then deallocated. This chapter, while tracing the execution of recursive functions, shows us that every (recursive) call has its own set of parameters and (automatic) local variables. That is, every (recursive) call requires the system to allocate memory space for its formal parameters and (automatic) local variables and then deallocate the memory space when the function exits. Thus, overhead is associated with executing a (recursive) function both in terms of memory space and computer time. Therefore, a recursive function executes more slowly than its iterative counterpart. On slower computers, especially those with limited memory space, the (slow) execution of a recursive function would be visible.

Today's computers, however, are fast and have inexpensive memory. Therefore, the execution of a recursive function is not noticeable. Keeping the power of today's computers in mind, the choice between the two alternatives—recursion or iteration—therefore depends on the nature of the problem. Of course, for problems such as mission control systems, efficiency is absolutely critical and, therefore, the efficiency factor would dictate the solution method.

As a general rule, if you think that an iterative solution is more obvious and easier to understand than a recursive solution, use the iterative solution; this would be more efficient. On the other hand, problems exist for which the recursive solution is more obvious or easier to construct, such as the Tower of Hanoi problem. (In fact, it is difficult to construct an iterative solution for the Tower of Hanoi problem.) Keeping the power of recursion in mind, if the definition of a problem is inherently recursive, then you should consider a recursive solution.

RECURSION AND BACKTRACKING: *N*-QUEENS PUZZLE

This section describes a problem-solving and algorithm design technique called backtracking. Let us consider the following 8-queens puzzle: place eight queens on a chessboard (8 × 8 square board) so that no two queens can attack each other. For any two queens to be nonattacking, they cannot be in the same row, same column, or same diagonal. Figure 6-11 gives one possible solution to the 8-queens puzzle.

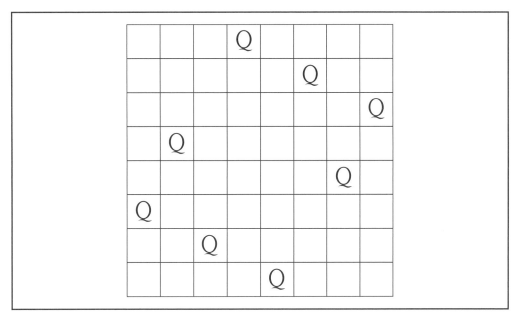

Figure 6-11   A solution to the 8-queens puzzle

In 1850, the 8-queens puzzle was considered by the great C. F. Gauss, who was unable to obtain a complete solution. The term backtrack was first coined by D. H. Lehmer in 1950. In 1960, R. J. Walker gave an algorithmic account of backtracking. A general description of backtracking with a variety of applications was presented by S. Golomb and L. Baumert.

Backtracking

The backtracking algorithm attempts to find solutions to a problem by constructing partial solutions, and then making sure that any partial solution does not violate the problem requirements. The algorithm tries to extend a partial solution towards completion. However, if it is determined that the partial solution would not lead to a solution, that is, the partial solution would end in a dead end, then the algorithm backs up by removing the most recently added part and trying other possibilities.

n-Queens Puzzle

In backtracking, the solution to the *n*-queens puzzle, because each queen must be placed in a different row, can be represented as an *n*-tuple $(x_1, x_2, ..., x_n)$, where x_i is an integer such that $1 \le x_i \le n$. In this tuple, x_i specifies the column number where to place the *i*th queen in the *i*th row. Therefore, for the 8-queens puzzle the solution is an 8-tuple $(x_1, x_2, x_3, x_4, x_5, x_6, x_7, x_8)$, where x_i is the column where to place the *i*th queen in the *i*th row. For example, the solution in Figure 6-11 can be represented as the 8-tuple $(4, 6, 8, 2, 7, 1, 3, 5)$. That is, the first queen is placed in the first row and fourth column, the second queen is placed in the second row and sixth column, and so on. Clearly, each x_i is an integer such that $1 \le x_i \le 8$.

Let us again consider the 8-tuple $(x_1, x_2, x_3, x_4, x_5, x_6, x_7, x_8)$, where x_i is an integer such that $1 \le x_i \le 8$. Because each x_i has eight choices, there are 8^8 such tuples, and so possibly 8^8 solutions. However, because no two queens can be placed in the same row, no two elements of the 8-tuple $(x_1, x_2, x_3, x_4, x_5, x_6, x_7, x_8)$ are the same. From this, it follows that the number of 8-tuples possibly representing solutions is 8!.

The solution that we develop can, in fact, be applied to any number of queens. Therefore, to illustrate the backtracking technique, we consider the 4-queens puzzle. That is, you are given a 4 × 4 square board (see Figure 6-12) and you are to place four queens on the board so that no two queens can attack each other.

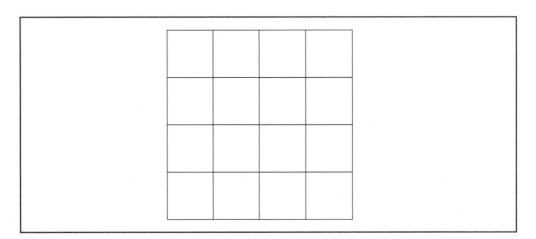

Figure 6-12   Square board for the 4-queens puzzle

We start by placing the first queen in the first row and first column as shown in Figure 6-13(a). (A cross in a box means that no other queen can be placed in that box.)

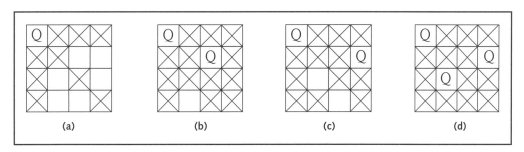

Figure 6-13   Finding a solution to the 4-queens puzzle

After placing the first queen, we try to place the second queen in the second row. Clearly, the first square in the second row where the second queen can be placed is the third column. So we place the second queen in that column; see Figure 6-13(b).

Next, we try to place the third queen in the third row. We find that the third queen cannot be placed in the third row and so we arrive at a dead end. At this point, we backtrack to the previous board configuration and place the second queen in the fourth column; see Figure 6-13(c). Next, we try to place the third queen in the third row. This time, we successfully place the third queen in the second column of the third row; see Figure 6-13(d). After placing the third queen in the third row, when we try to place the fourth queen, we discover that the fourth queen cannot be placed in the fourth row.

We backtrack to the third row and try placing the queen in any other column. Because no other column is available for queen three, we backtrack to row 2 and try placing the second queen in any other column, which cannot be done. We, therefore, backtrack to the first row and place the first queen in the next column. After placing the first queen in the second column, we place the remaining queens in the successive rows. This time we obtain the solution as shown in Figure 6-14.

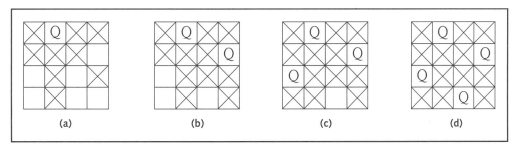

Figure 6-14   Solution to the 4-queens puzzle

Backtracking and 4-Queens Puzzle

Suppose that the rows of the square board of the 4-queens puzzle are numbered 0 through 3 and the columns are numbered 0 through 3. (Recall that, in C++, an array index starts at 0.)

For the 4-queens puzzle, we start by placing the first queen in the first row and first column, thus generating the tuple (0). We then place the second queen in the third column of the second row and so generate the tuple (0,2). When we try to place the third queen in the third row, we determined that the third queen cannot be placed in the third row. Therefore, we back up to the partial solution (0,2), remove 2 from the tuple and then generate the tuple (0,3); that is, the second queen is placed in the fourth column of the second row. With the partial solution (0,3), we then try to place the third queen in the third row and generate the tuple (0,3,1). Next, with the partial solution (0,3,1), when we try to place the fourth queen in the fourth row, it is determined that it cannot be done and so the partial solution (0,3,1) ends up in a dead end.

From the partial solution (0,3,1), the backtracking algorithm, in fact, backs up to placing the first queen and so removes all the elements of the tuple. The algorithm then places the first queen in the second column of the first row and thus generates the partial solution (1). In this case, the sequence of the partial solution generated is (1), (1,3), (1,3,0), and (1,3,0,2), which represents a solution to the 4-queens puzzle. The solutions generated by the backtracking algorithm can be represented by a tree, as shown in Figure 6–15.

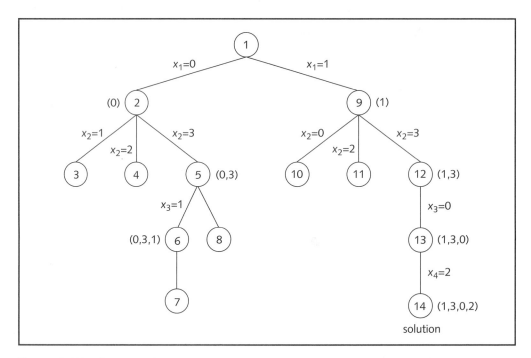

Figure 6-15   4-queens tree

8-Queens Puzzle

Let us now consider the 8-queens puzzle. Like the 4-queens puzzle, no two queens can be in the same row, same column, or same diagonal. Determining whether two queens are in the same row or column is easy because we can check their row and column positions. Let us describe how to determine whether two queens are in the same diagonal or not.

Consider the 8×8 square board shown in Figure 6-16. The rows are numbered 0 through 7; the columns are numbered 0 through 7. (Recall that, in C++, the array index starts at 0.)

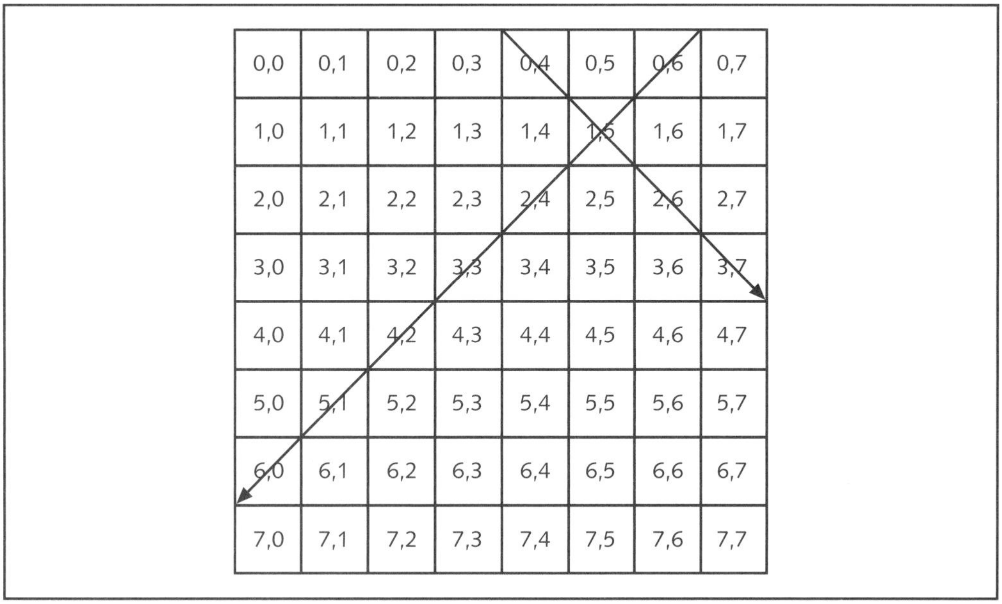

Figure 6-16   8 x 8 square board

Consider the diagonal from upper left to lower right, as indicated by the arrow. The positions of the squares on this diagonal are (0, 4), (1,5), (2,6), and (3,7). Notice that for these entries `rowPosition – columnPosition` is -4. For example, $0 - 4 = 1 - 5 = 2 - 6 = 3 - 7 = -4$. It can be shown that for each square on a diagonal from upper left to lower right, `rowPosition – columnPosition` is the same.

Now consider the diagonal from upper right to lower left as indicated by the arrow. The positions of the squares on this diagonal are (0,6), (1,5), (2,4), (3,3), (4,2), (5,1), and (6,0). Here `rowPosition + columnPosition = 6`. It can be shown that for each square on a diagonal from upper right to lower left, `rowPosition + columnPosition` is the same.

We can use these results to determine whether two queens are on the same diagonal or not. Suppose a queen is at position (i, j), (row i and column j), and another queen is at position (k, l), (row k and column l). These queens are on the same diagonal if either $i + j = k + l$ or $i - j = k - l$. The first equation implies that $j - l = k - i$; the second equation implies that $j - l = i - k$. From this it follows that the two queens are on the same diagonal if $|j - l| = |i - k|$, where $|j - l|$ is the absolute value of $j - l$ and so on.

Because a solution to the 8-queens puzzle is represented as an 8-tuple, we use the array `queensInRow` of size 8, where `queensInRow[k]` specifies the column position of the kth queen in row k. For example, `queensInRow[0]` = 3 means that the first queen is placed in column 3 (which is the fourth column) of row 0 (which is the first row).

Suppose that we place the first $k - 1$ queens in the first $k - 1$ rows. Next, we try to place the kth queen in a column of the kth row. We write the function `canPlaceQueen(k,i)`, which returns `true` if the kth queen can be placed in the ith column of row k; otherwise, it returns `false`.

The first $k - 1$ queens are in the first $k - 1$ rows and we are trying to place the kth queen in the kth row. The kth row, therefore, must first be empty. It thus follows that the kth queen can be placed in column i of row k, provided no other queen is in column i and no queens are on the diagonals on which square (k, i) lies. The general algorithm for the function `canPlaceQueen(k,i)` is

```
for(int j = 0; j < k; j++)
    if((queensInRow[j] == i)  //there is already a queen in column i
       || (abs(queensInRow[j] - i) == abs(j-k))) //there is already
                                //a queen in one of the diagonals
                                //on which square (k,i) lies

        return false

return true
```

The `for` loop checks whether there is already a queen either in column i or in one of the diagonals on which square (k, i) lies. If it finds a queen at any of such positions, the `for` loop returns the value `false`; otherwise, the value `true` is returned.

The following class defines the n-queens puzzle as an ADT.

```
class nQueensPuzzle
{
public:
    nQueensPuzzle(int queens = 8);
    //constructor
    //Postcondition: noOfSolutions = 0; noOfQueens = queens;
    //               queensInRow is a pointer to the array
    //               that stores the n-tuple.
    //    If the user does not specify any value for the
    //    parameter queens, then the default value, which is 8,
    //    is assigned to it.
    //    bool canPlaceQueen(int k, int i);
```

```
    //Function to determine whether a queen can be placed
    //in row k and column i.
    //Postcondition: Returns true if a queen can be placed in
    //               row k and column i; otherwise, returns false.

void queensConfiguration(int k);
    //Function to determine all the solutions to the n-queens
    //puzzle using backtracking.
    //The function is called with the value 0.
    //Postcondition: All n-tuples representing solutions to the
    //               n-queens puzzle are generated and printed.

void printConfiguration();
    //Function to output an n-tuple containing a solution
    //to the n-queens puzzle.

int solutionsCount();
    //Function to return the total number of solutions.
    //Postcondition: The value of noOfSolutions is returned.

private:
    int noOfSolutions;
    int noOfQueens;
    int *queensInRow;
};
```

The definitions of the member functions of the **class nQueensPuzzle** are given next.

```
nQueensPuzzle::nQueensPuzzle(int queens)
{
    noOfQueens = queens;
    queensInRow = new int[noOfQueens];
    noOfSolutions = 0;
}

bool nQueensPuzzle::canPlaceQueen(int k, int i)
{
    for(int j = 0; j < k; j++)
        if((queensInRow[j] == i
            || (abs(queensInRow[j] - i) == abs(j-k)))
            return false;
    return true;
}
```

Using recursion, the function **queensConfiguration** implements the backtracking technique to determine all the solutions to the *n*-queens puzzle. The parameter **k** specifies the queen to be placed in the *k*th row. Its definition is:

6

```
void nQueensPuzzle::queensConfiguration(int k)
{
   for(int i = 0; i < noOfQueens; i++)
   {
      if(canPlaceQueen(k, i))
      {
         queensInRow[k] = i;  //place the kth queen in column i
         if(k == noOfQueens - 1)  //all the queens are placed
            printConfiguration(); //print the n-tuple
         else
            queensConfiguration(k + 1)    //determine the place for
                                          //the (k+1)th queen
      }
   }
}

void nQueensPuzzle::printConfiguration()
{
   noOfSolutions++;
   cout<<"(";
   for(int i = 0; i < noOfQueens - 1; i++)
       cout<<queensInRow[i]<<", ";

   cout<<queensInRow[noOfQueens - 1]<<")"<<endl;
}

int nQueensPuzzle::solutionsCount()
{
   return noOfSolutions;
}
```

We leave it as an exercise for you to write a program to test the *n*–queens puzzle for various board sizes.

QUICK REVIEW

1. The process of solving a problem by reducing it to smaller versions of itself is called recursion.
2. A recursive definition defines the problem in terms of smaller versions of itself.
3. Every recursive definition has one or more base cases.
4. A recursive algorithm solves a problem by reducing it to smaller versions of itself.
5. Every recursive algorithm has one or more base cases.
6. The solution to the problem in a base case is obtained directly.
7. A function is called recursive if it calls itself.
8. Recursive algorithms are implemented using recursive functions.

9. Every recursive function must have one or more base cases.

10. The general solution breaks the problem into smaller versions of itself.

11. The general case must eventually be reduced to a base case.

12. The base case stops the recursion.

13. While tracing a recursive function:

    ■ Logically, you can think of a recursive function as having unlimited copies of itself.

    ■ Every call to a recursive function—that is, every recursive call—has its own code and its own set of parameters and local variables.

    ■ After completing a particular recursive call, the control goes back to the calling environment, which is the previous call. The current (recursive) call must execute completely before the control goes back to the previous call. The execution in the previous call begins from the point immediately following the recursive call.

14. A function is called directly recursive if it calls itself.

15. A function that calls another function and eventually results in the original function call is said to be indirectly recursive.

16. A recursive function in which the last statement executed is the recursive call is called a tail recursive function.

17. To design a recursive function, you must do the following:

    a. Understand the problem requirements.

    b. Determine the limiting condition(s). For example, the limiting condition for a list is determined by the number of elements in the list.

    c. Identify the base cases and provide a direct solution to each base case.

    d. Identify the general cases and provide a solution to each general case in terms of a smaller version of itself.

18. The backtracking algorithm attempts to find solutions to a problem by constructing partial solutions and then making sure that any partial solution does not violate the problem requirements. The algorithm tries to extend a partial solution towards completion. However, if it is determined that the partial solution would not lead to a solution, that is, the partial solution would end in a dead end, the algorithm backs up by removing the most recently added part and then tries other possibilities.

EXERCISES

1. Mark the following statements as true or false.

   a. Every recursive definition must have one or more base cases.

   b. Every recursive function must have one or more base cases.

   c. The general case stops the recursion.

   d. In the general case, the solution to the problem is obtained directly.

   e. A recursive function always returns a value.

2. What is a base case?

3. What is a recursive case?

4. What is direct recursion?

5. What is indirect recursion?

6. What is tail recursion?

7. Consider the following recursive function.

```
int mystery(int number)                                    //Line 1
{
    if(number == 0)                                        //Line 2
        return number;                                     //Line 3
    else                                                   //Line 4
        return(number + mystery(number - 1));              //Line 5
}
```

a. Identify the base case.

b. Identify the general case.

c. What valid values can be passed as parameters to the function `mystery`?

d. If `mystery(0)` is a valid call, what is its value? If not, explain why.

e. If `mystery(5)` is a valid call, what is its value? If not, explain why.

f. If `mystery(-3)` is a valid call, what is its value? If not, explain why.

8. Consider the following recursive function:

```
void funcRec(int u, char v)                                          //Line 1
{
    if(u == 0)                                                       //Line 2
        cout<<v;                                                     //Line 3
    else if(u == 1)                                                  //Line 4
            cout<<static_cast<char>(static_cast<int>(v) + 1); //Line 5
    else                                                             //Line 6
        funcRec(u - 1, v);                                           //Line 7
}
```

Answer the following:

a. Identify the base case.

b. Identify the general case.

c. What is the output of the following statement?

```
funcRec(5,'A');
```

9. Consider the following recursive function:

```
void exercise(int x)
{
    if(x > 0 && x < 10)
    {
        cout<<x<<" ";
        exercise(x+1);
    }
}
```

What is the output of the following statements?

a. `exercise(0);`

b. `exercise(5);`

c. `exercise(10);`

d. `exercise(-5);`

10. Consider the following function:

```
int test(int x, int y)
{
    if(x == y)
        return x;
    else if(x > y)
            return (x + y);
    else
        return test(x + 1, y - 1);
}
```

What is the output of the following statements?

a. `cout<<test(5,10)<<endl;`

b. `cout<<test(3,19)<<endl;`

11. Consider the following function:

```
int Func(int x)
{
    if(x == 0)
        return 2;
    else if(x == 1)
            return 3;
    else
        return (Func(x - 1) + Func(x - 2));
}
```

What is the output of the following statements?

a. `cout<<Func(0)<<endl;`

b. `cout<<Func(1)<<endl;`

c. `cout<<Func(2)<<endl;`

d. `cout<<Func(5)<<endl;`

12. Suppose that `intArray` is an array of integers, and `length` specifies the number of elements in `intArray`. Also suppose that `low` and `high` are two integers such that `0 <= low < length, 0 <= high < length`, and `low < high`. That is, `low` and `high` are two indices in `intArray`. Write a recursive definition that reverses the elements in `intArray` between `low` and `high`.

13. Write a recursive algorithm to multiply two positive integers m and n using repeated addition. Specify the base case and the recursive case.

14. Consider the following problem: How many ways can a committee of four people be selected from a group of 10 people? There are many other similar problems, where you are asked to find the number of ways to select a set of items from a given set of items. The general problem can be stated as follows: find the number of ways r different things can be chosen from a set of n items, where r and n are nonnegative integers and $r \le n$. Suppose $C(n, r)$ denotes the number of ways r different things can be chosen from a set of n items. Then $C(n, r)$ is given by the following formula:

$$C(n,r) = \frac{n!}{r! \ (n-r)!},$$

where the exclamation point denotes the factorial function. Moreover, $C(n, 0) = C(n, n) = 1$. It is also known that $C(n, r) = C(n - 1, r - 1) + C(n - 1, r)$.

a. Write a recursive algorithm to determine $C(n, r)$. Identify the base case(s) and the general case(s).

b. Using your recursive algorithm, determine $C(5, 3)$ and $C(9, 4)$.

PROGRAMMING EXERCISES

1. Write a recursive function that takes as a parameter a nonnegative integer and generates the following pattern of stars. If the nonnegative integer is 4, then the pattern generated is:

```
****
***
**
*
*
**
***
****
```

Also, write a program that prompts the user to enter the number of lines in the pattern and uses the recursive function to generate the pattern. For example, specifying 4 as the number of lines generates the above pattern.

2. Write a recursive function to generate a pattern of stars such as the following:

```
*
* *
* * *
* * * *
* * * *
* * *
* *
*
```

Also, write a program that prompts the user to enter the number of lines in the pattern and uses the recursive function to generate the pattern. For example, specifying 4 as the number of lines generates the above pattern.

3. Write a recursive function to generate the following pattern of stars.

```
    *
   * *
  * * *
 * * * *
  * * *
   * *
    *
```

Also, write a program that prompts the user to enter the number of lines in the pattern and uses the recursive function to generate the pattern. For example, specifying 4 as the number of lines generates the above pattern.

4. Write a recursive function, `vowels`, that returns the number of vowels in a string. Also, write a program to test your function.

5. Write a recursive function that finds and returns the sum of the elements of an `int` array. Also, write a program to test your function.

6. A palindrome is a string that reads the same both forward and backward. For example, the string `"madam"` is a palindrome. Write a program that uses a recursive function to check whether a string is a palindrome. Your program must contain a value-returning recursive function that returns `true` if the string is a palindrome, and `false` otherwise. Do not use any global variables; use the appropriate parameters.

7. Write a program that uses a recursive function to print a string backwards. Your program must contain a recursive function that prints the string backwards. Do not use any global variables; use appropriate parameters.

8. Write a recursive function, `reverseDigits`, that takes an integer as a parameter and returns the number with the digits reversed. Also, write a program to test your function.

9. Write a recursive function, `power`, that takes as parameters two integers x and y such that x is nonzero and returns x^y. You can use the following recursive definition to calculate x^y. If $y \geq 0$,

$$power(x, y) = \begin{cases} 1 & \text{if } y = 0 \\ x & \text{if } y = 1 \\ x * power(x, y-1) & \text{if } y > 1 \end{cases}$$

If $y < 0$,

$$power(x, y) = \frac{1}{power(x, -y)}$$

Also, write a program to test your function.

10. **(Greatest Common Divisor)** Given two integers x and y, the following recursive definition determines the greatest common divisor of x and y, written $gcd(x,y)$:

$$gcd(x, y) = \begin{cases} x & \text{if } y = 0 \\ gcd(y, x\%y) & \text{if } y \neq 0 \end{cases}$$

 Notice that in this definition, % is the mod operator.

Write a recursive function, gcd, that takes as parameters two integers and returns the greatest common divisor of the numbers. Also, write a program to test your function.

11. Write a recursive function to implement the recursive algorithm of Exercise 12 (reversing the elements of an array between two indices). Write a program to test your function.

12. Write a recursive function to implement the recursive algorithm of Exercise 13 (multiplying two positive integers using repeated addition). Write a program to test your function.

13. Write a recursive function to implement the recursive algorithm of Exercise 14 (determining the number of ways of selecting a set of things from a given set of things). Write a program to test your function.

14. In Example 6-5, "Converting a Number from Decimal to Binary," you learned how to convert a decimal number into the equivalent binary number. Two more number systems, octal (base 8) and hexadecimal (base 16), are of interest to computer scientists. In fact, in C++, you can instruct the computer to store a number in octal or hexadecimal.

The digits in the octal number system are 0, 1, 2, 3, 4, 5, 6, and 7. The digits in the hexadecimal number system are 0, 1, 2, 3, 4, 5, 6, 7, 8, 9, A, B, C, D, E, and F. So A in hexadecimal is 10 in decimal, B in hexadecimal is 11 in decimal, and so on.

The algorithm to convert a positive decimal number into an equivalent number in octal (or hexadecimal) is the same as discussed for binary numbers. Here we divide the decimal number by 8 (for octal) and by 16 (for hexadecimal). Suppose a_b represents the number a to the base b. For example, 75_{10} means 75 to the base 10 (that is decimal), and 83_{16} means 83 to the base 16 (that is, hexadecimal). Then

$$753_{10} = 1361_8$$
$$753_{10} = 2F1_{16}$$

The method of converting a decimal number to base 2, 8, or 16 can be extended to any arbitrary base. Suppose you want to convert a decimal number n into an equivalent number in base b, where b is between 2 and 36. You then divide the decimal number n by b as in the algorithm for converting decimal to binary.

Note that the digits in, say base 20, are 0, 1, 2, 3, 4, 5, 6, 7, 8, 9, A, B, C, D, E, F, G, H, I, and J.

Write a program that uses a recursive function to convert a number in decimal to a given base b, where b is between 2 and 36. Your program should prompt the user to enter the number in decimal and then enter the desired base.

Test your program on the following data:

9098 and base 20

692 and base 2

753 and base 16

15. **(Converting a Number from Binary to Decimal)** The language of a computer, called machine language, is a sequence of 0s and 1s. When you press the key A on the keyboard, 01000001 is stored in the computer. Also, the collating sequence of A in the ASCII character set is 65. In fact, the binary representation of A is 01000001 and the decimal representation of A is 65.

The numbering system we use is called the decimal system, or base 10 system. The numbering system that the computer uses is called the binary system, or base 2 system. Example 6-5 describes how to convert a decimal number into an equivalent binary number. The purpose of this exercise is to write a function to convert a number from base 2 to base 10.

To convert a number from base 2 to base 10, we first find the weight of each bit in the binary number. The weight of each bit in the binary number is assigned from right to left. The weight of the rightmost bit is 0. The weight of the bit immediately to the left of the rightmost bit is 1, the weight of the bit immediately to the left of it is 2, and so on. Consider the binary number 1001101. The weight of each bit is as follows:

```
weight   6  5  4  3  2  1  0
         1  0  0  1  1  0  1
```

We use the weight of each bit to find the equivalent decimal number. For each bit, we multiply the bit by 2 to the power of its weight, and then we add all of the numbers. For the binary number 1001101, the equivalent decimal number is

$$1 * 2^6 + 0 * 2^5 + 0 * 2^4 + 1 * 2^3 + 1 * 2^2 + 0 * 2^1 + 1 * 2^0$$
$$= 64 + 0 + 0 + 8 + 4 + 0 + 1$$
$$= 77$$

To write a program that converts a binary number into the equivalent decimal number, we note two things: (1) the weight of each bit in the binary number must be known, and (2) the weight is assigned from right to left. Because we do not know in advance how many bits are in the binary number, we must process the bits from right to left. After processing a bit, we can add 1 to its weight, giving the weight of the bit immediately to its left. Also, each bit must be extracted from the binary number and multiplied by 2 to the power of its weight. To extract a bit, you can use the mod operator.

Write a function that converts a binary number into an equivalent decimal number. Moreover, write a program and test your function for the following values: 11000101, 10101010, 11111111, 10000000, 1111100000.

16. The function `sqrt` from the header file `cmath` can be used to find the square root of a nonnegative real number. Using Newton's method, you can also write an algorithm to find the square root of a nonnegative real number within a given tolerance as follows: Suppose x is a nonnegative real number, a is the approximate square root of x, and *epsilon* is the tolerance. Start with $a = x$;

a. If $|a*a-x| \leq epsilon$, then a is the square root of x within the tolerance; otherwise

b. Replace a with $(a*a+x)/(2*a)$ and repeat Step a.

where $|a*a-x|$ denotes the absolute value of $a*a-x$.

Write a recursive function to implement this algorithm to find the square root of a nonnegative real number. Also, write a program to test your function.

17. Write a program to find solutions to the *n*-queens puzzle for various values of *n*. To be specific, test your program for $n = 4$ and $n = 8$.

18. (Knight's tour) This chapter described the backtracking algorithm and how to use recursion to implement it. Another well-known chessboard problem that can be solved using the backtracking algorithm is the knight's tour. Given an initial board position, determine a sequence of moves by a knight that visits every square of the chessboard exactly once. For example, for a 5 × 5 and 6 × 6 square board, Figure 6-17 shows the sequence of moves.

						1	16	7	26	11	14
1	6	15	10	21		34	25	12	15	6	27
14	9	20	5	16		17	2	33	8	13	10
19	2	7	22	11		32	35	24	21	28	5
8	13	24	17	4		23	18	3	30	9	20
25	18	3	12	23		36	31	22	19	4	29

Figure 6-17 Knight's tour

A knight moves by jumping two positions either vertically or horizontally and one position in the perpendicular direction. Write a recursive backtracking program that takes as input an initial board position and determines a sequence of moves by a knight that visits each square of the board exactly once.

STACKS

In this chapter, you will:

♦ Learn about stacks

♦ Examine various stack operations

♦ Learn how to implement a stack as an array

♦ Learn how to implement a stack as a linked list

♦ Discover stack applications

♦ Learn how to use a stack to remove recursion

♦ Become aware of the STL `class stack`

This chapter discusses a very useful data structure called the stack. It has numerous applications in computer science.

STACKS

Suppose that you have a program with several functions. To be specific, suppose that your program has the functions A, B, C, and D. Now suppose that function A calls function B, function B calls function C, and function C calls function D. When function D terminates, control goes back to function C; when function C terminates, control goes back to function B; and when function B terminates, control goes back to function A. During program execution, how do you think the computer keeps track of the function calls? What about recursive functions? How does the computer keep track of recursive calls? In Chapter 6, we designed a recursive function to print a linked list backwards. What if you want to write a nonrecursive algorithm to print a linked list backwards?

This section discusses the data structure called the **stack**. The computer uses the stack to implement function calls. You can also use stacks to convert recursive algorithms into nonrecursive algorithms, especially recursive algorithms that are not tail recursive. Stacks have numerous other applications in computer science. After developing the tools necessary to implement a stack, we will examine some applications of stacks.

A stack is a list of homogeneous elements, wherein the addition and deletion of elements occurs only at one end, called the **top** of the stack. For example, in a cafeteria, the second tray in a stack of trays can be removed only if the first tray has been removed. For another example, to get to your favorite computer science book, which is underneath your math and history books, you must first remove the math and history books. After removing these two books, the computer science book becomes the top book—that is, the top element of the stack. Figure 7-1 shows some examples of stacks.

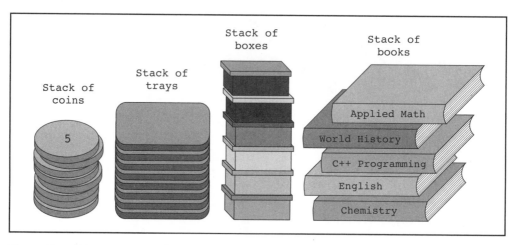

Figure 7-1 Various types of stacks

The elements at the bottom of the stack have been in the stack the longest. The top element of the stack is the last element added to the stack. Because elements are added and removed from one end (that is, the top), it follows that the item that is added last will be removed first. For this reason, a stack is also called a **Last In First Out (LIFO)** data structure.

Stack: A data structure in which the elements are added and removed from one end only; a Last In First Out (LIFO) data structure.

Now that you know what a stack is, let us see what kinds of operations can be performed on a stack. Because new items can be added to the stack, we can perform the add operation, called **push**, to add an element onto the stack. Similarly, because the top item can be retrieved and/or removed from the stack, we can perform the operation **top** to retrieve the top element of the stack, and the operation **pop** to remove the top element from the stack. Figures 7-2 and 7-3 illustrate the **push**, **top**, and **pop** operations.

The **push**, **top**, and **pop** operations work as follows: Suppose there are boxes lying on the floor that need to be stacked. Initially, all of the boxes are on the floor and the stack is empty. (See Figure 7-2.)

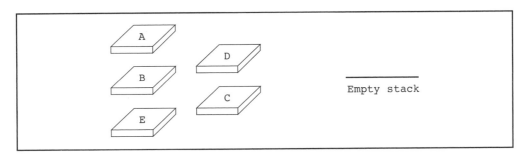

Figure 7-2   Empty stack

First we push box A onto the stack. After this **push** operation, the stack is as shown in Figure 7-3(a).

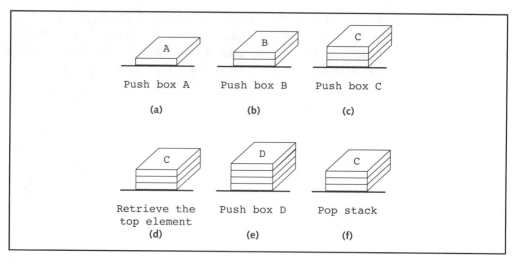

Figure 7-3 Stack operations

We then push box B onto the stack. After this **push** operation, the stack is as shown in Figure 7-3(b). Next, we push box C onto the stack. After this **push** operation, the stack is as shown in Figure 7-3(c). Next, we retrieve the top element of the stack. After this operation, the stack is unchanged and shown in Figure 7-3(d). We then push box D onto the stack. After this **push** operation, the stack is as shown in Figure 7-3(e). Next, we pop the stack. After the **pop** operation, the stack is as shown in Figure 7-3(f).

An element can be removed and/or retrieved from a stack only if there is something in the stack, and an element can be added to a stack only if there is room. The two operations that follow from the **push**, **top**, and **pop** operations are **isFullStack** (checks whether the stack is full) and **isEmptyStack** (checks whether the stack is empty). Because a stack keeps changing as we add and remove elements, the stack must be empty before we first start using it. Thus, we need another operation, called **initializeStack**, which initializes the stack to an empty state. Another useful operation is **destroyStack**. This operation usually removes all the elements from a stack, leaving the stack in an empty state. Therefore, to successfully implement a stack, we need at least these seven operations, as described in the next section. We might also need other operations on a stack, depending on the specific implementation.

Stack Operations

The basic operations on a stack are:

- **initializeStack**: Initializes the stack to an empty state.
- **destroyStack**: Removes all the elements from the stack, leaving the stack empty.
- **isEmptyStack**: Checks whether the stack is empty. If the stack is empty, it returns the value **true**; otherwise, it returns the value **false**.
- **isFullStack**: Checks whether the stack is full. If the stack is full, it returns the value **true**; otherwise, it returns the value **false**.

- **push**: Adds a new element to the top of the stack. The input to this operation consists of the stack and the new element. Prior to this operation, the stack must exist and must not be full.

- **top**: Returns the top element of the stack. Prior to this operation, the stack must exist and must not be empty.

- **pop**: Removes the top element of the stack. Prior to this operation, the stack must exist and must not be empty.

We now consider the implementation of an abstract stack data structure. Because all of the elements of a stack are of the same type, a stack can be implemented either as an array or as a linked structure. Both implementations are useful and are discussed in this chapter.

IMPLEMENTATION OF STACKS AS ARRAYS

Because all of the elements of a stack are of the same type, you can use an array to implement a stack. The first element of the stack can be put in the first array slot, the second element of the stack in the second array slot, and so on. The top of the stack is the index of the last element added to the stack.

In this implementation of a stack, the stack elements are stored in an array, and an array is a random access data structure; that is, you can directly access any element of the array. However, by definition, a stack is a data structure in which the elements are accessed (popped or pushed) at only one end—that is, a Last In First Out data structure. Thus, a stack element is accessed only through the top, not through the bottom or middle. This feature of a stack is extremely important and must be recognized in the beginning.

To keep track of the top position of the array, we can simply declare another variable, called **stackTop.**

The following **class**, **stackType**, defines a stack as an ADT. By using a pointer, we can dynamically allocate arrays, so we leave it for the user to specify the size of the array (that is, the stack size). We assume that the default stack size is **100**. Because the **class stackType** has a pointer data member (the pointer to the array that stores the stack elements), we must overload the assignment operator, include the copy constructor, and include the destructor. Moreover, we give a generic definition of the stack. Depending on the specific application, we can pass the stack element type when we declare a stack object.

```
template<class Type>
class stackType
{
public:
    const stackType<Type>& operator=(const stackType<Type>&);
      //Overload the assignment operator.
    void initializeStack();
      //Function to initialize the stack to an empty state.
      //Postcondition: stackTop = 0
```

```
bool isEmptyStack();
   //Function to determine whether the stack is empty.
   //Postcondition: Returns true if the stack is empty;
   //               otherwise, returns false.
bool isFullStack();
   //Function to determine whether the stack is full.
   //Postcondition: Returns true if the stack is full;
   //               otherwise, returns false.
void destroyStack();
   //Function to remove all the elements from the stack.
   //Postcondition: stackTop = 0

void push(const Type& newItem);
   //Function to add newItem to the stack.
   //Precondition: The stack exists and is not full.
   //Postcondition: The stack is changed and newItem
   //               is added to the top of stack.
Type top();
   //Function to return the top element of the stack.
   //Precondition: The stack exists and is not empty.
   //Postcondition: If the stack is empty, the program
   //               terminates; otherwise, the top element
   //               of the stack is returned.
void pop();
   //Function to remove the top element of the stack.
   //Precondition: The stack exists and is not empty.
   //Postcondition: The stack is changed and the top
   //               element is removed from the stack.

stackType(int stackSize = 100);
   //constructor
   //Creates an array of the size stackSize to hold the
   //stack elements. The default stack size is 100.
   //Postcondition: The variable list contains the base
   //               address of the array; stackTop = 0; and
   //               maxStackSize = stackSize.
stackType(const stackType<Type>& otherStack);
   //copy constructor
~stackType();
   //destructor
   //Removes all the elements from the stack.
   //Postcondition: The array (list) holding the stack
   //               elements is deleted.

private:
   int maxStackSize;  //variable to store the maximum stack size
   int stackTop;      //variable to point to the top of the stack
   Type *list;        //pointer to the array that holds the
                      //stack elements
```

```
void copyStack(const stackType<Type>& otherStack);
   //Function to make a copy of otherStack.
   //Postcondition: A copy of otherStack is created and
   //                assigned to this stack.
};
```

Because C++ arrays begin with the index 0, we need to distinguish between the value of `stackTop` and the array position indicated by `stackTop`. If `stackTop` is 0, the stack is empty; if `stackTop` is nonzero, then the stack is nonempty and the top element of the stack is given by `stackTop - 1`.

Notice that the function `copyStack` is included as a `private` member. This is because we want to use this function only to implement the copy constructor and overload the assignment operator. To copy a stack into another stack, the program can use the assignment operator.

Figure 7-4 shows this data structure, wherein `stack` is an object of the type `stackType`. Note that `stackTop` can range from 0 to `maxStackSize`. If `stackTop` is nonzero, then `stackTop - 1` is the index of the `stackTop` element of the stack. Suppose that `maxStackSize = 100`.

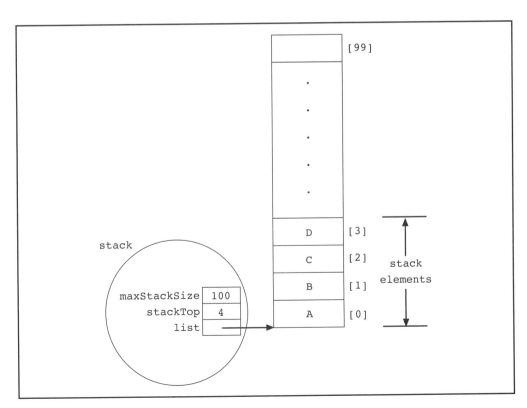

Figure 7-4   Example of a stack

Note that the pointer `list` contains the base address of the array (holding the stack elements)—that is, the address of the first array component. The next 11 sections of this chapter define the member functions of the `class stackType` that implement the stack operations.

Initialize Stack

Let us consider the `initializeStack` operation. Because the value of `stackTop` indicates whether a stack is empty, we can simply set `stackTop` to 0 to initialize the stack. (See Figure 7-5.)

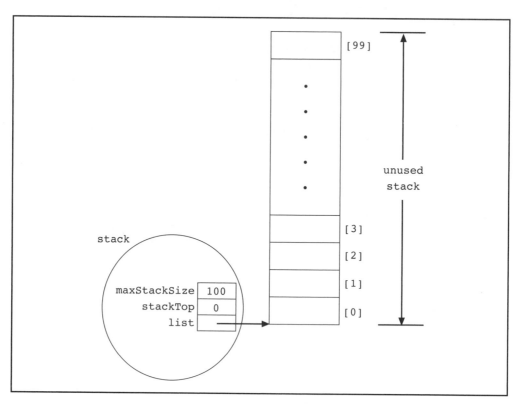

Figure 7-5 Empty stack

The definition of the function `initializeStack` is:

```
template<class Type>
void stackType<Type>::initializeStack()
{
     stackTop = 0;
}//end initializeStack
```

Destroy Stack

In the array implementation of a stack, the `destroyStack` operation is similar to the `initializeStack` operation. If we set the value of `stackTop` to 0, then all the elements of the stack are destroyed. Even though the elements are still in the stack (they are treated as garbage), the value of `stackTop` indicates whether the stack is empty. The definition of the function `destroyStack` is:

```
template<class Type>
void stackType<Type>::destroyStack()
{
    stackTop = 0;
}//end destroyStack
```

Empty Stack

We have seen that the value of `stackTop` indicates whether a stack is empty. If `stackTop` is 0, the stack is empty; otherwise, the stack is not empty. The definition of the function `isEmptyStack` is:

```
template<class Type>
bool stackType<Type>::isEmptyStack()
{
    return(stackTop == 0);
}//end isEmptyStack
```

Full Stack

Next, we consider the operation `isFullStack`. It follows that a stack is full if `stackTop` is equal to `maxStackSize`. The definition of the function `isFullStack` is:

```
template<class Type>
bool stackType<Type>::isFullStack()
{
    return(stackTop == maxStackSize);
}//end isFullStack
```

Push

Adding, or pushing, an element onto the stack is a two-step process. Recall that the value of `stackTop` indicates the number of elements in a stack, and `stackTop - 1` gives the position of the `stackTop` element of the stack. Therefore, the `push` operation is as follows:

    a. Store `newItem` in the array component indicated by `stackTop`.

    b. Increment `stackTop`.

Figures 7-6 and 7-7 illustrate the `push` operation.

Suppose that before the `push` operation, the stack is as shown in Figure 7-6.

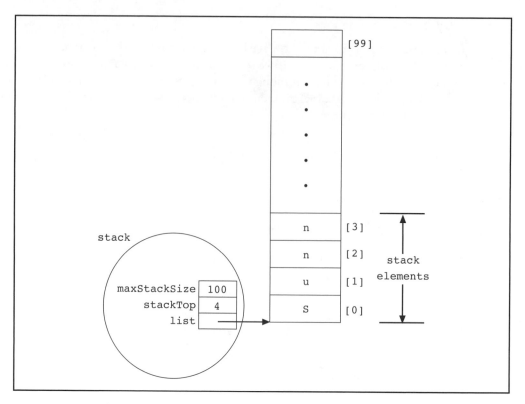

Figure 7-6   Stack before pushing y

Assume newItem is 'y'. After the push operation, the stack is as shown in Figure 7-7.

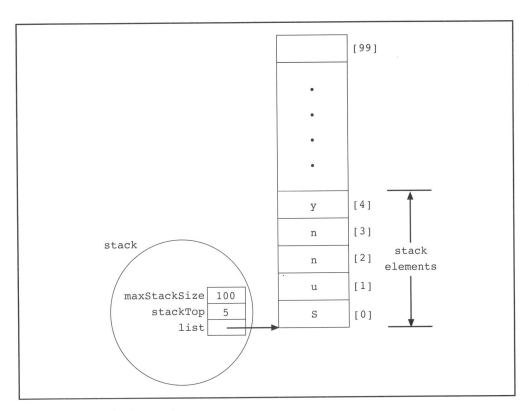

Figure 7-7   Stack after pushing y

If the stack is full, of course, we cannot add any elements to the stack. Therefore, before adding an element to the stack, the function **push** checks whether the stack is full. The definition of the function **push** is:

```
template<class Type>
void stackType<Type>::push(const Type& newItem)
{
    if(!isFullStack())
    {
        list[stackTop] = newItem;    //add newItem at the top
                                     //of the stack

        stackTop++;                  //increment stackTop
    }
    else
        cerr<<"Cannot add to a full stack."<<endl;
}//end push
```

If we try to add a new item to a full stack, the resulting condition is called an **overflow**. Error checking for an overflow can be handled in different ways. One way is as shown above.

Alternatively, we can check for an overflow before calling the function **push** as shown next (assuming **stack** is an object of the type **stackType**).

```
if(!stack.isFullStack())
    stack.push(name);
```

Return the Top Element

The operation **top** returns the top element of a stack. Its definition is given next.

```
template<class Type>
Type stackType<Type>::top()
{
    assert(stackTop != 0);          //if the stack is empty,
                                    //terminate the program
    return list[stackTop - 1];      //return the element of the
                                    //stack indicated by
                                    //stackTop - 1
}//end top
```

Pop

To remove, or pop, an element from a stack, we need to only decrement **stackTop** by 1.

Figures 7-8 and 7-9 illustrate the **pop** operation.

Suppose that before the **pop** operation, the stack is as shown in Figure 7-8.

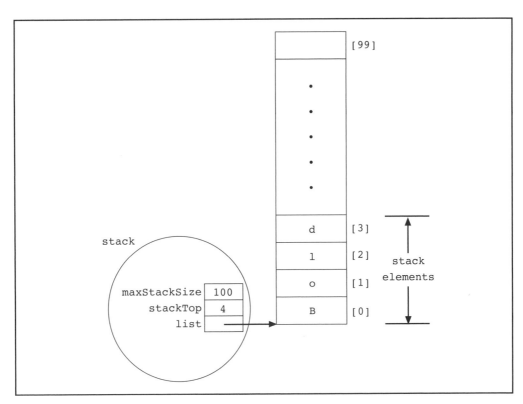

Figure 7-8   Stack before popping d

After the **pop** operation, the stack is as shown in Figure 7-9.

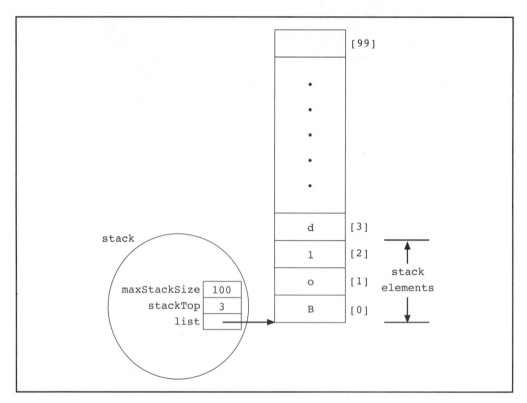

Figure 7-9 Stack after popping d

If the stack is empty, of course, we cannot remove any element from the stack. Therefore, before removing the top element from the stack, the function **pop** checks whether the stack is empty. Using the previous algorithm, the definition of the function **pop** is:

```
template<class Type>
void stackType<Type>::pop()
{
    if(!isEmptyStack())
        stackTop--;                    //decrement stackTop
    else
        cerr<<"Cannot remove from an empty stack."<<endl;
}//end pop
```

If we try to remove an item from an empty stack, the resulting condition is called an **underflow**. Error checking for an underflow can be handled in different ways. One way is as shown above. Alternatively, we can check for an underflow before calling the function **pop** as shown next (assuming **stack** is an object of the type **stackType**).

```
if(!stack.isEmptyStack())
    stack.pop();
```

Copy Stack

The function `copyStack` makes a copy of a stack. The stack to be copied is passed as a parameter to the function `copyStack`. We will, in fact, use this function to implement the copy constructor and overload the assignment operator. The definition of this function is:

```
template<class Type>
void stackType<Type>::copyStack(const stackType<Type>& otherStack)
{
        delete [] list;
        maxStackSize = otherStack.maxStackSize;
        stackTop = otherStack.stackTop;

        list = new Type[maxStackSize];
        assert(list != NULL);

                //copy otherStack into this stack
        for(int j = 0; j < stackTop; j++)
            list[j] = otherStack.list[j];
}//end copyStack
```

Constructor and Destructor

The functions to implement the constructor and the destructor are straightforward. The constructor sets the stack size to the size specified by the user, sets `stackTop` to 0, and creates an appropriate array in which to store the stack elements. If the user does not specify the size of the array in which to store the stack elements, the constructor uses the default value, which is 100, to create an array of size 100. The destructor simply deallocates the memory occupied by the array (that is, the stack) and sets `stackTop` to 0. The definitions of the constructor and destructor are as follows:

```
        //constructor
template<class Type>
stackType<Type>::stackType(int stackSize)
{
   if(stackSize <= 0)
   {
      cerr<<"The size of the array to hold the stack must "
         <<"be positive."<<endl;
      cerr<<"Creating an array of size 100."<<endl;

      maxStackSize = 100;
   }
   else
      maxStackSize = stackSize;  //set the stack size to
                                 //the value specified by
                                 //the parameter stackSize
```

7

```
    stackTop = 0;                       //set stackTop to 0
    list = new Type[maxStackSize]; //create the array to
                                        //hold the stack elements
    assert(list != NULL);
}//end constructor

template<class Type>
stackType<Type>::~stackType() //destructor
{
    delete [] list; //deallocate the memory occupied by the array
}//end destructor
```

Copy Constructor

Recall that one of the situations when the copy constructor executes is when an object is passed as a (value) parameter to a function. It copies the data members of the actual parameter into the corresponding data members of the formal parameter. Its definition is:

```
template<class Type>
stackType<Type>::stackType(const stackType<Type>& otherStack)
{
    list = NULL;

    copyStack(otherStack);
}//end copy constructor
```

Overloading the Assignment Operator (=)

Recall that for classes that have pointer data members, the assignment operator must be explicitly overloaded. The definition of the function to overload the assignment operator for the **class stackType** is:

```
template<class Type>
const stackType<Type>& stackType<Type>::operator=
                                (const stackType<Type>& otherStack)
{
    if(this != &otherStack) //avoid self-copy
        copyStack(otherStack);

    return *this;
}//end operator=
```

The analysis of the stack operations is similar to the operations of the **class arrayListType** (Chapter 3). We therefore provide only a summary in Table 7-1.

Table 7-1 summarizes the time-complexity of the operations of the **class stackType**.

Table 7-1 Time-Complexity of the Operations of the `class stackType`

Function	Time-Complexity
isEmptyStack	O(1)
isFullStack	O(1)
initializeStack	O(1)
destroyStack	O(1)
constructor	O(1)
top	O(1)
push	O(1)
pop	O(1)
copyStack	O(n)
destructor	O(1)
copy constructor	O(n)
Overload the assignment operator	O(n)

7

Stack Header File

Now that you know how to implement the stack operations, you can put the definitions of the class, and the functions to implement the stack operations, together to create the stack header file. For the sake of completeness, we next describe how to create the header file. Suppose that the name of the header file containing the definition of the `class stackType` is `myStack.h`. We will refer to this header file in any program that uses a stack.

```
//Header file: myStack.h

#ifndef H_StackType
#define H_StackType

#include <iostream>
#include <cassert>

using namespace std;

//Place the definition of the class template stackType, as given
//previously in this chapter, here.

//Place the definitions of the member functions, as discussed in
//this chapter, here.

#endif
```

Example 7-1

Before we give a programming example, let us first write a simple program that uses the class stackType and tests some of the stack operations. Among others, we will test the assignment operator. The program and its output are as follows. (We assume that the definitions of the class stackType and its member functions are in the header file myStack.h.)

```
//Program to test the various operations of a stack
#include <iostream>
#include "myStack.h"

using namespace std;

int main()
{
    stackType<int> intStack(50);
    stackType<int> tempStack;

    intStack.push(23);
    intStack.push(45);
    intStack.push(38);

    tempStack = intStack;  //copy intStack into tempStack

    cout<<"tempStack elements: ";

    while(!tempStack.isEmptyStack())  //print tempStack
    {
        cout<<tempStack.top()<<" ";
        tempStack.pop();
    }

    cout<<endl;

    cout<<"The top element of intStack: "<<intStack.top()<<endl;

    return 0;
}
```

Output

```
tempStack elements: 38 45 23
The top element of intStack: 38
```

It is recommended that you do a walk-through of this program.

Programming Example: Highest GPA

In this example, we write a C++ program that reads a data file consisting of each student's GPA followed by the student's name. The program then prints the highest GPA and the names of all the students who received that GPA. The program scans the input file only once.

Input   The program reads an input file consisting of each student's GPA, followed by the student's name. Sample data is:

```
3.8 Lisa
3.6 John
3.9 Susan
3.7 Kathy
3.4 Jason
3.9 David
3.4 Jack
```

Output   The result of the program will be the highest GPA and all the names associated with the highest GPA. For example, for the above data, the highest GPA is 3.9 and the students with that GPA are Susan and David.

Program Analysis and Algorithm Design

We read the first GPA and the name of the student. Because this data is the first item read, it is the highest GPA so far. Next, we read the second GPA and the name of the student. We then compare this (second) GPA with the highest GPA so far. Three cases arise:

1. The new GPA is greater than the highest GPA so far. In this case, we
   a. Update the value of the highest GPA so far.
   b. Destroy the stack—that is, remove the names of the students from the stack.
   c. Save the name of the student having the highest GPA so far in the stack.
2. The new GPA is equal to the highest GPA so far. In this case, we add the name of the new student to the stack.
3. The new GPA is less than the highest GPA so far. In this case, we discard the name of the student having this grade.

We then read the next GPA and the name of the student, and repeat Steps 1 through 3. We continue this process until we reach the end of the file.

From this discussion, it is clear that we need the following variables:

```
double GPA;              //variable to hold the current GPA
double highestGPA;       //variable to hold the highest GPA
newString name;          //variable to hold the name of the student
stackType<newString> stack; //object to implement the stack
```

Note that we use the `class newString` that we designed in Chapter 3 for the student name. We can use the assignment operator to store a name in a variable of the `newString` type.

The preceding discussion translates into the following algorithm:

1. Declare the variables.
2. Open the input file.
3. If the input file does not exist, exit the program.
4. Set the output of the floating-point numbers to a fixed decimal format with a decimal point and trailing zeroes. Also, set the precision to two decimal places.
5. Read the GPA and student name.
6. `highestGPA = GPA;`
7. Initialize the stack.
8. `while` (not end of file)

   ```
   {
     8.1 if (GPA > highestGPA)
         {
         8.1.1 destroyStack(stack);
         8.1.2 push(stack, student name);
         8.1.3 highestGPA = GPA;
         }
     8.2 else
         if(GPA is equal to highestGPA)
             push(stack, student name);
     8.3 Read the GPA and student name;
   }
   ```
9. Output the highest GPA.
10. Output the names of the students having the highest GPA.

Complete Program Listing

```cpp
//Program: Highest GPA

#include <iostream>
#include <iomanip>
#include <fstream>
#include "newString.h"
#include "myStack.h"

using namespace std;

int main()
{
            //Step 1
    double GPA;
    double highestGPA;
    newString name;
```

```
stackType<newString> stack(100);
ifstream infile;

infile.open("a:\\Ch7_HighestGPAData.txt");  //Step 2

if(!infile)                                 //Step 3
{
   cerr<<"The input file does not exist. "
       <<"Program terminates!"<<endl;
   return 1;
}

cout<<fixed<<showpoint;                     //Step 4
cout<<setprecision(2);                      //Step 4

infile>>GPA>>name;                          //Step 5

highestGPA = GPA;                           //Step 6

stack.initializeStack();                    //Step 7

while(infile)                               //Step 8
{
   if(GPA > highestGPA)                     //Step 8.1
   {
      stack.destroyStack();                 //Step 8.1.1

      if(!stack.isFullStack())              //Step 8.1.2
         stack.push(name);

      highestGPA = GPA;                     //Step 8.1.3
   }
   else
      if(GPA == highestGPA)                 //Step 8.2
         if(!stack.isFullStack())
            stack.push(name);
         else
         {
            cerr<<"Stack overflow. Program terminates."
                <<endl;
            return 1;  //exit the program
         }
   infile>>GPA>>name;                       //Step 8.3
}

cout<<"Highest GPA = "<<highestGPA<<endl;   //Step 9
cout<<"The students holding the highest GPA are:"
    <<endl;

while(!stack.isEmptyStack())                //Step 10
{
   name = stack.top();
```

```
        stack.pop();
        cout<<name<<endl;
    }

    cout<<endl;

    return 0;
}
```

Sample Run

Input File (Ch7_HighestGPAData.txt)

```
3.4 Holt
3.2 Bolt
2.5 Colt
3.4 Tom
3.8 Ron
3.8 Mickey
3.6 Pluto
3.5 Donald
3.8 Cindy
3.7 Dome
3.9 Andy
3.8 Fox
3.9 Minnie
2.7 Goofy
3.9 Doc
3.4 Danny
```

Output

```
Highest GPA = 3.90
The students holding the highest GPA are:
Doc
Minnie
Andy
```

LINKED IMPLEMENTATION OF STACKS

Because an array size is fixed, in the array (linear) representation of a stack, only a fixed number of elements can be pushed onto the stack. If in a program the number of elements to be pushed exceeds the size of the array, the program may terminate in an error. We must overcome these problems.

We have seen that by using pointer variables we can dynamically allocate and deallocate memory, and by using linked lists we can dynamically organize data (such as an ordered list). Next, we use these concepts to implement a stack dynamically.

Recall that in the linear representation of a stack, the value of stackTop indicates the number of elements in the stack, and the value of stackTop – 1 points to the top item in the stack. With the help of stackTop, we can do several things: find the top element, check whether the stack is empty, and so on.

Similar to the linear representation, in a linked representation stackTop is used to locate the top element of the stack. However, there is a slight difference. In the former case, stackTop gives the index of the array; in the latter case, stackTop gives the address (memory location) of the top element of the stack.

The following statements define a linked stack as an ADT:

```
//Definition of the node
template<class Type>
struct nodeType
{
    Type info;
    nodeType<Type> *link;
};

template<class Type>
class linkedStackType
{
public:
    const linkedStackType<Type>& operator=
                            (const linkedStackType<Type>&);
      //Overload the assignment operator.
    void initializeStack();
      //Function to initialize the stack to an empty state.
      //Postcondition: The stack elements are removed;
      //               stackTop = NULL.
    bool isEmptyStack();
      //Function to determine whether the stack is empty.
      //Postcondition: Returns true if the stack is empty;
      //               otherwise, returns false.
    bool isFullStack();
      //Function to determine whether the stack is full;
      //Postcondition: Returns false.

    void destroyStack();
      //Function to remove all the elements of the stack,
      //leaving the stack in an empty state.
      //Postcondition: stackTop = NULL

    void push(const Type& newItem);
      //Function to add newItem to the stack.
      //Precondition: The stack exists and is not full.
      //Postcondition: The stack is changed and newItem
      //               is added to the top of stack.
```

```
        Type top();
          //Function to return the top element of the stack.
          //Precondition: The stack exists and is not empty.
          //Postcondition: If the stack is empty, the program
          //                terminates; otherwise, the top element
          //                of the stack is returned.

        void pop();
          //Function to remove the top element of the stack.
          //Precondition: The stack exists and is not empty.
          //Postcondition: The stack is changed and the top element
          //                is removed from the stack.

        linkedStackType();
          //default constructor
          //Postcondition: stackTop = NULL
        linkedStackType(const linkedStackType<Type>& otherStack);
          //copy constructor
        ~linkedStackType();
          //destructor
          //Postcondition: All the elements of the stack are removed
          //                from the stack.

private:
        nodeType<Type> *stackTop; //pointer to the stack

        void copyStack(const linkedStackType<Type>& otherStack);
          //Function to make a copy of otherStack.
          //Postcondition: A copy of otherStack is created and
          //                assigned to this stack.
};
```

 In this linked implementation of stacks, the memory to store the stack elements is allocated dynamically. Therefore, logically the stack is never full. The stack is full only if we run out of memory space. Thus, it is not necessary to implement the operation isFullStack to determine whether the stack is full. However, the implementation of stacks as arrays does have the operation isFullStack to determine whether the stack is full. The user of a stack does not need to know the implementation details of the stack. Therefore, to be consistent, the implementation of stacks as linked lists also includes this operation.

The following example shows how both empty and nonempty linked stacks appear.

Example 7-2

Empty stack: Suppose that `stack` is an object of the type `linkedStackType`. (See Figure 7-10.)

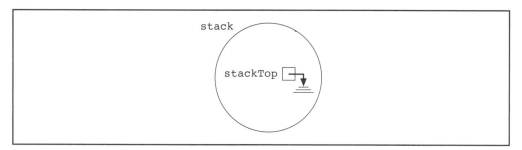

Figure 7-10   Empty linked stack

Nonempty stack: Figure 7-11 shows a nonempty stack.

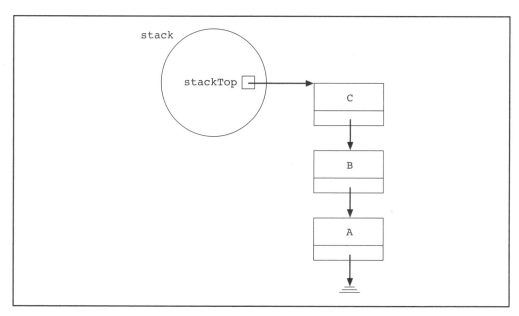

Figure 7-11   Nonempty linked stack

In Figure 7-11, the top element of the stack is C; that is, the last element pushed onto the stack is C.

Next, we discuss the definitions of the functions to implement the operations of a linked stack.

Default Constructor

The first operation that we consider is the default constructor. The default constructor initializes a stack to an empty state when a stack object is declared. Thus, this function sets `stackTop` to NULL. The definition of this function is:

```
template<class Type> //default constructor
linkedStackType<Type>::linkedStackType()
{
    stackTop = NULL;
}
```

Destroy Stack

In a linked representation, the function `destroyStack` does more work than it does in an array representation. In an array representation, a stack is destroyed simply by setting `stackTop` to 0. In a linked representation, memory for the stack elements is allocated dynamically. Thus, we need to set `stackTop` to NULL, and we must deallocate the memory occupied by the stack elements. The definition of this function is:

```
template<class Type>
void linkedStackType<Type>::destroyStack()
{
    nodeType<Type> *temp;    //pointer to delete the node

    while(stackTop != NULL)  //while there are elements
                             //in the stack
    {
        temp = stackTop;         //set temp to point to
                                 //the current node
        stackTop = stackTop->link; //advance stackTop
                                   //to the next node
        delete temp;             //deallocate the memory
                                 //occupied by temp
    }
}//end destroyStack
```

Initialize Stack

The operation `initializeStack` reinitializes a stack to an empty state. Because a stack may contain some elements and we are using a linked implementation of a stack, we must deallocate the memory occupied by the stack elements. This task can be accomplished by calling the member function `destroyStack`. Note that the function `destroyStack` also sets `stackTop` to NULL. The definition of `initializeStack` is:

```
template<class Type>
void linkedStackType<Type>:: initializeStack()
{
    destroyStack();
}
```

The operations `isEmptyStack` and `isFullStack` are considered next. The stack is empty if `stackTop` is NULL. Also, because the memory for a stack element is allocated and deallocated dynamically, the stack is never full. (The stack is full only if we run out of memory.) Thus, the function `isFullStack` always returns the value `false`. The definitions of the functions to implement these operations are:

```
template<class Type>
bool linkedStackType<Type>::isEmptyStack()
{
      return(stackTop == NULL);
}

template<class Type>
bool linkedStackType<Type>::isFullStack()
{
      return false;
}
```

Next, we consider the `push`, `top`, and `pop` operations. From Figure 7-11, it is clear that the new element is added (in the case of `push`) at the beginning of the linked list pointed to by `stackTop`. In the case of `pop`, the node pointed to by `stackTop` is removed. In both cases, the value of the pointer `stackTop` is updated.

push

Consider the stack shown in Figure 7-12.

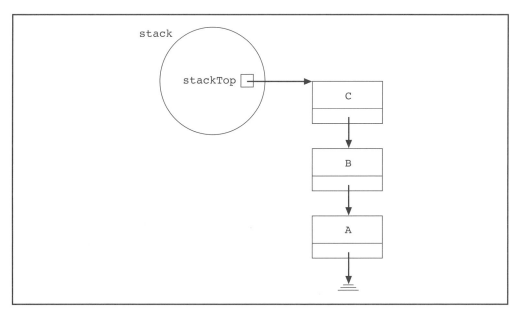

Figure 7-12   Stack before the `push` operation

Assume that the new element to be pushed is `'D'`. First, we allocate memory for the new node. We then store `'D'` in the new node and insert the new node at the beginning of the list. Finally, we update the value of **stackTop**. The statements

```
newNode = new nodeType<Type>; //create the new node
assert(newNode != NULL);   //if unable to allocate memory,
                           //terminate the program
newNode->info = newElement;
```

create a node, store the address of the node in the variable **newNode**, and store **newElement** in the **info** field of **newNode**. Thus, we have the situation shown in Figure 7-13.

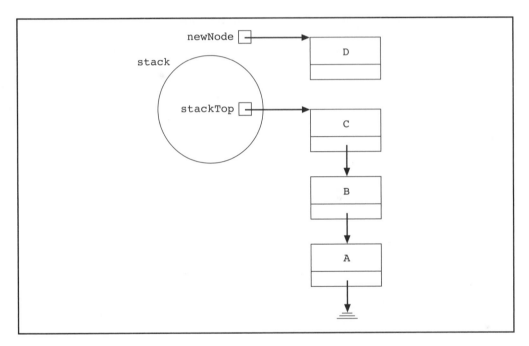

Figure 7-13   Stack and newNode

The statement

```
newNode->link = stackTop;
```

inserts **newNode** at the top of the stack, as shown in Figure 7-14.

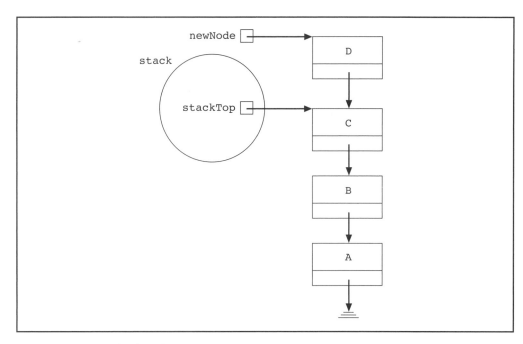

Figure 7-14 Stack after the statement `newNode->link = stackTop;` executes

Finally, the statement

`stackTop = newNode;`

updates the value of **stackTop**, which results in Figure 7–15.

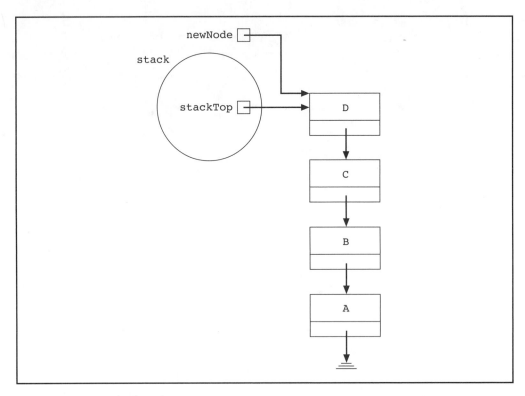

Figure 7-15 Stack after the statement `stackTop = newNode;` executes

The definition of the function **push** is:

```
template<class Type>
void linkedStackType<Type>::push(const Type& newElement)
{
    nodeType<Type> *newNode;      //pointer to create the new node

    newNode = new nodeType<Type>; //create the node
    assert(newNode != NULL);

    newNode->info = newElement;   //store newElement in the node
    newNode->link = stackTop;     //insert newNode before stackTop
    stackTop = newNode;           //set stackTop to point to the
                                  //top node
}//end push
```

We do not need to check whether the stack is full before we push an element onto the stack because in this implementation, logically, the stack is never full.

Return the Top Element

The operation to return the top element of a stack is quite straightforward. Its definition is:

```
template<class Type>
Type linkedStackType<Type>::top()
{
     assert(stackTop != NULL);        //if the stack is empty,
                                      //terminate the program
     return stackTop->info;           //return the top element
}//end top
```

pop

Now we consider the **pop** operation, which removes the top element of the stack. Consider the stack shown in Figure 7-16.

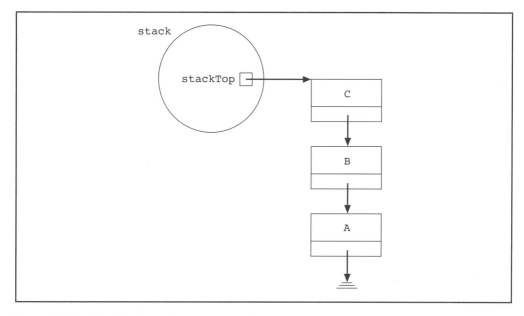

Figure 7-16   Stack before the pop operation

The statement

```
temp = stackTop;
```

makes **temp** point to the top of the stack, and the statement

```
stackTop = stackTop->link;
```

makes the second element of the stack become the top element of the stack. We then have the situation shown in Figure 7-17.

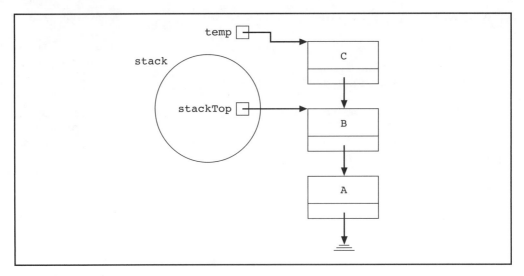

Figure 7-17 Stack after the statements `temp = stackTop;` and `stackTop = stackTop->link;` execute

Finally, the statement

```
delete temp;
```

deallocates the memory pointed to by **temp**. Figure 7-18 shows the resulting stack.

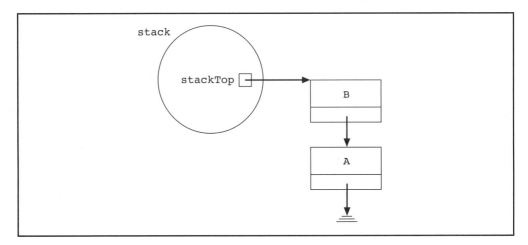

Figure 7-18 Stack after the statement `delete temp;` executes

The definition of the function pop is:

```
template<class Type>
void linkedStackType<Type>::pop()
{
   nodeType<Type> *temp;              //pointer to deallocate the memory

   if(stackTop != NULL)               //if stack is nonempty
   {
      temp = stackTop;                //set temp to point to the top node
      stackTop = stackTop->link;      //advance stackTop to the next node
      delete temp;                    //delete the top node
   }
   else
      cerr<<"Cannot remove from an empty stack."<<endl;
}//end pop
```

We have already discussed the default constructor. To complete the implementation of the stack operations, we need to write the definitions of the function copyStack, the copy constructor, the destructor, and the function to overload the assignment operator. These functions are similar to those discussed for linked lists in Chapter 5 and are, therefore, left as exercises for you.

The definition of a stack, and the functions to implement the stack operations discussed previously, are generic. Also, as in the case of an array representation of a stack, in the linked representation of a stack we must put the definition of the stack, and the functions to implement the stack operations, together in a (header) file. A client's program can include this header file via the include statement. Also, when we declare a stack object, we must pass the type of stack elements as a parameter to the type (name) linkedStackType. For example, the statement

```
linkedStackType<int> stack;
```

declares stack to be an object of the type linkedStackType, and the stack element type is int. Similarly, the statement

```
linkedStackType<newString> stringStack;
```

declares stringStack to be an object of the type linkedStackType, and the stack element type is newString.

Stack as Derived from the class linkedListType

If we compare the push function stack with the insertFirst function discussed for general lists in Chapter 5, we see that the algorithms to implement these operations are similar. A comparison of other functions, such as initializeStack and initializeList, isEmptyStack and isEmptyList, and so on, suggests that the class linkedStackType can be derived from the class linkedListType. Moreover, the functions pop and isFullStack can be implemented as in the previous section.

Next, we define the class linkedStackType that is derived from the class linkedListType. The definitions of the functions to implement the stack operations are also given.

```cpp
#ifndef H_derivedLinkedStack
#define H_derivedLinkedStack
#include <iostream>
#include "linkedList.h"

using namespace std;

template<class Type>
class linkedStackType: public linkedListType<Type>
{
public:
   void initializeStack();
   bool isEmptyStack();
   bool isFullStack();
   void push(const Type& newItem);
   Type top();
   void pop();
   void destroyStack();
};

template<class Type>
void linkedStackType<Type>::initializeStack()
{
      linkedListType<Type>::initializeList();
}

template<class Type>
bool linkedStackType<Type>::isEmptyStack()
{
      return linkedListType<Type>::isEmptyList();
}

template<class Type>
bool linkedStackType<Type>::isFullStack()
{
      return false;
}

template<class Type>
void linkedStackType<Type>::destroyStack()
{
      linkedListType<Type>::destroyList();
}

template<class Type>
void linkedStackType<Type>::push(const Type& newElement)
{
      linkedListType<Type>::insertFirst(newElement);
}

template<class Type>
Type linkedStackType<Type>::top()
{
      return linkedListType<Type>::front();
}
```

```
template<class Type>
void linkedStackType<Type>::pop()
{
    nodeType<Type> *temp;

    if(first != NULL)
    {
        temp = first;
        first = first->link;
        count--;
        delete temp;
        if(first == NULL)
            last = NULL;
    }
    else
        cerr<<"Cannot remove from an empty stack."<<endl;
}

#endif
```

7

APPLICATION OF STACKS: POSTFIX EXPRESSION CALCULATOR

The usual notation for writing arithmetic expressions (the notation we learned in elementary school) is called **infix** notation, in which the operator is written between the operands. For example, in the expression $a + b$, the operator + is between the operands a and b. In infix notation, the operators have precedence. That is, we evaluate expressions from left to right, and multiplication and division have higher precedence than addition and subtraction. If we want to evaluate an expression in a different order, we must include parentheses. For example, in the expression $a + b * c$, we first evaluate * using the operands b and c, and then we evaluate + using the operand a and the result of $b * c$.

In the early 1950s, the Polish mathematician Lukasiewicz discovered that if operators were written before the operands (**prefix** or **Polish** notation; for example, + a b) or after the operands (**suffix**, **postfix**, or **reverse Polish** notation; for example, a b +), the parentheses can be omitted. For example, the expression

$a + b * c$

in a postfix expression is

a b c * +

The following example shows infix expressions and their equivalent postfix expressions.

Example 7-3

Table 7-2 shows various infix expressions and their equivalent postfix expressions.

Table 7-2 Infix Expressions and Their Equivalent Postfix Expressions

Infix Expression	Equivalent Postfix Expression
$a + b$	$a\ b\ +$
$a + b * c$	$a\ b\ c\ *\ +$
$a * b + c$	$a\ b\ *\ c\ +$
$(a + b) * c$	$a\ b\ +\ c\ *$
$(a - b) * (c + d)$	$a\ b\ -\ c\ d\ +\ *$
$(a + b) * (c - d\ /\ e) + f$	$a\ b\ +\ c\ d\ e\ /\ -\ *\ f\ +$

Shortly after Lukasiewicz's discovery, it was realized that postfix notation had important applications in computer science. In fact, many compilers now first translate arithmetic expressions into some form of postfix notation and then translate this postfix expression into machine code. Postfix expressions can be evaluated using the following algorithm:

Scan the expression from left to right. When an operator is found, back up to get the required number of operands, perform the operation, and continue.

Consider the following postfix expression:

6 3 + 2 * =

Let us evaluate this expression using a stack and the previous algorithm. (In the following discussion, we list the postfix expression after each step. The shading indicates the part of the expression that has been processed.)

6 3 + 2 * =

　1. Read the first symbol, **6**, which is a number. Push the number onto the stack (see Figure 7-19).

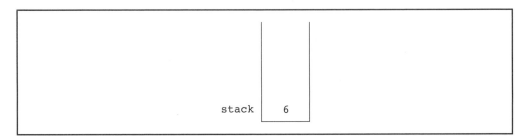

Figure 7-19   Stack after pushing 6

6 3 + 2 * =

2. Read the next symbol, 3, which is a number. Push the number onto the stack (see Figure 7–20).

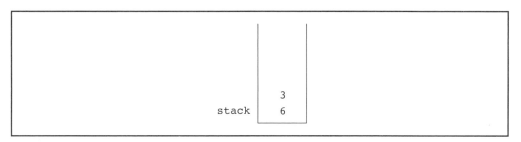

Figure 7-20   Stack after pushing 3

6 3 + 2 * =

3. Read the next symbol, +, which is an operator. Because an operator requires two operands to be evaluated, retrieve the top two elements and pop the stack twice. Perform the operation and put the result back onto the stack (see Figures 7–21 and 7–22).

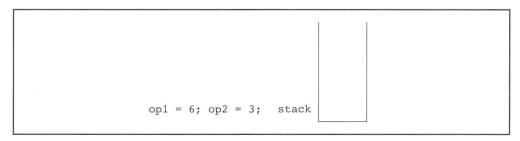

Figure 7-21   Stack after retrieving the top two elements and popping twice

Perform the operation: op1 + op2 = 6 + 3 = 9.
Push the result onto the stack (see Figure 7–22).

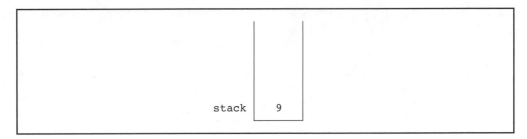

Figure 7-22   Stack after pushing the result of op1 + op2, which is 9

6 3 + 2 * =

4. Read the next symbol, 2, which is a number. Push the number onto the stack (see Figure 7-23).

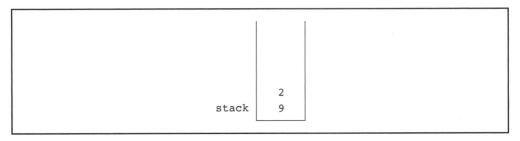

Figure 7-23   Stack after pushing 2

6 3 + 2 * =

5. Read the next symbol, *, which is an operator. Because an operator requires two operands to be evaluated, retrieve the top two elements and pop the stack twice. Perform the operation and put the result back onto the stack (see Figures 7-24 and 7-25).

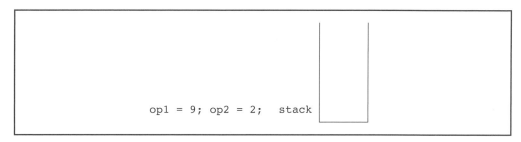

Figure 7-24   Stack after retrieving the top two elements and popping twice

Perform the operation: `op1 * op2 = 9 * 2 = 18`.
Push the result onto the stack (see Figure 7-25).

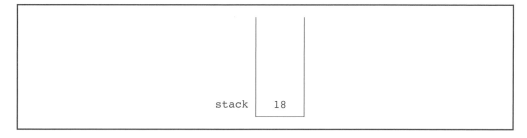

Figure 7-25   Stack after pushing the result of `op1 * op2`, which is 18

```
6 3 + 2 * =
```

6. Read the next symbol, =, which is the equal sign, indicating the end of the expression. Therefore, print the result. The result of the expression is in the stack, so retrieve the top element, pop the stack, and print the result. After the **pop** operation, the stack is as shown in Figure 7-26.

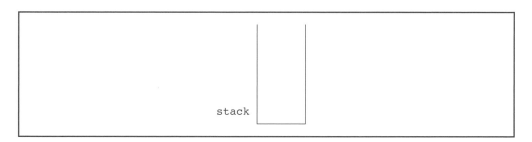

Figure 7-26   Stack after popping the element

The value of the expression 6 3 + 2 * = 18.

From this discussion, it is clear that when we read a symbol other than a number, the following cases arise:

1. The symbol we read is one of the following: +, −, *, /, or =.

   a. If the symbol is +, −, *, or /, the symbol is an operator and so we must evaluate it. Because an operator requires two operands, the stack must have at least two elements; otherwise, the expression has an error.

   b. If the symbol is = (an equal sign), the expression ends and we must print the answer. At this step, the stack must contain exactly one element; otherwise, the expression has an error.

2. The symbol we read is something other than +, −, *, /, or =. In this case, the expression contains an illegal operator.

It is also clear that when an operand (number) is encountered in an expression, it is pushed onto the stack because the operators come after the operands.

Consider the following expressions:

```
(i)    7 6 + 3 ; 6 - =
(ii)  14 + 2 3 * =
(iii) 14 2 3 + =
```

Expression (i) has an illegal operator, expression (ii) does not have enough operands for +, and expression (iii) has too many operands. In the case of expression (iii), when we encounter the equal sign (=), the stack has two elements and this error cannot be discovered until we are ready to print the value of the expression.

To make the input easier to read, we assume that the postfix expressions are in the following form:

```
#6 #3 + #2 * =
```

The symbol # precedes each number in the expression. If the symbol scanned is #, then the next input is a number (that is, an operand). If the symbol scanned is not #, then it is either an operator (may be illegal) or an equal sign (indicating the end of the expression). Furthermore, we assume that each expression contains only the +, −, *, and / operators.

This program outputs the entire postfix expression together with the answer. If the expression has an error, the expression is discarded. In this case, the program outputs the expression together with an appropriate error message. Because an expression may contain an error, we must clear the stack before processing the next expression. Also, the stack must be initialized; that is, the stack must be empty.

Main Algorithm

Pursuant to the previous discussion, the main algorithm in pseudocode is:

```
read the first ch;
while more data to process
{
    clear the stack;
    output ch;

    while(ch is not = '=') //process each expression
                            //= marks the end of an expression
    {
        switch(ch)
        {
        case '#': read a number;
                  output the number;
                  push the number onto the stack;
                  break;
        default: Assume that ch is an operation
                 evaluate the operation;
        }//end switch

        if no error is found, then
        {
            read next ch;
            output ch;
        }
    }   //end while

    if the expression does not contain any error(s), then
        output the result;
    else
      discard the result;

    start processing the next expression;
}
```

Evaluate: This function (if possible) evaluates an expression. Two operands are needed to evaluate an operation, and operands are saved in the stack. Therefore, the stack must contain at least two numbers. If the stack contains fewer than two numbers, then the expression has an error. In this case, the entire expression is discarded and an appropriate message is printed. This function also checks for any illegal operations. In pseudocode, this function is:

```
if stack is empty
{
   error in the expression
   set expressionOk to false
}
else
{
```

```
    retrieve the top element of stack into op2
    pop stack
    if stack is empty
    {
      error in the expression
      set expressionOk to false
    }
    else
    {
      retrieve the top element of stack into op1
      pop stack

          //If the operation is legal, perform the
          //operation and push the result onto stack.
      switch(ch)
      {
      case '+': //Perform the operation and push the result
                //onto stack.
                stack.push(op1 + op2);
                break;
      case '-': //Perform the operation and push the result
                //onto stack.
                stack.push(op1 - op2);
                break;
      case '*': //Perform the operation and push the result
                //onto stack.
                stack.push(op1 * op2);
                break;
      case '/': //If(op2 != 0), perform the operation and
                //push the result onto stack.
                stack.push(op1/op2);

                //Otherwise, report the error.
                //Set expressionOk to false.
                break;
      otherwise operation is illegal
          {
             output an appropriate message;
             set expressionOk to false
          }
      }//end switch
    }
```

Discard: This function is called whenever an error is discovered in an expression. It reads and writes the input data only until the input is =, the end of the expression. The following loop accomplishes this.

```
while(ch != '=')
{
    read ch;
    output ch;
}
```

Complete Program Listing

```cpp
//Postfix Calculator
#include <iostream>
#include <iomanip>
#include <fstream>
#include "mystack.h"

using namespace std;

void evaluate(ofstream& out, stackType<double>& stack,
              char& ch, bool& expressionOk);
void discard(ifstream& in, ofstream& out, char& ch);

int main()
{
    double num, result;
    bool expressionOk;
    char ch;
    stackType<double> stack(100);
    ifstream infile;
    ofstream outfile;

    infile.open("a:\\Ch7_RpnData.txt");

    if(!infile)
    {
        cerr<<"Cannot open the input file. "
            <<"Program terminates!"<<endl;
        return 1;
    }

    outfile.open("a:\\ch7_RpnOutput.txt");

    outfile<<fixed<<showpoint;
    outfile<<setprecision(2);

    infile>>ch;
    while(infile)
    {
        stack.initializeStack();
        expressionOk = true;
        outfile<<ch;

        while(ch != '=')
        {
            switch(ch)
            {
            case '#': infile>>num;
                    outfile<<num<<" ";
                    if(!stack.isFullStack())
                        stack.push(num);
                    else
                    {
```

7

```
                               cerr<<"Stack overflow. "
                                   <<"Program terminates!"<<endl;
                               return 1;
                       }

                       break;
            default: evaluate(outfile, stack, ch, expressionOk);

        }//end switch

        if(expressionOk) //if no error
        {
            infile>>ch;
            outfile<<ch;
            if(ch != '#')
                outfile<<" ";
        }
        else
            discard(infile, outfile, ch);
    }//end while (!= '=')

    if(expressionOk) //if no error, print the result
    {
        if(!stack.isEmptyStack())
        {
            result = stack.top();
            stack.pop();
            if(stack.isEmptyStack())
                outfile<<result<<endl;
            else
                outfile<<" (Error: Too many operands)"<<endl;
        }//end if
        else
            outfile<<" (Error in the expression)"<<endl;
    }
    else
        outfile<<" (Error in the expression)"<<endl;

    outfile<<"_____"<<endl<<endl;

    infile>>ch; //begin processing the next expression
    }//end while

    infile.close();
    outfile.close();

    return 0;

}//end main
```

```
void evaluate(ofstream& out, stackType<double>& stack,
              char& ch, bool& expressionOk)
{
    double op1, op2;

    if(stack.isEmptyStack())
    {
        out<<" (Not enough operands)";
        expressionOk = false;
    }
    else
    {
        op2 = stack.top();
        stack.pop();

        if(stack.isEmptyStack())
        {
            out<<" (Not enough operands)";
            expressionOk = false;
        }
        else
        {
            op1 = stack.top();
            stack.pop();

            switch(ch)
            {
            case '+': stack.push(op1 + op2);
                    break;
            case '-': stack.push(op1 - op2);
                    break;
            case '*': stack.push(op1 * op2);
                    break;
            case '/': if(op2 != 0)
                        stack.push(op1 / op2);
                    else
                    {
                        out<<" (Division by 0)";
                        expressionOk = false;
                    }
                    break;
            default:  out<<" (Illegal operator)";
                    expressionOk = false;
            }//end switch
        }//end else
    }//end else
}//end evaluate
```

7

```
void discard(ifstream& in, ofstream& out, char& ch)
{
    while(ch != '=')
    {
        in.get(ch);
        out<<ch;
    }
}//end discard
```

Sample Run

Input File

```
#35 #27 + #3 * =
#26 #28 + #32 #2 ; - #5 / =
#23 #30 #15 * / =
#2 #3 #4 + =
#20 #29 #9 * ; =
#25 #23 - + =
#34 #24 #12 #7 / * + #23 - =
```

Output

```
#35.00 #27.00 + #3.00 * = 186.00
```
_____

```
#26.00 #28.00 + #32.00 #2.00 ;   (Illegal operator) - #5 / = (Error
in the expression)
```
_____

```
#23.00 #30.00 #15.00 * / = 0.05
```
_____

```
#2.00 #3.00 #4.00 + =   (Error: Too many operands)
```
_____

```
#20.00 #29.00 #9.00 * ;   (Illegal operator) = (Error in the
expression)
```
_____

```
#25.00 #23.00 - +   (Not enough operands) = (Error in the expression)
```
_____

```
#34.00 #24.00 #12.00 #7.00 / * + #23.00 - = 52.14
```
_____

REMOVING RECURSION: NONRECURSIVE ALGORITHM TO PRINT A LINKED LIST BACKWARDS

In Chapter 6, we used recursion to print a linked list backwards. In this section, you learn how a stack can be used to design a nonrecursive algorithm to print a linked list backwards.

Consider the linked list shown in Figure 7-27.

Figure 7-27   Linked list

To print the list backwards, first we need to get to the last node of the list, which we can do by traversing the linked list starting at the first node. However, once we are at the last node, how do we get back to the previous node, especially given that links go in only one direction? You can again traverse the linked list with the appropriate loop termination condition, but this approach might waste a considerable amount of computer time, especially if the list is very large. Moreover, if we do this for every node in the list, the program might execute very slowly. Let us see how to use a stack effectively to print the list backwards.

After printing the `info` of a particular node, we need to move to the node immediately behind this node. For example, after printing 20, we need to move to the node with `info 15`. Thus, while initially traversing the list to move to the last node, we must save a pointer to each node. For example, for the list in Figure 7-27, we must save a pointer to each of the nodes with `info 5, 10,` and `15`. After printing 20, we go back to the node with `info 15`; after printing 15, we go back to the node with `info 10`, and so on. From this, it follows that we must save pointers to each node in a stack, so as to implement the Last In First Out principle.

Because the number of nodes in a linked list is usually not known, we use the linked implementation of a stack. Suppose that `stack` is an object of the type `linkedStackType`, and `current` is a pointer of the same type as the pointer `first`. Consider the following statements:

```
current = first;                    //Line 1
while(current != NULL)              //Line 2
{
    stack.push(current);           //Line 3
    current = current->link;       //Line 4
}
```

After the statement in Line 1 executes, `current` points to the first node (see Figure 7-28).

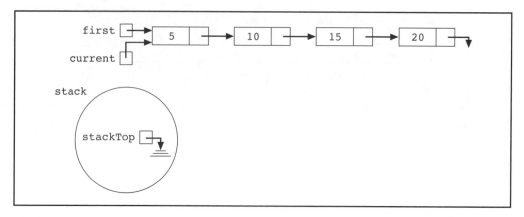

Figure 7-28 List after the statement `current = first;` executes

Because **current** is not **NULL**, the statements in Lines 3 and 4 execute (see Figure 7-29).

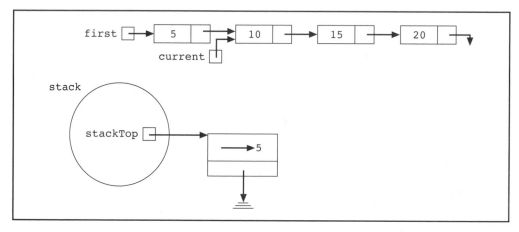

Figure 7-29 List and `stack` after the statements `stack.push(current);` and `current = current->link;` execute

After the statement in Line 4 executes, the loop condition, in Line ⁀ is reevaluated. Because **current** is not **NULL**, the loop condition evaluates to **true** and so the statements in Lines 3 and 4 execute (see Figure 7-30).

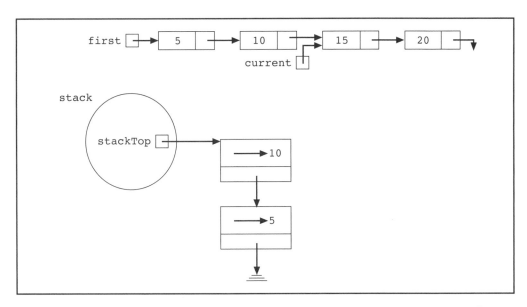

Figure 7-30 List and `stack` after the statements `stack.push(current);` and `current = current->link;` execute

After the statement in Line 4 executes, the loop condition, in Line 2, is evaluated again. Because `current` is not `NULL`, the loop condition evaluates to `true` and so the statements in Lines 3 and 4 execute (see Figure 7-31).

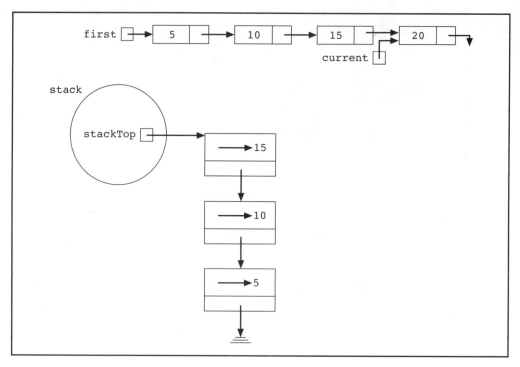

Figure 7-31 List and `stack` after the statements `stack.push(current);` and `current = current->link;` execute

After the statement in Line 4 executes, the loop condition, in Line 2, is evaluated again. Because **current** is not **NULL**, the loop condition evaluates to **true** and so the statements in Lines 3 and 4 execute (see Figure 7-32).

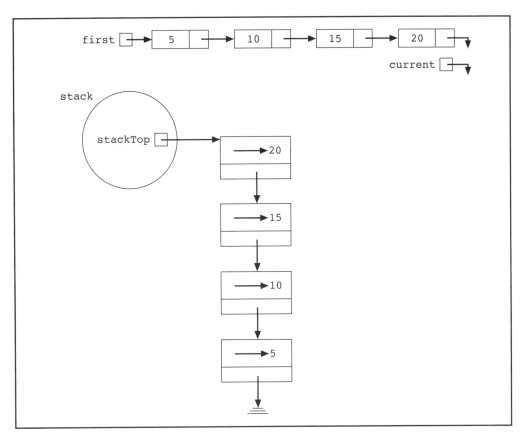

Figure 7-32   List and `stack` after the statements `stack.push(current);` and
`current = current->link;` execute

After the statement in Line 4 executes, the loop condition, in Line 2, is evaluated again. Because `current` is `NULL`, the loop condition evaluates to `false` and the `while` loop, in Line 2, terminates. From Figure 7-32, it follows that a pointer to each node in the linked list is saved in the stack. The top element of the stack contains a pointer to the last node in the list, and so on. Let us now execute the following statements:

```
while(!stack.isEmptyStack())          //Line 5
{
    current = stack.top();            //Line 6
    stack.pop();                      //Line 7
    cout<<current->info<<" ";         //Line 8
}
```

The loop condition in Line 5 evaluates to `true` because the stack is nonempty. Therefore, the statements in Lines 6, 7, and 8 execute. After the statement in Line 6 executes, `current` points to the last node; after the statement in Line 7 executes, the top element of the stack is removed (see Figure 7-33).

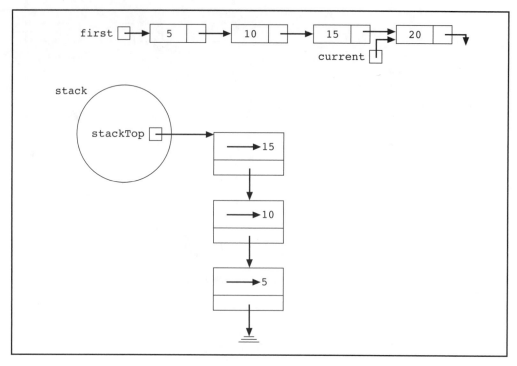

Figure 7-33   List and `stack` after the statements `current = stack.top();` and
`stack.pop();` execute

The statement in Line 8 outputs `current->info`, which is 20. Next, the loop condition in
Line 5 is evaluated. Because the loop condition evaluates to `true`, the statements in Lines 6,
7, and 8 execute. After the statements in Lines 6 and 7 execute, Figure 7–34 results.

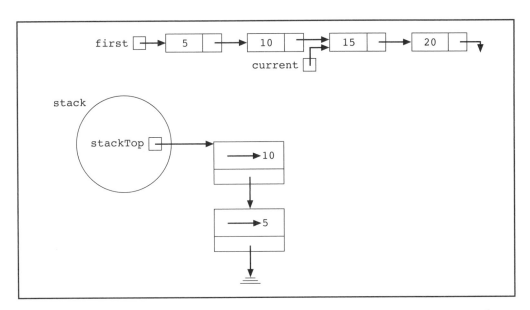

Figure 7-34   List and `stack` after the statements `current = stack.top();` and `stack.pop();` execute

The statement in Line 8 outputs `current->info`, which is 15. Next, the loop condition in Line 5 is evaluated. Because the loop condition evaluates to `true`, the statements in Lines 6, 7, and 8 execute. After the statements in Lines 6 and 7 execute, Figure 7-35 results.

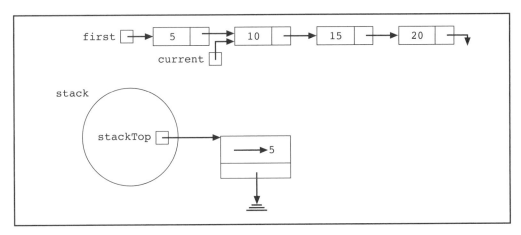

Figure 7-35   List and `stack` after the statements `current = stack.top();` and `stack.pop();` execute

The statement in Line 8 outputs `current->info`, which is `10`. Next, the loop condition in Line 5 is evaluated. Because the loop condition evaluates to `true`, the statements in Lines 6, 7, and 8 execute. After the statements in Lines 6 and 7 execute, Figure 7-36 results.

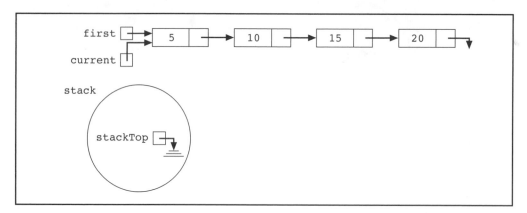

Figure 7-36   List and `stack` after the statements `current = stack.top();` and `stack.pop();` execute

The statement in Line 8 outputs `current->info`, which is `5`. Next, the loop condition in Line 5 is evaluated. Because the loop condition evaluates to `false`, the `while` loop terminates. The `while` loop in Line 5 produces the following output:

```
20 15 10 5
```

STL class `stack` (STACK CONTAINER ADAPTER)

The preceding sections discussed the data structure `stack` in detail. Because a stack is an important data structure, the Standard Template Library (STL) provides a class to implement a stack in a program. The name of the class defining a stack is `stack`; the name of the header file containing the definition of the `class stack` is `stack`. The implementation of the `class stack` provided by the STL is similar to the one described earlier in this chapter. Table 7-3 defines the various operations supported by the stack container class.

Table 7-3 Operations on a `stack` Object

Operation	Effect
size	Returns the actual number of elements in the stack.
empty	Returns `true` if the stack is empty, and `false` otherwise.
push(item)	Inserts a copy of `item` into the stack.
top	Returns the top element of the stack, but does not remove the top element from the stack. This operation is implemented as a value-returning function.
pop	Removes the top element of the stack.

In addition to the operations `size`, `empty`, `push`, `top`, and `pop`, the stack container class provides relational operators to compare two stacks. For example, the relational operator `==` can be used to determine whether two stacks are identical.

The program in Example 7-4 illustrates how to use the stack container class.

Example 7-4

```
#include <iostream>
#include <stack>

using namespace std;

int main()
{
    stack<int> intStack;                           //Line 1

    intStack.push(16);                             //Line 2
    intStack.push(8);                              //Line 3
    intStack.push(20);                             //Line 4
    intStack.push(3);                              //Line 5

    cout<<"Line 6: The top element of intStack: "
        <<intStack.top()<<endl;                    //Line 6

    intStack.pop();                                //Line 7

    cout<<"Line 8: After the pop operation, "
        <<"the top element of intStack: "
        <<intStack.top()<<endl;                    //Line 8

    cout<<"Line 9: intStack elements: ";           //Line 9

    while(!intStack.empty())                       //Line 10
    {
        cout<<intStack.top()<<" ";                 //Line 11
        intStack.pop();                            //Line 12
    }
```

```
        cout<<endl;                                  //Line 13
        return 0;
}
```

Output

```
Line 6: The top element of intStack: 3
Line 8: After the pop operation, the top element of intStack: 20
Line 9: intStack elements: 20 8 16
```

The preceding output is self-explanatory. The details are left as an exercise for you.

QUICK REVIEW

1. A stack is a data structure wherein the items are added and deleted from one end only.

2. A stack is a Last In First Out (LIFO) data structure.

3. The basic operations on a stack are: push an item onto the stack, pop an item from the stack, return the top element of the stack, initialize the stack, destroy the stack, check whether the stack is empty, and check whether the stack is full.

4. A stack can be implemented either as an array or as a linked list.

5. The middle elements of a stack should not be accessed directly.

6. Stacks are restricted versions of arrays and linked lists.

7. The postfix notation does not require the use of parentheses to enforce operator precedence.

8. In postfix notation, the operators are written after the operands.

9. Postfix expressions are evaluated according to the following rules:

   a. Scan the expression from left to right.

   b. If an operator is found, back up to get the required number of operands, evaluate the operator, and continue.

10. The STL `class stack` can be used to implement a stack in a program.

EXERCISES

1. Consider the following statements.

   ```
   stackType<int> stack;
   int x, y;
   ```

   Show what is output by the following segment of code.

   ```
   x = 4;
   stack.push(7);
   stack.push(x);
   stack.push(x + 5);
   y = stack.top();
   ```

```
stack.pop();
stack.push(x + y);
stack.push(y - 2);
stack.push(3);
x = stack.top();
stack.pop();
cout<<"x = "<<x<<endl;
cout<<"y = "<<y<<endl;

while(!stack.isEmptyStack())
{
    cout<<stack.top()<<endl;
    stack.pop();
}
```

2. Consider the following statements.

```
stackType<int> stack;
int x;
```

Suppose that the input is

```
14 45 34 23 10 5 -999
```

Show what is output by the following segment of code.

```
stack.push(5);
cin>>x;
while(x != -999)
{
    if(x % 2 == 0)
    {
        if(!stack.isFullStack())
            stack.push(x);
    }
    else
        cout<<"x = "<<x<<endl;
    cin>>x;
}
cout<<"Stack Elements: ";

while(!stack.isEmptyStack())
{
    cout<<" "<<stack.top();
    stack.pop();
}
cout<<endl;
```

3. Evaluate the following postfix expressions.

a. 6 4 + 3 * 16 4 / - =

b. 12 25 5 1 / / * 8 7 + - =

c. 70 14 4 5 15 3 / * - - / 6 + =

d. 3 5 6 * + 13 - 18 2 / + =

4. Convert the following infix expressions to postfix notations. (For an algorithm to convert an infix expression to an equivalent postfix expression, see Programming Exercise 10 of this chapter.)

   a. (A + B) * (C + D) - E

   b. A - (B + C) * D + E / F

   c. ((A + B) / (C - D) + E) * F - G

   d. A + B * (C + D) - E / F * G + H

5. Write the equivalent infix expressions for the following postfix expressions.

   a. a b * c +

   b. a b + c d - *

   c. a b - c - d *

6. What is the output of the following program?

```cpp
#include <iostream>
#include <stack>
#include <string>

using namespace std;

template<class type>
void mystery(stack<type> s, stack<type>& t);

int main()
{
    string list[] = {"Winter", "Spring", "Summer", "Fall",
                     "Cold", "Warm", "Hot"};

    stack<string> s1, s2;

    for(int i = 0; i < 7; i++)
        s1.push(list[i]);

    mystery(s1, s2);

    while(!s2.empty())
    {
        cout<<s2.top()<<" ";
        s2.pop();
    }
    cout<<endl;

    return 0;
}
```

```
template<class type>
void mystery(stack<type> s, stack<type>& t)
{
    while(!s.empty())
    {
        t.push(s.top());
        s.pop();
    }
}
```

7. What is the output of the following program?

```
#include <iostream>
#include <stack>

using namespace std;

void mystery(stack<int> s, stack<int>& t);

int main()
{
    int list[] = {5, 10, 15, 20, 25};

    stack<int> s1, s2;

    for(int i = 0; i < 5; i++)
        s1.push(list[i]);

    mystery(s1, s2);

    while(!s2.empty())
    {
        cout<<s2.top()<<" ";
        s2.pop();
    }
    cout<<endl;

    return 0;
}
void mystery(stack<int> s, stack<int>& t)
{
    while(!s.empty())
    {
        t.push(2 * s.top());
        s.pop();
    }
}
```

8. Write the definition of the function template `printListReverse` that uses a stack to print a linked list in reverse order. Assume that this function is a member of the `class linkedListType`, designed in Chapter 5.

9. Write the definition of the function template `second` that takes as a parameter a stack object and returns the second element of the stack. The original stack remains unchanged.

10. Write the definition of the function template `clear` that takes as a parameter a stack object of the type `stack` (STL class) and removes all the elements from the stack.

PROGRAMMING EXERCISES

1. Write the definitions of the function `copyStack`, the copy constructor, the destructor, and the function to overload the assignment operator for the `class linkedStackType`. Also, write a program to test your function.

2. Two stacks of the same type are the same if they have the same size and their elements at the corresponding positions are the same. Overload the relational operator `==` for the `class stackType` that returns `true` if two stacks of the same type are the same, and `false` otherwise. Also, write the definition of the function `template` to overload the operator `==`. Moreover, write a program to test your function.

3. Repeat Programming Exercise 2 for the `class linkedStackType`. (The definition of the class given in this chapter does not implement the `copyStack` function and the other functions as listed in Programming Exercise 1. Your program, at least, uses the destructor. Therefore, write the definition of the destructor before executing the program.)

4. a. Add the following operation to the `class stackType`:

```
void reverseStack(stackType<Type> &otherStack);
```

This operation copies the elements of a stack in reverse order onto another stack.

Consider the following statements.

```
stackType<int> stack1;
stackType<int> stack2;
```

The statement

```
stack1.reverseStack(stack2);
```

copies the elements of `stack1` onto `stack2` in reverse order. That is, the top element of `stack1` is the bottom element of `stack2`, and so on. The old contents of `stack2` are destroyed and `stack1` is unchanged.

b. Write the definition of the function `template` to implement the operation `reverseStack`. Also, write a program to test the function `reverseStack`.

5. Repeat Exercises 4a and 4b for the `class linkedStackType`. Also, write a program to test your function. (The definition of the class given in this chapter does not implement the `copyStack` function and the other functions as listed in Programming Exercise 1. Your program, at least, uses the destructor. Therefore, write the definition of the destructor before executing your program.)

6. Write a program that outputs an appropriate message for grouping symbols, such as parentheses and braces, if an arithmetic expression matches. For example, the expression `{25 + (3 - 6) * 8}` contains matching grouping symbols.

7. Write a program that uses a stack to print the prime factors of a positive integer in descending order.

8. Programming Exercise 15 in Chapter 6, Converting a Number from Binary to Decimal, uses recursion to convert a binary number into an equivalent decimal number. Write a program that uses a stack to convert a binary number into an equivalent decimal number.

9. Example 6-5 (in Chapter 6), Converting a Number from Decimal to Binary, contains a program that uses recursion to convert a decimal number into an equivalent binary number. Write a program that uses a stack to convert a decimal number into an equivalent binary number.

10. **(Infix to Postfix)** Write a program that converts an infix expression into an equivalent postfix expression.

The rules to convert an infix expression into an equivalent postfix expression are as follows:

a. Scan the expression from left to right. One pass is sufficient.

b. If the next scanned symbol is an operand, append it to the postfix expression.

c. If the next scanned symbol is a left parenthesis, push it onto the stack.

d. If the next scanned symbol is a right parenthesis, pop and append all the symbols from the stack until the most recent left parenthesis. Pop and discard the left parenthesis.

e. If the next scanned symbol is an operator:

    i. Pop and append to the postfix expression every operator from the stack that is above the most recently scanned left parenthesis and that has precedence greater than or equal to the new operator.

    ii. Push the new operator onto the stack.

f. After the infix string is completely processed, pop and append to the postfix string everything from the stack.

In this program, you are to consider the following (binary) arithmetic operators: +, −, *, and /. You may assume that the expressions you process are error free.

Design a class that stores the infix and postfix strings. The class must include the following operations:

    getInfix: Stores the infix expression.

    showInfix: Outputs the infix expression.

    showPostfix: Outputs the postfix expression.

Some other operations that you might need are the following:

    convertToPostfix: Converts the infix expression into a postfix expression. The resulting postfix expression is stored in **postfixString**.

    precedence: Determines the precedence between two operators. If the first operator is of higher or equal precedence than the second operator, it returns the value **true**; otherwise, it returns the value **false**.

Include the constructors and destructor for automatic initialization and dynamic memory deallocation.

7

Test your program on the following expressions.

```
1. A + B - C;
2. (A + B) * C;
3. (A + B) / (C - D);
4. A + ((B + C) * (E - F) - G) / (H - I);
5. A + B * (C + D) - E / F * G + H;
```

For each expression, your answer must be in the following form:

```
Infix Expression: A + B - C;
Postfix Expression: A B + C -
```

11. Redo the program in the section, Application of Stacks: Postfix Expression Calculator, of this chapter so that it uses the STL `class stack` to evaluate the postfix expressions.

12. Redo Programming Exercise 10 so that it uses the STL `class stack` to convert the infix expressions to postfix expressions.

CHAPTER

8

QUEUES

In this chapter, you will:

♦ Learn about queues

♦ Examine various queue operations

♦ Learn how to implement a queue as an array

♦ Learn how to implement a queue as a linked list

♦ Discover queue applications

♦ Examine the STL `class queue`

♦ Discover priority queues

This chapter discusses another important data structure: the **queue**. The notion of a queue in computer science is the same as the notion of the queues to which you are accustomed in everyday life. There are queues of customers in a bank or in a grocery store, and queues of cars waiting to pass through a tollbooth. Similarly, because a computer can send a print request faster than a printer can print, a queue of documents is often waiting to be printed at a printer. The general rule to process elements in a queue is that the customer at the front of the queue is served next and that when a new customer arrives, he or she stands at the end of the queue. That is, a queue is a First In First Out data structure.

Queues have numerous applications in computer science. Whenever a system is modeled on the First In First Out principle, queues are used. This chapter discusses one of the most widely used applications of queues, computer simulation. First, however, we need to develop the tools necessary to implement a queue. The next few sections discuss how to design classes to implement queues as an abstract data type (ADT).

QUEUES

A queue is a set of elements of the same type in which the elements are added at one end, called the **back** or **rear**, and deleted from the other end, called the **front** or **first**. For example, consider a line of customers in a bank, wherein customers are waiting to make a withdrawal, deposit money, or conduct some other business. Each new customer gets in the line at the rear. Whenever a teller is ready for a new customer, the customer at the front of the line is served.

The rear of the queue is accessed whenever a new element is added to the queue, and the front of the queue is accessed whenever an element is deleted from the queue. As in a stack, the middle elements of the queue are inaccessible, even if the queue elements are stored in an array.

Queue: A data structure in which the elements are added at one end, called the **rear**, and deleted from the other end, called the **front** or **first**; a First In First Out (FIFO) data structure.

Queue Operations

From the definition of queues, we see that the two key operations are add and delete. We call the add operation **addQueue** and the delete operation **deleteQueue**. Because elements can be neither deleted from an empty queue nor added to a full queue, we need two more operations to successfully implement the **addQueue** and **deleteQueue** operations: **isEmptyQueue** (determines whether the queue is empty) and **isFullQueue** (determines whether the queue is full).

We also need an operation, **initializeQueue**, to initialize the queue to an empty state, and—similar to stacks—we need an operation **destroyQueue** to destroy the queue, leaving it empty. Moreover, to retrieve the first and last elements of the queue, we include the operations **front** and **back** as described in the following list. Therefore, some of the queue operations are:

- **initializeQueue**: Initializes the queue to an empty state.
- **destroyQueue**: Removes all the elements from the queue, leaving the queue empty.
- **isEmptyQueue**: Determines whether the queue is empty. If the queue is empty, it returns the value **true**; otherwise, it returns the value **false**.
- **isFullQueue**: Determines whether the queue is full. If the queue is full, it returns the value **true**; otherwise, it returns the value **false**.
- **front**: Returns the front, that is, the first element of the queue. Prior to this operation, the queue must exist.

- **back**: Returns the last element of the queue. Prior to this operation, the queue must exist.

- **addQueue**: Adds a new element to the rear of the queue. Prior to this operation, the queue must exist and must not be full.

- **deleteQueue**: Removes the front element from the queue. Prior to this operation, the queue must exist and must not be empty.

As in the case of a stack, a queue can be stored either in an array or in a linked list. We will consider both implementations. Because the elements are added at one end and removed from the other end, we need two pointers to keep track of the front and rear of the queue, called **queueFront** and **queueRear**.

Implementation of Queues as Arrays

Before giving the definition of the class to implement a queue as an ADT, we need to decide how many data members are needed to implement the queue. Of course, we need an array to store the queue elements, the variables **queueFront** and **queueRear** to keep track of the first and last elements of the queue, and the variable **maxQueueSize** to specify the maximum size of the queue. Thus, we need at least four data members.

Before writing the algorithms to implement the queue operations, we need to decide how to use **queueFront** and **queueRear** to access the queue elements. How do **queueFront** and **queueRear** indicate that the queue is empty or full? Suppose that **queueFront** gives the index of the first element of the queue, and **queueRear** gives the index of the last element of the queue. To add an element to the queue, we first advance **queueRear** to the next array position and then add the new element at the position to which **queueRear** is pointing. To delete an element from the queue, we advance **queueFront** to the next element of the queue. Thus, **queueRear** changes after each **addQueue** operation and **queueFront** changes after each **deleteQueue** operation.

Let us see what happens when **queueRear** changes after an **addQueue** operation and **queueFront** changes after a **deleteQueue** operation. Assume that the array to hold the queue elements is of the size **100**.

Initially, the queue is empty. Assume that **queueFront** and **queueRear** directly point to the first and last elements of the queue, respectively. After the operation

```
addQueue('A');
```

the array is as shown in Figure 8-1.

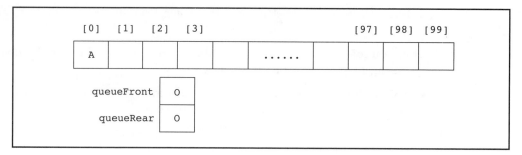

Figure 8-1 Queue after the first `addQueue` operation

After two more `addQueue` operations,

```
addQueue('B');
addQueue('C');
```

the array is as shown in Figure 8-2.

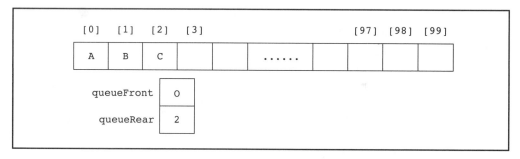

Figure 8-2 Queue after two more `addQueue` operations

Now consider the `deleteQueue` operation:

```
deleteQueue();
```

After this operation, the array containing the queue is as shown in Figure 8-3.

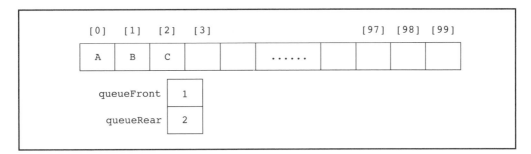

Figure 8-3   Queue after the `deleteQueue` operation

Will this queue design work? Suppose `A` stands for add (that is, `addQueue`) an element to the queue, and `D` stands for delete (that is, `deleteQueue`) an element from the queue. Consider the following sequence of operations:

`AAADADADADADADADADA...`

This sequence of operations would eventually set the index `queueRear` to point to the last array position, giving the impression that the queue is full. However, the queue has only two or three elements and the front of the array is empty (see Figure 8-4).

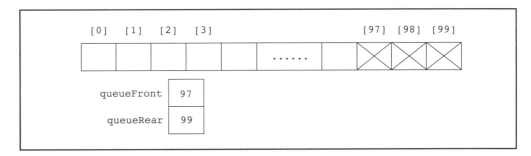

Figure 8-4   Queue after the sequence of operations `AAADADADADADADADA...`

One solution to this problem is that when the queue overflows to the rear (that is, `queueRear` points to the last array position), we can check the value of the index `queueFront`. If the value of `queueFront` indicates that there is room in the front of the array, then when the rear gets to the last array position, we can slide all of the queue elements toward the first array position. This solution is good if the queue size is very small; otherwise, the program may execute more slowly.

Another solution to this problem is to assume that the array is circular—that is, the first array position immediately follows the last array position (see Figure 8-5).

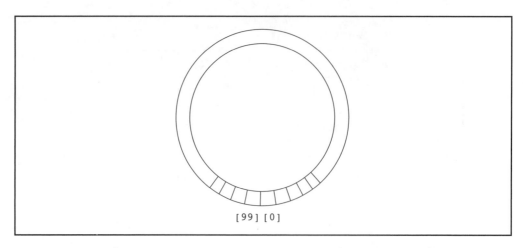

Figure 8-5 Circular queue

We consider the array containing the queue to be circular, although we draw the figures of the array holding the queue elements as before.

Suppose that we have the queue shown in Figure 8-6.

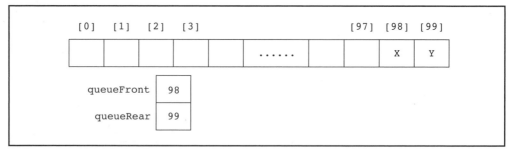

Figure 8-6 Queue with two elements at positions 98 and 99

After the operation

addQueue('Z');

the queue is as shown in Figure 8-7.

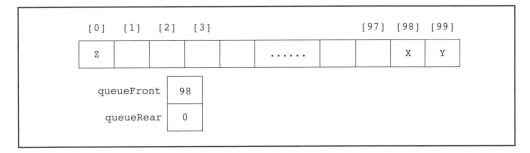

Figure 8-7   Queue after one more addQueue operation

Because the array containing the queue is circular, we can use the following statement to advance queueRear to the next array position:

queueRear = (queueRear + 1) % maxQueue;

If queueRear < maxQueue - 1, then queueRear + 1 <= maxQueue - 1 and so (queueRear + 1) % maxQueue = queueRear + 1. If queueRear == max Queue - 1 (that is, queueRear points to the last array position), then queueRear + 1 == maxQueue and so (queueRear + 1) % maxQueue == 0. In this case, queueRear is set to 0, which is the first array position. We can use a statement similar to the previous statement to advance queueFront to the next array position.

This queue design seems to work well. Before we write the algorithms to implement the queue operations, consider the following two cases.

Case 1: Suppose that after certain operations, the array containing the queue is as shown in Figure 8-8.

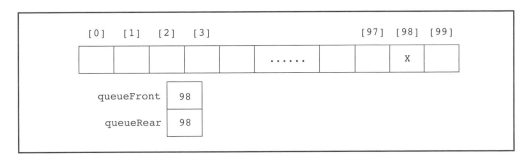

Figure 8-8   Queue with one element

After the operation

`deleteQueue();`

the resulting array is as shown in Figure 8-9.

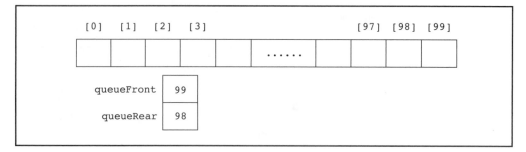

Figure 8-9   Queue after the `deleteQueue` operation

Case 2: Let us now consider the queue shown in Figure 8-10.

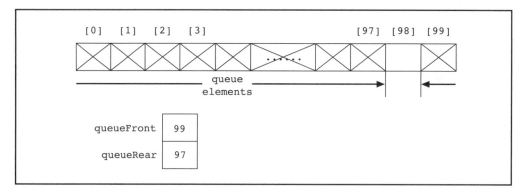

Figure 8-10   Queue with 99 elements

After the operation

`addQueue('Z');`

the resulting array is as shown in Figure 8-11.

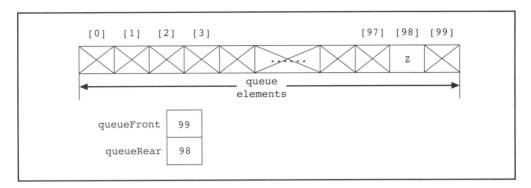

Figure 8-11   Queue after the addQueue operation

The arrays in Figures 8-9 and 8-11 have identical values for **queueFront** and **queueRear**. However, the resulting array in Figure 8-9 represents an empty queue, whereas the resulting array in Figure 8-11 represents a full queue. This latest queue design poses another problem: distinguishing between an empty and a full queue.

This problem has several possible solutions. One possible solution is to keep a count. In addition to **queueFront** and **queueRear**, we need another variable, **count**, to implement the queue. The value of **count** is incremented whenever a new element is added to the queue, and decremented whenever an element is removed from the queue. In this case, the functions **initializeQueue** and **destroyQueue** initialize **count** to 0. This solution is very useful if the user of the queue frequently needs to know the number of elements in the queue.

Another possible solution is to let **queueFront** indicate the index of the array position *preceding* the first element of the queue, rather than the index of the (actual) first element itself. In this case, assuming **queueRear** still indicates the index of the last element in the queue, the queue is empty if **queueFront == queueRear**. In this solution, the slot indicated by the index **queueFront** (that is, the slot preceding the first true element) is reserved. The queue is full if the next available space is this special reserved slot indicated by **queueFront**. Finally, because the array position indicated by **queueFront** is to be kept empty, if the array size is, say, **100**, then **99** elements can be stored in the queue (see Figure 8-12).

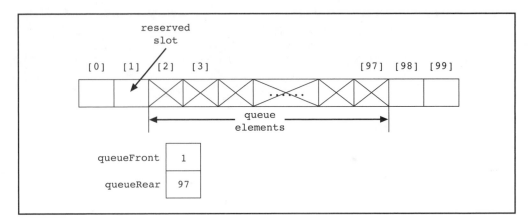

Figure 8-12 Array to store the queue elements with a reserved slot

Let us implement the queue using the first solution. That is, we use the variable `count` to indicate whether the queue is empty or full.

The following class defines the queue as an ADT (see also Figure 8-13). Because arrays can be allocated dynamically, we leave it for the user to specify the size of the array to implement the queue. The default size of the array is 100.

```
template<class Type>
class queueType
{
public:
    const queueType<Type>& operator=(const queueType<Type>&);
      //Overload the assignment operator.

    bool isEmptyQueue();
      //Function to determine whether the queue is empty.
      //Postcondition: Returns true if the queue is empty;
      //               otherwise, returns false.

    bool isFullQueue();
      //Function to determine whether the queue is full.
      //Postcondition: Returns true if the queue is full;
      //               otherwise, returns false.

    void initializeQueue();
      //Function to initialize the queue to an empty state.
      //Postcondition: count = 0; queueFront = 0;
      //               queueRear = maxQueueSize - 1
```

```
    void destroyQueue();
      //Function to remove all the elements from the queue.
      //Postcondition: count = 0; queueFront = 0;
      //               queueRear = maxQueueSize - 1

    Type front();
      //Function to return the first element of the queue.
      //Precondition: The queue exists and is not empty.
      //Postcondition: If the queue is empty, the program
      //               terminates; otherwise, the first
      //               element of the queue is returned.
    Type back();
      //Function to return the last element of the queue.
      //Precondition: The queue exists and is not empty.
      //Postcondition: If the queue is empty, the program
      //               terminates; otherwise, the last
      //               element of the queue is returned.

    void addQueue(const Type& queueElement);
      //Function to add queueElement to the queue.
      //Precondition: The queue exists and is not full.
      //Postcondition: The queue is changed and queueElement
      //               is added to the queue.

    void deleteQueue();
      //Function to remove the first element of the queue.
      //Precondition: The queue exists and is not empty.
      //Postcondition: The queue is changed and the first
      //               element is removed from the queue.

    queueType(int queueSize = 100);
      //constructor
    queueType(const queueType<Type>& otherQueue);
      //copy constructor
    ~queueType();
      //destructor

private:
    int maxQueueSize;
    int count;
    int queueFront;
    int queueRear;
    Type *list;    //pointer to the array that holds the
                   //queue elements
};
```

8

```
                        queueType<Type>

-maxQueueSize: int
-count: int
-queueFront: int
-queueRear: int
-*list: Type

+operator=(const queueType<Type>&): const queueType<Type>&
+initializeQueue(): void
+destroyQueue(): void
+isEmptyQueue(): bool
+isFullQueue(): bool
+addQueue(const Type&): void
+front(): Type
+back(): Type
+deleteQueue(): void
+queueType(int = 100)
+queueType(const queueType<Type>&)
+~queueType()
```

Figure 8-13 UML diagram of the `class queueType`

Next, we consider the implementation of the queue operations.

Initialize Queue

The first operation that we consider is `initializeQueue`. This operation initializes a queue to an empty state, and the first element is added at the first array position. Therefore, we initialize `queueFront` to 0, `queueRear` to `maxQueueSize - 1`, and `count` to 0. (See Figure 8-14.)

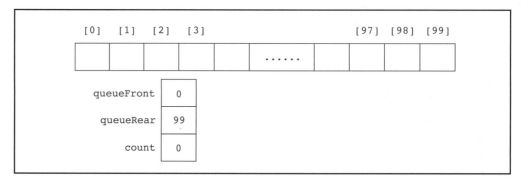

Figure 8-14 Empty queue

The definition of the function `initializeQueue` is:

```
template<class Type>
void queueType<Type>::initializeQueue()
{
    queueFront = 0;
    queueRear = maxQueueSize - 1;
    count = 0;
}
```

Empty Queue and Full Queue

As discussed earlier, the queue is empty if `count == 0`, and the queue is full if `count == maxQueueSize`. So the functions to implement `isEmptyQueue` and `isFullQueue` are:

```
template<class Type>
bool queueType<Type>::isEmptyQueue()
{
    return (count == 0);
}

template<class Type>
bool queueType<Type>::isFullQueue()
{
    return (count == maxQueueSize);
}
```

Destroy Queue

The `destroyQueue` operation removes all the elements from the queue, leaving the queue in an empty state. Because the queue is stored in an array, we can remove all the elements from the queue simply by resetting `queueFront`, `queueRear`, and `count`. So in this implementation of the queue, the `destroyQueue` operation is the same as the `initializeQueue` operation.

```
template<class Type>
void queueType<Type>::destroyQueue()
{
    queueFront = 0;
    queueRear = maxQueueSize - 1;
    count = 0;
}
```

front

This operation returns the first element of the queue. If the queue is nonempty, the element of the queue indicated by the index `queueFront` is returned; otherwise, the program terminates.

```
template<class Type>
Type queueType<Type>::front()
{
     assert(!isEmptyQueue());
     return list[queueFront];
}
```

back

This operation returns the last element of the queue. If the queue is nonempty, the element of the queue indicated by the index **queueRear** is returned; otherwise, the program terminates.

```
template<class Type>
Type queueType<Type>::back()
{
     assert(!isEmptyQueue());
     return list[queueRear];
}
```

Add Queue

Next, we implement the **addQueue** operation. Because **queueRear** directly points to the last element of the queue, to add a new element to the queue we first advance **queueRear** to the next array position and then add the new element to the array position to which **queueRear** is pointing. We also increment **count** by 1. So the function **addQueue** is:

```
template<class Type>
void queueType<Type>::addQueue(const Type& newElement)
{
     if(!isFullQueue())
     {
        queueRear = (queueRear + 1) % maxQueueSize; //use the mod
                                 //operator to advance queueRear
                                 //because the array is circular
        count++;
        list[queueRear] = newElement;
     }
     else
        cerr<<"Cannot add to a full queue."<<endl;
}
```

Delete Queue

To implement the **deleteQueue** operation, we advance **queueFront** to the next queue element. So the function **deleteQueue** is:

```
template<class Type>
void queueType<Type>::deleteQueue()
{
    if(!isEmptyQueue())
    {
        count--;
        queueFront = (queueFront + 1) % maxQueueSize; //use the mod
                                    //operator to advance queueFront
                                    //because the array is circular
    }
    else
        cerr<<"Cannot remove from an empty queue."<<endl;
}
```

Constructor and Destructor

To complete the implementation of the queue operations, we next consider the implementation of the constructor and the destructor. The constructor creates an array of the size specified by the user and sets the variable **maxQueueSize** to the size of the array. If the user does not specify the queue size, the constructor uses the default value, which is 100, to create an array of size 100. The constructor also initializes **queueFront** and **queueRear** to indicate that the queue is empty. The definition of the function to implement the constructor is:

```
    //constructor
template<class Type>
queueType<Type>::queueType(int queueSize)
{
    if(queueSize <= 0)
    {
        cerr<<"The size of the array to hold the queue must "
            <<"be positive."<<endl;
        cerr<<"Creating an array of size 100."<<endl;

        maxQueueSize = 100;
    }
    else
        maxQueueSize = queueSize;   //set maxQueueSize to queueSize

    queueFront = 0;                     //initialize queueFront
    queueRear = maxQueueSize - 1;       //initialize queueRear
    count = 0;
    list = new Type[maxQueueSize];      //create the array to
                                        //hold the queue elements

    assert(list != NULL);
}
```

The array to store the queue elements is created dynamically. Therefore, when the queue object goes out of scope, the destructor simply deallocates the memory occupied by the array that stores the queue elements. The definition of the function to implement the destructor is:

```
template<class Type>
queueType<Type>::~queueType()    //destructor
{
     delete [] list;
}
```

The implementation of the copy constructor and overloading the assignment operator are left as exercises for you. (The definitions of these functions are similar to those discussed for linked lists and stacks.)

LINKED IMPLEMENTATION OF QUEUES

Because the size of the array to store the queue elements is fixed, only a finite number of queue elements can be stored in the array. Also, the array implementation of the queue requires the array to be treated in a special way together with the values of the indices **queueFront** and **queueRear**. The linked implementation of a queue simplifies many of the special cases of the array implementation and, because the memory to store a queue element is allocated dynamically, the queue is never full. This section discusses the linked implementation of a queue.

Because elements are added at one end, **queueRear**, and removed from the other end, **queueFront**, we need to know the front of the queue and the rear of the queue. Thus, we need two pointers, **queueFront** and **queueRear**, to maintain the queue. The following class defines the linked queue as an ADT.

```
//Definition of the node
template<class Type>
struct nodeType
{
     Type info;
     nodeType<Type> *link;
};

template<class Type>
class linkedQueueType
{
public:
    const linkedQueueType<Type>& operator=
                  (const linkedQueueType<Type>&);
      //Overload the assignment operator.

    bool isEmptyQueue();
      //Function to determine whether the queue is empty.
      //Postcondition: Returns true if the queue is empty;
      //               otherwise, returns false.
```

```
    bool isFullQueue();
      //Function to determine whether the queue is full.
      //Postcondition: Returns true if the queue is full;
      //               otherwise, returns false.

    void destroyQueue();
      //Function to delete all the elements from the queue.
      //Postcondition: queueFront = NULL; queueRear = NULL

    void initializeQueue();
      //Function to initialize the queue to an empty state.
      //Postcondition: queueFront = NULL; queueRear = NULL

    Type front();
      //Function to return the first element of the queue.
      //Precondition: The queue exists and is not empty.
      //Postcondition: If the queue is empty, the program
      //               terminates; otherwise, the first
      //               element of the queue is returned.

    Type back();
      //Function to return the last element of the queue.
      //Precondition: The queue exists and is not empty.
      //Postcondition: If the queue is empty, the program
      //               terminates; otherwise, the last
      //               element of the queue is returned.

    void addQueue(const Type& queueElement);
      //Function to add queueElement to the queue.
      //Precondition: The queue exists and is not full.
      //Postcondition: The queue is changed and queueElement
      //               is added to the queue.

    void deleteQueue();
      //Function to remove the first element of the queue.
      //Precondition: The queue exists and is not empty.
      //Postcondition: The queue is changed and the first
      //               element is removed from the queue.

    linkedQueueType ();
      //default constructor
    linkedQueueType(const linkedQueueType<Type>& otherQueue);
      //copy constructor
    ~linkedQueueType();
      //destructor

private:
    nodeType<Type> *queueFront; //pointer to the front of the queue
    nodeType<Type> *queueRear;  //pointer to the rear of the queue
};
```

The UML diagram of the class linkedQueueType is left as an exercise for you.

The definitions of the functions to implement the queue operations are given next.

The queue is empty if `queueFront` is `NULL`. Memory to store the queue elements is allocated dynamically. Therefore, the queue is never full, and so the function to implement the `isFullQueue` operation returns the value `false`. (The queue is full only if we run out of memory.)

The operation `destroyQueue` removes all the elements of the queue, leaving the queue in an empty state. As stated previously, memory to store the queue elements is allocated dynamically. Therefore, this operation traverses the list containing the queue starting at the first node and deallocates the memory occupied by the queue elements.

The definitions of the functions to implement the operations `isEmptyQueue`, `isFullQueue`, and `destroyQueue` are given next:

```
template<class Type>
bool linkedQueueType<Type>::isEmptyQueue()
{
    return(queueFront == NULL);
}

template<class Type>
bool linkedQueueType<Type>::isFullQueue()
{
    return false;
}

template<class Type>
void linkedQueueType<Type>::destroyQueue()
{
    nodeType<Type> *temp;

    while(queueFront!= NULL)   //while there are elements left
                               //in the queue
    {
       temp = queueFront;      //set temp to point to
                               //the current node
       queueFront = queueFront->link;   //advance queueFront to
                                        //the next node
       delete temp;            //deallocate the memory
                               //occupied by temp
    }
    queueRear = NULL;          //set queueRear to NULL
}
```

The operation `initializeQueue` initializes the queue to an empty state. The queue is empty if there are no elements in the queue. As in the case of stacks, the function `initializeQueue` reinitializes the queue to an empty state. Note that the constructor initializes the queue when the queue object is declared. So this operation must remove all the elements from the queue. This task can be accomplished by calling the function destroyQueue.

```
template<class Type>
void linkedQueueType<Type>::initializeQueue()
{
     destroyQueue();
}
```

addQueue, front, back, and deleteQueue Operations

The addQueue operation adds a new element at the end of the queue. To implement this operation, we access the pointer queueRear.

If the queue is nonempty, the operation front returns the first element of the queue, and so the element of the queue indicated by the pointer queueFront is returned. If the queue is empty, the function front terminates the program.

If the queue is nonempty, the operation back returns the last element of the queue, and so the element of the queue indicated by the pointer queueRear is returned. If the queue is empty, the function back terminates the program. Similarly, if the queue is nonempty, the operation deleteQueue removes the first element of the queue, and so we access the pointer queueFront.

The definitions of the functions to implement these operations are:

```
template<class Type>
void linkedQueueType<Type>::addQueue(const Type& newElement)
{
     nodeType<Type> *newNode;

     newNode = new nodeType<Type>;  //create the node
     assert(newNode != NULL);

     newNode->info = newElement;  //store the info
     newNode->link = NULL;   //initialize the link field to NULL

     if(queueFront == NULL)   //if initially the queue is empty
     {
        queueFront = newNode;
        queueRear = newNode;
     }
     else                     //add newNode at the end
     {
        queueRear->link = newNode;
        queueRear = queueRear->link;
     }
}//end addQueue
```

```
template<class Type>
Type linkedQueueType<Type>::front()
{
      assert(queueFront != NULL);
      return queueFront->info;
}

template<class Type>
Type linkedQueueType<Type>::back()
{
      assert(queueRear != NULL);
      return queueRear->info;
}

template<class Type>
void linkedQueueType<Type>::deleteQueue()
{
   nodeType<Type> *temp;

   if(!isEmptyQueue())
   {
      temp = queueFront;          //make temp point to the first node
      queueFront = queueFront->link; //advance queueFront
      delete temp;                   //delete the first node

      if(queueFront == NULL)  //if after deletion the queue is empty,
         queueRear = NULL;//set queueRear to NULL
   }
   else
      cerr<<"Cannot remove from an empty queue."<<endl;
}//end deleteQueue
```

The definition of the function to implement the default constructor is similar to the definition of the function `initializeQueue`. When the queue object goes out of scope, the destructor destroys the queue; that is, it deallocates the memory occupied by the elements of the queue. The definition of the function to implement the destructor is similar to the definition of the function `destroyQueue`. Also, the functions to implement the copy constructor and overload the assignment operator are similar to the corresponding functions for stacks. Implementing these operations is left as an exercise for you.

QUEUE DERIVED FROM THE `class linkedListType`

From the definitions of the functions to implement the queue operations, it is clear that the linked implementation of a queue is similar to the implementation of a linked list created in a forward manner (see Chapter 5). The `addQueue` operation is similar to the operation `insertFirst`. Likewise, the operations `initializeQueue` and `initializeList`, `isEmptyQueue` and `isEmptyList`, and `destroyQueue` and `destroyList` are similar.

The operations **deleteQueue and isFullQueue** can be implemented as in the previous section. The pointer **queueFront** is the same as the pointer **first**, and the pointer **queueRear** is the same as the pointer **last**.This correspondence suggests that we can derive the class to implement the queue from the **class linkedListType** (see Chapter 5).

Next, we derive the **class linkedQueueType** from the **class linkedListType**, and we implement the queue operations using the operations defined for linked lists.

```
//Queue derived from the class linkedListType
//Header file: queueLinked.h
#ifndef H_QueueType
#define H_QueueType

#include <iostream>
#include "linkedList.h"

using namespace std;

template<class Type>
class linkedQueueType: public linkedListType<Type>
{
public:
    bool isEmptyQueue();
    bool isFullQueue();
    void destroyQueue();
    void initializeQueue();
    void addQueue(const Type& newElement);
    Type front();
    Type back();
    void deleteQueue();
};

template<class Type>
void linkedQueueType<Type>::initializeQueue()
{
    linkedListType<Type>::initializeList();
}

template<class Type>
void linkedQueueType<Type>::destroyQueue()
{
    linkedListType<Type>::destroyList();
}

template<class Type>
bool linkedQueueType<Type>::isEmptyQueue()
{
    return linkedListType<Type>::isEmptyList();
}
```

```
template<class Type>
bool linkedQueueType<Type>::isFullQueue()
{
    return false;
}

template<class Type>
void linkedQueueType<Type>::addQueue(const Type& newElement)
{
    linkedListType<Type>::insertLast(newElement);
}

template<class Type>
Type linkedQueueType<Type>::front()
{
    return linkedListType<Type>::front();
}

template<class Type>
Type linkedQueueType<Type>::back()
{
    return linkedListType<Type>::back();
}

template<class Type>
void linkedQueueType<Type>::deleteQueue()
{
    nodeType<Type> *temp;

    if(!isEmptyQueue())
    {
        temp = first;          //make temp point to the first node
        first = first->link;   //advance first to the next node
        delete temp;           //delete the first node
        count--;               //decrement count
        if(first == NULL)      //if after deletion the queue is empty,
            last = NULL;       //set last to NULL
    }
    else
        cerr<<"Cannot remove from an empty queue."<<endl;
}

#endif
```

The program in Example 8-1 tests various operations on a queue. It uses the linked version of the queue derived from the **class linkedListType**.

Example 8-1

```cpp
//Program to test the queue operations
#include <iostream>
#include "linkedList.h"
#include "queueLinked.h"

using namespace std;

int main()
{
    linkedQueueType<int> queue;
    linkedQueueType<int> copyQueue;

    int num;

    cout<<"Queue Operations"<<endl;
    cout<<"Enter numbers ending with -999"<<endl;
    cin>>num;

    while(num != -999)
    {
        queue.addQueue(num); //add an element to the queue
        cin>>num;
    }

    copyQueue = queue;        //copy the queue into copyQueue

    cout<<"Queue contains: ";
    while(!copyQueue.isEmptyQueue())
    {
        cout<<copyQueue.front()<<" ";
        copyQueue.deleteQueue();   //remove an element from
                                   //the queue
    }

    cout<<endl;

    return 0;
}
```

Sample Run: In this sample run, the user input is shaded.

```
Queue Operations
Enter numbers ending with -999
23 76 64 56 28 91 21 11 82 -999
Queue contains: 23 76 64 56 28 91 21 11 82
```

STL class queue (QUEUE CONTAINER ADAPTER)

The preceding sections discussed the data structure queue in detail. Because a queue is an important data structure, the Standard Template Library (STL) provides a class to implement queues in a program. The name of the class defining the queue is queue, and the name of the header file containing the definition of the **class queue** is queue. The **class queue** provided by the STL is implemented similarly to the classes discussed in this chapter. Table 8-1 defines various operations supported by the queue container class.

Table 8-1 Operations on a queue Object

Operation	Effect
size	Returns the actual number of elements in the queue.
empty	Returns true if the queue is empty, and false otherwise.
push(item)	Inserts a copy of item into the queue.
front	Returns the next—that is, first—element in the queue, but does not remove the element from the queue. This operation is implemented as a value-returning function.
back	Returns the last element in the queue, but does not remove the element from the queue. This operation is implemented as a value-returning function.
pop	Removes the next element in the queue.

In addition to the operations size, empty, push, front, back, and pop, the queue container class provides relational operators to compare two queues. For example, the relational operator == can be used to determine whether two queues are identical.

The program in Example 8-2 illustrates how to use the queue container class.

Example 8-2

```
#include <iostream>
#include <queue>

using namespace std;

int main()
{
    queue<int> intQueue;                          //Line 1

    intQueue.push(26);                            //Line 2
    intQueue.push(18);                            //Line 3
    intQueue.push(50);                            //Line 4
    intQueue.push(33);                            //Line 5
```

```
        cout<<"Line 6: The front element of intQueue: "
            <<intQueue.front()<<endl;          //Line 6

        cout<<"Line 7: The last element of intQueue: "
            <<intQueue.back()<<endl;           //Line 7

        intQueue.pop();                        //Line 8

        cout<<"Line 9: After the pop operation, "
            <<"the front element of intQueue: "
            <<intQueue.front()<<endl;          //Line 9

        cout<<"Line 10: intQueue elements: ";  //Line 10

        while(!intQueue.empty())               //Line 11
        {
            cout<<intQueue.front()<<" ";       //Line 12
            intQueue.pop();                    //Line 13
        }

        cout<<endl;                            //Line 14

        return 0;
}
```

Output

```
Line 6: The front element of intQueue: 26
Line 7: The last element of intQueue: 33
Line 9: After the pop operation, the front element of intQueue: 18
Line 10: intQueue elements: 18 50 33
```

The preceding output is self-explanatory. The details are left as an exercise for you.

PRIORITY QUEUES

The preceding sections described how to implement a queue in a program. The use of a queue structure ensures that the items are processed in the order they are received. For example, in a banking environment, the customers who arrive first are served first. However, there are certain situations when this First In First Out rule needs to be relaxed somewhat. In a hospital environment, patients are, usually, seen in the order they arrive. Therefore, you could use a queue to ensure that the patients are seen in the order they arrive. However, if a patient arrives with severe or life-threatening symptoms, they are treated first. In other words, these patients take priority over the patients who can wait to be seen, such as those awaiting their routine annual check-up. For another example, in a shared environment, when print requests are sent to the printer, interactive programs take priority over batch processing programs.

There are many other situations where some priority is assigned to the customers. To implement such a data structure in a program, we use special types of queues, called **priority queues**. In a priority queue, customers or jobs with higher priority are pushed to the front of the queue.

One way to implement a priority queue is to use an ordinary linked list, which keeps the items in order from the highest to lowest priority. However, an effective way to implement a priority queue is to use a treelike structure. (In Chapter 10, we discuss a special type of sorting algorithm, called the heap sort, which uses a treelike structure to sort a list.) After describing this algorithm, we then discuss how to effectively implement a priority queue.

STL class `priority_queue`

The STL provides the class template `priority_queue<elemType>`, where the data type of the queue elements is specified by `elemType`. This class template is contained in the STL header file `queue`. There are various ways to specify the priority of the elements of a priority queue. The default priority criteria for the queue elements uses the less than operator, `<`. For example, a program that implements a priority queue of numbers could use the operator `<` to assign the priority to the numbers so that the larger numbers are always at the front of the queue. If you design your own class to implement the queue elements, then you can specify your priority rule by overloading the less than operator, `<`, to compare the elements. You could also define a comparison function to specify the priority. The implementation of comparison functions is discussed in Chapter 13.

APPLICATION OF QUEUES: SIMULATION

A technique in which one system models the behavior of another system is called **simulation**. For example, physical simulators include wind tunnels used to experiment with the design of car bodies and flight simulators used to train airline pilots. Simulation techniques are used when it is too expensive or dangerous to experiment with real systems. You can also design computer models to study the behavior of real systems. (We describe some real systems modeled by computers shortly.) Simulating the behavior of an expensive or dangerous experiment using a computer model is usually less expensive than using the real system and a good way to gain insight without putting human life in danger. Moreover, computer simulations are particularly useful for complex systems where it is difficult to construct a mathematical model. For such systems, computer models can retain descriptive accuracy. In mathematical simulations, the steps of a program are used to model the behavior of a real system. Let us consider one such problem.

The manager of a local movie theater is hearing complaints from customers about the time they have to wait in line to buy tickets. The theater currently has only one cashier. Another theater is preparing to open in the neighborhood and the manager is afraid of losing customers. The manager wants to hire enough cashiers so that a customer does not have to wait too long to buy a ticket, but the manager does not want to hire extra cashiers on a trial basis and potentially waste time and money. One thing that the manager would like to know is the average time a customer has to wait for service. The manager wants someone to write a program to simulate the behavior of the theater.

In computer simulation, the objects being studied are usually represented as data. For the theater problem, some of the objects are the customers and the cashier. The cashier serves the customers, and we want to determine a customer's average waiting time. Actions are implemented by writing algorithms, which in a programming language are implemented with the help of functions. Thus, functions are used to implement the actions of the objects.

In C++, we can combine the data and the operations on that data into a single unit with the help of classes. Thus, objects can be represented as classes. The data members of the class describe the properties of the objects, and the function members describe the actions on that data. The change in simulation results can also occur if we change the values of the data or modify the definitions of the functions (that is, modify the algorithms implementing the actions). The main goal of a computer simulation is either to generate results showing the performance of an existing system or to predict the performance of a proposed system.

In the theater problem, when the cashier is serving a customer, the other customers must wait. Because customers are served on a first come, first served basis and queues are an effective way to implement a First In First Out system, queues are important data structures for use in this type of computer simulation. This section examines computer simulations in which queues are the basic data structure. These simulations model the behavior of systems, called **queuing systems**, in which queues of objects are waiting to be served by various servers. In other words, a queuing system consists of servers and queues of objects waiting to be served.

We deal with a variety of queuing systems on a daily basis. For example, a grocery store and a bank are both queuing systems. Furthermore, when you send a print request to a networked printer that is shared by many people, your print request goes into a queue. Print requests that arrived before your print request are usually completed before yours. Thus, the printer acts as the server when a queue of documents is waiting to be printed.

Designing a Queuing System

In this section, we describe a queuing system that can be used in a variety of applications, such as a grocery store, bank, movie theater, printer, or a mainframe environment in which several people are trying to use the same processors to execute their programs. To describe a queuing system, we use the term **server** for the object that provides the service. For example, in a bank, a teller is a server; in a grocery store or movie theater, a cashier is a server. We call the object receiving the service the **customer**, and the service time—the time it takes to serve a customer—the **transaction time**.

Because a queuing system consists of servers and a queue of waiting objects, we model a system that consists of a list of servers and a waiting queue holding the customers to be served. The customer at the front of the queue waits for the next available server. When a server becomes free, the customer at the front of the queue moves to the free server to be served.

When the first customer arrives, all servers are free and the customer moves to the first server. When the next customer arrives, if a server is available, the customer immediately moves to the available server; otherwise, the customer waits in the queue. To model a queuing system, we need to know the number of servers, the expected arrival time of a customer, the time between the arrivals of customers, and the number of events affecting the system.

Let us again consider the movie theater system. Suppose that the number of servers is 1, on average it takes 5 minutes to serve a customer, and on average a new customer arrives every 4 minutes. The performance of the system depends on how many servers are available, how long it takes to serve a customer, and how often a customer arrives. If it takes too long to serve a customer and customers arrive frequently, then more servers are needed. This system can be modeled as a time-driven simulation. In a **time-driven simulation**, the clock is implemented as a counter and the passage of, say, 1 minute can be implemented by incrementing the counter by 1. The simulation is run for a fixed amount of time. If the simulations need to be run for 100 minutes, the counter starts at 1 and goes up to 100, which can be implemented by using a loop.

For the simulation described in this section, we want to determine the average wait time for a customer. To calculate the average wait time for a customer, we need to add the waiting time of each customer, and then divide the sum by the number of customers who have arrived. When a customer arrives, he or she goes to the end of the queue and the customer's waiting time starts. If the queue is empty and a server is free, the customer is served immediately and so this customer's waiting time is zero. On the other hand, if when the customer arrives either the queue is nonempty or all the servers are busy, the customer must wait for the next available server and, therefore, this customer's waiting time starts. We can keep track of the customer's waiting time by using a timer for each customer. When a customer arrives, the timer is set to 0, which is incremented after each clock unit.

Suppose that, on average, it takes 5 minutes for a server to serve a customer. When a server becomes free and the waiting customers' queue is nonempty, the customer at the front of the queue proceeds to begin the transaction. Thus, we must keep track of the time a customer is with a server. When the customer arrives at a server, the transaction time is set to 5 and is decremented after each clock unit. When the transaction time becomes zero, the server is marked as free. Hence, the two objects needed to implement a time-driven computer simulation of a queuing system are the customer and the server.

Next, before designing the main algorithm to implement this simulation, we design the classes to implement each of the two objects: customer and server.

Customer

Every customer has a customer number, arrival time, waiting time, transaction time, and departure time. If we know the arrival, waiting, and transaction times, we can determine the departure time by adding the arrival time, waiting time, and transaction time. Let us call the class to implement the customer object `customerType`. It follows that the `class customerType` has four data members: `customerNumber`, `arrivalTime`, waitingTime, and transactionTime, each of the data type int. The basic operations that must be performed on an object of the type customerType are as follows: set the customer's number, arrival time, and waiting time; increment the waiting time by one clock unit; return the waiting time; return the arrival time; return the transaction time; and return the customer number. The following class, customerType, implements the customer as an ADT (also see Figure 8-15):

```
class customerType
{
public:
    customerType(int customerN = 0, int arrvTime = 0, int wTime = 0,
                int tTime = 0);
    //constructor to initialize the data members
    //according to the parameters
    //In the object declaration if no value is specified,
    //the default is assigned.
    //Postcondition: customerNumber = customerN;
    //               arrivalTime = arrvTime;
    //               waitingTime = wTime;
    //               transactionTime = tTime
    void setCustomerInfo(int customerN, int arrvTime,
                        int wTime, int tTime);
      //Function to set the data members according
      //to the parameters.
      //Postcondition: customerNumber = customerN;
      //               arrivalTime = arrvTime;
      //               waitingTime = wTime;
      //               transactionTime = tTime
    int getWaitingTime() const;
      //Function to return the waiting time of a customer.
      //Postcondition: The value of waitingTime is returned.
    void setWaitingTime(int time);
      //Function to set the waiting time of a customer.
      //Postcondition: waitingTime = time
    void incrementWaitingTime();
      //Function to increment the waiting time.
      //Postcondition: waitingTime++
    int getArrivalTime();
      //Function to return the arrival time of a customer.
      //Postcondition: The value of arrivalTime is returned.
    int getTransactionTime();
      //Function to return the transaction time of a customer.
      //Postcondition: The value of transactionTime is returned.
    int getCustomerNumber();
      //Function to return the customer number.
      //Postcondition: The value of customerNumber is returned.
```

```
private:
    int customerNumber;
    int arrivalTime;
    int waitingTime;
    int transactionTime;
};
```

```
                              customerType

-customerNumber: int
-arrivalTime: int
-waitingTime: int
-transactionTime: int

+setCustomerInfo(int, int, int, int): void
+getWaitingTime(): int
+setWaitingTime(int): void
+incrementWaitingTime(): void
+getArrivalTime(): int
+getTransactionTime(): int
+getCustomerNumber(): int
+customerType(int = 0, int = 0, int = 0, int = 0)
```

Figure 8-15 UML diagram of the `class customerType`

Next, we give the definitions of the member functions of the **class customerType**.

The function `setCustomerInfo` uses the values of the parameters to initialize `customerNumber`, `arrivalTime`, `waitingTime`, and `transactionTime`. Its definition is:

```
void customerType::setCustomerInfo(int customerN, int arrvTime,
                                   int wTime, int tTime)
{
    customerNumber = customerN;
    arrivalTime = arrvTime;
    waitingTime = wTime;
    transactionTime = tTime;
}
```

The definition of the constructor is similar to the definition of the function `setCustomerInfo`. It uses the values of the parameters to initialize `customerNumber`, `arrivalTime`, `waitingTime`, and `transactionTime`. To make debugging easier, we use the function `setCustomerInfo` to write the definition of the constructor, which is given next.

```
customerType::customerType(int customerN, int arrvTime, int wTime,
                          int tTime)
{
    setCustomerInfo(customerN, arrvTime, wTime, tTime);
}
```

The function `getWaitingTime` returns the current waiting time. Because the waiting time is stored in the **private** data member `waitingTime`, the function `getWaitingTime` returns the value of `waitingTime`. The definition of the function `getWaitingTime` is:

```
int customerType::getWaitingTime() const
{
    return waitingTime;
}
```

The function `incrementWaitingTime` increments the value of `waitingTime`. Its definition is:

```
void customerType::incrementWaitingTime()
{
    waitingTime++;
}
```

The definitions of the functions `setWaitingTime`, `getArrivalTime`, `getTransactionTime`, and `getCustomerNumber` are left as an exercise for you.

Server

At any given time unit, the server is either busy serving a customer or is free. We use the string variable `status` to set the status of the server. Every server has a timer, and, because the program might need to know which server serves which customer, the server also stores the information of the customer being served. Thus, three data members are associated with a server: `status` of the type `string`, `transactionTime` of the type `int`, and `currentCustomer` of the type `customerType`. Some of the basic operations that must be performed on a server are as follows: check whether the server is free; set the server as free; set the server as busy; set the transaction time (that is, how long it takes to serve the customer); return the remaining transaction time (to determine whether the server should be set to free); if the server is busy after each time unit, decrement the transaction time by one time unit; and so on. The following **class**, `serverType`, implements the server as an ADT (see also Figure 8-16):

```
class serverType
{
public:
    serverType();
        //default constructor
        //Set the values of the data members to their default
        //values.
```

```
    //Postcondition: currentCustomer is initialized by its
    //                 default constructor; status = "free";
    //                 the transaction time is initialized to 0.
bool isFree() const;
  //Function to determine whether a server is free.
    //Postcondition: Returns true if the server is free;
    //                 otherwise, returns false.
void setBusy();
  //Function to set the status of a server to "busy".
    //Postcondition: status = "busy".
void setFree();
  //Function to set the status of a server to "free".
    //Postcondition: status = "free".
void setTransactionTime(int t);
  //Function to set the transaction time according
    //to the parameter t.
    //Postcondition: transactionTime = t
void setTransactionTime();
  //Function to set the transaction time according
    //to the transaction time of the current customer.
    //Postcondition:
    //   transactionTime = currentCustomer.transactionTime
int getRemainingTransactionTime();
  //Function to return the remaining transaction time.
    //Postcondition: The value of the data member
    //                 transactionTime is returned.
void decreaseTransactionTime();
  //Function to decrease the transaction time by 1.
    //Postcondition: transactionTime--
void setCurrentCustomer(customerType cCustomer);
  //Function to set the info of the current customer
    //according to the parameter cCustomer.
    //Postcondition: currentCustomer = cCustomer.
int getCurrentCustomerNumber();
  //Function to return the customer number of the
    //current customer.
    //Postcondition: The value of the data member
    //                 customerNumber of the current customer
    //                 is returned.
int getCurrentCustomerArrivalTime();
  //Function to return the arrival time of the current customer.
    //Postcondition: The value of the data member arrivalTime
    //                 of the current customer is returned.
int getCurrentCustomerWaitingTime();
  //Function to return the current waiting time of the
    //current customer.
    //Postcondition: The value of the data member
    //                 waitingTime of the current
    //                 customer is returned.
```

```
    int getCurrentCustomerTransactionTime();
      //Function to return the transaction time of the
        //current customer.
        //Postcondition: The value of the data member
        //                transactionTime of the current customer
        //                is returned.

private:
   customerType currentCustomer;
   string status;
   int transactionTime;
};
```

Figure 8-16   UML diagram of the class serverType

The definitions of the member functions of the **class serverType** are as follows:

```
serverType::serverType()
{
      status = "free";
      transactionTime = 0;
}

bool serverType::isFree() const
{
      return (status == "free");
}
```

```
void serverType::setBusy()
{
     status = "busy";
}

void serverType::setFree()
{
     status = "free";
}

void serverType::setTransactionTime(int t)
{
     transactionTime = t;
}

void serverType::setTransactionTime()
{
     int time;

     time = currentCustomer.getTransactionTime();

     transactionTime = time;
}

void serverType::decreaseTransactionTime()
{
     transactionTime--;
}
```

We leave the definitions of the functions `getRemainingTransactionTime`, `setCurrentCustomer`, `getCurrentCustomerNumber`, `getCurrentCustomerArrivalTime`, `getCurrentCustomerWaitingTime`, and `getCurrentCustomerTransactionTime` as an exercise for you.

Because we are designing a simulation program that can be used in a variety of applications, we need to design two more classes: a class to create and process a list of servers, and a class to create and process a queue of waiting customers. The next two sections describe each of these classes.

Server List

A server list is a set of servers, like a row of bank tellers. At any given time, a server is either free or busy. For the customer at the front of the queue, we need to find a server in the list that is free. If all the servers are busy, then the customer must wait until one of the servers becomes free. Thus, the class that implements a list of servers has two data members: one to store the number of servers, and one to maintain a list of servers. Using dynamic arrays, and depending on the number of servers specified by the user, a list of servers is created during program execution. Some of the operations that must be performed on a server list are as follows: return the server number of a free server; when a customer gets ready to conduct business and a server is available, set the server to "busy"; when the simulation ends, some of the servers might still be busy, so return the number of busy servers; after each time unit, reduce `transactionTime` of each busy server by one time unit; and if `transactionTime` of a server becomes zero, set the server to "free". The following `class`, `serverListType`, implements the list of servers as an ADT (see also Figure 8-17):

```
class serverListType
{
public:
    serverListType(int num = 1);
      //constructor to create a list of servers
      //Postcondition: numOfServers = num
      //   A list of servers, specified by num, is created.
      //   If no value is specified for num, its default
      //   value is assumed.
    ~serverListType();
      //destructor
      //Postcondition: The list of servers is destroyed.
    int getFreeServerID();
      //Function to search the list of servers.
      //Postcondition: If a free server is found, return its ID;
      //   otherwise, return -1.
    int getNumberOfBusyServers();
      //Function to return the number of busy servers.
      //Postcondition: The number of busy servers is returned.
    void setServerBusy(int serverID, customerType cCustomer,
                       int tTime);
      //Function to set a server to "busy".
      //Postcondition: To serve the customer specified by
      //   cCustomer, the server specified by serverID is set
      //   to "busy", and the transaction time is set according
      //   to the parameter tTime.
    void setServerBusy(int serverID, customerType cCustomer);
      //Function to set a server to "busy".
      //Postcondition: To serve the customer specified by
      //   cCustomer, the server specified by serverID is
      //   set to "busy", and the transaction time is set
      //   according to the customer's transaction time.
    void updateServers();
      //Function to update the transaction time of each
      //busy server.
      //Postcondition: The transaction time of each busy
      //   server is decremented by one time unit. If the
      //   transaction time of a busy server is reduced to
      //   zero, the server is set to "free" and a message
      //   indicating which customer was served, together
```

8

```
//    with the customer's departing time, is printed
//    on the screen.
void updateServers(ofstream& outFile);
    //Function to update the transaction time of each
    //busy server.
    //Postcondition: The transaction time of each busy
    //    server is decremented by one time unit. If the
    //    transaction time of a busy server is reduced to
    //    zero, the server is set to "free" and a message
    //    indicating which customer was served, together
    //    with the customer's departing time, is sent to
    //    a file specified by outFile.

private:
    int numOfServers;
    serverType *servers;
};
```

serverListType
-numOfServers: int
-*servers: serverType
+getFreeServerID(): int
+getNumberOfBusyServers(): int
+setServerBusy(int, customerType, int): void
+setServerBusy(int, customerType): void
+updateServers(): void
+updateServers(ofstream&): void
+serverListType(int = 1)
+~serverListType()

Figure 8-17 UML diagram of the class serverListType

Following are the definitions of the member functions of the **class serverListType**. The definitions of the constructor and destructor are as follows:

```
serverListType::serverListType(int num)
{
    numOfServers = num;
    servers = new serverType[num]; //create a list of servers
}
```

```
serverListType::~serverListType()
{
    delete [] servers;
}
```

The function **getFreeServerID** searches the list of servers. If a free server is found, it returns the server's ID; otherwise, the value **-1** is returned, which indicates that all of the servers are busy. The definition of this function is:

```
int serverListType::getFreeServerID()
{
    int serverID = -1;

    int i;

    for(i = 0; i < numOfServers; i++)
        if(servers[i].isFree())
        {
            serverID = i;
            break;
        }

    return serverID;
}
```

The function **getNumberOfBusyServers** searches the list of servers and determines the number of busy servers. The number of busy servers is returned. The definition of this function is:

```
int serverListType::getNumberOfBusyServers()
{
    int busyServers = 0;

    int i;

    for(i = 0; i < numOfServers; i++)
        if(!servers[i].isFree())
            busyServers++;

    return busyServers;
}
```

The function **setServerBusy** sets a server to **"busy"**. This function is overloaded. The **serverID** of the server that is set to **"busy"** is passed as a parameter to this function. One function sets the server's transaction time according to the parameter **tTime**; the other function sets it by using the transaction time stored in the object **cCustomer**. The transaction time is later needed to determine the average wait time. The definitions of these functions are as follows:

```
void serverListType::setServerBusy(int serverID,
                                   customerType cCustomer,
                                   int tTime)
{
    servers[serverID].setBusy();
    servers[serverID].setTransactionTime(tTime);
    servers[serverID].setCurrentCustomer(cCustomer);
}

void serverListType::setServerBusy(int serverID,
                                   customerType cCustomer)
{
    int time;

    time = cCustomer.getTransactionTime();

    servers[serverID].setBusy();
    servers[serverID].setTransactionTime(time);
    servers[serverID].setCurrentCustomer(cCustomer);

}
```

Next, we consider the definition of the function `updateServers`. Starting at the first server, it searches the list of servers for busy servers. When a busy server is found, its `transactionTime` is decremented by 1. If `transactionTime` reduces to zero, the server is set to `"free"`. If `transactionTime` of a busy server reduces to zero, then the transaction of the customer being served by this server is completed. A message indicating the customer's server number, customer number, and departure time is then printed. The function `updateServers` is overloaded. One function sends the output to the screen; the other sends the output to a file. The definitions of these functions are as follows:

```
void serverListType::updateServers()
{
    int i;

    for(i = 0; i < numOfServers; i++)
        if(!servers[i].isFree())
        {
            servers[i].decreaseTransactionTime();

            if(servers[i].getRemainingTransactionTime() == 0)
            {
                cout<<"Server No: "<<(i + 1)<<" Customer number "
                    <<servers[i].getCurrentCustomerNumber()
```

```
                        <<" departed at "<<endl
                        <<"              clock unit "
                        <<servers[i].getCurrentCustomerArrivalTime()
                           + servers[i].getCurrentCustomerWaitingTime()
                           + servers[i].getCurrentCustomerTransactionTime()
                        <<endl;
                  servers[i].setFree();
              }
          }
    }

void serverListType::updateServers(ofstream& outFile)
{
    int i;

    for(i = 0; i < numOfServers; i++)
        if(!servers[i].isFree())
        {
            servers[i].decreaseTransactionTime();

            if(servers[i].getRemainingTransactionTime() == 0)
            {
                outFile<<"Server No: "<<(i + 1)<<" Customer number "
                        <<servers[i].getCurrentCustomerNumber()
                        <<" departed at "<<endl
                        <<"               clock unit "
                        <<servers[i].getCurrentCustomerArrivalTime()
                         + servers[i].getCurrentCustomerWaitingTime()
                         + servers[i].getCurrentCustomerTransactionTime()
                        <<endl;
                  servers[i].setFree();
            }
        }
}
```

Waiting Customers' Queue

When a customer arrives, he or she goes to the end of the queue. When a server becomes available, the customer at the front of the queue leaves to conduct the transaction. After each time unit, the waiting time of each customer in the queue is incremented by 1. The ADT queueType designed in this chapter has all the operations needed to implement a queue, except the operation of incrementing the waiting time of each customer in the queue by one time unit. Thus, we derive the class waitingCustomerQueueType from the class queueType and add the additional operations to implement the customers' queue. The definition of the class waitingCustomerQueueType is:

```
class waitingCustomerQueueType: public queueType<customerType>
{
public:
    waitingCustomerQueueType(int size = 100);
      //constructor
      //Postcondition: The queue is initialized
      //   according to the parameter size. The value of
      //   size is passed to the constructor of queueType.
      //   If no value is specified for size, its default
      //   value is assumed.
    ~waitingCustomerQueueType();
      //destructor
      //Postcondition: The queue is destroyed
  void updateWaitingQueue();
      //Function to increment the waiting time of each
      //customer in the queue by one time unit.
      //Postcondition: The waiting time of each customer in
      //   the queue is incremented by one time unit.
};
```

 Notice that the class waitingCustomerQueueType is derived from the class queueType, which implements the queue in an array. You can also derive the class waitingCustomerQueueType from the class linkedQueueType, which implements the queue in a linked list. We leave the details as an exercise for you.

The definitions of the member functions are given next. The definitions of the constructor and the destructor are as follows:

```
waitingCustomerQueueType::waitingCustomerQueueType(int size)
                        :queueType<customerType>(size)
{
}

waitingCustomerQueueType::~waitingCustomerQueueType()
{
}
```

The function updateWaitingQueue increments the waiting time of each customer in the queue by one time unit. The class waitingCustomerQueueType is derived from the class queueType. Because the data members of queueType are private, the function updateWaitingQueue cannot directly access the elements of the queue. The only way to access the elements of the queue is to use the front and deleteQueue operations. After incrementing the waiting time, the element can be put back into the queue by using the addQueue operation.

The addQueue operation inserts the element at the end of the queue. If we perform the front and deleteQueue operations followed by the addQueue operation for each element of the queue, then eventually the front element again becomes the front element. Given that each front and deleteQueue operation is followed by an addQueue operation, how do we determine that all the elements of the queue have been processed? We cannot use the isEmptyQueue or isFullQueue operations on the queue, because the queue will never be empty or full.

One solution to this problem is to create a temporary queue. Every element of the original queue is removed, processed, and inserted into the temporary queue. When the original queue becomes empty, all of the elements in the queue are processed. We can then copy the elements from the temporary queue back into the original queue. However, this solution requires us to use extra memory space, which could be significant. Also, if the queue is large, extra computer time is needed to copy the elements from the temporary queue back into the original queue. Let us look into another solution.

Before starting to update the elements of the queue, we can insert a dummy customer with a waiting time of, say, -1. During the update process, when we arrive at the customer with the waiting time of -1, we can stop the update process without processing this customer. If we do not process the customer with the waiting time of -1, this customer is removed from the queue and, after processing all the elements of the queue, the queue contains no extra elements. This solution does not require us to create a temporary queue, so we do not need extra computer time to copy the elements back into the original queue. We will use this solution to update the queue. Therefore, the definition of the function updateWaitingQueue is:

```cpp
void waitingCustomerQueueType::updateWaitingQueue()
{
    customerType cust;

    cust.setWaitingTime(-1);
    int wTime = 0;

    addQueue(cust);

    while(wTime != -1)
    {
        cust = front();
        deleteQueue();
        wTime = cust.getWaitingTime();

        if(wTime == -1)
            break;

        cust.incrementWaitingTime();
        addQueue(cust);
    }
}
```

8

Main Program

To run the simulation, we first need to get the following information:

- The number of time units the simulation should run. Assume that each time unit is one minute.

- The number of servers.

- The amount of time it takes to serve a customer—that is, the transaction time.

- The approximate time between customer arrivals.

These pieces of information are called simulation parameters. By changing the values of these parameters, we can observe the changes in the performance of the system. We can write a function, `setSimulationParameters`, to prompt the user to specify these values. The definition of this function is:

```cpp
void setSimulationParameters(int& sTime, int& numOfServers,
                             int& transTime,
                             int& tBetweenCArrival)
{
    cout<<"Enter the simulation time: "<<flush;
    cin>>sTime;
    cout<<endl;

    cout<<"Enter the number of servers: "<<flush;
    cin>>numOfServers;
    cout<<endl;

    cout<<"Enter the transaction time: "<<flush;
    cin>>transTime;
    cout<<endl;

    cout<<"Enter the time between customer arrivals: "<<flush;
    cin>>tBetweenCArrival;
    cout<<endl;
}
```

When a server becomes free and the customer queue is nonempty, we can move the customer at the front of the queue to the free server to be served. Moreover, when a customer starts the transaction, the waiting time ends. The waiting time of the customer is added to the total waiting time. The general algorithm to start the transaction (supposing that `serverID` denotes the ID of the free server) is:

1. Retrieve and remove the customer from the front of the queue.

   ```cpp
   customer = customerQueue.front();
   customerQueue.deleteQueue();
   ```

2. Update the total waiting time by adding the current customer's waiting time to the previous total waiting time.

   ```cpp
   totalWait = totalWait + customer.getWaitingTime();
   ```

3. Set the free server to begin the transaction.

```
serverList.setServerBusy(serverID, customer, transTime);
```

To run the simulation, we need to know the number of customers arriving at a given time unit and how long it takes to serve the customer. We use the Poisson distribution from statistics, which says that the probability of y events occurring at a given time is given by the formula:

$$P(y) = \frac{\lambda^y e^{-\lambda}}{y!}, y = 0, 1, 2, \ldots,$$

where λ is the expected value that y events occur at that time. Suppose that, on average, a customer arrives every 4 minutes. During this 4-minute period, the customer can arrive at any one of the 4 minutes. Assuming an equal likelihood of each of the 4 minutes, the expected value that a customer arrives in each of the 4 minutes is, therefore, $1 / 4 = .25$. Next, we need to determine whether or not the customer actually arrives at a given minute.

Now $P(0) = e^{-\lambda}$ is the probability that no event occurs at a given time. One of the basic assumptions of the Poisson distribution is that more than one outcome will occur in a short time interval is negligible. For simplicity, we assume that only one customer arrives at a given time unit. Thus, we use $e^{-\lambda}$ as the cutoff point to determine whether a customer arrives at a given time unit. Suppose that, on average, a customer arrives every 4 minutes. Then $\lambda = 0.25$. We can use an algorithm to generate a number between 0 and 1. If the value of the number generated is $> e^{-0.25}$, we can assume that the customer arrived at a particular time unit. For example, suppose that $rNum$ is a random number such that $0 \leq rNum \leq 1$. If $rNum > e^{-0.25}$, the customer arrived at the given time unit.

We now describe the function `runSimulation` to implement the simulation. Suppose that we run the simulation for 100 time units and customers arrive at time units 93, 96, and 100. The average transaction time is 5 minutes—that is, 5 time units. For simplicity, assume that we have only one server and the server becomes free at time unit 97, and that all customers arriving before time unit 93 have been served. When the server becomes free at time unit 97, the customer who arrived at time unit 93 starts the transaction. Because the transaction of the customer arriving at time unit 93 starts at time unit 97 and it takes 5 minutes to complete a transaction, when the simulation loop ends, this customer is still at the server. Moreover, customers who arrive at time units 96 and 100 are in the queue. For simplicity, we assume that when the simulation loop ends, the customers at the servers are considered served. The general algorithm for this function is:

1. Declare and initialize the variables, such as the simulation parameters, customer number, clock, total and average waiting times, number of customers arrived, number of customers served, number of customers left in the waiting queue, number of customers left with the servers, `waitingCustomersQueue`, and a list of servers.

2. The main loop is:

```
for(clock = 1; clock <= simulationTime; clock++)
{
```

a. Update the server list to decrement the transaction time of each busy server by one time unit.

b. If the customers' queue is nonempty, increment the waiting time of each customer by one time unit.

c. If a customer arrives, increment the number of customers by 1 and add the new customer to the queue.

d. If a server is free and the customers' queue is nonempty, remove the customer from the front of the queue and send the customer to the free server.

```
}
```

3. Print the appropriate results. Your results must include the number of customers left in the queue, the number of customers still with servers, the number of customers arrived, and the number of customers who actually completed a transaction.

Once you have designed the function `runSimulation`, the definition of the function `main` is simple and straightforward because the function `main` calls only the function `runSimulation`. (See Programming Exercise 6 at the end of this chapter.)

When we tested our version of the simulation program, we generated the following results. We assumed that the average transaction time is 5 minutes and that, on average, a customer arrives every 4 minutes. We used a random number generator to generate a number between 0 and 1 to decide whether a customer arrived at a given time unit.

Sample Runs:

Sample Run 1:

```
Customer number 1 arrived at time unit 4
Customer number 2 arrived at time unit 8
Server No: 1 Customer number 1 departed at
           clock unit 9
Customer number 3 arrived at time unit 9
Customer number 4 arrived at time unit 12
Server No: 1 Customer number 2 departed at
           clock unit 14
Server No: 1 Customer number 3 departed at
           clock unit 19
Customer number 5 arrived at time unit 21
Server No: 1 Customer number 4 departed at
           clock unit 24
Server No: 1 Customer number 5 departed at
           clock unit 29
Customer number 6 arrived at time unit 37
```

```
Customer number 7 arrived at time unit 38
Customer number 8 arrived at time unit 41
Server No: 1 Customer number 6 departed at
            clock unit 42
Customer number 9 arrived at time unit 43
Customer number 10 arrived at time unit 44
Server No: 1 Customer number 7 departed at
            clock unit 47
Customer number 11 arrived at time unit 49
Customer number 12 arrived at time unit 51
Server No: 1 Customer number 8 departed at
            clock unit 52
Customer number 13 arrived at time unit 52
Customer number 14 arrived at time unit 53
Customer number 15 arrived at time unit 54
Server No: 1 Customer number 9 departed at
            clock unit 57
Customer number 16 arrived at time unit 59
Server No: 1 Customer number 10 departed at
            clock unit 62
Customer number 17 arrived at time unit 66
Server No: 1 Customer number 11 departed at
            clock unit 67
Customer number 18 arrived at time unit 71
Server No: 1 Customer number 12 departed at
            clock unit 72
Server No: 1 Customer number 13 departed at
            clock unit 77
Customer number 19 arrived at time unit 78
Server No: 1 Customer number 14 departed at
            clock unit 82
Server No: 1 Customer number 15 departed at
            clock unit 87
Customer number 20 arrived at time unit 90
Server No: 1 Customer number 16 departed at
            clock unit 92
Customer number 21 arrived at time unit 92
Server No: 1 Customer number 17 departed at
            clock unit 97

Simulation ran for 100 time units
Number of servers: 1
Average transaction time: 5
Average arrival time difference between customers: 4
Total wait time: 269
Number of customers who completed a transaction: 17
Number of customers left in the servers: 1
Number of customers left in the queue: 3
Average wait time: 12.81
************* END SIMULATION *************
```

Sample Run 2:

```
Customer number 1 arrived at time unit 4
Customer number 2 arrived at time unit 8
Server No: 1 Customer number 1 departed at
             clock unit 9
Customer number 3 arrived at time unit 9
Customer number 4 arrived at time unit 12
Server No: 2 Customer number 2 departed at
             clock unit 13
Server No: 1 Customer number 3 departed at
             clock unit 14
Server No: 2 Customer number 4 departed at
             clock unit 18
Customer number 5 arrived at time unit 21
Server No: 1 Customer number 5 departed at
             clock unit 26
Customer number 6 arrived at time unit 37
Customer number 7 arrived at time unit 38
Customer number 8 arrived at time unit 41
Server No: 1 Customer number 6 departed at
             clock unit 42
Server No: 2 Customer number 7 departed at
             clock unit 43
Customer number 9 arrived at time unit 43
Customer number 10 arrived at time unit 44
Server No: 1 Customer number 8 departed at
             clock unit 47
Server No: 2 Customer number 9 departed at
             clock unit 48
Customer number 11 arrived at time unit 49
Customer number 12 arrived at time unit 51
Server No: 1 Customer number 10 departed at
             clock unit 52
Customer number 13 arrived at time unit 52
Customer number 14 arrived at time unit 53
Server No: 2 Customer number 11 departed at
             clock unit 54
Customer number 15 arrived at time unit 54
Server No: 1 Customer number 12 departed at
             clock unit 57
Server No: 2 Customer number 13 departed at
             clock unit 59
Customer number 16 arrived at time unit 59
Server No: 1 Customer number 14 departed at
             clock unit 62
Server No: 2 Customer number 15 departed at
             clock unit 64
Customer number 17 arrived at time unit 66
```

```
Server No: 1 Customer number 16 departed at
            clock unit 67
Server No: 2 Customer number 17 departed at
            clock unit 71
Customer number 18 arrived at time unit 71
Server No: 1 Customer number 18 departed at
            clock unit 76
Customer number 19 arrived at time unit 78
Server No: 1 Customer number 19 departed at
            clock unit 83
Customer number 20 arrived at time unit 90
Customer number 21 arrived at time unit 92
Server No: 1 Customer number 20 departed at
            clock unit 95
Server No: 2 Customer number 21 departed at
            clock unit 97

Simulation ran for 100 time units
Number of servers: 2
Average transaction time: 5
Average arrival time difference between customers: 4
Total wait time: 20
Number of customers who completed a transaction: 21
Number of customers left in the servers: 0
Number of customers left in the queue: 0
Average wait time: 0.95
************* END SIMULATION *************
```

Sample Run 3: (In this output, to save space the details of the output of the customer's arrival and departure times are omitted.)

```
Customer number 1 arrived at time unit 4
Customer number 2 arrived at time unit 8
Server No: 1 Customer number 1 departed at
            clock unit 9
Customer number 3 arrived at time unit 9
Customer number 4 arrived at time unit 12
Server No: 1 Customer number 2 departed at
            clock unit 14
Server No: 1 Customer number 3 departed at
            clock unit 19
Customer number 5 arrived at time unit 21
Server No: 1 Customer number 4 departed at
            clock unit 24
Server No: 1 Customer number 5 departed at
            clock unit 29
Customer number 6 arrived at time unit 37
Customer number 7 arrived at time unit 38
Customer number 8 arrived at time unit 41
```

```
Server No: 1 Customer number 6 departed at
             clock unit 42
Customer number 9 arrived at time unit 43
Customer number 10 arrived at time unit 44
...

Simulation ran for 1000 time units
Number of servers: 1
Average transaction time: 5
Average arrival time difference between customers: 4
Total wait time: 8008
Number of customers who completed a transaction: 197
Number of customers left in the servers: 1
Number of customers left in the queue: 15
Average wait time: 37.60
************** END SIMULATION *************
```

Sample Run 4: (In this output, to save space the details of the output of the customer's arrival and departure times are omitted.)

```
Customer number 1 arrived at time unit 4
Customer number 2 arrived at time unit 8
Server No: 1 Customer number 1 departed at
             clock unit 9
Customer number 3 arrived at time unit 9
Customer number 4 arrived at time unit 12
Server No: 2 Customer number 2 departed at
             clock unit 13
Server No: 1 Customer number 3 departed at
             clock unit 14
Server No: 3 Customer number 4 departed at
             clock unit 17
Customer number 5 arrived at time unit 21
Server No: 1 Customer number 5 departed at
             clock unit 26
Customer number 6 arrived at time unit 37
Customer number 7 arrived at time unit 38
Customer number 8 arrived at time unit 41
Server No: 1 Customer number 6 departed at
             clock unit 42
Server No: 2 Customer number 7 departed at
             clock unit 43
Customer number 9 arrived at time unit 43
Customer number 10 arrived at time unit 44
Server No: 3 Customer number 8 departed at
             clock unit 46

...
```

```
Simulation ran for 1000 time units
Number of servers: 3
Average transaction time: 5
Average arrival time difference between customers: 4
Total wait time: 13
Number of customers who completed a transaction: 212
Number of customers left in the servers: 1
Number of customers left in the queue: 0
Average wait time: 0.06
************* END SIMULATION *************
```

QUICK REVIEW

1. A queue is a data structure wherein the items are added at one end and removed from the other end.

2. A queue is a First In First Out (FIFO) data structure.

3. The basic operations on a queue are: initialize the queue, destroy the queue, check whether the queue is empty, check whether the queue is full, add an item to the queue, and remove an item from the queue.

4. A queue can be implemented either as an array or as a linked list.

5. The middle elements of a queue should not be accessed directly.

6. If the queue is nonempty, the function `front` returns the front element of the queue, and the function `back` returns the last element of the queue.

7. Queues are restricted versions of arrays and linked lists.

EXERCISES

1. Suppose that `queue` is a `queueType` object and the size of the array implementing `queue` is 100. Also suppose that the value of `queueFront` is 50 and the value of `queueRear` is 99?

   a. What are the values of `queueFront` and `queueRear` after adding an element to `queue`?

   b. What are the values of `queueFront` and `queueRear` after removing an element from `queue`?

2. Suppose that `queue` is a `queueType` object and the size of the array implementing `queue` is 100. Also suppose that the value of `queueFront` is 99 and the value of `queueRear` is 25.

   a. What are the values of `queueFront` and `queueRear` after adding an element to `queue`?

   b. What are the values of `queueFront` and `queueRear` after removing an element from `queue`?

3. Suppose that **queue** is a **queueType** object and the size of the array implementing queue is 100. Also suppose that the value of **queueFront** is 25 and the value of **queueRear** is 75.

    a. What are the values of **queueFront** and **queueRear** after adding an element to **queue**?

    b. What are the values of **queueFront** and **queueRear** after removing an element from **queue**?

4. Suppose that **queue** is a **queueType** object and the size of the array implementing queue is 100. Also suppose that the value of **queueFront** is 99 and the value of **queueRear** is 25.

    a. What are the values of **queueFront** and **queueRear** after adding an element to **queue**?

    b. What are the values of **queueFront** and **queueRear** after removing an element from **queue**?

5. Suppose that **queue** is implemented as an array with the special reserved slot, as described in this chapter. Also suppose that the size of the array implementing **queue** is 100. If the value of **queueFront** is 50, what is the position of the first **queue** element?

6. Suppose that **queue** is implemented as an array with the special reserved slot, as described in this chapter. Also suppose that the value of **queueFront** is 74 and the value of **queueRear** is 99.

    a. What are the values of **queueFront** and **queueRear** after adding an element to **queue**?

    b. What are the values of **queueFront** and **queueRear** after removing an element from the **queue**? Also what was the position of the removed **queue** element?

7. Consider the following statements:

```
queueType<int> queue;
int x, y;
```

Show what is output by the following segment of code.

```
queue.initializeQueue();
x = 4;
y = 5;
queue.addQueue(x);
queue.addQueue(y);
x = queue.front();
queue.deleteQueue();
queue.addQueue(x + 5);
queue.addQueue(16);
queue.addQueue(x);
queue.addQueue(y - 3);
```

```
cout<<"Queue Elements: ";

while(!queue.isEmptyQueue())
{
    cout<<" "<<queue.front();
    queue.deleteQueue();
}

cout<<endl;
```

8. Consider the following statements:

```
stackType<int> stack;
queueType<int> queue;
int x;
```

Suppose the input is:

```
15 28 14 22 64 35 19 32 7 11 13 30 -999
```

Show what is output by the following segment of code.

```
stack.initializeStack();
queue.initializeQueue();
stack.push(0);
queue.addQueue(0);
cin>>x;

while(x != -999)
{
    switch(x % 4)
    {
    case 0: stack.push(x);
            break;
    case 1: if(!stack.isEmptyStack())
            {
                cout<<"Stack Element = "<<stack.top()<<endl;
                stack.pop();
            }
            else
                cout<<"Sorry, the stack is empty."<<endl;
            break;
    case 2: queue.addQueue(x);
            break;
    case 3: if(!queue.isEmptyQueue())
            {
                cout<<"Queue Element = "<<queue.front()<<endl;
                queue.deleteQueue();
```

8

```
        }
        else
            cout<<"Sorry, the queue is empty."<<endl;
        break;
   }//end switch

   cin>>x;
}//end while

cout<<"Stack Elements: ";
while(!stack.isEmptyStack())
{
   cout<<stack.top()<<" ";
   stack.pop();
}

cout<<endl;
cout<<"Queue Elements: ";
while(!queue.isEmptyQueue())
{
    cout<<queue.front()<<" ";
    queue.deleteQueue();
}
cout<<endl;
```

9. What is the output of the following program segment? (In this C++ code, `queue` is the STL `class queue`.)

```
queue<int> q;
int x, y;

x = 2;
q.push(8);
q.push(x + 3);
y = q.front();
q.push(2 * y);
q.pop();
x = q.front();
q.push(q.front());

while(!q.empty())
{
   cout<<q.front()<<" ";
   q.pop();
}

cout<<endl;
```

10. What does the following function do?

```
void mystery(queue<int>& q)
{
    stack<int> s;

    while(!q.empty())
    {
        s.push(q.front());
        q.pop();
    }

    while(!s.empty())
    {
        q.push(2 * s.top());
        s.pop();
    }
}
```

11. Write the definition of the function template `moveNthFront` that takes as a parameter a queue and a positive integer, *n*. The function moves the *n*th element of the queue to the front. The order of the remaining elements remains unchanged. For example, suppose

`queue = {5, 11, 34, 67, 43, 55}` and *n* = 3.

After a call to the function `moveNthFront`,

`queue = {34, 5, 11, 67, 43, 55}`.

12. Write a function template, `reverseStack`, that takes as a parameter a stack object and a queue object whose elements are of the same type. The function `reverseStack` uses the queue to reverse the elements of the stack.

13. Write a function template, `reverseQueue`, that takes as a parameter a stack object and a queue object whose elements are of the same type. The function `reverseQueue` uses the stack to reverse the elements of the queue.

14. Add the operation `queueCount` to the `class queueType` (the array implementation of queues), which returns the number of elements in the queue. Write the definition of the function template to implement this operation.

PROGRAMMING EXERCISES

1. Write the definitions of the functions to overload the assignment operator and copy constructor for the `class queueType`. Also, write a program to test these operations.

2. Write the definitions of the functions to overload the assignment operator and copy constructor for the `class linkedQueueType`. Also, write a program to test these operations.

3. The array implementation of queues given in this chapter uses a special array slot—a reserved slot—to distinguish between an empty queue and a full queue. Write the array implementation of queues as an ADT, in which a variable count is used to keep track of the number of elements in the queue. Write the definitions of the function members of this queue design. Also, write a program to test various operations on the queue.

4. Write a program that reads a line of text, changes each uppercase letter to lowercase, and places each letter both in a queue and onto a stack. The program should then verify whether the line of text is a palindrome.

5. The implementation of a queue in an array, as given in this chapter, uses the variable count to determine whether the queue is empty or full. You can also use the variable count to return the number of elements in the queue; see Exercise 8 of this chapter. On the other hand, the class linkedQueueType does not use such a variable to keep track of the number of elements in the queue. Redefine the class linkedQueueType by adding a variable count to keep track of the number of elements in the queue. Modify the definitions of the functions addQueue and deleteQueue as necessary. Also add the function queueCount, to return the number of elements in the queue. Moreover, write a program to test various operations of the class you defined.

6. a. Write the definitions of the functions setWaitingTime, getArrivalTime, getTransactionTime, and getCustomerNumber of the class customerType defined in the section "Application of Queues: Simulation."

   b. Write the definitions of the functions getRemainingTransactionTime, setCurrentCustomer, getCurrentCustomerNumber, getCurrentCustomerArrivalTime, getCurrentCustomerWaitingTime, and getCurrentCustomerTransactionTime of the class serverType defined in the section "Application of Queues: Simulation."

   c. Write the definition of the function runSimulation to complete the design of the computer simulation program in the section "Application of Queues: Simulation." Test run your program for a variety of data. Moreover, use a random number generator to decide whether a customer arrived at a given time unit.

7. Redo the simulation program of this chapter so that it uses the STL class queue to maintain the list of waiting customers.

SEARCH ALGORITHMS

Chapter 3 described how to organize data into computer memory using an array and how to perform basic operations on that data. Chapter 5 then described how to organize data using linked lists. The most important operation performed on a list is the search algorithm. Using the search algorithm, you can:

■ Determine whether a particular item is in the list.

■ If the data is specially organized (for example, sorted), find the location in the list where a new item can be inserted.

■ Find the location of an item to be deleted.

The search algorithm's performance, therefore, is crucial. If the search is slow, it takes a large amount of computer time to accomplish your task; if the search is fast, you can accomplish your task quickly.

SEARCH ALGORITHMS

Chapters 3 and 5 described how to implement the sequential search algorithm. This chapter discusses other search algorithms and also analyzes the algorithms. Analysis of the algorithms enables programmers to decide which algorithm to use for a specific application. Before describing these algorithms, let us make the following observations.

Associated with each item in a data set is a special member that uniquely identifies the item in the data set. For example, if you have a data set consisting of student records, then the student ID uniquely identifies each student in a particular school. This unique member of the item is called the **key** of the item. The keys of the item in the data set are used in such operations as searching, sorting, insertion, and deletion. For instance, when we search the data set for a particular item, we compare the key of the item for which we are searching with the keys of the items in the data set.

As previously remarked, this chapter, in addition to describing the searching and sorting algorithms, analyzes these algorithms. In the analysis of an algorithm, the key comparisons refer to comparing the key of the search item with the key of an item in the list. Moreover, the number of key comparisons refers to the number of times the key of the item (in algorithms such as searching and sorting) is compared with the keys of the items in the list.

In Chapter 3, we designed and implemented the **class arrayListType** to implement a list and the basic operations on a list. Because this chapter refers to this class, for easy reference we give its definition here:

```cpp
template<class elemType>
class arrayListType
{
public:
    const arrayListType<elemType>&
                  operator=(const arrayListType<elemType>&);
      //Overload the assignment operator.

    bool isEmpty();
      //Function to determine whether the list is empty.
      //Postcondition: Returns true if the list is empty;
      //               otherwise, returns false.
    bool isFull();
      //Function to determine whether the list is full.
      //Postcondition: Returns true if the list is full;
      //               otherwise, returns false.
    int listSize();
      //Function to determine the number of elements in list.
      //Postcondition: Returns the value of the length.
    int maxListSize();
      //Function to determine the size of the list.
      //Postcondition: Returns the value of maxSize.
```

```
void print() const;
   //Function to output the elements of the list.
   //Postcondition: Elements of the list are output on the
   //               standard output device.
bool isItemAtEqual(int location, const elemType& item);
   //Function to determine whether item is the same as the
   //item in the list at the position specified by location.
   //Postcondition: Returns true if list[location] is the
   //               same as item; otherwise, returns false.
void insertAt(int location, const elemType& insertItem);
   //Function to insert an item in the list at the
   //location specified by location. The item to be inserted
   //and the list are passed as parameters to the function.
   //Postcondition: Starting at location, the elements of the
   //               list are shifted down, list[location] =
   //               insertItem; and length++
   //    If the list is full or location is out of range,
   //    an appropriate message is displayed.
void insertEnd(const elemType& insertItem);
   //Function to insert an item at the end of the list.
   //The parameter insertItem specifies the item to be inserted.
   //Postcondition: list[length] = insertItem; and length++
   //    If the list is full, an appropriate message is
   //    displayed.
void removeAt(int location);
   //Function to remove the item from the list at the position
   //specified by location.
   //Postcondition: The list element at list[location] is removed
   //    and the length is decremented by 1.
   //    If location is out of range, an appropriate message
   //    is displayed.
void retrieveAt(int location, elemType& retItem);
   //Function to retrieve the element from the list at the
   //position specified by location.
   //Postcondition: retItem = list[location]
   //    If location is out of range, an appropriate message
   //    is displayed.
void replaceAt(int location, const elemType& repItem);
   //Function to replace the element in the list at the
   //position specified by location. The item to be replaced
   //is specified by the parameter repItem.
   //Postcondition: list[location] = repItem
   //    If location is out of range, an appropriate message
   //    is displayed.
void clearList();
   //Function to remove all the elements from the list.
   //After this operation, the size of the list is zero.
   //Postcondition: length = 0
```

9

```
    int seqSearch(const elemType& item);
       //Function to search the list for a given item.
       //Postcondition: If item is found, returns the location
       //                in the array where item is found;
       //                otherwise, returns -1.
    void insert(const elemType& insertItem);
       //Function to insert the item specified by the parameter
       //insertItem at the end of the list. However, first the
       //list is searched to see whether the item to be inserted
       //is already in the list.
       //Postcondition: list[length] = insertItem; and length++
       //   If the item is already in the list or the list is
       //   full, an appropriate message is displayed.
    void remove(const elemType& removeItem);
       //Function to remove an item from the list. The parameter
       //removeItem specifies the item to be removed.
       //Postcondition: If removeItem is found in the list, it is
       //                removed from the list and length is
       //                decremented by one.

    arrayListType(int size = 100);
       //constructor
       //Creates an array of the size specified by the parameter
       //size. The default array size is 100.
       //Postcondition: list points to the array; length = 0;
       //                and maxSize = size

    arrayListType(const arrayListType<elemType>& otherList);
       //copy constructor

    ~arrayListType();
       //destructor
       //Deallocates the memory occupied by the array.

protected:
    elemType *list;     //array to hold the list elements
    int length;         //variable to store the length of the list
    int maxSize;        //variable to store the maximum size of
                        //the list
};
```

Sequential Search

The sequential search (also called the linear search) on array-based lists was described in Chapter 3, and the sequential search on linked lists was covered in Chapter 5. The sequential search works the same for both array-based and linked lists. The search always starts at the first element in the list and continues until either the item is found in the list or the entire list is searched.

Because we are interested in the performance of the sequential search (that is, the analysis of this type of search), for easy reference, next we give the sequential search algorithm for array-based lists (as described in Chapter 3). If the search item is found, its index (that is, its location in the array) is returned. If the search is unsuccessful, −1 is returned. Note that the following sequential search does not require the list elements to be in any particular order.

```
template<class elemType>
int arrayListType<elemType>::seqSearch(const elemType& item)
{
    int loc;
    bool found = false;

    for(loc = 0; loc < length; loc++)
        if(list[loc] == item)
        {
            found = true;
            break;
        }

    if(found)
        return loc;
    else
        return -1;
}//end seqSearch
```

 The sequential search algorithm, as given here, uses an iterative control structure (the for loop) to compare the search item with the list elements. You can also write a recursive algorithm to implement the sequential search algorithm. (See Programming Exercise 1 at the end of this chapter.)

Sequential Search Analysis

This section analyzes the performance of the sequential search algorithm in both the worst case and the average case.

The statements before and after the loop are executed only once, and hence require very little computer time. The statements in the **for** loop are the ones that are repeated several times. For each iteration of the loop, the search item is compared with an element in the list, and a few other statements are executed, including some other comparisons. Clearly, the loop terminates as soon as the search item is found in the list. Therefore, the execution of the other statements in the loop is directly related to the outcome of the key comparison. Also, different programmers might implement the same algorithm differently, although the number of key comparisons would typically be the same. The speed of a computer can also easily affect the time an algorithm takes to perform, but not the number of key comparisons.

Therefore, when analyzing a search algorithm, we count the number of key comparisons because this number gives us the most useful information. Furthermore, the criteria for counting the number of key comparisons can be applied equally well to other search algorithms.

Suppose that the length of the list, say L, is n. We want to determine the number of key comparisons made by the sequential search when the list L is searched for a given item.

If the search item is not in the list, we then compare the search item with every element in the list, making n comparisons. This is an unsuccessful case.

Suppose that the search item is in the list. Then the number of key comparisons depends on where in the list the search item is located. If the search item is the first element of L, we make only one key comparison. This is the best case. On the other hand, if the search item is the last element in the list, the algorithm makes n comparisons. This is the worst case. The best and worst cases are not likely to occur every time we apply the sequential search on L, so it would be more helpful if we could determine the average behavior of the algorithm. That is, we need to determine the average number of key comparisons that the sequential search algorithm makes in the successful case.

To determine the average number of comparisons in the successful case of the sequential search algorithm:

1. Consider all possible cases.

2. Find the number of comparisons for each case.

3. Add the number of comparisons and divide by the number of cases.

If the search item, called the **target**, is the first element in the list, one comparison is required. If the target is the second element in the list, two comparisons are required. Similarly, if the target is the kth element in the list, k comparisons are required. We assume that the target can be any element in the list; that is, all list elements are equally likely to be the target. Suppose that there are n elements in the list. The following expression gives the average number of comparisons:

$$\frac{1 + 2 + \ldots + n}{n}$$

It is known that

$$1 + 2 + \ldots + n = \frac{n(n + 1)}{2}$$

Therefore, the following expression gives the average number of comparisons made by the sequential search in the successful case:

$$\frac{1 + 2 + \ldots + n}{n} = \frac{1}{n} \frac{n(n + 1)}{2} = \frac{n + 1}{2}$$

This expression shows that, on average, the sequential search searches half the list. It thus follows that if the list size is 1,000,000, on average, the sequential search makes 500,000 comparisons. As a result, the sequential search is not efficient for large lists.

Ordered Lists

A list is ordered if its elements are ordered according to some criteria. The elements of a list are usually in ascending order. Several operations that can be performed on an ordered list are similar to the operations performed on an arbitrary list. For example, the operations to determine whether the list is empty or full, determine the length of the list, print the list, and clear the list are the same operations on an ordered list as those on an unordered list. Therefore, to define an ordered list as an ADT, by using the mechanism of inheritance, we can derive the class to implement the ordered lists from the `class arrayListType` discussed in the previous section. Depending on whether a specific application of a list can be stored in either an array or a linked list, we define two classes.

The following `class`, `orderedArrayListType`, defines an ordered list stored in an array as an ADT:

```
template<class elemType>
class orderedArrayListType: public arrayListType<elemType>
{
public:
    orderedArrayListType(int size = 100);
        //constructor

        ...
        //We will add the necessary members as needed.

private:
        //We will add the necessary members as needed.
}
```

Chapter 5 defined the following class to implement ordered linked lists:

```
template<class elemType>
class orderedLinkedListType: public linkedListType<elemType>
{
public:
        ...

}
```

Binary Search

As you can see, the sequential search is not efficient for large lists because, on average, the sequential search searches half the list. We therefore describe another search algorithm, called the **binary search**, which is very fast. However, a binary search can be performed only on ordered lists. We therefore assume that the list is ordered.

The binary search algorithm uses the "divide and conquer" technique to search the list. First, the search item is compared with the middle element of the list. If the search item is less than the middle element of the list, we restrict the search to the first half of the list; otherwise, we search the second half of the list.

Consider the sorted list of length = 12 in Figure 9-1.

	[0]	[1]	[2]	[3]	[4]	[5]	[6]	[7]	[8]	[9]	[10]	[11]
list	4	8	19	25	34	39	45	48	66	75	89	95

Figure 9-1   List of length 12

Suppose that we want to determine whether 75 is in the list. Initially, the entire list is the search list (see Figure 9-2).

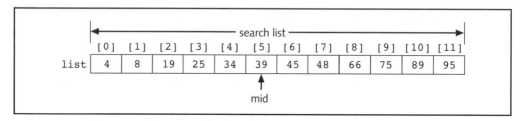

Figure 9-2   Search list, list[0]...list[11]

First, we compare 75 with the middle element in this list, list[5] (which is 39). Because 75 ≠ list[5] and 75 > list[5], we then restrict our search to the list list[6]...list[11], as shown in Figure 9-3.

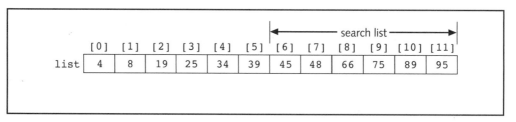

Figure 9-3   Search list, list[6]...list[11]

This process is now repeated on the list list[6]...list[11], which is a list of length = 6.

Because we need to frequently determine the middle element of the list, the binary search algorithm is typically implemented for array-based lists. To determine the middle element of the list, we add the starting index, first, and the ending index, last, of the search list and then divide by 2 to calculate its index. That is,

$$mid = \frac{first + last}{2}.$$

Initially, first = 0 and (because an array index in C++ starts at 0 and length denotes the number of elements in the list) last = length − 1.

The following C++ function implements the binary search algorithm. If the search item is found in the list, its location is returned; if the item is not in the list, −1 is returned.

```
template<class elemType>
int orderedArrayListType<elemType>::binarySearch
                                    (const elemType& item)
{
    int first = 0;
    int last = length - 1;
    int mid;

    bool found = false;

    while(first <= last && !found)
    {
        mid = (first + last) / 2;

        if(list[mid] == item)
            found = true;
        else
            if(list[mid] > item)
                last = mid - 1;
            else
                first = mid + 1;
    }

    if(found)
        return mid;
    else
        return -1;
}//end binarySearch
```

In the binary search algorithm, each time through the loop we make two key comparisons. The only exception is in the successful case; the last time through the loop only one key (item) comparison is made.

 NOTE The binary search algorithm, as given previously, uses an iterative control structure (the while loop) to compare the search item with the list elements. You can also write a recursive algorithm to implement the binary search algorithm. (See Programming Exercise 2 at the end of this chapter.)

The following example further illustrates how the binary search algorithm works.

Example 9-1

Consider the list given in Figure 9-4.

	[0]	[1]	[2]	[3]	[4]	[5]	[6]	[7]	[8]	[9]	[10]	[11]
list	4	8	19	25	34	39	45	48	66	75	89	95

Figure 9-4   Sorted list for a binary search

The size of this list is 12; that is, the length is 12. Table 9-1 shows the values of first, last, and middle each time through the loop. It also shows the number of times the item is compared with an element in the list each time through the loop.

Suppose that we are searching for item 89.

Table 9-1   Values of first, last, and middle and the Number of Comparisons for Search Item 89

Iteration	first	last	mid	list[mid]	Number of Comparisons
1	0	11	5	39	2
2	6	11	8	66	2
3	9	11	10	89	1 (found is true)

The item is found at location 10, and the total number of comparisons is 5.

Next, let us search the list for item 34. As in Table 9-1, Table 9-2 shows the values of first, last, and middle each time through the loop. It also shows the number of times the item is compared with an element in the list each time through the loop.

Table 9-2   Values of first, last, and middle and the Number of Comparisons for Search Item 34

Iteration	first	last	mid	list[mid]	Number of Comparisons
1	0	11	5	39	2
2	0	4	2	19	2
3	3	4	3	25	2
4	4	4	4	34	1 (found is true)

The item is found at location 4, and the total number of comparisons is 7.

Let us now search for item 22, as shown in Table 9-3.

Table 9-3 Values of first, last, and middle and the Number of Comparisons for Search Item 22

Iteration	first	last	mid	list[mid]	Number of Comparisons
1	0	11	5	39	2
2	0	4	2	19	2
3	3	4	3	25	2
4	3	2	the loop stops (because first > last)		

This is an unsuccessful search. The total number of comparisons is 6.

Performance of Binary Search

9

Suppose that L is a sorted list of 1000 elements, and you want to determine whether x is in L. Because L is sorted, you can apply the binary search algorithm to search for x. Suppose that L is as shown in Figure 9-5.

```
[0] [1]        [249]           [499]                            [999]
┌───┬───┬───┬───┬───┬───┬───┬───┬───┬───┬───┬───┬───┬───┬───┐
│   │   │...│   │   │...│   │   │...│   │   │   │...│   │   │
└───┴───┴───┴───┴───┴───┴───┴───┴───┴───┴───┴───┴───┴───┴───┘
```

Figure 9-5   List L

The first iteration of the while loop searches for x in L[0]...L[999], which is a list of 1000 items. This iteration of the while loop compares x with L[499] (see Figure 9-6).

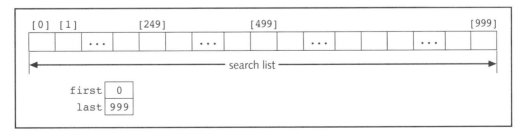

Figure 9-6   Search list

Suppose that x ≠ L[499]. If x < L[499], then the next iteration of the while loop looks for x in L[0]...L[498]; otherwise, the while loop looks for x in L[500]...L[999]. Suppose that x < L[499]. Then the next iteration of the while loop looks for x in L[0]...L[498], which is a list of 499 items, as shown in Figure 9-7.

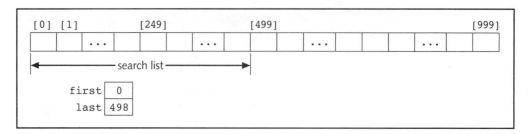

Figure 9-7   Search list after the first iteration

The second iteration of the while loop compares x with L[249]. Once again, suppose that x ≠ L[249]. Further suppose that x > L[249]. The next iteration of the while loop then searches for x in L[250]...L[498], which is a list of 249 items, as shown in Figure 9-8.

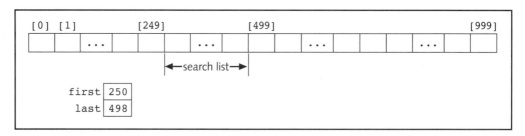

Figure 9-8   Search list after the second iteration

From these observations, it follows that every iteration of the while loop cuts the size of the search list in half. Because $1000 \approx 1024 = 2^{10}$, the while loop has at most 11 iterations to determine whether x is in L. (The symbol ≈ stands for "approximately equal to.") Because every iteration of the while loop makes 2 key comparisons—that is, x is compared twice with the elements of L—the binary search makes at most 22 comparisons to determine whether x is in L. By contrast, recall that the sequential search, on average, makes 500 comparisons to determine whether x is in L.

To have a better idea of how fast a binary search is as compared to a sequential search, suppose that L is of the size 1000000. Because $1000000 \approx 1048576 = 2^{20}$, it follows that the `while` loop in a binary search has at most 21 iterations to determine whether an element is in `L`. Every iteration of the `while` loop makes 2 item (that is, key) comparisons. Therefore, to determine whether an element is in `L`, a binary search makes at most 42 item comparisons. By contrast, on average, the sequential search makes 500,000 item (key) comparisons to determine whether an element is in `L`.

Note that

$$40 = 2 * 20 = 2 * \log_2 2^{20} = 2 * \log_2(1048576) \approx 2 * \log_2(1000000)$$

In general, if L is a sorted list of size n, to determine whether or not an element is in L, a binary search makes at most $2*\log_2 n + 2$ key comparisons.

Unsuccessful Search

In the case of an unsuccessful search, it can be shown that for a list of length n, a binary search makes approximately $2*\log_2(n + 1)$ key comparisons.

Successful Search

In the case of a successful search, it can be shown that for a list of length n, on average, a binary search makes $2*\log_2 n - 4$ key comparisons.

Now that we know how to effectively search an ordered list stored in an array, let us discuss how to insert an item into an ordered list.

Insertion into an Ordered List

Suppose that you have an ordered list and want to insert an item into the list. After insertion, the resulting list must also be ordered. Chapter 5 described how to insert an item into an ordered linked list. This section describes how to insert an item into an ordered list stored in an array.

To store the item in the ordered list, first we must find the place in the list where the item is to be inserted. Then we slide the list elements one array position down to make room for the item to be inserted, and then insert the item. Because the list is sorted and stored in an array, we can use an algorithm similar to the binary search algorithm to find the place in the list where the item is to be inserted. We can then use the function `insertAt` (of the `class arrayListType`) to insert the item. (Note that we cannot use the binary search algorithm as designed previously because it returns `-1` if the item is not in the list. Of course, we can write another function using the binary search technique to find the position in the array where the item is to be inserted.) Therefore, the algorithm to insert the item is:

Use an algorithm similar to the binary search algorithm to find the place where the item is to be inserted. (The special cases, such as inserting an item into an empty list or into a full list, are handled separately.)

if the item is already in this list

output an appropriate message

else

use the function insertAt to insert the item in the list.

The following function, insertOrd, implements this algorithm:

```cpp
template<class elemType>
void orderedArrayListType<elemType>::insertOrd(const elemType& item)
{
    int first = 0;
    int last = length - 1;
    int mid;

    bool found = false;

    if(length == 0)   //the list is empty
    {
        list[0] = item;
        length++;
    }
    else
        if(length == maxSize)
            cerr<<"Cannot insert into a full list."<<endl;
        else
        {
            while(first <= last && !found)
            {
                mid = (first + last) / 2;

                if(list[mid] == item)
                    found = true;
                else
                    if(list[mid] > item)
                        last = mid - 1;
                    else
                        first = mid + 1;
            }//end while

            if(found)
                cerr<<"The insert item is already in the list. "
                    <<"Duplicates are not allowed.";
            else
            {
                if(list[mid] < item)
                    mid++;
```

```
            insertAt(mid, item);
        }
    }
}//end insertOrd
```

Similarly, you can write a function to remove an element from an ordered list; see Programming Exercise 6 at the end of this chapter.

If we add the binary search algorithm and the `insertOrd` algorithm to the `class` `orderedArrayListType`, then the definition of this class is:

```
template<class elemType>
class orderedArrayListType: public arrayListType<elemType>
{
public:
    void insertOrd(const elemType&);
    int binarySearch(const elemType& item);
    orderedArrayListType(int size = 100);
};
```

Table 9-4 summarizes the algorithm analysis of the search algorithms discussed earlier.

Table 9-4 Number of Comparisons for a List of Length n

Algorithm	Successful Search	Unsuccessful Search
Sequential search	$\dfrac{n+1}{2} = O(n)$	$n = O(n)$
Binary search	$2 * \log_2 n - 4 = O(\log_2 n)$	$2 * \log_2 (n + 1) = O(\log_2 n)$

LOWER BOUND ON COMPARISON-BASED SEARCH ALGORITHMS

Sequential and binary search algorithms search the list by comparing the target element with the list elements. For this reason, these algorithms are called **comparison-based search algorithms**. Earlier sections of this chapter showed that a sequential search is of the order n, and a binary search is of the order $\log_2 n$, where n is the size of the list. The obvious question is: Can we devise a search algorithm that has an order less than $\log_2 n$? Before we answer this question, first we obtain the lower bound on the number of comparisons for the comparison-based search algorithms.

Theorem: Let L be a list of size $n > 1$. Suppose that the elements of L are sorted. If SRH(n) denotes the minimum number of comparisons needed, in the worst case, by using a comparison-based algorithm to recognize whether an element x is in L, then SRH(n) $\geq \log_2(n + 1)$.

Corollary: The binary search algorithm is the optimal worst-case algorithm for solving search problems by the comparison method.

From these results, it follows that if we want to design a search algorithm that is of an order less than $\log_2 n$, then it cannot be comparison based.

HASHING

Previous sections of this chapter discussed two search algorithms: binary and sequential. In a binary search, the data must be sorted; in a sequential search, the data does not need to be in any particular order. We also analyzed both these algorithms and showed that a sequential search is of the order n, and a binary search is of the order $\log_2 n$, where n is the length of the list. The obvious question is: Can we construct a search algorithm that is of the order less than $\log_2 n$? Recall that both search algorithms, binary and sequential, are comparison-based algorithms. We obtained a lower bound on comparison-based search algorithms, which shows that comparison-based search algorithms are at least of the order $\log_2 n$. Therefore, if we want to construct a search algorithm that is of the order less than $\log_2 n$, it cannot be comparison based. This section describes an algorithm that, on average, is of the order 1.

The previous section showed that for comparison-based algorithms, a binary search achieves the lower bound. However, a binary search requires the data to be specially organized, that is, the data must be sorted. The search algorithm that we now describe, called **hashing**, also requires the data to be specially organized.

In hashing, the data is organized with the help of a table, called the **hash table**, denoted by **HT**, and the hash table is stored in an array. To determine whether a particular item with a key, say X, is in the table, we apply a function h, called the **hash function**, to the key X; that is, we compute $h(X)$, read as h of X. The function h is an arithmetic function, and $h(X)$ gives the address of the item in the hash table. Suppose that the size of the hash table, HT, is m. Then $0 \leq h(X) < m$. Thus, to determine whether the item with key X is in the table, we look at the entry $HT[h(X)]$ in the hash table. Because the address of an item is computed with the help of a function, it follows that the items are stored in no particular order. Before continuing with this discussion, let us consider the following questions:

- How do we choose a hash function?

- How do we organize the data with the help of the hash table?

First, we discuss how to organize the data in the hash table.

There are two ways that data is organized with the help of the hash table. In the first approach, the data is stored within the hash table, that is, in an array. In the second approach, the data is stored in linked lists and the hash table is an array of pointers to those linked lists. Each approach has its own advantages and disadvantages, and we discuss both approaches in detail. However, first we introduce some more terminology that is used in this section.

The hash table HT is usually divided into, say, b buckets $HT[0]$, $HT[1]$, ..., $HT[b-1]$. Each bucket is capable of holding, say, r items. It thus follows that $br = m$, where m is the size of HT. Generally, $r = 1$ and so each bucket can hold one item.

The hash function h maps the key X onto an integer t, that is, $h(X) = t$, such that $0 \leq h(X) \leq b - 1$. Two keys, X_1 and X_2, such that $X_1 \neq X_2$, are called **synonyms** if $h(X_1) = h(X_2)$. Let X be a key and $h(X) = t$. If bucket t is full, we say that an **overflow** occurs. Let X_1 and X_2 be two nonidentical keys, that is, $X_1 \neq X_2$. If $h(X_1) = h(X_2)$, we say that a **collision** occurs. If $r = 1$, that is, the bucket size is 1, an overflow and a collision occur at the same time.

When choosing a hash function, the main objectives are to:

- Choose a hash function that is easy to compute.
- Minimize the number of collisions.

Next, we consider some examples of hash functions.

Suppose that *HTSize* denotes the size of the hash table, that is, the size of the array holding the hash table. We assume that the bucket size is 1. Thus, each bucket can hold one item and, therefore, overflow and collision occur simultaneously.

Hash Functions: Some Examples

Several hash functions are described in the literature. Here we describe some of the commonly used hash functions.

Mid–Square: In this method, the hash function, h, is computed by squaring the identifier, and then using the appropriate number of bits from the middle of the square to obtain the bucket address. Because the middle bits of a square usually depend on all the characters, it is expected that different keys will yield different hash addresses with high probability, even if some of the characters are the same.

Folding: In folding, the key X is partitioned into parts such that all the parts, except possibly the last parts, are of equal length. The parts are then added, in some convenient way, to obtain the hash address.

Division (Modular arithmetic): In this method, the key X is converted into an integer i_X. This integer is then divided by the size of the hash table to get the remainder, giving the address of X in HT. That is, (in C++)

$h(X) = i_X \% HTSize;$

Suppose that each **key** is a string. The following C++ function uses the division method to compute the address of the **key**:

```
int hashFunction(char *key, int keyLength)
{
    int sum = 0;

    for(int j = 0; j <= keyLength; j++)
        sum = sum + static_cast<int>(key[j]);

    return (sum % HTSize);
}//end hashFunction
```

Collision Resolution

As noted previously, the hash function that we choose not only should be easy to compute, but it is most desirable that the number of collisions is minimized. However, in reality, collisions are unavoidable. Thus, in hashing, we must include algorithms to handle collisions. Collision resolution techniques are classified into two categories: **open addressing** (also called **closed hashing**), and **chaining** (also called **open hashing**). In open addressing, the data is stored within the hash table. In chaining, the data is organized in linked lists and the hash table is an array of pointers to the linked lists. First we discuss collision resolution by open addressing.

Collision Resolution: Open Addressing

As described previously, in open addressing, the data is stored within the hash table. Therefore, for each key X, $h(X)$ gives the index in the array where the item with key X is likely to be stored. Open addressing can be implemented in several ways. Next, we describe some of the common ways to implement open addressing.

Linear Probing

Suppose that an item with key X is to be inserted in HT. We use the hash function to compute the index $h(X)$ of this item in HT. Suppose that $h(X) = t$. Then $0 \leq h(X) \leq HTSize - 1$. If $HT[t]$ is empty, we store this item into this array slot. Suppose that $HT[t]$ is already occupied by another item; therefore, we have a collision. In linear probing, starting at location t, we search the array sequentially to find the next available array slot.

In linear probing, we assume that the array is circular so that if the lower portion of the array is full, we can continue the search in the top portion of the array. This can be easily accomplished by using the mod operator. That is, starting at t, we check the array locations t, $(t + 1) \% HTSize$, $(t + 2) \% HTSize, ..., (t + j) \% HTSize$. This is called the **probe sequence**.

The next array slot is given by

$(h(X) + j) \% HTSize$

where j is the jth probe.

The following C++ pseudocode implements linear probing:

```
hIndex = hashFunction(insertKey);
found = false;

while(HT[hIndex] != emptyKey && !found)
    if(HT[hIndex].key == key)
        found = true;
    else
        hIndex = (hIndex + 1) % HTSize;
```

```
if(found)
   cerr<<"Duplicate items are not allowed."<<endl;
else
   HT[hIndex] = newItem;
```

From the definition of linear probing, we see that linear probing is easy to implement. However, linear probing causes **clustering**; that is, more and more new keys would likely be hashed to the array slots that are already occupied. For example, consider the hash table of size 20, as shown in Figure 9-9.

Figure 9-9   Hash table of size 20

Initially, all the array positions are available. Because all the array positions are available, the probability of any position being probed is (1/20). Suppose that after storing some of the items, the hash table is as shown in Figure 9-10.

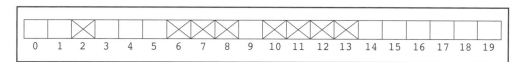

Figure 9-10   Hash table of size 20 with certain positions occupied

In this figure, a cross indicates that this array slot is occupied. Slot 9 will be occupied next if, for the next key, the hash address is 6, 7, 8 or 9. Thus, the probability that slot 9 will be occupied next is 4/20. Similarly, in this hash table, the probability that array position 14 will be occupied next is 5/20.

Now consider the hash table of Figure 9-11.

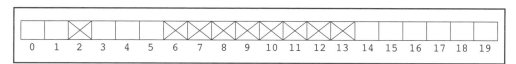

Figure 9-11   Hash table of size 20 with certain positions occupied

In this hash table, the probability that the array position 14 will be occupied next is 9/20, while the probability that the array positions, say, 15 or 16 or 17 will be occupied next is 1/20. We see that items tend to cluster, which would increase the search length. Linear probing, therefore, causes clustering. This clustering is called **primary clustering**.

One way to improve linear probing is to skip array positions by a fixed constant, say c, rather than 1. In this case, the hash address is:

$(h(X) + i * c)$ % $HTSize$

If $c = 2$ and $h(X) = 2k$, that is, $h(X)$ is even, only the even numbered array positions are visited. Similarly, if $c = 2$ and $h(X) = 2k + 1$, that is, $h(X)$ is odd, only the odd numbered array positions are visited. To visit all the array positions, the constant c must be relatively prime to $HTSize$.

Random Probing

This method uses a random number generator to find the next available slot. The ith slot in the probe sequence is:

$(h(X) + r_i)$ % $HTSize$

where r_i is the ith value in a random permutation of the numbers 1 to $HTSize - 1$. All insertions and searches use the same sequence of random numbers.

Example 9-2 illustrates how to create the probe sequence using random probing.

Example 9-2

Suppose that the size of the hash table is 101, and for the keys X_1 and X_2, $h(X_1) = 26$, and $h(X_2) = 35$. Also suppose that $r_1 = 2$, $r_2 = 5$, and $r_3 = 8$. Then the probe sequence of X_1 has the elements 26, 28, 31, and 34. Similarly, the probe sequence of X_2 has the elements 35, 37, 40, and 43.

Rehashing

In this method, if a collision occurs with the hash function h, we use a series of hash functions, $h_1, h_2, ..., h_s$. That is, if the collision occurs at $h(X)$, the array slots $h_i(X)$, $1 \le h_i(X) \le s$ are examined.

Quadratic Probing

Suppose that an item with key X is hashed at t, that is, $h(X) = t$, and $0 \le t \le HTSize - 1$. Further suppose that position t is already occupied. In quadratic probing, starting at position t, we linearly search the array at locations $(t + 1)$ % $HTSize$, $(t + 2^2)$ % $HTSize = (t + 4)$ % $HTSize$, $(t + 3^2)$ % $HTSize = (t + 9)$ % $HTSize$, ..., $(t + i^2)$ % $HTSize$. That is, the probe sequence is: t, $(t + 1)$ % $HTSize$, $(t + 2^2)$ % $HTSize$, $(t + 3^2)$ % $HTSize$, ..., $(t + i^2)$ % $HTSize$.

Example 9-3 illustrates how to create the probe sequence using quadratic probing.

Example 9-3

Suppose that the size of the hash table is 101 and for the keys X_1, X_2, and X_3, $h(X_1) = 25$, $h(X_2) = 96$, and $h(X_3) = 34$. Then the probe sequence for X_1 is 25, 26, 29, 34, 41, and so on. The probe sequence for X_2 is 96, 97, 100, 4, 11, and so on. (Notice that $(96 + 3^2) \% 101 = 105 \% 101 = 4$.)

The probe sequence for X_3 is 34, 35, 38, 43, 50, 59, and so on. Even though element 34 of the probe sequence of X_3 is the same as the fourth element of the probe sequence of X_1, both the probe sequences after 34 are different.

Although quadratic probing reduces primary clustering, we do not know if it probes all the positions in the table. In reality, it does not probe all the positions in the table. However, when *HTSize* is a prime, quadratic probing probes about half the table before repeating the probe sequence. Let us prove this observation.

Suppose that *HTSize* is a prime and for $0 \le i < j \le HTSize$,

$(t + i^2) \% HTSize = (t + j^2) \% HTSize.$

This implies that

$HTSize \mid (j^2 - i^2)$ or $HTSize \mid (j - i)(j + i)$

(Here the symbol $\mid$ means divide. For example, $a \mid b$ means a divides b.) Because *HTSize* is a prime, we get

$HTSize \mid (j - i)$ or $HTSize \mid (j + i)$

Now since $0 < j - i < HTSize$, it follows that *HTSize* does not divide $(j - i)$. Hence, $HTSize \mid (j + i)$. This implies that $j + i \ge HTSize$ and so

$$j \ge \frac{HTSize}{2}$$

Hence, quadratic probing probes half the table before repeating the probe sequence. It thus follows that if the size of *HTSize* is a prime at least twice the number of items, we can resolve all the collisions.

Because probing half the table is already a considerable number of probes, after making this many probes we assume that the table is full and stop the insertion (and search). (This can occur when the table is actually half full; in practice, it seldom happens unless the table is nearly full.)

Next, we describe how to generate the probe sequence.

Note that

$$2^2 = 1 + (2 \cdot 2 - 1)$$
$$3^2 = 1 + 3 + (2 \cdot 3 - 1)$$
$$4^2 = 1 + 3 + 5 + (2 \cdot 4 - 1)$$
$$\vdots$$
$$i^2 = 1 + 3 + 5 + 7 + \ldots + (2 \cdot i - 1), \ i \geq 1.$$

It thus follows that

$$(t + i^2) \ \% \ HTSize = (t + 1 + 3 + 5 + 7 + \ldots + (2 \cdot i - 1)) \ \% \ HTSize$$

Consider the probe sequence:

$$t, (t+1)\% \ HTSize, (t + 2^2)\% \ HTSize, (t + 3^2)\% \ HTSize, \ldots, (t + i^2) \ \% \ HTSize$$

The following C++ code computes the ith probe, that is, $(t + i^2) \ \% \ HTSize$.

```
int inc = 1;
int pCount = 0;

while(p < i)
{
    t = (t + inc) % HTSize;
    inc = inc + 2;
    pCount++;
}
```

The following pseudocode implements quadratic probing. (Assume that *HTSize* is a prime.)

```
int pCount;
int inc;
int hIndex;

hIndex = hashFunction(insertKey);

pCount = 0;
inc = 1;

while(HT[hIndex] is not empty
    && HT[hIndex] is not the same as the insert item
    && pCount < HTSize / 2)
{
    pCount++;
    hIndex = (hIndex + inc ) % HTSize;
    inc = inc + 2;
}

if(HT[hIndex] is empty)
    HT[hIndex] = newItem;
```

```
else
   if(HT[hIndex] is the same as the insert item)
      cerr<<"Error: No duplicates are allowed."<<endl;
   else
      cerr<<"Error: The table is full. "
            <<"Unable to resolve the collision."<<endl;
```

Both random and quadratic probings eliminate primary clustering. However, if two nonidentical keys, say X_1 and X_2, are hashed to the same home position, that is, $h(X_1) = h(X_2)$, then the same probe sequence is followed for both keys. The same probe sequence is used for both keys because random probing and quadratic probing are functions of the home positions, not the original key. It follows that if the hash function causes a cluster at a particular home position, the cluster remains under these probings. This is called **secondary clustering**.

One way to solve secondary clustering is to use linear probing, with the increment value a function of the key. This is called **double hashing**. In double hashing, if a collision occurs at $h(X)$, the probe sequence is generated by using the rule:

$$(h(X) + i * h'(X)) \% HTSize$$

where h' is the second hash function.

Example 9-4 illustrates how to create the probe sequence using double hashing.

Example 9-4

Suppose that the size of the hash table is 101 and for the keys X_1 and X_2, $h(X_1) = 35$ and $h(X_2) = 83$. Also suppose that $h'(X_1) = 3$ and $h'(X_2) = 6$. Then the probe sequence for X_1 is 35, 38, 41, 44, 47, and so on. The probe sequence for X_2 is 83, 89, 95, 0, 6, and so on. (Notice that $(83 + 3 * 6) \% 101 = 101 \% 101 = 0$.)

Deletion: Open Addressing

Suppose that an item, say R, is to be deleted from the hash table, HT. Clearly, we first must find the index of R in HT. To find the index of R, we apply the same criteria that was applied to R when R was inserted in HT. Let us further assume that after inserting R another item, R', was inserted in HT, and the home position of R and R' is the same. The probe sequence of R is contained in the probe sequence of R' because R' was inserted in the hash table after R. Suppose that we delete R simply by marking the array slot containing R as empty. If this array position stays empty, then while searching for R' and following its probe sequence, the search terminates at this empty array position. This gives the impression that R' is not in the table, which, of course, is incorrect. The item R cannot be deleted simply by marking its position as empty from the hash table.

One way to solve this problem is to create a special key to be stored in the keys of the items to be deleted. The special key in any slot indicates that this array slot is available for a new item to be inserted. However, during the search, the search should not terminate at this location. This, unfortunately, makes the deletion algorithm slow and complicated.

Another solution is to use another array, say `indexStatusList` of `int`, of the same size as the hash table as follows: initialize each position of `indexStatusList` to 0, indicating that the corresponding position in the hash table is empty. When an item is added to the hash table at position, say, `i`, we set `indexStatusList[i]` to 1. When an item is deleted from the hash table at position, say, k, we set `indexStatusList[k]` to −1. Therefore, each entry in the array `indexStatusList` is −1, 0, or 1.

For example, suppose that you have the hash table as shown in Figure 9-12.

	indexStatusList		HashTable
[0]	1	[0]	Mickey
[1]	1	[1]	Goofy
[2]	0	[2]	
[3]	1	[3]	Grumpy
[4]	0	[4]	
[5]	1	[5]	Balto
[6]	1	[6]	Duckey
[7]	0	[7]	
[8]	1	[8]	Minnie
[9]	0	[9]	

Figure 9-12   Hash table and `indexStatusList`

In Figure 9-12, the hash table positions 0, 1, 3, 5, 6, and 8 are occupied. Suppose that the entries at positions 3 and 6 are removed. To remove these entries from the hash table, we store −1 at positions 3 and 6 in the array `indexStatusList` (see Figure 9-13).

               indexStatusList   HashTable

[0]	1	[0]	Mickey
[1]	1	[1]	Goofy
[2]	0	[2]	
[3]	-1	[3]	Grumpy
[4]	0	[4]	
[5]	1	[5]	Balto
[6]	-1	[6]	Duckey
[7]	0	[7]	
[8]	1	[8]	Minnie
[9]	0	[9]	

Figure 9-13   Hash table and `indexStatusList` after removing the entries at positions 3 and 6

Hashing: Implementation Using Quadratic Probing

This section briefly describes how to design a class, as an ADT, to implement hashing using quadratic probing. To implement hashing, we use two arrays. One is used to store the data, and the other, `indexStatusList` as described in the previous section, is used to indicate whether a position in the hash table is free, occupied, or used previously. The following class template defines hashing as an ADT:

```
template<class elemType>
class hashT
{
public:
    void insert(int hashIndex, const elemType& rec);
      //Function to insert an item in the hash table.
      //The first parameter specifies the initial hash index
      //of the item to be inserted.
      //The item to be inserted is specified by the parameter rec.
      //Postcondition: If an empty position is found in the
      //   hash table, rec is inserted and the length is
      //   incremented by one; otherwise, an appropriate error
      //   message is displayed.

    void search(int& hashIndex, const elemType& rec, bool& found);
      //Function to determine whether the item specified by the
      //parameter rec is in the hash table.
      //The parameter hashIndex specifies the initial hash index
      //of rec.
```

```
        //Postcondition: If rec is found, found is set to true and
        //    hashIndex specifies the position where rec is found;
        //    otherwise, found is set to false.

    bool isItemAtEqual(int hashIndex, const elemType& rec);
        //Function to determine whether the item specified by the
        //parameter rec is the same as the item in the hash table
        //at position hashIndex.
        //Postcondition: Returns true if HTable[hashIndex] == rec;
        //    otherwise, returns false.

    void retrieve(int hashIndex, elemType& rec);
        //Function to retrieve the item at position hashIndex.
        //Postcondition: If the table has an item at position
        //    hashIndex, it is copied into rec.

    void remove(int hashIndex, const elemType& rec);
        //Function to remove an item from the hash table.
        //Postcondition: Given the initial hashIndex, if rec
        //    is found in the table it is removed; otherwise,
        //    an appropriate error message is displayed.

    void print() const;
        //Function to output the data.

    hashT(int size = 101);
        //constructor
        //Postcondition: Create the arrays HTable and
        //    indexStatusList; initialize the array
        //    indexStatusList to 0; length = 0; HTSize =
        //    size; and the default array size is 101.

    ~hashT();
        //destructor
        //Postcondition: Array HTable and indexStatusList
        //    are deleted.

private:
    elemType *HTable;           //pointer to the hash table
    int *indexStatusList;       //pointer to the array indicating
                                //the status of a position in the
                                //hash table
    int length;                 //number of items in the hash table
    int HTSize;                 //maximum size of the hash table
};
```

We give the definition of only the function **insert** and leave the others as an exercise for you.

The definition of the function `insert` using quadratic probing is as follows:

```
template<class elemType>
void hashT<elemType>::insert(int hashIndex, const elemType& rec)
{
    int pCount;
    int inc;

    pCount = 0;
    inc = 1;

    while(indexStatusList[hashIndex] == 1
            && HTable[hashIndex] != rec
            && pCount < HTSize / 2)
    {
        pCount++;
        hashIndex = (hashIndex + inc) % HTSize;
        inc = inc + 2;
    }


    if(indexStatusList[hashIndex] != 1)
    {
        HTable[hashIndex] = rec;
        indexStatusList[hashIndex] = 1;
        length++;
    }
    else
        if(HTable[hashIndex] == rec)
            cerr<<"Error: No duplicates are allowed."<<endl;
        else
            cerr<<"Error: The table is full. "
                <<"Unable to resolve the collision."<<endl;
}
```

Collision Resolution: Chaining (Open Hashing)

In chaining, the hash table, *HT*, is an array of pointers (see Figure 9-14). Therefore, for each *j*, where $0 \leq j \leq HTSize - 1$, $HT[j]$ is a pointer to a linked list. The size of the hash table, *HTSize*, is less than or equal to the number of items.

9

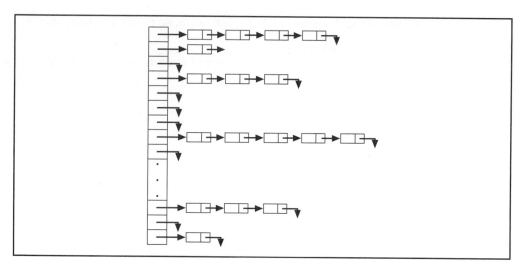

Figure 9-14 Linked hash table

Item Insertion and Collision

For each key X (in the item), we first find $h(X) = t$, where $0 \leq t \leq HTSize - 1$. The item with this key is then inserted in the linked list (which may be empty) pointed to by $HT[t]$. It then follows that for nonidentical keys X_1 and X_2, if $h(X_1) = h(X_2)$, the items with keys X_1 and X_2 are inserted in the same linked list and so collision is handled quickly and effectively. (A new item can be inserted at the beginning of the linked list because the data in a linked list is in no particular order.)

Search

Suppose that we want to determine whether an item R with key X is in the hash table. As usual, first we calculate $h(X)$. Suppose $h(X) = t$. Then the linked list pointed to by $HT[t]$ is searched sequentially.

Deletion

To delete an item, say R, from the hash table, first we search the hash table to find where in a linked list R exists. We then adjust the pointers at the appropriate locations and deallocate the memory occupied by R.

Overflow

Because data is stored in linked lists, overflow is no longer a concern because memory space to store the data is allocated dynamically. Furthermore, the size of the hash table no longer needs to be greater than the number of items. If the size of the hash table is less than the number of items, some of the linked lists contain more than one item. However, with a good hash function, the average length of a linked list is still small and so the search is efficient.

Advantages of Chaining

From the construction of the hash table using chaining, we see that item insertion and deletion are straightforward. If the hash function is efficient, few keys are hashed to the same home position. Thus, on average, a linked list is short, which results in a shorter search length. If the item size is large, it saves a considerable amount of space. For example, suppose there are 1000 items and each item requires 10 words of storage. (Typically, 1 word is equal to 4 bytes.) Further suppose that each pointer requires one word of storage. We then need 1000 words for the hash table, 10000 words for the items, and 1000 words for the link in each node. A total of 12000 words of storage space, therefore, is required to implement chaining. On the other hand, if we use quadratic probing, if the hash table size is twice the number of items, we need 20000 words of storage.

Disadvantages of Chaining

If the item size is small, a considerable amount of space is wasted. For example, suppose there are 1000 items, each requiring 1 word of storage. Chaining then requires a total of 3000 words of storage. On the other hand, with quadratic probing, if the hash table size is twice the number of items, only 2000 words are required for the hash table. Also, if the table size is three times the number of items, then in quadratic probing the keys are reasonably spread out. This results in fewer collisions and so the search is fast.

Hashing Analysis

Let

$$\alpha = \frac{\text{Number of records in the table}}{HTSize}$$

Then α is called the **load factor**.

The proofs of the following results about hashing analysis are left as exercises for you.

Linear Probing

The average number of comparisons for a successful search and an unsuccessful search are as follows:

1. Successful search

$$\frac{1}{2}\left\{1 + \frac{1}{1-\alpha}\right\}$$

2. Unsuccessful search

$$\frac{1}{2}\left\{1 + \frac{1}{(1-\alpha)^2}\right\}$$

Quadratic Probing

The average number of comparisons for a successful search and an unsuccessful search are as follows:

     1. Successful search

$$\frac{-\log_2(1-\alpha)}{\alpha}$$

     2. Unsuccessful search

$$\frac{1}{1-\alpha}$$

Chaining

The average number of comparisons for a successful search and an unsuccessful search are as follows:

     1. Successful search

$$1+\frac{\alpha}{2}$$

     2. Unsuccessful search

$$\alpha$$

Quick Review

1. A list is a set of elements of the same type.

2. The length of a list is the number of elements in the list.

3. A one-dimensional array is a convenient place to store and process lists.

4. The sequential search algorithm searches the list for a given item, starting with the first element in the list. It continues to compare the search item with the elements in the list until either the item is found or no more elements are left in the list with which it can be compared.

5. On average, the sequential search algorithm searches half the list.

6. For a list of length n, in a successful search, on average, the sequential search makes $\frac{n+1}{2} = O(n)$ comparisons.

7. A sequential search is not efficient for large lists.

8. A binary search is much faster than a sequential search.

9. A binary search requires the list elements to be in order—that is, sorted.

10. For a list of length 1024, to search for an item in the list, a binary search requires no more than 11 iterations of the loop, and so no more than 22 comparisons.

11. For a list of length n, in a successful search, on average, a binary search makes $2\log_2 n - 4 = O(\log_2 n)$ key comparisons.

12. Let L be a list of size $n > 1$. Suppose that the elements of L are sorted. If $SRH(n)$ is the minimum number of comparisons needed, in the worst case, by using a comparison-based algorithm to recognize whether an element x is in L, then $SRH(n) \geq \log_2(n + 1)$.

13. The binary search algorithm is the optimal worst-case algorithm for solving search problems by using the comparison method.

14. To construct a search algorithm of the order less than $\log_2 n$, it cannot be comparison based.

15. In hashing, the data is organized with the help of a table, called the hash table, denoted by HT. The hash table is stored in an array.

16. To determine whether a particular item with the key, say, X, is in the hash table, we apply a function h, called the hash function, to the key X; that is, we compute $h(X)$, read as h of X. The function h is an arithmetic function, and $h(X)$ gives the address of the item in the hash table.

17. In hashing, because the address of an item is computed with the help of a function, it follows that the items are stored in no particular order.

18. Two keys X_1 and X_2, such that $X_1 \neq X_2$, are called synonyms if $h(X_1) = h(X_2)$.

19. Let X be a key and $h(X) = t$. If bucket t is full, we say that an overflow has occurred.

20. Let X_1 and X_2 be two nonidentical keys. If $h(X_1) = h(X_2)$, we say that a collision has occurred. If $r = 1$, that is, the bucket size is 1, an overflow and a collision occur at the same time.

21. Collision resolution techniques are classified into two categories: open addressing (also called closed hashing), and chaining (also called open hashing).

22. In open addressing, data is stored within the hash table.

23. In chaining, the data is organized in linked lists, and the hash table is an array of pointers to the linked lists.

24. In linear probing, if a collision occurs at location t, then, starting at location t, we search the array sequentially to find the next available array slot.

25. In linear probing, we assume that the array is circular so that if the lower portion of the array is full we can continue the search in the top portion of the array. If a collision occurs at location t, then starting at t, we check the array locations t, $(t + 1)$ %$HTSize$, $(t + 2)$ %$HTSize$, ..., $(t + j)$ % $HTSize$. This is called the probe sequence.

26. Linear probing causes clustering, called primary clustering.

27. In random probing, a random number generator is used to find the next available slot.

9

28. In rehashing, if a collision occurs with the hash function h, we use a series of hash functions.

29. In quadratic probing, if a collision occurs at position t, then starting at position t we linearly search the array at locations $(t + 1)$ % $HTSize$, $(t + 2^2)$ % $HTSize = (t + 4)$ % $HTSize$, $(t + 3^2)$ % $HTSize = (t + 9)$ % $HTSize$, ..., $(t + i^2)$ % $HTSize$. The probe sequence is: t, $(t + 1)$ % $HTSize$, $(t + 2^2)$ % $HTSize$, $(t + 3^2)$ % $HTSize$, ..., $(t + i^2)$ % $HTSize$.

30. Both random and quadratic probing eliminate primary clustering. However, if two nonidentical keys, say X_1 and X_2, are hashed to the same home position, that is, $h(X_1) = h(X_2)$, the same probe sequence is followed for both keys. This is because random probing and quadratic probing are functions of the home positions, not the original key. If the hash function causes a cluster at a particular home position, the cluster remains under these probings. This is called secondary clustering.

31. One way to solve secondary clustering is to use linear probing, wherein the increment value is a function of the key. This is called double hashing. In double hashing, if a collision occurs at $h(X)$, the probe sequence is generated by using the rule:

$(h(X) + i * h'(X))$ % $HTSize$

where h' is the second hash function.

32. In open addressing, when an item is deleted, its position in the array cannot be marked as empty.

33. In chaining, for each key X (in the item), first we find $h(X) = t$, where $0 \le t \le HTSize - 1$. The item with this key is then inserted in the linked list (which may be empty) pointed to by $HT[t]$.

34. In chaining, for nonidentical keys X_1 and X_2, if $h(X_1) = h(X_2)$, the items with keys X_1 and X_2 are inserted in the same linked list.

35. In chaining, to delete an item, say R, from the hash table, first we search the hash table to find where in the linked list R exists. Then we adjust the pointers at the appropriate locations and deallocate the memory occupied by R.

36. Let

$$\alpha = \frac{\text{Number of records in the table}}{HTSize}$$

Then α is called the **load factor**.

37. Linear probing: Average number of comparisons:

Successful search: $\dfrac{1}{2}\left\{1 + \dfrac{1}{1 - \alpha}\right\}$

Unsuccessful search: $\dfrac{1}{2}\left\{1 + \dfrac{1}{(1 - \alpha)^2}\right\}$

38. Quadratic probing: Average number of comparisons:

Successful search: $\dfrac{-\log_2(1-\alpha)}{\alpha}$

Unsuccessful search: $\dfrac{1}{1-\alpha}$

39. Chaining: Average number of comparisons:

Successful search: $1 + \dfrac{\alpha}{2}$

Unsuccessful search: α

EXERCISES

1. Mark the following statements as true or false.

a. A sequential search of a list assumes that the list is in ascending order.

b. A binary search of a list assumes that the list is sorted.

c. A binary search is faster on ordered lists and slower on unordered lists.

d. A binary search is faster on large lists, but a sequential search is faster on small lists.

2. Consider the following list:

```
63 45 32 98 46 57 28 100
```

Using the sequential search as described in this chapter, how many comparisons are required to find whether the following items are in the list? (Recall that by comparisons we mean item comparisons, not index comparisons.)

a. 90

b. 57

c. 63

d. 120

3. Consider the following list:

```
2 10 17 45 49 55 68 85 92 98 110
```

Using the binary search as described in this chapter, how many comparisons are required to find whether the following items are in the list? Show the values of `first`, `last`, and `middle` and the number of comparisons after each iteration of the loop.

a. 15

b. 49

c. 98

d. 99

9

4. Write the definition of the **class orderedArrayListType** that implements the search algorithms for array-based lists as discussed in this chapter.

5. Suppose that the size of the hash table is 150 and the bucket size is 5. How many buckets are in the hash table, and how many items can a bucket hold?

6. Explain how collision is resolved using linear probing.

7. Explain how collision is resolved using quadratic probing.

8. What is double hashing?

9. Suppose that the size of the hash table is 101 and items are inserted in the table using quadratic probing. Also, suppose that a new item is to be inserted in the table and its hash address is 30. If position 30 in the hash table is occupied and the next 4 positions given by the probe sequence are also occupied, determine where in the table the item will be inserted.

10. Suppose that the size of the hash table is 101. Further suppose that certain keys with the indices 15, 101, 116, 0, and 217 are to be inserted in this order into an initially empty hash table. Using modular arithmetic, find the indices in the hash table if:

    a. Linear probing is used.

    b. Quadratic probing is used.

11. Suppose that 50 keys are to be inserted into an initially empty hash table using quadratic probing. What should be the size of the hash table to guarantee that all the collisions are resolved?

12. Suppose that an item is to be removed from a hash table that was implemented using linear or quadratic probing. Why wouldn't you mark the position of the item to be deleted as empty?

13. What are the advantages of open hashing?

14. Give a numerical example to show that collision resolution by quadratic probing is better that chaining.

15. Give a numerical example to show that collision resolution by chaining is better that quadratic probing.

16. Suppose that the size of the hash table is 1001 and the table has 850 items. What is the load factor?

17. Suppose that the size of the hash table is 1001 and the table has 500 items. On average, how many comparisons are made to determine whether an item is in the list if:

    a. Linear probing is used?

    b. Quadratic probing is used?

    c. Chaining is used?

18. Suppose that 550 items are to be stored in a hash table. If, on average, three key comparisons are needed to determine whether an item is in the table, what should be the size of the hash table if:

a. Linear probing is used?

b. Chaining is used?

PROGRAMMING EXERCISES

1. **(Recursive sequential search)** The sequential search algorithm given in this chapter is nonrecursive. Write and implement a recursive version of the sequential search algorithm.

2. **(Recursive binary search)** The binary search algorithm given in this chapter is non-recursive. Write and implement a recursive version of the binary search algorithm. Also, write a version of the sequential search algorithm that can be applied to sorted lists. Add this operation to the **class orderedArrayListType** for array-based lists. Moreover, write a test program to test your algorithm.

3. The sequential search algorithm as given in this chapter does not assume that the list is in order. Therefore, it usually works the same for both sorted and unsorted lists. However, if the elements of the list are sorted, then you can somewhat improve the performance of the sequential search algorithm. For example, if the search item is not in the list, you can stop the search as soon as you find an element in the list that is larger than the search item. Write the function **seqOrdSearch** to implement a version of the sequential search algorithm for sorted lists. Add this function to the **class orderedArrayListType** and write a program to test it.

4. Write a program to find the number of comparisons using **binarySearch** and the sequential search algorithm as follows:

Suppose **list** is an array of **1000** elements.

a. Use a random number generator to fill **list**.

b. Use any sorting algorithm to sort **list**. Alternatively, you can use the function **insertOrd**, to initially insert all the elements in the list.

c. Search **list** for some items as follows:

i. Use the binary search algorithm to search the list. (You may need to modify the algorithm given in this chapter to count the number of comparisons.)

ii. Use the binary search algorithm to search the list, switching to a sequential search when the size of the search list reduces to less than 15. (Use the sequential search algorithm for a sorted list.)

d. Print the number of comparisons for Steps c.i and c.ii. If the item is found in the list, then print its position.

9

5. Write a program to test the function `insertOrd` that inserts an item into an array-based ordered list.

6. Write the function `removeOrd` that removes an item from an array-based ordered list. The item to be removed is passed as a parameter to this function. After removing the item, the resulting list must be ordered with no empty array positions between the elements. Add this function to the **class `orderedArrayListType`** and write a program to test it.

7. Write the definitions of the functions `search`, `isItemAtEqual`, `retrieve`, `remove`, and `print`, the constructor, and the destructor for the **class `hashT`**, as described in the section "Hashing: Implementation Using Quadratic Probing" of this chapter. Also, write a program to test various hashing operations.

8. a. Some of the attributes of a state in the United States are its name, capital, area, year of admission to the union, and the order of admission to the union. Design the **class `stateData`** to keep track of the information for a state. Your class must include appropriate functions to manipulate the state's data, such as the functions `setStateInfo`, `getStateInfo`, and so on. Also, overload the relational operators to compare two states by their names. For easy input and output, overload the stream operators.

   b. Use the **class `hashT`** as described in the section "Hashing: Implementation Using Quadratic Probing," which uses quadratic probing to resolve collision, to create a hash table to keep track of each state's information. Use the state's name as the key to determine the hash address. You may assume that a state's name is a string of no more than 15 characters.

   Test your program by searching for and removing certain states from the hash table.

   You may use the following hash function to determine the hash address of an item:

```
int hashFunc(string name)
{
    int i, k, sum;
    int len;

    i = 0;
    sum = 0;

    len = name.length();

    for(k = 0; k < 15 - len; k++)
        name = name + ' ';   //increase the length of the name
                             //to 15 characters

    for(k = 0; k < 5; k++)
    {
        sum = sum + static_cast<int>(name[i]) * 128 * 128
                  + static_cast<int>(name[i + 1]) * 128
                  + static_cast<int>(name[i + 2]);
        i = i + 3;
    }

    return sum % HTSize;
}
```

SORTING ALGORITHMS

> ## In this chapter, you will:
>
> - Learn the various sorting algorithms
> - Explore how to implement the selection, insertion, quick, merge, and heap sorting algorithms
> - Discover how the sorting algorithms discussed in this chapter perform
> - Learn how priority queues are implemented

Chapter 9 discussed the search algorithms on lists. A sequential search does not assume that the data is in any particular order; however, as noted, this search does not work efficiently for large lists. By contrast, a binary search is very fast for array-based lists, but requires that the data be in order. Because a binary search requires the data to be in order and its performance is good for array-based lists, this chapter focuses on sorting algorithms.

SORTING ALGORITHMS

There are several sorting algorithms in the literature; in this chapter we discuss some of the commonly used ones. To compare the performance of these algorithms, we also provide some analysis of these algorithms. These sorting algorithms can be applied to either array-based lists or linked lists. We will specify whether the algorithm being developed is for array-based lists or linked lists.

The functions implementing these sorting algorithms are included as **public** members of the related class. (For example, for an array-based list, these are the members of the **class orderedArrayListType**.) By doing so, the algorithms have direct access to the list elements.

Suppose that the sorting algorithm selection sort (described in the next section) is to be applied to array-based lists. The following statements show how to include a selection sort as a member of the **class orderedArrayListType**:

```
template<class elemType>
class orderedArrayListType: public arrayListType
{
public:
    void selectionSort();
    ...
};
```

SELECTION SORT: ARRAY-BASED LISTS

The selection sort algorithm sorts a list by selecting the smallest element in the (unsorted portion of the) list, and then moving this smallest element to the top of the (unsorted) list. The first time we locate the smallest item in the entire list; the second time we locate the smallest item in the list starting from the second element in the list, and so on. The selection sort algorithm described here is designed for array-based lists.

For example, suppose that you have the list as shown in Figure 10-1.

	[0]	[1]	[2]	[3]	[4]	[5]	[6]	[7]	[8]	[9]
list	16	30	24	7	25	62	45	5	65	50

Figure 10-1 List of 10 elements

Initially, the entire list is unsorted. So we find the smallest item in the list, which is at position 7, as shown in Figure 10-2.

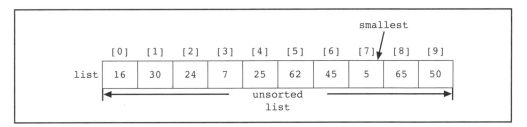

Figure 10-2   Smallest element of the unsorted list

Because this is the smallest item, it must be moved to position 0. We therefore swap **16** (that is, `list[0]`) with **5** (that is, `list[7]`), as shown in Figure 10-3.

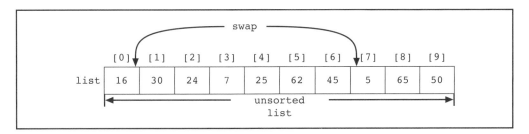

Figure 10-3   Swap elements `list[0]` and `list[7]`

After swapping these elements, Figure 10-4 shows the resulting list.

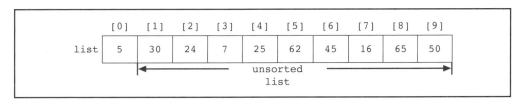

Figure 10-4   List after swapping `list[0]` and `list[7]`

Now the unsorted list is `list[1]...list[9]`. Next, we find the smallest element in the unsorted portion of the list. The smallest element is at position **3**, as shown in Figure 10-5.

10

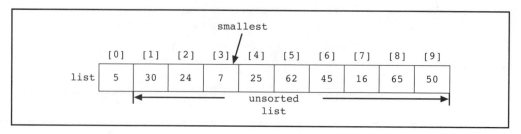

Figure 10-5 Smallest element in the unsorted portion of list

Because the smallest element in the unsorted list is at position 3, it must be moved to position 1. That is, we swap 7 (that is, list[3]) with 30 (that is, list[1]), as shown in Figure 10-6.

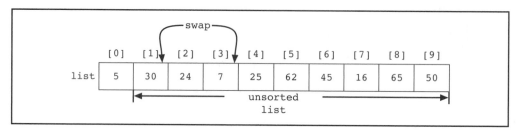

Figure 10-6 Swap list[1] with list[3]

After swapping list[1] with list[3], Figure 10-7 shows the resulting list.

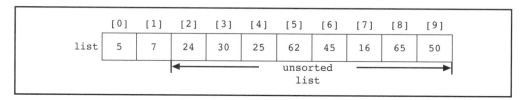

Figure 10-7 list after swapping list[1] with list[3]

Now the unsorted list is list[2]...list[9]. We repeat this process of finding the (position of the) smallest element in the unsorted portion of the list and moving it to the beginning of the unsorted portion of the list. The selection sort algorithm thus involves the following steps. In the unsorted portion of the list:

a. Find the location of the smallest element.

b. Move the smallest element to the beginning of the unsorted list.

Initially, the entire list, `list[0]...list[length - 1]`, is the unsorted list. After executing Steps a and b once, the unsorted list is `list[1]...list[length - 1]`. After executing Steps a and b a second time, the unsorted list is `list[2]...list[length - 1]`, and so on. We can keep track of the unsorted portion of the list and repeat Steps a and b with the help of a **for** loop as follows:

```
for(index = 0; index < length - 1; index++)
{
    a. Find the location, smallestIndex, of the smallest element in
       list[index]...list[length - 1].
    b. Swap the smallest element with list[index]. That is, swap
       list[smallestIndex] with list[index].
}
```

The first time through the loop, we locate the smallest element in `list[0]...list[length - 1]` and swap this smallest element with `list[0]`. The second time through the loop, we locate the smallest element in `list[1]...list[length - 1]` and swap this smallest element with `list[1]`, and so on. This process continues until the length of the unsorted list is 1. (Note that a list of length 1 is sorted.) It therefore follows that to implement the selection sort algorithm, we need to implement Steps a and b.

Given the starting index, `first`, and the ending index, `last`, of the list, the following C++ function returns the index of the smallest element in `list[first]...list[last]`:

```
template<class elemType>
int orderedArrayListType<elemType>::minLocation(int first, int last)
{
    int loc, minIndex;
    minIndex = first;

    for(loc = first + 1; loc <= last; loc++)
        if(list[loc] < list[minIndex])
            minIndex = loc;

    return minIndex;
}//end minLocation
```

Given the locations in the list of the elements to be swapped, the following C++ function, `swap`, swaps those elements:

```
template<class elemType>
void orderedArrayListType<elemType>::swap(int first, int second)
{
    elemType temp;

    temp = list[first];
    list[first] = list[second];
    list[second] = temp;
}//end swap
```

10

We can now complete the definition of the function `selectionSort`.

```
template<class elemType>
void orderedArrayListType<elemType>::selectionSort()
{
    int loc, minIndex;

    for(loc = 0; loc < length - 1; loc++)
    {
        minIndex = minLocation(loc, length - 1);
        swap(loc, minIndex);
    }
}
```

The definition of the **class orderedArrayListType** to implement the selection sort algorithm is as follows:

```
template<class elemType>
class orderedArrayListType: public arrayListType<elemType>
{
public:
    void insertOrd(const elemType&);
    int binarySearch(const elemType& item);
    void selectionSort();

    orderedArrayListType(int size = 100);

private:
    void swap(int first, int second);
    int minLocation(int first, int last);
};
```

Example 10-1

The following program tests the selection sort algorithm. We assume that the definition of the **class orderedArrayListType** is in the header file **orderedArrayListType.h**.

```
#include <iostream>
#include "orderedArrayListType.h"

using namespace std;

int main()
{
    orderedArrayListType<int> list;              //Line 1
    int num;                                     //Line 2

    cout<<"Line 3: Enter numbers ending with -999"
        <<endl;                                  //Line 3

    cin>>num;                                    //Line 4
```

```
    while(num != -999)                          //Line 5
    {
        list.insert(num);                       //Line 6
        cin>>num;                               //Line 7
    }

    cout<<"Line 8: The list before sorting:"<<endl; //Line 8
    list.print();                               //Line 9
    cout<<endl;                                 //Line 10

    list.selectionSort();                       //Line 11

    cout<<"Line 12: The list after sorting:"<<endl; //Line 12
    list.print();                               //Line 13
    cout<<endl;                                 //Line 14

    return 0;

}
```

Sample Run: In this sample run, the user input is shaded.

```
Line 3: Enter numbers ending with -999
34 67 23 12 78 56 36 79 5 32 66 -999
Line 8: The list before sorting:
34 67 23 12 78 56 36 79 5 32 66

Line 12: The list after sorting:
5 12 23 32 34 36 56 66 67 78 79
```

For the most part, the preceding output is self-explanatory. Notice that the statement in Line 6 calls the function **insert** of the **class arrayListType**, which is the base class of the **class orderedArrayListType**. Similarly, the statements in Lines 9 and 13 call the function **print** of the **class arrayListType**. The statement in Line 11 calls the function **selectionSort** of the **class orderedArrayListType** to sort the list.

---

1. A selection sort can also be implemented by selecting the largest element in the (unsorted portion of the) list and moving it to the bottom of the list. You can easily implement this form of selection sort by altering the **if** statement in the function **minLocation**, and passing the appropriate parameters to the corresponding function and the function **swap**, when these functions are called in the function **selectionSort**.

2. A selection sort can also be applied to linked lists. The general algorithm is the same, and the details are left as an exercise for you. See Programming Exercise 1 at the end of this chapter.

Analysis: Selection Sort

In the case of search algorithms (Chapter 9), our only concern was with the number of key (item) comparisons. A sorting algorithm makes key comparisons and also moves the data. Therefore, in analyzing a sorting algorithm, we look at the number of key comparisons as well as the number of data movements. Let us look at the performance of a selection sort.

Suppose that the length of the list is n. The function `swap` does three item assignments and is executed $n - 1$ times. Hence, the number of item assignments is $3(n - 1)$.

The key comparisons are made by the function `minLocation`. For a list of length k, the function `minLocation` makes $k - 1$ key comparisons. Also, the function `minLocation` is executed $n - 1$ times (by the function `selectionSort`). The first time, the function `minLocation` finds the index of the smallest key item in the entire list and therefore makes $n - 1$ comparisons. The second time, the function `minLocation` finds the index of the smallest element in the sublist of length $n - 1$ and therefore makes $n - 2$ comparisons, and so on. Hence, the number of key comparisons is as follows:

$$
\begin{aligned}
(n-1)+(n-2)+\ldots+2+1 &= \frac{n(n-1)}{2} \\
&= \frac{1}{2}n^2 - \frac{1}{2}n \\
&= \frac{1}{2}n^2 + O(n) \\
&= O(n^2).
\end{aligned}
$$

It thus follows that if $n = 1000$, the number of key comparisons that the selection sort algorithm makes is $\frac{1}{2}(1000)^2 - \frac{1}{2}(1000) = 499500 \approx 500000$.

INSERTION SORT: ARRAY-BASED LISTS

The previous section described and analyzed the selection sort algorithm. It was shown that if $n = 1000$, the number of key comparisons is approximately 500,000, which is quite high. This section describes the sorting algorithm called the insertion sort, which tries to improve—that is, reduce—the number of key comparisons.

The insertion sort algorithm sorts the list by moving each element to its proper place. Consider the list given in Figure 10-8.

	[0]	[1]	[2]	[3]	[4]	[5]	[6]	[7]
list	10	18	25	30	23	17	45	35

Figure 10-8   `list`

The length of the list is 8. In this list, the elements list[0], list[1], list[2], and list[3] are in order. That is, list[0]...list[3] is sorted (see Figure 10-9).

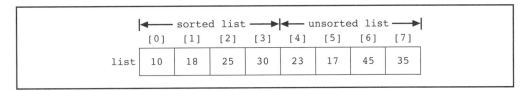

Figure 10-9 Sorted and unsorted portion of list

Next, we consider the element list[4], the first element of the unsorted list. Because list[4] < list[3], we need to move the element list[4] to its proper location. It thus follows that element list[4] should be moved to list[2] (see Figure 10-10).

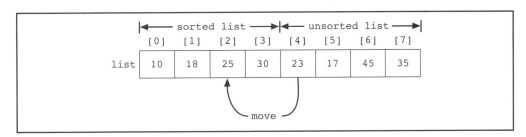

Figure 10-10 Move list[4] into list[2]

To move list[4] into list[2], first we copy list[4] into temp, a temporary memory space (see Figure 10-11).

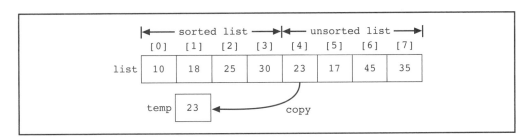

Figure 10-11 Copy list[4] into temp

Next, we copy `list[3]` into `list[4]`, and then `list[2]` into `list[3]` (see Figure 10-12).

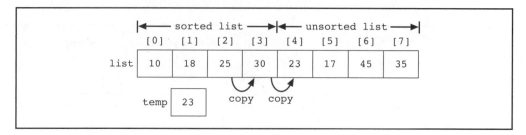

Figure 10-12 List before copying `list[3]` into `list[4]` and then `list[2]` into `list[3]`

After copying `list[3]` into `list[4]` and `list[2]` into `list[3]`, the list is as shown in Figure 10-13.

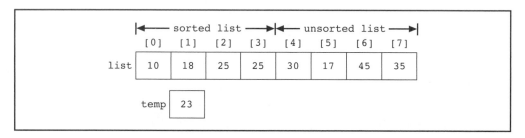

Figure 10-13 List after copying `list[3]` into `list[4]` and then `list[2]` into `list[3]`

We now copy `temp` into `list[2]`. Figure 10-14 shows the resulting list.

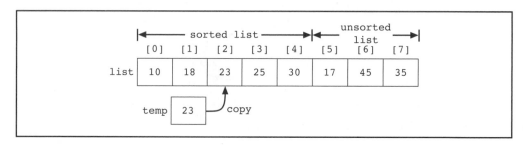

Figure 10-14 List after copying `temp` into `list[2]`

Now `list[0]...list[4]` is sorted and `list[5]...list[7]` is unsorted. We repeat this process on the resulting list by moving the first element of the unsorted list into the sorted list in the proper place.

From this discussion, we see that during the sorting phase the array containing the list is divided into two sublists, upper and lower. Elements in the upper sublist are sorted; elements in the lower sublist are to be moved to the upper sublist in their proper places one at a time. We use an index—say, `firstOutOfOrder`—to point to the first element in the lower sublist; that is, `firstOutOfOrder` gives the index of the first element in the unsorted portion of the array. Initially, `firstOutOfOrder` is initialized to 1.

This discussion translates into the following pseudoalgorithm:

```
for(firstOutOfOrder = 1; firstOutOfOrder < length; firstOutOfOrder++)
  if(list[firstOutOfOrder] is less than list[firstOutOfOrder - 1])
  {
     copy list[firstOutOfOrder] into temp

     initialize location to firstOutOfOrder

     do
     {
        a. move list[location - 1] one array slot down
        b. decrement location by 1 to consider the next element
           of the sorted portion of the array
     }
     while(location > 0 && the element in the upper sublist at
                           location - 1 is greater than temp)

  }
copy temp into list[location]
```

Let us trace the execution of this algorithm on the list given in Figure 10-15.

	[0]	[1]	[2]	[3]	[4]	[5]	[6]	[7]
list	13	7	15	8	12	30	3	20

Figure 10-15   Unsorted list

The length of this list is 8; that is, `length` = 8. We initialize `firstOutOfOrder` to 1 (see Figure 10-16).

10

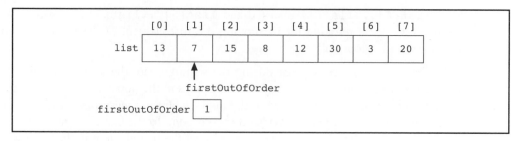

Figure 10-16 `firstOutOfOrder = 1`

Now `list[firstOutOfOrder] = 7`, `list[firstOutOfOrder - 1] = 13` and 7 < 13, and the expression in the `if` statement evaluates to `true`, so we execute the body of the `if` statement.

```
temp = list[firstOutOfOrder] = 7
location = firstOutOfOrder = 1
```

Next, we execute the do...while loop.

```
list[1] = list.[0] = 13    (copy list[0] into list[1])
location = 0               (decrement location)
```

The do...while loop terminates because `location = 0`. We copy `temp` into `list[location]`—that is, into `list[0]`.

Figure 10-17 shows the resulting list.

	[0]	[1]	[2]	[3]	[4]	[5]	[6]	[7]
list	7	13	15	8	12	30	3	20

Figure 10-17 List after the first iteration of the insertion sort algorithm

Now suppose that we have the list given in Figure 10-18.

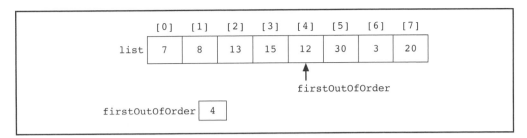

Figure 10-18   First out-of-order element is at position 4

Here `list[0]...list[3]`, or the elements `list[0]`, `list[1]`, `list[2]`, and `list[3]`, are in order. Now `firstOutOfOrder = 4`. Because `list[4] < list[3]`, the element `list[4]`, which is 12, needs to be moved to its proper location.

As before,

```
temp = list[firstOutOfOrder] = 12
location = firstOutOfOrder   =  4
```

First, we copy `list[3]` into `list[4]` and decrement `location` by 1. Then we copy `list[2]` into `list[3]` and again decrement `location` by 1. Now the value of `location` is 2. At this point, the list is as shown in Figure 10-19.

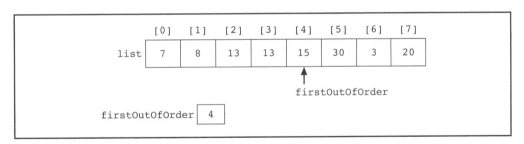

Figure 10-19   List after copying `list[3]` into `list[4]` and then `list[2]` into `list[3]`

Because `list[1] < temp`, the do...while loop terminates. Because at this point `location` is 2, we copy `temp` into `list[2]`. That is,

```
list[2] = temp = 12
```

Figure 10-20 shows the resulting list.

	[0]	[1]	[2]	[3]	[4]	[5]	[6]	[7]
list	7	8	12	13	15	30	3	20

Figure 10-20 List after copying `temp` into `list[2]`

We can repeat this process for the remaining elements of `list` to sort `list`.

The following C++ function implements the previous algorithm:

```
template<class elemType>
void orderedArrayListType<elemType>::insertionSort()
{
    int firstOutOfOrder, location;
    elemType temp;

    for(firstOutOfOrder = 1; firstOutOfOrder < length;
                              firstOutOfOrder++)
        if(list[firstOutOfOrder] < list[firstOutOfOrder - 1])
        {
            temp = list[firstOutOfOrder];
            location = firstOutOfOrder;

            do
            {
                list[location] = list[location - 1];
                location--;
            }while(location > 0 && list[location - 1] > temp);

            list[location] = temp;
        }
}//end insertionSort
```

INSERTION SORT: LINKED LIST-BASED LISTS

The insertion sort algorithm can also be applied to linked lists. Therefore, this section describes the insertion algorithm for linked lists. Consider the linked list shown in Figure 10-21.

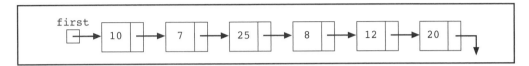

Figure 10-21   Linked list

In Figure 10-21, `first` is a pointer to the first node of the linked list.

If the list is stored in an array, we can traverse the list in either direction using an index variable. However, if the list is stored in a linked list, we can traverse the list in only one direction starting at the first node because the links are in only one direction, as shown in Figure 10-21. Therefore, in the case of a linked list, to find the location of the node to be inserted, we do the following. Suppose that `firstOutOfOrder` is a pointer to the node that is to be moved to its proper location, and `lastInOrder` is a pointer to the last node of the sorted portion of the list. For example, see the linked list in Figure 10-22.

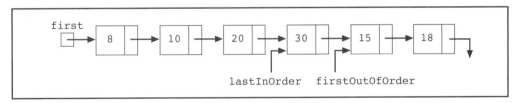

Figure 10-22   Linked list and pointers `lastInOrder` and `firstOutOfOrder`

First, we compare the `info` of `firstOutOfOrder` with the `info` of the first node. If the `info` of `firstOutOfOrder` is smaller than the `info` of `first`, then the node `firstOutOfOrder` is to be moved before the first node of the list; otherwise, we search the list starting at the second node to find the location where to move `firstOutOfOrder`. As usual, we search the list using two pointers, say, `current` and `trailCurrent`. The pointer `trailCurrent` points to the node just before `current`. In this case, the node `firstOutOfOrder` is to be moved between `trailCurrent` and `current`. Of course, we also handle any special cases such as an empty list, a list with only one node, or a list in which the node `firstOutOfOrder` is already in the proper place.

This discussion translates into the following algorithm:

```
if(firstOutOfOrder->info is less than first->info)
   move firstOutOfOrder before first
else
{
   set trailCurrent to first
   set current to the second node in the list

     //search the list
   while(current->info is less than firstOutOfOrder->info)
   {
        advance trailCurrent;
        advance current;
   }

   if(current is not equal to firstOutOfOrder)
   {      //insert firstOutOfOrder between current and trailCurrent
      lastInOrder->link = firstOutOfOrder->link;
      firstOutOfOrder->link = current;
      trailCurrent->link = firstOutOfOrder;
   }
   else       //firstOutOfOrder is already at the first place
      lastInOrder = lastInOrder->link;
}
```

Let us illustrate this algorithm on the list shown in Figure 10-23. We consider several cases.

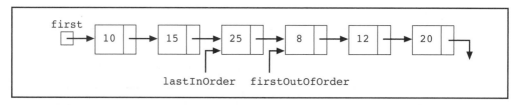

Figure 10-23 Linked list and pointers `lastInOrder` and `firstOutOfOrder`

Case 1: Because `firstOutOfOrder->info` is less than `first->info`, the node `firstOutOfOrder` is to be moved before `first`. So we adjust the necessary links, and Figure 10-24 shows the resulting list.

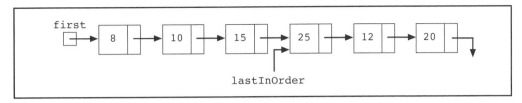

Figure 10-24   Linked list after moving the node with `info` 8 to the beginning

Case 2: Consider the list shown in Figure 10-25.

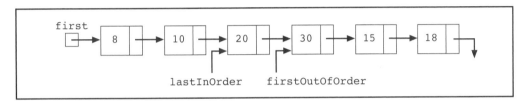

Figure 10-25   Linked list and pointers `lastInOrder` and `firstOutOfOrder`

Because `firstOutOfOrder->info` is greater than `first->info`, we search the list to find the place where `firstOutOfOrder` is to be moved. As previously explained, we use the pointers `trailCurrent` and `current` to traverse the list. For this list, these pointers end up at the nodes as shown in Figure 10-26.

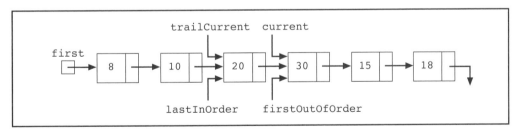

Figure 10-26   Linked list and pointers `trailCurrent` and `current`

Because `current` is the same as `firstOutOfOrder`, the node `firstOutOfOrder` is in the right place. So no adjustment of the links is necessary.

Case 3: Consider the list in Figure 10-27.

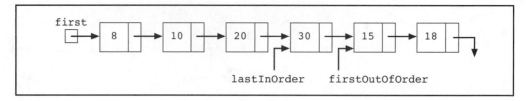

Figure 10-27 Linked list and pointers `lastInOrder` and `firstOutOfOrder`

Because `firstOutOfOrder->info` is greater than `first->info`, we search the list to find the place where `firstOutOfOrder` is to be moved. As in Case 2, we use the pointers `trailCurrent` and `current` to traverse the list. For this list, these pointers end up at the nodes as shown in Figure 10-28.

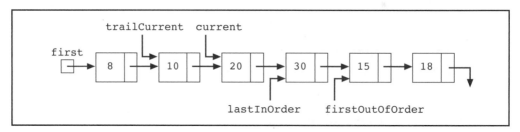

Figure 10-28 Linked list and pointers `trailCurrent` and `current`

Now, `firstOutOfOrder` is to be moved between `trailCurrent` and `current`. So we adjust the necessary links and obtain the list as shown in Figure 10-29.

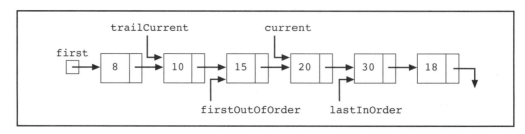

Figure 10-29 Linked list after moving `firstOutOfOrder` between `trailCurrent` and `current`

We now write the C++ function, linkedInsertionSort, to implement the previous algorithm.

```cpp
template<class elemType>
void orderedLinkedListType<elemType>::linkedInsertionSort()
{
    nodeType<elemType> *lastInOrder;
    nodeType<elemType> *firstOutOfOrder;
    nodeType<elemType> *current;
    nodeType<elemType> *trailCurrent;

    lastInOrder = first;

    if(first == NULL)
        cerr<<"Cannot sort an empty list."<<endl;
    else
        if(first->link == NULL)
            cout<<"The list is of length 1. "
                <<"It is already in order."<<endl;
        else
            while(lastInOrder->link != NULL)
            {
                firstOutOfOrder = lastInOrder->link;

                if(firstOutOfOrder->info < first->info)
                {
                    lastInOrder->link = firstOutOfOrder->link;
                    firstOutOfOrder->link = first;
                    first = firstOutOfOrder;
                }
                else
                {
                    trailCurrent = first;
                    current = first->link;
                    while(current->info < firstOutOfOrder->info)
                    {
                        trailCurrent = current;
                        current = current->link;
                    }

                    if(current != firstOutOfOrder)
                    {
                        lastInOrder->link = firstOutOfOrder->link;
                        firstOutOfOrder->link = current;
                        trailCurrent->link = firstOutOfOrder;
                    }
                    else
                        lastInOrder = lastInOrder->link;
                }
            }//end while
}//end linkedInsertionSort
```

10

We leave it as an exercise for you to write a program to test the insertion sort algorithm. See Programming Exercises 2 and 3 at the end of this chapter.

Analysis: Insertion Sort

It can be shown that the average number of key comparisons and the average number of item assignments in an insertion sort algorithm are

$$\frac{1}{4}n^2 + O(n) = O(n^2)$$

Table 10-1 summarizes the behavior of the selection and insertion sort algorithms.

Table 10-1   Average Case Behavior of the Selection and Insertion Sort Algorithms for a List of Length n

Algorithm	Number of Comparisons	Number of Swaps
Selection sort	$\frac{n(n-1)}{2} = O(n^2)$	$3(n-1) = O(n)$
Insertion sort	$\frac{1}{4}n^2 + O(n) = O(n^2)$	$\frac{1}{4}n^2 + O(n) = O(n^2)$

LOWER BOUND ON COMPARISON-BASED SORT ALGORITHMS

The previous sections discussed the selection and insertion sort algorithms, and noted that the average-case behavior of these algorithms is $O(n^2)$. Both of these algorithms are comparison-based algorithms; that is, the lists are sorted by comparing their respective keys. Before discussing any additional sorting algorithms, let us discuss the best-case scenario for the comparison-based sorting algorithms.

We can trace the execution of a comparison-based algorithm by using a graph called a **comparison tree**. Let L be a list of n distinct elements, where $n > 0$. For any j and k, where $1 \leq j, k \leq n$, either $L[j] < L[k]$ or $L[j] > L[k]$. Because each comparison of the keys has two outcomes, the comparison tree is a binary tree. While drawing this figure, we draw each comparison as a circle, called a **node**. The node is labeled as $j{:}k$, representing the comparison of $L[j]$ with $L[k]$. If $L[j] < L[k]$, follow the left branch; otherwise, follow the right branch. Figure 10-30 shows the comparison tree for a list of length 3. (In Figure 10-30, the rectangle, called a **leaf**, represents the final ordering of the nodes.)

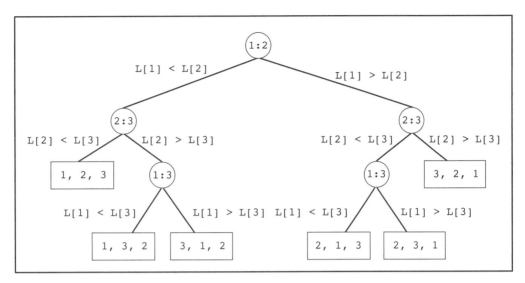

Figure 10-30   Comparison tree for sorting three items

We call the top node in the figure the **root** node. The straight line that connects the two nodes is called a **branch**. A sequence of branches from a node, x, to another node, y, is called a **path** from x to y.

Associated with each path from the root to a leaf is a unique permutation of the elements of L. This uniqueness follows because the sort algorithm only moves the data and makes comparisons. Furthermore, the data movement on any path from the root to a leaf is the same regardless of the initial inputs. For a list of n elements, $n > 0$, there are $n!$ different permutations. Any one of these $n!$ permutations might be the correct ordering of L. Thus, the comparison tree must have at least $n!$ leaves.

Let us consider the worst case for all comparison-based sorting algorithms. We state the following result without proof.

Theorem: Let L be a list of n distinct elements. Any sorting algorithm that sorts L by comparison of the keys only, in its worst case, makes at least $O(n*\log_2 n)$ key comparisons.

As analyzed in the previous sections, both the selection and insertion sort algorithms are of the order $O(n^2)$. The remainder of this chapter discusses sorting algorithms that, on average, are of the order $O(n*\log_2 n)$.

QUICK SORT: ARRAY-BASED LISTS

The previous section noted that the lower bound on comparison-based algorithms is $O(n*\log_2 n)$. Both the selection sort and insertion sort algorithms discussed earlier in this chapter are $O(n^2)$. This and the next two sections discuss sorting algorithms that are of the order $O(n*\log_2 n)$. The first algorithm is the quick sort algorithm.

The quick sort algorithm uses the divide-and-conquer technique to sort a list. The list is partitioned into two sublists, and the two sublists are then sorted and combined into one list in such a way so that the combined list is sorted. Thus, the general algorithm is:

```
if(the list size is greater than 1)
{
    a. Partition the list into two sublists, say lowerSublist and
       upperSublist.
    b. Quick sort lowerSublist.
    c. Quick sort upperSublist.
    d. Combine the sorted lowerSublist and sorted upperSublist.
}
```

After partitioning the list into two sublists—`lowerSublist` and `upperSublist`—these two sublists are sorted using the quick sort algorithm. In other words, we use *recursion* to implement the quick sort algorithm.

The quick sort algorithm described here is for array-based lists. The algorithm for linked lists can be developed in a similar manner and is left as an exercise for you. See Programming Exercise 4 at the end of this chapter.

In the quick sort algorithm, the list is partitioned in such way that combining the sorted `lowerSublist` and `upperSublist` is trivial. Therefore, in a quick sort, all the sorting work is done in partitioning the list. Because all the sorting work occurs during the partitioning of the list, we first describe the partition procedure in detail.

To partition the list into two sublists, first we choose an element of the list called **pivot**. The pivot is used to divide the list into two sublists: `lowerSublist` and `upperSublist`. The elements in `lowerSublist` are smaller than `pivot`; the elements in `upperSublist` are greater than `pivot`. For example, consider the list in Figure 10-31.

	[0]	[1]	[2]	[3]	[4]	[5]	[6]	[7]	[8]
list	45	82	25	94	50	60	78	32	92

Figure 10-31 `list` before the partition

There are several ways to determine **pivot**. However, **pivot** is chosen so that, it is hoped, `lowerSublist` and `upperSublist` are of nearly equal size. For illustration purposes, let us choose the middle element of the list as **pivot**. The partition procedure that we describe partitions this list using **pivot** as the middle element, in our case **50**, as shown in Figure 10-32.

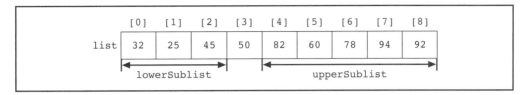

Figure 10-32   `list` after the partition

From Figure 10-32, it follows that after partitioning `list` into `lowerSublist` and `upperSublist`, `pivot` is in the right place. Thus, after sorting `lowerSublist` and `upperSublist`, combining the two sorted sublists is trivial.

The partition algorithm is as follows (we assume that `pivot` is chosen as the middle element of the list):

1. Determine `pivot`, and swap `pivot` with the first element of the list.

   Suppose that the index `smallIndex` points to the last element less than `pivot`. The index `smallIndex` is initialized to the first element of the list.

2. For the remaining elements in the list (starting at the second element):

   If the current element is less than `pivot`

   a. Increment `smallIndex`.

   b. Swap the current element with the array element pointed to by `smallIndex`.

3. Swap the first element, that is, `pivot`, with the array element pointed to by `smallIndex`.

Step 2 can be implemented using a `for` loop, with the loop starting at the second element of the list.

Step 1 determines the pivot and moves `pivot` to the first array position. During the execution of Step 2, the list elements get arranged as shown in Figure 10-33. (Suppose the name of the array containing the list elements is `list`.)

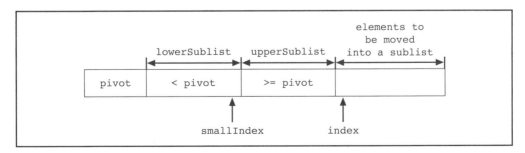

Figure 10-33   List during the execution of Step 2

As shown in Figure 10-33, `pivot` is in the first array position. Elements in the lower sublist are less than `pivot`; elements in the upper sublist are greater than or equal to `pivot`. The variable `smallIndex` contains the index of the last element of the lower sublist; the variable `index` contains the index of the next element that needs to be moved either into the lower sublist or into the upper sublist. As explained in Step 2, if the next element of the list (that is, `list[index]`) is less than `pivot`, we advance `smallIndex` to the next array position and swap `list[index]` with `list[smallIndex]`). Next, we illustrate Step 2.

Suppose that the list is as given in Figure 10-34.

[0]	[1]	[2]	[3]	[4]	[5]	[6]	[7]	[8]	[9]	[10]	[11]	[12]	[13]
32	55	87	13	78	96	52	48	22	11	58	66	88	45

Figure 10-34   List before sorting

For the list in Figure 10-34, `pivot` is at position 6. After moving `pivot` to the first array position, the list is as shown in Figure 10-35. (Notice that in Figure 10-35, 52 is swapped with 32.)

[0]	[1]	[2]	[3]	[4]	[5]	[6]	[7]	[8]	[9]	[10]	[11]	[12]	[13]
52	55	87	13	78	96	32	48	22	11	58	66	88	45

pivot

Figure 10-35   List after moving `pivot` to the first array position

Suppose that after executing Step 2 a few times, the list is as shown in Figure 10-36.

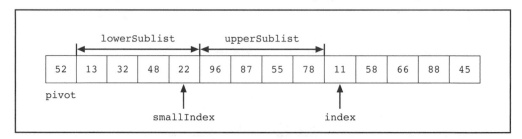

Figure 10-36   List after a few iterations of Step 2

As shown in Figure 10-36, the next element of the list that needs to be moved into a sublist is indicated by `index`. Because `list[index] < pivot`, we need to move the element `list[index]` into the lower sublist. To do so, we first advance `smallIndex` to the next array position and then swap `list[smallIndex]` with `list[index]`. The resulting list is as shown in Figure 10-37. (Notice that **11** is swapped with **96**.)

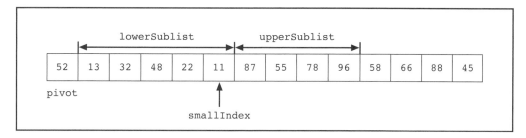

Figure 10-37   List after moving `11` into the lower sublist

Now consider the list in Figure 10-38.

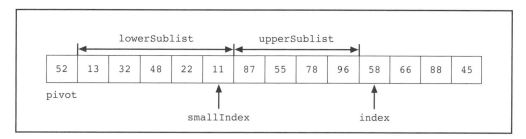

Figure 10-38   List before moving `58` into a sublist

For the list in Figure 10-38, `list[index]` is **58**, which is greater than `pivot`. Therefore, `list[index]` is to be moved into the upper sublist. This is accomplished by leaving **58** at its position and increasing the size of the upper sublist, by one, to the next array position. After moving **58** into the upper sublist, the list is shown in Figure 10-39.

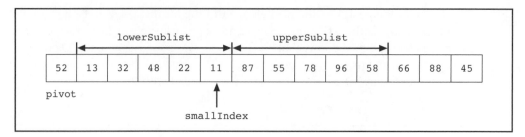

Figure 10-39   List after moving 58 into the upper sublist

After moving all the elements that are less than **pivot** into the lower sublist and all the elements that are greater than **pivot** into the upper sublist (that is, after completely executing Step 2), Figure 10-40 shows the resulting list.

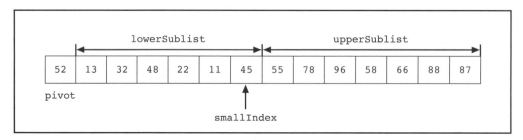

Figure 10-40   List elements after arranging into the lower sublist and upper sublist

Next, we execute Step 3 and move 52, **pivot**, to the proper position in the list. This is accomplished by swapping 52 with 45. The resulting list is as shown in Figure 10-41.

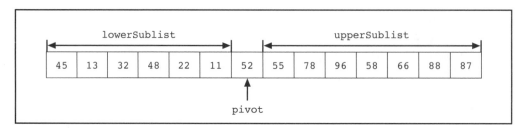

Figure 10-41   List after swapping 52 with 45

As shown in Figure 10-41, Steps 1, 2, and 3 in the preceding algorithm partition the list into two sublists. The elements less than **pivot** are in the lower sublist; the elements greater than or equal to **pivot** are in the upper sublist.

To partition the list into the lower and upper sublists, we need to keep track of only the last element of the lower sublist and the next element of the list that needs to be moved into either the lower sublist or the upper sublist. In fact, the upper sublist is between the two indices smallIndex and index.

We now write the function, partition, to implement the preceding partition algorithm. After rearranging the elements of the list, the function returns the location of pivot so that we can determine the starting and ending locations of the sublists. Also, because the function partition is a member of the class, it has direct access to the array containing the list. Thus, to partition a list, we need to pass only the starting and ending indices of the list.

```
template<class elemType>
int orderedArrayListType<elemType>::partition(int first, int last)
{
    elemType pivot;

    int index, smallIndex;

    swap(first, (first + last) / 2);

    pivot = list[first];
    smallIndex = first;

    for(index = first + 1; index <= last; index++)
        if(list[index] < pivot)
        {
            smallIndex++;
            swap(smallIndex, index);
        }

    swap(first, smallIndex);

    return smallIndex;
}
```

As you can see from the definition of the function partition, certain elements of the list need to be swapped. The following function, swap, accomplishes this task. (Notice that this swap function is the same as the one given earlier in this chapter for the selection sort algorithm.)

```
template<class elemType>
void orderedArrayListType<elemType>::swap(int first, int second)
{
    elemType temp;

    temp = list[first];
    list[first] = list[second];
    list[second] = temp;
}
```

Once the list is partitioned into lowerSublist and upperSublist, we again apply the quick sort method to sort the two sublists. Because both sublists are sorted using the same quick sort algorithm, the easiest way to implement this algorithm is to use recursion. Therefore, this section gives the recursive version of the quick sort algorithm. As explained previously, after rearranging the elements of the list, the function `partition` returns the index of `pivot` so that the starting and ending indices of the sublists can be determined.

Given the starting and ending indices of a list, the following function, `recQuickSort`, implements the recursive version of the quick sort algorithm:

```
template<class elemType>
void orderedArrayListType<elemType>::recQuickSort(int first, int last)
{
    int pivotLocation;

    if(first < last)
    {
        pivotLocation = partition(first, last);
        recQuickSort(first, pivotLocation - 1);
        recQuickSort(pivotLocation + 1, last);
    }
}
```

Finally, we write the quick sort function, `quickSort`, that calls the function `recQuickSort` on the original list.

```
template<class elemType>
void orderedArrayListType<elemType>::quickSort()
{
    recQuickSort(0, length - 1);
}
```

We leave it as an exercise for you to write a program to test the quick sort algorithm. See Programming Exercise 5 at the end of this chapter.

Analysis: Quick Sort

Table 10-2 summarizes the behavior of the quick sort algorithm for a list of length n. (The proofs of these results are beyond the scope of this book.)

Table 10-2 Analysis of the Quick Sort Algorithm for a List of Length n

	Number of Comparisons	Number of Swaps
Average case	$(1.39)*n*\log_2 n + O(n) = O(n*\log_2 n)$	$(0.69)*n*\log_2 n + O(n) = O(n*\log_2 n)$
Worst case	$\dfrac{n^2}{2} - \dfrac{n}{2} = O(n^2)$	$\dfrac{n^2}{2} + \dfrac{3n}{2} - 2 = O(n^2)$

MERGE SORT: LINKED LIST-BASED LISTS

The previous section described the quick sort algorithm and stated that the average-case behavior of a quick sort is $O(n*\log_2 n)$. However, the worst-case behavior of a quick sort is $O(n^2)$. This section describes the sorting algorithm whose behavior is always $O(n*\log_2 n)$.

Like the quick sort algorithm, the merge sort algorithm uses the divide-and-conquer technique to sort a list. A merge sort algorithm also partitions the list into two sublists, sorts the sublists, and then combines the sorted sublists into one sorted list. This section describes the merge sort algorithm for linked lists. We leave it for you to develop the merge sort algorithm for array-based lists, which can be done by using the techniques described for linked lists.

The merge sort and the quick sort algorithms differ in how they partition the list. As discussed earlier, a quick sort first selects an element in the list, called `pivot`, and then partitions the list so that the elements in one sublist are smaller than `pivot` and the elements in the other sublist are larger than `pivot`. By contrast, a merge sort chops the list into two sublists of nearly equal size. For example, consider the list whose elements are as follows:

```
list: 35   28   18   45   62   48   30   38
```

The merge sort algorithm partitions this list into two sublists as follows:

```
first sublist: 35   28   18   45
second sublist: 62   48   30   38
```

The two sublists are sorted using the same algorithm (that is, a merge sort), used on the original list. Suppose that we have sorted the sublist. That is, suppose that:

```
first sublist: 18   28   35   45
second sublist: 30   38   48   62
```

Next, the merge sort algorithm combines, that is, merges, the two sorted sublists into one sorted list.

Figure 10-42 further illustrates the merge sort process.

10

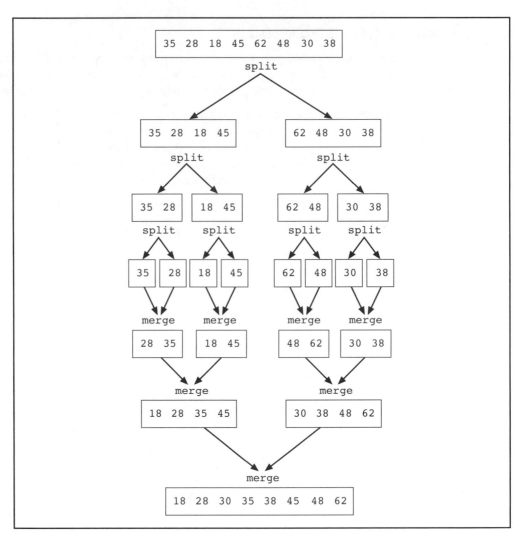

Figure 10-42 Merge sort algorithm

From Figure 10-42, it is clear that in the merge sort algorithm, most of the sorting work is done in merging the sorted sublists.

The general algorithm for the merge sort is as follows:

```
if the list is of a size greater than 1
{
    a. Divide the list into two sublists.
    b. Merge sort the first sublist.
```

```
        c. Merge sort the second sublist.
        d. Merge the first sublist and the second sublist.
}
```

As remarked previously, after dividing the list into two sublists—the first sublist and the second sublist—these two sublists are sorted using the merge sort algorithm. In other words, we use *recursion* to implement the merge sort algorithm.

We next describe the necessary algorithm to:

- Divide the list into two sublists of nearly equal size

- Merge sort both sublists

- Merge the sorted sublists.

Divide

Because the data is stored in a linked list, we do not know the length of the list. Furthermore, a linked list is not a random access data structure. Therefore, to divide the list into two sublists, we need to find the middle node of the list.

Consider the list in Figure 10-43.

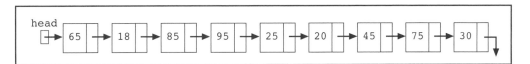

Figure 10-43   Unsorted linked list

To find the middle of the list, we traverse the list with two pointers—say, `middle` and `current`. The pointer `middle` is initialized to the first node of the list. Because this list has more than two nodes, we initialize the pointer `current` to the third node. (Recall that we sort the list only if it has more than one element because a list of size 1 is already sorted. Furthermore, if the list has only two nodes, we set `current` to `NULL`.) Consider the list shown in Figure 10-44.

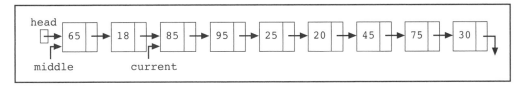

Figure 10-44   `middle` and `current` before traversing the list

Every time we advance `middle` by one node, we advance `current` by one node. After advancing `current` by one node, if `current` is not `NULL`, we again advance `current` by one node. That is, for the most part, every time `middle` advances by one node, `current` advances by two nodes. Eventually, `current` becomes `NULL` and `middle` points to the last node of the first sublist. For example, for the list in Figure 10-44, when `current` becomes `NULL`, `middle` points to the node with `info 25` (see Figure 10-45).

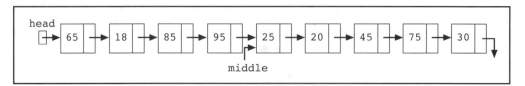

Figure 10-45   `middle` after traversing the list

It is now easy to divide the list into two sublists. First, using the link of `middle`, we assign a pointer to the node following `middle`. Then we set the link of `middle` to `NULL`. Figure 10-46 shows the resulting sublists.

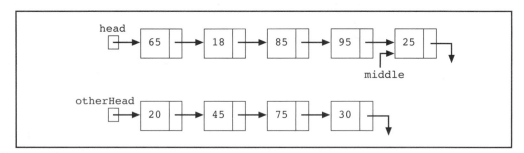

Figure 10-46   List after dividing it into two lists

This discussion translates into the following C++ function, `divideList`:

```
template<class elemType>
void orderedLinkedListType<elemType>::divideList
                                (nodeType<elemType>* first1,
                                 nodeType<elemType>* &first2)
{
    nodeType<elemType>* middle;
    nodeType<elemType>* current;

    if(first1 == NULL)    //the list is empty
        first2 = NULL;
```

```
      else
         if(first1->link == NULL)   //the list has only one node
            first2 = NULL;
      else
      {
         middle = first1;
         current = first1->link;
         if(current != NULL)      //the list has more than two nodes
            current = current->link;

         while(current != NULL)
         {
            middle = middle->link;
            current = current->link;
            if(current != NULL)
               current = current->link;
         }//end while

         first2 = middle->link;   //first2 points to the first
                                  //node of the second sublist
         middle->link = NULL;     //set the link of the last node
                                  //of the first sublist to NULL
      }//end else
}//end divideList
```

Now that we know how to divide a list into two sublists of nearly equal size, next we focus on merging the sorted sublists. Recall that, in a merge sort, most of the sorting work is done in merging the sorted sublists.

Merge

Once the sublists are sorted, the next step in the merge sort algorithm is to merge the sorted sublists. Sorted sublists are merged into a sorted list by comparing the elements of the sublists, and then adjusting the pointer of the nodes with the smaller `info`. Let us illustrate this procedure on the sublists shown in Figure 10-47. Suppose that `first1` points to the first node of the first sublist, and `first2` points to the first node of the second sublist.

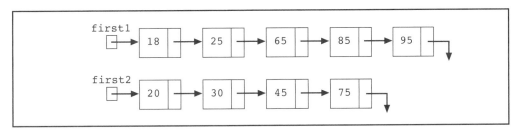

Figure 10-47   Sublists before merging

We first compare the **info** of the first node of each of the two sublists to determine the first node of the merged list. We assign a pointer, **newHead**, to point to the first node of the merged list. We also use a pointer, **lastSmall**, to keep track of the last node of the merged list. The head pointer of the sublist with the smaller node then advances to the next node of that sublist. Figure 10-48 shows the sublists of Figure 10-47 after setting **newHead** and **lastSmall**, and advancing **first1**.

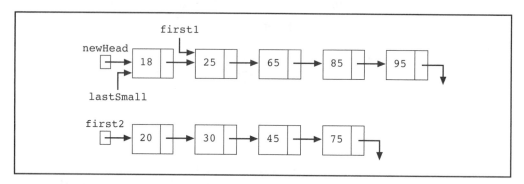

Figure 10-48   Sublists after setting **newHead** and **lastSmall** and advancing **first1**

In Figure 10-48, **first1** points to the first node of the first sublist that is yet to be merged with the second sublist. So we again compare the nodes pointed to by **first1** and **first2**, and adjust the link of the smaller node and the last node of the merged list so as to move the smaller node to the end of the merged list. For the sublists shown in Figure 10-48, after adjusting the necessary links, we have Figure 10-49.

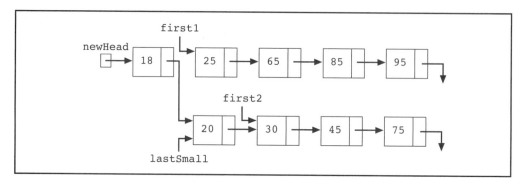

Figure 10-49   Merged list after putting the node with **info** 20 at the end of the merged list

We continue this process for the remaining elements of both sublists. Every time we move a node to the merged list, we advance either `first1` or `first2` to the next node. Eventually, either `first1` or `first2` becomes `NULL`. If `first1` becomes `NULL`, the first sublist is exhausted first, and so we attach the remaining nodes of the second sublist at the end of the partially merged list. If `first2` becomes `NULL`, the second sublist is exhausted first, and so we attach the remaining nodes of the first sublist at the end of the partially merged list.

Following this discussion, we can now write the C++ function, `mergeList`, to merge the two sorted sublists. The head pointers of the sublists are passed as parameters to the function `mergeList`.

```cpp
template<class elemType>
nodeType<elemType>* orderedLinkedListType<elemType>::mergeList
                       (nodeType<elemType>* first1,
                        nodeType<elemType>* first2)
{
    nodeType<elemType> *lastSmall;  //pointer to the last node of
                                    //the merged list
    nodeType<elemType> *newHead;    //pointer to the merged list

    if(first1 == NULL)   //the first sublist is empty
        return first2;
    else
        if(first2 == NULL)   //the second sublist is empty
            return first1;
        else
        {
            if(first1->info < first2->info) //compare the first nodes
            {
                newHead = first1;
                first1 = first1->link;
                lastSmall = newHead;
            }
            else
                if(first2->info < first1->info)
                {
                    newHead = first2;
                    first2 = first2->link;
                    lastSmall = newHead;
                }

            while(first1 != NULL && first2 != NULL)
            {
                if(first1->info < first2->info)
                {
                    lastSmall->link = first1;
                    lastSmall = lastSmall->link;
                    first1 = first1->link;
                }
```

```
        else
        {
           lastSmall->link = first2;
           lastSmall = lastSmall->link;
           first2 = first2->link;
        }
     }//end while

     if(first1 == NULL)      //first sublist is exhausted first
        lastSmall->link = first2;
     else                    //second sublist is exhausted first
        lastSmall->link = first1;

     return newHead;
  }
}//end mergeList
```

Finally, we write the recursive merge sort function, recMergeSort, which uses the divideList and mergeList functions to sort a list. The head pointer of the list to be sorted is passed as a parameter to the function recMergeSort.

```
template<class elemType>
void orderedLinkedListType<elemType>::recMergeSort
                                    (nodeType<elemType>* &head)
{
    nodeType<elemType> *otherHead;

    if(head != NULL)  //if the list is not empty
       if(head->link != NULL)  //if the list has more than one node
       {
          divideList(head, otherHead);
          recMergeSort(head);
          recMergeSort(otherHead);
          head = mergeList(head, otherHead);
       }
}//end recMergeSort
```

We can now give the definition of the function mergeSort, which should be included as a public member of the class orderedLinkedListType. (Note that the functions divideList, merge, and recMergesort can be included as private members of the class orderedLinkedListType because these functions are used only to implement the function mergeSort.) The function mergeSort simply calls the function recMergeSort and passes the pointer first to this function. The definition of the function mergeSort is:

```
template<class elemType>
void orderedLinkedListType<elemType>::mergeSort()
{
    recMergeSort(first);
}//end mergeSort
```

We leave it as an exercise for you to write a program to test the merge sort algorithm. See Programming Exercise 8 at the end of this chapter.

Analysis: Merge Sort

Suppose that L is a list of n elements, where $n > 0$. Let $A(n)$ denote the number of key comparisons in the average case, and $W(n)$ denote the number of key comparisons in the worst case to sort L. It can be shown that

$$A(n) = n*\log_2 n - 1.26n = O(n*\log_2 n)$$
$$W(n) = n*\log_2 n - (n-1) = O(n*\log_2 n)$$

HEAP SORT: ARRAY-BASED LISTS

In an earlier section, we described the quick sort algorithm for contiguous lists, that is, array-based lists. We remarked that, on average, the quick sort is of the order $O(n*\log_2 n)$. However, in the worst case, the quick sort is of the order $O(n^2)$. This section describes another algorithm, the **heap sort**, for array-based lists. This algorithm is of the order $O(n*\log_2 n)$ even in the worst case, therefore overcoming the worst case of the quick sort.

Definition: A **heap** is a list in which each element contains a key, such that the key in the element at position k in the list is at least as large as the key in the element at position $2k + 1$ (if it exists), and $2k + 2$ (if it exists).

Recall that in C++ the array index starts at 0. Therefore, the element at position k is in fact the $k + 1$th element of the list.

Consider the list in Figure 10–50.

	[0]	[1]	[2]	[3]	[4]	[5]	[6]	[7]	[8]	[9]	[10]	[11]	[12]
	85	70	80	50	40	75	30	20	10	35	15	62	58

Figure 10-50   A list that is a heap

It can be checked that the list in Figure 10–50 is a heap.

Given a heap, we can construct a complete binary tree as follows: The root node of the tree is the first element of the list. The left child of the root is the second element of the list; the right child of the root node is the third element of the list. Thus, in general, for the node k, which is the $k - 1$th element of the list, its left child is the $2k$th (if it exists) element of the list, which is at position $2k - 1$ in the list, and the right child is the $2k + 1$st (if it exists) element of the list, which is at position $2k$ in the list.

The diagram in Figure 10–51 represents the complete binary tree corresponding to the list in Figure 10–50.

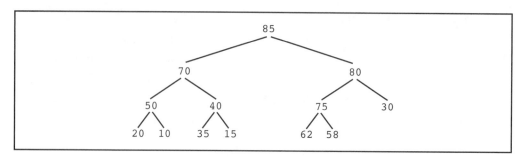

Figure 10-51   Complete binary tree corresponding to the list in Figure 10-50

Figure 10-51 shows that the list in Figure 10-50 is in a heap. In fact, to demonstrate the heap sort algorithm, we will always draw the complete binary tree corresponding to a list.

We now describe the heap sort algorithm.

The first step in the heap sort algorithm is to convert the list into a heap, called `buildHeap`. After we convert the array into a heap, the sorting phase begins.

Build Heap

This section describes the build heap algorithm.

The general algorithm is as follows: suppose `length` denotes the length of the list. Let `index = length / 2 - 1`. Then `list[index]` is the last element in the list that is not a leaf; that is, this element has at least one child. Thus, elements `list[index + 1]...list[length - 1]` are leaves.

First, we convert the subtree with the root node `list[index]` into a heap. Note that this subtree has at most three nodes. We then convert the subtree with the root node `list[index - 1]` into a heap, and so on.

To convert a subtree into a heap, we perform the following steps: suppose that `list[a]` is the root node of the subtree, `list[b]` is the left child, and `list[c]`, if it exists, is the right child of `list[a]`.

Compare `list[b]` with `list[c]` to determine the larger child. If `list[c]` does not exist, then `list[b]` is the larger child. Suppose that `largerIndex` indicates the larger child. (Notice that `largerIndex` is either b or c.)

Compare `list[a]` with `list[largerIndex]`. If `list[a] < list[largerIndex]`, then swap `list[a]` with `list[largerIndex]`; otherwise, the subtree with the root node `list[a]` is already in a heap.

Suppose that `list[a] < list[largerIndex]` and we swap the elements `list[a]` with `list[largerIndex]`. After making this swap, the subtree with the root node `list[largerIndex]` might not be in a heap. If this is the case, then we repeat Steps 1 and 2 at the subtree with the root node `list[largerIndex]`, and continue this process until either the heaps in the subtrees are restored or we arrive at an empty subtree. This step is implemented using a loop, which is described when we write the algorithm.

Consider the list in Figure 10-52. Let us call this `list`.

	[0]	[1]	[2]	[3]	[4]	[5]	[6]	[7]	[8]	[9]	[10]
list	15	60	72	70	56	32	62	92	45	30	65

Figure 10-52   Array `list`

Figure 10-53 shows the complete binary tree corresponding to the list in Figure 10-52.

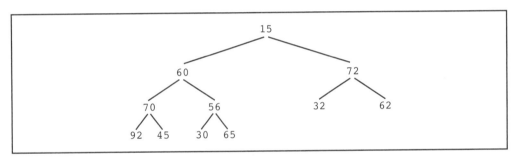

Figure 10-53   Complete binary tree corresponding to the list in Figure 10-52

To facilitate this discussion, when we say node 56 we mean the node with info 56.

This list has 11 elements and so the length of the list is 11. To convert the array into a heap, we start at the list element n/2 − 1 = 11/2 − 1 = 5 − 1 = 4, which is the fifth element of the list.

Now `list[4]` = 56. The children of `list[4]` are `list[4 * 2 + 1]` and `list[4 * 2 + 2]`, that is, `list[9]` and `list[10]`. In the previous list, both `list[9]` and `list[10]` exist. To convert the tree with the root node `list[4]`, we perform the following three steps:

1. Find the larger of `list[9]` and `list[10]`, that is, the largest child of `list[4]`. In this case, `list[10]` is larger than `list[9]`.

2. Compare the larger child with the parent node. If the larger child is larger than the parent, swap the larger child with the parent. Because `list[4]` < `list[10]`, we swap `list[4]` with `list[10]`.

3. Because `list[10]` does not have a subtree, Step 3 does not execute.

Figure 10-54 shows the resulting binary tree.

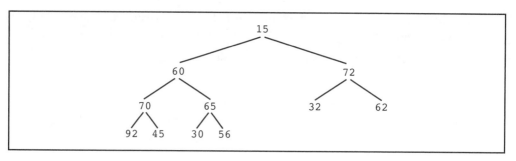

Figure 10-54 Binary tree after swapping `list[4]` with `list[10]`

Next, we consider the subtree with the root node `list[3]`, that is, 70, and repeat the three steps given previously to obtain the complete binary tree as given in Figure 10-55. (Notice that here, also, Step 3 does not execute.)

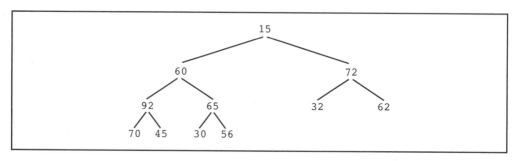

Figure 10-55 Binary tree after repeating Steps 1, 2, and 3 at the root node `list[3]`

Now we consider the subtree with the root node `list[2]`, that is, 72, and apply the three steps given earlier. Figure 10-56 shows the resulting binary tree. (Note that in this case, because the parent is larger than both children, this subtree is already in a heap.)

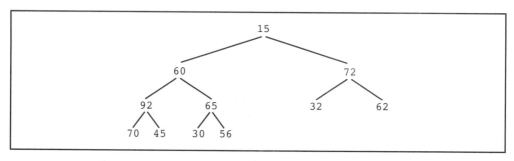

Figure 10-56 Binary tree after repeating Steps 1 and 2 at the root node `list[2]`

Next, we consider the subtree with the root node `list[1]`, that is, `60`. First we apply Steps 1 and 2. Because `list[1]` = `60` < `list[3]` = `92` (the larger child), we swap `list[1]` with `list[3]`, to obtain the tree as given in Figure 10-57.

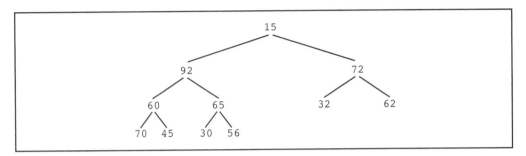

Figure 10-57   Binary tree after swapping `list[1]` with `list[3]`

However, after swapping `list[1]` with `list[3]`, the subtree with the root node `list[3]`, that is, `60`, is no longer a heap. Thus, we must restore the heap in this subtree. To do this, we apply Step 3 and find the larger child of `60` and swap it with `60`. We then obtain the binary tree as given in Figure 10-58.

10

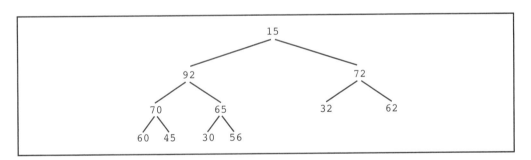

Figure 10-58   Binary tree after restoring the heap at `list[3]`

Once again, the subtree with the root node `list[1]`, that is, `92`, is in a heap (see Figure 10-58).

Finally, we consider the tree with the root node `list[0]`, that is, `15`. We repeat the previous three steps to obtain the binary tree as given in Figure 10-59.

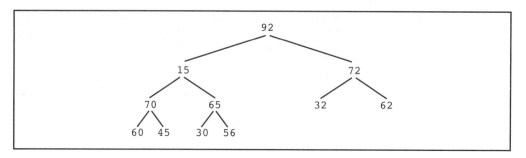

Figure 10-59 Binary tree after applying Steps 1 and 2 at `list[0]`

We see that the subtree with the root node `list[1]`, that is, 15, is no longer in a heap. So we must apply Step 3 to restore the heap in this subtree. (This requires us to repeat Steps 1 and 2 at the subtree with the root node `list[1]`.) We swap `list[1]` with the larger child, `list[3]`, that is, 70. We then get the binary tree of Figure 10-60.

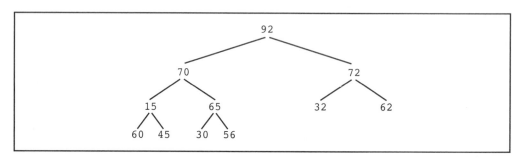

Figure 10-60 Binary tree after applying Steps 1 and 2 at `list[1]`

The subtree with the root node `list[3]` = 15 is not in a heap, and so we must restore the heap in this subtree. To do so, we apply Steps 1 and 2 at the subtree with the root node `list[3]`. We swap `list[3]` with the larger child, `list[7]`, that is, 60. Figure 10-61 shows the resulting binary tree.

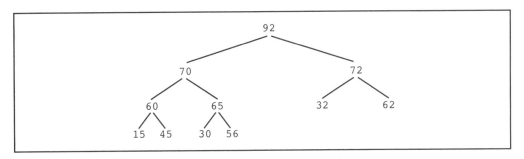

Figure 10-61   Binary tree after restoring the heap at `list[3]`

The resulting binary tree (in Figure 10-61) is in a heap, and so the list corresponding to this complete binary tree is in a heap.

Thus, in general, starting at the lowest level from right to left, we look at a subtree and convert the subtree into a heap as follows: if the root node of the subtree is smaller than the larger child, we swap the root node with the larger child. After swapping the root node with the larger child, we must restore the heap in the subtree whose root node was swapped.

Suppose `low` contains the index of the root node of the subtree, and `high` contains the index of the last item in the list. The heap is to be restored in the subtree rooted at `list[low]`. The preceding discussion translates into the following C++ algorithm:

```
int largeIndex = 2 * low + 1;    //the index of the left child

while(largeIndex <= high)
{
   if(largeIndex < high)
      if(list[largeIndex] < list[largeIndex + 1])
         largeIndex = largeIndex + 1; //the index of the larger child
   if(list[low] > list[largeIndex])   //the subtree is already in
                                      //a heap
      break;
   else
   {
      swap(list[low], list[largeIndex]);   //Line **
      low = largeIndex;  //go to the subtree to further
                         //restore the heap
      largeIndex = 2 * low + 1;
   }//end else
}//end while
```

The **swap** statement at the line marked **Line ** swaps the parent with the larger child. Because a **swap** statement makes three item assignments to swap the contents of two variables, each time through the loop three item assignments are made. The **while** loop moves the parent node to a place in the tree so that the resulting subtree with the root node `list[low]` is in a heap. We can easily reduce the number of assignments each time through the loop from three to one by first storing the root node in a temporary location, say `temp`. Then each time through the loop the larger child is compared with `temp`. If the larger child is larger than `temp`, we move the larger child to the root node of the subtree under consideration.

Next, we describe the function `heapify`, which restores the heap in a subtree by making one item assignment each time through the loop. The index of the root node of the list, and the index of the last element of the list, are passed as parameters to this function.

```
template<class elemType>
void orderedArrayListType<elemType>::heapify(int low, int high)
{
    int largeIndex;

    elemType temp = list[low]; //copy the root node of the subtree

    largeIndex = 2 * low + 1;   //index of the left child

    while(largeIndex <= high)
    {
        if(largeIndex < high)
            if(list[largeIndex] < list[largeIndex + 1])
                largeIndex = largeIndex + 1; //index of the
                                             //largest child

        if(temp > list[largeIndex]) //subtree is already in a heap
            break;
        else
        {
            list[low] = list[largeIndex]; //move the larger child
                                          //to the root
            low = largeIndex;       //go to the subtree to
                                    //restore the heap
            largeIndex = 2 * low + 1;
        }
    }//end while

    list[low] = temp; //insert temp into the tree, that is, list

}//end heapify
```

Next, we use the function `heapify` to implement the `buildHeap` function to convert the list into a heap.

```
template<class elemType>
void orderedArrayListType<elemType>::buildHeap()
{
    int index;
    for(index = length / 2 - 1; index >= 0; index--)
        heapify(index, length - 1);
}
```

We now describe the heap sort algorithm.

Suppose the list is in a heap. Consider the complete binary tree representing the list as given in Figure 10-62.

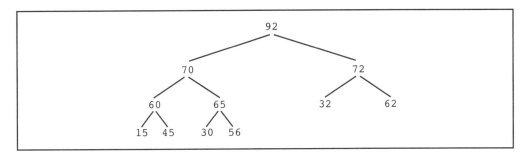

Figure 10-62   A heap

Because this is a heap, the root node is the largest element of the tree, that is, the largest element of the list. So it must be moved to the end of the list. We swap the root node of the tree, that is, the first element of the list, with the last node in the tree (which is the last element of the list). We then obtain the binary tree as shown in Figure 10-63.

10

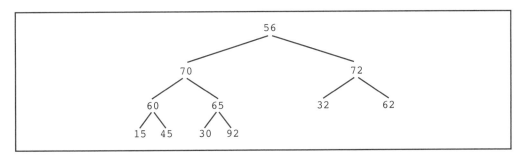

Figure 10-63   Binary tree after moving the root node to the end

Because the largest element is now in its proper place, we consider the remaining elements of the list, that is, elements `list[0]...list[9]`. The complete binary tree representing this list is no longer a heap, and so we must restore the heap in this portion of the complete binary tree. We use the function `heapify` to restore the heap. A call to this function is:

`heapify(list, 0, 9);`

We thus obtain the binary tree as shown in Figure 10-64.

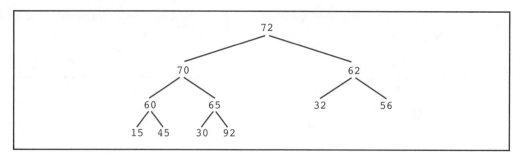

Figure 10-64 Binary tree after the statement `heapify (list, 0, 9);` executes

We repeat this process for the complete binary tree corresponding to the list elements `list[0]...list[9]`. We swap `list[0]` with `list[9]`, and then restore the heap in the complete binary tree corresponding to the list elements `list[0]...list[8]`. We continue this process.

The following C++ function describes this algorithm:

```
template<class elemType>
void orderedArrayListType<elemType>::heapSort()
{
    int lastOutOfOrder;
    elemType temp;

    buildHeap();

    for(lastOutOfOrder = length - 1; lastOutOfOrder >= 0;
                                     lastOutOfOrder--)
    {
        temp = list[lastOutOfOrder];
        list[lastOutOfOrder] = list[0];
        list[0] = temp;
        heapify(0, lastOutOfOrder - 1);
    }//end for
}//end heapSort
```

We leave it as an exercise for you to write a program to test the heap sort algorithm. See Programming Exercise 9 at the end of this chapter.

Analysis: Heap Sort

Suppose that L is a list of n elements, where $n > 0$. In the worst case, the number of key comparisons in the heap sort algorithm to sort L (the number of comparisons in `heapSort` and the number of comparisons in `buildHeap`) is $2n*\log_2 n + O(n)$. Also, in the worst case, the number of item assignments in the heap sort algorithm to sort L is $n*\log_2 n + O(n)$. On average, the number of comparisons made by the heap sort algorithm to sort L is of $O(n*\log_2 n)$.

In the average case of the quick sort algorithm, the number of key comparisons is $1.39n*\log_2 n + O(n)$ and the number of swaps is $0.69*\log_2 n + O(n)$. Because each swap is three assignments, the number of item assignments in the average case of the quick sort algorithm is at least $1.39n*\log_2 n + O(n)$. It now follows that for the key comparisons, the average case of the quick sort algorithm is somewhat better than the worst case of the heap sort algorithm. On the other hand, for the item assignments, the average case of the quick sort algorithm is somewhat poorer than the worst case of the heap sort algorithm. However, the worst case of the quick sort algorithm is of $O(n^2)$. Empirical studies have shown that the heap sort algorithm usually takes twice as long as the quick sort algorithm, but avoids the slight possibility of poor performance.

PRIORITY QUEUES (REVISITED)

Chapter 8 introduced priority queues. Recall that in a priority queue, customers or jobs with higher priorities are pushed to the front of the queue. Chapter 8 stated that we would discuss the implementation of priority queues after describing the heap sort algorithm. For simplicity, we assume that the priority of the queue elements is assigned using the relational operators.

In a heap, the largest element of the list is always the first element of the list. After removing the largest element of the list, the function `heapify` restores the heap in the list. To ensure that the largest element of the priority queue is always the first element of the queue, we can implement priority queues as heaps. We can write algorithms similar to the ones used in the function `heapify` to insert (`addQueue` operation) an element in the priority queue, and remove (`deleteQueue` operation) an element from the queue. The next two sections describe these algorithms.

Insert an Element in the Priority Queue

Assuming the priority queue is implemented as a heap, we perform the following steps:

1. Insert the new element in the first available position in the list. (This ensures that the array holding the list is a complete binary tree.)
2. After inserting the new element in the heap, the list may no longer be a heap. So to restore the heap:

    `while` (the parent of the new entry is smaller than the new entry)

    swap the parent with the new entry.

Notice that restoring the heap might result in moving the new entry to the root node.

Remove an Element from the Priority Queue

Assuming the priority queue is implemented as a heap, to remove the first element of the priority queue, we perform the following steps:

1. Copy the last element of the list into the first array position.
2. Reduce the length of the list by 1.
3. Restore the heap in the list.

The other operations for priority queues can be implemented in the same way as implemented for queues. We leave the implementation of the priority queues as an exercise for you.

PROGRAMMING EXAMPLE: ELECTION RESULTS

The presidential election for the student council of your local university is about to be held. Due to confidentiality, the chair of the election committee wants to computerize the voting. The chair is looking for someone to write a program to analyze the data and report the winner. Let us write a program to help the election committee.

The university has four major divisions, and each division has several departments. For the election, the four divisions are labeled as region 1, region 2, region 3, and region 4. Each department in each division handles its own voting and directly reports the votes received by each candidate to the election committee. The voting is reported in the following form:

```
firstName lastName regionNumber numberOfVotes
```

The election committee wants the output in the following tabular form:

```
          --------------------Election Results--------------------

                                         Votes
        Candidate Name    Region1  Region2  Region3  Region4   Total
        ----------------  -------  -------  -------  -------   ------
Buddy        Balto              0        0        0      272      272
Doctor       Doc               25       71      156       97      349
Ducky        Donald           110      158        0        0      268
     .
     .
     .

Winner: ???,  Votes Received: ???
Total votes polled: ???
```

The names of the candidates must be in alphabetical order in the output.

For this program, we assume that six candidates are seeking the student council's president post. This program can be enhanced to handle any number of candidates.

The data is provided in two files. One file, **candData.txt**, consists of the names of the candidates seeking the president's post. The names of the candidates in this file are in no particular order. In the second file, **voteData.txt**, each line consists of the voting results in the following form:

```
firstName lastName regionNumber numberOfVotes
```

That is, each line in the file **voteData.txt** consists of the candidate's name, the region number, and the number of votes received by the candidate in that region. There is one entry per line. For example, the input file containing the voting data looks like the following:

```
Ducky Donald 1 23
Peter Pluto 2 56
Doctor Doc 1 25
Peter Pluto 4 23
.
.
.
```

The first line indicates that **Ducky Donald** received **23** votes from region **1**.

Input   Two files: one containing the candidates' names, and the other containing the voting data as described previously

Output   The election results in a tabular form as described previously, and the winner

Problem Analysis and Algorithm Design

From the output, it is clear that the program must organize the voting data by region, and calculate the total votes both received by each candidate and polled for the election. Furthermore, the names of the candidates must appear in alphabetical order.

The main component of this program is a candidate. Therefore, first we design the **class candidateType** to implement a candidate object. Every candidate has a name and receives votes. Because there are four regions, we can use an array of four components. In Example 1-6 (Chapter 1), we designed the **class personType** to implement the name of a person. Recall that an object of the type **personType** can store the first name and the last name. Now that we have discussed operator overloading (see Chapter 2), we can redesign the **class personType** and define the relational operators so that the names of two people can be compared. We can also overload the assignment operator for easy assignment, and use the stream insertion and extraction operators for input/output. Because every candidate is a person, we derive the **class candidateType** from the **class personType**.

personType

The **class personType** implements the first name and last name of a person. Therefore, the **class personType** has two data members: a data member, **firstName**, to store the first name; and a data member, **lastName**, to store the last name. We declare these as **protected** so that the definition of the **class personType** can be easily extended to accommodate the requirements of a specific application needed to implement a person's name. The definition of the **class personType** is given next (see also Figure 10-65).

```cpp
#include <iostream>
#include <string>

using namespace std;

class personType
{
        //Overload the stream insertion and extraction operators.
    friend istream& operator>>(istream&, personType&);
    friend ostream& operator<<(ostream&, const personType&);

public:
    const personType& operator=(const personType&);
      //Overload the assignment operator.

    void setName(string first, string last);
      //Function to set firstName and lastName according to
      //the parameters.
      //Postcondition: firstName = first; lastName = last

    void getName(string& first, string& last);
      //Function to return firstName and lastName via the
      //parameters.
      //Postcondition: first = firstName; last = lastName

    personType(string first = "", string last = "");
      //constructor with parameters
      //Set firstName and lastName according to the parameters.
      //Postcondition: firstName = first; lastName = last


        //Overload the relational operators.
    bool operator==(const personType& right) const;
    bool operator!=(const personType& right) const;
    bool operator<=(const personType& right) const;
    bool operator<(const personType& right) const;
    bool operator>=(const personType& right) const;
    bool operator>(const personType& right) const;

protected:
    string firstName; //variable to store the first name
    string lastName;  //variable to store the last name
};
```

```
                              personType

#firstName: string
#lastName: string

+setName(string, string): void
+getName(string&, string&): void
+operator==(const personType&) const: bool
+operator!=(const personType&) const: bool
+operator<=(const personType&) const: bool
+operator<(const personType&) const: bool
+operator>=(const personType&) const: bool
+operator>(const personType&) const: bool
+operator=(const personType&) const personType&
+operator>>(istream&, personType&): istream&
+opeartor<<(ostream&, const personType&): ostream&
+personType(string = "", string = "")
```

Figure 10-65   UML diagram of the class `personType`

We give the definitions of the functions only to overload the operators **==** and **>>** and leave the others as an exercise for you. See Programming Exercise 11 at the end of this chapter.

```
        //Overload the operator ==
bool personType::operator==(const personType& right) const
{
   return(firstName == right.firstName
        && lastName == right.lastName);
}

        //Overload the stream extraction operator.
istream& operator>>(istream& isObject, personType& pName)
{
      isObject>>pName.firstName>>pName.lastName;

      return isObject;
}
```

candidateType

The main component of this program is the candidate, which is described and implemented in this section. Every candidate has a first and a last name and receives votes. Because there are four regions, we declare an array of four components to keep track of the votes for each region. We also need a data member to store the total number of votes received by each candidate. Because every candidate is a person and we have designed a class to implement the first and last name, we derive the `class candidateType` from the `class personType`. Because the data members of the `class personType` are `protected`, these data members can be accessed directly in the `class candidateType`.

There are six candidates. Therefore, we declare a list of six candidates of the type `candidateType`. This chapter defines and implements the `class orderedArrayListType` to implement a sorted list; we use this class to maintain the list of candidates. This list of candidates will be sorted and searched. Therefore, we must define (that is, overload) the assignment and relational operators for the `class candidateType` because these operators are used by the sorting and searching algorithms.

Data in the file containing the candidates' data consists of only the names of the candidates. Therefore, in addition to overloading the assignment operator so that the value of one object can be assigned to another object, we also overload the assignment operator for the `class candidateType`, so that only the name (of the `personType`) of the candidate can be assigned to a candidate object. That is, we overload the assignment operator twice: once for objects of the type `candidateType`, and another for objects of the types `candidateType` and `personType` (see also Figure 10-66).

```
#include <string>
#include "personType.h"

using namespace std;

const int noOfRegions = 4;

class candidateType: public personType
{
public:
   const candidateType& operator=(const candidateType&);
     //Overload the assignment operator for the objects of the
     //type candidateType.

   const candidateType& operator=(const personType&);
     //Overload the assignment operator for the objects so
     //that the value of an object of the type personType can
     //be assigned to an object of the type candidateType.

   void setVotes(int region, int votes);
     //Function to set the votes of a candidate for a
     //particular region.
     //Postcondition: The votes specified by the parameter votes
     //               are assigned to the region specified by the
     //               parameter region.

   void updateVotesByRegion(int region, int votes);
     //Function to update the votes of a candidate for a
     //particular region.
     //Postcondition: The votes specified by the parameter votes
     //               are added to the region specified by the
     //               parameter region.
```

```
   void calculateTotalVotes();
     //Function to calculate the total votes received by a
     //candidate.
     //Postcondition: The votes received in each region are added.

   int getTotalVotes();
     //Function to return the total votes received by a
     //candidate.
     //Postcondition: The total votes received by the candidate
     //               are returned.

   void printData() const;
     //Function to output the candidate's name, the votes
     //received in each region, and the total votes received.

   candidateType();
     //default constructor
     //Postcondition: Initialize the votes received in each
     //               region, and the total votes received, to zero.

     //Overload the relational operators.
   bool operator==(const candidateType& right) const;
   bool operator!=(const candidateType& right) const;
   bool operator<=(const candidateType& right) const;
   bool operator<(const candidateType& right) const;
   bool operator>=(const candidateType& right) const;
   bool operator>(const candidateType& right) const;

private:
   int votesByRegion[noOfRegions];
   int totalVotes;
};
```

```
                        candidateType

 -votesByRegion[]: int
 -totalVotes: int

 +operator=(const candidateType&): const candidateType&
 +operator=(const personType&): const candidateType&
 +updateVotesByRegion(int, int): void
 +setVotes(int, int): void
 +calculateTotalVotes(): void
 +getTotalVotes(): int
 +printData()const: void
 +operator==(const candidateType&) const: bool
 +operator!=(const candidateType&) const: bool
 +operator<=(const candidateType&) const: bool
 +operator<(const candidateType&) const: bool
 +operator>=(const candidateType&) const: bool
 +operator>(const candidateType&) const: bool
 +candidateType()
```

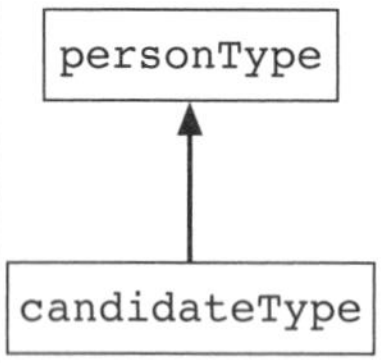

```
personType
```

```
candidateType
```

Figure 10-66 UML diagram of the `class candidateType`

The definitions of the member functions of the **class candidateType** are given next.

To set the votes of a particular region, the region number and the number of votes are passed as parameters to the function **setVotes**. Because an array index starts at 0, region 1 corresponds to the array component at position 0, and so on. Therefore, to set the value of the correct array component, 1 is subtracted from the region. The definition of the function **setVotes** is:

```
void candidateType::setVotes(int region, int votes)
{
      votesByRegion[region - 1] = votes;
}
```

To update the votes for a particular region, the region number and the number of votes for that region are passed as parameters. The votes are then added to the region's previous value. The definition of the function **updateVotesByRegion** is:

```
void candidateType::updateVotesByRegion(int region, int votes)
{
      votesByRegion[region - 1] = votesByRegion[region - 1]
                                   + votes;
}
```

The definitions of the functions calculateTotalVotes, getTotalVotes, printData, the default constructor, and getName are given next.

```
void candidateType::calculateTotalVotes()
{
    int i;

    totalVotes = 0;

    for(i = 0; i < noOfRegions; i++)
        totalVotes += votesByRegion[i];
}

int candidateType::getTotalVotes()
{
    return totalVotes;
}

void candidateType::printData() const
{
    cout<<left
        <<setw(10)<<firstName<<" "
        <<setw(10)<<lastName<<" ";

    cout<<right;

    for(int i = 0; i < noOfRegions; i++)
        cout<<setw(7)<<votesByRegion[i]<<"   ";
    cout<<setw(7)<<totalVotes<<endl;
}

candidateType::candidateType()
{
    for(int i = 0; i < noOfRegions; i++)
        votesByRegion[i] = 0;

    totalVotes = 0;
}
```

To overload the relational operators for the **class candidateType**, the names of the candidates are compared. For example, two candidates are the same if they have the same name. The definitions of these functions are similar to the definitions of the functions to overload the relational operators for the **class personType**. We give the definition of the function to overload the operator ==, and leave the others as an exercise for you. See Programming Exercise 11.

```
bool candidateType::operator==(const candidateType& right) const
{
    return(firstName == right.firstName
        && lastName == right.lastName);
}
```

The definitions of the functions to overload the assignment operators for the `class candidateType` are also left as an exercise for you; see Programming Exercise 11.

Main Program

Now that the `class candidateType` has been designed, we focus on designing the main program.

Because there are six candidates, we create a list, `candidateList`, containing six components of the type `candidateType`. The first thing that the program should do is read each candidate's name from the file `candData.txt` into the list `candidateList`. Next, we sort `candidateList`.

The next step is to process the voting data from the file `voteData.txt`, which holds the voting data. After processing the voting data, the program should calculate the total votes received by each candidate and then print the data as shown previously. Thus, the general algorithm is:

1. Read each candidate's name into `candidateList`.
2. Sort `candidateList`.
3. Process the voting data.
4. Calculate the total votes received by each candidate.
5. Print the results.

The following statement creates the object `candidateList` of the type `orderedArrayListType`:

```
orderedArrayListType<candidateType> candidateList(noOfCandidates);
```

Figure 10-67 shows the object `candidateList`. Every component of the array `list` is an object of the type `candidateType`.

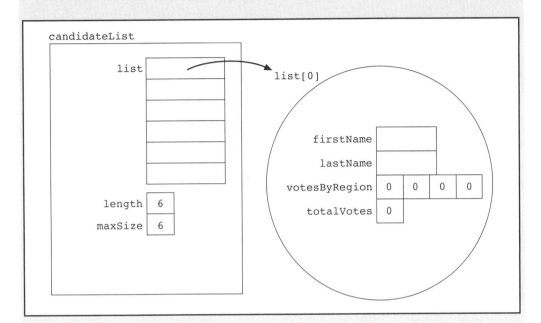

Figure 10-67   `candidateList`

In Figure 10-67, the array `votesByRegion` and the variable `totalVotes` are initialized to 0 by the default constructor of the `class candidateType`. To save space, whenever needed, we will draw the object `candidateList` as shown in Figure 10-68.

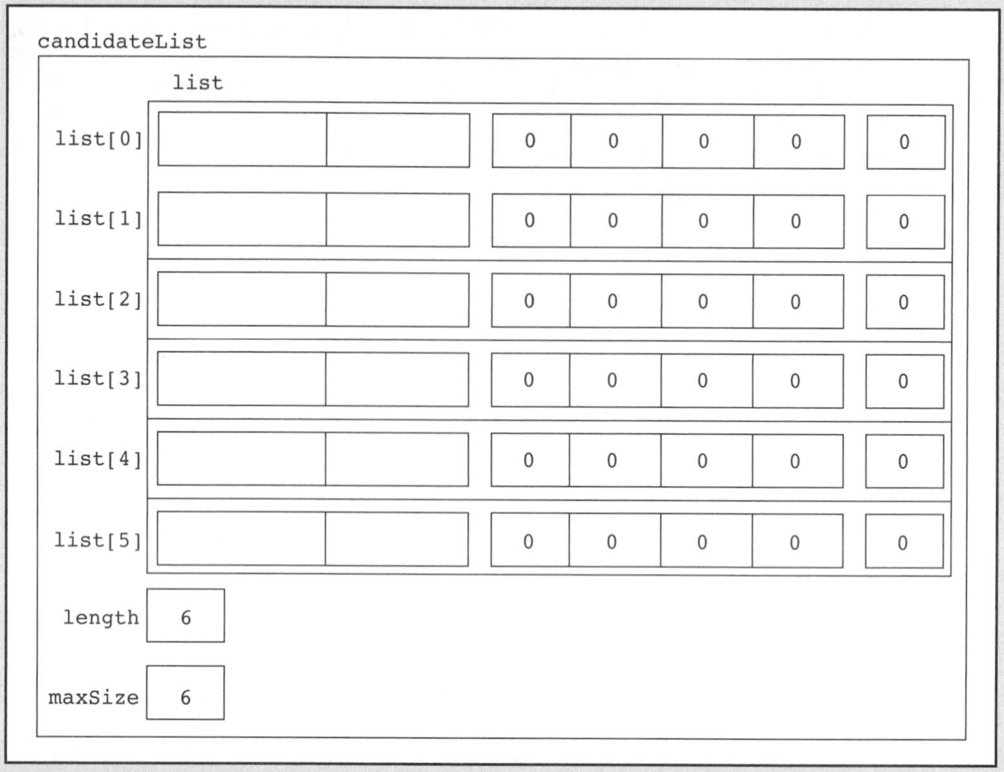

Figure 10-68   Object `candidateList`

fillNames

The first thing that the program must do is to read the candidates' names into
`candidateList`. Therefore, we write a function to accomplish this task. The file
`candData.txt` is opened in the function `main`. The name of the input file and
`candidateList` are therefore passed as parameters to the function `fillNames`.
Because the data member `list` of the object `candidateList` is a `protected` data
member, it cannot be accessed directly. We therefore create an object, `temp`, of the type
`candidateType`, to store the candidates' names, and use the function `insertAt`
(of the `class ArrayListType`) to store each candidate's name in the object
`candidateList`. The definition of the function `fillNames` is as follows:

```
void fillNames(ifstream& inFile,
               orderedArrayListType<candidateType>& cList)
{
    string firstN;
    string lastN;
    int i;

    candidateType temp;
```

```
    for(i = 0; i < noOfCandidates; i++)
    {
        inFile>>firstN>>lastN;
        temp.setName(firstN, lastN);
        cList.insertAt(i, temp);
    }
}
```

After a call to the function `fillNames`, Figure 10-69 shows the object `candidateList`.

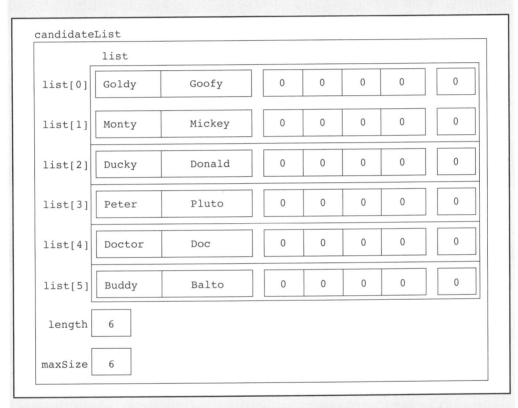

Figure 10-69   Object `candidateList` after a call to the function `fillNames`

Sort Names

After reading the candidates' names, next we sort the array `list` of the object `candidateList` using any of the (array-based) sorting algorithms discussed in this chapter. Because `candidateList` is an object of the type `orderedArrayListType`, all sorting algorithms discussed in this chapter are available to it. For illustration purposes, we use a selection sort. The following statement accomplishes this task:

```
candidateList.selectionSort();
```

After this statement executes, `candidateList` is as shown in Figure 10-70.

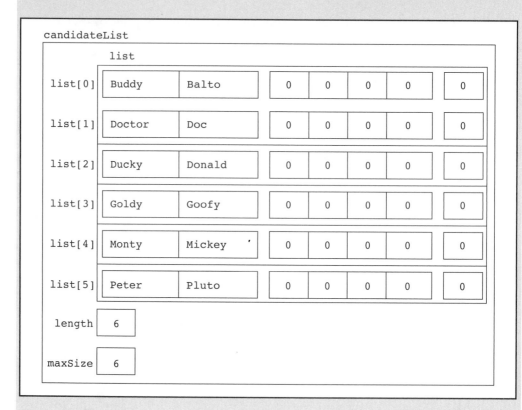

Figure 10-70 Object `candidateList` after the statement `candidateList.selectionSort();` executes

Process Voting Data

We now discuss how to process the voting data. Each entry in the file **voteData.txt** is of the form:

```
firstName lastName regionNumber numberOfVotes
```

After reading an entry from the file **voteData.txt**, we locate the row in the array `list` (of the object `candidateList`) corresponding to the specific candidate, and update the entry specified by `regionNumber`.

The component **votesByRegion** is a **private** data member of each component of the array **list**. Moreover, **list** is a **private** data member of **candidateList**. The only way that we can update the votes of a candidate is to make a copy of that candidate's record into a temporary object, update the object, and then copy the temporary object back into **list** by replacing the old value with new value of the temporary object. We use the member function **retrieveAt** to make a copy of the candidate whose votes need to be updated. After updating the temporary object, we use the member function **replaceAt** to copy the temporary object back into the list. Suppose the next entry read is:

```
Ducky Donald 2 35
```

This entry says that **Ducky Donald** received 35 votes from region 2. Suppose that before processing this entry, **candidateList** is as shown in Figure 10-71.

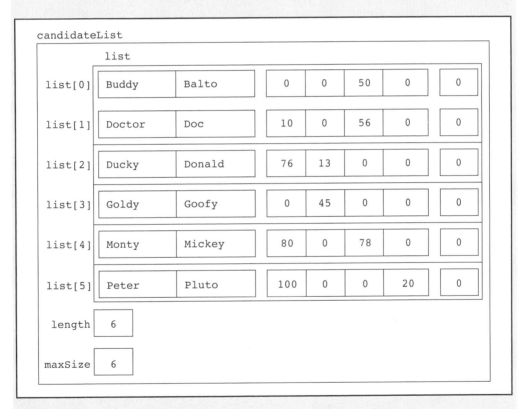

Figure 10-71   Object candidateList before processing the entry
Ducky Donald 2 35

We make a copy of the row corresponding to **Ducky Donald** (see Figure 10-72).

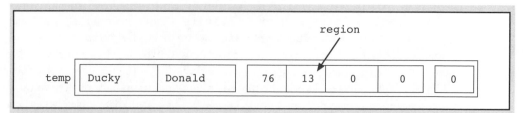

Figure 10-72 Object `temp`

Next, the following statement updates the voting data for region 2. (Here `region` = 2 and `votes` = 35.)

```
temp.updateVotesByRegion(region, votes);
```

After this statement executes, the object `temp` is as shown in Figure 10-73.

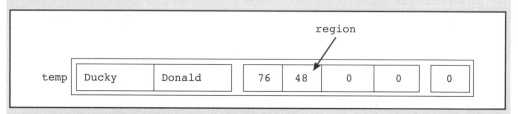

Figure 10-73 Object `temp` after the statement
`temp.updateVotesByRegion(region, votes);` executes

Now we copy the object `temp` into `list` (see Figure 10-74).

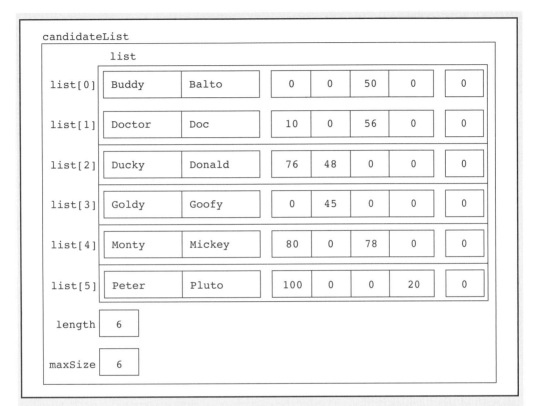

Figure 10-74   `candidateList` after copying `temp`

Because the member `list` of `candidateList` is sorted, we can use the binary search algorithm to find the row position in `list` corresponding to the candidate whose votes need to be updated. Also, the function `binarySearch` is a member of the **class** `orderedArrayListType`, so we can use this function to search the array `list`. We leave the definition of the function `processVotes` to process the voting data as an exercise for you (see Programming Exercise 11 at the end of this chapter).

Add Votes

After processing the voting data, the next step is to find the total votes received by each candidate. This is done by adding the votes received in each region. Now `votesByRegion` is a **private** data member of `candidateType` and `list` is a **protected** data member of `candidateList`. Therefore, to add the votes for each candidate, we use the `retrieveAt` function to make a temporary copy of each candidate's data, add the votes in the temporary object, and then copy the temporary object back into `candidateList`. The following function does this:

```
void addVotes(orderedArrayListType<candidateType>& cList)
{
    int i;

    candidateType temp;

    for(i = 0; i < noOfCandidates; i++)
    {
        cList.retrieveAt(i, temp);
        temp.calculateTotalVotes();
        cList.replaceAt(i, temp);
    }
}
```

Figure 10-75 shows **candidateList** after adding the votes for each candidate—that is, after a call to the function **addVotes**.

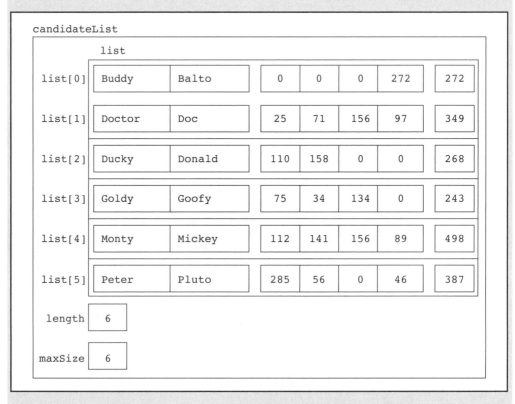

Figure 10-75 candidateList after a call to the function addVotes

Print Heading and Print Results

To complete the program, we include a function to print the heading, which is the first four lines of the output. The following function accomplishes this task:

```
void printHeading()
{
    cout<<"          --------------------Election Results---------"
        <<"-----------"<<endl<<endl;
    cout<<"                                        Votes"<<endl;
    cout<<"      Candidate Name      Region1  Region2  Region3  "
        <<"Region4    Total"<<endl;
    cout<<"--------------------    -------  -------   "
        <<"-------   -------  ------"<<endl;
}
```

We now describe the function `printResults`, which prints the results. Suppose that the variable `sumVotes` holds the total votes polled for the election, the variable `largestVotes` holds the largest number of votes received by a candidate, and the variable `winLoc` holds the index of the winning candidate in the array `list`. Further suppose that `temp` is an object of the type `candidateType`. The algorithm for this function is:

1. Initialize `sumVotes`, `largestVotes`, and `winLoc` to 0.
2. For each candidate,
   a. Retrieve the candidate's data into `temp`.
   b. Print the candidate's name and relevant data.
   c. Retrieve the total votes received by the candidate and update `sumVotes`.

   ```
   if(largestVotes < temp.getTotalVotes())
   {
       largestVotes = temp.getTotalVotes();
       winLoc = i;
   }
   ```
3. Output the final lines of the output.

We leave the definition of the function `printResults` to print the results as an exercise for you; see Programming Exercise 11 at the end of this chapter.

Program Listing (Main Program)

```
#include <iostream>
#include <string>
#include <fstream>
#include "candidateType.h"
#include "orderedArrayListType.h"

using namespace std;

const int noOfCandidates = 6;
```

```
void fillNames(ifstream& inFile,
               orderedArrayListType<candidateType>& cList);
void processVotes(ifstream& inFile,
                  orderedArrayListType<candidateType>& cList);
void addVotes(orderedArrayListType<candidateType>& cList);

void printHeading();

void printResults(orderedArrayListType<candidateType>& cList);

int main()
{
  orderedArrayListType<candidateType> candidateList(noOfCandidates);

  candidateType temp;

  ifstream inFile;

  inFile.open("a:\\candData.txt");

  fillNames(inFile, candidateList);

  candidateList.selectionSort();

  inFile.close();

  inFile.open("a:\\voteData.txt");

  processVotes(inFile, candidateList);

  addVotes(candidateList);

  printHeading();

  printResults(candidateList);

  return 0;
}
//Place the definitions of the functions fillNames, addVotes,
//and printHeading here. Also, write and place the definitions
//of the functions processVotes and printResults here.
```

Sample Output (After you have written the definitions of the functions of the classes
personType and candidateType, and of the functions processVotes and
printResults, and then run your program, it should produce the following output.
See Programming Exercise 11.)

```
-------------------Election Results-------------------

                                        Votes
   Candidate Name       Region1  Region2  Region3  Region4   Total
-------------------     -------  -------  -------  -------   ------
Buddy      Balto              0        0        0      272      272
Doctor     Doc               25       71      156       97      349
```

Ducky	Donald	110	158	0	0	268
Goldy	Goofy	75	34	134	0	243
Monty	Mickey	112	141	156	89	498
Peter	Pluto	285	56	0	46	387

Winner: Monty Mickey, Votes Received: 498

Total votes polled: 2017

Input Files

candData.txt

```
Goldy Goofy
Monty Mickey
Ducky Donald
Peter Pluto
Doctor Doc
Buddy Balto
```

voteData.txt

```
Goldy Goofy 2 34
Monty Mickey 1 56
Ducky Donald 2 56
Peter Pluto 1 78
Doctor Doc 4 29
Buddy Balto 4 78
Monty Mickey 2 63
Ducky Donald 1 23
Peter Pluto 2 56
Doctor Doc 1 25
Peter Pluto 4 23
Doctor Doc 4 12
Goldy Goofy 3 134
Buddy Balto 4 82
Monty Mickey 3 67
Ducky Donald 2 67
Doctor Doc 3 67
Buddy Balto 4 23
Monty Mickey 1 56
Ducky Donald 2 35
Peter Pluto 1 27
Doctor Doc 2 34
Goldy Goofy 1 75
Peter Pluto 4 23
Monty Mickey 4 89
Peter Pluto 1 23
Doctor Doc 3 89
Monty Mickey 3 89
Peter Pluto 1 67
```

```
Doctor Doc 2 37
Buddy Balto 4 89
Monty Mickey 2 78
Ducky Donald 1 87
Peter Pluto 1 90
Doctor Doc 4 56
```

QUICK REVIEW

1. The selection sort algorithm sorts a list by finding the smallest (or equivalently largest) element in the list, and then moving it to the beginning (or end) of the list.

2. For a list of length n, where $n > 0$, the selection sort algorithm makes $\frac{1}{2}n^2 - \frac{1}{2}n$ key comparisons and $3(n-1)$ item assignments.

3. For a list of length n, where $n > 0$, on average, the insertion sort algorithm makes $\frac{1}{4}n^2 + O(n)$ key comparisons and $\frac{1}{4}n^2 + O(n)$ item assignments.

4. Let L be a list of n distinct elements. Any sorting algorithm that sorts L by comparison of the keys only, in its worst case, makes at least $O(n*\log_2 n)$ key comparisons.

5. Both the quick sort and merge sort algorithms sort a list by partitioning the list.

6. To partition a list, the quick sort algorithm first selects an item from the list, called `pivot`. The algorithm then rearranges the elements so that the elements in one of the sublists are less than `pivot`, and the elements in the other sublist are greater than or equal to `pivot`.

7. In a quick sort, the sorting work is done in partitioning the list.

8. On average, the number of key comparisons in a quick sort is $O(n*\log_2 n)$. In the worst case, the number of key comparisons in a quick sort is $O(n^2)$.

9. The merge sort algorithm partitions the list by dividing it in the middle.

10. In a merge sort, the sorting work is done in merging the list.

11. The number of key comparisons in a merge sort is $O(n*\log_2 n)$.

12. A heap is a list in which each element contains a key, such that the key in the element at position k in the list is at least as large as the key in the element at position $2k + 1$ (if it exists), and $2k + 2$ (if it exists).

13. The first step in the heap sort algorithm is to convert the list into a heap, called `buildHeap`. After we convert the array into a heap, the sorting phase begins.

14. Suppose that L is a list of n elements, where $n > 0$. In the worst case, the number of key comparisons in the heap sort algorithm to sort L is $2n*\log_2 n + O(n)$. Also, in the worst case, the number of item assignments in the heap sort algorithm to sort L is $n*\log_2 n + O(n)$.

1. Assume the following list of keys:

   5, 18, 21, 10, 55, 20

   The first three keys are in order. To move 10 to its proper position using the insertion sort algorithm as described in this chapter, exactly how many key comparisons are executed?

2. Assume the following list of keys:

   7, 28, 31, 40, 5, 20

   The first four keys are in order. To move 5 to its proper position using the insertion sort algorithm as described in this chapter, exactly how many key comparisons are executed?

3. Assume the following list of keys:

   28, 18, 21, 10, 25, 30, 12, 71, 32, 58, 15

   This list is to be sorted using the insertion sort algorithm as described in this chapter for array-based lists. Show the resulting list after 6 passes of the sorting phase—that is, after 6 iterations of the for loop.

4. Recall the insertion sort algorithm (contiguous version) as discussed in this chapter. Assume the following list of keys:

   18, 8, 11, 9, 15, 20, 32, 61, 22, 48, 75, 83, 35, 3

   Exactly how many key comparisons are executed to sort this list using the insertion sort algorithm?

5. Both the merge sort and quick sort algorithms sort a list by partitioning the list. Explain how the merge sort algorithm differs from the quick sort algorithm in partitioning the list.

6. Assume the following list of keys:

   16, 38, 54, 80, 22, 65, 55, 48, 64, 95, 5, 100, 58, 25, 36

   This list is to be sorted using the quick sort algorithm as discussed in this chapter. Use pivot as the middle element of the list.

   a. Give the resulting list after one call to the partition procedure.

   b. Give the resulting list after two calls to the partition procedure.

7. Assume the following list of keys:

   18, 40, 16, 82, 64, 67, 57, 50, 37, 47, 72, 14, 17, 27, 35

   This list is to be sorted using the quick sort algorithm as discussed in this chapter. Use pivot as the median of the first, last, and middle elements of the list.

   a. What is pivot?

   b. Give the resulting list after one call to the partition procedure.

10

8. Use the function `buildHeap` as given in this chapter to convert the following array into a heap. Show the final form of the array.

   47, 78, 81, 52, 50, 82, 58, 42, 65, 80, 92, 53, 63, 87, 95, 59, 34, 37, 7, 20

9. Suppose that the following list was created by the function `buildHeap` during the heap creation phase of the heap sort algorithm:

   100, 85, 94, 47, 72, 82, 76, 30, 20, 60, 65, 50, 45, 17, 35, 14, 28, 5

   Show the resulting array after two passes of the heap sort algorithm. (Use the `heapify` function as given in this chapter.) Exactly how many key comparisons are executed during the first pass?

10. Write the definition of the `class orderedArrayListType` that implements the searching (described in Chapter 9) and sorting algorithms for array-based lists as discussed in this chapter.

11. Write the definition of the `class orderedLinkedListType` that implements the searching (described in Chapter 5) and sorting algorithms for linked lists as discussed in this chapter.

PROGRAMMING EXERCISES

1. Write and test a version of the selection sort algorithm for linked lists.

2. Write a program to test the insertion sort algorithm for array-based lists as given in this chapter.

3. Write a program to test the insertion sort algorithm for linked lists as given in this chapter.

4. Write a program to test the quick sort algorithm for array-based lists as given in this chapter.

5. Write and test a version of the quick sort algorithm for linked lists.

6. **(C. A. R. Hoare)** Let L be a list of size n. The quick sort algorithm can be used to find the kth smallest item in L, where $0 < k < n - 1$, without completely sorting L. Write and implement a C++ function, `kThSmallestItem`, that uses a version of the quick sort algorithm to determine the kth smallest item in L without completely sorting L.

7. Sort an array of 10,000 elements using the quick sort algorithm as follows:

   a. Sort the array using `pivot` as the middle element of the array.

   b. Sort the array using `pivot` as the median of the first, last, and middle elements of the array.

   c. Sort the array using `pivot` as the middle element of the array. However, when the size of any sublist reduces to less than 20, sort the sublist using an insertion sort.

    d. Sort the array using **pivot** as the median of the first, last, and middle elements of the array. When the size of any sublist reduces to less than 20, sort the sublist using an insertion sort.

    e. Calculate and print the CPU time for each of the preceding four steps.

       To find the current CPU time, declare a variable, say **x**, of the type **clock_t**. The statement **x = clock();** stores the current CPU time in **x**. You can check the current CPU time before and after a particular phase of a program. Then to find the CPU time for that particular phase of the program, subtract the before time from the after time. Moreover, you must include the header file **ctime** to use the data type **clock_t** and the function **clock**. Use a random generator to initially fill the array.

8. Write a program to test the merge sort algorithm for linked lists as given in this chapter.

9. Write a program to test the heap sort algorithm for linked lists as given in this chapter.

10. a. Write the definition of the class template to define the priority queues, as discussed in this chapter, as an abstract data type (ADT).

    b. Write the definitions of the function templates to implement the operations of the priority queues as defined in (a).

    c. Write a program to test various operations of the priority queues.

11. a. Write the definitions of the functions of the **class personType**, of the Programming Example Election Results, not given in the programming example.

    b. Write the definitions of the functions of the **class candidateType**, of the Programming Example Election Results, not given in the programming example.

    c. Write the definitions of the functions **processVotes** and **printResults** of the Programming Example Election Results.

    d. After completing a, b, and c, write a program to produce the output shown in the Sample Run of the Programming Example Election Results.

12. In the Programming Example Election Results, the **class candidateType** contains the function **calculateTotalVotes**. After processing the voting data, this function calculates the total number of votes received by a candidate. The function **updateVotesByRegion** (of the **class candidateType**) updates only the number of votes for a particular region. Modify the definition of this function so that it also updates the total number of votes received by the candidate. By doing so, the function **addVotes** in the main program is no longer needed. Modify and run your program with the modified definition of the function **updateVotesByRegion**.

10

13. In the Programming Example Election Results, the object `candidateList` of the type `orderedArrayListType` is declared to process the voting data. The operations of inserting a candidate's data and updating and retrieving the votes were somewhat complicated. To update the candidate's votes, we copied that candidate's data from `candidateList` into a temporary object of the type `candidateType`, updated the temporary object, and then replaced the candidate's data with the temporary object. This is due to the fact that the data member's `list` is a `protected` member of `candidateList`, and each component of `list` is a `private` data member. In this exercise, you are to modify the Programming Example Election Results to simplify accessing a candidate's data as follows: derive the `class candidateListType` from the `class orderedArrayListType`.

```
class candidateListType: public orderedArrayListType<candidateType>
{
public:
    candidateListType();
      //default constructor
    candidateListType(int size);
      //constructor
    void processVotes(string fName, string lName, int region,
                      int votes);
      //Function to update the number of votes for a
      //particular candidate for a particular region.
      //Postcondition: The name of the candidate, the region
      //               number, and the number of votes are
      //               passed as parameters.
    void addVotes();
      //Function to find the total number of votes
      //received by each candidate.
    void printResult();
      //Function to output the voting data.
};
```

Because the `class candidateListType` is derived from the `class orderedArrayListType`, and `list` is a `protected` data member of the `class orderedArrayListType` (inherited from the `class arrayListType`), `list` can be directly accessed by any member of the `class candidateListType`.

Write the definitions of the member functions of the `class candidateListType`. Rewrite and run your program using the `class candidateListType`.

BINARY TREES

When data is being organized, a programmer's highest priority is to organize it in such a way that item insertion, deletion, and lookups (searches) are fast. You have already seen how to store and process data in an array. Because an array is a random access data structure, if the data is properly organized (say, sorted), then we can use a search algorithm, such as a binary search, to effectively find and retrieve an item from the list. However, we know that storing data in an array has its limitations. For example, item insertion (especially if the array is sorted) and item deletion can be very time consuming, especially if the list size is very large, because each of these operations requires data movement. To speed up item insertion and deletion, we used linked lists. Item insertion and deletion in a linked list do not require any data movement; we simply adjust some of the pointers in the list. However, one of the drawbacks of linked lists is that they must be processed sequentially. That is, to insert or delete an item, or simply search the list for a particular item, we must begin our search at the first node in the list. As you know, a sequential search is good only for very small lists because the average search length of a sequential search is half the size of the list.

BINARY TREES

This chapter discusses how to dynamically organize data so that item insertion, deletion, and lookups are more efficient.

We first introduce some definitions to facilitate our discussion.

Definition: A **binary tree**, T, is either empty or such that:

  i. T has a special node called the **root** node;

  ii. T has two sets of nodes, L_T and R_T, called the left subtree and right subtree of T, respectively; and

  iii. L_T and R_T are binary trees.

A binary tree can be shown pictorially. Suppose that T is a binary tree with the root node A. Let L_A denote the left subtree of A and R_A denote the right subtree of A. Now L_A and R_A are binary trees. Suppose that B is the root node of L_A and C is the root node of R_A. B is called the **left child** of A; C is called the **right child** of A. Moreover, A is called the **parent** of B and C.

In the diagram of a binary tree, each node of the binary tree is represented as a circle and the circle is labeled by the node. The root node of the binary tree is drawn at the top. The left child of the root node (if any) is drawn below and to the left of the root node. Similarly, the right child of the root node (if any) is drawn below and to the right of the root node. Children are connected to the parent by an *arrow* from the parent to the child. An arrow is usually called a **directed edge** or a **directed branch** (or simply a **branch**). Because the root node, B, of L_A is already drawn, we apply the same procedure to draw the remaining parts of L_A. R_A is drawn similarly. If a node has no left child, for example, when we draw an arrow from the node to the left we end the arrow with three lines. That is, three lines at the end of an arrow indicate that the subtree is empty.

The diagram in Figure 11-1 is an example of a binary tree. The root node of this binary tree is A. The left subtree of the root node, which we denote by L_A, is the set L_A = {B, D, E, G} and the right subtree of the root node, which we denote by R_A, is the set R_A = {C, F, H}. The root node of the left subtree of A—that is, the root node of L_A—is node B. The root node of R_A is C, and so on. Clearly, L_A and R_A are binary trees. Because three lines at the end of an arrow mean that the subtree is empty, it follows that the left subtree of D is empty.

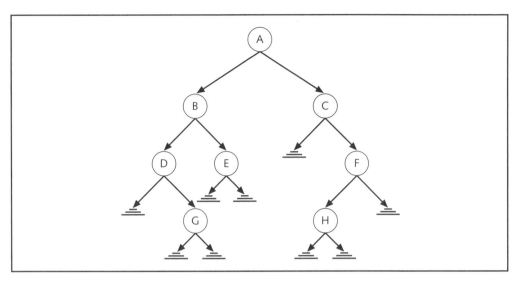

Figure 11-1 Binary tree

In Figure 11-1, the left child of A is B and the right child of A is C. Similarly, for node F, the left child is H and node F has no right child.

Examples 11-1 to 11-5 show nonempty binary trees.

Example 11-1

This example shows a binary tree with one node. See Figure 11-2.

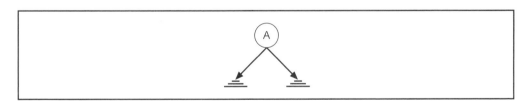

Figure 11-2 Binary tree with one node

In the binary tree of Figure 11-2:

The root node of the binary tree = A

L_A = empty

R_A = empty

Example 11-2

This example shows a binary tree with two nodes. See Figure 11-3.

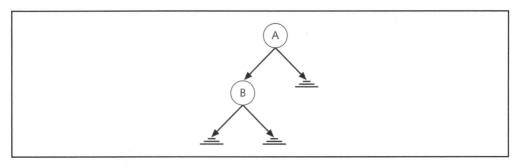

Figure 11-3   Binary tree with two nodes; the right subtree of the root node is empty

In the binary tree of Figure 11-3:

The root node of the binary tree = A

L_A = {B}

R_A = empty

The root node of L_A = B

L_B = empty

R_B = empty

Example 11-3

This example shows a binary tree with two nodes. See Figure 11-4.

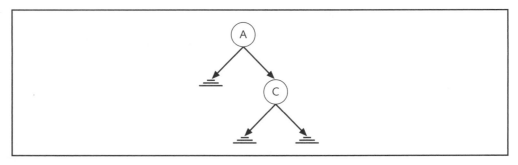

Figure 11-4   Binary tree with two nodes; the left subtree of the root node is empty

In the binary tree of Figure 11-4:

The root node of the binary tree = A.

L_A = empty

R_A = {C}

The root node of R_A = C.

L_C = empty

R_C = empty

Example 11-4

This example shows a binary tree with three nodes. See Figure 11-5.

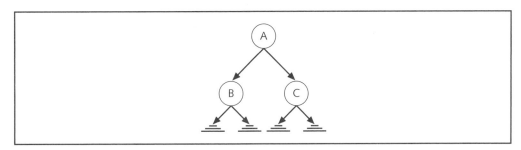

Figure 11-5 Binary tree with three nodes

In the binary tree of Figure 11-5:

The root node of the binary tree = A.

L_A = {B}

R_A = {C}

The root node of L_A = B.

L_B = empty

R_B = empty

The root node of R_A = C.

L_C = empty

R_C = empty

Example 11-5

This example shows other cases of nonempty binary trees with three nodes. See Figure 11-6.

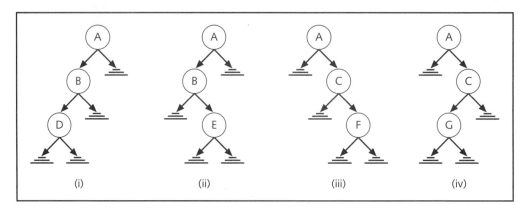

Figure 11-6 Various binary trees with three nodes

As you can see from the preceding examples, every node in a binary tree has at most two children. Thus, every node, other than storing its own information, must keep track of its left subtree and right subtree. This implies that every node has two pointers, say `llink` and `rlink`. The pointer `llink` points to the root node of the left subtree; the pointer `rlink` points to the root node of the right subtree.

The following `struct` defines the node of a binary tree:

```
template<class elemType>
struct nodeType
{
    elemType info;
    nodeType<elemType> *llink;
    nodeType<elemType> *rlink;
};
```

From the definition of the node it is clear that for each node:

- The data is stored in `info`.

- The pointer to the left child is stored in `llink`.

- The pointer to the right child is stored in `rlink`.

Furthermore, the pointer to the root node of a binary tree is stored outside the binary tree in a pointer variable, usually called the **root**, of the type `nodeType`. Thus, in general, a binary tree looks like the diagram in Figure 11-7.

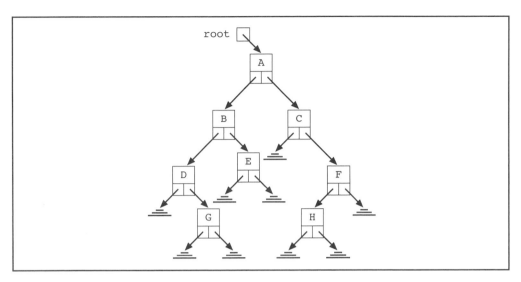

Figure 11-7   Binary tree

For simplicity, we will continue to draw binary trees as before. That is, we will use circles to represent nodes, and left and right arrows to represent links. As before, three lines at the end of an arrow mean that the subtree is empty.

Before we leave this section, let us define a few more terms.

A node in a binary tree is called a **leaf** if it has no left and right children. Let U and V be two nodes in the binary tree T. U is called the **parent** of V if there is a branch from U to V. A **path** from a node X to a node Y in a binary tree is a sequence of nodes $X_0, X_1, ..., X_n$ such that

   i. $X = X_0, X_n = Y$

  ii. X_{i-1} is the parent of X_i for all $i = 1, 2, ..., n$. That is, there is a branch from X_0 to X_1, X_1 to $X_2, ..., X_{i-1}$ to $X_i, ..., X_{n-1}$ to X_n.

Because the branches go only from a parent to its children, from the previous discussion it is clear that in a binary tree, there is a unique path from the root to every node in the binary tree.

Definition: The **level of a node** in a binary tree is the number of branches on the path from the root to the node.

Clearly, the level of the root node of a binary tree is 0, and the level of the children of the root node is 1.

Definition: The **height of a binary tree** is the number of nodes on the longest path from the root to a leaf.

Suppose that a pointer, **p**, to the root node of a binary tree is given. We next describe the C++ function **height** to find the height of the binary tree. The pointer to the root node is passed as a parameter to the function **height**.

If the binary tree is empty, then **height** is 0. Suppose that the binary tree is nonempty. To find the height of the binary tree, we first find the height of the left subtree and the height of the right subtree. We then take the maximum of these two heights and add 1 to find the height of the binary tree. To find the height of the left (right) subtree, we apply the same procedure because the left (right) subtree is a binary tree. Therefore, the general algorithm to find the height of a binary tree is as follows (suppose **height(p)** denotes the height of the binary tree with root **p**):

```
if(p is NULL)
   height(p) = 0
else
   height(p) = 1 + max(height(p->llink), height(p->rlink))
```

Clearly, this is a recursive algorithm. The following function implements this algorithm:

```
template<class elemType>
int height(nodeType<elemType> *p)
{
    if(p == NULL)
       return 0;
    else
       return 1 + max(height(p->llink), height(p->rlink));
}
```

The definition of the function **height** uses the function **max** to determine the larger of two integers. The function **max** can be easily implemented.

Similarly, we can implement algorithms to find the number of nodes and number of leaves in a binary tree.

Copy Tree

One useful operation on binary trees is to make an identical copy of a binary tree. A binary tree is a dynamic data structure; that is, memory for its nodes is allocated and deallocated during program execution. Therefore, if we use just the value of the pointer of the root node to make a copy of a binary tree, we get a shallow copy of the data. To make an identical copy of a binary tree, we need to create as many nodes as there are in the binary tree to be copied. Moreover, in the copied tree, these nodes must appear in the same order as they are in the original binary tree.

Given the pointer to the root node of a binary tree, we next describe the function **copyTree**, which makes a copy of a given binary tree. This function is also useful in implementing the copy constructor and overloading the assignment operator, as described later in this chapter (see the section "Implementing Binary Trees").

```
template<class elemType>
void copyTree(nodeType<elemType>* &copiedTreeRoot,
              nodeType<elemType>* otherTreeRoot)
{
    if(otherTreeRoot == NULL)
       copiedTreeRoot = NULL;
    else
    {
       copiedTreeRoot = new nodeType<elemType>;
       copiedTreeRoot->info = otherTreeRoot->info;
       copyTree(copiedTreeRoot->llink, otherTreeRoot->llink);
       copyTree(copiedTreeRoot->rlink, otherTreeRoot->rlink);
    }
}//end copyTree
```

We use the function `copyTree` when we overload the assignment operator and implement the copy constructor.

BINARY TREE TRAVERSAL

The item insertion, deletion, and lookup operations require that the binary tree be traversed. Thus, the most common operation performed on a binary tree is to traverse the binary tree, or visit each node of the binary tree. As you can see from the diagram of a binary tree (for example, Figure 11-7), the traversal must start at the root node because there is a pointer to the root node. For each node, we have two choices:

- Visit the node first.

- Visit the subtrees first.

These choices lead to three different traversals of a binary tree, as described in the ensuing three sections:

- Inorder traversal

- Preorder traversal

- Postorder traversal

Inorder Traversal

In an inorder traversal, the binary tree is traversed as follows:

1. Traverse the left subtree.

2. Visit the node.

3. Traverse the right subtree.

Preorder Traversal

In a preorder traversal, the binary tree is traversed as follows:

1. Visit the node.

2. Traverse the left subtree.

3. Traverse the right subtree.

Postorder Traversal

In a postorder traversal, the binary tree is traversed as follows:

1. Traverse the left subtree.

2. Traverse the right subtree.

3. Visit the node.

Clearly, each of these traversal algorithms is recursive.

The listing of the nodes produced by the inorder traversal of a binary tree is called the **inorder sequence**. The listing of the nodes produced by the preorder traversal of a binary tree is called the **preorder sequence**. The listing of the nodes produced by the postorder traversal of a binary tree is called the **postorder sequence**.

Before giving the C++ code for each of these traversals, let us illustrate the inorder traversal of the binary tree in Figure 11-8. For simplicity, we assume that visiting a node means to output the data stored in the node. The section "Binary Tree Traversal and Functions as Parameters," located later in this chapter, explains how to modify the binary tree traversal algorithms so that by using a function, the user can specify the action to be performed on a node when the node is visited.

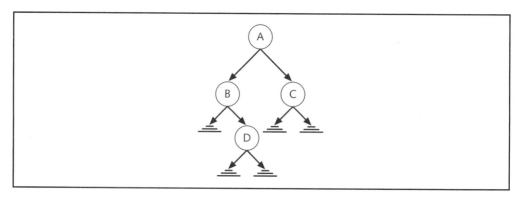

Figure 11-8 Binary tree for an inorder traversal

A pointer to the binary tree in Figure 11-8 is stored in the pointer variable `root` (which points to the node with info A). Therefore, we start the traversal at A.

1. Traverse the left subtree of A; that is, traverse $L_A = \{B, D\}$.

2. Visit A.

3. Traverse the right subtree of A; that is, traverse $R_A = \{C\}$.

Now we cannot do Step 2 until we have finished Step 1.

1. Traverse the left subtree of A; that is, traverse $L_A = \{B, D\}$. Now L_A is a binary tree with the root node B. Because L_A is a binary tree, we apply the inorder traversal criteria to L_A.

    1.1 Traverse the left subtree of B; that is, traverse L_B = empty.

    1.2 Visit B.

    1.3 Traverse the right subtree of B; that is, traverse $R_B = \{D\}$.

As before, first we complete Step 1.1 before going to Step 1.2.

1.1. Because the left subtree of B is empty, there is nothing to traverse. Step 1.1 is completed, so we proceed to Step 1.2.

1.2. Visit B. That is, output B on an output device. Clearly, the first node printed is B. This completes Step 1.2, so we proceed to Step 1.3.

1.3. Traverse the right subtree of B; that is, traverse $R_B = \{D\}$. Now R_B is a binary tree with the root node D. Because R_B is a binary tree, we apply the inorder traversal criteria to R_B.

    1.3.1. Traverse the left subtree of D; that is, traverse L_D = empty.

    1.3.2. Visit D.

    1.3.3. Traverse the right subtree of D; that is, traverse R_D = empty.

1.3.1. Because the left subtree of D is empty, there is nothing to traverse. Step 1.3.1 is completed, so we proceed to Step 1.3.2.

1.3.2. Visit D. That is, output D on an output device. This completes Step 1.3.2, so we proceed to Step 1.3.3.

1.3.3. Because the right subtree of D is empty, there is nothing to traverse. Step 1.3.3 is completed.

This completes Step 1.3. Because Steps 1.1, 1.2, and 1.3 are completed, Step 1 is completed, and so we go to Step 2.

2. Visit A. That is, output A on an output device. This completes Step 2, so we proceed to Step 3.

11

3. Traverse the right subtree of A; that is, traverse $R_A = \{C\}$. Now R_A is a binary tree with the root node C. Because R_A is a binary tree, we apply the inorder traversal criteria to R_A.

3.1 Traverse the left subtree of C; that is, traverse L_C = empty.

3.2 Visit C.

3.3 Traverse the right subtree of C; that is, traverse R_C = empty.

3.1. Because the left subtree of C is empty, there is nothing to traverse. Step 3.1 is completed, so we proceed to Step 3.2.

3.2. Visit C. That is, output C on an output device. This completes Step 3.2, so we proceed to Step 3.3.

3.3. Because the right subtree of C is empty, there is nothing to traverse. Step 3.3 is completed.

This completes Step 3, which in turn completes the traversal of the binary tree.

Clearly, the inorder traversal of the previous binary tree outputs the nodes in the following order:

Inorder sequence: B D A C

Similarly, the preorder and postorder traversals output the nodes in the following order:

Preorder sequence: A B D C

Postorder sequence: D B C A

As you can see from the walk-through of the inorder traversal, after visiting the left subtree of a node we must come back to the node itself. The links are in only one direction; that is, the parent node points to the left and right children, but there is no pointer from each child to the parent. Therefore, before going to a child, we must somehow save a pointer to the parent node. A convenient way to do this is to write a recursive inorder function; this is because in a recursive call, after completing a particular call, the control goes back to the caller. (Later we discuss how to write nonrecursive traversal functions.) The recursive definition of the function to implement the inorder traversal algorithm is:

```
template<class elemType>
void inorder(nodeType<elemType> *p)
{
    if(p != NULL)
    {
        inorder(p->llink);
        cout<<p->info<<" ";
        inorder(p->rlink);
    }
}
```

To do the inorder traversal of a binary tree, the root node of the binary tree is passed as a parameter to the function `inorder`. For example, if the root points to the root node of the binary tree, a call to the function `inorder` is:

```
inorder(root);
```

Similarly, we can write the functions to implement the preorder and postorder traversals. The definitions of these functions are given next.

```
template<class elemType>
void preorder(nodeType<elemType> *p)
{
    if(p != NULL)
    {
        cout<<p->info<<" ";
        preorder(p->llink);
        preorder(p->rlink);
    }
}

template<class elemType>
void postorder(nodeType<elemType> *p)
{
    if(p != NULL)
    {
        postorder(p->llink);
        postorder(p->rlink);
        cout<<p->info<<" ";
    }
}
```

Implementing Binary Trees

The preceding sections described various operations that can be performed on a binary tree, as well as the functions to implement these operations. This section describes binary trees as an ADT. Before designing the class to implement a binary tree as an ADT, let us list various operations that are typically performed on a binary tree.

1. Determine whether the binary tree is empty.

2. Search the binary tree for a particular item.

3. Insert an item in the binary tree.

4. Delete an item from the binary tree.

5. Find the height of the binary tree.

6. Find the number of nodes in the binary tree.

7. Find the number of leaves in the binary tree.

11

8. Traverse the binary tree.

9. Copy the binary tree.

The item search, insertion, and deletion operations all require the binary tree to be traversed. However, because the nodes of a binary tree are in no particular order, these algorithms are not very efficient on arbitrary binary trees. That is, no criteria exist to guide the search on these binary trees, as we will see in the next section. Therefore, we will discuss these algorithms when we discuss special types of binary trees.

Other than the search, insertion, and deletion operations, the following class defines binary trees as an ADT. The definition of the node is the same as before. However, for the sake of completeness and easy reference, we give the definition of the node followed by the definition of the class:

```
    //Definition of the node
template<class elemType>
struct nodeType
{
    elemType info;
    nodeType<elemType> *llink;
    nodeType<elemType> *rlink;
};


    //Definition of the class
template<class elemType>
class binaryTreeType
{
public:
    const binaryTreeType<elemType>& operator=
                (const binaryTreeType<elemType>&);
    //Overload the assignment operator.
    bool isEmpty();
    //Function to determine whether the binary tree is empty.
    //Postcondition: Returns true if the binary tree is empty;
    //               otherwise, returns false.
    void inorderTraversal();
    //Function to do an inorder traversal of the binary tree.
    //Postcondition: The nodes of the binary tree are output
    //               in the inorder sequence.
    void preorderTraversal();
    //Function to do a preorder traversal of the binary tree.
    //Postcondition: The nodes of the binary tree are output
    //               in the preorder sequence.
    void postorderTraversal();
    //Function to do a postorder traversal of the binary tree.
    //Postcondition: The nodes of the binary tree are output
    //               in the postorder sequence.
```

```
   int treeHeight();
     //Function to determine the height of the binary tree.
     //Postcondition: The height of the binary tree is returned.
   int treeNodeCount();
     //Function to determine the number of nodes in the
     //binary tree.
     //Postcondition: The number of nodes in the binary tree
     //               is returned.
   int treeLeavesCount();
     //Function to determine the number of leaves in the
     //binary tree.
     //Postcondition: The number of leaves in the binary tree
     //               is returned.
   void destroyTree();
     //Deallocates the memory space occupied by the binary tree.
     //Postcondition: root = NULL

   binaryTreeType(const binaryTreeType<elemType>& otherTree);
     //copy constructor

   binaryTreeType();
     //default constructor

   ~binaryTreeType();
     //destructor

protected:
   nodeType<elemType> *root;

private:
   void copyTree(nodeType<elemType>* &copiedTreeRoot,
                 nodeType<elemType>* otherTreeRoot);
     //Function to make a copy of the binary tree to
     //which otherTreeRoot points.
     //Postcondition: The pointer copiedTreeRoot points to
     //               the root of the copied binary tree.

   void destroy(nodeType<elemType>* &p);
     //Function to destroy the binary tree to which p points.
     //Postcondition: The nodes of the binary tree to which
     //               p points are deallocated; p = NULL.

   void inorder(nodeType<elemType> *p);
     //Function to do an inorder traversal of the binary
     //tree to which p points.
     //Postcondition: The nodes of the binary tree to which p
     //               points are output in the inorder sequence.
```

11

```
void preorder(nodeType<elemType> *p);
  //Function to do a preorder traversal of the binary
  //tree to which p points.
  //Postcondition: The nodes of the binary tree to which p
  //               points are output in the preorder sequence.
void postorder(nodeType<elemType> *p);
  //Function to do a postorder traversal of the binary
  //tree to which p points.
  //Postcondition: The nodes of the binary tree to which p
  //               points are output in the postorder sequence.

int height(nodeType<elemType> *p);
  //Function to determine the height of the binary tree
  //to which p points.
  //Postcondition: The height of the binary tree to which p
  //               points is returned.

int max(int x, int y);
  //Function to determine the larger of x and y.
  //Postcondition: The larger of x and y is returned.

int nodeCount(nodeType<elemType> *p);
  //Function to determine the number of nodes in the binary
  //tree to which p points.
  //Postcondition: The number of nodes in the binary tree
  //               to which p points is returned.

int leavesCount(nodeType<elemType> *p);
  //Function to determine the number of leaves in the binary
  //tree to which p points.
  //Postcondition: The number of leaves in the binary tree
  //               to which p points is returned.
};
```

Notice that the definition of the **class binaryTreeType** contains the statement to overload the assignment operator, copy constructor, and destructor. This is because the **class binaryTreeType** contains pointer data members. Recall that for classes with pointer data members, the three things that we must do are explicitly overload the assignment operator, include the copy constructor, and include the destructor.

The definition of the **class binaryTreeType** contains several member functions that are **private** members of the class. These functions are used to implement the **public** member functions of the class and the user need not know of their existence. For example, to do an inorder traversal, the function **inorderTraversal** calls the function **inorder** and passes the pointer **root** as a parameter to this function. Suppose that you have the following statement:

```
binaryTreeType<int> myTree;
```

The following statement does an inorder traversal of `myTree`:

```
myTree.inorderTraversal();
```

Also, note that in the definition of the **class binaryTreeType**, the pointer `root` is declared as a **protected** member so that we can later derive special binary trees.

Next, we give the definitions of the member functions of the **class binaryTreeType**.

The binary tree is empty if `root` is NULL. So the definition of the function `isEmpty` is:

```
template<class elemType>
bool binaryTreeType<elemType>::isEmpty()
{
    return (root == NULL);
}
```

The default constructor initializes the binary tree to an empty state; that is, it sets the pointer `root` to NULL. Therefore, the definition of the default constructor is:

```
template<class elemType>
binaryTreeType<elemType>::binaryTreeType()
{
    root = NULL;
}
```

The definitions of the other functions are:

```
template<class elemType>
void binaryTreeType<elemType>::inorderTraversal()
{
    inorder(root);
}

template<class elemType>
void binaryTreeType<elemType>::preorderTraversal()
{
    preorder(root);
}

template<class elemType>
void binaryTreeType<elemType>::postorderTraversal()
{
    postorder(root);
}

template<class elemType>
int binaryTreeType<elemType>::treeHeight()
{
    return height(root);
}
```

11

```cpp
template<class elemType>
int binaryTreeType<elemType>::treeNodeCount()
{
    return nodeCount(root);
}

template<class elemType>
int binaryTreeType<elemType>::treeLeavesCount()
{
    return leavesCount(root);
}

template<class elemType>
void binaryTreeType<elemType>::inorder(nodeType<elemType> *p)
{
    if(p != NULL)
    {
        inorder(p->llink);
        cout<<p->info<<" ";
        inorder(p->rlink);
    }
}

template<class elemType>
void binaryTreeType<elemType>::preorder(nodeType<elemType> *p)
{
    if(p != NULL)
    {
        cout<<p->info<<" ";
        preorder(p->llink);
        preorder(p->rlink);
    }
}

template<class elemType>
void binaryTreeType<elemType>::postorder(nodeType<elemType> *p)
{
    if(p != NULL)
    {
        postorder(p->llink);
        postorder(p->rlink);
        cout<<p->info<<" ";
    }
}
```

```
template<class elemType>
int binaryTreeType<elemType>::height(nodeType<elemType> *p)
{
    if(p == NULL)
        return 0;
    else
        return 1 + max(height(p->llink), height(p->rlink));
}

template<class elemType>
int binaryTreeType<elemType>::max(int x, int y)
{
    if(x >= y)
        return x;
    else
        return y;
}
```

The definitions of the functions `nodeCount` and `leavesCount` are left as exercises for you. (See Programming Exercises 1 and 2 at the end of this chapter.)

Next, we give the definitions of the functions `copyTree`, `destroy`, and `destroyTree`, the copy constructor and the destructor, as well as overload the assignment operator.

The definition of the function `copyTree` is the same as before; here this function is a member of the **class binaryTreeType**.

```
template<class elemType>
void binaryTreeType<elemType>::copyTree
                    (nodeType<elemType>* &copiedTreeRoot,
                     nodeType<elemType>* otherTreeRoot)
{
    if(otherTreeRoot == NULL)
        copiedTreeRoot = NULL;
    else
    {
        copiedTreeRoot = new nodeType<elemType>;
        copiedTreeRoot->info = otherTreeRoot->info;
        copyTree(copiedTreeRoot->llink, otherTreeRoot->llink);
        copyTree(copiedTreeRoot->rlink, otherTreeRoot->rlink);
    }
}//end copyTree
```

11

To destroy a binary tree, for each node, first we destroy its left subtree, then its right subtree, and then the node itself. We must use the operator `delete` to deallocate the memory occupied by each node. The definition of the function `destroy` is:

```
template<class elemType>
void binaryTreeType<elemType>::destroy(nodeType<elemType>* &p)
{
    if(p != NULL)
    {
        destroy(p->llink);
        destroy(p->rlink);
        delete p;
        p = NULL;
    }
}
```

To implement the function `destroyTree`, we use the function `destroy` and pass the pointer `root` of the root node of the binary tree to the function `destroy`. The definition of the function `destroyTree` is:

```
template<class elemType>
void binaryTreeType<elemType>::destroyTree()
{
    destroy(root);
}
```

Recall that when a class object is passed by value, the copy constructor copies the values of the actual parameters into the formal parameters. Because the **class binaryTreeType** has pointer data members, which create dynamic memory, we must provide the definition of the copy constructor to avoid the shallow copying of data. The definition of the copy constructor, given next, uses the function `copyTree` to make an identical copy of the binary tree that is passed as a parameter.

```
    //copy constructor
template<class elemType>
binaryTreeType<elemType>::binaryTreeType
            (const binaryTreeType<elemType>& otherTree)
{
    if(otherTree.root == NULL) //otherTree is empty
        root = NULL;
    else
        copyTree(root, otherTree.root);
}
```

The definition of the destructor is given next. When an object of the type `binaryTreeType` goes out of scope, the destructor deallocates the memory occupied by the nodes of the binary tree. The definition of the destructor uses the function `destroy` to accomplish this task.

```
        //destructor
template<class elemType>
binaryTreeType<elemType>::~binaryTreeType()
{
    destroy(root);
}
```

Next, we discuss the function to overload the assignment operator. To assign the value of one binary tree to another binary tree, we make an identical copy of the binary tree to be assigned by using the function **copyTree**. The definition of the function to overload the assignment operator is:

```
        //Overload the assignment operator.
template<class elemType>
const binaryTreeType<elemType>& binaryTreeType<elemType>::operator=
            (const binaryTreeType<elemType>& otherTree)
{

    if(this != &otherTree) //avoid self-copy
    {
        if(root != NULL)    //if the binary tree is not empty,
                            //destroy the binary tree
            destroy(root);

        if(otherTree.root == NULL) //otherTree is empty
            root = NULL;
        else
            copyTree(root, otherTree.root);
    }//end else

    return *this;
}
```

BINARY SEARCH TREES

Now that you know the basic operations on a binary tree, this section discusses a special type of binary tree, called a binary search tree.

Consider the binary tree in Figure 11-9.

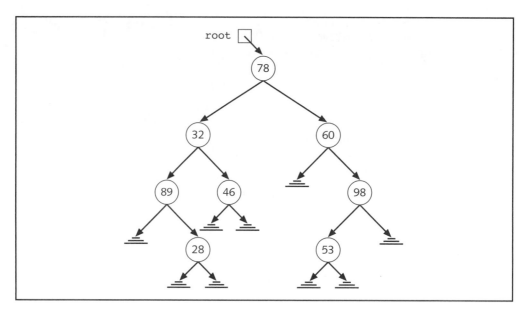

Figure 11-9 Arbitrary binary tree

Suppose that we want to determine whether **50** is in the binary tree. To do so, we can use any of the previous traversal algorithms to visit each node and compare the search item with the data stored in the node. However, this could require us to traverse a large part of the binary tree, so the search would be slow. We need to visit each node in the binary tree until either the item is found or we have traversed the entire binary tree because no criteria exist to guide our search. This case is like an arbitrary linked list where we must start our search at the first node, and continue looking at each node until either the item is found or the entire list is searched.

On the other hand, consider the binary tree in Figure 11-10.

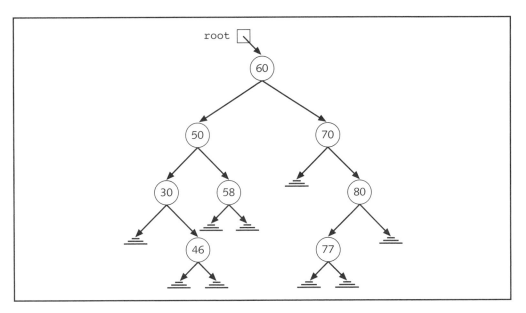

Figure 11-10   Binary search tree

In the binary tree in Figure 11-10, the data in each node is:

- Larger than the data in its left child
- Smaller than the data in its right child

The binary tree in Figure 11-10 has some structure. Suppose that we want to determine whether 58 is in this binary tree. As before, we must start our search at the root node. We compare 58 with the data in the root node; that is, we compare 58 with 60. Because 58 ≠ 60 and 58 < 60, it is guaranteed that 58 is not in the right subtree of the root node. Therefore, if 58 is in the binary tree, then it must be in the left subtree of the root node. We follow the left pointer of the root node and go to the node with info 50. We now apply the same criteria at this node. Because 58 > 50, we must follow the right pointer of this node and go to the node with info 58. At this node we find item 58.

This example shows that every time we move down to a child, we eliminate one of the subtrees of the node from our search. If the binary tree is nicely constructed, then the search is very similar to the binary search on arrays.

The binary tree given in Figure 11-10 is a special type of binary tree, called a binary search tree. (In the following definition, by the term key of a node we mean the key of the data item that uniquely identifies the item.)

Definition: A **binary search tree**, T, is either empty or:

i. T has a special node called the **root** node;

ii. T has two sets of nodes, L_T and R_T, called the left subtree and right subtree of T, respectively;

iii. The key in the root node is larger than every key in the left subtree and smaller than every key in the right subtree; and

iv. L_T and R_T are binary search trees.

 In this definition, because the left and right subtrees of the root node are again binary search trees, (iii) is equivalent to (iii)'. The key in the root node is larger than the key in its left child (if any) and smaller than the key in its right child (if any).

The following operations are typically performed on a binary search tree:

1. Determine whether the binary search tree is empty.

2. Search the binary search tree for a particular item.

3. Insert an item in the binary search tree.

4. Delete an item from the binary search tree.

5. Find the height of the binary search tree.

6. Find the number of nodes in the binary search tree.

7. Find the number of leaves in the binary search tree.

8. Traverse the binary search tree.

9. Copy the binary search tree.

Clearly, every binary search tree is a binary tree. The height of a binary search tree is determined the same way as the height of a binary tree. Similarly, the operations to find the number of nodes, find the number of leaves, and to do inorder, preorder, and postorder traversals of a binary search tree are the same as those for a binary tree. Therefore, we can inherit all of these operations from the binary tree. That is, we can extend the definition of the binary tree by using the principle of inheritance and hence define the binary search tree.

The following class defines a binary search tree as an ADT by extending the definition of the binary tree:

```
template<class elemType>
class bSearchTreeType: public binaryTreeType<elemType>
{
public:
    bool search(const elemType& searchItem);
      //Function to determine whether searchItem is in the binary
      //search tree.
```

```
        //Postcondition: Returns true if searchItem is found in the
        //                binary search tree; otherwise, returns false.

    void insert(const elemType& insertItem);
        //Function to insert insertItem in the binary search tree.
        //Postcondition: If no node in the binary search tree has
        //               the same info as insertItem, a node with
        //               the info insertItem is created and inserted
        //               in the binary search tree.

    void deleteNode(const elemType& deleteItem);
        //Function to delete deleteItem from the binary search tree.
        //Postcondition: If a node with the same info as deleteItem
        //               is found, it is deleted from the binary
        //               search tree.

private:
    void deleteFromTree(nodeType<elemType>* &p);
        //Function to delete the node, to which p points, from the
        //binary search tree.
        //Postcondition: The node to which p points is deleted
        //               from the binary search tree.
};
```

Next, we describe each of these operations.

Search

The function **search** searches the binary search tree for a given item. If the item is found in the binary search tree, it returns **true**; otherwise, it returns **false**. Because the pointer **root** points to the root node of the binary search tree, we must begin our search at the root node. Furthermore, because **root** must always point to the root node, we need a pointer, say **current**, to traverse the binary search tree. The pointer **current** is initialized to **root**.

If the binary search tree is nonempty, we first compare the search item with the info in the root node. If they are the same, we stop the search and return **true**. Otherwise, if the search item is smaller than the info in the node, we follow **llink** to go to the left subtree; otherwise, we follow **rlink** to go to the right subtree. We repeat this process for the next node. If the search item is in the binary search tree, our search ends at the node containing the search item; otherwise, the search ends at an empty subtree. Thus, the general algorithm is:

```
if root is NULL
   Cannot search an empty tree, returns false.
else
{
   current = root;
   while(current is not NULL and not found)
     if(current->info is the same as the search item)
```

```
            set found to true;
        else
            if(current->info is greater than the search item)
                follow the llink of current
            else
                follow the rlink of current
}
```

This pseudocode algorithm translates into the following C++ function:

```
template<class elemType>
bool bSearchTreeType<elemType>::search(const elemType& searchItem)
{
    nodeType<elemType> *current;
    bool found = false;

    if(root == NULL)
        cerr<<"Cannot search an empty tree."<<endl;
    else
    {
        current = root;

        while(current != NULL && !found)
        {
            if(current->info == searchItem)
                found = true;
            else
                if(current->info > searchItem)
                    current = current->llink;
                else
                    current = current->rlink;
        }//end while
    }//end else

    return found;
}//end search
```

Insert

The function **insert** inserts a new item in the binary search tree. After inserting an item in
a binary search tree, the resulting binary tree must also be a binary search tree. To insert a new
item, first we search the binary search tree and find the place where the new item is to be
inserted. The search algorithm is similar to the search algorithm of the function **search**.
Here we traverse the binary search tree with two pointers—a pointer, say **current**, to check
the current node and a pointer, say **trailCurrent**, pointing to the parent of **current**.
Because duplicate items are not allowed, our search must end at an empty subtree. We can

then use the pointer `trailCurrent` to insert the new item at the proper place. The item to be inserted, `insertItem`, is passed as a parameter to the function `insert`. The general algorithm is:

    a. Create a new node and copy `insertItem` into the new node. Also set `llink` and `rlink` of the new node to `NULL`.

    b. `if` `root` is `NULL`, the tree is empty so make `root` point to the new node.

```
else
{
    current = root;
    while(current is not NULL)      //search the binary tree
    {
        trailCurrent = current;
        if(current->info is the same as insertItem)
           Error: Cannot insert duplicate items.
           exit
        else
           if(current->info > insertItem)
               Follow llink of current
           else
               Follow rlink of current
    }

    //insert the new node in the binary tree

    if(trailCurrent->info > insertItem)
       make the new node the left child of trailCurrent
    else
       make the new node the right child of trailCurrent
}
```

This pseudocode algorithm translates into the following C++ function:

```
template<class elemType>
void bSearchTreeType<elemType>::insert(const elemType& insertItem)
{
    nodeType<elemType> *current;   //pointer to traverse the tree
    nodeType<elemType> *trailCurrent; //pointer behind current
    nodeType<elemType> *newNode;   //pointer to create the node

    newNode = new nodeType<elemType>;
    assert(newNode != NULL);
    newNode->info = insertItem;
    newNode->llink = NULL;
    newNode->rlink = NULL;
```

11

```
        if(root == NULL)
            root = newNode;
        else
        {
            current = root;

            while(current != NULL)
            {
                trailCurrent = current;

                if(current->info == insertItem)
                {
                    cerr<<"The insert item is already in the list - ";
                    cerr<<"duplicates are not allowed."<<endl;
                    return;
                }
                else
                    if(current->info > insertItem)
                        current = current->llink;
                    else
                        current = current->rlink;
            }//end while

            if(trailCurrent->info > insertItem)
                trailCurrent->llink = newNode;
            else
                trailCurrent->rlink = newNode;
        }
}//end insert
```

Delete

The function `deleteNode` deletes an item from the binary search tree. After deleting the item, the resulting binary tree must be a binary search tree. As before, first we search the binary search tree to find the node to be deleted. To help you better understand the delete operation, before describing the function to delete an item from the binary search tree, let us consider the binary search tree given in Figure 11-11.

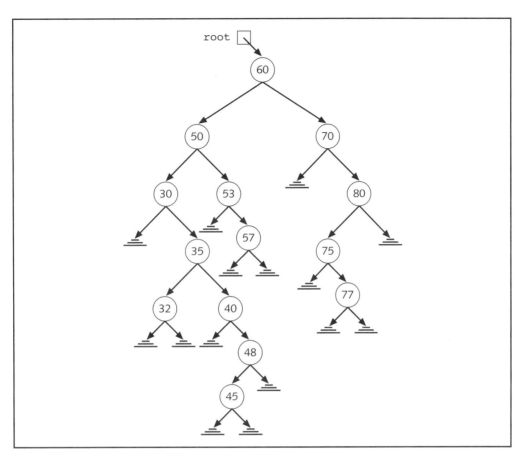

Figure 11-11 Binary search tree before deleting a node

After deleting the desired item (if it exists in the binary search tree), the resulting tree must be a binary search tree. The delete operation has four cases:

Case 1: The node to be deleted has no left and right subtrees; that is, the node to be deleted is a leaf. For example, the node with info 45 is a leaf.

Case 2: The node to be deleted has no left subtree; that is, the left subtree is empty, but it has a nonempty right subtree. For example, the left subtree of the node with info 40 is empty and its right subtree is nonempty.

Case 3: The node to be deleted has no right subtree; that is, the right subtree is empty, but it has a nonempty left subtree. For example, the right subtree of the node with info 80 is empty and its left subtree is nonempty.

Case 4: The node to be deleted has nonempty left and right subtrees. For example, the left and right subtrees of the node with info 50 are nonempty.

Case 1: Suppose that we want to delete 45 from the binary search tree in Figure 11-11. We search the binary search tree and arrive at the node containing 45. Because this node is a leaf and is the left child of its parent, we can simply set the llink of the parent node of 45 to NULL and deallocate the memory occupied by this node. After deleting this node, Figure 11-12 shows the resulting binary search tree.

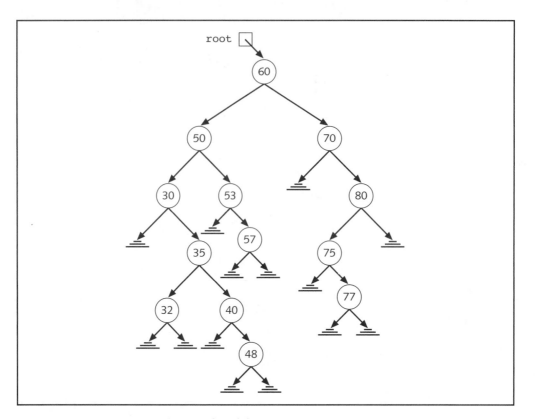

Figure 11-12 Binary search tree after deleting 45

Case 2: Suppose that we want to delete 30 from the binary search tree in Figure 11-11. In this case, the node to be deleted has no left subtree. Because 30 is the left child of its parent node, we make the llink of the parent node, of 30, point to the right child of 30—that is, 35—and then deallocate the memory occupied by 30. Figure 11-13 shows the resulting binary search tree.

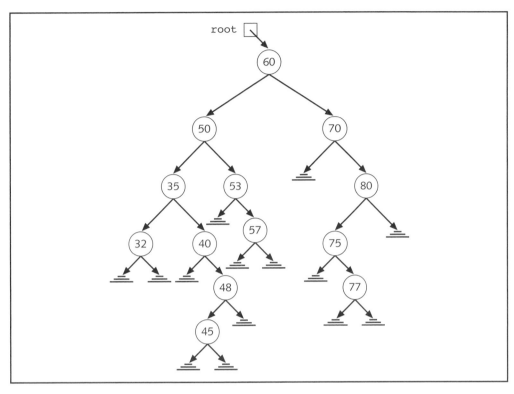

Figure 11-13   Binary search tree after deleting 30

Case 3: Suppose that we want to delete 80 from the binary search tree in Figure 11-11. The node containing 80 has no right child and is the right child of its parent. Thus, we make the `rlink` of the parent of 80—that is, 70—point to the left child of 80. Figure 11-14 shows the resulting binary search tree.

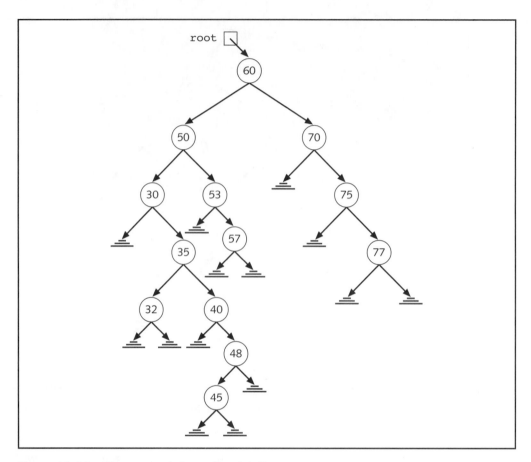

Figure 11-14 Binary search tree after deleting 80

Case 4: Suppose that we want to delete 50 from the binary search tree in Figure 11-11. The node with info 50 has a nonempty left subtree and a nonempty right subtree. Here, we first reduce this case to either Case 2 or Case 3 as follows. To be specific, suppose that we reduce it to Case 3—that is, the node to be deleted has no right subtree. For this case, we find the immediate predecessor of 50 in this binary tree, which is 48. This is done by first going to the left child of 50 and then locating the rightmost node of the left subtree of 50. To do so, we follow the `rlink` of the nodes. Because the binary search tree is finite, we eventually arrive at a node that has no right subtree. Next, we swap the info of the node to be deleted with the info of its immediate predecessor. In this case, we swap 48 with 50. This reduces to the case wherein the node to be deleted has no right subtree. We now apply Case 3 to delete the node. (Note that because we delete the immediate predecessor from the binary search tree, we, in fact, copy only the info of the immediate predecessor into the node to be deleted.) After deleting 50 from the binary search tree in Figure 11-11, the resulting binary tree is as shown in Figure 11-15.

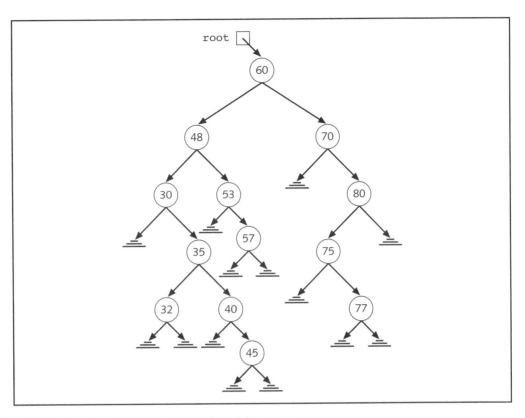

Figure 11-15 Binary search tree after deleting 50

In each case, we see that the resulting binary tree is again a binary search tree.

From this discussion, it follows that to delete an item from a binary search tree, we must do the following:

1. Find the node containing the item (if any) to be deleted.

2. Delete the node.

We accomplish the second step by a separate function, which we call `deleteFromTree`. Given a pointer to the node to be deleted, this function deletes the node by taking into account the previous four cases.

The preceding examples show that whenever we delete a node from a binary tree, we adjust one of the pointers of the parent node. Because the adjustment has to be made in the parent node, we must call the function `deleteFromTree` by using an appropriate pointer of the parent node. For example, suppose that the node to be deleted is 35, which is the right child of its parent node. Further suppose that `trailCurrent` points to the node containing 30, the parent node of 35. A call to the function `deleteFromTree` is:

```
deleteFromTree(trailCurrent->rlink);
```

Of course, if the node to be deleted is the root node, then the call to the function `deleteFromTree` is:

```
deleteFromTree(root);
```

We now define the C++ function `deleteFromTree`.

```
template<class elemType>
void bSearchTreeType<elemType>::deleteFromTree
                                (nodeType<elemType>* &p)
{
    nodeType<elemType> *current;      //pointer to traverse
                                      //the tree
    nodeType<elemType> *trailCurrent;   //pointer behind current
    nodeType<elemType> *temp;         //pointer to delete the node

    if(p == NULL)
       cerr<<"Error: The node to be deleted is NULL."
          <<endl;
    else if(p->llink == NULL && p->rlink == NULL)
        {
            temp = p;
            p = NULL;
            delete temp;
        }
    else if(p->llink == NULL)
        {
            temp = p;
            p = temp->rlink;
            delete temp;
        }
    else if(p->rlink == NULL)
        {
            temp = p;
            p = temp->llink;
            delete temp;
        }
    else
    {
        current = p->llink;
        trailCurrent = NULL;
```

```
        while(current->rlink != NULL)
        {
            trailCurrent = current;
            current = current->rlink;
        }//end while

        p->info = current->info;

        if(trailCurrent == NULL) //current did not move;
                                 //current == p->llink; adjust p
            p->llink = current->llink;
        else
            trailCurrent->rlink = current->llink;

        delete current;
    }//end else
}//end deleteFromTree
```

Next, we describe the function `deleteNode`. The function `deleteNode` first searches the binary search tree to find the node containing the item to be deleted. The item to be deleted, `deleteItem`, is passed as a parameter to the function. If the node containing `deleteItem` is found in the binary search tree, the function `deleteNode` calls the function `deleteFromTree` to delete the node. The definition of the function `deleteNode` is given next.

```
template<class elemType>
void bSearchTreeType<elemType>::deleteNode
                                (const elemType& deleteItem)
{
    nodeType<elemType> *current;   //pointer to traverse the tree
    nodeType<elemType> *trailCurrent; //pointer behind current
    bool found = false;

    if(root == NULL)
        cerr<<"Cannot delete from the empty tree."<<endl;
    else
    {
        current = root;
        trailCurrent = root;

        while(current != NULL && !found)
        {
            if(current->info == deleteItem)
                found = true;
            else
            {
                trailCurrent = current;
```

11

```
                    if(current->info > deleteItem)
                        current = current->llink;
                    else
                        current = current->rlink;
                }
            }//end while

            if(current == NULL)
                cout<<"The delete item is not in the list."<<endl;
            else
                if(found)
                {
                    if(current == root)
                        deleteFromTree(root);
                    else
                        if(trailCurrent->info > deleteItem)
                            deleteFromTree(trailCurrent->llink);
                        else
                            deleteFromTree(trailCurrent->rlink);
                }//end if
    }
}//end deleteNode
```

BINARY SEARCH TREE: ANALYSIS

This section provides an analysis of the performance of binary search trees. Let T be a binary search tree with n nodes, where $n > 0$. Suppose that we want to determine whether an item, x, is in T. The performance of the search algorithm depends on the shape of T. Let us first consider the worst case. In the worst case, T is linear. That is, T is one of the forms shown in Figure 11-16.

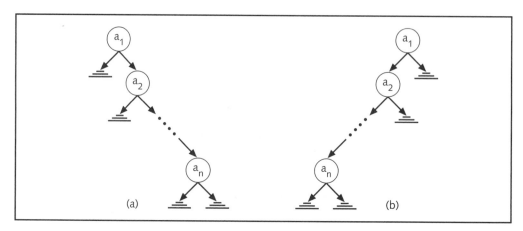

Figure 11-16 Linear binary search trees

Because T is linear, the performance of the search algorithm on T is the same as its performance on a linear list. Therefore, in the successful case, on average, the search algorithm makes $\frac{n+1}{2}$ key comparisons. In the unsuccessful case, it makes n comparisons.

Let us now consider the average-case behavior. In the successful case, the search would end at a node. Because there are n items, there are $n!$ possible orderings of the keys. We assume that all $n!$ orderings of the keys are possible. Let $S(n)$ denote the number of comparisons in the average successful case, and $U(n)$ denote the number of comparisons in the average unsuccessful case.

The number of comparisons required to determine whether x is in T is one more than the number of comparisons required to insert x in T. Furthermore, the number of comparisons required to insert x in T is the same as the number of comparisons made in the unsuccessful search, reflecting that x is not in T. From this, it follows that

$$S(n) = 1 + \frac{U(0) + U(1) + \ldots + U(n-1)}{n} \qquad (11\text{-}1)$$

It is also known that

$$S(n) = \left(1 + \frac{1}{n}\right)U(n) - 3 \qquad (11\text{-}2)$$

Solving Equations (11-1) and (11-2), it can be shown that

$$U(n) \approx 2.77\log_2 n$$

and

$$S(n) \approx 1.39\log_2 n$$

We can now formulate the following result.

Theorem: Let T be a binary search tree with n nodes, where $n > 0$. The average number of nodes visited in a search of T is approximately $1.39\log_2 n$.

11

NONRECURSIVE BINARY TREE TRAVERSAL ALGORITHMS

The previous sections described how to do the following:

- Traverse a binary tree using the inorder, preorder, and postorder methods.
- Construct a binary search tree.
- Insert an item in a binary search tree.
- Delete an item from a binary search tree.

The traversal algorithms—inorder, preorder, and postorder—discussed earlier are recursive. Because traversing a binary tree is a fundamental operation and recursive functions are somewhat less efficient then their iterative versions, this section discusses the nonrecursive inorder, preorder, and postorder traversal algorithms.

Nonrecursive Inorder Traversal

In an inorder traversal of a binary tree, for each node, the left subtree is visited first, then the node, and then the right subtree. It follows that in an inorder traversal, the first node visited is the leftmost node of the binary tree. For example, in the binary tree in Figure 11-17, the leftmost node is the node with info 28.

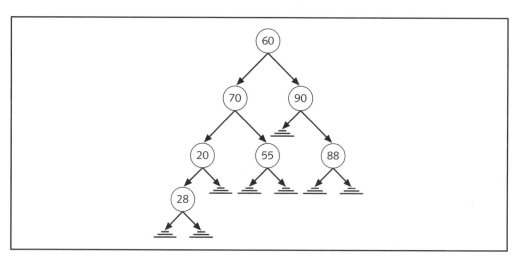

Figure 11-17 Binary tree; the leftmost node is 28

To get to the leftmost node of the binary tree, we start by traversing the binary tree at the root node and then follow the left link of each node until the left link of a node becomes NULL. We then back up to the parent node, visit the node, and then move to the right node. Because links go in only one direction, to get back to a node we must save a pointer to the node before moving to the child node. Moreover, the nodes must be backtracked in the order they were traversed. It follows that while backtracking, the nodes must be visited in a Last In First Out manner. This can be done by using a stack. We, therefore, save a pointer to a node in a stack. The general algorithm is as follows:

```
1. current = root;   //start traversing the binary tree at the
                     //root node

2. while(current is not NULL or stack is nonempty)
       if(current is not NULL)
       {
           push current onto stack;
           current = current->llink;
       }
       else
       {
           pop stack into current;
           visit current;     //visit the node
           current = current->rlink;     //move to the
                                         //right child
       }
```

The following function implements the nonrecursive inorder traversal of a binary tree:

```
template<class elemType>
void binaryTreeType<elemType>::nonRecursiveInTraversal()
{
    stackType<nodeType<elemType>* > stack;
    nodeType<elemType> *current;
    current = root;

    while((current != NULL) || (!stack.isEmptyStack()))
        if(current != NULL)
        {
            stack.push(current);
            current = current->llink;
        }
        else
        {
            current = stack.top();
            stack.pop();
            cout<<current->info<<" ";
            current = current->rlink;
        }

    cout<<endl;
}
```

11

Nonrecursive Preorder Traversal

In a preorder traversal of a binary tree, for each node, first the node is visited, then the left subtree is visited, and then the right subtree is visited. As in the case of an inorder traversal, after visiting a node and before moving to the left subtree, we must save a pointer to the node so that after visiting the left subtree, we can visit the right subtree. The general algorithm is as follows:

```
1. current = root;   //start the traversal at the root node

2. while(current is not NULL or stack is nonempty)
       if(current is not NULL)
       {
           visit current;
           push current onto stack;
           current = current->llink;
       }
       else
       {
           pop stack into current;
           current = current->rlink;       //prepare to visit
                                           //the right subtree

       }
```

The following function implements the nonrecursive preorder traversal algorithm:

```cpp
template<class elemType>
void binaryTreeType<elemType>::nonRecursivePreTraversal()
{

    stackType<nodeType<elemType>* > stack;
    nodeType<elemType> *current;

    current = root;

    while((current != NULL) || (!stack.isEmptyStack()))
        if(current != NULL)
        {
            cout<<current->info<<" ";
            stack.push(current);
            current = current->llink;
        }
        else
        {
            current = stack.top();
            stack.pop();
            current = current->rlink;
        }

    cout<<endl;
}
```

Nonrecursive Postorder Traversal

In a postorder traversal of a binary tree, for each node, first the left subtree is visited, then the right subtree is visited, and then the node is visited. As in the case of an inorder traversal, in a postorder traversal, the first node visited is the leftmost node of the binary tree. Because—for each node—the left and right subtrees are visited before visiting the node, we must indicate to the node whether the left and right subtrees have been visited. After visiting the left subtree of a node and before visiting the node, we must visit its right subtree. Therefore, after returning from a left subtree, we must tell the node that the right subtree needs to be visited, and after visiting the right subtree we must tell the node that it can now be visited. To do this, other than saving a pointer to the node (to get back to the right subtree and to the node itself), we also save an integer value of 1 before moving to the left subtree and an integer value of 2 before moving to the right subtree. Whenever the stack is popped, the integer value associated with that pointer is popped as well. This integer value tells whether the left and right subtrees of a node have been visited.

The general algorithm is:

1. `current = root;` `//start the traversal at the root node`

2. `v = 0;`

3. `if(current is NULL)`
   the binary tree is empty

4. `if(current is not NULL)`

   a. `push current into stack;`

   b. `push 1 onto stack;`

   c. `current = current->llink;`

   d. `while(stack is not empty)`
   ```
               if(current is not NULL and v is 0)
               {
                   push current and 1 onto stack;
                   current = current->llink;
               }
               else
               {
                   pop stack into current and v;
                   if(v == 1)
                   {
                       push current and 2 onto stack;
                       current = current->rlink;
                       v = 0;
                   }
                   else
                       visit current;
               }
   ```

11

We use two (parallel) stacks: one to save a pointer to a node, and another to save the integer value (1 or 2) associated with this pointer. We leave it as an exercise for you to write the definition of a C++ function to implement the preceding postorder traversal algorithm. (See Programming Exercise 6 at the end of this chapter.)

BINARY TREE TRAVERSAL AND FUNCTIONS AS PARAMETERS

Suppose that you have stored employee data in a binary search tree, and at the end of the year pay increases or bonuses are to be awarded to each employee. This task requires that each node in the binary search tree be visited and that the salary of each employee be updated. The preceding sections discussed various ways to traverse a binary tree. However, in these traversal algorithms—inorder, preorder, and postorder—whenever we visited a node, for simplicity and for illustration purposes, we only output the data contained in each node. How do we use a traversal algorithm to visit each node and update the data in each node? One way to do this is to first create another binary tree in which the data in each node is the updated data of the original binary tree, and then destroy the old binary tree. This would require extra computer time and perhaps extra memory, and therefore is not efficient. Another solution is to write separate traversal algorithms to update the data. This solution requires you to frequently modify the definition of the class implementing the binary search tree. However, if the user can write an appropriate function to update the data of each employee and then pass this function as a parameter to the traversal algorithms, we can considerably enhance the program's flexibility. This section describes how to pass functions as parameters to other functions.

In C++, a function name without any parentheses is considered a pointer to the function. To specify a function as a formal parameter to another function, we specify the function type, followed by the function name as a pointer, followed by the parameter types of the function. For example, consider the following statements:

```
void fParamFunc1(void (*visit) (int));        //Line 1
void fParamFunc2(void (*visit) (elemType&));  //Line 2
```

The statement in Line 1 declares `fParamFunc1` to be a function that takes as a parameter any `void` function that has one value parameter of the type `int`. The statement in Line 2 declares `fParamFunc2` to be a function that takes as a parameter any `void` function that has one reference parameter of the type `elemType`.

We can now rewrite, say, the inorder traversal function of the **class binaryTreeType**. Alternatively, we can overload the existing inorder traversal functions. To further illustrate function overloading, we will overload the inorder traversal functions. Therefore, we include the following statements in the definition of the **class binaryTreeType**:

```
void inorderTraversal(void (*visit) (elemType&));
  //Function to do an inorder traversal of the binary tree.
  //The parameter visit, which is a function, specifies the
  //action to be taken at each node.
```

```
void inorder(nodeType<elemType> *p, void (*visit) (elemType&));
  //Function to do an inorder traversal of the binary tree,
  //starting at the node specified by the parameter p.
  //The parameter visit, which is a function, specifies the
  //action to be taken at each node.
```

The definitions of these functions are as follows:

```
template<class elemType>
void binaryTreeType<elemType>::inorderTraversal
                            (void (*visit) (elemType& item))
{
    inorder(root, *visit);
}

template<class elemType>
void binaryTreeType<elemType>::inorder(nodeType<elemType>* p,
                            void (*visit) (elemType& item))
{
    if(p != NULL)
    {
        inorder(p->llink, *visit);
        (*visit)(p->info);
        inorder(p->rlink, *visit);
    }
}
```

The statement

```
(*visit)(p->info);
```

in the definition of the function **inorder** makes a call to the function with one reference parameter of the type **elemType** pointed to by the pointer **visit**.

Example 11-6 further illustrates how functions are passed as parameters to other functions.

Example 11-6

This example shows how to pass a user-defined function as a parameter to the binary tree traversal algorithms. For illustration purposes, we show how to use only the inorder traversal function.

The following program uses the **class bSearchTreeType**, which is derived from the **class binaryTreeType**, to build the binary tree. The traversal functions are included in the **class binaryTreeType**, which are then inherited by the **class bSearchTreeType**.

```
#include <iostream>
#include "binarySearchTree.h"

using namespace std;
```

```
void print(int& x);
void update(int& x);

int main()
{
    bSearchTreeType<int> treeRoot;                          //Line 1

    int num;                                                //Line 2

    cout<<"Line 3: Enter numbers ending with -999"
        <<endl;                                             //Line 3
    cin>>num;                                               //Line 4

    while(num != -999)                                      //Line 5
    {
        treeRoot.insert(num);                               //Line 6
        cin>>num;                                           //Line 7
    }

    cout<<endl<<"Line 8: Tree nodes in inorder: ";          //Line 8
    treeRoot.inorderTraversal(print);                       //Line 9
    cout<<endl<<"Line 10: Tree Height: "
        <<treeRoot.treeHeight()
        <<endl<<endl;                                       //Line 10

    cout<<"Line 11: ******* Update Nodes *******"
        <<endl;                                             //Line 11
    treeRoot.inorderTraversal(update);                      //Line 12

    cout<<"Line 13: Tree nodes in inorder after "
        <<"the update: "<<endl<<"            ";             //Line 13
    treeRoot.inorderTraversal(print);                       //Line 14
    cout<<endl<<"Line 15: Tree Height: "
        <<treeRoot.treeHeight()
        <<endl;                                             //Line 15

    return 0;                                               //Line 16
}

void print(int& x)                                          //Line 17
{
    cout<<x<<" ";                                           //Line 18
}

void update(int& x)                                         //Line 19
{
    x = 2 * x;                                              //Line 20
}
```

Sample Run: In this sample run, the user input is shaded.

```
Line 3: Enter numbers ending with -999
56 87 23 65 34 45 12 90 66 -999

Line 8: Tree nodes in inorder: 12 23 34 45 56 65 66 87 90
Line 10: Tree Height: 4

Line 11: ******* Update Nodes *******
Line 13: Tree nodes in inorder after the update:
        24 46 68 90 112 130 132 174 180
Line 15: Tree Height: 4
```

This program works as follows. The statement in Line 1 declares `treeRoot` to be a binary search tree object, in which the data in each node is of the type `int`. The statements in Lines 4 through 7 build the binary search tree. The statement in Line 9 uses the member function `inorderTraversal` of `treeRoot` to traverse the binary search tree `treeRoot`. The parameter to the function `inorderTraversal`, in Line 9, is the function `print` (defined in Line 17). Because the function `print` outputs the value of its argument, the statement in Line 9 outputs the data of the nodes of the binary search tree `treeNode`. The statement in Line 10 outputs the height of the binary search tree.

The statement in Line 12 uses the member function `inorderTraversal` to traverse the binary search tree `treeRoot`. In Line 12, the actual parameter of the function `inorderTraversal` is the function `update` (defined in Line 19). The function `update` doubles the value of its argument. Therefore, the statement in Line 12 updates the data of each node of the binary search tree by doubling the value. The statements in Lines 14 and 15 output the nodes and the height of the binary search tree.

11

AVL (Height-Balanced) Trees

In the previous sections, you learned how to build and manipulate a binary search tree. The performance of the search algorithm on a binary search tree depends on how the binary tree is built. The shape of the binary search tree depends on the data set. If the data set is sorted, then the binary search tree is linear and so the search algorithm would not be efficient. On the other hand, if the tree is nicely built, then the search would be fast. In fact, the smaller the height of the tree, the faster the search. Therefore, we want the height of the binary search tree to be as small as possible. This section describes a special type of binary search tree, called the **AVL tree** (also called the **height-balanced tree**), in which the resulting binary search tree is nearly balanced. AVL trees were introduced by the mathematicians G. M. Adelson-Veĺskiĭ and E. M. Landis in 1962 and are so named in their honor.

We begin by defining the following terms:

Definition: A **perfectly balanced** binary tree is a binary tree such that:

  i. The height of the left and right subtrees of the root are equal.

  ii. The left and right subtrees of the root are perfectly balanced binary trees.

Figure 11-18 shows a perfectly balanced binary tree.

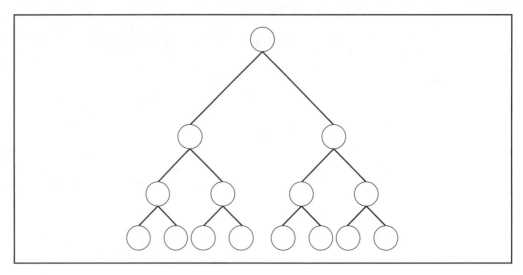

Figure 11-18 Perfectly balanced binary tree

Let T be a binary tree and x be a node in T. If T is perfectly balanced, then from the definition of the perfectly balanced tree it follows that the height of the left subtree of x is the same as the height of the right subtree of x.

It can be proved that if T is a perfectly balanced binary tree of height h, then the number of nodes in T is 2^{h-1}. From this it follows that if the number of items in the data set is not a power of 2, then we cannot construct a perfectly balanced binary tree. Moreover, perfectly balanced binary trees are a too stringent refinement.

Definition: An **AVL tree** (or **height-balanced tree**) is a binary search tree such that:

  i. The height of the left and right subtrees of the root differ by at most 1.

  ii. The left and right subtrees of the root are AVL trees.

Figures 11-19 and 11-20 give examples of AVL and non-AVL trees.

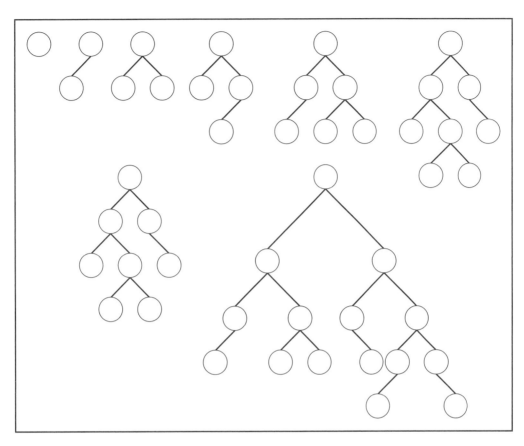

Figure 11-19 AVL trees

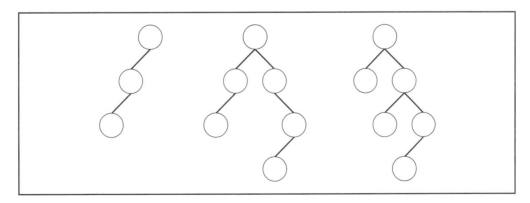

Figure 11-20 Non-AVL trees

Let x be a node in a binary tree. Let x_l denote the height of the left subtree of x, and x_r denote the height of the right subtree of x.

Proposition: Let T be an AVL tree and x be a node in T. Then $|x_r - x_l| \le 1$, where $|x_r - x_l|$ denotes the absolute value of $x_r - x_l$.

Let x be a node in the AVL tree T. Then:

1. If $x_l > x_r$, we say that x is **left high**. In this case, $x_l = x_r + 1$.

2. If $x_l = x_r$, we say that x is **equal high**.

3. If $x_r > x_l$, we say that x is **right high**. In this case, $x_r = x_l + 1$.

Definition: The **balance factor** of x, written $bf(x)$, is defined by $bf(x) = x_r - x_l$.

Let x be a node in the AVL tree T. Then:

1. If x is left high, then $bf(x) = -1$.

2. If x is equal high, then $bf(x) = 0$.

3. If x is right high, then $bf(x) = 1$.

Definition: Let x be a node in a binary tree. We say that the node x **violates the balance criteria** if $|x_r - x_l| > 1$, that is, the height of the left and right subtrees of x differ by more that 1.

From the previous discussion, it follows that in addition to the data and pointers to the left and right subtrees, one more thing associated with each node x in the AVL tree T is the balance factor of x. Thus, every node must keep track of its balance factor. To make the algorithms efficient, we store the balance factor of each node in the node itself. Hence the definition of a node in an AVL tree is:

```
template<class elemType>
struct AVLNode
{
    elemType  info;
    int     bfactor;                //balance factor
    AVLNode<elemType> *llink;
    AVLNode<elemType> *rlink;
};
```

Because an AVL tree is a binary search tree, the search algorithm for an AVL tree is the same as the search algorithm for a binary search tree. Other operations, such as finding the height, determining the number of nodes, checking whether the tree is empty, tree traversal, and so on, on AVL trees can be implemented exactly the same way they are implemented on binary trees. However, item insertion and deletion operations on AVL trees are somewhat different than the ones discussed for binary search trees. This is because after inserting (or deleting) a node in an AVL tree, the resulting binary tree must be an AVL tree. Next, we describe these operations.

Insertion into AVL Trees

To insert an item in an AVL tree, first we search the tree and find the place where the new item is to be inserted. Because an AVL tree is a binary search tree, to find the place for the new item we can search the AVL tree using a search algorithm similar to the search algorithm designed for binary search trees. If the item to be inserted is already in the tree, then the search ends at a nonempty subtree. Because duplicates are not allowed, in this case, we can output an appropriate error message. Suppose that the item to be inserted is not in the AVL tree. Then the search ends at an empty subtree and we insert the item in that subtree. After inserting the new item in the tree, the resulting tree might not be an AVL tree. Thus, we must restore the tree's balance criteria. This is accomplished by traveling the same path, back to the root node, which was followed when the new item was inserted in the AVL tree. The nodes on this path (back to the root node) are visited and either their balance factors are changed, or we might have to reconstruct part of the tree. We illustrate these cases with the help of the following examples.

 In Figures 11-21 through 11-32, for each node we show only the data stored in the node. Moreover, an equal sign (=) on the top of a node indicates that the balance factor of this node is 0, the less than symbol (<) indicates that the balance factor of this node is −1, and the greater than symbol (>) indicates that the balance factor of this node is 1.

Consider the AVL tree of Figure 11-21.

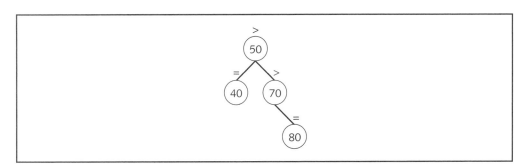

Figure 11-21   AVL tree before inserting 90

Let us insert 90 into this AVL tree. We search the tree starting at the root node to find the place for 90. The dotted arrow shows the path traversed. We insert the node with info 90 and obtain the binary search tree of Figure 11-22.

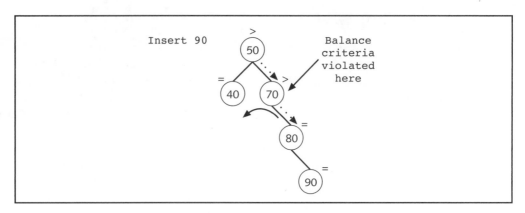

Figure 11-22   Binary tree of Figure 11-21 after inserting 90; nodes other than 90 show their balance factors before insertion

The binary search tree of Figure 11-22 is not an AVL tree. So we backtrack and go to node 80. Prior to insertion, bf(80) was 0. Because the new node was inserted into the (empty) right subtree of 80, we change its balance factor to 1 (not shown in the figure). Now we go back to node 70. Prior to insertion, bf(70) was 1. After insertion, the height of the right subtree of 70 is increased; thus, we see that the subtree with the root node 70 is not an AVL tree. In this case, we reconstruct this subtree (this is called rotating the tree at root node 70). We thus obtain the AVL tree as shown in Figure 11-23.

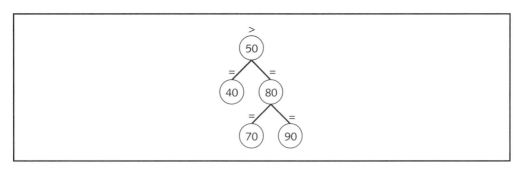

Figure 11-23   AVL tree of Figure 11-21 after inserting 90 and adjusting the balance factors

The binary search tree of Figure 11-23 is an AVL tree.

Now consider the AVL tree of Figure 11-24.

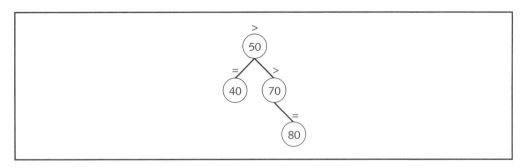

Figure 11-24   AVL tree before inserting 75

Let us insert 75 into the AVL tree of Figure 11-24.

As before, we search the tree starting at the root node. The dotted arrows show the path traversed. After inserting 75, the resulting binary search tree is as shown in Figure 11-25.

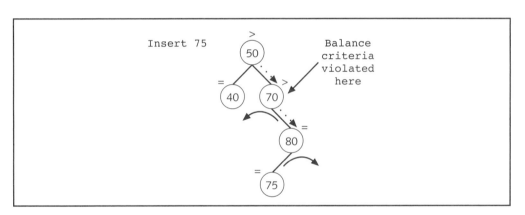

Figure 11-25   Binary tree of Figure 11-24 after inserting 75; nodes other than 75 show their balance factors before insertion

After inserting 75, we backtrack. First we go to node 80 and change its balance factor to −1. The subtree with the root node 80 is an AVL tree. Now we go back to 70. Clearly, the subtree with the root node 70 is not an AVL tree. So we reconstruct this subtree. In this case, we first reconstruct the subtree at root node 80, and then reconstruct the subtree at root node 70 to obtain the binary search tree as shown in Figure 11-26. (These constructions, that is, rotations, are explained in the next section, "AVL Tree Rotations.")

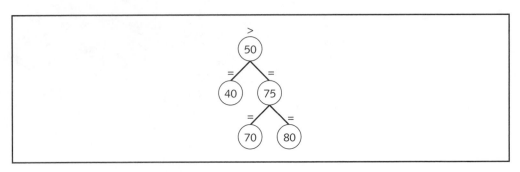

Figure 11-26   AVL tree of Figure 11-24 after inserting 75 and adjusting the balance factors

After reconstruction, the root of the constructed subtree is 75.

Notice that in Figures 11-23 and 11-26, after reconstructing the subtrees at the nodes, the subtrees no longer grew in height. At this point, we usually send the message, stating that overall the tree did not gain any height, to the remaining nodes on the path back to the root node of the tree. Thus, the remaining nodes on the path do not need to do anything.

Next, consider the AVL tree of Figure 11-27.

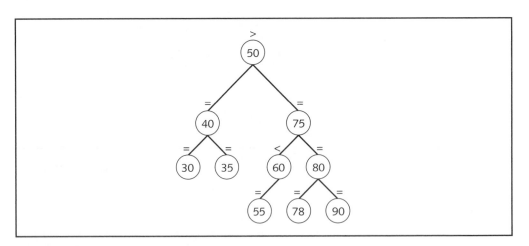

Figure 11-27   AVL tree before inserting 95

Let us insert 95 into this AVL tree. We search the tree and insert 95, as shown in Figure 11-28.

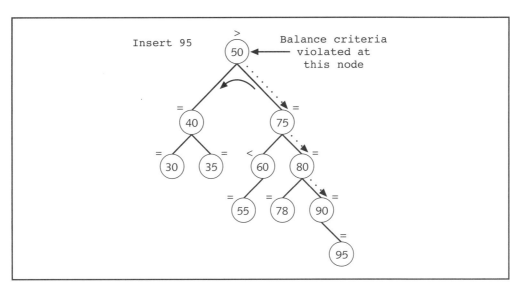

Figure 11-28 Binary tree of Figure 11-27 after inserting 95; nodes other than 95 show their balance factors before insertion

After inserting 95, we see that the subtrees with the root nodes 90, 80, and 75 are still AVL trees. When backtracking the path, we simply adjust the balance factors of these nodes (if needed). However, when we backtrack to the root node, we discover that the tree at this node is no longer an AVL tree. Prior to insertion, bf(50) was 1, that is, its right subtree was higher than its left subtree. After insertion, the subtree grew in height, thus violating the balance criteria at 50. So we reconstruct the binary search tree at node 50. In this case, the tree is reconstructed as shown in Figure 11-29.

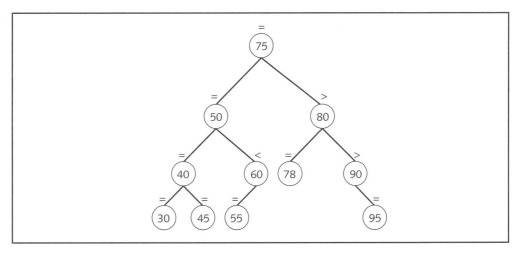

Figure 11-29 AVL tree of Figure 11-27 after inserting 95 and adjusting the balance factors

Before discussing the general algorithms for reconstructing (rotating) a subtree, let us consider one more case. Consider the AVL tree as shown in Figure 11-30.

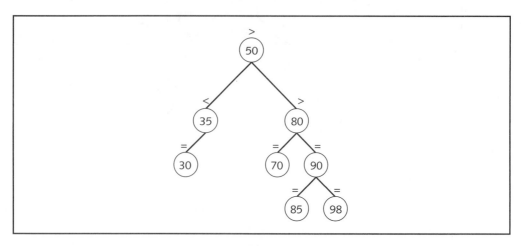

Figure 11-30 AVL tree before inserting 88

Let us insert 88 into the tree of Figure 11-30. Following the insertion procedure as described previously, we obtain the binary search tree as shown in Figure 11-31.

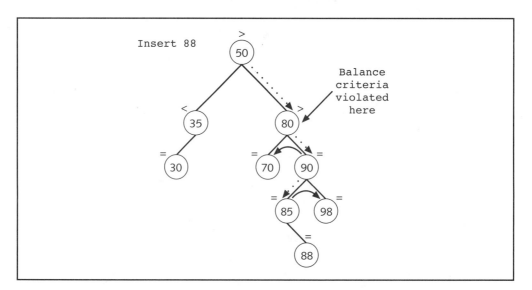

Figure 11-31 Binary tree of Figure 11-30 after inserting 88; nodes other than 88 show their balance factors before insertion

As before, we now backtrack to the root node. We adjust the balance factors of nodes 85 and 90. When we visit node 80, we discover that at this node we need to reconstruct the subtree. In this case, the subtree is reconstructed as shown in Figure 11-32.

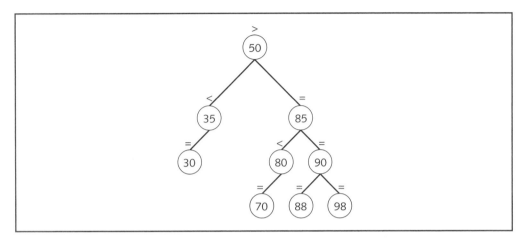

Figure 11-32   AVL tree of Figure 11-30 after inserting 88 and adjusting the balance factors

As before, after reconstructing the subtree, the entire tree is balanced. So for the remaining nodes on the path back to the root node, we do not do anything.

The previous examples indicate that if part of the binary search tree requires reconstruction, then after reconstructing that part of the binary search tree, we can ignore the remaining nodes on the path back to the root node. (This is, indeed, the case.) Also, after inserting the node, the reconstruction can occur at any node on the path back to the root node.

AVL Tree Rotations

We now describe the reconstruction procedure, called **rotating** the tree. There are two types of rotations, **left rotation** and **right rotation**. Suppose that the rotation occurs at node x. If it is a left rotation, then certain nodes from the right subtree of x move to its left subtree; the root of the right subtree of x becomes the new root of the reconstructed subtree. Similarly, if it is a right rotation at x, certain nodes from the left subtree of x move to its right subtree; the root of the left subtree of x becomes the new root of the reconstructed subtree.

Case 1: Consider Figure 11-33.

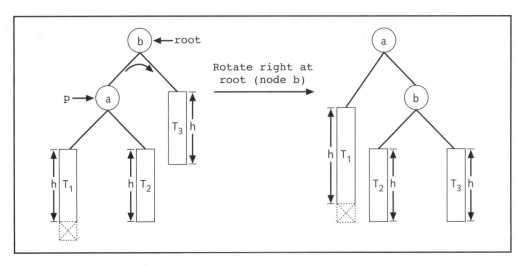

Figure 11-33 Right rotation at *b*

In Figure 11-33, subtrees T_1, T_2, and T_3 are of equal height, say h. The dotted rectangle shows an item insertion in T_1, causing the height of the subtree T_1 to increase by 1. The subtree at node *a* is still an AVL tree, but the balance criteria is violated at the root node. We note the following in this tree. Because the tree is a binary search tree:

- Every key in T_1 is smaller than the key in node *a*.

- Every key in T_2 is larger than the key in node *a*.

- Every key in T_2 is smaller than the key in node *b*.

Therefore:

1. We make T_2 (the right subtree of node *a*) the left subtree of node *b*.

2. We make node *b* the right child of node *a*.

3. Node *a* becomes the root node of the reconstructed tree, as shown in Figure 11-33.

Case 2: This case is a mirror image of Case 1. See Figure 11-34.

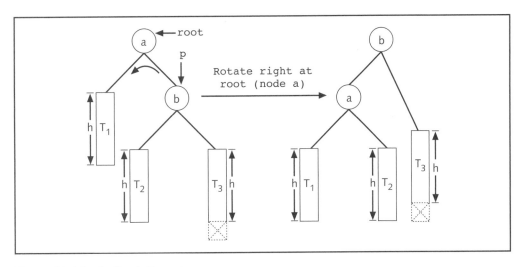

Figure 11-34   Left rotation at *a*

Case 3: Consider Figure 11-35.

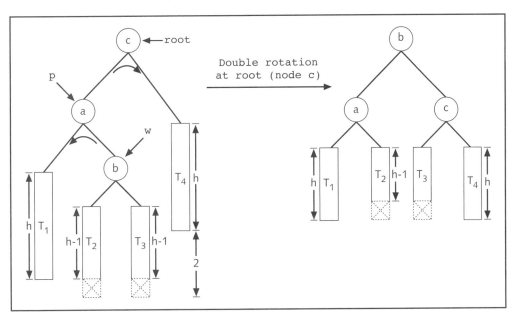

Figure 11-35   Double rotation: first rotate left at *a*, then rotate right at *c*

In Figure 11-35, the tree on the left is the tree prior to the reconstruction. The heights of the subtrees are shown in the figure. The dotted rectangle shows that a new item is inserted in the subtree, T_2 or T_3, causing the subtree to grow in height. We note the following (in the tree prior to reconstruction):

- All keys in T_3 are smaller than the key in node c.

- All keys in T_3 are larger than the key in node b.

- All keys in T_2 are smaller than the key in node b.

- All keys in T_2 are larger than the key in node a.

- After insertion, the subtrees with root nodes a and b are still AVL trees.

- The balance criteria is violated at the root node, c, of the tree.

- The balance factors of node c, $bf(c) = -1$, and node a, $bf(a) = 1$, are opposite.

This is an example of double rotation. One rotation is required at node a, and another rotation is required at node c. If the balance factor of the node where the tree is to be reconstructed and the balance factor of the higher subtree are opposite, that node requires a double rotation. First we rotate the tree at node a and then at node c. Now the tree at node a is right high and so we make a left rotation at a. Next, because the tree at node c is left high, we make a right rotation at c. Figure 11-35 shows the resulting tree (which is to the right of the tree after insertion). Figure 11-36, however, shows both rotations in sequence.

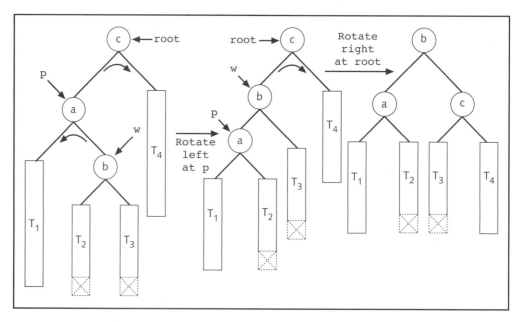

Figure 11-36 Left rotation at a followed by a right rotation at c

Case 4: This is a mirror image of Case 3. We illustrate this with the help of Figure 11-37.

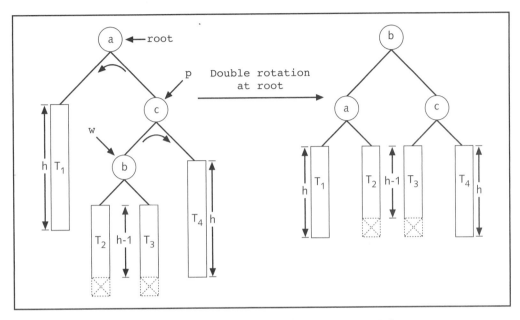

Figure 11-37   Double rotation: first rotate right at c, then rotate left at a

Using these four cases, we now describe what type of rotation might be required at a node.

Suppose that the tree is to be reconstructed, by rotation, at node x. Then the subtree with the root node x requires either a single or a double rotation.

1. Suppose that the balance factor of the node x and the balance factor of the root node of the higher subtree of x have the same sign, that is, both positive or both negative.

    a. If these balance factors are positive, make a single *left* rotation at x. (Prior to insertion, the right subtree of x was higher than its left subtree. The new item was inserted in the right subtree of x, causing the height of the right subtree to increase, which in turn violated the balance criteria at x.)

    b. If these balance factors are negative, make a single *right* rotation at x. (Prior to insertion, the left subtree of x was higher than its right subtree. The new item was inserted in the left subtree of x, causing the height of the left subtree to increase, which in turn violated the balance criteria at x.)

2. Suppose that the balance factor of the node x and the balance factor of the higher subtree of x are opposite in sign. To be specific, suppose that the balance factor of the node x prior to insertion was -1 and suppose that y is the root node of the left subtree of x. After insertion, the balance factor of the node y is 1. That is, after insertion, the right subtree of node y grew in height. In this case, we require a *double* rotation at x. First we make a left rotation at y (because y is right high). Then we make a right rotation at x. The other case, which is a mirror image of this case, is handled similarly.

The following C++ functions implement the left and right rotations of a node. The pointer of the node requiring the rotation is passed as a parameter to the function.

```
template<class elemType>
void rotateToLeft(AVLNode<elemType>* &root)
{
    AVLNode<elemType> *p; //pointer to the root of the
                          //right subtree of root
    if(root == NULL)
       cerr<<"Error in the tree."<<endl;
    else
       if(root->rlink == NULL)
          cerr<<"Error in the tree:"
              <<" No right subtree to rotate."<<endl;
       else
       {
          p = root->rlink;
          root->rlink = p->llink; //the left subtree of p
                          //becomes the right subtree of root
          p->llink = root;
          root = p;    //make p the new root node
       }
}//end rotateToLeft

template<class elemType>
void rotateToRight(AVLNode<elemType>* &root)
{
    AVLNode<elemType> *p;   //pointer to the root of the
                            //left subtree of root

    if(root == NULL)
       cerr<<"Error in the tree."<<endl;
    else
       if(root->llink == NULL)
          cerr<<"Error in the tree:"
              <<" No left subtree to rotate."<<endl;
```

```
        else
        {
            p = root->llink;
            root->llink = p->rlink; //the right subtree of p
                              //becomes the left subtree of root
            p->rlink = root;
            root = p;        //make p the new root node
        }
}//end rotateToRight
```

Now that we know how to implement both rotations, we next write the C++ functions, `balanceFromLeft` and `balanceFromRight`, which are used to reconstruct the tree at a particular node. The pointer of the node where the reconstruction occurs is passed as a parameter to this function. These functions use the functions `rotateToLeft` and `rotateToRight` to reconstruct the tree, and also adjust the balance factors of the nodes affected by the reconstruction. The function `balanceFromLeft` is called when the subtree is left double high and certain nodes need to be moved to the right subtree. The function `balanceFromRight` has similar conventions.

```
template<class elemType>
void balanceFromLeft(AVLNode<elemType>* &root)
{
    AVLNode<elemType> *p;
    AVLNode<elemType> *w;

    p = root->llink;    //p points to the left subtree of root

    switch(p->bfactor)
    {
    case -1: root->bfactor = 0;
             p->bfactor = 0;
             rotateToRight(root);
             break;
    case 0:  cerr<<"Error: Cannot balance from the left."<<endl;
             break;
    case 1:  w = p->rlink;
             switch(w->bfactor)  //adjust the balance factors
             {
             case -1: root->bfactor = 1;
                      p->bfactor = 0;
                      break;
             case 0:  root->bfactor = 0;
                      p->bfactor = 0;
                      break;
             case 1:  root->bfactor = 0;
                      p->bfactor = -1;
             }//end switch
```

```
            w->bfactor = 0;
            rotateToLeft(p);
            root->llink = p;
            rotateToRight(root);
    }//end switch;
}//end balanceFromLeft
```

For the sake of completeness, we also give the definition of the function balanceFromRight.

```
template<class elemType>
void balanceFromRight(AVLNode<elemType>* &root)
{
    AVLNode<elemType> *p;
    AVLNode<elemType> *w;

    p = root->rlink;    //p points to the right subtree of root

    switch(p->bfactor)
    {
    case -1: w = p->llink;
            switch(w->bfactor)  //adjust the balance factors
            {
            case -1: root->bfactor = 0;
                    p->bfactor = 1;
                    break;
            case 0:  root->bfactor = 0;
                    p->bfactor = 0;
                    break;
            case 1:  root->bfactor = -1;
                    p->bfactor = 0;
            }//end switch

            w->bfactor = 0;
            rotateToRight(p);
            root->rlink = p;
            rotateToLeft(root);
            break;
    case 0:  cerr<<"Error: Cannot balance from the right."<<endl;
            break;
    case 1:  root->bfactor = 0;
            p->bfactor = 0;
            rotateToLeft(root);
    }//end switch;
}//end balanceFromRight
```

We now focus our attention on the function insertIntoAVL. The function insertIntoAVL inserts a new item into an AVL tree. The item to be inserted and the pointer of the root node of the AVL tree are passed as parameters to this function.

The following steps describe the function `insertIntoAVL`:

1. Create a node and copy the item to be inserted into the newly created node.

2. Search the tree and find the place for the new node in the tree.

3. Insert the new node in the tree.

4. Backtrack the path, which was constructed to find the place for the new node in the tree, to the root node. If necessary, adjust the balance factors of the nodes, or reconstruct the tree at a node on the path.

Because Step 4 requires us to backtrack the path to the root node, and in a binary tree we have links only from the parent to the children, the easiest way to implement the function `insertIntoAVL` is to use recursion. (Recall that recursion automatically takes care of the backtracking.) This is exactly what we do. The function `insertIntoAVL` also uses a reference `bool` parameter, `isTaller`, to indicate to the parent whether the subtree grew in height or not.

```
template<class elemType>
void insertIntoAVL(AVLNode<elemType>* &root,
                   AVLNode<elemType>  *newNode,
                   bool& isTaller)
{
    if(root == NULL)
    {
        root = newNode;
        isTaller = true;
    }
    else
        if(root->info == newNode->info)
            cerr<<"No duplicates are allowed."<<endl;
        else
            if(root->info > newNode->info) //newItem goes in
                                           //the left subtree
            {
                insertIntoAVL(root->llink, newNode, isTaller);

                if(isTaller)               //after insertion, the
                                           //subtree grew in height
                    switch(root->bfactor)
                    {
                    case -1: balanceFromLeft(root);
                             isTaller = false;
                             break;
                    case 0:  root->bfactor = -1;
                             isTaller = true;
                             break;
```

```
                      case 1:   root->bfactor = 0;
                                isTaller = false;
                    }//end switch
            }//end if
            else
            {
                insertIntoAVL(root->rlink, newNode, isTaller);

                if(isTaller)                    //after insertion, the
                                                //subtree grew in height
                    switch(root->bfactor)
                    {
                    case -1: root->bfactor = 0;
                             isTaller = false;
                             break;
                    case 0:   root->bfactor = 1;
                             isTaller = true;
                             break;
                    case 1:   balanceFromRight(root);
                             isTaller = false;
                    }//end switch
            }//end else
}//end insertIntoAVL
```

Next, we illustrate how the function `insertIntoAVL` works and build an AVL tree from scratch. Initially the tree is empty. Each figure (Figures 11-37 through 11-45) shows the item to be inserted as well as the balance factor of each node. An equal sign (=) on the top of a node indicates that the balance factor of this node is 0; the less than symbol (<) indicates that the balance factor of this node is −1; and the greater-than symbol (>) indicates that the balance factor of this node is 1.

Initially, the AVL tree is empty. Let us insert 40 into the empty AVL tree. See Figure 11-38.

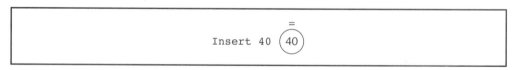

Figure 11-38   AVL tree after inserting 40

Next, we insert 30 into the AVL tree. See Figure 11-39.

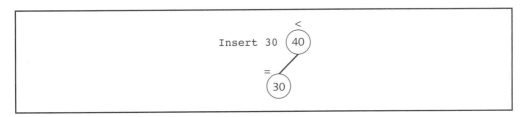

Figure 11-39   AVL tree after inserting 30

Item 30 is inserted into the left subtree of node 40, causing the left subtree of 40 to grow in height. After insertion, the balance factor of node 40 is −1.

Next, we insert 20 into the AVL tree. See Figure 11-40.

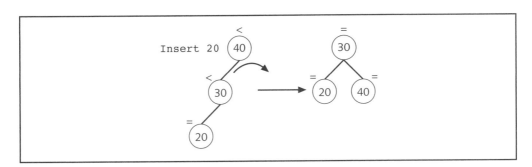

Figure 11-40   AVL tree after inserting 20

The insertion of 20 violates the balance criteria at node 40. The tree is reconstructed at node 40 by making a single right rotation.

Next, we insert 60 into the AVL tree. See Figure 11-41.

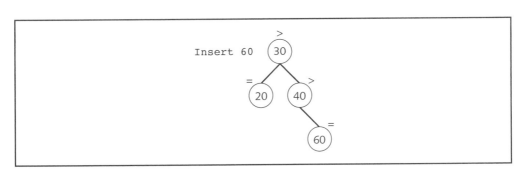

Figure 11-41   AVL tree after inserting 60

The insertion of 60 does not require reconstruction; only the balance factor is adjusted at nodes 40 and 30.

Next, we insert 50. See Figure 11-42.

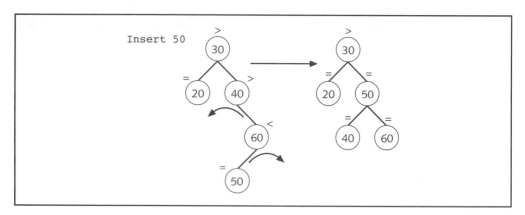

Figure 11-42   AVL tree after inserting 50

The insertion of 50 requires the tree to be reconstructed at 40. Notice that a double rotation is made at node 40.

Next, we insert 80. See Figure 11-43.

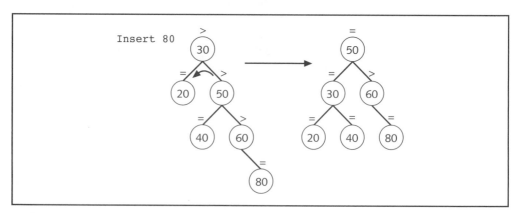

Figure 11-43   AVL tree after inserting 80

The insertion of 80 requires the tree to be reconstructed at node 30. Next, we insert 15. See Figure 11-44.

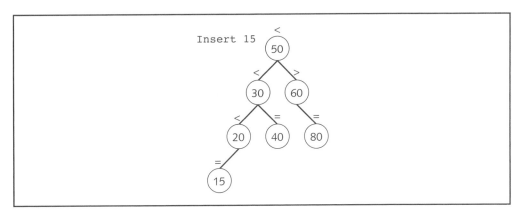

Figure 11-44   AVL tree after inserting 15

The insertion of node 15 does not require any part of the tree to be reconstructed. We need to only adjust the balance factors of nodes 20, 30, and 50.

Next, we insert 28. See Figure 11-45.

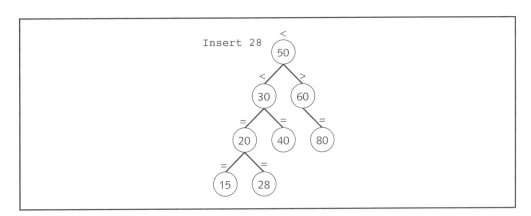

Figure 11-45   AVL tree after inserting 28

The insertion of node 28 also does not require any part of the tree to be reconstructed. We need only to adjust the balance factor of node 20.

Next, we insert 25. The insertion of 25 requires a double rotation at node 30. Figure 11-46 shows both rotations in sequence.

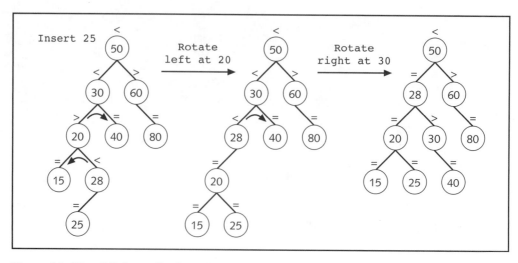

Figure 11-46 AVL tree after inserting 25

In Figure 11-46, the tree is first rotated left at node 20 and then right at node 30.

The following function creates a node, stores the info in the node, and calls the function `insertIntoAVL` to insert the new node into the AVL tree:

```
template<class elemType>
void insert(const elemType &newItem)
{
    bool isTaller = false;
    AVLNode<elemType> *newNode;

    newNode = new AVLNode<elemType>;
    newNode->info = newItem;
    newNode->bfactor = 0;
    newNode->llink = NULL;
    newNode->rlink = NULL;

    insertIntoAVL(root, newNode, isTaller);
}
```

We leave it as an exercise for you to design the class to implement AVL trees as an ADT. See Programming Exercise 9 at the end of this chapter. (Notice that because the structure of the node of an AVL tree is different than the structure of the node of a binary tree discussed in the beginning of this chapter, you cannot use inheritance to derive the class to implement AVL trees from the **class binaryTreeType**.)

Deletion from AVL Trees

To delete an item from an AVL tree, first we find the node containing the item to be deleted. The following four cases arise:

Case 1: The node to be deleted is a leaf.

Case 2: The node to be deleted has no right child, that is, its right subtree is empty.

Case 3: The node to be deleted has no left child, that is, its left subtree is empty.

Case 4: The node to be deleted has a left child and a right child.

Cases 1 through 3 are easier to handle than Case 4. Let us first discuss Case 4.

Suppose that the node to be deleted, say x, has a left and a right child. As in the case of deletion from a binary search tree, we reduce Case 4 to Case 2. That is, we find the immediate predecessor, say y, of x. Then the data of y is copied into x and now the node to be deleted is y. Clearly, y has no right child.

To delete the node, we adjust one of the pointers of the parent node. After deleting the node, the resulting tree may no longer be an AVL tree. As in the case of insertion into an AVL tree, we traverse the path (from the parent node) back to the root node. For each node on this path, sometimes we need to change only the balance factor, while other times the tree at a particular node is reconstructed. The following steps describe what to do at a node on the path back to the root node. (As in the case of insertion, we use the `bool` variable `shorter` to indicate whether the height of the subtree is reduced.) Let p be a node on the path back to the root node. We look at the current balance factor of p.

11

1. If the current balance factor of p is equal high, then the balance factor of p is changed according to whether the left subtree of p was shortened or the right subtree of p was shortened. The variable `shorter` is set to `false`.

2. Suppose that the balance factor of p is not equal and the taller subtree of p is shortened. The balance factor of p is changed to equal high, and the variable `shorter` is left as `true`.

3. Suppose that the balance factor of p is not equal high and the shorter subtree of p is shortened. Further suppose that q points to the root of the taller subtree of p.

   a. If the balance factor of q is equal high, a single rotation is required at p and `shorter` is set to `false`.

   b. If the balance factor of q is the same as p, a single rotation is required at p and `shorter` is set to `true`.

   c. Suppose that the balance factors of p and q are opposite. A double rotation is required at p (a single rotation at q and then a single rotation at p). We adjust the balance factors and set `shorter` to `true`.

Analysis: AVL Trees

Consider all the possible AVL trees of height h. Let T_h be an AVL tree of height h such that T_h has the fewest number of nodes. Let T_{hl} denote the left subtree of T_h and T_{hr} denote the right subtree of T_h. Then

$$|T_h| = |T_{hl}| + |T_{hr}| + 1$$

where $|T_h|$ denotes the number of nodes in T_h.

Because T_h is an AVL tree of height h such that T_h has the fewest number of nodes, it follows that one of the subtrees of T_h is of height $h - 1$ and the other is of height $h - 2$. To be specific, suppose that T_{hl} is of height $h - 1$ and T_{hr} is of height $h - 2$. From the definition of T_h, it follows that T_{hl} is an AVL tree of height $h - 1$ such that T_{hl} has the fewest number of nodes among all AVL trees of height $h - 1$. Similarly, T_{hr} is an AVL tree of height $h - 2$ that has the fewest number of nodes among all AVL trees of height $h - 2$. Thus, T_{hl} is of the form T_{h-1} and T_{hr} is of the form T_{h-2}. Hence

$$|T_h| = |T_{h-1}| + |T_{h-2}| + 1$$

Clearly,

$$|T_0| = 1$$
$$|T_1| = 2$$

Let $F_{h+2} = |T_h| + 1$. Then,
$$F_{h+2} = F_{h+1} + F_h$$
$$F_2 = 2$$
$$F_3 = 3.$$

This is called a Fibonacci sequence. The solution to F_h is given by

$$F_h \approx \frac{\phi^h}{\sqrt{5}}, \quad \text{where } \phi = \frac{1+\sqrt{5}}{2}$$

Hence

$$|T_h| \approx \frac{\phi^{h+2}}{\sqrt{5}} = \frac{1}{\sqrt{5}} \left[\frac{1+\sqrt{5}}{2} \right]^{h+2}$$

From this it can be concluded that

$$h \approx (1.44)\log_2 |T_h|$$

This implies that, in the worst case, the height of an AVL tree with n nodes is approximately $(1.44)\log_2 n$. Because the height of a perfectly balanced binary tree with n nodes is $\log_2 n$, it follows that, in the worst case, the time to manipulate an AVL tree is no more than 44% of the optimum time. However, in general, AVL trees are not as sparse as in the worst case. It can be shown that the average search time of an AVL tree is about 4% more than the optimum.

PROGRAMMING EXAMPLE: VIDEO STORE (REVISITED)

In Chapter 5, we designed a program to help a video store automate its video rental process. That program used an (unordered) linked list to keep track of the video inventory in the store. Because the search algorithm on a linked list is sequential and the list is fairly large, the search could be time consuming. In this chapter, you learned how to organize data into a binary tree. If the binary tree is nicely constructed (that is, it is not linear), then the search algorithm can be improved considerably. Moreover, in general, item insertion and deletion in a binary search tree is faster than in a linked list. We will, therefore, redesign the video store program so that the video inventory can be maintained in a binary tree. As in Chapter 5, we leave the design of the customer list in a binary tree as an exercise for you.

Video Object

In Chapter 5, a linked list was used to maintain a list of videos in the store. Because the linked list was unordered, to see whether a particular video was in stock, the sequential search algorithm used the equality operator for comparison. However, in the case of a binary tree, we need other relational operators for the search, insertion, and deletion operations. We, therefore, overload all of the relational operators. Other than this difference, the **class videoType** is the same as before. However, we give its definition, without the documentation, here for easy reference and for the sake of completeness.

```
#include <iostream>
#include <string>

using namespace std;

class videoType
{
    friend ostream& operator<<(ostream&, const videoType&);
public:
    void setVideoInfo(string title, string star1,
                      string star2, string producer,
                      string director, string productionCo,
                      int setInStock);
    int getNoOfCopiesInStock() const;
    void checkOut();
    void checkIn();
    void printTitle() const;
    void printInfo() const;
    bool checkTitle(string title);
    void updateInStock(int num);
```

```
    void setCopiesInStock(int num);
    string getTitle();
    videoType(string title = "", string star1 = "",
             string star2 = "", string producer = "",
             string director = "", string productionCo = "",
             int setInStock = 0);

    bool operator==(const videoType&) const;
    bool operator!=(const videoType&) const;
    bool operator<(const videoType&) const;
    bool operator<=(const videoType&) const;
    bool operator>(const videoType&) const;
    bool operator>=(const videoType&) const;

private:
    string videoTitle;
    string movieStar1;
    string movieStar2;
    string movieProducer;
    string movieDirector;
    string movieProductionCo;
    int copiesInStock;
};
```

The definitions of the member functions of the **class videoType** are the same as in Chapter 5. Because here we are overloading all of the relational operators, we give only the definitions of these member functions.

```
    //Overload the relational operators.
bool videoType::operator==(const videoType& right) const
{
     return (videoTitle == right.videoTitle);
}

bool videoType::operator!=(const videoType& right) const
{
     return (videoTitle != right.videoTitle);
}

bool videoType::operator<(const videoType& right) const
{
     return (videoTitle < right.videoTitle);
}

bool videoType::operator<=(const videoType& right) const
{
     return (videoTitle <= right.videoTitle);
}
```

```
bool videoType::operator>(const videoType& right) const
{
     return (videoTitle > right.videoTitle);
}

bool videoType::operator>=(const videoType& right) const
{
     return (videoTitle >= right.videoTitle);
}
```

Video List

The video list is maintained in a binary search tree. Therefore, we derive the class videoBinaryTree from the class bSearchTreeType. The definition of the class videoBinaryTree is as follows:

```
#include <iostream>
#include <string>
#include "binarySearchTree.h"
#include "videoType.h"

using namespace std;

class videoBinaryTree: public bSearchTreeType<videoType>
{
public:
   bool videoSearch(string title);
     //Function to search the list to see whether a
     //particular title, specified by the parameter
     //title, is in stock.
     //Postcondition: Returns true if the title is found,
     //               false otherwise.
   bool isVideoAvailable(string title);
     //Function to determine whether at least one copy of
     //a particular video is in stock.
     //Postcondition: Returns true if at least one copy is
     //               in stock, false otherwise.
   void videoCheckOut(string title);
     //Function to check out a video, that is, rent a video.
     //Postcondition: copiesInStock is decremented by 1.
   void videoCheckIn(string title);
     //Function to check in a video returned by a customer.
     //Postcondition: copiesInstock is incremented by 1.
   bool videoCheckTitle(string title);
     //Function to determine whether a particular video is
     //in stock.
     //Postcondition: Returns true if the video is in stock,
     //               false otherwise.
```

```
    void videoUpdateInStock(string title, int num);
        //Function to update the number of copies of a video
        //by adding the value of the parameter num. The
        //parameter title specifies the name of the video
        //for which the number of copies is to be updated.
        //Postcondition: copiesInStock = copiesInStock + num

    void videoSetCopiesInStock(string title, int num);
        //Function to reset the number of copies of a video.
        //The parameter title specifies the name of the video
        //for which the number of copies is to be reset; the
        //parameter num specifies the number of copies.
        //Postcondition: copiesInStock = num

    void videoPrintTitle();
        //Function to print the titles of all the videos in
        //stock.

private:
    void searchVideoList(string title, bool& found,
                         nodeType<videoType>* &current);
        //Function to search the video list for a
        //particular video, specified by the parameter title.
        //Postcondition: If the video is found, the parameter
        //               found is set to true, false otherwise.
        //               The parameter current points to the
        //               node containing the video.

    void inorderTitle(nodeType<videoType> *p);
        //Function to print the titles of all the videos in stock.
};
```

The definitions of the member functions of the **class videoBinaryTree** are similar to the ones given in Chapter 5. We give the definitions of only the functions **searchVideoList**, **inorderTitle**, and **videoPrintTitle**. (See Programming Exercise 10 at the end of the chapter.)

The function **searchVideoList** uses a search algorithm similar to the search algorithm for a binary search tree given earlier in this chapter. It returns **true** if the search item is found in the list, and **false** otherwise. It also returns a pointer to the node containing the search item. Note that the function **searchVideoList** is a **private** member of the **class videoBinaryTree**. So the user cannot directly use this function in a program. Therefore, even though this function returns a pointer to a node in the tree, the user cannot directly access the node. The function **searchVideoList** is used only to implement the other functions of the `class videoBinaryTree`. The definition of this function is as follows:

```
void videoBinaryTree::searchVideoList(string title,
                                      bool& found,
                                      nodeType<videoType>* &current)
{
    found = false;

    videoType temp;

    temp.setVideoInfo(title, "", "", "", "", "", 0);

    if(root == NULL)  //the tree is empty
       cout<<"Cannot search an empty list. "<<endl;
    else
    {
       current = root;   //set current to point to the root node
                         //of the binary tree
       found = false;    //set found to false

       while(current != NULL && !found)  //search the tree
            if(current->info == temp)       //the item is found
               found = true;
            else
               if(current->info > temp)
                  current = current->llink;
               else
                  current = current->rlink;
    }//end else
}
```

Given a pointer to the root node of the binary tree containing the videos, the function `inorderTitle` uses the inorder traversal algorithm to print the titles of the videos. Notice that this function outputs only the video titles. The definition of this function is as follows:

```
void videoBinaryTree::inorderTitle(nodeType<videoType> *p)
{
    if(p != NULL)
    {
       inorderTitle(p->llink);
       p->info.printTitle();
       inorderTitle(p->rlink);
    }
}
```

The function `videoPrintTitle` uses the function `inorderTitle` to print the titles of all the videos in the store. The definition of this function is:

```
void videoBinaryTree::videoPrintTitle()
{
     inorderTitle(root);
}
```

Main Program

The main program is the same as before. Here we give only the listing of this program. We assume that the name of the header file containing the definition of the **class** `videoBinaryTree` is `videoBinaryTree.h`, and so on.

```
#include <iostream>
#include <fstream>
#include <string>
#include "binarySearchTree.h"
#include "videoType.h"
#include "videoBinaryTree.h"

using namespace std;

void createVideoList(ifstream& infile,
                     videoBinaryTree& videoList);
void displayMenu();

int main()
{
    videoBinaryTree videoList;
    int choice;
    char ch;
    string title;

    ifstream infile;

    infile.open("a:\\videoDat.txt");
    if(!infile)
    {
       cout<<"The input file does not exist."<<endl;
       return 1;
    }

    createVideoList(infile, videoList);
    infile.close();
```

```cpp
    displayMenu();                      //show the menu
    cout<<"Enter your choice: ";
    cin>>choice;                        //get the request
    cin.get(ch);
    cout<<endl;

        //process the request
    while(choice != 9)
    {
        switch(choice)
        {
        case 1: cout<<"Enter the title: ";
                getline(cin, title);
                cout<<endl;
                if(videoList.videoSearch(title))
                    cout<<"Title found."<<endl;
                else
                    cout<<"The store does not carry "
                        <<"this title."<<endl;
                break;
        case 2: cout<<"Enter the title: ";
                getline(cin, title);
                cout<<endl;
                if(videoList.videoSearch(title))
                {
                    if(videoList.isVideoAvailable(title))
                    {
                        videoList.videoCheckOut(title);
                        cout<<"Enjoy your movie: "<<title<<endl;
                    }
                    else
                        cout<<"The video is currently "
                            <<"out of stock."<<endl;
                }
                else
                    cout<<"The video is not in the store."<<endl;

                break;
        case 3: cout<<"Enter the title: ";
                getline(cin,title);
                cout<<endl;
                if(videoList.videoSearch(title))
                {
                    videoList.videoCheckIn(title);
                    cout<<"Thanks for returning "<<title<<endl;
                }
```

```
                 else
                    cout<<"This video is not from our store."
                        <<endl;

                 break;
        case 4: cout<<"Enter the title: ";
                getline(cin, title);
                cout<<endl;
                if(videoList.videoSearch(title))
                {
                    if(videoList.isVideoAvailable(title))
                        cout<<"The video is currently in stock."
                            <<endl;
                    else
                        cout<<"The video is out of stock."<<endl;
                }
                else
                    cout<<"The video is not in the store."<<endl;

                break;
        case 5: videoList.videoPrintTitle();
                break;
        case 6: videoList.inorderTraversal();
                break;
        default: cout<<"Bad Selection."<<endl;
        }//end switch

        displayMenu();                    //display the menu
        cout<<"Enter your choice: ";
        cin>>choice;                      //get the next request
        cin.get(ch);
        cout<<endl;
    }//end while

    return 0;
}

void createVideoList(ifstream& infile,
                     videoBinaryTree& videoList)
{
    string Title;
    string Star1;
    string Star2;
    string Producer;
    string Director;
    string ProductionCo;
    char   ch;
    int    InStock;
```

```
      videoType newVideo;

      getline(infile, Title);
      while(infile)
      {
          getline(infile, Star1);
          getline(infile, Star2);
          getline(infile, Producer);
          getline(infile, Director);
          getline(infile, ProductionCo);
          infile>>InStock;
          infile.get(ch);
          newVideo.setVideoInfo(Title, Star1, Star2, Producer,
                              Director, ProductionCo, InStock);
          videoList.insert(newVideo);

          getline(infile, Title);
      }//end while

}//end createVideoList

void displayMenu()
{
    cout<<"Select one of the following "<<endl;
    cout<<"1: To check whether a particular video is in "
        <<"the store"<<endl;
    cout<<"2: To check out a video"<<endl;
    cout<<"3: To check in a video"<<endl;
    cout<<"4: To check whether a particular video is in stock"
        <<endl;
    cout<<"5: To print the titles of all the videos"<<endl;
    cout<<"6: To print a list of all the videos"<<endl;
    cout<<"9: To exit"<<endl;
}
```

QUICK REVIEW

1. A binary tree is either empty or it has a special node called the root node. If the tree is nonempty, the root node has two sets of nodes, called the left and right subtrees, such that the left and right subtrees are also binary trees.

2. The node of a binary tree has two links in it.

3. A node in a binary tree is called a leaf if it has no left and right children.

4. A node U is called the parent of a node V if there is a branch from U to V.

5. A path from a node X to a node Y in a binary tree is a sequence of nodes $X_0, X_1, ..., X_n$ such that (a) $X = X_0$, $X_n = Y$, and (b) X_{i-1} is the parent of X_i for all $i = 1, 2, ..., n$. That is, there is a branch from X_0 to X_1, X_1 to X_2, ..., X_{i-1} to X_i, ..., X_{n-1} to X_n.

6. The level of a node in a binary tree is the number of branches on the path from the root to the node.

7. The level of the root node of a binary tree is 0; the level of the children of the root node is 1.

8. The height of a binary tree is the number of nodes on the longest path from the root to a leaf.

9. In an inorder traversal, the binary tree is traversed as follows:
   a. Traverse the left subtree.
   b. Visit the node.
   c. Traverse the right subtree.

10. In a preorder traversal, the binary tree is traversed as follows:
    a. Visit the node.
    b. Traverse the left subtree.
    c. Traverse the right subtree.

11. In a postorder traversal, the binary tree is traversed as follows:
    a. Traverse the left subtree.
    b. Traverse the right subtree.
    c. Visit the node.

12. A binary search tree T is either empty or:
    i. T has a special node called the root node;
    ii. T has two sets of nodes, L_T and R_T, called the left subtree and the right subtree of T, respectively;
    iii. The key in the root node is larger than every key in the left subtree and smaller than every key in the right subtree; and
    iv. L_T and R_T are binary search trees.

13. To delete a node from a binary search tree that has both left and right nonempty subtrees, first its immediate predecessor is located, then the predecessor's info is copied into the node, and finally the predecessor is deleted.

14. A perfectly balanced binary tree is a binary tree such that:

    (i) The height of the left and right subtrees of the root are equal.

    (ii) The left and right subtrees of the root are perfectly balanced binary trees.

15. An AVL (or height-balanced) tree is a binary search tree such that:

    (i) The height of the left and right subtrees of the root differ by at most 1.

    (ii) The left and right subtrees of the root are AVL trees.

16. Let x be a node in a binary tree. Then x_l denotes the height of the left subtree of x and x_r denotes the height of the right subtree of x.

17. Let T be an AVL tree and x be a node in T. Then $|x_r - x_l| \le 1$, where $|x_r - x_l|$ denotes the absolute value of $x_r - x_l$.

18. Let x be a node in the AVL tree T.

    a. If $x_l > x_r$, we say that x is left high. In this case, $x_l = x_r + 1$.

    b. If $x_l = x_r$, we say that x is equal high.

    c. If $x_r > x_l$, we say that x is right high. In this case, $x_r = x_l + 1$.

19. The balance factor of x, written $bf(x)$, is defined as $bf(x) = x_r - x_l$.

20. Let x be a node in the AVL tree T. Then,

    a. If x is left high, then $bf(x) = -1$.

    b. If x is equal high, then $bf(x) = 0$.

    c. If x is right high, then $bf(x) = 1$.

21. Let x be a node in a binary tree. We say that node x violates the balance criteria if $|x_r - x_l| > 1$, that is, the height of the left and right subtrees of x differ by more that 1.

22. Every node x in the AVL tree T, in addition to the data and pointers to the left and right subtrees, must keep track of its balance factor.

23. In an AVL tree, there are two types of rotations, left rotation and right rotation. Suppose that the rotation occurs at node x. If it is a left rotation, then certain nodes from the right subtree of x move to its left subtree; the root of the right subtree of x becomes the new root of the reconstructed subtree. Similarly, if it is a right rotation at x, certain nodes from the left subtree of x move to its right subtree; the root of the left subtree of x becomes the new root of the reconstructed subtree.

11

1. Mark the following statements as true or false.

   a. A binary tree must be nonempty.

   b. The level of the root node is 0.

   c. If a tree has only one node, the height of the tree is 0 because the number of levels is 0.

   d. The inorder traversal of a binary tree always outputs the data in ascending order.

2. There are 14 different binary trees with four nodes. Draw all of them.

The binary tree of Figure 11-47 is to be used for Exercises 3 through 8.

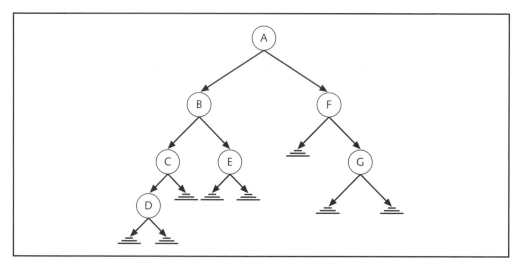

Figure 11-47 Figure for Exercises 3 through 8

3. Find L_A, the node in the left subtree of A.

4. Find R_A, the node in the right subtree of A.

5. Find R_B, the node in the right subtree of B.

6. List the nodes of this binary tree in an inorder sequence.

7. List the nodes of this binary tree in a preorder sequence.

8. List the nodes of this binary tree in a postorder sequence.

The binary tree of Figure 11-48 is to be used for Exercises 9 through 13.

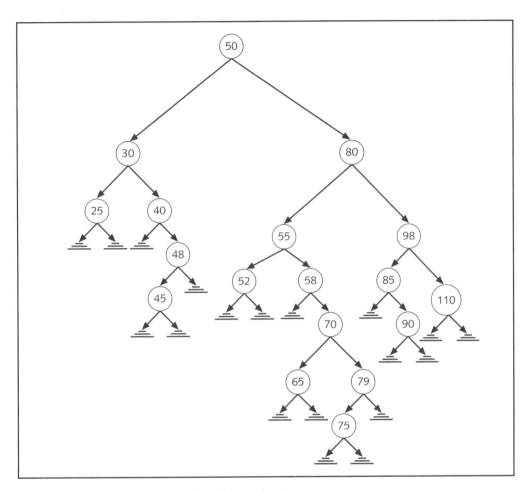

Figure 11-48   Figure for Exercises 9 through 13

9. List the path from the node with info 80 to the node with `info` 79.

10. A node with info 35 is to be inserted in the tree. List the nodes that are visited by the function `insert` to insert 35. Redraw the tree after inserting 35.

11. Delete node 52 and redraw the binary tree.

12. Delete node 40 and redraw the binary tree.

13. Delete nodes 80 and 58 in that order. Redraw the binary tree after each deletion.

14. Suppose that you are given two sequences of elements corresponding to the inorder sequence and the preorder sequence. Prove that it is possible to reconstruct a unique binary tree.

15. The following code lists the nodes in a binary tree in two different orders:

    ```
    preorder:    ABCDEFGHIJKLM
    inorder:     CEDFBAHJIKGML
    ```

    Draw the binary tree.

16. Given the preorder sequence and the postorder sequence, show that it may not be possible to reconstruct the binary tree.

17. Insert 100 in the AVL tree of Figure 11-49. The resulting tree must be an AVL tree. What is the balance factor at the root node after the insertion?

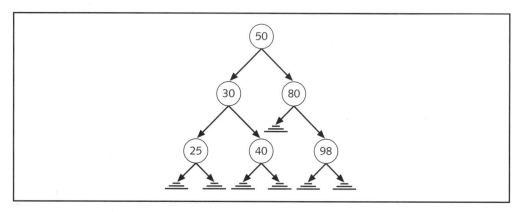

Figure 11-49   AVL tree for Exercise 17

18. Insert 45 in the AVL tree of Figure 11-50. The resulting tree must be an AVL tree. What is the balance factor at the root node after the insertion?

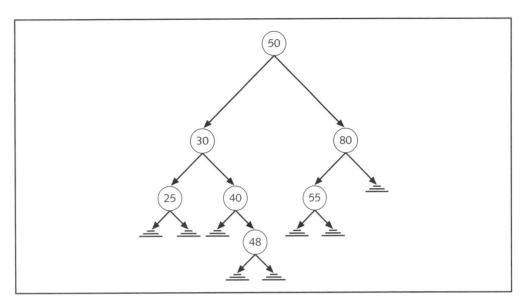

Figure 11-50   AVL tree for Exercise 18

19. Insert 42 in the AVL tree of Figure 11-51. The resulting tree must be an AVL tree. What is the balance factor at the root node after the insertion?

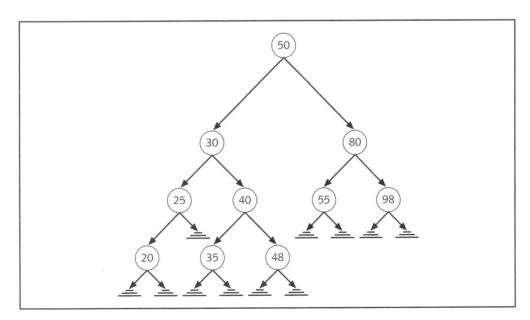

Figure 11-51   AVL tree for Exercise 19

20. The following keys are inserted (in the order given) into an initially empty AVL tree. Show the AVL tree after each insertion.

24, 39, 31, 46, 48, 34, 19, 5, 29

PROGRAMMING EXERCISES

1. Write the definition of the function `nodeCount` that returns the number of nodes in a binary tree. Add this function to the `class binaryTreeType` and create a program to test this function.

2. Write the definition of the function `leavesCount` that takes as a parameter a pointer to the root node of a binary tree and returns the number of leaves in a binary tree. Add this function to the `class binaryTreeType` and create a program to test this function.

3. Write a function, `swapSubtrees`, that swaps all of the left and right subtrees of a binary tree. Add this function to the `class binaryTreeType` and create a program to test this function.

4. Write a function, `singleParent`, that returns the number of nodes in a binary tree that have only one child. Add this function to the `class binaryTreeType` and create a program to test this function. (Note: first create a binary search tree.)

5. Write a program to test various operations on a binary search tree.

6. a. Write the definition of the function to implement the nonrecursive postorder traversal algorithm.

b. Write a program to test the nonrecursive inorder, preorder, and postorder traversal algorithms. (Note: first create a binary search tree.)

7. Write a version of the preorder traversal algorithm in which a user-defined function can be passed as a parameter to specify the visiting criteria at a node.

8. Write a version of the postorder traversal algorithm in which a user-defined function can be passed as a parameter to specify the visiting criteria at a node.

9. a. Write the definition of the class template that implements an AVL tree as an ADT. (You do not need to implement the delete operation.)

b. Write the definitions of the member functions of the class that you defined in (a).

c. Write a program to test various operations of an AVL tree.

10. Write the definitions of the functions of the `class videoBinaryTree` not given in the Programming Example Video Store.

11. **(Video Store Program)** In Programming Exercise 14 in Chapter 5, you were asked to design and implement a class to maintain customer data in a linked list. Because the search on a linked list is sequential and therefore can be time consuming, design and implement the **class customerBTreeType** so that this customer data can be stored in a binary search tree. The **class customerBTreeType** must be derived from the **class bSearchTreeType** as designed in this chapter. Write a program to test the customer component. Moreover, write the definition of the function **nodeCount** of the **class binaryTreeType** before executing the program.

12. **(Video Store Program)** Using classes to implement the video data, video list data, customer data, and customer list data, as designed in this chapter and in Programming Exercises 10 and 11, design and complete the program to put the video store into operation. Write the definition of the function **nodeCount** of the **class binaryTreeType** before executing the program.

11

12

GRAPHS

In this chapter, you will:

♦ Learn about graphs

♦ Become familiar with the basic terminology of graph theory

♦ Discover how to represent graphs in computer memory

♦ Explore graphs as ADTs

♦ Examine and implement various graph traversal algorithms

♦ Learn how to implement the shortest path algorithm

♦ Examine and implement the minimal spanning tree algorithm

♦ Explore the topological sort

In previous chapters, you learned various ways to represent and manipulate data. This chapter discusses how to implement and manipulate graphs, which have numerous applications in computer science.

INTRODUCTION

In 1736, the following problem was posed. In the town of Königsberg (now called Kalin-ingrad), the river Pregel (Pregolya) flows around the island Kneiphof and then divides into two. See Figure 12-1.

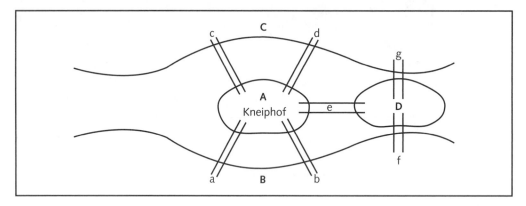

Figure 12-1   Königsberg bridge problem

The river has four land areas (A, B, C, D), as shown in the figure. These land areas are con-nected using seven bridges as shown in Figure 12-1. The bridges are labeled a, b, c, d, e, f, and g. The Königsberg bridge problem is as follows: Starting at one land area, is it possible to walk across all the bridges exactly once and return to the starting land area? In 1736, Euler repre-sented the Königsberg bridge problem as a graph, as shown in Figure 12-2, and answered the question in the negative. This marked (as recorded) the birth of graph theory.

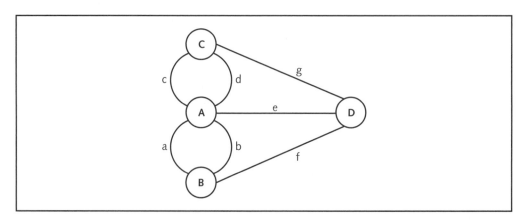

Figure 12-2   Graph representation of the Königsberg bridge problem

Over the past 200 years, graph theory has been applied to a variety of applications. Graphs are used to model electrical circuits, chemical compounds, highway maps, and so on. They are also used in the analysis of electrical circuits, finding the shortest route, project planning, linguistics, genetics, social science, and so forth. In this chapter, you learn about graphs and their applications in computer science.

GRAPH DEFINITIONS AND NOTATIONS

To facilitate and simplify our discussion, we borrow a few definitions and terminology from the set theory. Let X be a set. If a is an element of X, then we write $a \in X$. (The symbol "$\in$" means "belongs to.") A set Y is called a subset of X if every element of Y is also an element of X. If Y is a subset of X, we write $Y \subseteq X$. (The symbol "$\subseteq$" means "is a subset of.") The **intersection** of sets A and B, written $A \cap B$, is the set of all the elements that are in A and B; that is, $A \cap B = \{x \mid x \in A \text{ and } x \in B\}$. (The symbol "$\cap$" means "intersection.") The **union** of sets A and B, written $A \cup B$, is the set of all the elements that are in A or in B; that is, $A \cup B = \{x \mid x \in A \text{ or } x \in B\}$. (The symbol "$\cup$" means "union.") For sets A and B, the set $A \times B$ is the set of all the ordered pairs of elements of A and B; that is, $A \times B = \{(a, b) \mid a \in A, b \in B\}$.

A **graph** G is a pair, $G = (V, E)$, where V is a finite nonempty set, called the set of **vertices** of G, and $E \subseteq V \times V$. That is, the elements of E are the pair of elements of V. E is called the set of **edges**.

Let $V(G)$ denote the set of vertices, and $E(G)$ denote the set of edges of a graph G. If the elements of $E(G)$ are ordered pairs, G is called a **directed graph** or **digraph**; otherwise, G is called an **undirected graph**. In an undirected graph, the pairs (u, v) and (v, u) represent the same edge.

Let G be a graph. A graph H is called a **subgraph** of G if $V(H) \subseteq V(G)$ and $E(H) \subseteq E(G)$; that is, every vertex of H is a vertex of G, and every edge in H is an edge in G.

A graph can be shown pictorially. The vertices are drawn as circles, and a label inside the circle represents the vertex. In an undirected graph, the edges are drawn using lines. In a directed graph, the edges are drawn using arrows.

12

Example 12-1

Figure 12-3 shows some examples of undirected graphs.

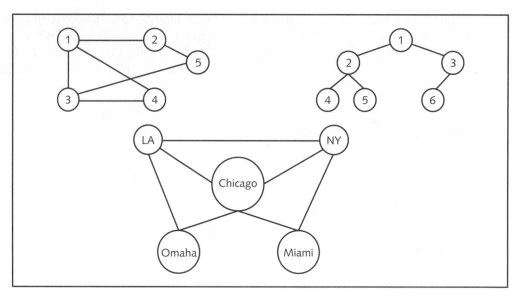

Figure 12-3 Various undirected graphs

Example 12-2

Figure 12-4 shows some examples of directed graphs.

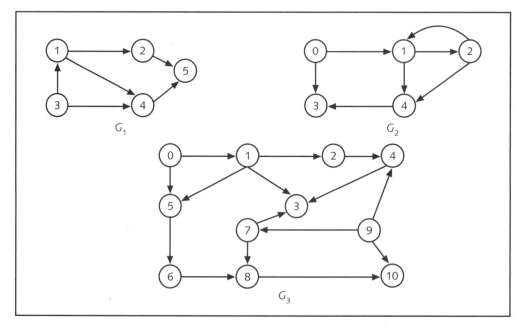

Figure 12-4 Various directed graphs

For the graphs of Figure 12-4, we have:

$V(G_1) = \{1, 2, 3, 4, 5\}$ $E(G_1) = \{(1, 2), (1, 4), (2, 5), (3, 1), (3, 4), (4, 5)\}$

$V(G_2) = \{0, 1, 2, 3, 4\}$ $E(G_2) = \{(0, 1), (0, 3), (1, 2), (1, 4), (2, 1), (2, 4), (4, 3)\}$

$V(G_3) = \{0, 1, 2, 3, 4, 5, 6, 7, 8, 9, 10\}$ $E(G_3) = \{(0, 1), (0, 5), (1, 2), (1, 3), (1, 5), (2, 4), (4, 3), (5, 6), (6, 8), (7, 3),$
                                       $(7, 8), (8, 10), (9, 4), (9, 7), (9, 10)\}$

Let G be an undirected graph. Let u and v be two vertices in G. Then u and v are called **adjacent** if there is an edge from one to the other; that is, $(u, v) \in E$. Let $e = (u, v)$ be an edge in G. We then say that edge e is **incident** on the vertices u and v. An edge incident on a single vertex is called a **loop**. If two edges, e_1 and e_2, are associated with the same pair of vertices, then e_1 and e_2 are called **parallel edges**. A graph is called a **simple graph** if it has no loops and no parallel edges. There is a **path** from u to v if there is a sequence of vertices $u_1, u_2, ..., u_n$ such that $u = u_1, u_n = v$, and (u_i, u_{i+1}) is an edge for all $i = 1, 2, ..., n - 1$. Vertices u and v are called **connected** if there is a path from u to v. A **simple path** is a path in which all the vertices, except possibly the first and last vertices, are distinct. A **cycle** in G is a simple path in which the first and last vertices are the same. G is called **connected** if there is a path from any vertex to any other vertex. A maximal subset of connected vertices is called a **component** of G.

Let G be a directed graph, and let u and v be two vertices in G. If there is an edge from u to v, that is, $(u, v) \in E$, then we say that u is **adjacent to** v and v is **adjacent from** u. The definitions of the paths and cycles in G are similar to those for undirected graphs. G is called **strongly connected** if any two vertices in G are connected.

Consider the directed graphs of Figure 12-4. In G_1, **1–4–5** is a path from vertex 1 to vertex 5. There are no cycles in G_1. In G_2, **1–2–1** is a cycle. In G_3, **0–1–2–4–3** is a path from vertex 0 to vertex 3; **1–5–6–8–10** is a path from vertex 1 to vertex 10. There are no cycles in G_3.

GRAPH REPRESENTATION

To write programs that process and manipulate graphs, the graphs must be stored—that is, represented—in computer memory. A graph can be represented (in computer memory) in several ways. We now discuss two commonly used ways: adjacency matrices and adjacency lists.

Adjacency Matrix

Let G be a graph with n vertices, where $n > 0$. Let $V(G) = \{v_1, v_2, ..., v_n\}$. The adjacency matrix A_G is a two-dimensional $n \times n$ matrix such that the (i, j)th entry of A_G is 1 if there is an edge from v_i to v_j; otherwise, the (i, j)th entry is zero. That is,

$$A_G(i, j) = \begin{cases} 1 & \text{if } (v_i, v_j) \in E(G) \\ 0 & \text{otherwise} \end{cases}$$

Example 12-3

Consider the directed graphs of Figure 12-4. The adjacency matrices of the directed graphs G_1, G_2, and G_3 are as follows:

$$A_{G_1} = \begin{bmatrix} 0 & 1 & 0 & 1 & 0 \\ 0 & 0 & 0 & 0 & 1 \\ 1 & 0 & 0 & 1 & 0 \\ 0 & 0 & 0 & 0 & 1 \\ 0 & 0 & 0 & 0 & 0 \end{bmatrix}$$

$$A_{G_2} = \begin{bmatrix} 0 & 1 & 0 & 1 & 0 \\ 0 & 0 & 1 & 0 & 1 \\ 0 & 1 & 0 & 0 & 1 \\ 0 & 0 & 0 & 0 & 0 \\ 0 & 0 & 0 & 1 & 0 \end{bmatrix}$$

$$A_{G_3} = \begin{matrix} 0 \\ 1 \\ 2 \\ 3 \\ 4 \\ 5 \\ 6 \\ 7 \\ 8 \\ 9 \\ 10 \end{matrix} \begin{bmatrix} 0 & 1 & 0 & 0 & 0 & 1 & 0 & 0 & 0 & 0 & 0 \\ 0 & 0 & 1 & 1 & 0 & 1 & 0 & 0 & 0 & 0 & 0 \\ 0 & 0 & 0 & 0 & 1 & 0 & 0 & 0 & 0 & 0 & 0 \\ 0 & 0 & 0 & 0 & 0 & 0 & 0 & 0 & 0 & 0 & 0 \\ 0 & 0 & 0 & 1 & 0 & 0 & 0 & 0 & 0 & 0 & 0 \\ 0 & 0 & 0 & 0 & 0 & 0 & 1 & 0 & 0 & 0 & 0 \\ 0 & 0 & 0 & 0 & 0 & 0 & 0 & 0 & 1 & 0 & 0 \\ 0 & 0 & 0 & 1 & 0 & 0 & 0 & 0 & 1 & 0 & 0 \\ 0 & 0 & 0 & 0 & 0 & 0 & 0 & 0 & 0 & 0 & 1 \\ 0 & 0 & 0 & 0 & 1 & 0 & 0 & 1 & 0 & 0 & 1 \\ 0 & 0 & 0 & 0 & 0 & 0 & 0 & 0 & 0 & 0 & 0 \end{bmatrix}$$

Adjacency Lists

Let G be a graph with n vertices, where $n > 0$. Let $V(G) = \{v_1, v_2, ..., v_n\}$. In the adjacency list representation, corresponding to each vertex, v, there is a linked list such that each node of the linked list contains the vertex u, such that $(v, u) \in E(G)$. Because there are n nodes, we use an array, A, of size n, such that $A[i]$ is a pointer to the linked list containing the vertices to which v_i is adjacent. Clearly, each node has two components, say **vertex** and **link**. The component **vertex** contains the index of the vertex adjacent to vertex i.

Example 12-4

Consider the directed graphs of Figure 12-4. Figure 12-5 shows the adjacency list of the directed graph G_2.

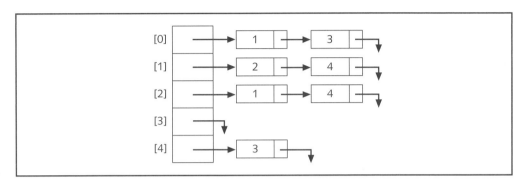

Figure 12-5 Adjacency list of graph G_2 of Figure 12-4

Figure 12-6 shows the adjacency list of the directed graph G_3.

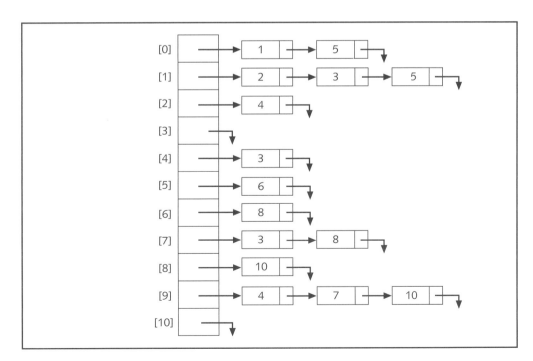

Figure 12-6 Adjacency list of graph G_3 of Figure 12-4

OPERATIONS ON GRAPHS

Now that you know how to represent graphs in computer memory, the next obvious step is to learn the basic operations on a graph. The operations commonly performed on a graph are as follows:

1. Create the graph. That is, store the graph in computer memory using a particular graph representation.

2. Clear the graph. This operation makes the graph empty.

3. Determine whether the graph is empty.

4. Traverse the graph.

5. Print the graph.

We will add more operations on a graph when we discuss a specific application or a particular graph later in this chapter.

How a graph is represented in computer memory depends on the specific application. For illustration purposes, we use the adjacency list (linked list) representation of graphs. Therefore, for each vertex, v, the vertices adjacent to v (in a directed graph, also called the **immediate successors**) are stored in the linked list associated with v.

To manage the data in a linked list, we use the **class linkedListType**, discussed in Chapter 5. Graph traversal algorithms, and the algorithms that we will add and discuss in later sections, all require the linked list associated with each node to be traversed and to retrieve the vertex contained in each node. The **class linkedListType** does not contain any function that can traverse the linked list and retrieve the data stored in each node one by one. (Note that the **print** function simply outputs the data to an output device.) Therefore, we first extend the definition of the **class linkedListType** (using the inheritance mechanism) so that the vertices adjacent to a given vertex can be retrieved in an array. This simplifies the processing of vertices. Let us call this **class linkedListGraph**. The definition of this class is:

```
template<class vType>
class linkedListGraph: public linkedListType<vType>
{
public:
    void getAdjacentVertices(vType adjacencyList[],
                             int& length);
    //Function to retrieve the vertices adjacent to a given
    //vertex.
    //Postcondition: The vertices adjacent to a given vertex
    //               are retrieved in the array adjacencyList.
    //               The parameter length specifies the number
    //               of vertices adjacent to a given vertex.
};
```

The definition of the member function **getAdjacentVertices** is given next.

```
template<class vType>
void linkedListGraph<vType>::getAdjacentVertices
                              (vType adjacencyList[], int& length)
{
    nodeType<vType> *current;

    length = 0;
    current = first;

    while(current != NULL)
    {
        adjacencyList[length++] = current->info;
        current = current->link;
    }
}
```

Next, we extend the definition of the class templates to include constant expressions as parameters.

Templates (Revisited)

Until now, we have passed only data types as parameters to templates. Just like types (data types), constant expressions can also be passed as parameters to templates. For example, consider the following class template:

```
template<class elemType, int size>
class listType
{
public:
    .
    .
    .
private:
    int maxSize;
    int length;
    elemType listElem[size];
};
```

This class template contains an array data member. The array element type and the size of the array are passed as parameters to the class template. To create a list of 100 components of int elements, we use the following statement:

```
listType<int, 100> intList;
```

The element type and the size of the array are both passed to the class template listType. Note that the element type (that is, int) and the array size, 100, are enclosed in angular brackets following the name of the class template.

12

Because the previous class definition no longer contains pointer data members, we may not need to include the destructor. However, we include the default constructor to set the values of the data members `maxSize` and `length`.

In this chapter, we will use this method to declare the array data members. This is quite helpful if we need to declare two-dimensional or larger arrays.

GRAPHS AS ADTS

In this section, we describe the class to implement graphs as an ADT and provide the definitions of the functions to implement the operations on a graph.

The following class defines a graph as an ADT:

```
const int infinity = 10000000;    //This will be used in later
                                  //sections of this chapter, when
                                  //we discuss weighted graphs.

template<class vType, int size>
class graphType
{
public:
    bool isEmpty()
      //Function to determine whether the graph is empty.
      //Postcondition: Returns true if the graph is empty;
      //               otherwise, returns false.
    void createGraph();
      //Function to create the graph using the adjacency list
      //representation.
      //Postcondition: The graph is created in the form of
      //               adjacency lists.
    void clearGraph();
      //Function to deallocate the memory occupied by the linked
      //lists and the array of pointers pointing to the linked
      //lists.
    void printGraph() const;
      //Function to print the graph.

    graphType();
      //default constructor
      //Postcondition: The graph size is set to 0, that is,
      //               gSize = 0 and maxSize = size.

    ~graphType();
      //destructor
      //Postcondition: The storage occupied by the graph
      //               is deallocated.
```

```
protected:
    int maxSize;   //maximum number of vertices
    int gSize;     //current number of vertices

    linkedListGraph<vType> graph[size];   //array of pointers to
                                          //create the adjacency
                                          //lists (linked lists)
};
```

 In the rest of this chapter, whenever we write graph algorithms in C++, we assume that the *n* vertices of the graphs are numbered 0, 1, ..., *n* − 1. Therefore, the vertex type is an integer. We will continue to use templates in case the user wants another way to specify the vertex type, and leave it for the user to make the necessary modifications to the algorithms.

The definitions of the member functions of the **class graphType** are discussed next.

A graph is empty if the number of vertices is zero—that is, if **gSize** is zero. Therefore, the definition of the function **isEmpty** is:

```
template<class vType, int size>
bool graphType<vType, size>::isEmpty()
{
    return(gSize == 0);
}
```

The definition of the function **createGraph** depends on how the data is input into the program. For illustration purposes, we assume that the data for the program is input from a file. The user is prompted for the input file. The data in the file appears in the following form:

```
5
0 2 4 ... -999
1 3 6 8 ... -999
...
```

The first line of input specifies the number of vertices in the graph. The first entry in the remaining lines specifies the vertex, and all of the remaining entries in the line (except the last) specify the vertices that are adjacent to the vertex. Each line ends with the number **-999**.

Using these conventions, the definition of the function `createGraph` is:

```
template<class vType, int size>
void graphType<vType, size>::createGraph()
{
    ifstream infile;
    char fileName[50];

    vType vertex;
    vType adjacentVertex;

    if(gSize != 0)  //if the graph is not empty, make it empty
        clearGraph();

    cout<<"Enter the input file name: ";
    cin>>fileName;
    cout<<endl;

    infile.open(fileName);

    if(!infile)
    {
        cerr<<"Cannot open the input file."<<endl;
        return;
    }

    infile>>gSize;   //get the number of vertices

    for(int index = 0; index < gSize; index++)
    {
        infile>>vertex;
        infile>>adjacentVertex;

        while(adjacentVertex != -999)
        {
            graph[vertex].insertLast(adjacentVertex);
            infile>>adjacentVertex;
        }//end while
    }//end for

    infile.close();
}//end createGraph
```

The function `clearGraph` empties the graph by deallocating the storage occupied by each linked list and then setting the number of vertices to zero.

```
template<class vType, int size>
void graphType<vType, size>::clearGraph()
{
    int index;

    for(index = 0; index < gSize; index++)
        graph[index].destroyList();

    gSize = 0;
}
```

The definition of the function `printGraph` is given next.

```
template<class vType, int size>
void graphType<vType, size>::printGraph() const
{
    int index;

    for(index = 0; index < gSize; index++)
        cout<<index<<" "<<graph[index]<<endl;

    cout<<endl;
}//end printGraph
```

The definitions of the default constructor and the destructor are given next.

```
    //default constructor
template<class vType, int size>
graphType<vType, size>::graphType()
{
    maxSize = size;
    gSize = 0;
}

    //destructor
template<class vType, int size>
graphType<vType, size>::~graphType()
{
    clearGraph();
}
```

12

GRAPH TRAVERSALS

Processing a graph requires the ability to traverse the graph. This section discusses the graph traversal algorithms.

Traversing a graph is similar to traversing a binary tree, except that traversing a graph is a bit more complicated. Recall that a binary tree has no cycles. Also, starting at the root node, we can traverse the entire tree. On the other hand, a graph might have cycles and we might not be able to traverse the entire graph from a single vertex (for example, if the graph is not connected). Therefore, we must keep track of the vertices that have been visited. We must also traverse the graph from each vertex (that has not been visited) of the graph. This ensures that the entire graph is traversed.

The two most common graph traversal algorithms are the **depth first traversal** and **breadth first traversal**, which are described next. For simplicity, we assume that when a vertex is visited, its index is output. Moreover, each vertex is visited only once. We use the bool array visited to keep track of the visited vertices.

Depth First Traversal

The **depth first traversal** is similar to the preorder traversal of a binary tree. The general algorithm is:

```
for each vertex v in the graph
   if v is not visited
      start the depth first traversal at v
```

Consider the graph G_3 of Figure 12-4. It is shown here again as Figure 12-7 for easy reference.

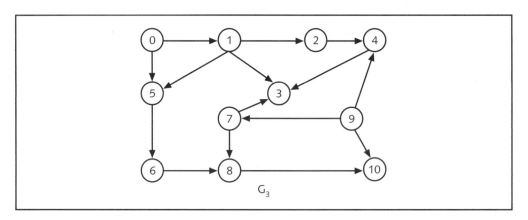

Figure 12-7   Directed graph G_3

The depth first ordering of the vertices of the graph G_3 in Figure 12-7 is:

```
0  1  2  4  3  5  6  8  10  7  9
```

The general algorithm to do a depth first traversal *at a given node v* is:

```
1. Mark node v as visited
2. Visit the node
3. For each vertex u adjacent to v
      if u is not visited
         start the depth first traversal at u
```

Clearly, this is a recursive algorithm. We use a recursive function, `dft`, to implement this algorithm. The vertex at which the depth first traversal is to be started, and the `bool` array `visited`, are passed as parameters to this function.

```
template<class vType, int size>
void graphType<vType, size>::dft(vType v, bool visited[])
{
    vType w;

    vType *adjacencyList;      //array to retrieve the
                               //adjacent vertices
    adjacencyList = new vType[gSize];

    int alLength = 0;   //the number of adjacent vertices

    visited[v] = true;
    cout<<" "<<v<<" ";   //visit the vertex

    graph[v].getAdjacentVertices(adjacencyList, alLength);
            //retrieve the adjacent vertices into adjacencyList

    for(int index = 0; index < alLength; index++) //for each
    {                                      //vertex adjacent to v
        w = adjacencyList[index];
        if(!visited[w])
            dft(w, visited);
    }//end for

    delete [] adjacencyList;
}//end dft
```

Next, we give the definition of the function **depthFirstTraversal** to implement the depth first traversal of the graph.

```
template<class vType, int size>
void graphType<vType, size>::depthFirstTraversal()
{
    bool *visited;      //array to keep track of the visited
                        //vertices
    visited = new bool[gSize];

    int index;

    for(index = 0; index < gSize; index++)
        visited[index] = false;

    for(index = 0; index < gSize; index++) //for each vertex
        if(!visited[index])                //that is not visited,
            dft(index, visited);       //do a depth first
                                       //traversal
    delete [] visited;
}//end depthFirstTraversal
```

The function **depthFirstTraversal** performs a depth first traversal of the entire graph. The definition of the function **dftAtVertex**, which performs a depth first traversal at a given vertex, is as follows:

```
template<class vType, int size>
void graphType<vType, size>::dftAtVertex(vType vertex)
```

12

```
{
    bool *visited;

    visited = new bool[gSize];

    for(int index = 0; index < gSize; index++)
        visited[index] = false;

     dft(vertex, visited);

    delete [] visited;

}//end dftAtVertex
```

Breadth First Traversal

The **breadth first traversal** of a graph is similar to traversing a binary tree level by level (the nodes at each level are visited from left to right). All the nodes at any level, i, are visited before visiting the nodes at level $i + 1$.

The breadth first ordering of the vertices of the graph G_3 (Figure 12-7) is:

```
0   1   5   2   3   6   4   8   10   7   9
```

For the graph G_3, we start the breadth traversal at vertex 0. After visiting vertex 0, next we visit the vertices that are directly connected to it and are not visited, which are 1 and 5. Next, we visit the vertices that are directly connected to 1 and are not visited, which are 2 and 3. After this, we visit the vertices that are directly connected to 5 and are not visited, which is 6. After this, we visit the vertices that are directly connected to 2 and are not visited, and so on.

As in the case of the depth first traversal, because it might not be possible to traverse the entire graph from a single vertex, the breadth first traversal also traverses the graph from each vertex that is not visited. Starting at the first vertex, the graph is traversed as much as possible; we then go to the next vertex that has not been visited. To implement the breadth first search algorithm, we use a queue. The general algorithm is:

```
a. for each vertex v in the graph
        if v is not visited
            add v to the queue   //start the breadth first search at v
b. Mark v as visited
c. while the queue is not empty
    c.1. Remove vertex u from the queue
    c.2. Retrieve the vertices adjacent to u
    c.3. for each vertex w that is adjacent to u
            if w is not visited
                c.3.1. Add w to the queue
                c.3.2. Mark w as visited
```

The following C++ function, `breadthFirstTraversal`, implements this algorithm:

```
template<class vType, int size>
void graphType<vType, size>::breadthFirstTraversal()
```

```
{
    linkedQueueType<vType> queue;
    vType u;

    bool *visited;
    visited = new bool[gSize];

    for(int ind = 0; ind < gSize; ind++)
        visited[ind] = false;      //initialize the array
                                   //visited to false

    vType *adjacencyList;
    adjacencyList = new vType[gSize];

    int alLength = 0;

    for(int index = 0; index < gSize; index++)
        if(!visited[index])
        {
            queue.addQueue(index);
            visited[index] = true;
            cout<<" "<<index<<" ";

            while(!queue.isEmptyQueue())
            {
                u = queue.front();
                queue.deleteQueue();
                graph[u].getAdjacentVertices(adjacencyList, alLength);
                for(int w = 0; w < alLength; w++)
                    if(!visited[adjacencyList[w]])
                    {
                        queue.addQueue(adjacencyList[w]);
                        visited[adjacencyList[w]] = true;
                        cout<<" "<<adjacencyList[w]<<" ";
                    }//end if
            }//end while
        }//end if

    delete [] visited;
    delete [] adjacencyList;
}//end breadthFirstTraversal
```

After including the previous graph traversal algorithms, the definition of the class graphType is:

```
template<class vType, int size>
class graphType
{
public:
    bool isEmpty();
        //Function to determine whether the graph is empty.
        //Postcondition: Returns true if the graph is empty;
        //               otherwise, returns false.
```

```
        void createGraph();
          //Function to create the graph using the adjacency list
          //representation.
          //Postcondition: The graph is created in the form of
          //               adjacency lists.
        void clearGraph();
          //Function to deallocate the memory occupied by the linked
          //lists and the array of pointers pointing to the linked
          //lists.
        void printGraph() const;
          //Function to print the graph.

        void depthFirstTraversal();
          //Function to perform the depth first traversal of
          //the entire graph.
        void dftAtVertex(vType vertex);
          //Function to perform the depth first traversal of
          //the graph at a node specified by the parameter vertex.

        void breadthFirstTraversal();
          //Function to perform the breadth first traversal of
          //the entire graph.

        graphType();
          //default constructor
          //Postcondition: The graph size is set to 0, that is,
          //               gSize = 0; maxSize = size.

        ~graphType();
          //destructor
          //Postcondition: The storage occupied by the graph
          //               is deallocated.
    protected:
        int maxSize;      //maximum number of vertices
        int gSize;        //current number of vertices
        linkedListGraph<vType> graph[size]; //array of pointers
                    //to create the adjacency lists (linked lists)
    private:
        void dft(vType v, bool visited[]);
          //Function to perform the depth first traversal of
          //the graph at a particular node.
};
```

As we continue to discuss graph algorithms, we will be writing C++ functions to implement specific algorithms, and so we will derive (using inheritance) new classes from the **class graphType**.

SHORTEST PATH ALGORITHM

The graph theory has many applications. For example, we can use graphs to show how different chemicals are related or to show airline routes. They can also be used to show the highway structure of a city, state, or country. The edges connecting two vertices can be assigned a non-negative real number, called the **weight of the edge**. If the graph represents a highway structure, the weight can represent the distance between two places, or the travel time from one place to another. Such graphs are called **weighted graphs**.

Let G be a weighted graph. Let u and v be two vertices in G, and let P be a path in G from u to v. The **weight of the path** P is the sum of the weights of all the edges on the path P, which is also called the **weight** of v from u via P.

Let G be a weighted graph representing a highway structure. Suppose that the weight of an edge represents the travel time. For example, to plan monthly business trips, a salesperson wants to find the **shortest path** (that is, the path with the smallest weight) from her or his city to every other city in the graph. Many such problems exist in which we want to find the shortest path from a given vertex, called the **source**, to every other vertex in the graph.

This section describes the **shortest path algorithm**, also called the **greedy algorithm**, developed by Dijkstra.

Let G be a graph with n vertices, where $n > 0$. Let $V(G) = \{v_1, v_2, ..., v_n\}$. Let W be a two-dimensional $n \times n$ matrix such that

$$W(i, j) = \begin{cases} w_{ij} & \text{if } (v_i, v_j) \text{ is an edge in G and } w_{ij} \text{ is the weight of the edge } (v_i, v_j) \\ \infty & \text{if there is no edge from } v_i \text{ to } v_j \end{cases}$$

The input to the program is the graph and the weight matrix associated with the graph. To make inputting the data easier, we extend the definition of the **class graphType** (using inheritance), and add the function **createWeightedGraph** to create the graph and the weight matrix associated with the graph. Let us call this **class weightedGraphType**. The functions to implement the shortest path algorithm will also be added to this class. The definition of the **class weightedGraphType** is:

```
template<class vType, int size>
class weightedGraphType: public graphType<vType, size>
{
public:
    void createWeightedGraph();
      //Function to create the graph and the weight matrix.
    void shortestPath(vType vertex);
      //Function to determine the smallest weight from the
      //vertex, that is, the source, to every other vertex
      //in the graph.
    void printShortestDistance(vType vertex);
      //Function to print the smallest weight from the
      //source to all the other vertices in the graph.
```

12

```
protected:
    double weights[size][size];  //weight matrix
    double smallestWeight[size]; //smallest weight from the
                                 //source to the other
                                 //vertices
};
```

The definition of the function `createWeightedGraph` is left as an exercise for you. Next, we describe the shortest path algorithm.

Shortest Path

Given a vertex, say `vertex` (that is, a source), this section describes the shortest path algorithm.

The general algorithm is:

1. Initialize the array `smallestWeight` so that

   `smallestWeight[u] = weights[vertex, u]`.

2. Set `smallestWeight[vertex] = 0`.

3. Find the vertex, **v**, that is closest to `vertex` for which the shortest path has not been determined.

4. Mark **v** as the (next) vertex for which the smallest weight is found.

5. For each vertex **w** in **G**, such that the shortest path from `vertex` to **w** has not been determined and an edge (**v, w**) exists, if the weight of the path to **w** via **v** is smaller than its current weight, update the weight of **w** to the weight of **v** + the weight of the edge (**v, w**).

Because there are **n** vertices, repeat Steps 3 through 5 $n - 1$ times.

Example 12-5 illustrates the shortest path algorithm. (We use the `bool` array `weightFound` to keep track of the vertices for which the smallest weight from the source vertex has been found. If the smallest weight for a vertex, from the source, has been found, then this vertex's corresponding entry in the array `weightFound` is set to `true`; otherwise, the corresponding entry is `false`.)

Example 12-5

Let G be the graph shown in Figure 12-8.

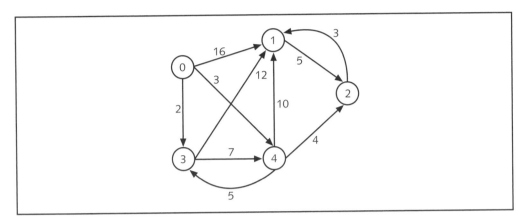

Figure 12-8 Weighted graph G

Suppose that the source vertex of G is 0. The graph shows the weight of each edge. After Steps 1 and 2 execute, the resulting graph is as shown in Figure 12-9. (In Figure 12-9, the symbol Θ means ∞.)

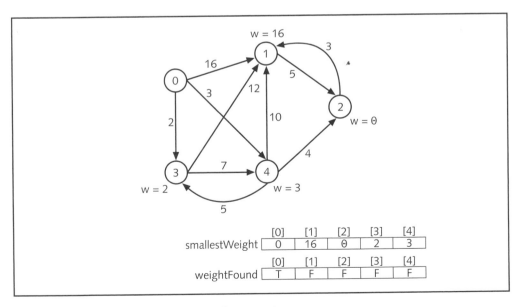

Figure 12-9 Graph after Steps 1 and 2 execute

First we select vertex 3 and mark `weightFound[3]` as `true`. Clearly, the weight of the path `0-3-1`, which is `14`, from 0 to 1 is less than the weight of the path `0-1`. So we update `smallestWeight[1]` to `14`. Figure 12-10 shows the resulting graph. (The dotted arrow shows the shortest path from the source—that is, from 0—to the vertex.)

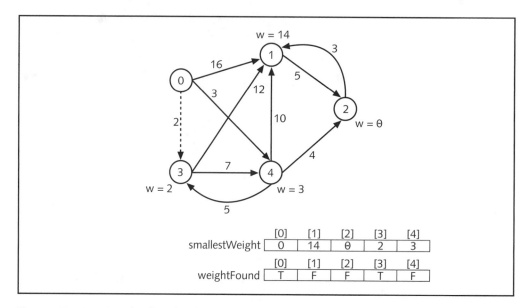

	[0]	[1]	[2]	[3]	[4]
smallestWeight	0	14	0	2	3

	[0]	[1]	[2]	[3]	[4]
weightFound	T	F	F	T	F

Figure 12-10   Graph after the first iteration of Steps 3, 4, and 5

Now we select vertex 4 because this is the vertex in the array `smallestWeight` that has the smallest weight and its corresponding entry in the array `weightFound` is `false`. Then we repeat the previous steps. We set `weightFound[4]` to `true`. Clearly, the weight of the path `0-4-1`, which is `13`, is smaller than the current weight of vertex 1, which is `14`. So we update `smallestWeight[1]`. Similarly, we update `smallestWeight[2]`. Figure 12-11 shows the resulting graph.

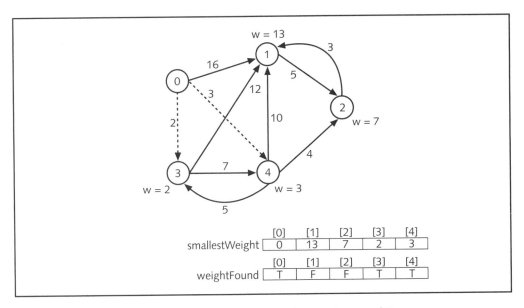

Figure 12-11   Graph after the second iteration of Steps 3, 4, and 5

The next vertex selected is 2. We set `weightFound[2]` to `true`. Clearly, the weight of the path 0-4-2-1, which is 10, from 0 to 1 is smaller than the current weight of vertex 1 (which is 13). So we update `smallestWeight[1]`. Figure 12-12 shows the resulting graph.

12

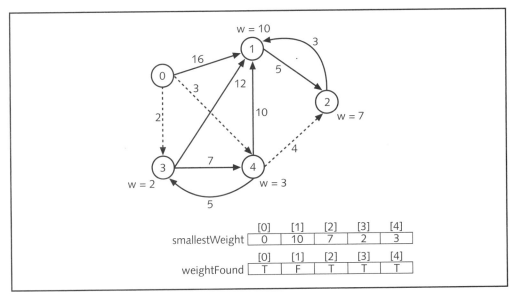

Figure 12-12   Graph after the third iteration of Steps 3, 4, and 5

Finally, vertex 1 is selected and the path is marked. Figure 12-13 shows the resulting graph.

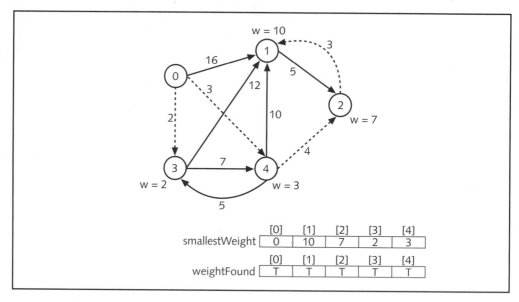

	[0]	[1]	[2]	[3]	[4]
smallestWeight	0	10	7	2	3

	[0]	[1]	[2]	[3]	[4]
weightFound	T	T	T	T	T

Figure 12-13   Graph after the fourth iteration of Steps 3, 4, and 5

The following C++ function, shortestPath, implements the previous algorithm:

```
template<class vType, int size>
void weightedGraphType<vType, size>::shortestPath(vType vertex)
{
    int i, j;
    int v;
    double minWeight;

    for(j = 0; j < gSize; j++)
        smallestWeight[j] = weights[vertex][j];

    bool weightFound[size];
    for(j = 0; j < gSize; j++)
        weightFound[j] = false;

    weightFound[vertex] = true;
    smallestWeight[vertex] = 0;
```

```
    for(i = 0; i < gSize - 1; i++)
    {
        minWeight = infinity;

        for(j = 0; j < gSize; j++)
            if(!weightFound[j])
                if(smallestWeight[j] < minWeight)
                {
                    v = j;
                    minWeight = smallestWeight[v];
                }

        weightFound[v] = true;

        for(j = 0; j < gSize; j++)
            if(!weightFound[j])
                if(minWeight + weights[v][j] < smallestWeight[j])
                    smallestWeight[j] = minWeight + weights[v][j];
    }//end for
}//end shortestPath
```

Note that the function `shortestPath` records only the weight of the shortest path from the source to a vertex. We leave it for you to modify this function so that the shortest path from the source to a vertex is also recorded.

The definition of the function `printShortestDistance` is:

```
template<class vType, int size>
void weightedGraphType<vType, size>::printShortestDistance
                                    (vType vertex)
{
    cout<<fixed<<showpoint<<setprecision(2);
    cout<<"Source vertex: "<<vertex<<endl;
    cout<<"Shortest distance from the source to each vertex."
        <<endl;
    cout<<"Vertex Shortest_Distance"<<endl;

    for(int j = 0; j < gSize; j++)
        cout<<setw(4)<<j<<setw(12)<<smallestWeight[j]<<endl;
    cout<<endl;
}
```

12

MINIMAL SPANNING TREE

Consider the graph of Figure 12-14, which represents the airline connections of a company between seven cities. The number on each edge represents some cost factor of maintaining the connection between the cities.

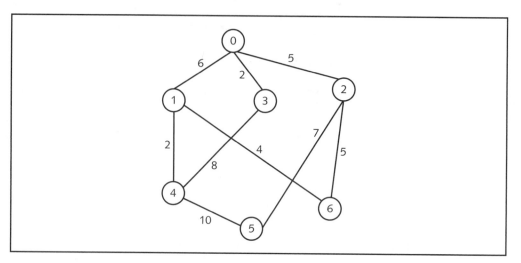

Figure 12-14   Airline connections between cities and the cost factor of maintaining the connections

Due to financial hardship, the company needs to shut down the maximum number of connections and still be able to fly from one city to another (may not be directly). The graphs of Figure 12-15(a), (b), and (c) show three different solutions.

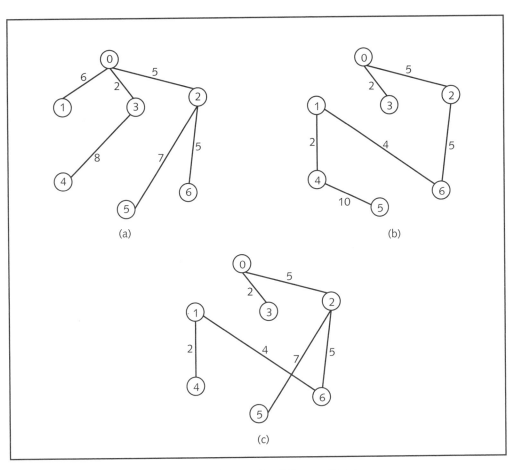

Figure 12-15   Possible solutions to the graph of Figure 12-14

The total cost factor of maintaining the remaining connections in Figure 12-15(a) is **33**, in Figure 12-15(b) it is **28**, and in Figure 12-15(c) it is **25**. Out of these three solutions, obviously, the desired solution is the one shown by the graph of Figure 12-15(c) because it gives the lowest cost factor. The graphs of Figure 12-15 are called spanning trees of the graph of Figure 12-14.

Let us note the following from the graphs of Figure 12-15. Each of the graphs of Figure 12-15 is a subgraph of the graph of Figure 12-14, and there is a unique path from a node to any other node. Such graphs are called trees. There are many other situations where, given a weighted graph, we need to determine a graph such as in Figure 12-15 with the smallest weight. In this section, we give an algorithm to determine such graphs. However, first we introduce some terminology.

A **(free) tree** T is a simple graph such that if u and v are two vertices in T, then there is a unique path from u to v. A tree in which a particular vertex is designated as a root is called a **rooted tree**. If a weight is assigned to the edges in T, T is called a **weighted tree**. If T is a weighted tree, the **weight** of T, denoted by $W(T)$, is the sum of the weights of all the edges in T.

A tree T is called a **spanning tree** of graph G if T is a subgraph of G such that $V(T) = V(G)$, that is, all the vertices of G are in T.

Suppose G denotes the graph of Figure 12-14. Then the graphs of Figure 12-15 show three spanning trees of G. Let us note the following theorem:

Theorem: A graph G has a spanning tree if and only if G is connected.

From this theorem, it follows that in order to determine a spanning tree of a graph, the graph must be connected.

Let G be a weighted graph. A **minimal spanning tree** of G is a spanning tree with the minimum weight.

There are two well-known algorithms, Prim's algorithm and Kruskal's algorithm, to find the minimal spanning tree of a graph. This section discusses Prim's algorithm to find a minimal spanning tree.

Prim's algorithm builds the tree iteratively by adding edges until a minimal spanning tree is obtained. We start with a designated vertex, which we call the source vertex. At each iteration, a new edge that does not complete a cycle is added to the tree.

Let G be a weighted graph such that $V(G) = \{v_0, v_1, ..., v_{n-1}\}$, where n, the number of vertices, is positive. Let v_0 be the source vertex. Let T be the partially built tree. Initially, $V(T)$ contains the source vertex and $E(T)$ is empty. At the next iteration, a new vertex that is not in $V(T)$ is added to $V(T)$, such that an edge exists from a vertex in T to the new vertex so that the corresponding edge has the smallest weight. The corresponding edge is added to $E(T)$.

The general form of Prim's algorithm is as follows (let n be the number of vertices in G):

```
1. Set V(T) = {source}
2. Set E(T) = empty
3. for i = 1 to n
      3.1 minWeight = infinity;
      3.2 for j = 1 to n
          if v_j is in V(T)
              for k = 1 to n
                  if v_k is not in T and weight[v_j][v_k] < minWeight
                  {
                      endVertex = v_k;
                      edge = (v_j, v_k);
                      minWeight = weight[v_j][v_k];
                  }
      3.3 V(T) = V(T) ∪ {endVertex};
      3.4 E(T) = E(T) ∪ {edge};
```

Let us illustrate Prim's algorithm using the graph G of Figure 12-16 (which is the same as the graph of Figure 12-14).

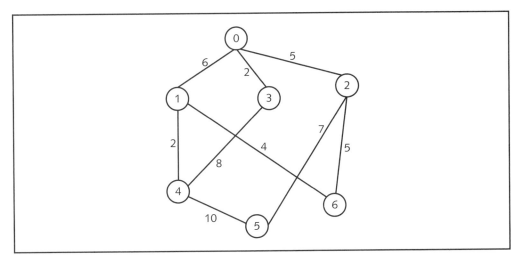

Figure 12-16   Weighted graph G

Let N denote the set of vertices of G that are not in T. Suppose that the source vertex is 0. After Steps 1 and 2 execute, $V(T), E(T)$, and N are as shown in Figure 12-17.

12

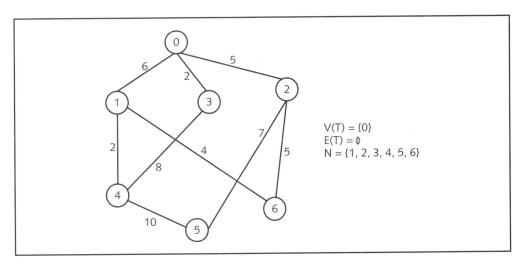

Figure 12-17   Graph G, $V(T)$, $E(T)$, and N after Steps 1 and 2 execute

Step 3.2 checks the following edges:

Edge	Weight of the Edge
(0,1)	6
(0,2)	5
(0,3)	2

Clearly, the edge (0,3) has the smallest weight. Therefore, vertex 3 is added to $V(T)$ and the edge (0,3) is added to $E(T)$. Figure 12-18 shows the resulting graph, $V(T)$, $E(T)$, and N. (The dotted line shows the edge in T.)

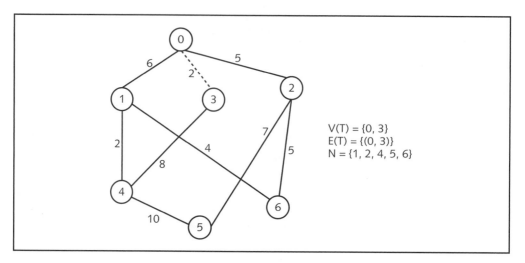

Figure 12-18   Graph G, V(T), E(T), and N after the first iteration of Step 3

Next, Step 3.2 checks the following edges:

Edge	Weight of the Edge
(0,1)	6
(0,2)	5
(3,4)	8

Clearly, the edge (0,2) has the smallest weight. Therefore, vertex 2 is added to $V(T)$ and the edge (0,2) is added to $E(T)$. Figure 12-19 shows the resulting graph, $V(T)$, $E(T)$, and N.

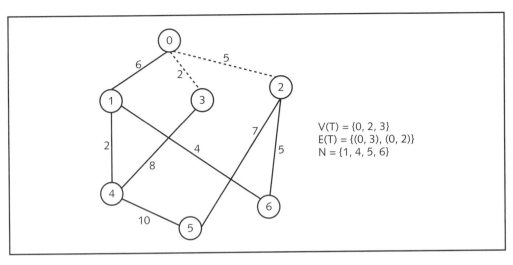

Figure 12-19   Graph G, V(T), E(T), and N after the second iteration of Step 3

At the next iteration, Step 3.2 checks the following edges:

Edge	Weight of the Edge
(0,1)	6
(2,5)	7
(2,6)	5
(3,4)	8

Clearly, the edge (2,6) has the smallest weight. Therefore, vertex 6 is added to V(T) and the edge (2,6) is added to E(T). Figure 12-20 shows the resulting graph, V(T), E(T), and N. (The dotted lines show the edges in T.)

12

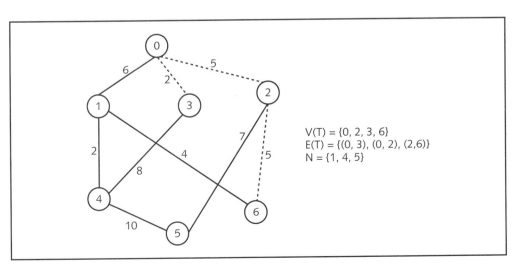

Figure 12-20   Graph G, V(T), E(T), and N after the third iteration of Step 3

At the next iteration, Step 3.2 checks the following edges:

Edge	Weight of the Edge
(0,1)	6
(2,5)	7
(3,4)	8
(6,1)	4

Clearly, the edge (**6,1**) has the smallest weight. Therefore, vertex **1** is added to $V(T)$ and the edge (**6,1**) is added to $E(T)$. Figure 12-21 shows the resulting graph, $V(T)$, $E(T)$, and N. (The dotted lines show the edges in T.)

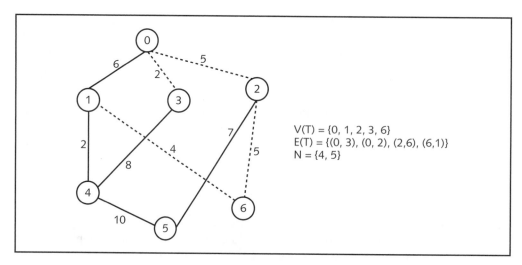

Figure 12-21   Graph G, $V(T)$, $E(T)$, and N after the fourth iteration of Step 3

At the next iteration, Step 3.2 checks the following edges:

Edge	Weight of the Edge
(1,4)	2
(2,5)	7
(3,4)	8

Clearly, the edge (**1,4**) has the smallest weight. Therefore, vertex **4** is added to $V(T)$ and the edge (**1,4**) is added to $E(T)$. Figure 12-22 shows the resulting graph, $V(T)$, $E(T)$, and N. (The dotted lines show the edges in T.)

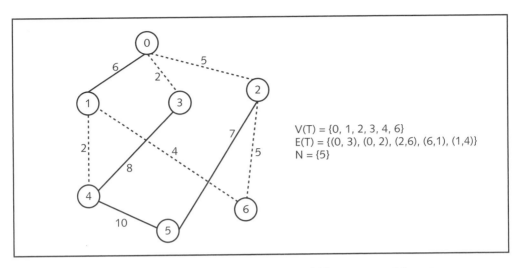

Figure 12-22 Graph G, V(T), E(T), and N after the fifth iteration of Step 3

At the next iteration, Step 3.2 checks the following edges:

Edge   **Weight of the Edge**

(2,5)   7
(4,5)   10

Clearly, the edge (2,5) has the smallest weight. Therefore, vertex 5 is added to $V(T)$ and the edge (2,5) is added to $E(T)$. Figure 12-23 shows the resulting graph, $V(T)$, $E(T)$, and N. (The dotted lines show the edges in T.)

12

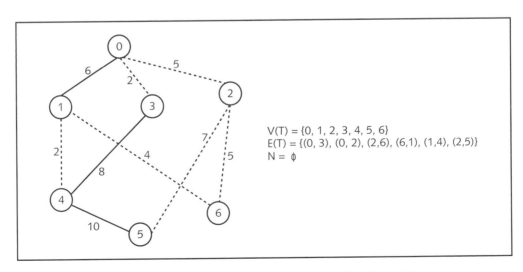

Figure 12-23 Graph G, V(T), E(T), and N after the sixth iteration of Step 3

The dotted lines show a minimal spanning tree of G of weight 25.

Before we give the definition of the function to implement Prim's algorithm, let us first define the spanning tree as an ADT.

Let msvt be the bool array such that msvt[j] is true if the vertex v_i is in T, and false otherwise. Let edges be an array such that edges[j] = k, if there is an edge connecting vertices v_j and v_k. Suppose that the edge (v_i, v_j) is in the minimal spanning tree. Let edgeWeights be an array such that edgeWeights[j] is the weight of the edge (v_i, v_j).

Using these conventions, the following class defines a spanning tree as an ADT:

```
template<class vType, int size>
class msTreeType: public graphType<vType, size>
{
public:
    void createSpanningGraph();
      //Function to create the graph and the weight matrix.
    void minimalSpanning(vType sVertex);
      //Function to create the edges of the minimal
      //spanning tree. The weight of the edges is also
      //saved in the array edgeWeights.
    void printTreeAndWeight();
      //Function to output the edges and the weight of the
      //minimal spanning tree.

protected:
    vType source;
    double weights[size][size];
    int edges[size];
    double edgeWeights[size];
};
```

The definition of the function createSpanningGraph is left as an exercise for you. This function creates the graph and the weight matrix associated with the graph.

The following C++ function, minimalSpanning, implements Prim's algorithm, as described previously:

```
template<class vType, int size>
void msTreeType<vType, size>::minimalSpanning(vType sVertex)
{
    int i, j, k;
    vType startVertex, endVertex;
    double minWeight;

    source = sVertex;

    bool mstv[size];
```

```
    for(j = 0; j < gSize; j++)
    {
        mstv[j] = false;
        edges[j] = source;
        edgeWeights[j] = weights[source][j];
    }

    mstv[source] = true;
    edgeWeights[source] = 0;

    for(i = 0; i < gSize - 1; i++)
    {
        minWeight = infinity;

        for(j = 0; j < gSize; j++)
            if(mstv[j])
                for(k = 0; k < gSize; k++)
                    if(!mstv[k] && weights[j][k] < minWeight)
                    {
                        endVertex = k;
                        startVertex = j;
                        minWeight = weights[j][k];
                    }
        mstv[endVertex] = true;
        edges[endVertex] = startVertex;
        edgeWeights[endVertex] = minWeight;
    }//end for
}//end minimalSpanning
```

The definition of the function `minimalSpanning` contains three nested `for` loops. Therefore, in the worst case, Prim's algorithm given in this section is of the order $O(n^3)$. It is possible to design Prim's algorithm so that it is of the order $O(n^2)$; Programming Exercise 5 at the end of this chapter asks you to do so.

The definition of the function `printTreeAndWeight` is given next.

```
template<class vType, int size>
void msTreeType<vType, size>::printTreeAndWeight()
{
    double treeWeight = 0;

    cout<<fixed<<showpoint<<setprecision(2);

    cout<<"Source Vertex: "<<source<<endl;
    cout<<"Edges    Weight"<<endl;

    for(int j = 0; j < gSize; j++)
    {
        if(edges[j] != j)
        {
```

12

```
        treeWeight = treeWeight + edgeWeights[j];
        cout<<"("<<edges[j]<<", "<<j<<")      "
            <<edgeWeights[j]<<endl;
    }
}

cout<<endl;
cout<<"Tree Weight: "<<treeWeight<<endl;
}//end printTreeAndWeight
```

TOPOLOGICAL ORDER

In college, before taking a particular course, students usually must take all its prerequisite courses, if any. For example, before taking the Programming II course, students must take the Programming I course. However, certain courses can be taken independently of each other. The courses within a department can be represented as a directed graph. A directed edge from, say, vertex u to vertex v means that the course represented by the vertex u is a prerequisite of the course represented by the vertex v. It would be helpful for students to know, before starting a major, the sequence in which they can take the courses so that before taking a course they take all its prerequisite courses and fulfill the graduation requirements on time. This section describes an algorithm that can be used to output the vertices of a directed graph in such a sequence. Let us first introduce some terminology.

Let G be a directed graph and $V(G) = \{v_1, v_2, ..., v_n\}$, where $n > 0$. A **topological ordering** of $V(G)$ is a linear ordering $v_{i1}, v_{i2}, ..., v_{in}$ of the vertices such that if v_{ij} is a predecessor of $v_{ik}, j \neq k$, $1 \leq j \leq n$, and $1 \leq k \leq n$, then v_{ij} precedes v_{ik}, that is, $j < k$ in this linear ordering.

This section describes an algorithm, that outputs the vertices of a directed graph in topological order. We assume that the graph has no cycles. We leave it for the reader, as an exercise, to modify the algorithm for the graphs that have cycles.

Because the graph has no cycles:

- There exists a vertex u in G such that u has no predecessor.

- There exists a vertex v in G such that v has no successor.

Suppose that the array `topologicalOrder` (of size n, the number of vertices) is used to store the vertices of G in topological order. Thus, if a vertex, say `u`, is a successor of the vertex `v` and `topologicalOrder[j]` = `v` and `topologicalOrder[k]` = `u`, then `j < k`.

The topological sort algorithm can be implemented using either the depth first traversal or the breadth first traversal. This section discusses how to implement topological ordering using the breadth first traversal. Programming Exercise 7 at the end of this chapter describes how to implement the topological sort using the depth first traversal.

We extend the definition of the **class graphType** (using inheritance) to implement the breadth first topological ordering algorithm. Let us call this **class topologicalOrderT**.

The definition of the class that includes the functions to implement the topological ordering algorithm is given next.

```
template<class vType, int size>
class topologicalOrderT: public graphType<vType, size>
{
public:
    void bfTopOrder();
        //Function to output the vertices in breadth first
        //topological order

};
```

Next, we discuss how to implement the function `bfTopOrder`.

Breadth First Topological Ordering

Recall that the breadth first traversal algorithm is similar to traversing a binary tree level by level, and so the root node (which has no predecessor) is visited first. Therefore, in the breadth first topological ordering we first find a vertex that has no predecessor vertex and place it first in the topological ordering. We next find the vertex, say **v**, all of whose predecessors have been placed in the topological ordering and place **v** next in the topological ordering. To keep track of the number of vertices of a vertex we use the array `predCount`. Initially, `predCount[j]` is the number of predecessors of the vertex v_j. The queue used to guide the breadth first traversal is initialized to those vertices v_k such that `predCount[k]` is zero. In essence, the general algorithm is:

1. Create the array `predCount` and initialize it so that `predCount[i]` is the number of predecessors of the vertex v_i.

2. Initialize the queue, say `queue`, to all those vertices v_k so that `predCount[k]` is zero. (Clearly, `queue` is not empty because the graph has no cycles.)

3. `while` the queue is not empty

    3.1   Remove the front element, **u**, of the queue.

    3.2   Put u in the next available position, say `topologicalOrder[topIndex]`, and increment `topIndex`.

    3.3   For all the immediate successors **w** of **u**

        3.3.1   Decrement the predecessor count of **w** by 1.

        3.3.2   `if` the predecessor count of **w** is zero, add **w** to `queue`.

The graph G_3 of Figure 12-7 has no cycles. The vertices of G_3 in breadth first topological ordering are:

```
Breadth First Topological order: 0 9 1 7 2 5 4 6 3 8 10
```

Next, we illustrate the breadth first topological ordering of the graph G_3.

12

After Steps 1 and 2 execute, the arrays `predCount`, `topologicalOrder`, and `queue` are as shown in Figure 12-24. (Notice that for simplicity, we show only the elements of the queue.)

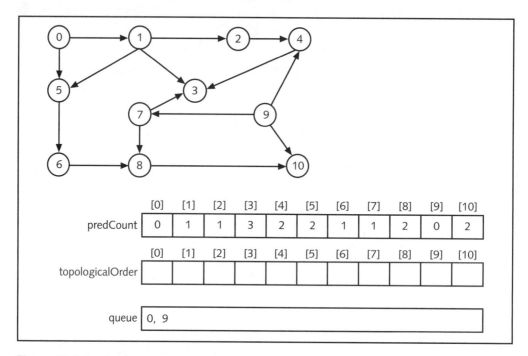

Figure 12-24 Arrays `predCount`, `topologicalOrder`, and `queue` after Steps 1 and 2 execute

Step 3 executes as long as the queue is nonempty.

Step3: Iteration 1: After Step 3.1 executes, the value of u is 0. Step 3.2 stores the value of u, which is 0, in the next available position in the array `topologicalOrder`. Notice that 0 is stored at position 0 in this array. Step 3.3 reduces the predecessor count of all the successors of 0 by 1, and if the predecessor count of any successor node of 0 reduces to 0, that node is added to `queue`. The successor nodes of the node 0 are the nodes 1 and 5. The predecessor count of the node 1 reduces to 0, and the predecessor count of the node 5 reduces to 1. The node 1 is added to `queue`. After the first iteration of Step 3, the arrays `predCount`, `topologicalOrder`, and `queue` are as shown in Figure 12-25.

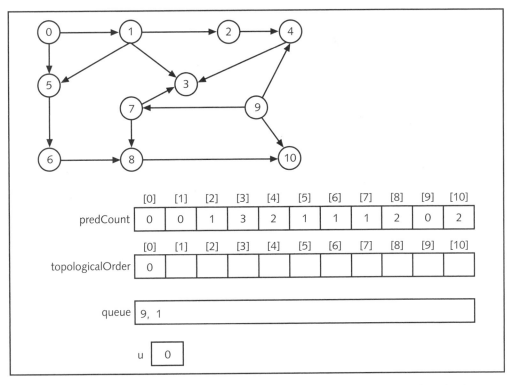

Figure 12-25 Arrays predCount, topologicalOrder, and queue after the first iteration of Step 3

12

Step3: Iteration 2: The queue is nonempty. After Step 3.1 executes, the value of u is 9. Step 3.2 stores the value of u, which is 9, in the next available position in the array topologicalOrder. Notice that 9 is stored at position 1 in this array. Step 3.3 reduces the predecessor count of all the successors of 9 by 1, and if the predecessor count of any successor node of 9 reduces to 0, that node is added to queue. The successor nodes of the node 9 are the nodes 4, 7, and 10. The predecessor count of the node 7 reduces to 0 and the predecessor count of the nodes 4 and 10 reduces to 1. The node 7 is added to queue. After the second iteration of Step 3, the arrays predCount, topologicalOrder, and queue are as shown in Figure 12-26.

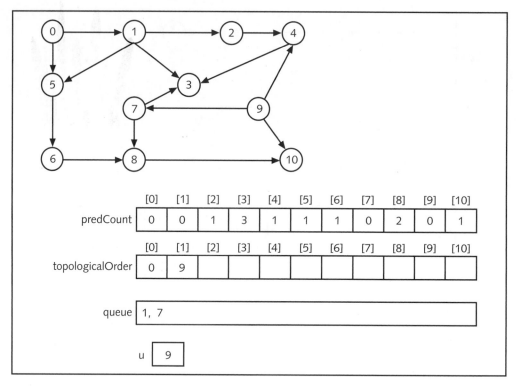

Figure 12-26 Arrays `predCount`, `topologicalOrder`, and `queue` after the second iteration of Step 3

Step3: Iteration 3: The queue is nonempty. After Step 3.1 executes, the value of u is 1. Step 3.2 stores the value of u, which is 1, in the next available position in the array `topologicalOrder`. Notice that 1 is stored at position 2 in this array. Step 3.3 reduces the predecessor count of all the successors of 1 by 1, and if the predecessor count of any successor node of 1 reduces to 0, that node is added to `queue`. The successor nodes of the node 1 are the nodes 2, 3, and 5. The predecessor count of the nodes 2 and 5 reduces to 0 and the predecessor count of the node 3 reduces to 2. The nodes 2 and 5, in this order, are added to `queue`. After the third iteration of Step 3, the arrays `predCount`, `topologicalOrder`, and `queue` are as shown in Figure 12-27.

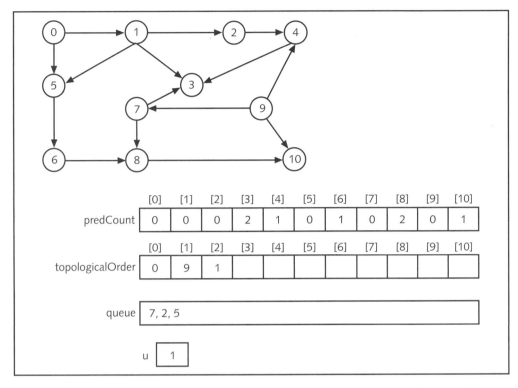

Figure 12-27   Arrays predCount, topologicalOrder, and queue after the third
iteration of Step 3

12

If you repeat Step 3 eight more times, the arrays predCount, topologicalOrder, and
queue are as shown in Figure 12-28.

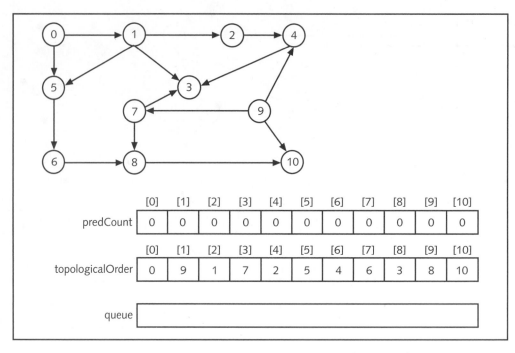

Figure 12-28   Arrays `predCount`, `topologicalOrder`, and `queue` after Step 3 executes eight more times

In Figure 12-28, the array `topologicalOrder` shows the breadth first topological ordering of the nodes of the graph G_3.

The following C++ function implements this breadth first topological ordering algorithm:

```
template<class vType, int size>
void topologicalOrderT<vType, size>::bfTopOrder()
{
    linkedQueueType<vType> queue;

    vType u;
    int ind, j;

    int *topologicalOrder;
    topologicalOrder = new int[gSize];

    for(ind = 0; ind < gSize; ind++)
        topologicalOrder[ind] = -1;

    int topIndex = 0;

    vType *adjacencyList; //array to store the adjacent vertices
    adjacencyList = new vType[gSize];
    int alLength = 0;
```

```
    int *predCount;
    predCount = new int[gSize];

    for(ind = 0; ind < gSize; ind++)
        predCount[ind] = 0;

    for(ind = 0; ind < gSize; ind++)
    {
        graph[ind].getAdjacentVertices(adjacencyList, alLength);

        for(j = 0; j < alLength; j++)
            predCount[adjacencyList[j]]++;
    }

    for(ind = 0; ind < gSize; ind++)
        if(predCount[ind] == 0)
            queue.addQueue(ind);

    while(!queue.isEmptyQueue())
    {
        u = queue.front();
        queue.deleteQueue();
        topologicalOrder[topIndex++] = u;

        graph[u].getAdjacentVertices(adjacencyList, alLength);
        for(int w = 0; w < alLength; w++)
        {
            predCount[adjacencyList[w]]--;
            if(predCount[adjacencyList[w]] == 0)
                queue.addQueue(adjacencyList[w]);
        }
    }//end while

        //output the vertices in breadth first topological order
    for(ind = 0; ind < gSize; ind++)
        cout<<topologicalOrder[ind]<<" ";
    cout<<endl;

    delete [] topologicalOrder;
    delete [] predCount;
    delete [] adjacencyList;

}//bfTopOrder
```

12

QUICK REVIEW

1. A graph G is a pair, $G = (V, E)$, where V is a finite nonempty set, called the set of vertices of G, and $E \subseteq V \times V$, called the set of edges.

2. In an undirected graph $G = (V, E)$, the elements of E are unordered pairs.

3. In a directed graph $G = (V, E)$, the elements of E are ordered pairs.

4. Let G be a graph. A graph H is called a subgraph of G if every vertex of H is a vertex of G and every edge in H is an edge in G.

5. Two vertices u and v in an undirected graph are called adjacent if there is an edge from one to the other.

6. Let $e = (u, v)$ be an edge in an undirected graph G. The edge e is said to be incident on the vertices u and v.

7. An edge incident on a single vertex is called a loop.

8. In an undirected graph, if two edges e_1 and e_2 are associated with the same pair of vertices, then e_1 and e_2 are called parallel edges.

9. A graph is called a simple graph if it has no loops and no parallel edges.

10. A path from a vertex u to a vertex v is a sequence of vertices $u_1, u_2, ..., u_n$ such that $u = u_1$, $u_n = v$, and (u_i, u_{i+1}) is an edge for all $i = 1, 2, ..., n - 1$.

11. The vertices u and v are called connected if there is a path from u to v.

12. A simple path is a path in which all the vertices, except possibly the first and last vertices, are distinct.

13. A cycle in G is a simple path in which the first and last vertices are the same.

14. An undirected graph G is called connected if there is a path from any vertex to any other vertex.

15. A maximal subset of connected vertices is called a component of G.

16. Suppose that u and v are vertices in a directed graph G. If there is an edge from u to v, that is, $(u, v) \in E$, we say that u is adjacent to v and v is adjacent from u.

17. A directed graph G is called strongly connected if any two vertices in G are connected.

18. Let G be a graph with n vertices, where $n > 0$. Let $V(G) = \{v_1, v_2, ..., v_n\}$. The adjacency matrix A_G is a two-dimensional $n \times n$ matrix such that the (i, j)th entry of A_G is 1 if there is an edge from v_i to v_j; otherwise, the (i, j)th entry is zero.

19. In an adjacency list representation, corresponding to each vertex v is a linked list such that each node of the linked list contains the vertex u, and $(v, u) \in E(G)$.

20. The depth first traversal of a graph is similar to the preorder traversal of a binary tree.

21. The breadth first traversal of a graph is similar to the level-by-level traversal of a binary tree.

22. The shortest path algorithm gives the shortest distance for a given node to every other node in the graph.

23. In a weighted graph, every edge has a nonnegative weight.

24. The weight of the path P is the sum of the weights of all the edges on the path P, which is also called the weight of v from u via P.

25. A (free) tree T is a simple graph such that if u and v are two vertices in T, there is a unique path from u to v.

26. A tree in which a particular vertex is designated as a root is called a rooted tree.

27. Suppose T is a tree. If a weight is assigned to the edges in T, T is called a weighted tree.

28. If T is a weighted tree, the weight of T, denoted by $W(T)$, is the sum of the weights of all the edges in T.

29. A tree T is called a spanning tree of graph G if T is a subgraph of G such that $V(T) = V(G)$, that is, if all the vertices of G are in T.

30. Let G be a graph and $V(G) = \{v_1, v_2, ..., v_n\}$, where $n > 0$. A topological ordering of $V(G)$ is a linear ordering $v_{i1}, v_{i2}, ..., v_{in}$ of the vertices such that if v_{ij} is a predecessor of $v_{ik}, j \neq k, 1 \leq j \leq n$, and $1 \leq k \leq n$, then v_{ij} precedes v_{ik}, that is, $j < k$ in this linear ordering.

EXERCISES

Use the graph in Figure 12-29 for Exercises 1 through 4.

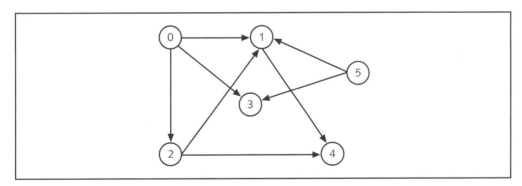

Figure 12-29 Graph for Exercises 1 through 4

1. Find the adjacency matrix of the graph.

2. Draw the adjacency list of the graph.

3. List the nodes of the graph in a depth first traversal.

4. List the nodes of the graph in a breadth first traversal.

5. Find the weight matrix of the graph in Figure 12-30.

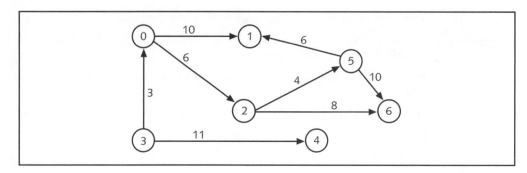

Figure 12-30 Graph for Exercise 5

6. Consider the graph in Figure 12-31. Find the shortest distance from node 0 to every other node in the graph.

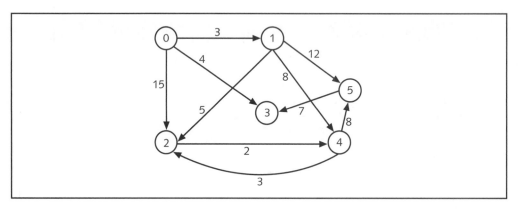

Figure 12-31 Graph for Exercise 6

7. Find a spanning tree in the graph in Figure 12-32.

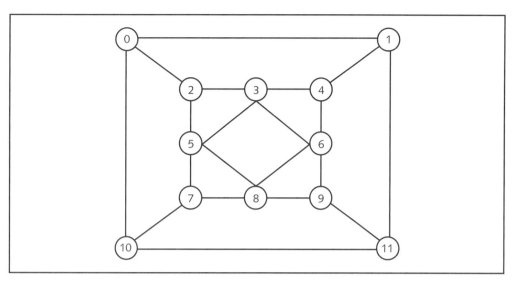

Figure 12-32   Graph for Exercise 7

8. Find a spanning tree in the graph in Figure 12-33.

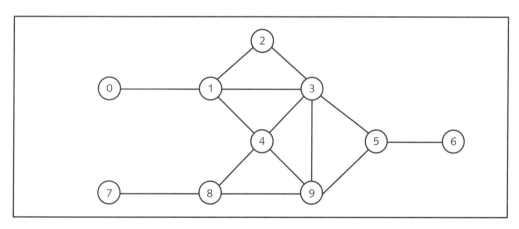

12

Figure 12-33   Graph for Exercise 8

9. Find the minimal spanning tree for the graph in Figure 12-34 using the algorithm given in this chapter.

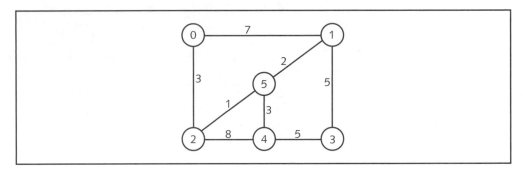

Figure 12-34   Graph for Exercise 9

10. List the nodes of the graph of Figure 12–35 in a breadth first topological ordering.

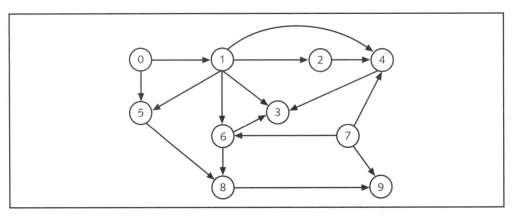

Figure 12-35   Graph for Exercise 10

PROGRAMMING EXERCISES

1. Write a program that outputs the nodes of a graph in a depth first traversal.

2. Write a program that outputs the nodes of a graph in a breadth first traversal.

3. Write a program that outputs the shortest distance from a given node to every other node in the graph.

4. Write a program that outputs the minimal spanning tree for a given graph.

5. The algorithm to determine the minimal spanning tree given in this chapter is of the order $O(n^3)$. The following is an alternative to Prim's algorithm that is of the order $O(n^2)$.

   Input: A connected weighted graph $G = (V, E)$ of n vertices, numbered $0, 1, ..., n - 1$; starting with vertex s, with a weight matrix of W

Output: The minimal spanning tree

```
Prim2(G, W, n, s)
Let T = (V, E), where E = φ.
for(j = 0; j < n; j++)
{
    edgeWeight[j] = W[s][j];
    edges[j] = s;
    visited[s] = false;
}
edgeWeight[s] = 0;
visited[s] = true;
while(not all nodes are visited)
{
    Choose the node that is not visited and has the smallest weight, and call it k.
    visited[k] = true;
    E = E ∪ {(k, edges[k])}
    V = V ∪ {k}
    for each node j that is not visited
        if(W[k][j] < edgeWeight[k])
        {
            edgeWeight[k] = W[k][j];
            edges[j] = k;
        }
}
return T
```

Write a definition of the function **Prim2** to implement this algorithm, and also add this function to the **class msTreeType**. Furthermore, write a program to test this version of Prim's algorithm.

6. Write a program to test the breadth first topological ordering algorithm.

7. Let G be a graph and $V(G) = \{v_1, v_2, ..., v_n\}$, where $n > 0$. Recall that a topological ordering of $V(G)$ is a linear ordering $v_{i1}, v_{i2}, ..., v_{in}$ of the vertices such that if v_{ij} is a predecessor of $v_{ik}, j \neq k, 1 \leq j \leq n$, and $1 \leq k \leq n$, then v_{ij} precedes v_{ik}, that is, $j < k$ in this linear ordering. Suppose that G has no cycles. The following algorithm, a depth first topological, lists the nodes of the graph in a topological ordering.

In a depth first topological ordering, we first find a vertex that has no successors (such a vertex exists because the graph has no cycles), and place it last in the topological order. After we have placed all the successors of a vertex in topological order, we place the vertex in the topological order before any of its successors. Clearly, in the depth first topological ordering, first we find the vertex to be placed in **topologicalOrder[n-1]**, then **topologicalOrder[n-2]**, and so on.

Write the definitions of the C++ functions to implement the depth first topological ordering. Add these functions to the **class topologicalOrderT**, which is derived from the **class graphType**. Also, write a program to test your depth first topological ordering.

12

13

STANDARD TEMPLATE LIBRARY (STL) II

In this chapter, you will:

♦ Learn more about the Standard Template Library (STL)

♦ Become familiar with the associative containers

♦ Explore how associative containers are used to manipulate data in a program

♦ Learn about various generic algorithms

Chapter 4 introduced the Standard Template Library (STL). Recall that the basic components of the STL are containers, iterators, and algorithms. The three categories of containers are sequence containers, associative containers, and container adapters. Chapter 4 described the sequence containers `vector` and `deque`; Chapter 5 described the sequence container `list`. The container adapter `stack` is described in Chapter 7, and the container adapters `queue` and `priority_queue` are described in Chapter 8. Chapter 4 discussed iterators. This chapter discusses the components of the STL not discussed in the previous chapters, specifically, the associative containers and algorithms.

Before discussing the associative containers, first we discuss the `class pair`, which is used by some of the associative containers.

Class pair

With the help of the **class pair**, two values can be combined into a single unit and can, therefore, be treated as one unit. Thus, a function can return two values by using the **class pair**. This class is used in several other places in the STL. For example, the **classes map** and **multimap**, described later in this chapter, use the **class pair** to manage their elements.

The definition of the **class pair** is contained in the header file **utility**. Thus, to use the **class pair** in a program, the program must include the following statement:

#include <utility>

The **class pair** has two constructors: the default constructor, and a constructor with two parameters. Thus, the general syntax to declare an object of the type **pair** is:

```
pair<Type1, Type2> pElement;
```

or:

```
pair<Type1, Type2> pElement(expr1, expr2);
```

where **expr1** is of the type **Type1** and **expr2** is of the type **Type2**.

Every object of the type **pair** has two data members, **first** and **second**, and these two data members are **public**. Because the data members **first** and **second** of an object of the type **pair** are **public**, each object of the type **pair** can directly access these data members in a program.

Example 13-1 illustrates the use of the **class pair**.

Example 13-1

Consider the following statements.

```
pair<int, double> x;                                //Line 1
pair<int, double> y(13, 45.9);                      //Line 2
pair<int, int> z(10, 20);                           //Line 3
pair<string, string> name("Bill", "Brown");         //Line 4
pair<string, double> employee("John Smith", 45678.50);  //Line 5
```

The statement in Line 1 declares x to be an object of the type **pair**. The first component of x is of the type **int**; the second component is of the type **double**. Because no values are specified in the declaration of x, the default constructor of the **class pair** executes and the data members, **first** and **second**, are initialized to their default values, which in this case are 0.

The statement in Line 2 declares `y` to be an object of the type `pair`. The first component of `y` is of the type `int`; the second component is of the type `double`. The first component of `y`, that is, `first`, is initialized to `13`; the second component, that is, `second`, is initialized to `45.9`.

The statement in Line 3 declares `z` to be an object of the type `pair`. Both components of `z` are of the type `int`. The first component of `z`, `first`, is initialized to `10`; the second component, `second`, is initialized to `20`.

The statement in Line 4 declares `name` to be an object of the type `pair`. Both components of `name` are of the type `string`. The first component of `name`, `first`, is initialized to `"Bill"`; the second component, `second`, is initialized to `"Brown"`.

The statement in Line 5 declares `employee` to be an object of the type `pair`. The first component of `employee` is of the type `string`; the second component is of the type `double`. The first component of `employee`, `first`, is initialized to `"John Smith"`; the second component, `second`, is initialized to `45678.50`.

The statement:

```
x.first = 50;
```

assigns `50` to the data member `first` of `x`. Similarly, the statement:

```
name.second = "Calvert";
```

assigns `"Calvert"` to the data member `second` of `name`.

The following statements show how to output the value of an object of the type `pair`. Assume that we have the declarations of Lines 1 through 5.

Statement	Effect
`cout<<y.first<<" "<<y.second<<endl;`	Outputs: `13 45.9`
`cout<<name.first<<" "` `<<name.second<<endl;`	Outputs: `Bill Brown`
`cout<<employee.first<<" "` `<<employee.second<<endl;`	Outputs: `John Smith 45678.50`

13

Comparing Objects of the Type `pair`

The relational operators have been overloaded for the `class pair`. Similar objects of the type `pair` are compared as follows.

Suppose `x` and `y` are objects of the type `pair`, and the corresponding data members of `x` and `y` are of the same type. (If the data members of `x` and `y` are not of the built-in type, then the relational operators must be properly defined for `x` and `y`.) Table 13-1 describes how the relational operators are defined for the `class pair`.

Table 13-1 Relational Operators for the `class pair`

Comparison	Description
`x == y`	`if (x.first == y.first)` and `(x.second == y.second)`
`x < y`	`if (x.first < y.first)` or `((x.first >= y.first)` and `(x.second < y.second))`
`x <= y`	`if (x < y)` or `(x == y)`
`x > y`	`if not(x <= y)`
`x >= y`	`if not(x < y)`
`x != y`	`if not(x == y)`

Type `pair` and Function `make_pair`

The header file `utility` also contains the definition of the function template `make_pair`. With the help of the function `make_pair`, we can create pairs without explicitly specifying the type `pair`. The definition of the function template `make_pair` is similar to the following:

```
template<class T1, class T2>
pair<T1, T2> make_pair(const T1& X, const T2& Y)
{
      return (pair<T1, T2>(X, Y));
}
```

From the definition of the function template `make_pair`, it is clear that the function template `make_pair` is a value-returning function and returns a value of the type `pair`. The components of the value returned by the function template `make_pair` are passed as parameters to the function template `make_pair`.

The expression:

```
make_pair(75, 'A')
```

returns a value of the type `pair`. The value of the first component is 75; the value of the second component is the character `'A'`.

The function `make_pair` is especially useful if a pair is to be passed as an argument to a function. Example 13-2 illustrates the use of `make_pair`.

Example 13-2

```cpp
#include <iostream>
#include <utility>
#include <string>

using namespace std;

void funcExp(pair<int, int>);
void funcExp1(pair<int, char>);
void funcExp2(pair<int, string> x);
void funcExp3(pair<int, char *> x);

int main()
{
    pair<int, double> x(50, 87.67);                      //Line 1
    pair<string, string> name("John", "Johnson");        //Line 2

    cout<<"Line 3: "<<x.first<<" "<<x.second<<endl;      //Line 3
    cout<<"Line 4: "<<name.first<<" "<<name.second
        <<endl;                                          //Line 4

    pair<int, int> y;                                    //Line 5
    cout<<"Line 6: "<<y.first<<" "<<y.second<<endl;      //Line 6

    pair<string, string> name2;                          //Line 7
    cout<<"Line 8: "<<name2.first<<"***"
        <<name2.second<<endl;                            //Line 8

    funcExp(make_pair(75, 80));                          //Line 9
    funcExp1(make_pair(87, 'H'));                        //Line 10
    funcExp1(pair<int, char>(198, 'K'));                 //Line 11
    funcExp2(pair<int, string>(250, "Hello"));           //Line 12
    funcExp2(make_pair(65,string("Hello There")));       //Line 13
    funcExp3(pair<int, char *>(35, "Hello World"));      //Line 14
    funcExp3(make_pair(22, (char *)("Sunny")));          //Line 15

    return 0;                                            //Line 16
}

void funcExp(pair<int, int> x)
{
    cout<<"Line 17: "<<"In funcExp: "<<x.first
        <<" "<<x.second<<endl;                           //Line 17
}

void funcExp1(pair<int, char> x)
{
    cout<<"Line 18: "<<"In funcExp1: "<<x.first
        <<" "<<x.second<<endl;                           //Line 18
}
```

13

```
void funcExp2(pair<int, string> x)
{
    cout<<"Line 19: "<<"In funcExp2: "<<x.first
        <<" "<<x.second<<endl;                        //Line 19
}

void funcExp3(pair<int, char *> x)
{
    cout<<"Line 20: "<<"In funcExp3: "<<x.first
        <<" "<<x.second<<endl;                        //Line 20
}
```

Output

```
Line 3: 50 87.67
Line 4: John Johnson
Line 6: 0 0
Line 8: ***
Line 17: In funcExp: 75 80
Line 18: In funcExp1: 87 H
Line 18: In funcExp1: 198 K
Line 19: In funcExp2: 250 Hello
Line 19: In funcExp2: 65 Hello There
Line 20: In funcExp3: 35 Hello World
Line 20: In funcExp3: 22 Sunny
```

ASSOCIATIVE CONTAINERS

Elements in an associative container are automatically sorted according to some ordering criteria. The default ordering criterion is the relational operator < (less than). Users also have the option of specifying their own ordering criterion.

Because elements in an associative container are sorted automatically, when a new element is inserted in the container, it is inserted at the proper place. A convenient and fast way to implement this type of data structure is to use a binary search tree. This is, in fact, how associative containers are implemented. Thus, every element in the container has a parent node (except the root node) and at most two children. For each element, the key in the parent node is larger than the key in the left child and smaller than the key in the right child.

The predefined associative containers in the STL are:

- sets
- multisets
- maps
- multimaps

The following sections describe these containers.

Associative Containers: `set` and `multiset`

As described earlier, both the containers `set` and `multiset` automatically sort their elements according to some sort criteria. The default sorting criterion is the relational operator < (less than); that is, the elements are arranged in ascending order. The user can also specify other sorting criteria. For user-defined data types, such as classes, the relational operators must be properly overloaded.

The only difference between the containers `set` and `multiset` is that the container `multiset` allows duplicates, whereas the container `set` does not.

The name of the class defining the container `set` is `set`; the name of the class defining the container `multiset` is `multiset`. The name of the header file containing the definitions of the classes `set` and `multiset`, and the definitions of the functions to implement various operations on these containers, is `set`. Thus, to use any of these containers, the program must include the following statement:

```
#include <set>
```

Declaring `set` or `multiset` Associative Containers

The classes `set` and `multiset` contain several constructors to declare and initialize containers of these types. This section discusses the various ways that these types of associative containers are declared and initialized. Table 13-2 describes how a `set/multiset` container of a specific type can be declared and initialized. (In Table 13-2, `ctType` is either a `set` or a `multiset`.)

Table 13-2 Various Ways to Declare a `set/multiset` Container

Statement	Effect
`ctType<elmType> ct;`	Creates an empty `set/multiset` container, `ct`. The sort criterion is <.
`ctType<elmType, sortOp> ct;`	Creates an empty `set/multiset` container, `ct`. The sort criterion is specified by `sortOp`.
`ctType<elmType> ct(otherCt);`	Creates a `set/multiset` container, `ct`. The elements of `otherCt` are copied into `ct`. The sort criterion is <. Both `ct` and `otherCt` are of the same type.
`ctType<elmType, sortOp> ct(otherCt);`	Creates a `set/multiset` container, `ct`. The elements of `otherCt` are copied into `ct`. The sort criterion is specified by `sortOp`. Both `ct` and `otherCt` are of the same type. Note that the sort criteria of `ct` and `otherCt` must be the same.

13

Table 13-2 Various Ways to Declare a `set`/`multiset` Container (continued)

Statement	Effect
`ctType<elmType> ct(beg, end);`	Creates a `set`/`multiset` container, `ct`. The elements starting at the position `beg` until the position `end-1` are copied into `ct`. Both `beg` and `end` are iterators.
`ctType<elmType, sortOp> ct(beg, end);`	Creates a `set`/`multiset` container, `ct`. The elements starting at the position `beg` until the position `end-1` are copied into `ct`. Both `beg` and `end` are iterators. The sort criterion is specified by `sortOp`.

If you want to use a sort criterion other than the default, you must specify this option when the container is declared. For example, consider the following statements:

```
set<int> intSet;                                           //Line 1
set<int, greater<int> > otherIntSet;                       //Line 2
multiset<string> stringMultiSet;                           //Line 3
multiset<string, greater<string> > otherStringMultiSet;    //Line 4
```

The statement in Line 1 declares **intSet** to be an empty **set** container, the element type is **int**, and the sort criterion is the default sort criterion. The statement in Line 2 declares **otherIntSet** to be an empty **set** container, the element type is **int**, and the sort criterion is greater than (that is, the elements in the container **otherIntSet** will be arranged in descending order). The statements in Lines 3 and 4 have similar conventions. The statements in Lines 2 and 4 illustrate how to specify the descending sorting criterion.

In the statements in Lines 2 and 4, note the space between the two >s—that is, the space between `greater<int>` and >. This space is important because >> is also a shift operator in C++. Moreover, `greater`, in Lines 2 and 4, is a function object, described in the section "Function Objects" later in this chapter.

Item Insertion and Deletion from `set`/`multiset`

Suppose that **ct** is of either the type **set** or **multiset**. Table 13-3 describes the operations that can be used to insert, delete, or find elements in a set. Table 13-3 also illustrates how to use these operations. The name of the function is shown in bold. In this table, **ct** is either a **set** or **multiset** container.

Table 13-3 Operations to Insert, Delete, or Find Elements in a `set` or `multiset`

Expression	Effect
`ct.insert(elem);`	Inserts a copy of `elem` into `ct`. In the case of sets, it also returns whether the `insert` operation succeeded.
`ct.insert(position, elem);`	Inserts a copy of `elem` into `ct`. The position where `elem` is inserted is returned. The first parameter, `position`, hints at where to begin the search for `insert`. The parameter `position` is an iterator.
`ct.insert(beg, end);`	Inserts a copy of all the elements into `ct` starting at the position `beg` until `end-1`. Both `beg` and `end` are iterators.
`ct.erase(elem);`	Deletes all the elements with the value `elem`. The number of deleted elements is returned.
`ct.erase(position);`	Deletes the element at the position specified by the iterator `position`. No value is returned.
`ct.erase(beg, end);`	Deletes all the elements starting at the position `beg` until the position `end-1`. Both `beg` and `end` are iterators. No value is returned.
`ct.clear();`	Deletes all the elements from the container `ct`. After this operation, the container `ct` is empty.
`ct.find(elem)`	Returns an iterator to the first element in `ct` that is equal to `elem`. If no such element is found, it returns `ct.end()`.

Example 13-3 illustrates various operations on a `set`/`multiset` container.

Example 13-3

```cpp
#include <iostream>
#include <set>
#include <string>
#include <iterator>
#include <algorithm>

using namespace std;

int main()
{
    set<int> intSet;                               //Line 1
    set<int, greater<int> > intSetA;               //Line 2

    set<int, greater<int> >::iterator intGtIt;     //Line 3

    ostream_iterator<int> screen(cout, " ");       //Line 4

    intSet.insert(16);                             //Line 5
    intSet.insert(8);                              //Line 6
```

13

```
intSet.insert(20);                                        //Line 7
intSet.insert(3);                                         //Line 8

cout<<"Line 9: intSet: ";                                 //Line 9
copy(intSet.begin(), intSet.end(), screen);               //Line 10
cout<<endl;                                                //Line 11

intSetA.insert(36);                                       //Line 12
intSetA.insert(84);                                       //Line 13
intSetA.insert(30);                                       //Line 14
intSetA.insert(39);                                       //Line 15
intSetA.insert(59);                                       //Line 16
intSetA.insert(238);                                      //Line 17
intSetA.insert(156);                                      //Line 18

cout<<"Line 19: intSetA: ";                               //Line 19
copy(intSetA.begin(), intSetA.end(), screen);             //Line 20
cout<<endl;                                                //Line 21

intSetA.erase(59);                                        //Line 22

cout<<"Line 23: After removing 59, intSetA: ";            //Line 23
copy(intSetA.begin(), intSetA.end(), screen);             //Line 24
cout<<endl;                                                //Line 25

intGtIt = intSetA.begin();                                //Line 26
++intGtIt;                                                 //Line 27
++intGtIt;                                                 //Line 28
++intGtIt;                                                 //Line 29

intSetA.erase(intGtIt);                                   //Line 30

cout<<"Line 31: After removing the fourth element, "
    <<endl<<"              intSetA: ";                     //Line 31
copy(intSetA.begin(), intSetA.end(), screen);             //Line 32
cout<<endl;                                                //Line 33

set<int, greater<int> > intSetB(intSetA);                 //Line 34

cout<<"Line 35: intSetB: ";                               //Line 35
copy(intSetB.begin(), intSetB.end(), screen);             //Line 36
cout<<endl;                                                //Line 37

intSetB.clear();                                          //Line 38

cout<<"Line 39: After removing all the elements, "
    <<endl<<"              intSetB: ";                     //Line 39
copy(intSetB.begin(), intSetB.end(), screen);             //Line 40
cout<<endl;                                                //Line 41
```

```
    multiset<string, greater<string> > namesMultiSet;   //Line 42
    multiset<string, greater<string> >::iterator iter;  //Line 43

    ostream_iterator<string> pScreen(cout, " ");        //Line 44

    namesMultiSet.insert("Donny");                      //Line 45
    namesMultiSet.insert("Zippy");                      //Line 46
    namesMultiSet.insert("Goofy");                      //Line 47
    namesMultiSet.insert("Hungry");                     //Line 48
    namesMultiSet.insert("Goofy");                      //Line 49
    namesMultiSet.insert("Donny");                      //Line 50

    cout<<"Line 51: namesMultiSet: ";                   //Line 51
    copy(namesMultiSet.begin(), namesMultiSet.end(),
         pScreen);                                      //Line 52
    cout<<endl;                                         //Line 53

    return 0;
}
```

Output

```
Line 9: intSet: 3 8 16 20
Line 19: intSetA: 238 156 84 59 39 36 30
Line 23: After removing 59, intSetA: 238 156 84 39 36 30
Line 31: After removing the fourth element,
         intSetA: 238 156 84 36 30
Line 35: intSetB: 238 156 84 36 30
Line 39: After removing all the elements,
         intSetB:
Line 51: namesMultiSet: Zippy Hungry Goofy Goofy Donny Donny
```

13

The statement in Line 1 declares `intSet` to be a set container. The statement in Line 2 declares `intSetA` to be a set container whose elements are to be arranged in descending order. The statement in Line 3 declares `intGtIt` to be a `set` iterator. The iterator `intGtIt` can process the elements of any set container whose elements are of the type `int` and arranged in descending order. The statement in Line 4 declares `screen` to be an `ostream` iterator that outputs the elements of any container whose elements are of the type `int`.

The statements in Lines 5 through 8 insert 16, 8, 20, and 3 into `intSet`; the statement in Line 10 outputs the elements of `intSet`. In the output, see the line marked Line 9, which contains the output of the statements in Lines 9 through 11 of the program.

The statements in Lines 12 through 18 insert 36, 84, 30, 39, 59, 238, and 156 into `intSetA`; the statement in Line 20 outputs the elements of `intSetA`. In the output, see the line marked Line 19, which contains the output of the statements in Lines 19 through 21 of the program. Notice that the elements of `intSetA` appear in descending order.

The statement in Line 22 removes 59 from `intSetA`. After the statement in Line 26 executes, `intGtIt` points to the first element of `intSetA`. The statements in Lines 27, 28, and 29 each advance `intGtIt` to the next element of `intSetA`. After the statement in Line 29 executes, `intGtIt` points to the fourth element of `intSetA`. The statement in Line 30 removes the element of `intSetA` pointed to by `intGtIt`. The meanings of the statements in Lines 34 through 41 are similar.

The statement in Line 42 declares `namesMultiSet` to be a container of the type `multiset`. The elements in `namesMultiSet` are of the type `string` and are arranged in descending order. The statement in Line 43 declares `iter` to be a `multiset` iterator.

The statements in Lines 45 through 50 insert `Donny`, `Zippy`, `Goofy`, `Hungry`, `Goofy`, and `Donny` into `namesMultiSet`. The statement in Line 52 outputs the elements of `namesMultiSet`.

Associative Containers: `map` and `multimap`

The containers `map` and `multimap` manage their elements in the form key/value. The elements are automatically sorted according to some sort criteria applied on the key. The default sorting criterion is the relational operator <(less than); that is, the elements are arranged in ascending order. The user can also specify other sorting criteria. For user-defined data types, such as classes, the relational operators must be properly overloaded.

The only difference between the containers `map` and `multimap` is that the container `multimap` allows duplicates, whereas the container `map` does not.

The name of the class defining the container `map` is `map`; the name of the class defining the container `multimap` is `multimap`. The name of the header file containing the definitions of the `class`es `map` and `multimap`, and the definitions of the functions to implement various operations on these containers, is `map`. Therefore, to use any of these containers, the program must include the following statement:

```
#include <map>
```

Declaring `map` or `multimap` Associative Containers

The `class`es `map` and `multimap` contain several constructors to declare and initialize containers of these types. This section discusses the various ways that these types of associative containers are declared and initialized. Table 13-4 describes how a `map/multimap` container of a specific type can be declared and initialized. (In Table 13-4, `ctType` is either a `map` or a `multimap`.)

Table 13-4 Various Ways to Declare a `map/multimap` Container

Statement	Effect
`ctType<key, elmType> ct;`	Creates an empty map/multimap container, ct. The sort criterion is <.
`ctType<key, elmType, sortOp> ct;`	Creates an empty map/multimap container, ct. The sort criterion is specified by sortOp.

Table 13-4 Various Ways to Declare a `map`/`multimap` Container (continued)

Statement	Effect
`ctType<key, elmType> ct(otherCt);`	Creates a map/multimap container, `ct`. The elements of `otherCt` are copied into `ct`. The sort criterion is <. Both `ct` and `otherCt` are of the same type.
`ctType<key, elmType, sortOp> ct(otherCt);`	Creates a map/multimap container, `ct`. The elements of `otherCt` are copied into `ct`. The sort criterion is specified by `sortOp`. Both `ct` and `otherCt` are of the same type. Note that the sort criteria of `ct` and `otherCt` must be the same.
`ctType<key, elmType> ct(beg, end);`	Creates a map/multimap container, `ct`. The elements starting at the position `beg` until the position `end-1` are copied into `ct`. Both `beg` and `end` are iterators.
`ctType<key, elmType, sortOp> ct(beg, end);`	Creates a map/multimap container, `ct`. The elements starting at the position `beg` until the position `end-1` are copied into `ct`. Both `beg` and `end` are iterators. The sort criterion is specified by `sortOp`.

13

If you want to use a sort criterion other than the default, you must specify this option when the container is declared. For example, consider the following statements:

```
map<int, int> intMap;                                      //Line 1
map<int, int, greater<int> > otherIntMap;                  //Line 2
multimap<int, string> stringMultiMap;                      //Line 3
multimap<int, string, greater<string> > otherStringMultiMap; //Line 4
```

The statement in Line 1 declares `intMap` to be an empty `map` container, the key type and the value type are `int`, and the sort criterion is the default sort criterion. The statement in Line 2 declares `otherIntMap` to be an empty `map` container, the key type and the value type are `int`, and the sort criterion is greater than (that is, the elements in the container `otherIntMap` will be arranged in descending order). The statements in Lines 3 and 4 have similar conventions. The statements in Lines 2 and 4 illustrate how to specify the descending sorting criterion.

In the statements in Lines 2 and 4, note the space between the two >s—that is, the space between `greater<int>` and `>`. This space is important because `>>` is also a shift operator in C++. Moreover, `greater`, in Lines 2 and 4, is a function object, described in the section "Function Objects" later in this chapter.

Item Insertion and Deletion from `map`/`multimap`

Suppose that `ct` is either of the type `map` or `multimap`. Table 13-5 describes the operations that can be used to insert, delete, or find elements in a `map` or `multimap`. Table 13-5 also illustrates how to use these operations. The name of the function is shown in bold. In this table, `ct` is either a `map` or `multimap` container.

Table 13-5 Operations to Insert, Delete, or Find Elements in a `map` or `multimap`

Expression	Effect
`ct.insert(elem);`	Inserts a copy of `elem` into `ct`. In the case of maps, it also returns whether the `insert` operation succeeded.
`ct.insert(position, elem);`	Inserts a copy of `elem` into `ct`. The position where `elem` is inserted is returned. The first parameter, `position`, hints at where to begin the search for `insert`. The parameter `position` is an iterator.
`ct.insert(beg, end);`	Inserts a copy of all the elements into `ct` starting at the position `beg` until `end-1`. Both `beg` and `end` are iterators.
`ct.erase(elem);`	Deletes all the elements with the value `elem`. The number of deleted elements is returned.
`ct.erase(position);`	Deletes the element at the position specified by the iterator `position`. No value is returned.
`ct.erase(beg, end);`	Deletes all the elements starting at the position `beg` until the position `end-1`. Both `beg` and `end` are iterators. No value is returned.
`ct.clear();`	Deletes all the elements from the container `ct`. After this operation, the container `ct` is empty.
`ct.find(key)`	Returns an iterator to the first element in `ct` that has the key equal to `key`. If no such element is found, it returns `ct.end()`.

Example 13-4 illustrates various operations on a `map`/`multimap` container.

Example 13-4

```
#include <iostream>
#include <map>
#include <utility>
#include <string>
#include <iterator>
```

```cpp
using namespace std;

int main()
{
    map<int, int> intMap;                               //Line 1
    map<int, int>::iterator mapItr;                     //Line 2

    intMap.insert(make_pair(1, 16));                    //Line 3
    intMap.insert(make_pair(2, 8));                     //Line 4
    intMap.insert(make_pair(4, 20));                    //Line 5
    intMap.insert(make_pair(3, 3));                     //Line 6
    intMap.insert(make_pair(1, 23));                    //Line 7
    intMap.insert(make_pair(20, 18));                   //Line 8
    intMap.insert(make_pair(8, 28));                    //Line 9
    intMap.insert(make_pair(15, 60));                   //Line 10
    intMap.insert(make_pair(6, 43));                    //Line 11
    intMap.insert(pair<int, int>(12, 16));              //Line 12

    cout<<"Line 13: The elements of intMap:"<<endl;     //Line 13
    for(mapItr = intMap.begin(); mapItr != intMap.end();
                                 mapItr++)               //Line 14
        cout<<mapItr->first<<"\t"<<mapItr->second
            <<endl;                                     //Line 15
    cout<<endl;                                         //Line 16

    intMap.erase(12);                                   //Line 17

    mapItr = intMap.begin();                            //Line 18
    ++mapItr;                                           //Line 19
    ++mapItr;                                           //Line 20
    intMap.erase(mapItr);                               //Line 21

    cout<<"Line 22: After deleting, the elements of intMap:"
        <<endl;                                         //Line 22
    for(mapItr = intMap.begin(); mapItr != intMap.end();
                                 mapItr++)               //Line 23
        cout<<mapItr->first<<"\t"<<mapItr->second
            <<endl;                                     //Line 24
    cout<<endl;                                         //Line 25

    multimap<string, string> namesMultiMap;             //Line 26
    multimap<string, string>::iterator nameItr;         //Line 27

    namesMultiMap.insert(make_pair("A1", "Donny"));     //Line 28
    namesMultiMap.insert(make_pair("B1", "Zippy"));     //Line 29
    namesMultiMap.insert(make_pair("K1", "Goofy"));     //Line 30
    namesMultiMap.insert(make_pair("A2", "Hungry"));    //Line 31
    namesMultiMap.insert(make_pair("D1", "Goofy"));     //Line 32
    namesMultiMap.insert(make_pair("A1", "Dumpy"));     //Line 33
```

13

```
    cout<<"Line 34: namesMultiMap: "<<endl;          //Line 34
    for(nameItr = namesMultiMap.begin();
              nameItr != namesMultiMap.end();
              nameItr++)                              //Line 35
        cout<<nameItr->first<<"\t"<<nameItr->second
            <<endl;                                   //Line 36
    cout<<endl;                                       //Line 37

    return 0;                                         //Line 38
}
```

Output

```
Line 13: The elements of intMap:
1       16
2       8
3       3
4       20
6       43
8       28
12      16
15      60
20      18

Line 22: After deleting, the elements of intMap:
1       16
2       8
4       20
6       43
8       28
15      60
20      18

Line 34: namesMultiMap:
A1      Donny
A1      Dumpy
A2      Hungry
B1      Zippy
D1      Goofy
K1      Goofy
```

The statement in Line 1 declares `intMap` to be a `map` container. The statement in Line 2 declares `mapItr` to be a `map` iterator. The iterator `mapItr` can process the elements of any `map` container whose elements have the key type and the value type `int`.

The statements in Lines 3 through 12 insert the elements with their keys. For example, `16` is inserted with the key 1. The statements in Lines 3 through 11 use the function `make_pair` to insert the elements; the statement in Line 12 uses the **class pair** as the cast operator to insert the elements.

The `for` loop in Line 14 outputs the elements of the container `intMap`.

The statement in Line 17 removes the element with key 12 from `intMap`. The statement in Line 18 initializes `mapItr` to the first element in the container `intMap`. The statements in Line 19 and 20 each advance `mapItr` to the next element in `intMap`. After the statement in Line 20 executes, `mapItr` points to the third element of `intMap`. The statement in Line 21 removes the element of `intMap` pointed to by `mapItr`. The `for` loop in Line 23 outputs the elements of the container `intMap`.

The statement in Line 26 declares `namesMultiMap` to be a container of the type `multimap`. The keys and the values in `namesMultiMap` are of the type `string`. The statement in Line 27 declares `nameItr` to be a `multimap` iterator.

The statements in Lines 28 through 33 insert the elements into `namesMultiMap`. The `for` loop in Line 35 outputs the elements of the container `namesMultiMap`.

CONTAINERS, ASSOCIATED HEADER FILES, AND ITERATOR SUPPORT

Chapters 4 and 5 and the previous sections discussed various types of containers. Recall that every container is a class. The definition of the class implementing a specific container is contained in the header file. Table 13-6 describes the container, its associated header file, and the type of iterator supported by the container.

Table 13-6 Containers, Associated Header Files, and the Type of Iterator Supported by Each Container

Sequence Containers	Associated Header File	Type of Iterator Support
`vector`	`<vector>`	Random access
`deque`	`<deque>`	Random access
`list`	`<list>`	Bidirectional
Associative Containers	**Associated Header File**	**Type of Iterator Support**
`set`	`<set>`	Bidirectional
`multiset`	`<set>`	Bidirectional
`map`	`<map>`	Bidirectional
`multimap`	`<map>`	Bidirectional
Adapters	**Associated Header File**	**Type of Iterator Support**
`stack`	`<stack>`	No iterator support
`queue`	`<queue>`	No iterator support
`priority_queue`	`<queue>`	No iterator support

13

ALGORITHMS

Several operations can be defined for a container. Some of the operations are very specific to a container and, therefore, are provided as part of the container definition (that is, as member functions of the class implementing the container). However, several operations—such as `find`, `sort`, and `merge`—are common to all containers. These operations are provided as generic algorithms and can be applied to all containers as well as the built-in array type. The algorithms are bound to a particular container through an iterator pair.

The generic algorithms are contained in the header file `algorithm`. The ensuing sections describe several of these algorithms and show how to use them in a program. Because algorithms are implemented with the help of functions, in the following sections, the terms *function* and *algorithm* mean the same thing.

STL ALGORITHM CLASSIFICATION

In Chapters 4 and 5 and in earlier sections of this chapter, we applied various operations on the sequence containers, such as `clear`, `sort`, and `merge`. However, those algorithms were tied to a specific container in terms of the members of a specific class. All those algorithms and a few more are also available in more general forms, called **generic algorithms**, and can be applied in a variety of situations. This section discusses some of these generic algorithms.

The STL contains algorithms that only look at the elements in a container and that move the elements of a container. The STL also has algorithms that can perform specific calculations, such as finding the sum of the elements of a numeric container. In addition, the STL contains algorithms for basic set theory operations such as set union and intersection. You have already encountered some of the generic algorithms such as the `copy` algorithm, which copies the elements from a given range of elements to another place such as another container or the screen. The algorithms in the STL can be classified into the following categories:

- Nonmodifying algorithms
- Modifying algorithms
- Numeric algorithms
- Heap algorithms

The next four sections describe these algorithms. Most of the generic algorithms are contained in the header file `algorithm`. Certain algorithms, such as the numeric algorithms, are contained in the header file `numeric`.

Nonmodifying Algorithms

Nonmodifying algorithms do not modify the elements of a container; they merely investigate the elements. Table 13-7 lists the nonmodifying algorithms.

Table 13-7 Nonmodifying Algorithms

adjacent_find	find_end	max_element
binary_search	find_first_of	min
count	find_if	min_element
count_if	for_each	mismatch
equal	includes	search
equal_range	lower_bound	search_n
find	max	upper_bound

Modifying Algorithms

Modifying algorithms, as the name implies, modify the elements of a container by rearranging, removing, or changing the values of the elements. Table 13-8 lists the modifying algorithms.

Table 13-8 Modifying Algorithms

copy	prev_permutation	rotate_copy
copy_backward	random_shuffle	set_difference
fill	remove	set_intersection
fill_n	remove_copy	set_symmetric_difference
generate	remove_copy_if	set_union
generate_n	remove_if	sort
inplace_merge	replace	stable_partition
iter_swap	replace_copy	stable_sort
merge	replace_copy_if	swap
next_permutation	replace_if	swap_ranges
nth_element	reverse	transform
partial_sort	reverse_copy	unique
partial_sort_copy	rotate	unique_copy
partition		

Modifying algorithms that change the order of the elements, not their values, are also called **mutating algorithms**. For example, next_permutation, partition, `prev_permutation`, `random_shuffle`, `reverse`, `reverse_copy`, `rotate`, `rotate_copy`, and `stable_partition` are mutating algorithms.

Numeric Algorithms

Numeric algorithms are designed to perform numeric calculations on the elements of a container. Table 13-9 lists these algorithms.

Table 13-9 Numeric Algorithms

`accumulate`	`inner_product`
`adjacent_difference`	`partial_sum`

Heap Algorithms

Chapter 10 described the heap sort algorithm. Recall that in the heap sort algorithm, the array containing the data is viewed as a binary tree. Therefore, a heap is a form of a binary tree represented as an array. In a heap, the first element is the largest element, and the element at the ith position (if it exists) is larger than the elements at positions $2i$ and $2i + 1$ (if they exist). In the heap sort algorithm, the array containing the data is first converted into a heap, and then the array is sorted using a special type of sorting algorithm. Table 13-10 lists the algorithms provided by the STL to implement the heap sort algorithm.

Table 13-10 Heap Algorithms

`make_heap`	`push_heap`
`pop_heap`	`sort_heap`

Most of the STL algorithms are explained toward the end of this section. For the most part, the function prototypes of these algorithms are given along with a brief explanation of what each algorithm does. You then learn how to use these algorithms with the help of an example or a C++ program. The STL algorithms are very powerful and accomplish wonderful results. Furthermore, they have been made general, in the sense that other than using the natural operations to manipulate containers, they allow the user to specify the manipulating criteria. For example, the natural sorting order is ascending, but the user can specify criteria to sort the container in descending order. Thus, every algorithm is typically implemented with the help of overloaded functions. Before starting to describe these algorithms, we discuss **function objects**, which allow the user to specify the manipulating criteria.

Function Objects

To make the generic algorithms flexible, the STL usually provides two forms of an algorithm using the mechanism of function overloading. The first form of an algorithm uses the natural operation to accomplish this goal. In the second form, the user can specify the criteria based on which the algorithm processes the elements. For example, the algorithm `adjacent_find` searches the container and returns the position of the first two elements that are equal. In the second form of this algorithm, we can specify the criteria (say, less than) to look for the first two elements in which the second element is less than the first element. These criteria are passed as function objects. More formally, a **function object** contains a function that can be treated as a function using the function call operator, ( ). In fact, a function object is a class template that overloads the function call operator, ( ).

In addition to allowing you to create your own function objects, the STL provides arithmetic, relational, and logical function objects, which are described in Table 13-11. The STL's function objects are contained in the header file `functional`.

Table 13-11 Arithmetic STL Function Objects

Function Object Name	Description
plus<Type>	plus<int> addNum; int sum = addNum(12, 35); The value of sum is 47.
minus<Type>	minus<int> subtractNum; int difference = subtractNum(56, 35); The value of difference is 21.
multiplies<Type>	multiplies<int> multiplyNum; int product = multiplyNum(6, 3); The value of product is 18.
divides<Type>	divides<int> divideNum; int quotient = divideNum(16, 3); The value of quotient is 5.
modulus<Type>	modulus<int> remainder; int rem = remainder(16, 7); The value of rem is 2.
negate<Type>	negate<int> opposite; int num = opposite(-25); The value of opposite is 25.

13

Example 13-5 illustrates how to use the STL's function objects.

Example 13-5

```
//Function Objects

#include <iostream>
#include <string>
#include <algorithm>
#include <numeric>
#include <iterator>
#include <vector>
#include <functional>

using namespace std;

int funcAdd(plus<int>, int, int);

int main()
{
    plus<int> addNum;                                       //Line 1
    int num = addNum(34, 56);                               //Line 2

    cout<<"Line 3: num = "<<num<<endl;                      //Line 3

    plus<string> joinString;                                //Line 4

    string str1 = "Hello ";                                 //Line 5
    string str2 = "There";                                  //Line 6

    string str = joinString(str1, str2);                    //Line 7

    cout<<"Line 8: str = "<<str<<endl;                      //Line 8

    cout<<"Line 9: Sum of 34 and 26 = "
        <<funcAdd(addNum, 34, 26)<<endl;                    //Line 9

    int list[8] = {1, 2, 3, 4, 5, 6, 7, 8};                 //Line 10

    vector<int> intList(list, list + 8);                    //Line 11
    ostream_iterator<int> screenOut(cout, " ");             //Line 12

    cout<<"Line 13: intList: ";                             //Line 13
    copy(intList.begin(), intList.end(), screenOut);        //Line 14
    cout<<endl;                                             //Line 15

        //accumulate
    int sum = accumulate(intList.begin(),
                        intList.end(), 0);                  //Line 16
```

```
    cout<<"Line 17: Sum of the elements of intList = "
        <<sum<<endl;                                    //Line 17

    int product = accumulate(intList.begin(),
                             intList.end(),
                             1, multiplies<int>());   //Line 18

    cout<<"Line 19: Product of the elements of intList = "
        <<product<<endl;                                //Line 19

    return 0;
}

int funcAdd(plus<int> sum, int x, int y)
{
    return sum(x, y);
}
```

Output

```
Line 3: num = 90
Line 8: str = Hello There
Line 9: Sum of 34 and 26 = 60
Line 13: intList: 1 2 3 4 5 6 7 8
Line 17: Sum of the elements of intList = 36
Line 19: Product of the elements of intList = 40320
```

Table 13-12 describes the relational STL function objects.

13

Table 13-12 Relational STL Function Objects

Function Object Name	Description
equal_to<Type>	Returns true if the two arguments are equal, and false otherwise. For example, equal_to<int> compare; bool isEqual = compare(5,5); The value of isEqual is true.
not_equal_to<Type>	Returns true if the two arguments are not equal, and false otherwise. For example, not_equal_to<int> compare; bool isNotEqual = compare(5,6); The value of isNotEqual is true.
greater<Type>	Returns true if the first argument is greater than the second argument, and false otherwise. For example, greater<int> compare; bool isGreater = compare(8,5); The value of isGreater is true.

Table 13-12 Relational STL Function Objects (continued)

Function Object Name	Description
greater_equal<Type>	Returns `true` if the first argument is greater than or equal to the second argument, and `false` otherwise. For example, `greater_equal<int> compare;` `bool isGreaterEqual = compare(8,5);` The value of `isGreaterEqual` is `true`.
less<Type>	Returns `true` if the first argument is less than the second argument, and `false` otherwise. For example, `less<int> compare;` `bool isLess = compare(3,5);` The value of `isLess` is `true`.
less_equal<Type>	Returns `true` if the first argument is less than or equal to the second argument, and `false` otherwise. For example, `less_equal<int> compare;` `bool isLessEqual = compare(8,15);` The value of `isLessEqual` is `true`.

The STL relational function objects can also be applied to containers, as shown next. The STL algorithm `adjacent_find` searches a container and returns the position in the container where the two elements are equal. This algorithm has a second form that allows the user to specify the comparison criteria. For example, consider the following vector, **vecList**:

```
vecList = {2, 3, 4, 5, 1, 7, 8, 9};
```

The elements of **vecList** are supposed to be in ascending order. To see if the elements are out of order, we can use the algorithm **adjacent_find** as follows:

```
intItr = adjacent_find{vecList.begin(), vecList.end(),
                       greater<int>());
```

where **intItr** is an iterator of the type **vector**. The function **adjacent_find** starts at the position **vecList.begin()**—that is, at the first element of **vecList**—and looks for the first set of consecutive elements in which the first element is greater than the second. The function returns a pointer to element 5, which is stored in **intItr**.

The program in Example 13-6 further illustrates how to use the relational function objects.

Example 13-6

```
//STL Predicates

#include <iostream>
#include <string>
#include <algorithm>
#include <iterator>
```

```
#include <vector>
#include <functional>

using namespace std;

int main()
{
    equal_to<int> compare;                              //Line 1
    bool isEqual = compare(6, 6);                       //Line 2

    cout<<"Line 3: isEqual = "<<isEqual<<endl;          //Line 3

    greater<string> greaterStr;                         //Line 4

    string str1 = "Hello";                              //Line 5
    string str2 = "There";                              //Line 6

    if(greaterStr(str1, str2))                          //Line 7
        cout<<"Line 8: \""<<str1<<"\" is greater "
            <<"than \""<<str2<<"\""<<endl;              //Line 8
    else                                                //Line 9
        cout<<"Line 10: \""<<str1<<"\" is not "
            <<"greater than \""<<str2<<"\""<<endl;      //Line 10

    int temp[8] = {2, 3, 4, 5, 1, 7, 8, 9};             //Line 11

    vector<int> vecList(temp, temp+8);                  //Line 12
    vector<int>::iterator intItr1, intItr2;             //Line 13
    ostream_iterator<int> screen(cout, " ");            //Line 14

    cout<<"Line 15: vecList: ";                         //Line 15
    copy(vecList.begin(), vecList.end(), screen);       //Line 16
    cout<<endl;                                         //Line 17

    intItr1 = adjacent_find(vecList.begin(),
                            vecList.end(),
                            greater<int>());             //Line 18
    intItr2 = intItr1 + 1;                              //Line 19

    cout<<"Line 20: In vecList, the first set of "
        <<"out of order elements are: "<<*intItr1
        <<" "<<*intItr2<<endl;                          //Line 20
    cout<<"Line 21: In vecList, the first out of "
        <<"order element is at position: "
        <<vecList.end() - intItr2<<endl;                //Line 21

    return 0;
}
```

13

Output

```
Line 3: isEqual = 1
Line 10: "Hello" is not greater than "There"
Line 15: vecList: 2 3 4 5 1 7 8 9
Line 20: In vecList, the first set of out of order elements are: 5 1
Line 21: In vecList, the first out of order element is at
position: 4
```

Table 13-13 describes the logical STL function objects.

Table 13-13 Logical STL Function Objects

Function Object Name	Effect
logical_not<Type>	Returns true if its operand evaluates to false, and false otherwise. This is a unary function object.
logical_and<Type>	Returns true if both of its operands evaluate to true, and false otherwise. This is a binary function object.
logical_or<Type>	Returns true if at least one of its operands evaluates to true, and false otherwise. This is a binary function object.

Predicates

Predicates are special types of function objects that return boolean values. There are two types of predicates—unary and binary. Unary predicates check a specific property for a single argument; binary predicates check a specific property for a pair of—that is, two—arguments. Predicates are typically used to specify searching or sorting criteria. In the STL, a predicate must always return the same result for the same value. Therefore, the functions that modify their internal states *cannot* be considered predicates.

Insert Iterator

Consider the following statements:

```
int list[5] = {1, 3, 6, 9, 12};   //Line 1
vector<int> vList;                 //Line 2
```

The statement in Line 1 declares and initializes list to be an array of 5 components; the statement in Line 2 declares vList to be a vector. Because no size is specified for vList, no memory space is reserved for the elements of vList. Now suppose that we want to copy the elements of list into vList. The statement:

```
copy(list, list + 8, vList.begin());
```

will not work because no memory space is allocated for the elements of vList, and the copy function uses the assignment operator to copy the elements from the source to the destination. One solution to this problem is to use a `for` loop to step through the elements of `list` and use the function `push_back` of `vList` to copy the elements of `list`. However, there is a better solution, which is convenient and applicable whenever no memory space is allocated at the destination. The STL provides three iterators, called **insert iterators**, to insert the elements at the destination: `back_inserter`, `front_inserter`, and `inserter`.

- `back_inserter`: This inserter uses the **push_back** operation of the container in place of the assignment operator. The argument to this iterator is the container itself. For example, for the preceding problem, we can copy the elements of `list` into `vList` by using `back_inserter` as follows:

```
copy(list, list + 5, back_inserter(vList));
```

- `front_inserter`: This inserter uses the **push_front** operation of the container in place of the assignment operator. The argument to this iterator is the container itself. Because the **class vector** does not support the **push_front** operation, this iterator cannot be used for the **vector** container.

- `inserter`: This inserter uses the container's **insert** operation in place of the assignment operator. This iterator has two arguments: the first argument is the container itself; the second argument is an iterator to the container specifying the position at which the insertion should begin.

The program in Example 13-7 illustrates the effect of inserters on a container.

Example 13-7

```
//Inserters

#include <iostream>
#include <algorithm>
#include <iterator>
#include <vector>
#include <list>

using namespace std;

int main()
{
    int temp[8] = {1, 2, 3, 4, 5, 6, 7, 8};        //Line 1

    vector<int> vecList1;                           //Line 2
    vector<int> vecList2;                           //Line 3

    ostream_iterator<int> screenOut(cout, " ");     //Line 4

    copy(temp, temp + 8, back_inserter(vecList1));  //Line 5
```

13

```
    cout<<"Line 6: vecList1: ";                          //Line 6
    copy(vecList1.begin(), vecList1.end(),
                       screenOut);                        //Line 7
    cout<<endl;                                           //Line 8

    copy(vecList1.begin(), vecList1.end(),
         inserter(vecList2, vecList2.begin()));           //Line 9

    cout<<"Line 10: vecList2: ";                          //Line 10
    copy(vecList2.begin(), vecList2.end(),
                       screenOut);                        //Line 11
    cout<<endl;                                           //Line 12

    list<int> tempList;                                  //Line 13

    copy(vecList2.begin(), vecList2.end(),
         front_inserter(tempList));                       //Line 14

    cout<<"Line 15: tempList: ";                          //Line 15
    copy(tempList.begin(), tempList.end(),
                       screenOut);                        //Line 16
    cout<<endl;                                           //Line 17

    return 0;
}
```

Output

```
Line 6: vecList1: 1 2 3 4 5 6 7 8
Line 10: vecList2: 1 2 3 4 5 6 7 8
Line 15: tempList: 8 7 6 5 4 3 2 1
```

STL Algorithms

This section describes most of the STL algorithms. Each algorithm also includes the function prototypes, a brief description of what the algorithm does, and an example or a program showing how to use it. In the function prototypes, the parameter types indicate for which type of container the algorithm is applicable. For example, if a parameter is of the type `randomAccessIterator`, then the algorithm is applicable only for random access type containers such as vectors. Throughout, we use abbreviations such as `outputItr` to mean output iterator, `inputItr` to mean input iterator, `forwardItr` to mean forward iterator, and so on.

Functions `fill` and `fill_n`

The function `fill` is used to fill a container with elements; the function `fill_n` is used to fill in the next n elements. The element that is used as a filling element is passed as a parameter to these functions. Both of these functions are defined in the header file `algorithm`. The prototypes of these functions are:

```
template<class forwardItr, class Type>
void fill(forwardItr first, forwardItr last, const Type& value);

template<class forwardItr, class size, class Type>
void fill_n(forwardItr first, size n, const Type& value);
```

The first two parameters of the function `fill` are forward iterators specifying the starting and ending positions of the container; the third parameter is the filling element. The first parameter of the function `fill_n` is a forward iterator that specifies the starting position of the container, the second parameter specifies the number of elements to be filled, and the third parameter specifies the filling element. The program in Example 13-8 illustrates how to use these functions.

Example 13-8

```
//STL functions fill and fill_n

#include <iostream>
#include <algorithm>
#include <iterator>
#include <vector>

using namespace std;

int main()
{
    vector<int> vecList(8);                             //Line 1
    ostream_iterator<int> screen(cout, " ");            //Line 2

    fill(vecList.begin(), vecList.end(), 2);            //Line 3

    cout<<"Line 4: After filling vecList with 2's: "; //Line 4
    copy(vecList.begin(), vecList.end(), screen);       //Line 5
    cout<<endl;                                          //Line 6

    fill_n(vecList.begin(), 3, 5);                      //Line 7

    cout<<"Line 8: After filling the first three "
        <<"elements with 5's: "<<endl<<"          "; //Line 8
    copy(vecList.begin(), vecList.end(), screen);       //Line 9
    cout<<endl;                                          //Line 10

    return 0;
}
```

13

Output

```
Line 4: After filling vecList with 2's: 2 2 2 2 2 2 2 2
Line 8: After filling the first three elements with 5's:
        5 5 5 2 2 2 2 2
```

The statements in Lines 1 and 2 declare **vecList** to be a sequence container of size 8, and **screen** to be an **ostream** iterator initialized to **cout** with the delimit character space. The statement in Line 3 uses the function **fill** to fill **vecList** with 2; that is, all eight elements of **vecList** are set to 2. Recall that **vecList.begin()** returns an iterator to the first element of **vecList**, and **vecList.end()** returns an iterator to the last element of **vecList**. The statement in Line 5 outputs the elements of **vecList** using the **copy** function. The statement in Line 7 uses the function **fill_n** to store 5 in the elements of **vecList**. The first parameter of **fill_n** is **vecList.begin()**, which specifies the starting position of where to begin copying. The second parameter of **fill_n** is 3, which specifies the number of elements to be filled. The third parameter, 5, specifies the filling character. Therefore, 5 is copied into the first three elements of **vecList**. The statement in Line 9 outputs the elements of **vecList**.

Functions `generate` and `generate_n`

The functions **generate** and **generate_n** are used to generate elements and fill a sequence. These functions are defined in the header file **algorithm**. The prototypes of these functions follow:

```
template<class forwardItr, class function>
void generate(forwardItr first, forwardItr last, function gen);

template<class forwardItr, class size, class function>
void generate_n(forwardItr first, size n, function gen);
```

The function **generate** fills a sequence in the range **first...last-1**, with successive calls to the function **gen()**. The function **generate_n** fills a sequence in the range **first...first+n-1**—that is, starting at the position **first**, with n successive calls to the function **gen()**. Note that **gen** can also be a pointer to a function. Moreover, if **gen** is a function, it must be a value-returning function without parameters. The program in Example 13-9 illustrates how to use these functions.

Example 13-9

```
//STL Functions generate and generate_n

#include <iostream>
#include <algorithm>
#include <iterator>
#include <vector>

using namespace std;
```

```
int nextNum();

int main()
{
    vector<int> vecList(8);                                   //Line 1

    ostream_iterator<int> screen(cout, " ");                  //Line 2

    generate(vecList.begin(), vecList.end(), nextNum);  //Line 3

    cout<<"Line 4: vecList after filling with "
        <<"numbers: ";                                        //Line 4

    copy(vecList.begin(), vecList.end(), screen);             //Line 5
    cout<<endl;                                                //Line 6

    generate_n(vecList.begin(), 3, nextNum);                  //Line 7

    cout<<"Line 8: vecList after filling the first three "
        <<"elements "<<endl
        <<"          with the next number: ";                 //Line 8
    copy(vecList.begin(), vecList.end(), screen);             //Line 9
    cout<<endl;                                                //Line 10

    return 0;
}

int nextNum()
{
    static int n = 1;

    return n++;
}
```

Output

```
Line 4: vecList after filling with numbers: 1 2 3 4 5 6 7 8
Line 8: vecList after filling the first three elements
        with the next number: 9 10 11 4 5 6 7 8
```

This program contains the value-returning function nextNum, which contains a static variable n initialized to 1. A call to this function returns the current value of n, and then increments the value of n. Therefore, the first call of nextNum returns 1, the second call returns 2, and so on.

The statements in Lines 1 and 2 declare vecList to be a sequence container of size 8, and screen to be an ostream iterator initialized to cout with the delimit character space. The statement in Line 3 uses the function generate to fill vecList by successively calling the function nextNum. Notice that after the statement in Line 3 executes, the value of the static variable n of nextNum is 9. The statement in Line 5 outputs the elements of vecList.

13

The statement in Line 7 calls the function `generate_n` to fill the first three elements of `vecList` by calling the function `nextNum` three times. The starting position is `vecList.begin()`, which is the first element of `vecList`, and the number of elements to be filled is 3, given by the second parameter of `generate_n` (see Line 7). The statement in Line 9 outputs the elements of `vecList`.

Functions `find`, `find_if`, `find_end`, and `find_first_of`

The functions `find`, `find_if`, `find_end`, and `find_first_of` are used to find the elements in a given range. These functions are defined in the header file `algorithm`. The prototypes of the functions `find` and `find_if` are:

```
template<class inputItr, class size, class Type>
inputItr find(inputItr first, inputItr last,
              const Type& searchValue);


template<class inputItr, class unaryPredicate>
inputItr find_if(inputItr first, inputItr last, unaryPredicate op);
```

The function `find` searches the range of elements `first...last-1` for the element `searchValue`. If `searchValue` is found in the range, the function returns the position in the range where `searchValue` is found; otherwise, it returns `last`. The function `find_if` searches the range of elements `first...last-1` for the element for which `op(rangeElement)` is `true`. If an element satisfying `op(rangeElement)` is `true` is found, it returns the position in the given range where such an element is found; otherwise, it returns `last`.

Example 13-10 illustrates how to use the functions `find` and `find_if`.

Example 13-10

Consider the following statements:

```
char cList[10] = {'a', 'i', 'C', 'd', 'e', 'f',
                  'o', 'H', 'u', 'j'};             //Line 1
vector<char> charList(cList, cList + 10);          //Line 2
vector<char>::iterator position;                   //Line 3
```

After the statement in Line 2 executes, the vector container `charList` is:

```
charList = {'a', 'i', 'C', 'd', 'e', 'f', 'o', 'H', 'u', 'j'};
```

Consider the following statement:

```
position = find(charList.begin(), charList.end(), 'd');
```

This statement searches `charList` for the first occurrence of `'d'` and returns an iterator, which is stored in `position`. Because `'d'` is the fourth character in `charList`, its position is 3. Therefore, `position` points to the element at position 3 in `charList`.

Now consider the following statement:

```
position = find_if(charList.begin(), charList.end(), isupper);
```

This statement uses the function `find_if` to find the first uppercase character in `charList`. Note that the function `isupper`, from the header file `cctype`, is passed as the third parameter to the function `find_if`. The first uppercase character in `charList` is the third element. Therefore, after this statement executes, `position` points to the third element of `charList`.

We leave it as an exercise for you to write a program that tests the functions `find` and `find_if` (see Programming Exercise 1 at the end of this chapter).

Next, we describe the functions `find_end` and `find_first_of`. These functions both have two forms. The prototypes of the function `find_end` are:

```
template<class forwardItr1, class forwardItr2>
forwardItr1 find_end(forwardItr1 first1, forwardItr1 last1,
                  forwardItr2 first2, forwardItr2 last2);


template<class forwardItr1, class forwardItr2,
        class binaryPredicate>
forwardItr1 find_end(forwardItr1 first1, forwardItr1 last1,
                  forwardItr2 first2, forwardItr2 last2,
                  binaryPredicate op);
```

Both forms of the function `find_end` search the range `first1...last1-1` for the last occurrence of the range `first2...last2-1`. If the search is successful, the function returns the position in `first1..last1-1` where the match occurs; otherwise, it returns `last1`. That is, the function `find_end` returns the position of the last element in the range `first1...last1-1` where the range `first2...last2-1` is a subrange of `first1...last1-1`. In the first form, the elements are compared for equality; in the second form, the comparison `op(elementFirstRange, elementSecondRange)` must be `true`.

The prototypes of the function `find_first_of` are:

```
template<class forwardItr1, class forwardItr2>
forwardItr1 find_first_of(forwardItr1 first1, forwardItr1 last1,
                        forwardItr2 first2, forwardItr2 last2);

template<class forwardItr1, class forwardItr2,
        class binaryPredicate>
forwardItr1 find_first_of(forwardItr1 first1, forwardItr1 last1,
                        forwardItr2 first2, forwardItr2 last2,
                        binaryPredicate op);
```

The first form returns the position, within the range `first1...last1-1`, of the first element of `first2...last2-1` that is also in the range `first1...last1-1`. The second

13

form returns the position, within the range `first1...last1-1`, of the first element of `first2...last2-1` for which `op(elemRange1, elemRange2)` is `true`. If no match is found, both forms return `last1-1`.

Example 13-11 illustrates how to use the functions `find_end` and `find_first_of`.

Example 13-11

Suppose that you have the following statements:

```
int list1[10] = {12, 34, 56, 21, 34, 78, 34, 56, 12, 25};
int list2[2] = {34, 56};
int list3[5] = {33, 48, 21, 34, 73};
vector<int>::iterator location;
```

Consider the following statement:

```
location = find_end(list1, list1 + 10, list2, list2 + 2);
```

This statement uses the function `find_end` to find the last occurrence of `list2` as a subsequence within `list1`. The last occurrence of `list2` in `list1` starts at position 6 (that is, at the seventh element). Therefore, after this statement executes, `location` points to the element at position 6 in `list1`, which is the seventh element of `list1`.

Now consider the following statement:

```
location = find_first_of(list1, list1 + 10, list3, list3 + 5);
```

This statement uses the function `find_first_of` to find the position in `list1` where the first element of `list3` is also an element of `list1`. The first element of `list3`, which is also an element of `list1`, is `34`; its position in `list1` is 1, the second element of `list1`. Therefore, after this statement executes, `location` points to the element at position 1 in `list1`, which is the second element of `list1`.

We leave it as an exercise for you to write a program that tests the functions `find_end` and `find_first_of` (see Programming Exercise 2 at the end of this chapter).

Functions `remove`, `remove_if`, `remove_copy`, and `remove_copy_if`

The function `remove` is used to remove certain elements from a sequence; the function `remove_if` is used to remove the elements from a sequence by using some criteria. The function `remove_copy` copies the elements of a sequence into another sequence by excluding certain elements of the first sequence. Similarly, the function `remove_copy_if` copies the elements of a sequence into another sequence by excluding certain elements, using some criteria, of the first sequence. These functions are defined in the header file `algorithm`.

The prototypes of the functions **remove** and **remove_if** are:

```
template<class forwardItr, class Type>
forwardItr remove(forwardItr first, forwardItr last,
                  const Type& value);

template<class forwardItr, class unaryPredicate>
forwardItr remove_if(forwardItr first, forwardItr last,
                     unaryPredicate op);
```

The function **remove** removes each occurrence of a given element in the range `first...last-1`. The element to be removed is passed as the third parameter to this function. The function **remove_if** removes those elements, in the range `first...last-1`, for which the predicate `op(element)` is **true**. These functions both return **forwardItr**, which points to the position after the last element of the new range of elements. These functions do not modify the size of the container; in fact, the elements are moved to the beginning of the container. For example, if the sequence is {3, 7, 2, 5, 7, 9} and the element to be removed is 7, then after removing 7, the resulting sequence is {3, 2, 5, 9, 7, 9}. The function returns a pointer to element 9 (which is after 5).

The program in Example 13-12 further illustrates the importance of this returned **forwardItr**. (See Lines 8, 10, 12, and 14.)

Let us now look at the prototypes of the functions **remove_copy** and **remove_copy_if**.

```
template<class inputItr, class outputItr, class Type>
outputItr remove_copy(inputItr first1, inputItr last1,
                      outputItr destFirst, const Type& value);

template<class inputItr, class outputItr, class unaryPredicate>
outputItr remove_copy_if(inputItr first1, inputItr last1,
                         outputItr destFirst,
                         unaryPredicate op);
```

The function **remove_copy** copies all the elements in the range `first1...last1-1`, except the elements specified by **value**, into the sequence starting at the position **destFirst**. Similarly, the function **remove_copy_if** copies all the elements in the range `first1...last1-1`, except the elements for which `op(element)` is **true**, into the sequence starting at the position **destFirst**. Both of these functions return an **outputItr**, which points to the position after the last copied element.

The program in Example 13-12 shows how to use the functions **remove**, **remove_if**, **remove_copy**, and **remove_copy_if**.

Example 13-12

```
//STL Functions remove, remove_if, remove_copy, and
//remove_copy_if

#include <iostream>
#include <cctype>
```

```
#include <algorithm>
#include <iterator>
#include <vector>

using namespace std;

bool lessThanEqualTo50(int num);
int main()
{
    char cList[10] = {'A', 'a', 'A', 'B', 'A',
                      'c', 'D', 'e', 'F', 'A'};          //Line 1

    vector<char> charList(cList, cList + 10);            //Line 2
    vector<char>::iterator lastElem, newLastElem;        //Line 3

    ostream_iterator<char> screen(cout, " ");            //Line 4

    cout<<"Line 6: Character list: ";                    //Line 5
    copy(charList.begin(), charList.end(), screen);      //Line 6
    cout<<endl;                                          //Line 7

       //remove
    lastElem = remove(charList.begin(),
                      charList.end(), 'A');              //Line 8

    cout<<"Line 9: Character list after removing A: ";   //Line 9
    copy(charList.begin(), lastElem, screen);            //Line 10
    cout<<endl;                                          //Line 11

      //remove_if
    newLastElem = remove_if(charList.begin(),
                            lastElem, isupper);          //Line 12
    cout<<"Line 13: Character list after removing "
        <<"the uppercase letters: "<<endl;              //Line 13
    copy(charList.begin(), newLastElem, screen);         //Line 14
    cout<<endl<<endl;                                    //Line 15

    int list[10] = {12, 34, 56, 21, 34,
                    78, 34, 55, 12, 25};                 //Line 16

    vector<int> intList(list, list + 10);                //Line 17
    vector<int>::iterator endElement;                    //Line 18

    ostream_iterator<int> screenOut(cout, " ");          //Line 19

    cout<<"Line 20: intList: ";                          //Line 20
    copy(intList.begin(), intList.end(), screenOut);     //Line 21
    cout<<endl;                                          //Line 22
```

```
    vector<int> temp1(10);                                      //Line 23

        //remove_copy
    endElement = remove_copy(intList.begin(), intList.end(),
                        temp1.begin(), 34);                     //Line 24

    cout<<"Line 25: temp1 after copying all the "
        <<"elements of intList except 34: "<<endl;              //Line 25
    copy(temp1.begin(), endElement, screenOut);                 //Line 26
    cout<<endl;                                                 //Line 27

    vector<int> temp2(10, 0);                                   //Line 28

        //remove_copy_if
    remove_copy_if(intList.begin(), intList.end(),
                temp2.begin(), lessThanEqualTo50);              //Line 29

    cout<<"Line 30: temp2 after copying all the elements of "
        <<"intList except \nnumbers less than 50: ";           //Line 30
    copy(temp2.begin(), temp2.end(), screenOut);                //Line 31
    cout<<endl;                                                 //Line 32

    return 0;
}

bool lessThanEqualTo50(int num)
{
    return (num <= 50);
}
```

Output

```
Line 6: Character list: A a A B A c D e F A
Line 9: Character list after removing A: a B c D e F
Line 13: Character list after removing the uppercase letters:
a c e

Line 20: intList: 12 34 56 21 34 78 34 55 12 25
Line 25: temp1 after copying all the elements of intList except 34:
12 56 21 78 55 12 25
Line 30: temp2 after copying all the elements of intList except
numbers less than 50: 56 78 55 0 0 0 0 0 0 0
```

The statement in Line 2 creates a vector list, charList, of the type char, and initializes charList using the array cList created in Line 1. The statement in Line 3 declares two vector iterators, lastElem and newLastElem. The statement in Line 4 declares an ostream iterator, screen. The statement in Line 6 outputs the value of charList. The statement in Line 8 uses the function remove to remove all the occurrences of 'A' from charList. The function returns an iterator positioned one past the last element of the new range, which is stored in lastElem. The statement in Line 10 outputs the elements of the new range. (Note that the statement in Line 10 outputs the elements in the range `charList.begin()...lastElem-1`.) The statement in Line 12 uses the function `remove_if` to remove the uppercase letters from the list `charList`, and stores the pointer returned by the function `remove_if` in `newLastElem`. The statement in Line 14 outputs the elements of the new range.

The statement in Line 17 creates a vector, `intList`, of the type `int` and initializes `intList` using the array `list`, created in Line 16. The statement in Line 21 outputs the elements of `intList`. The statement in Line 24 copies all the elements, except the occurrences of 34, of `intList` into `temp1`. The list `intList` is not modified. The statement in Line 26 outputs the elements of `temp1`. The statement in Line 28 creates a vector, `temp2`, of the type `int` of 10 components and initializes all the elements of `temp2` to 0. The statement in Line 29 uses the function `remove_copy_if` to copy those elements of `intList` that are less than or equal to 50. The statement in Line 31 outputs the elements of `temp2`.

Functions `replace`, `replace_if`, `replace_copy`, and `replace_copy_if`

The function `replace` is used to replace all the occurrences, within a specified range, of a given element with a new value. The function `replace_if` is used to replace the values of the elements, within a specified range, that satisfy certain criteria with a new value. The prototypes of these functions are:

```
template<class forwardItr, class Type>
void replace(forwardItr first, forwardItr last,
             const Type& oldValue, const Type& newValue);

template<class forwardItr, class unaryPredicate, class Type>
void replace_if(forwardItr first, forwardItr last,
                unaryPredicate op, const Type& newValue);
```

The function `replace` replaces all the elements in the range `first...last-1` whose values are equal to `oldValue` with the value specified by `newValue`. The function `replace_if` replaces all the elements in the range `first...last-1`, for which `op(element)` is `true`, with the value specified by `newValue`.

The function `replace_copy` is a combination of `replace` and `copy`. Similarly, the function `replace_copy_if` is a combination of `replace_if` and `copy`. Let us first look at the prototypes of the functions `replace_copy` and `replace_copy_if`:

```
template<class inputItr, class outputItr, class Type>
outputItr replace_copy(forwardItr first, forwardItr last,
                       outputItr destFirst,
                       const Type& oldValue,
                       const Type& newValue);

template<class forwardItr, class outputItr,
         class unaryPredicate, class Type>
```

```
outputItr replace_copy_if(forwardItr first, forwardItr last,
                          outputItr destFirst,
                          unaryPredicate op,
                          const Type& newValue);
```

The function `replace_copy` copies all the elements in the range `first...last-1` into the container starting at `destFirst`. If the value of an element in this range is equal to `oldValue`, it is replaced by `newValue`. The function `replace_copy_if` copies all the elements in the range `first...last-1` into the container starting at `destFirst`. If for any element in this range `op(element)` is `true`, at the destination its value is replaced by `newValue`. These functions both return an `outputItr` (a pointer) positioned one past the last element copied at the destination.

Example 13-13 illustrates how to use the functions `replace`, `replace_if`, `replace_copy`, and `replace_copy_if`.

Example 13-13

Consider the following statements:

```
char cList[10] = {'A', 'a', 'A', 'B', 'A',
                  'c', 'D', 'e', 'F', 'A'};        //Line 1
vector<char> charList(cList, cList + 10);          //Line 2
```

After the statement in Line 2 executes, the vector container `charList` is:

```
charList = {'A', 'a', 'A', 'B', 'A', 'c',
            'D', 'e', 'F', 'A'}                    //Line 3
```

Now consider the following statement:

```
replace(charList.begin(), charList.end(), 'A', 'Z');    //Line 4
```

This statement uses the function `replace` to replace all the occurrences of `'A'` with `'Z'` in `charList`. After this statement executes, `charList` is:

```
charList ={'Z', 'a', 'Z', 'B', 'Z', 'c', 'D',
           'e', 'F', 'Z'}                          //Line 5
```

Now consider the following statement:

```
replace_if(charList.begin(), charList.end(),
                            isupper, '*');         //Line 6
```

This statement uses the function `replace_if` to replace the uppercase letters with `'*'` in the list `charList`. After this statement executes, `charList` is:

```
charList ={'*', 'a', '*', '*', '*', 'c', '*',
           'e', '*', '*'}                          //Line 7
```

Next, suppose that you have the following statements:

```
int list[10] = {12, 34, 56, 21, 34, 78, 34, 55, 12, 25}; //Line 8
vector<int> intList(list, list + 10);                    //Line 9
vector<int> temp(10);                                    //Line 10
```

13

The statement in Line 9 creates a vector, `intList`, of the type `int` and initializes `intList` using the array `list`, created in Line 8. After the statement in Line 9 executes, `intList` is:

`intList = {12, 34, 56, 21, 34, 78, 34, 55, 12, 25}`

The statement in Line 10 declares a vector `temp` of the type `int`. Next, consider the following statement:

```
replace_copy(intList.begin(), intList.end(),
            temp.begin(), 34, 0);                            //Line 11
```

This statement copies all the elements of `intList` into `temp`; 34 is replaced with 0. The list `intList` is not modified. After this statement executes, `temp` is:

`temp = {12, 0, 56, 21, 0, 78, 0, 55, 12, 25}`

Next, suppose that you have the following function definition:

```
bool lessThanEqualTo50(int num)                              //Line 12
{
    return (num <= 50);
}
```

The function `lessThanEqualTo50` returns `true` if `num` is less than or equal to `50`; otherwise, it returns `false`. Consider the following statement:

```
replace_copy_if(intList.begin(), intList.end(),
               temp.begin(), lessThanEqualTo50, 50);     //Line 13
```

This statement uses the function `replace_copy_if` to copy the elements of `intList` into `temp`, and replaces all the elements that are less than or equal to `50` with `50`. Notice that the fourth parameter of the function `replace_copy_if` is the function `lessThanEqualTo50`. After the statement in Line 13 executes, `temp` is:

`temp = {50, 50, 56, 50, 50, 78, 50, 55, 50, 50}`

We leave it as an exercise for you to write a program that further illustrates how to use the functions `replace`, `replace_if`, `replace_copy`, and `replace_copy_if` (see Programming Exercise 3 at the end of this chapter).

Functions `swap`, `iter_swap`, and `swap_ranges`

The functions `swap`, `iter_swap`, and `swap_ranges` are used to swap elements. These functions are defined in the header file `algorithm`. The prototypes of these functions are:

```
template<class Type>
void swap(Type& object1, Type& object2);

template<class forwardItr1, class forwardItr2>
void iter_swap(forwardItr1 first, forwardItr2 second);
```

```
template<class forwardItr1, class forwardItr2>
forwardItr2 swap_ranges(forwardItr1 first1, forwardItr1 last1,
                        forwardItr2 first2);
```

The function **swap** swaps the values of **object1** and **object2**. The function **iter_swap** swaps the values to which the iterators **first** and **second** point. The function **swap_ranges** swaps the elements of the range **first1...last1-1** with the consecutive elements starting at position **first2**. It returns the iterator of the second range positioned one past the last element swapped.

The program in Example 13-14 illustrates how to use these functions.

Example 13-14

```
//STL functions swap, iter_swap, and swap_ranges

#include <iostream>
#include <algorithm>
#include <vector>
#include <iterator>

using namespace std;

int main()
{
    char cList[10] = {'A', 'B', 'C', 'D', 'F',
                      'G', 'H', 'I', 'J', 'K'};      //Line 1

    vector<char> charList(cList, cList + 10);         //Line 2
    vector<char>::iterator charItr;                   //Line 3

    ostream_iterator<char> screen(cout, " ");         //Line 4

    cout<<"Line 5: Character list: ";                 //Line 5
    copy(charList.begin(), charList.end(), screen);   //Line 6
    cout<<endl;                                        //Line 7

        //swap
    swap(charList[0], charList[1]);                   //Line 8

    cout<<"Line 9: Character list after swapping the "
        <<"first and second elements: "<<endl;        //Line 9
    copy(charList.begin(), charList.end(), screen);   //Line 10
    cout<<endl;                                        //Line 11

        //iter_swap
    iter_swap(charList.begin() + 2,
              charList.begin() + 3);                  //Line 12

    cout<<"Line 13: Character list after swapping the "
        <<"third and fourth elements: "<<endl;        //Line 13
```

13

```
        copy(charList.begin(), charList.end(), screen);     //Line 14
        cout<<endl;                                          //Line 15

        charItr = charList.begin() + 4;                      //Line 16
        iter_swap(charItr, charItr + 1);                     //Line 17

        cout<<"Line 18: Character list after swapping the "
            <<"fifth and sixth elements: "<<endl;            //Line 18
        copy(charList.begin(), charList.end(), screen);      //Line 19
        cout<<endl<<endl;                                    //Line 20

        int list[10] = {1, 2, 3, 4, 5, 6, 7, 8, 9, 10};      //Line 21

        vector<int> intList(list, list + 10);                //Line 22

        ostream_iterator<int> screenOut(cout, " ");          //Line 23

        cout<<"Line 24: intList: ";                          //Line 24
        copy(intList.begin(), intList.end(), screenOut);     //Line 25
        cout<<endl;                                          //Line 26

            //swap_ranges
        swap_ranges(intList.begin(), intList.begin() + 4,
                    intList.begin() + 5);                    //Line 27

        cout<<"Line 28: intList after swapping the first "
            <<"four elements with the \n          four elements "
            <<"starting at the sixth element of intList: "
            <<endl;                                          //Line 28
        copy(intList.begin(), intList.end(), screenOut);     //Line 29
        cout<<endl;                                          //Line 30

        swap_ranges(list, list + 10, intList.begin());       //Line 31

        cout<<"Line 32: list and intList after swapping "
            <<"the elements with each other: "<<endl;        //Line 32
        cout<<"Line 33: list: ";                             //Line 33
        copy(list, list + 10, screenOut);                    //Line 34
        cout<<endl;                                          //Line 35
        cout<<"Line 36: intList: ";                          //Line 36
        copy(intList.begin(), intList.end(), screenOut);     //Line 37
        cout<<endl;                                          //Line 38

        return 0;
    }
```

Output

```
Line 5: Character list: A B C D F G H I J K
Line 9: Character list after swapping the first and second elements:
B A C D F G H I J K
```

```
Line 13: Character list after swapping the third and fourth
elements: B A D C F G H I J K
Line 18: Character list after swapping the fifth and sixth elements:
B A D C G F H I J K

Line 24: intList: 1 2 3 4 5 6 7 8 9 10
Line 28: intList after swapping the first four elements with the
         four elements starting at the sixth element of intList:
6 7 8 9 5 1 2 3 4 10
Line 32: list and intList after swapping the elements with each other:
Line 33: list: 6 7 8 9 5 1 2 3 4 10
Line 36: intList: 1 2 3 4 5 6 7 8 9 10
```

The statement in Line 2 creates the vector `charList` and initializes it using the array `cList` declared in Line 1. The statement in Line 6 outputs the values of `charList`. The statement in Line 8 swaps the first and second elements of `charList`. The statement in Line 12, using the function `iter_swap`, swaps the third and fourth elements of `charList`. (Recall that the position of the first element in `charList` is 0.) After the statement in Line 16 executes, `charItr` points to the fifth element of `charList`. The statement in Line 17 uses the iterator `charItr` to swap the fifth and sixth elements of `charList`. The statement in Line 19 outputs the values of the elements of `charList`. (In the output, the line marked Line 18 contains the output of Lines 18 through 20 of the program.)

The statement in Line 22 creates the vector `intList` and initializes it using the array declared in Line 21. The statement in Line 25 outputs the values of the elements of `intList`. The statement in Line 27 uses the function `swap_ranges` to swap the first four elements of `intList` with the four elements of `intList` starting at the sixth element of `intList`. The statement in Line 29 outputs the elements of `intList`. (In the output, the line marked Line 28 contains the output of Lines 28 through 30 of the program.)

The statement in Line 31 swaps the elements of the array `list` with the elements of the vector `intList`. The statement in Line 34 outputs the elements of the array `list`; the statement in Line 37 outputs `intList`.

13

Functions search, search_n, sort, and binary_search

The functions `search`, `search_n`, `sort`, and `binary_search` are used to search elements. These functions are defined in the header file `algorithm`.

The prototypes of the function `search` are:

```
template<class forwardItr1, class forwardItr2>
forwardItr1 search(forwardItr1 first1, forwardItr1 last1,
                   forwardItr2 first2, forwardItr2 last2);

template<class forwardItr1, class forwardItr2,
         class binaryPredicate>
```

```
forwardItr1 search(forwardItr1 first1, forwardItr1 last1,
                   forwardItr2 first2, forwardItr2 last2,
                   binaryPredicate op);
```

Given two ranges of elements, `first1...last1-1` and `first2...last2-1`, the function `search` searches the first element in the range `first1...last1-1` where the range `first2...last2-1` occurs as a subrange of `first1...last1-1`. The first form makes the equality comparison between the elements of the two ranges. For the second form, the comparison `op(elemFirstRange, elemSecondRange)` must be `true`. If a match is found, the function returns the position in the range `first1...last1-1` where the match occurs; otherwise, the function returns `last1`.

The prototypes of the function `search_n` are:

```
template<class forwardItr, class size, class Type>
forwardItr search_n(forwardItr first, forwardItr last,
                    size count, const Type& value);
```

```
template<class forwardItr, class size, class Type,
         class binaryPredicate>
forwardItr search_n(forwardItr first, forwardItr last,
                    size count, const Type& value,
                    binaryPredicate op);
```

Given a range of elements `first...last-1`, the function `search_n` searches for `count` consecutive occurrences of `value`. The first form returns the position in the range `first...last-1` where a subsequence of `count` consecutive elements have values equal to `value`. The second form returns the position in the range `first...last-1` where a subsequence of `count` consecutive elements exists for which `op(elemRange, value)` is `true`. If no match is found, both forms return `last`.

The prototypes of the function `sort` are:

```
template<class randomAccessItr>
void sort(randomAccessItr first, randomAccessItr last);
```

```
template<class randomAccessItr, class compare>
void sort(randomAccessItr first, randomAccessItr last,
          compare op);
```

The first form of the function `sort` reorders the elements in the range `first...last-1` in ascending order. The second form reorders the elements according to the criteria specified by `op`.

The prototypes of the function `binary_search` are:

```
template<class forwardItr, class Type>
bool binary_search(forwardItr first, forwardItr last,
                   const Type& searchValue);
```

```
template<class forwardItr, class Type, class compare>
bool binary_search(forwardItr first, forwardItr last,
                   const Type& searchValue, compare op);
```

The first form returns `true` if `searchValue` is found in the range `first...last-1`, and `false` otherwise. The second form uses a function object, `op`, that specifies the search criteria.

Example 13-15 illustrates how to use these searching and sorting functions.

Example 13-15

```cpp
//STL Functions search, search_n, sort, and binary_search

#include <iostream>
#include <algorithm>
#include <iterator>
#include <vector>

using namespace std;

int main()
{
    int intList[15] = {12, 34, 56, 34, 34,
                       78, 38, 43, 12, 25,
                       34, 56, 62, 5, 49};            //Line 1

    vector<int> vecList(intList, intList + 15);       //Line 2
    int list[2] = {34, 56};                           //Line 3

    vector<int>::iterator location;                   //Line 4

    ostream_iterator<int> screenOut(cout, " ");       //Line 5

    cout<<"Line 6: vecList: ";                        //Line 6
    copy(vecList.begin(), vecList.end(), screenOut);  //Line 7
    cout<<endl;                                        //Line 8

    cout<<"Line 9: list: ";                           //Line 9
    copy(list, list + 2, screenOut);                  //Line 10
    cout<<endl;                                        //Line 11

        //search
    location = search(vecList.begin(), vecList.end(),
                      list, list + 2);                //Line 12

    if(location != vecList.end())                     //Line 13
        cout<<"Line 14: list found in vecList. The "
            <<"first occurrence of \n    list in vecList "
            <<"is at position: "
            <<(location - vecList.begin())<<endl;     //Line 14
```

13

```
        else                                                    //Line 15
           cout<<"Line 16: list is not in vecList"<<endl;       //Line 16

           //search_n
        location = search_n(vecList.begin(), vecList.end(),
                               2, 34);                           //Line 17

        if(location != vecList.end())                           //Line 18
           cout<<"Line 19: Two consecutive occurrences of "
              <<"34 found in \n    vecList at position: "
              <<(location - vecList.begin())<<endl;             //Line 19
        else                                                    //Line 20
           cout<<"Line 21: Two consecutive occurrences of "
              <<"34 not in vecList." <<endl;                    //Line 21

           //sort
        sort(vecList.begin(), vecList.end());                   //Line 22

        cout<<"Line 23: vecList after sorting:"
           <<endl<<"     ";                                     //Line 23
        copy(vecList.begin(), vecList.end(), screenOut);        //Line 24
        cout<<endl;                                             //Line 25

           //binary_search
        bool found;                                             //Line 26

        found = binary_search(vecList.begin(),
                             vecList.end(), 43);                //Line 27

        if(found)                                               //Line 28
           cout<<"Line 29: 43 found in vecList"<<endl;          //Line 29
        else                                                    //Line 30
           cout<<"Line 31: 43 not in vecList"<<endl;            //Line 31

        return 0;
    }
```

Output

```
Line 6: vecList: 12 34 56 34 34 78 38 43 12 25 34 56 62 5 49
Line 9: list: 34 56
Line 14: list found in vecList. The first occurrence of
   list in vecList is at position: 1
Line 19: Two consecutive occurrences of 34 found in
   vecList at position: 3
Line 23: vecList after sorting:
     5 12 12 25 34 34 34 34 38 43 49 56 56 62 78
Line 29: 43 found in vecList
```

The statement in Line 2 creates a vector, **vecList**, and initializes it using the array **intList** created in Line 1. The statement in Line 3 creates an array, **list**, of two components and initializes `list`. The statement in Line 7 outputs `vecList`. The statement in Line 12 uses the function `search` and searches `vecList` to find the position (of the first occurrence) in `vecList` where `list` occurs as a subsequence. The statements in Lines 13 through 16 output the result of the search; see the line marked Line 14 in the output.

The statement in Line 17 uses the function `search_n` to find the position in `vecList` where two consecutive instances of `34` occur. The statements in Lines 18 through 21 output the result of the search.

The statement in Line 22 uses the function `sort` to sort `vecList`. The statement in Line 24 outputs `vecList`. In the output, the line marked Line 23 contains the output of the statements in Lines 23 through 25 of the program.

The statement in Line 27 uses the function `binary_search` to search `vecList`. The statements in Lines 28 through 31 output the search result.

Functions `adjacent_find`, `merge`, and `inplace_merge`

The algorithm `adjacent_find` is used to find the first occurrence of consecutive elements that meet certain criteria. The prototypes of the functions implementing this algorithm are:

```
template<class forwardItr>
forwardItr adjacent_find(forwardItr first, forwardItr last);

template<class forwardItr, class binaryPredicate>
forwardItr adjacent_find(forwardItr first, forwardItr last,
                         binaryPredicate op);
```

The first form of `adjacent_find` uses the equality criteria; that is, it looks for the first consecutive occurrence of the same element. In the second form, the algorithm returns an iterator to the element in the range `first...last-1` for which `op(elem, nextElem)` is `true`, where `elem` is an element in the range `first...last-1` and `nextElem` is an element in this range next to `elem`. If no matching elements are found, both algorithms return `last`.

Suppose that `intList` is a list container of the type `int`. Further assume that `intList` is

```
intList = {0, 1, 1, 2, 3, 4, 4, 5, 6, 6};              //Line 1
```

Consider the following statements:

```
list<int>::iterator listItr;                            //Line 2
listItr = adjacent_find(intList.begin(), intList.end()); //Line 3
```

The statement in Line 2 declares `listItr` to be a `list` iterator that can point to any `list` container of the type `int`. The statement in Line 3 uses the function `adjacent_find` to find the position of the (first set of) consecutive identical elements. The function returns a pointer to the first set of consecutive elements, which is stored in `listItr`. After the statement in Line 3 executes, `listItr` points to the second element of `intList`.

13

Now suppose that `vecList` is a `vector` container of the type `int`. Further assume that `vecList` is

```
vecList = {1, 3, 5, 7, 9, 0, 2, 4, 6, 8};                 //Line 4
```

Consider the following statements:

```
vector<int>::iterator intItr;                             //Line 5
intItr = adjacent_find(vecList.begin(), vecList.end(),
                       greater<int>());                   //Line 6
```

The statement in Line 5 declares `intItr` to be a `vector` iterator that can point to any `vector` container of the type `int`. The statement in Line 6 uses the second form of the function `adjacent_find` to find the first element of `vecList` that is greater than the following element of `vecList`. Notice that the third parameter of the function `adjacent_find` is the binary predicate `greater`, which returns the position in `vecList` where the first element is greater than the second element. The returned position is stored in the iterator `intItr`. After the statement in Line 6 executes, `intItr` points to the element **9**.

Next, we discuss the algorithm `merge`. The algorithm `merge` merges the sorted lists. The result is a sorted list. Both lists must be sorted according to the same criteria. For example, both lists should be in ascending order. The prototypes of the functions to implement the `merge` algorithms are:

```
template<class inputItr1, class inputItr2,
        class outputItr>
outputItr merge(inputItr1 first1, inputItr1 last1,
                inputItr2 first2, inputItr2 last2,
                outputItr destFirst);

template<class inputItr1, class inputItr2,
        class outputItr, class binaryPredicate>
outputItr merge(inputItr1 first1, inputItr1 last1,
                inputItr2 first2, inputItr2 last2,
                outputItr destFirst, binaryPredicate op);
```

Both forms of the algorithm `merge` merge the elements of the sorted ranges `first1...last1-1` and `first2...last2-1`. The destination range beginning with the iterator `destFirst` contains the merged elements. The first form uses the less-than operator, `<`, to order the elements. The second form uses the binary predicate `op` to order the elements; that is, `op(elemRange1, elemRange2)` must be `true`. Both forms return the position after the last copied element in the destination range. Moreover, the source ranges are not modified and the destination range should not overlap with the source ranges.

Consider the following statements:

```
int list1[5] = {0, 2, 4, 6, 8};              //Line 7
int list2[5] = {1, 3, 5, 7, 9};              //Line 8
```

```
list<int> intList;                              //Line 9
merge(list1, list1 + 5, list2, list2 + 5,
      back_inserter(intList));                  //Line 10
```

The statements in Lines 7 and 8 create the sorted arrays `list1` and `list2`. The statement in Line 9 declares `intList` to be a `list` container of the type `int`. The statement in Line 10 uses the function `merge` to merge `list1` and `list2`. The fifth parameter of the function `merge`, in Line 10, is a call to `back_inserter`, which places the merged list into `intList`. After the statement in Line 10 executes, `intList` contains the merged list, that is,

```
intList = {0, 1, 2, 3, 4, 5, 6, 7, 8, 9}
```

The algorithm `inplace_merge` is used to combine two sorted consecutive sequences. The prototypes of the functions implementing this algorithm are:

```
template<class biDirectionalItr>
void inplace_merge(biDirectionalItr first,
                   biDirectionalItr middle,
                   biDirectionalItr last);

template<class biDirectionalItr, class binaryPredicate>
void inplace_merge(biDirectionalItr first,
                   biDirectionalItr middle,
                   biDirectionalItr last,
                   binaryPredicate op);
```

Both forms merge the sorted consecutive sequences `first...middle-1` and `middle...last-1`. The merged elements overwrite the two ranges beginning at `first`. The first form uses the less-than criterion to merge the two consecutive sequences. The second form uses the binary predicate `op` to merge the sequences; that is, for the elements of the two sequences, `op(elemSeq1, elemSeq2)` must be `true`. For example, suppose that:

```
vecList = {1, 3, 5, 7, 9, 2, 4, 6, 8}
```

where `vecList` is a vector container. Further suppose that `vecItr` is a vector iterator pointing to the element 2. Then, after the execution of the statement:

```
inplace_merge(vecList.begin(), vecItr, vecList.end());
```

the elements in `vecList` are in the following order

```
vecList = {1, 2, 3, 4, 5, 6, 7, 8, 9}
```

We leave it as an exercise for you to write a program that further illustrates how to use the functions `adjacent_find`, `merge`, and `inplace_merge` (see Programming Exercise 4 at the end of this chapter).

13

Functions `reverse`, `reverse_copy`, `rotate`, and `rotate_copy`

The algorithm **reverse** reverses the order of the elements in a given range. The prototype of the function to implement the algorithm **reverse** is:

```
template<class biDirectionalItr>
void reverse(biDirectionalItr first, biDirectionalItr last);
```

The elements in the range `first...last-1` are reversed. For example, if `vecList = {1, 2, 5, 3, 4}`, then the elements in reverse order are `vecList = {4, 3, 5, 2, 1}`.

The algorithm **reverse_copy** reverses the order of the elements of a given range while copying them into a destination range. The source is not modified. The prototype of the function implementing the **reverse_copy** algorithm is:

```
template<class biDirectionalItr, class outputItr>
outputItr reverse_copy(biDirectionalItr first,
                       biDirectionalItr last,
                       outputItr destFirst);
```

The elements in the range `first...last-1` are copied in reverse order at the destination beginning with `destFirst`. The function also returns an iterator positioned one past the last element copied at the destination.

The algorithm **rotate** rotates the elements of a given range. Its prototype is:

```
template<class forwardItr>
void rotate(forwardItr first, forwardItr newFirst,
            forwardItr last);
```

The elements in the range `first...newFirst-1` are moved to the end of the range. The element specified by **newFirst** becomes the first element of the range. For example, suppose that:

```
vecList = {3, 5, 4, 0, 7, 8, 2, 5}
```

and the iterator **vecItr** points to 0. Then, after the statement:

```
rotate(vecList.begin(), vecItr, vecList.end());
```

executes, **vecList** is as follows:

```
vecList = {0, 7, 8, 2, 5, 3, 5, 4}
```

The algorithm **rotate_copy** is a combination of **rotate** and **copy**. That is, the elements of the source are copied at the destination in a rotated order. The source is not modified. The prototype of the function implementing this algorithm is:

```
template<class forwardItr, class outputItr>
outputItr rotate_copy(forwardItr first, forwardItr middle,
                      forwardItr last,
                      outputItr destFirst);
```

The elements in the range `first...last-1` are copied into the destination range beginning with **destFirst** in the rotated order so that the element specified by **middle** in the range `first...last-1` becomes the first element of the destination. The function also returns an iterator positioned one past the last element copied at the destination.

The algorithms `reverse`, `reverse_copy`, `rotate`, and `rotate_copy` are contained in the header file `algorithm`. The program in Example 13-16 illustrates how to use these algorithms.

Example 13-16

```cpp
//STL Functions reverse, reverse_copy, rotate, and
//rotate_copy

#include <iostream>
#include <algorithm>
#include <iterator>
#include <list>

using namespace std;

int main()
{
    int temp[10] = {1, 3, 5, 7, 9, 0, 2, 4, 6, 8};      //Line 1

    list<int> intList(temp, temp + 10);                 //Line 2
    list<int> resultList;                               //List 3
    list<int>::iterator listItr;                        //Line 4

    ostream_iterator<int> screen(cout, " ");            //Line 5

    cout<<"Line 6: intList: ";                          //Line 6
    copy(intList.begin(), intList.end(), screen);       //Line 7
    cout<<endl;                                          //Line 8

        //reverse
    reverse(intList.begin(), intList.end());            //Line 9

    cout<<"Line 10: intList after reversal: ";          //Line 10
    copy(intList.begin(), intList.end(), screen);       //Line 11
    cout<<endl;                                          //Line 12

        //reverse_copy
    reverse_copy(intList.begin(), intList.end(),
                back_inserter(resultList));             //Line 13

    cout<<"Line 14: resultList: ";                      //Line 14
    copy(resultList.begin(), resultList.end(),
        screen);                                        //Line 15
    cout<<endl;                                          //Line 16
```

13

```
    listItr = intList.begin();                              //Line 17
    listItr++;                                              //Line 18
    listItr++;                                              //Line 19

    cout<<"Line 20: intList before rotating: ";             //Line 20
    copy(intList.begin(), intList.end(), screen);           //Line 21
    cout<<endl;                                             //Line 22

        //rotate
    rotate(intList.begin(), listItr, intList.end());        //Line 23

    cout<<"Line 24: intList after rotating: ";              //Line 24
    copy(intList.begin(), intList.end(), screen);           //Line 25
    cout<<endl;                                             //Line 26

    resultList.clear();                                     //Line 27

        //rotate_copy
    rotate_copy(intList.begin(), listItr, intList.end(),
            back_inserter(resultList));                      //Line 28

    cout<<"Line 29: intList after rotating and "
        <<"copying: ";                                      //Line 29
    copy(intList.begin(), intList.end(), screen);           //Line 30
    cout<<endl;                                             //Line 31

    cout<<"Line 32: resultList after rotating and "
        <<"copying: ";                                      //Line 32
    copy(resultList.begin(), resultList.end(),
        screen);                                            //Line 33
    cout<<endl;                                             //Line 34

    resultList.clear();                                     //Line 35

    rotate_copy(intList.begin(),
            find(intList.begin(), intList.end(), 6),
            intList.end(),
            back_inserter(resultList));                     //Line 36

    cout<<"Line 37: resultList after rotating and "
        <<"copying: ";                                      //Line 37
    copy(resultList.begin(), resultList.end(),
        screen);                                            //Line 38
    cout<<endl;                                             //Line 39

    return 0;
}
```

Output

```
Line 6: intList: 1 3 5 7 9 0 2 4 6 8
Line 10: intList after reversal: 8 6 4 2 0 9 7 5 3 1
Line 14: resultList: 1 3 5 7 9 0 2 4 6 8
Line 20: intList before rotating: 8 6 4 2 0 9 7 5 3 1
Line 24: intList after rotating: 4 2 0 9 7 5 3 1 8 6
Line 29: intList after rotating and copying: 4 2 0 9 7 5 3 1 8 6
Line 32: resultList after rotating and copying: 0 9 7 5 3 1 8 6 4 2
Line 37: resultList after rotating and copying: 6 4 2 0 9 7 5 3 1 8
```

The preceding output is self-explanatory. The details are left as an exercise for you.

Functions count, count_if, max, max_element, min, min_element, and random_shuffle

The algorithm count counts the occurrences of a specified value in a given range. The prototype of the function implementing this algorithm is:

```
template<class inputItr, class type>
iterator_traits<inputItr>::difference_type
    count(inputItr first, inputItr last, const Type& value);
```

The function count returns the number of times the value specified by the parameter value occurs in the range first...last-1.

The algorithm count_if counts the occurrences of a specified value in a given range satisfying a certain criterion. The prototype of the function implementing this algorithm is:

```
template<class inputItr, class unaryPredicate>
iterator_traits<inputItr>::difference_type
    count_if(inputItr first, inputItr last, unaryPredicate op);
```

The function count_if returns the number of elements in the range first...last-1 for which op(elemRange) is true.

The algorithm max is used to determine the maximum of two values. It has two forms, as shown by the following prototypes:

```
template<class Type>
const Type& max(const Type& aVal, const Type& bVal);

template<class Type, class compare>
const Type& max(const Type& aVal, const Type& bVal, compare comp);
```

In the first form, the greater-than operator associated with Type is used. In the second form, the comparison operation specified by comp is used.

13

The algorithm `max_element` is used to determine the largest element in a given range. This algorithm has two forms, as shown by the following prototypes:

```
template<class forwardItr>
forwardItr max_element(forwardItr first, forwardItr last);

template<class forwardItr, class compare>
forwardItr max_element(forwardItr first, forwardItr last,
                       compare comp);
```

The first form uses the greater-than operator associated with the data type of the elements in the range `first...last-1`. In the second form, the comparison operation specified by `comp` is used. Both forms return an iterator to the element containing the largest value in the range `first...last-1`.

The algorithm `min` is used to determine the minimum of two values. It has two forms, as shown by the following prototypes:

```
template<class Type>
const Type& min(const Type& aVal, const Type& bVal);

template<class Type, class compare>
const Type& min(const Type& aVal, const Type& bVal, compare comp);
```

In the first form, the less-than operator associated with `Type` is used. In the second form, the comparison operation specified by `comp` is used.

The algorithm `min_element` is used to determine the smallest element in a given range. This algorithm has two forms, as shown by the following prototypes:

```
template<class forwardItr>
forwardItr min_element(forwardItr first, forwardItr last);

template<class forwardItr, class compare>
forwardItr min_element(forwardItr first, forwardItr last,
                       compare comp);
```

The first form uses the less-than operator associated with the data type of the elements in the range `first...last-1`. In the second form, the comparison operation specified by `comp` is used. Both forms return an iterator to the element containing the smallest value in the range `first...last-1`.

The algorithm `random_shuffle` is used to randomly order the elements in a given range. There are two forms of this algorithm, as shown by the following prototypes:

```
template<class randomAccessItr>
void random_shuffle(randomAccessItr first,
                    randomAccessItr last);

template<class randomAccessItr, class randomAccessGenerator>
void random_shuffle(randomAccessItr first,
                    randomAccessItr last,
                    randomAccessGenerator rand);
```

The first form reorders the elements in the range `first...last-1` using a uniform distribution random number generator. The second form reorders the elements in the range `first...last-1` using a random number-generating function object or a pointer to a function specified by `rand`.

Example 13-17 illustrates how to use these functions.

Example 13-17

```cpp
//STL Functions count, count_if, max_element,
//min_element, and random_shuffle

#include <iostream>
#include <cctype>
#include <algorithm>
#include <iterator>
#include <vector>

using namespace std;

int main ()
{
    char cList[10] = {'Z', 'a', 'Z', 'B', 'Z',
                      'c', 'D', 'e', 'F', 'Z'};          //Line 1

    vector<char> charList(cList, cList + 10);            //Line 2

    ostream_iterator<char> screen(cout, " ");            //Line 3

    cout<<"Line 4: charList: ";                          //Line 4
    copy(charList.begin(), charList.end(), screen);      //Line 5
    cout<<endl;                                          //Line 6

        //count
    int noOfZs = count(charList.begin(), charList.end(),
                       'Z');                             //Line 7

    cout<<"Line 8: Number of Z\'s in charList:"
        <<noOfZs<<endl;                                  //Line 8

        //count_if
    int noOfUpper = count_if(charList.begin(),
                         charList.end(), isupper);       //Line 9

    cout<<"Line 10: Number of uppercase letters in "
        <<"charList: "<<noOfUpper<<endl;                 //Line 10
```

13

```
int list[10] = {12, 34, 56, 21, 34,
                78, 34, 55, 12, 25};            //Line 11

ostream_iterator<int> screenOut(cout, " ");     //Line 12

cout<<"Line 13: list: ";                        //Line 13
copy(list, list + 10, screenOut);               //Line 14
cout<<endl;                                      //Line 15

    //max_element
int *maxLoc = max_element(list, list + 10);     //Line 16

cout<<"Line 17: Largest element in list: "
    <<*maxLoc<<endl;                             //Line 17

    //min_element
int *minLoc = min_element(list, list + 10);     //Line 18

cout<<"Line 19: Smallest element in list: "
    <<*minLoc<<endl;                             //Line 19

    //random_shuffle
random_shuffle(list, list + 10);                //Line 20

cout<<"Line 21: list after random shuffle: ";   //Line 21
copy(list, list + 10, screenOut);               //Line 22
cout<<endl;                                      //Line 23

return 0;
}
```

Output

```
Line 4: charList: Z a Z B Z c D e F Z
Line 8: Number of Z's in charList:4
Line 10: Number of uppercase letters in charList: 7
Line 13: list: 12 34 56 21 34 78 34 55 12 25
Line 17: Largest element in list: 78
Line 19: Smallest element in list: 12
Line 21: list after random shuffle: 12 34 25 56 12 78 55 21 34 34
```

The preceding output is self-explanatory. The details are left as an exercise for you.

Functions `for_each` and `transform`

The algorithm `for_each` is used to access and process each element in a given range by applying a function, which is passed as a parameter. The prototype of the function implementing this algorithm is

```
template<class inputItr, class function>
function for_each(inputItr first, inputItr last, function func);
```

The function specified by the parameter `func` is applied to each element in the range `first...last-1`. The function `func` can modify the element. The returned value of the function `for_each` is usually ignored.

The algorithm `transform` has two forms. The prototypes of the functions implementing this algorithm are:

```
template<class inputItr, class outputItr,
         class unaryOperation>
outputItr transform(inputItr first, inputItr last,
                    outputItr destFirst,
                    unaryOperation op);

template<class inputItr1, class inputItr2,
         class outputItr, class binaryOperation>
outputItr transform(inputItr1 first1, inputItr1 last,
                    inputItr2 first2,
                    outputItr destFirst,
                    binaryOperation bOp);
```

The first form of the function `transform` has four parameters. This function creates a sequence of elements at the destination, beginning with `destFirst`, by applying the unary operation `op` to each element in the range `first1...last-1`. This function returns an iterator positioned one past the last element copied at the destination.

The second form of the function `transform` has five parameters. The function creates a sequence of elements by applying the binary operation `bOp`—that is, `bOp(elemRange1, elemRange2)`—to the corresponding elements in the range `first1...last1-1` and the range beginning with `first2`. The resulting sequence is placed at the destination beginning with `destFirst`. The function returns an iterator positioned one past the last element copied at the destination.

Example 13-18 illustrates how to use these functions.

Example 13-18

```
//STL Functions for_each and transform

#include <iostream>
#include <cctype>
#include <algorithm>
#include <iterator>
#include <vector>
```

13

```
using namespace std;

void doubleNum(int& num);

int main()
{
    char cList[5] = {'a', 'b', 'c', 'd', 'e'};           //Line 1

    vector<char> charList(cList, cList + 5);             //Line 2

    ostream_iterator<char> screen(cout, " ");           //Line 3

    cout<<"Line 4: charList: ";                          //Line 4
    copy(charList.begin(), charList.end(), screen);      //Line 5
    cout<<endl;                                          //Line 6

    transform(charList.begin(), charList.end(),
              charList.begin(), toupper);                //Line 7

    cout<<"Line 8: charList after changing all lowercase"
        <<" letters to \n           uppercase: ";       //Line 8
    copy(charList.begin(), charList.end(), screen);      //Line 9
    cout<<endl;                                          //Line 10


    int list[7] = {2, 8, 5, 1, 7, 11, 3};               //Line 11

    ostream_iterator<int> screenOut(cout, " ");         //Line 12

    cout<<"Line 13: list: ";                            //Line 13
    copy(list, list + 7, screenOut);                    //Line 14
    cout<<endl;                                          //Line 15

    cout<<"Line 16: The effect of the for_each "
        <<"function: ";                                 //Line 16
    for_each(list, list + 7, doubleNum);                //Line 17
    cout<<endl;                                          //Line 18

    cout<<"Line 19: list after a call to the for_each "
        <<"function: ";                                 //Line 19
    copy(list, list + 7, screenOut);                    //Line 20
    cout<<endl;                                          //Line 21

    return 0;
}

void doubleNum(int& num)
```

```
{
    num = 2 * num;
    cout<<num<<" ";
}
```

Output

```
Line 4: charList: a b c d e
Line 8: charList after changing all lowercase letters to
        uppercase: A B C D E
Line 13: list: 2 8 5 1 7 11 3
Line 16: The effect of the for_each function: 4 16 10 2 14 22 6
Line 19: list after a call to the for_each function: 4 16 10 2 14 22 6
```

The statement in Line 7 uses the function `transform` to change every lowercase letter of `charList` into its uppercase counterpart. In the output, the line marked Line 8 contains the output of the statements in Lines 8 through 10 of the program. Notice that the fourth parameter of the function `transform` (in Line 7) is the function `toupper` from the header file `cctype`.

The statement in Line 17 calls the function `for_each` to process each element in the list using the function `doubleNum`. The function `doubleNum` has a reference parameter, `num`, of the type `int`. Moreover, this function doubles the value of `num`, and then outputs the value of `num`. Because `num` is a reference parameter, the value of the actual parameter is changed. In the output, the line marked Line 16 contains the output produced by the `cout` statement in the function `doubleNum`, which is passed as the third parameter of the function `for_each` (see Line 17). The statement in Line 20 outputs the values of the elements of `list`. In the output, Line 19 contains the output of the statements in Lines 19 through 20 of the program.

13

Functions `includes`, `set_intersection`, `set_union`, `set_difference`, and `set_symmetric_difference`

This section describes the set theory operations `includes` (subset), `set_intersection`, `set_union`, `set_difference`, and `set_symmetric_difference`. These algorithms assume that the elements within each given range are *already sorted*.

The algorithm `includes` determines whether the elements in one range appear in another range. This function has two forms, as shown by the following prototypes:

```
template<class inputItr1, class inputItr2>
bool includes(inputItr1 first1, inputItr1 last1,
              inputItr2 first2, inputItr2 last2);

template<class inputItr1, class inputItr2,
         class binaryPredicate>
bool includes(inputItr1 first1, inputItr1 last1,
              inputItr2 first2, inputItr2 last2,
              binaryPredicate op);
```

Both forms of the function `includes` assume that the elements in the ranges `first1...last1-1` and `first2...last2-1` are sorted according to the same sorting criterion. The function returns `true` if all the elements in the range `first2...last2-1` are also in `first1...last1-1`. In other words, the function returns `true` if `first1...last1-1` contains all the elements in the range `first2...last2-1`. The first form assumes that the elements in both ranges are in ascending order. The second form uses the operation `op` to determine the ordering of the elements.

Example 13-19 illustrates how the function `includes` works.

Example 13-19

```
//STL function includes
//This function assumes that the elements in the given ranges
//are ordered according to some sorting criterion.

#include <iostream>
#include <algorithm>

using namespace std;

int main()
{
    char setA[5] = {'A', 'B', 'C', 'D', 'E'};          //Line 1
    char setB[10] = {'A', 'B', 'C', 'D', 'E',
                     'F', 'I', 'J', 'K', 'L'};          //Line 2
    char setC[5] = {'A', 'E', 'I', 'O', 'U'};           //Line 3

    ostream_iterator<char> screen(cout, " ");           //Line 4

    cout<<"Line 5: setA: ";                             //Line 5
    copy(setA, setA + 5, screen);                       //Line 6
    cout<<endl;                                         //Line 7

    cout<<"Line 8: setB: ";                             //Line 8
    copy(setB, setB + 10, screen);                      //Line 9
    cout<<endl;                                         //Line 10

    cout<<"Line 11: setC: ";                            //Line 11
    copy(setC, setC + 5, screen);                       //Line 12
    cout<<endl;                                         //Line 13

    if(includes(setB, setB + 10, setA, setA + 5))       //Line 14
        cout<<"Line 15: setA is a subset of setB"
            <<endl;                                     //Line 15
    else                                               //Line 16
        cout<<"Line 17: setA is not a subset of setB"
            <<endl;                                     //Line 17
```

```
    if(includes(setB, setB + 10, setC, setC + 5))      //Line 18
        cout<<"Line 19: setC is a subset of setB"
            <<endl;                                      //Line 19
    else                                                 //Line 20
        cout<<"Line 21: setC is not a subset of setB"
            <<endl;                                      //Line 21

    return 0;
}
```

Output

```
Line 5: setA: A B C D E
Line 8: setB: A B C D E F I J K L
Line 11: setC: A E I O U
Line 15: setA is a subset of setB
Line 21: setC is not a subset of setB
```

The preceding output is self-explanatory. The details are left as an exercise for you.

The algorithm `set_intersection` is used to find the elements that are common to two ranges of elements. This algorithm has two forms, as shown by the following prototypes:

```
template<class inputItr1, class inputItr2,
        class outputItr>
outputItr set_intersection(inputItr1 first1, inputItr1 last1,
                           inputItr2 first2, inputItr2 last2,
                           outputItr destFirst);

template<class inputItr1, class inputItr2,
        class outputItr, class binaryPredicate>
outputItr set_intersection(inputItr1 first1, inputItr1 last1,
                           inputItr2 first2, inputItr2 last2,
                           outputItr destFirst,
                           binaryPredicate op);
```

13

Both forms create a sequence of sorted elements that are common to two sorted ranges, `first1...last1-1` and `first2...last2-1`. The created sequence is placed in the container beginning with `destFirst`. Both forms return an iterator positioned one past the last element copied at the destination range. The first form assumes that the elements in both ranges are in ascending order. The second form assumes that both ranges are sorted using the operation specified by **op**. The elements in the source ranges are not modified.

Suppose that:

```
setA = {2, 4, 5, 7, 8}
setB = {1, 2, 3, 4, 5, 6, 7}
setC = {2, 5, 8, 8, 15}
setD = {1, 4, 4, 6, 7, 12}
setE = {2, 3, 4, 4, 5, 6, 10}
```

Then:

```
AintersectB = {2, 4, 5, 7}
AintersectC = {2, 5, 8}
DintersectE = {4, 4, 6}
```

Notice that because 8 appears only once in `setA`, 8 appears only once in `AintersectC`, even though 8 appears twice in `setC`. However, because 4 appears twice in both `setD` and `setE`, 4 also appears twice in `DintersectE`.

The algorithm `set_union` is used to find the elements that are contained in two ranges of elements. This algorithm has two forms, as shown by the following prototypes:

```
template<class inputItr1, class inputItr2,
        class outputItr>
outputItr set_union(inputItr1 first1, inputItr1 last1,
                    inputItr2 first2, inputItr2 last2,
                    outputItr destFirst);

template<class inputItr1, class inputItr2,
        class outputItr, class binaryPredicate>
outputItr set_union(inputItr1 first1, inputItr1 last1,
                    inputItr2 first2, inputItr2 last2,
                    outputItr result,
                    binaryPredicate op);
```

Both forms create a sequence of sorted elements that appear in either of the two sorted ranges, `first1...last1 - 1` or `first2...last2 - 1`. The created sequence is placed in the container beginning with `destFirst`. Both forms return an iterator positioned one past the last element copied at the destination range. The first form assumes that the elements in both ranges are in ascending order. The second form assumes that both ranges are sorted using the operation specified by `op`. The elements in the source ranges are not modified.

Suppose that you have `setA`, `setB`, `setC`, `setD`, and `setE` as defined previously. Then:

```
AunionB = {1, 2, 3, 4, 5, 6, 7, 8}
AunionC = {2, 4, 5, 7, 8, 8, 15}
BunionD = {1, 2, 3, 4, 4, 5, 6, 7, 12}
DunionE = {1, 2, 3, 4, 4, 5, 6, 7, 10, 12}
```

Notice that because 8 appears twice in `setC`, it appears twice in `AunionC`. Because 4 appears twice in `setD` and in `setE`, it appears twice in `DunionE`.

Example 13-20 illustrates how the functions `set_union` and `set_intersection` work.

Example 13-20

```
//STL functions set_union and set_intersection
//These functions assume that the elements in the given ranges
//are ordered according to the same sorting criterion.
```

```cpp
#include <iostream>
#include <algorithm>

using namespace std;

int main()
{
    int setA[5] = {2, 4, 5, 7, 8};                     //Line 1
    int setB[7] = {1, 2, 3, 4, 5, 6, 7};               //Line 2
    int setC[5] = {2, 5, 8, 8, 15};                    //Line 3
    int setD[6] = {1, 4, 4, 6, 7, 12};                 //Line 4

    int AunionB[10];                                   //Line 5
    int AunionC[10];                                   //Line 6
    int BunionD[15];                                   //Line 7
    int AintersectB[10];                               //Line 8
    int AintersectC[10];                               //Line 9

    int *lastElem;                                     //Line 10

    ostream_iterator<int> screen(cout, " ");           //Line 11

    cout<<"Line 12: setA = ";                          //Line 12
    copy(setA, setA + 5, screen);                      //Line 13
    cout<<endl;                                         //Line 14

    cout<<"Line 15: setB = ";                          //Line 15
    copy(setB, setB + 7, screen);                      //Line 16
    cout<<endl;                                         //Line 17

    cout<<"Line 18: setC = ";                          //Line 18
    copy(setC, setC + 5, screen);                      //Line 19
    cout<<endl;                                         //Line 20

    cout<<"Line 21: setD = ";                          //Line 21
    copy(setD, setD + 6, screen);                      //Line 22
    cout<<endl;                                         //Line 23

    lastElem = set_union(setA, setA + 5,
                         setB, setB + 7,
                         AunionB);                     //Line 24

    cout<<"Line 25: Set AunionB: ";                    //Line 25
    copy(AunionB, lastElem, screen);                   //Line 26
    cout<<endl;                                         //Line 27

    lastElem = set_union(setA, setA + 5,
                         setC, setC + 5,
                         AunionC);                     //Line 28
```

13

```
        cout<<"Line 29: Set AunionC: ";              //Line 29
        copy(AunionC, lastElem, screen);             //Line 30
        cout<<endl;                                  //Line 31

        lastElem = set_union(setB, setB + 7,
                             setD, setD + 6,
                             BunionD);                //Line 32

        cout<<"Line 33: Set BunionD: ";              //Line 33
        copy(BunionD, lastElem, screen);             //Line 34
        cout<<endl;                                  //Line 35

        lastElem = set_intersection(setA, setA + 5,
                                    setB, setB + 7,
                                    AintersectB);     //Line 36

        cout<<"Line 37: Set AintersectB: ";          //Line 37
        copy(AintersectB, lastElem, screen);         //Line 38
        cout<<endl;                                  //Line 39

        lastElem = set_intersection(setA, setA + 5,
                                    setC, setC + 5,
                                    AintersectC);     //Line 40

        cout<<"Line 41: Set AintersectC: ";          //Line 41
        copy(AintersectC, lastElem, screen);         //Line 42
        cout<<endl;                                  //Line 43

        return 0;
}
```

Output

```
Line 12: setA = 2 4 5 7 8
Line 15: setB = 1 2 3 4 5 6 7
Line 18: setC = 2 5 8 8 15
Line 21: setD = 1 4 4 6 7 12
Line 25: Set AunionB: 1 2 3 4 5 6 7 8
Line 29: Set AunionC: 2 4 5 7 8 8 15
Line 33: Set BunionD: 1 2 3 4 4 5 6 7 12
Line 37: Set AintersectB: 2 4 5 7
Line 41: Set AintersectC: 2 5 8
```

The preceding output is self-explanatory. The details are left as an exercise for you.

The algorithm `set_difference` is used to find the elements in one range of elements that do not appear in another range of elements. This algorithm has two forms, as shown by the following prototypes:

```
template<class inputItr1, class inputItr2,
         class outputItr>
outputItr set_difference(inputItr1 first1, inputItr1 last1,
                         inputItr2 first2, inputItr2 last2,
                         outputItr destFirst);


template<class inputItr1, class inputItr2,
         class outputItr, class binaryPredicate>
outputItr set_difference(inputItr1 first1, inputItr1 last1,
                         inputItr2 first2, inputItr2 last2,
                         outputItr destFirst,
                         binaryPredicate op);
```

Both forms create a sequence of sorted elements that are in the sorted range
`first1...last1-1`, but not in the sorted range `first2...last2-1`. The created
sequence is placed in the container beginning with `destFirst`. Both forms return an iterator positioned one past the last element copied at the destination range. The first form assumes
that the elements are in ascending order. The second form assumes that both ranges are sorted
using the operation specified by `op`. The elements in the source ranges are not modified.

Suppose that:

```
setA = {2, 4, 5, 7, 8}
setC = {1, 5, 6, 8, 15}
setD = {2, 5, 5, 6, 9}
setE = {1, 5, 7, 9, 12}
```

Then:

```
AdifferenceC = {2, 4, 7}
DdifferenceE = {2, 5, 6}
```

Because 5 appears twice in `setD` but only once in `setE`, 5 appears once in `DdifferenceE`.

The algorithm `set_symmetric_difference` has two forms, as shown by the following
prototypes:

```
template<class inputItr1, class inputItr2,
         class outputItr>
outputItr set_symmetric_difference(inputItr1 first1,
                                   inputItr1 last1,
                                   inputItr2 first2,
                                   inputItr2 last2,
                                   outputItr destFirst);


template<class inputItr1, class inputItr2,
         class outputItr, class binaryPredicate>
outputItr set_symmetric_difference(inputItr1 first1,
                                   inputItr1 last1,
                                   inputItr2 first2,
                                   inputItr2 last2,
                                   outputItr destFirst,
                                   binaryPredicate op);
```

13

Both forms create a sequence of sorted elements that are in the sorted range `first1...last1-1` but not in `first2...last2-1`, or elements that are in the sorted range `first2...last2-1`, but not in `first1...last1-1`. In other words, the sequence of elements created by `set_symmetric_difference` contains the elements that are in `range1_difference_range2` union `range2_difference_range1`. The created sequence is placed in the container beginning with `destFirst`. Both forms return an iterator positioned one past the last element copied at the destination range. The first form assumes that the elements are in ascending order. The second form assumes that both ranges are sorted using the operation specified by `op`. The elements in the source ranges are not modified. It can be shown that the sequence created by `set_symmetric_difference` contains elements that are in `range1_union_range2`, but not in `range1_intersection_range2`.

Suppose that:

```
setB = {3, 4, 5, 6, 7, 8, 10}
setC = {1, 5, 6, 8, 15}
setD = {2, 5, 5, 6, 9}
```

Notice that `BdifferenceC = {3, 4, 7, 10}` and `CdifferenceB = {1, 15}`. Therefore,

`BsymDiffC = {1, 3, 4, 7, 10, 15}`

Now `DdifferenceC = {2, 5, 9}` and `CdifferenceD = {1, 8, 15}`. Therefore,

`DsymDiffC = {1, 2, 5, 8, 9, 15}`

Example 13-21 further illustrates how the functions `set_difference` and `set_symmetric_difference` work.

Example 13-21

Suppose that we have the following statements:

```
int setA[5] = {2, 4, 5, 7, 8};                          //Line 1
int setB[7] = {3, 4, 5, 6, 7, 8, 10};                   //Line 2
int setC[5] = {1, 5, 6, 8, 15};                         //Line 3

int AdifferenceC[5];                                    //Line 4
int BsymDiffC[10];                                      //Line 5
```

Consider the following statement:

```
set_difference(setA, setA + 5, setC, setC + 5,
               AdifferenceC);                           //Line 6
```

After this statement executes, `AdifferenceC` contains the elements that are in `setA` but not in `setC`, that is,

`AdifferenceC = {2, 4, 7}`   //Line 7

Now consider the following statement:

```
set_symmetric_difference(setB, setB + 7, setC, setC + 5,
                         BsymDiffC);                    //Line 8
```

After this statement executes, `BsymDiffC` contains the elements that are in `setB` but not in `setC`, or the elements that are in `setC` but not in `setB`, that is,

```
BsymDiffC = {1, 3, 4, 7, 10, 15}                       //Line 9
```

We leave it as an exercise for you to write a program that further illustrates how to use the functions `set_difference` and `set_symmetric_difference` (see Programming Exercise 5, at the end of this chapter).

Functions `accumulate`, `adjacent_difference`, `inner_product`, and `partial_sum`

The algorithms `accumulate`, `adjacent_difference`, `inner_product`, and `partial_sum` are numerical functions and thus manipulate numeric data. Each of these functions has two forms. The first form uses the natural operation to manipulate the data. For example, the algorithm `accumulate` finds the sum of all the elements in a given range. In the second form, we can specify the operation to be applied to the elements of the range. For example, rather than add the elements of a given range, we can specify the multiplication operation to the algorithm `accumulate` to multiply the elements of the range. Next, as usual, we give the prototypes of each of these algorithms followed by a brief explanation. The algorithms are contained in the header file `numeric`.

```
template<class inputItr, class Type>
Type accumulate(inputItr first, inputItr last, Type init);

template<class inputItr, class Type, class binaryOperation>
Type accumulate(inputItr first, inputItr last,
                Type init, binaryOperation op);
```

The first form of the algorithm `accumulate` adds all the elements to an initial value specified by the parameter `init`, in the range `first...last-1`. For example, if the value of `init` is 0, the algorithm returns the sum of all the elements. In the second form, we can specify a binary operation, such as multiplication, to be applied to the elements of the range. For example, if the value of `init` is 1 and the binary operation is multiplication, the algorithm returns the product of the elements in the range.

Next, we describe the algorithm `adjacent_difference`. Its prototypes are:

```
template<class inputItr, class outputItr>
outputItr adjacent_difference(inputItr first, inputItr last,
                              outputItr destFirst);
```

13

```
template<class inputItr, class outputItr,
         class binaryOperation>
outputItr adjacent_difference(inputItr first, inputItr last,
                              outputItr destFirst,
                              binaryOperation op);
```

The first form creates a sequence of elements in which the first element is the same as the first element in the range `first...last-1`, and all the other elements are the differences of the current and previous elements. For example, if the range of elements is

```
{2, 5, 6, 8, 3, 7}
```

then the sequence created by the function `adjacent_difference` is

```
{2, 3, 1, 2, -5, 4}
```

The first element is the same as the first element in the original range. The second element is equal to the second element in the original range minus the first element in the original range. Similarly, the third element is equal to the third element in the original range minus the second element in the original range, and so on.

In the second form of `adjacent_difference`, the binary operation `op` is applied to the elements in the range. The resulting sequence is copied at the destination specified by `destFirst`. For example, if the sequence is {2, 5, 6, 8, 3, 7} and the operation is multiplication, the resulting sequence is {2, 10, 30, 48, 24, 21}.

Both forms return an iterator positioned one past the last element copied at the destination.

Example 13-22 illustrates how the functions **accumulate** and `adjacent_difference` work.

Example 13-22

```
//Numeric algorithms accumulate and adjacent_difference

#include <iostream>
#include <algorithm>
#include <numeric>
#include <iterator>
#include <vector>
#include <functional>

using namespace std;

void print(vector<int> vList);

int main()
{
    int list[8] = {1, 2, 3, 4, 5, 6, 7, 8};          //Line 1

    vector<int> vecList(list, list + 8);             //Line 2
    vector<int> newVList(8);                         //Line 3

    cout<<"Line 4: vecList: ";                       //Line 4
```

```
    print(vecList);                                    //Line 5

        //accumulate
    int sum = accumulate(vecList.begin(),
                         vecList.end(), 0);            //Line 6

    cout<<"Line 7: Sum of the elements of vecList = "
        <<sum<<endl;                                   //Line 7

    int product = accumulate(vecList.begin(),
                             vecList.end(),
                             1, multiplies<int>());     //Line 8

    cout<<"Line 9: Product of the elements of "
        <<"vecList = "<<product<<endl;                 //Line 9

        //adjacent_difference
    adjacent_difference(vecList.begin(),
                        vecList.end(),
                        newVList.begin());             //Line 10

    cout<<"Line 11: newVList: ";                       //Line 11
    print(newVList);                                   //Line 12

    adjacent_difference(vecList.begin(), vecList.end(),
                        newVList.begin(),
                        multiplies<int>());            //Line 13

    cout<<"Line 14: newVList: ";                       //Line 14
    print(newVList);                                   //Line 15

    return 0;
}

void print(vector<int> vList)
{
    ostream_iterator<int> screenOut(cout, " ");        //Line 16

    copy(vList.begin(), vList.end(), screenOut);       //Line 17
    cout<<endl;                                         //Line 18
}
```

Output

```
Line 4: vecList: 1 2 3 4 5 6 7 8
Line 7: Sum of the elements of vecList = 36
Line 9: Product of the elements of vecList = 40320
Line 11: newVList: 1 1 1 1 1 1 1 1
Line 14: newVList: 1 2 6 12 20 30 42 56
```

The preceding output is self-explanatory. The details are left as an exercise for you.

The algorithm `inner_product` is used to manipulate the elements of two ranges. The prototypes of this algorithm are:

```
template<class inputItr1, class inputItr2, class Type>
Type inner_product(inputItr1 first1, inputItr1 last,
                   inputItr2 first2, Type init);


template<class inputItr1, class inputItr2, class Type
        class binaryOperation1, class binaryOperation2>
Type inner_product(inputItr1 first1, inputItr1 last,
                   inputItr2 first2, Type init,
                   binaryOperation1 op1, binaryOperation2 op2);
```

The first form multiplies the corresponding elements in the range `first1...last - 1` and the range of elements starting with `first2`; the products of these elements are then added to the value specified by the parameter `init`. To be specific, suppose that `elem1` ranges over the first range and `elem2` ranges over the second range starting with `first2`. The first form computes:

```
init = init + elem1 * elem2
```

for all the corresponding elements. For example, suppose that the two ranges are {2, 4, 7, 8} and {1, 4, 6, 9}, and that `init` is 0. The function computes and returns:

```
0 + 2 * 1 + 4 * 4 + 7 * 6 + 8 * 9 = 132
```

In the second form, the default addition can be replaced by the operation specified by `op1`, and the default multiplication can be replaced by the operation specified by `op2`. This form, in fact, computes:

```
init = init op1 (elem1 op2 elem2);
```

The algorithm `partial_sum` has two forms, as shown by the following prototypes:

```
template<class inputItr, class outputItr>
outputItr partial_sum(inputItr first, inputItr last,
                      outputItr destFirst);


template<class inputItr, class randomAccessItr,
        class binaryOperation>
outputItr partial_sum(inputItr first, inputItr last,
                      outputItr destFirst, binaryOperation op);
```

The first form creates a sequence of elements in which each element is the sum of all the previous elements in the range `first...last-1` up to the position of the element. For example, the first element of the new sequence is the same as the first element in the range `first...last-1`, the second element is the sum of the first two elements in the range `first...last-1`, the third element of the new sequence is the sum of the first three elements in the range `first...last-1`, and so on. For example, for the sequence of elements:

```
{1, 3, 4, 6}
```

the function `partial_sum` generates the following sequence:

`{1, 4, 8, 14}`

In the second form, the default addition can be replaced by the operation specified by op. For example, if the sequence is:

`{1, 3, 4, 6}`

and the operation is multiplication, the function `partial_sum` generates the following sequence:

`{1, 3, 12, 72}`

The created sequence is copied at the destination specified by `destFirst`, and returns an iterator positioned one past the last copied element at the destination.

Example 13-23 further illustrates how the functions `inner_product` and `partial_sum` work.

Example 13-23

Suppose that you have the following statements:

```
int list1[8] = {1, 2, 3, 4, 5, 6, 7, 8};          //Line 1
int list2[8] = {2, 4, 5, 7, -9, 11, 12, 14};      //Line 2

vector<int> vecList(list1, list1 + 8);            //Line 3
vector<int> newVList(list2, list2 + 8);           //Line 4

int sum;                                          //Line 5
```

After the statements in Lines 3 and 4 execute,

```
vecList = {1, 2, 3, 4, 5, 6, 7, 8}               //Line 6
newVList = {2, 4, 5, 7, -9, 11, 12, 14}          //Line 7
```

Now consider the following statement:

```
sum = inner_product(vecList.begin(), vecList.end(),
                    newVList.begin(), 0);         //Line 8
```

This statement calculates the inner product of `vecList` and `newVList`, and the result is stored in `sum`, that is,

```
sum = 0 + 1 * 2 + 2 * 4 + 3 * 5 + 4 * 7 + 5 * (-9)
        + 6 * 11 + 7 * 12 + 8 * 14
    = 270
```

Now consider the following statement:

```
sum = inner_product(vecList.begin(), vecList.end(),
                    newVList.begin(), 0,
                    plus<int>(), minus<int>());      //Line 9
```

This statement calculates the inner product of **vecList** and **newVList**. The multiplication, *, is replaced with minus, −, and the result is stored in **sum**, that is,

```
sum = 0 + (1 − 2) + (2 − 4) + (3 − 5) + (4 − 7) + (5 − (−9))
      + (6 − 11) + (7 − 12) + (8 − 14)
    = −10
```

Next, consider the following statement:

```
partial_sum(vecList.begin(), vecList.end(),
            newVList.begin());                      //Line 10
```

This statement uses the function **partial_sum** to generate the sequence of elements 1, 3, 6, 10, 15, 21, 28, 36. These elements are assigned to **newVList**, that is,

```
newVList = {1, 3, 6, 10, 15, 21, 28, 36}
```

Next, consider the following statement:

```
partial_sum(vecList.begin(), vecList.end(),
            newVList.begin(), multiplies<int>());   //Line 11
```

This statement uses the function **partial_sum** to generate the sequence of elements 1, 2, 6, 24, 120, 720, 5040, 40320. Notice that the statement in Line 11 calculates the partial multiplication of the elements of **vecList** by replacing the plus, +, with multiplication, *. These elements are assigned to **newVList**, that is,

```
newVList = {1, 2, 6, 24, 120, 720, 5040, 40320}
```

We leave it as an exercise for you to write a program that further illustrates how to use the functions **inner_product** and **partial_sum** (see Programming Exercise 6, at the end of this chapter).

QUICK REVIEW

1. The STL provides class templates that process lists, stacks, and queues.
2. The three main components of the STL are containers, iterators, and algorithms.
3. Algorithms are used to manipulate the elements in a container.
4. The main categories of containers are sequence containers, associative containers, and container adapters.
5. The **class pair** allows you to combine two values into a single unit. A function can return two values by using the **class pair**. The **class**es **map** and **multimap** use the **class pair** to manage their elements.

6. The definition of the `class pair` is contained in the header file `utility`.

7. The function `make_pair` allows you to create pairs without explicitly specifying the type `pair`.

8. The definition of the function `make_pair` is contained in the header file `utility`.

9. Elements in an associative container are automatically sorted according to some ordering criterion. The default ordering criterion is the relational operator < (less than).

10. The predefined associative containers in the STL are `sets`, `multisets`, `maps`, and `multimaps`.

11. Containers of the type `set` do not allow duplicates.

12. Containers of the type `multiset` allow duplicates.

13. The name of the class defining the container `set` is `set`.

14. The name of the class defining the container `multiset` is `multiset`.

15. The name of the header file containing the definitions of the `class`es `set` and `multiset`, and the definitions of the functions to implement various operations on these containers, is `set`.

16. The operations `insert`, `erase`, and `clear` can be used to insert or delete elements from sets.

17. The containers `map` and `multimap` manage their elements in the form key/value. The elements are automatically sorted according to some sort criteria applied on the key.

18. The default sorting criterion for the key of the containers `map` and `multimap` is the relational operator < (less than). The user can also specify other sorting criteria. For user-defined data types, such as classes, the relational operators must be properly overloaded.

19. The only difference between the containers `map` and `multimap` is that the container `multimap` allows duplicates, whereas the container `map` does not.

20. The name of the class defining the container `map` is `map`.

21. The name of the class defining the container `multimap` is `multimap`.

22. The name of the header file containing the definitions of the `class`es `map` and `multimap`, and the definitions of the functions to implement various operations on these containers, is `map`.

23. Most of the generic algorithms are contained in the header file `algorithm`.

24. The main categories of the STL algorithms are nonmodifying, modifying, numeric, and heap.

25. Nonmodifying algorithms do not modify the elements of the container.

26. Modifying algorithms modify the elements of the container by rearranging, removing, and/or changing the values of the elements.

27. Modifying algorithms that change the order of the elements, not their values, are also called mutating algorithms.

28. Numeric algorithms are designed to perform numeric calculations on the elements of a container.

13

29. A function object is a class template that overloads the function call operator, `operator()`.

30. The predefined arithmetic function objects are `plus`, `minus`, `multiplies`, `divides`, `modulus`, and `negate`.

31. The predefined relational function objects are `equal_to`, `not_equal_to`, `greater`, `greater_equal`, `less`, and `less_equal`.

32. The predefined logical function objects are `logical_not`, `logical_and`, and `logical_or`.

33. Predicates are special types of function objects that return boolean values.

34. Unary predicates check a specific property for a single argument; binary predicates check a specific property for a pair of—that is, two—arguments.

35. Predicates are typically used to specify a searching or sorting criterion.

36. In the STL, a predicate must always return the same result for the same value.

37. The functions that modify their internal states cannot be considered predicates.

38. The STL provides three iterators—`back_inserter`, `front_inserter`, and `inserter`—called insert iterators, to insert the elements at the destination.

39. `back_inserter` uses the `push_back` operation of the container in place of the assignment operator.

40. `front_inserter` uses the `push_front` operation of the container in place of the assignment operator.

41. Because the `class vector` does not support the `push_front` operation, this iterator cannot be used for a vector container.

42. The `inserter` iterator uses the container's `insert` operation in place of the assignment operator.

43. The function `fill` is used to fill a container with elements; the function `fill_n` is used to fill in the next **n** elements.

44. The functions `generate` and `generate_n` are used to generate elements and fill a sequence.

45. The functions `find`, `find_if`, `find_end`, and `find_first_of` are used to find the elements in a given range.

46. The function `remove` is used to remove certain elements from a sequence.

47. The function `remove_if` is used to remove certain elements from a sequence using some criterion.

48. The function `remove_copy` copies the elements in a sequence into another sequence by excluding certain elements from the first sequence.

49. The function `remove_copy_if` copies the elements in a sequence into another sequence by excluding certain elements, using some criterion, from the first sequence.

50. The functions `swap`, `iter_swap`, and `swap_ranges` are used to swap elements.

51. The functions `search`, `search_n`, `sort`, and `binary_search` are used to search elements.

52. The function `adjacent_find` is used to find the first occurrence of consecutive elements satisfying a certain criterion.

53. The algorithm `merge` merges two sorted lists.

54. The algorithm `inplace_merge` is used to combine two sorted, consecutive sequences.

55. The algorithm `reverse` reverses the order of the elements in a given range.

56. The algorithm `reverse_copy` reverses the order of the elements in a given range while copying into a destination range. The source is not modified.

57. The algorithm `rotate` rotates the elements in a given range.

58. The algorithm `rotate_copy` copies the elements of the source at the destination in a rotated order.

59. The algorithm `count` counts the occurrences of a specified value in a given range.

60. The algorithm `count_if` counts the occurrences of a specified value in a given range satisfying a certain criterion.

61. The algorithm `max` is used to determine the maximum of two values.

62. The algorithm `max_element` is used to determine the largest element in a given range.

63. The algorithm `min` is used to determine the minimum of two values.

64. The algorithm `min_element` is used to determine the smallest element in a given range.

65. The algorithm `random_shuffle` is used to randomly order the elements in a given range.

66. The algorithm `for_each` is used to access and process each element in a given range by applying a function, which is passed as a parameter.

67. The function `transform` creates a sequence of elements by applying certain operations to each element in a given range.

68. The algorithm `includes` determines whether the elements of one range appear in another range.

69. The algorithm `set_intersection` is used to find the elements that are common to two ranges of elements.

70. The algorithm `set_union` is used to find the elements that are contained in two ranges of elements.

71. The algorithm `set_difference` is used to find the elements in one range of elements that do not appear in another range of elements.

72. Given two ranges of elements, the algorithm `set_symmetric_difference` determines the elements that are in the first range but not the second range, or the elements that are in the second range but not the first range.

13

73. The algorithms `accumulate`, `adjacent_difference`, `inner_product`, and `partial_sum` are numerical functions that manipulate numeric data.

EXERCISES

1. What is the difference between an STL container and an STL algorithm?

2. Suppose that you have the following statement:

   ```
   pair<int, string> temp;
   ```

   a. Write a C++ statement that stores the pair (`1, "Hello"`) into `temp`.

   b. Write a C++ statement that outputs the pair stored in `temp` onto the standard output device.

3. Suppose that you have the following statement:

   ```
   pair<string, string> name;
   ```

   What is the output, if any, of the following statements?

   ```
   name = make_pair("Duckey", "Donald");
   cout<<name.first<<" "<<name.second<<endl;
   ```

4. Explain how a `set` container differs from a `map` container.

5. a. Declare the `map` container `stateDataMap` to store pairs of the form (`stateName, capitalName`), where `stateName` and `capitalName` are variables of the form `string`.

   b. Write C++ statements that add the following pairs to `stateDataMap`: (`Nebraska, Lincoln`), (`New York, Albany`), (`Ohio, Columbus`), (`California, Sacramento`), (`Massachusetts, Boston`), and (`Texas, Austin`).

   c. Write a C++ code that outputs the data stored in `stateDataMap`.

   d. Write a C++ code that changes the capital of `California` to `Los Angeles`.

6. What is the difference between a `set` and a `multiset`?

7. What is an STL function object?

8. Suppose that `charList` is a vector container and:

   ```
   charList = {a, A, B, b, c, d, A, e, f, K}
   ```

   Further suppose that:

   ```
   lastElem = remove_if(charList.begin(), charList.end(), islower);
   ostream_iterator<char> screen(cout, " ");
   ```

   where `lastElem` is a vector iterator into a vector container of the type `char`. What is the output of the following statement?

   ```
   copy(charList.begin(), lastElem, screen);
   ```

9. Suppose that `intList` is a vector container and

   `intList = {18, 24, 24, 5, 11, 56, 27, 24, 2, 24}`

   Furthermore, suppose that:

   ```
   vector<int>::iterator lastElem;
   ostream_iterator<int> screen(cout, " ");
   vector<int> otherList(10);
   ```

   ```
   lastElem = remove_copy(intList.begin(), intList.end(),
                          otherList.begin(), 24);
   ```

   What is the output of the following statement?

   ```
   copy(otherList.begin(), lastElem, screenOut);
   ```

10. Suppose that `intList` is a vector container and

    `intList = {2, 4, 6, 8, 10, 12, 14, 16}`

    What is the value of **result** after the following statement executes?

    ```
    result = accumulate(intList.begin(), intList.end(), 0);
    ```

11. Suppose that `intList` is a vector container and

    `intList = {2, 4, 6, 8, 10, 12, 14, 16}`

    What is the value of **result** after the following statement executes?

    ```
    result = accumulate(intList.begin(), intList.end(),
                        0, multiplies<int>());
    ```

12. Suppose that `setA`, `setB`, `setC`, and `setD` are defined as follows:

    ```
    int setA[] = {3, 4, 5, 8, 9, 12, 14};
    int setB[] = {2, 3, 4, 5, 6, 7, 8};
    int setC[] = {2, 5, 5, 9};
    int setD[] = {4, 4, 4, 6, 7, 12};
    ```

    Further suppose that you have the following declarations:

    ```
    int AunionB[10];
    int AunionC[9];
    int BunionD[10];
    int AintersectB[4];
    int AintersectC[2];
    ```

    What is stored in `AunionB`, `AunionC`, `BunionD`, `AintersectB`, and `AintersectC` after the following statements execute?

    ```
    set_union(setA, setA + 7, setB, setB + 7, AunionB);
    set_union(setA, setA + 7, setC, setC + 4, AunionC);
    set_union(setB, setB + 7, setD, setD + 6, BunionD);
    set_intersection(setA, setA + 7, setB, setB + 7, AintersectB);
    set_intersection(setA, setA + 7, setC, setC + 4, AintersectC);
    ```

13

PROGRAMMING EXERCISES

1. Write a program that illustrates how to use the functions `find` and `find_if`.

2. Write a program that illustrates how to use the functions `find_end` and `find_first_of`.

3. Write a program that illustrates how to use the functions `replace`, `replace_if`, `replace_copy`, and `replace_copy_if`. Your program must use the function `lessThanEqualTo50` as shown in Example 13-13.

4. Write a program that illustrates how to use the functions `adjacent_find`, `merge`, and `inplace_merge`.

5. Write a program that illustrates how to use the functions `set_difference` and `set_symmetric_difference`.

6. Write a program that illustrates how to use the functions `inner_product` and `partial_sum`.

7. **(Stock Market Revisited)** In Programming Exercise 8 of Chapter 4, you were asked to design a program that analyzes the performance of the stocks managed by a local stock-trading company, and at the end of each day produces a listing of those stocks, ordered by the stock symbol. The company's investors would now like to see another listing of the stocks that is ordered by the percent gained by each stock.

   The company also requests that you produce the list ordered by the percent gain/loss. Therefore, you need to sort the stock list by this component. However, you are not to physically sort the list by the component percent gain/loss; instead, you are to provide a logical ordering with respect to this component.

   To do so, add a data member (a vector) to hold the indices of the stock list ordered by the component percent gain/loss. Call this vector `indexByGain`. When printing the list ordered by the component percent gain/loss, use the vector `indexByGain` to print the list. The elements of the array `indexByGain` will tell which component of the stock list to print next.

8. Redo the Programming Example: Video Store of Chapter 5 so that it uses the STL `class set` to process a list of videos.

9. Redo Programming Exercise 14 of Chapter 5 so that it uses the STL `class set` to process the list of videos rented by the customer and the list of store members.

10. Redo Programming Exercise 15 of Chapter 5 so that it uses the STL `class set` to process the list of videos owned by the store, the list of videos rented by the customer, and the list of store members.

RESERVED WORDS

and	and_eq	asm	auto
bitand	bitor	bool	break
case	catch	char	class
compl	const	const_cast	continue
default	delete	do	double
dynamic_case	else	enum	explicit
export	extern	false	float
for	friend	goto	if
inline	int	long	mutable
namespace	new	not	not_eq
operator	or	or_eq	private
protected	public	register	reinterpret_cast
return	short	signed	sizeof
static	static_cast	struct	switch
template	this	throw	true
try	typedef	typeid	typename
union	unsigned	using	virtual
void	volatile	wchar_t	while
xor	xor_eq		

B

OPERATOR PRECEDENCE

Precedence (highest to lowest)

Operator	Associativity
:: (binary scope resolution)	Left to right
:: (unary scope resolution)	Right to left
()	Left to right
[] -> .	Left to right
++ -- (as postfix operators)	Right to left
typeid dynamic_cast	Right to left
static_cast const_cast	Right to left
reinterpret_cast	Right to left
++ -- (as prefix operators) ! + (Unary) – (Unary)	Right to left
~ & (address of) * (dereference)	Right to left
new delete sizeof	Right to left
->* .*	Left to right
* / %	Left to right
+ –	Left to right
<< >>	Left to right
< <= > >=	Left to right
== !	Left to right
&	Left to right
^	Left to right
|	Left to right
&&	Left to right
||	Left to right
?:	Right to left
= += -= *= /= %=	Right to left
<<= >>= &= |= ^=	Right to left
throw	Right to left
, (the sequencing operator)	Left to right

C

CHARACTER SETS

ASCII (American Standard Code for Information Interchange)

ASCII										
	0	1	2	3	4	5	6	7	8	9
0	nul	soh	stx	etx	eot	enq	ack	bel	bs	ht
1	lf	vt	ff	cr	so	si	dle	dc1	dc2	dc3
2	dc4	nak	syn	etb	can	em	sub	esc	fs	gs
3	rs	us	b̲	!	"	#	$	%	&	'
4	(	)	*	+	,	-	.	/	0	1
5	2	3	4	5	6	7	8	9	:	;
6	<	=	>	?	@	A	B	C	D	E
7	F	G	H	I	J	K	L	M	N	O
8	P	Q	R	S	T	U	V	W	X	Y
9	Z	[	\	]	^	_	`		a	b	c
10	d	e	f	g	h	i	j	k	l	m
11	n	o	p	q	r	s	t	u	v	w
12	x	y	z	{	|	}	~	del		

The numbers 0–12 in the first column specify the left digit(s); the numbers 0–9 in the second row specify the right digit of each character in the ASCII data set. For example, the character in the row marked 6 (the number in the first column) and the column marked 5 (the number in the second row) is A. Therefore, the character at position 65 (which is the 66th character) is A. Moreover, the character b̲ at position 32 represents the blank character.

The first 32 characters, that is, the characters at positions 00–31 and at position 127, are nonprintable characters. This table shows the abbreviations of these characters. The meanings of these abbreviations are as follows:

nul	Null character	vt	Vertical tab	syn	Synchronous idle
soh	Start of header	ff	Form feed	etb	End of transmitted block
stx	Start of text	cr	Carriage return	can	Cancel
etx	End of text	so	Shift out	em	End of medium
eot	End of transmission	si	Shift in	sub	Substitute
enq	Enquiry	dle	Data link escape	esc	Escape
ack	Acknowledge	dc1	Device control 1	fs	File separator
bel	Bell character (beep)	dc2	Device control 2	gs	Group separator
bs	Back space	dc3	Device control 3	rs	Record separator
ht	Horizontal tab	dc4	Device control 4	us	Unit separator
lf	Line feed	nak	Negative acknowledge	del	Delete

EBCDIC (Extended Binary Coded Decimal Interchange Code)

EBCDIC	0	1	2	3	4	5	6	7	8	9
6					b̲					
7					.	<	(	+	|	
8	&									
9	!	$	*	)	;	¬	-	/		
10							^	,	%	_
11	>	?								
12		`	:	#	@	'	=	"		a
13	b	c	d	e	f	g	h	i		
14						j	k	l	m	n
15	o	p	q	r						
16		~	s	t	u	v	w	x	y	z
17								\	{	}
18	[	]								
19				A	B	C	D	E	F	G
20	H	I								J
21	K	L	M	N	O	P	Q	R		
22							S	T	U	V
23	W	X	Y	Z						
24	0	1	2	3	4	5	6	7	8	9

The numbers 6–24 in the first column specify the left digit(s); the numbers 0–9 in the second row specify the right digit of the characters in the EBCDIC data set. For example, the character in the row marked 19 (the number in the first column) and the column marked 3 (the number in the second row) is A. Therefore, the character at position 193 (which is the 194th character) is A. Moreover, the character b̲ at position 64 represents the blank character. This table does not show all the characters in the EBCDIC character set. In fact, the characters at positions 00–63 and 250–255 are nonprintable control characters.

D

OPERATOR OVERLOADING

The following table lists the operators that can be overloaded.

Operators that can be overloaded							
+	−	*	/	%	^	&	|
!	&&	||	=	==	<	<=	>
>=	!=	+=	−=	*=	/=	%=	^=
|=	&=	<<	>>	>>=	<<=	++	−−
->*	,	->	[]	()	~	new	delete

The following table lists the operators that cannot be overloaded.

Operators that cannot be overloaded				
.	.*	::	?:	sizeof

E

HEADER FILES

The C++ standard library contains many predefined functions, named constants, and specialized data types. This appendix discusses some of the most widely used library routines. It is a good idea to consult the manual for your particular system for additional explanation and to see what other routines the standard library provides.

Header File `cassert`

Function Name and Parameter	Parameter Type	Function Return Value
assert(expression)	expression is any int procession; expression is usually a logical expression	If the value of the expression is nonzero (true), the program continues to execute. If the value of the expression is 0 (false), the execution of the program terminates immediately. The expression, the name of the file containing the source code, and the line number in the source code are displayed.

 If the preprocessor directive #define NDEBUG is placed before the directive #include <cassert>, all the assert statements are ignored.

Header File `cctype`

Function Name and Parameter	Parameter Types	Function Return Value
isalnum(ch)	ch is a char value	The function returns an int value as follows: If ch is a letter or a digit character, that is ('A'-'Z', 'a'-'z', or '0'-'9'), it returns a nonzero value (true), 0 (false) otherwise.
iscntrl(ch)	ch is a char value	The function returns an int value as follows: If ch is a control character (in ASCII, a character value 0–31 or 127), it returns a nonzero value (true), 0 (false) otherwise.

Function Name and Parameter	Parameter Types	Function Return Value
`isdigit(ch)`	ch is a char value	The function returns an int value as follows: If ch is a digit (`'0'-'9'`), it returns a nonzero value (`true`), 0 (`false`) otherwise.
`isgraph(ch)`	ch is a char value	The function returns an int value as follows: If ch is a nonblank printable character (in ASCII, `'!'` through `'~'`), it returns a nonzero value (`true`), 0 (`false`) otherwise.
`islower(ch)`	ch is a char value	The function returns an int value as follows: If ch is a lowercase letter (`'a'-'z'`), it returns a nonzero value (`true`), 0 (`false`) otherwise.
`isprint(ch)`	ch is a char value	The function returns an int value as follows: If ch is a printable character, including blank (in ASCII, `' '` through `'~'`), it returns a nonzero value (`true`), 0 (`false`) otherwise.
`ispunct(ch)`	ch is a char value	The function returns an int value as follows: If ch is a punctuation character, it returns a nonzero value (`true`), 0 (`false`) otherwise.
`isspace(ch)`	ch is a char value	The function returns an int value as follows: If ch is a whitespace character (blank, newline, tab, carriage return, form feed), it returns a nonzero value (`true`), 0 (`false`) otherwise.
`isupper(ch)`	ch is a char value	The function returns an int value as follows: If ch is an uppercase letter (`'A'-'Z'`), it returns a nonzero value (`true`), 0 (`false`) otherwise.
`isxdigit(ch)`	ch is a char value	The function returns an int value as follows: If ch is a hexadecimal digit (`'0'-'9'`, `'A'-'Z'`, `'a'-'z'`), it returns a nonzero value (`true`), 0 (`false`) otherwise.
`tolower(ch)`	ch is a char value	The function returns an int value as follows: If ch is an uppercase letter, it returns the int value of the lowercase equivalent of ch; otherwise, it returns the int value of ch.

Function Name and Parameter	Parameter Types	Function Return Value
toupper(ch)	ch is a char value	The function returns an int value as follows: If ch is a lowercase letter, it returns the int value of the uppercase equivalent of ch; otherwise, it returns the int value of ch.

Header File cmath

E

Function Name and Parameters	Parameter(s) Type	Function Return Value
acos(x)	x is a floating-point expression, $-1.0 \leq x \leq 1.0$	Arc cosine of x, a value between 0.0 and π
asin(x)	x is a floating-point expression, $-1.0 \leq x \leq 1.0$	Arc sine of x, a value between $-\pi/2$ and $\pi/2$
atan(x)	x is a floating-point expression	Arc tan of x, a value between $-\pi/2$ and $\pi/2$
ceil(x)	x is a floating-point expression	The smallest whole number $\geq$ x ("ceiling" of x)
cos(x)	x is a floating-point expression; x is measured in radians	Trigonometric cosine of the angle; for example, if x = 90, cos(x) is 0
cosh(x)	x is a floating-point expression	Hyperbolic cosine of x
exp(x)	x is a floating-point expression	The value of e raised to the power of x; (e = 2.718...)
fabs(x)	x is a floating-point expression	Absolute value of x
floor(x)	x is a floating-point expression	The largest whole number $\leq$ x; ("floor" of x)
log(x)	x is a floating-point expression, where x > 0.0	Natural logarithm (base e) of x
log10(x)	x is a floating-point expression, where x > 0.0	Common logarithm (base 10) of x

Function Name and Parameters	Parameter(s) Type	Function Return Value
pow(x, y)	x and y are floating-point expressions. If x = 0.0, y must be positive; if x ≤ 0.0, y must be a whole number.	x raised to the power of y
sin(x)	x is a floating-point expression; x is measured in radians	Trigonometric sine of the angle; for example, if x = 90, sin(x) is 1
sinh(x)	x is a floating-point expression	Hyperbolic sine of x
sqrt(x)	x is a floating-point expression; x ≥ 0.0	Square root of x
tan(x)	x is a floating-point expression; x is measured in radians	Trigonometric tangent of the angle; for example, if x = 45, tan(x) is 1
tanh(x)	x is a floating-point expression	Hyperbolic tangent of x

Header File `cstddef`

Among others, this header file contains the definition of following symbolic constant:

`NULL`: The system–dependent null pointer (usually 0).

Header File `cstring`

Function Name and Parameters	Parameter(s) Type	Function Return Value
strcat(destStr, srcStr)	destStr and srcStr are null-terminated char arrays; destStr must be large enough to hold the result	The base address of destStr, srcStr, including the null character '\0', is concatenated (joined) to the end of destStr
strcmp(str1, str2)	str1 and str2 are null-terminated char arrays	The returned value is as follows: An int value < 0, if str1 < str2 An int value 0, if str1 == str2 An int value > 0, if str1 > str2

Function Name and Parameters	Parameter(s) Type	Function Return Value
strcpy(destStr, srcStr)	destStr and srcStr are null-terminated char arrays	The base address of destStr is returned; srcStr is copied into destStr
strlen(str)	str is a null-terminated char array	An int value ≥ 0 that is the length of str (excluding the '\0')

Header File string

This header file, not to be confused with the header file **cstring**, supplies a programmer-defined data type named **string**. Associated with the **string** type is a data type **string::size_type** and a named constant **string::npos**. These are defined as follows:

string::size_type   An unsigned integer type related to the number of characters in a string.

string::npos   The maximum value of the type **string::size_type**.

Several functions are associated with the **string** type. Some of these functions are given below. Unless stated otherwise, **str**, **str1**, and **str2** are variables (objects) of the type **string**. The position of the first character in a **string** variable (such as **str**) is 0, the second character is 1, and so on.

Function Name and Parameters	Arguments	Effect and Function Return Value
str.c_str()	None	The base address of a C-string (null-terminated char array) corresponding to the characters in str.
getline(istreamVar, str)	istreamVar is an input stream variable (of the type istream or ifstream). str is a string object (variable).	Characters are input from istreamVar and stored in str until the newline character is encountered. (The newline character is consumed but not stored in str.) The value returned by this function is typically ignored because programmers usually invoke this as a void function.
str.empty()	None	Returns true if str is empty, that is, the number of characters in str is zero, false otherwise.

Function Name and Parameters	Arguments	Effect and Function Return Value
str.length()	None	A value of the type string::size_type giving the number of characters in the string.
str.size()	None	A value of the type string::size_type giving the number of characters in the string.
str.find(strExp)	str is a string object and strExp is a string expression evaluating to a string. The string expression, strExp, can also be a character.	The find function searches str to find the first occurrence of the string or the character specified by strExp. If the search is successful, the find function returns the position in str where the match begins; if the search is unsuccessful, the function returns the special value string::npos.
str.substr(pos, len)	Two unsigned integers, pos and len.pos represents the starting position (of the substring in str); len represents the length (of the substring). The value of pos must be less than str.length()	A temporary string object that holds a substring of str starting at pos. The length of the substring is at most len characters. If len is too large, it means "to the end" of the string in str.
str1.swap(str2);	One parameter of the type string.str1 and str2 are objects of the type string.	The contents of str1 and str2 are swapped.
str.clear();	None	Removes all the characters from str.
str.erase();	None	Removes all the characters from str.
str.erase(m);	One parameter of the type string::size_type.	Removes all the characters from str starting at the index m.
str.erase(m, n);	Two parameters of the type int.	Starting at the index m, removes the next n characters from str. If n > length of str, removes all the characters starting at the mth.
str.insert(m, c);	Parameter m is of the type string::size_type; c is a character.	Inserts the character c at the index m into str.

Function Name and Parameters	Arguments	Effect and Function Return Value
`str.insert(m, n, c);`	Parameters m and n are of the type `string::size_type`; c is a character.	Inserts n occurrences of the character c at the index m into `str`.
`str1.insert(m, str2);`	Parameters m and n are of the type `string::size_type`; str2 is a string.	Inserts all the characters of `str2` at the index m into `str`.
`str1.replace(m, n, str2);`	Parameters m and n are of the type `string::size_type`; str2 is a string.	Starting at the index m, replaces the next n characters of `str1` with all the characters of `str2`. If n > length of `str1`, then all the characters until the end of `str1` are replaced.

E

F

ADDITIONAL C++ TOPICS

INHERITANCE, POINTERS, AND VIRTUAL FUNCTIONS

Chapter 2 discussed polymorphism via operator overloading and templates. This section describes a third type of polymorphism—via virtual functions.

As a parameter, a class object can be passed either by value or by reference. Moreover, usually the types of the actual and formal parameters must match. However, in the case of classes, C++ allows the user to pass an object of a derived class to a formal parameter of the base class type.

First, let us discuss the case when the formal parameter is either a reference parameter or a pointer. To be specific, let us consider the following classes:

```
class baseClass
{
public:
    void print();
    baseClass(int u = 0);

private:
    int x;
};

class derivedClass: public baseClass
{
public:
    void print();
    derivedClass(int u = 0, int v = 0);

private:
    int a;
};
```

The class baseClass is a class that has three members. The class derivedClass is derived from the class baseClass and it also has three members of its own. Both classes have a member function print. Suppose that the definitions of the member functions of both classes are as follows:

```
void baseClass::print()
{
    cout<<"In baseClass x = "<<x<<endl;
}
```

```
baseClass::baseClass(int u)
{
    x = u;
}

void derivedClass::print()
{
    cout<<"In derivedClass ***: ";
    baseClass::print();
    cout<<"In derivedClass a = "<<a<<endl;
}

derivedClass::derivedClass(int u, int v)
            : baseClass(u)
{
    a = v;
}
```

Consider the following function:

```
void callPrint(baseClass& p)
{
    p.print();
}
```

The function `callPrint` has a formal parameter p of the type `baseClass`. You can call the function `callPrint` by using an object of either the type `baseClass` or the type `derivedClass` as a parameter. Moreover, the body of the function `callPrint` calls the member function `print`. Consider the following function `main`:

```
int main()
{
    baseClass one(5);                       //Line 1
    derivedClass two(3, 15);                //Line 2

    one.print();                            //Line 3
    two.print();                            //Line 4

    cout<<"*** Calling the function callPrint ***"
        <<endl;                             //Line 5
    callPrint(one);                         //Line 6
    callPrint(two);                         //Line 7

    return 0;
}
```

Output

```
In baseClass x = 5
In derivedClass ***: In baseClass x = 3
In derivedClass a = 15
*** Calling the function callPrint  ***
In baseClass x = 5
In baseClass x = 3
```

The statements in Lines 1 through 5 are quite straightforward. Let us look at the statements in Lines 6 and 7. The statement in Line 6 calls the function `callPrint` and passes the object one as the parameter; it generates the fifth line of the output. The statement in Line 7 also calls the function `callPrint`, but passes the object `two` as the parameter; it generates the sixth line of the output. The output generated by the statements in Lines 6 and 7 shows only the value of `x`, even though each time a different class object was passed as a parameter. (Because in Line 7 object `two` is passed as a parameter to the function `callPrint`, the output generated by the statement in Line 7 should be the same as the second and third lines of the output.) This is because for both statements (Lines 6 and 7), the member function `print` of the `class baseClass` is executed. This is due to the fact that the binding of the member function `print`, in the body of the function `callPrint`, occurred at compile time. Because the formal parameter `p` of the function `callPrint` is of the type `baseClass`, for the statement `p.print();`, the compiler associates the function `print` of the `class baseClass`. More specifically, in **compile-time binding,** the necessary code to call a specific function is generated by the compiler. (Compile-time binding is also known as **static binding**.)

For the statement in Line 7, the actual parameter is of the type `derivedClass`. Thus, when the body of function `two` executes, logically the `print` function of object `two` should execute, which is not the case. So, during program execution, how does C++ correct this problem of making the call to the appropriate function? C++ corrects this problem by providing the mechanism of **virtual functions**. The binding of virtual functions occurs at program execution time, not at compile time. This kind of binding is called **run-time binding**. More formally, in run-time binding, the compiler does not generate the code to call a specific function; instead, it generates enough information to enable the run-time system to generate the specific code for the appropriate function call. Run-time binding is also known as **dynamic binding**.

In C++, virtual functions are declared using the reserved word `virtual`. Let us redefine the previous classes using this feature:

```
class baseClass
{
public:
    virtual void print();         //virtual function
    baseClass(int u = 0);

private:
    int x;
};
```

F

```
class derivedClass: public baseClass
{
public:
    void print();
    derivedClass(int u = 0, int v = 0);

private:
    int a;
};
```

Note that we need to declare a **virtual** function only in the base class.

The **definition** of the member function print is the same as before. If we execute the previous program with these modifications, the output is as follows.

Output

```
In baseClass x = 5
In derivedClass ***: In baseClass x = 3
In derivedClass a = 15
*** Calling the function callPrint  ***
In baseClass x = 5
In derivedClass ***: In baseClass x = 3
In derivedClass a = 15
```

This output shows that for the statement in Line 7, the print function of derivedClass is executed (see the last two lines of the output).

The previous discussion also applies when a formal parameter is a pointer to a class, and a pointer of the derived class is passed as an actual parameter. To illustrate this feature, suppose we have the previous classes. (We assume that the definition of the **class baseClass** is in the header file baseClass.h, and the definition of the **class derivedClass** is in the header file derivedClass.h.) Consider the following program:

```
//Virtual Functions

#include <iostream>

#include "derivedClass.h"

using namespace std;

void callPrint(baseClass *p);

int main()
{
    baseClass *q;                         //Line 1
    derivedClass *r;                      //Line 2

    q = new baseClass(5);                 //Line 3
    r = new derivedClass(3, 15);          //Line 4
```

```
    q->print();                        //Line 5
    r->print();                        //Line 6

    cout<<"*** Calling the function callPrint   ***"
        <<endl;                        //Line 7
    callPrint(q);                      //Line 8
    callPrint(r);                      //Line 9

    return 0;
}

void callPrint(baseClass *p)
{
    p->print();
}
```

F

Output

```
In baseClass x = 5
In derivedClass ***: In baseClass x = 3
In derivedClass a = 15
*** Calling the function callPrint   ***
In baseClass x = 5
In derivedClass ***: In baseClass x = 3
In derivedClass a = 15
```

Passing an object of a derived class as a parameter to a formal parameter of the base class type works well only if the formal parameter is either a reference parameter or a pointer. If the formal parameter is a value parameter, passing an object of a derived class type to a formal parameter of the base class type does not work well, even in the case of a virtual function. Recall that, if a formal parameter is a value parameter, the value of the actual parameter is copied into the formal parameter. If the formal parameter is of the type class, the data members of the actual object are copied into the corresponding data members of the formal parameter.

Suppose that we have the previous classes—that is, baseClass and derivedClass. Consider the following function definition:

```
void callPrint(baseClass p)   //p is a value parameter
{
    p.print();
}
```

Further suppose that we have the following declaration:

```
derivedClass two;
```

The object two has two data members, x and a. The data member x is inherited from the base class. Consider the following function call:

```
callPrint(two);
```

In this statement, because the formal parameter **p** is a value parameter, the data members of **two** are copied into the data members of **p**. However, because **p** is an object of the type **baseClass**, it has only one data member. Consequently, only the data member **x** of **two** is copied into the data member **x** of **p**. Also, the statement:

```
p.print();
```

in the body of the function causes the member function **print** of the **class baseClass** to execute.

The output of the following program further illustrates this concept. (As before, we assume that the definition of the **class baseClass** is in the header file **baseClass.h**, and the definition of the **class derivedClass** is in the header file **derivedClass.h**.)

```
//Virtual Functions and value parameters

#include <iostream>

#include "derivedClass.h"

using namespace std;

void callPrint(baseClass p);

int main()
{
    baseClass one(5);                       //Line 1
    derivedClass two(3, 15);                //Line 2

    one.print();                            //Line 3
    two.print();                            //Line 4

    cout<<"*** Calling the function callPrint  ***"
        <<endl;                             //Line 5
    callPrint(one);                         //Line 6
    callPrint(two);                         //Line 7

    return 0;
}

void callPrint(baseClass p) //p is a value parameter
{
    p.print();
}
```

Output

```
In baseClass x = 5
In derivedClass ***: In baseClass x = 3
In derivedClass a = 15
*** Calling the function callPrint  ***
In baseClass x = 5
In baseClass x = 3
```

Look closely at the output of the statements in Lines 6 and 7 (the last two lines of the output). In Line 7, because the formal parameter **p** is a value parameter, the data members of **two** are copied into the data members of **p**. However, because **p** is an object of the type **baseClass**, it has only one data member. Consequently, only the data member **x** of **two** is copied into the data member **x** of **p**. Moreover, the statement **p.print();** in the function **callPrint** executes the function **print** of the **class baseClass**, not the **class derivedClass**. Therefore, the last line of the output shows only the value of **x** (the data member of **two**).

An object of the base class type cannot be passed to a formal parameter of the derived class type.

Classes and Virtual Destructors

One thing recommended for classes with pointer data members is that these classes have the destructor. The destructor is automatically executed when the class object goes out of scope. Thus, if the object creates dynamic objects, the destructor can be designed to deallocate the storage for them. If a derived class object is passed to a formal parameter of the base class type, the destructor of the base class executes regardless of whether the derived class object is passed by reference or by value. Logically, however, the destructor of the derived class should be executed when the derived class object goes out of scope.

To correct this problem, the destructor of the base class must be virtual. The **virtual destructor** of a base class automatically makes the destructor of a derived class be virtual. When a derived class object is passed to a formal parameter of the base class type, then when the object goes out of scope, the destructor of the derived class executes. After executing the destructor of the derived class, the destructor of the base class automatically executes. Therefore, when the derived class object is destroyed, the base class part (that is, the members inherited from the base class) of the derived class object are also destroyed.

If a base class contains virtual functions, you need to make the destructor of the base class virtual.

ADDRESS OF OPERATOR AND CLASSES

Chapter 3 used the address of operator, &, to store the address of a variable in a pointer variable. The address of operator is also used to create aliases to an object. Consider the following statements:

```
int x;
int &y = x;
```

The first statement declares x to be an int variable; the second statement declares y to be an alias of x. That is, both x and y refer to the same memory location. Thus, y is like a constant pointer variable. The statement:

```
y = 25;
```

sets the value of y (and hence) the value of x to 25. Similarly, the statement:

```
x = 2 * x + 30;
```

updates the value of x (and hence) the value of y.

The address of operator can also be used to return the address of a **private** data member of a class. However, if you are not careful, this operation can result in serious errors in the program. The following example helps illustrate this idea.

Consider the following class definition:

```
//Header file testadd.h

#ifndef H_testAdd
#define H_testAdd

class testAddress
{
public:
    void setX(int);
    void printX() const;
    int& addressOfX();      //this function returns the
                            //address of the private data member

private:
    int x;
};

#endif
```

The definitions of the functions to implement the member functions are as follows:

```
//Implementation file testAdd.cpp

#include <iostream>
#include "testAdd.h"
```

```
using namespace std;

void testAddress::setX(int inX)
{
    x = inX;
}

void testAddress::printX() const
{
    cout<<x;
}

int& testAddress::addressOfX()
{
    return x;
}
```

F

Because the return type of the function **addressOfX** is an address of an int memory location, the statement:

```
return x;
```

returns the address of **x**.

Next, let us write a simple program that uses the **class testAddress** and illustrates what can go wrong. Later, we will show how to fix the problem.

```
//Test program

#include <iostream>
#include "testAdd.h"

using namespace std;

int main()
{
    testAddress a;
    int &y = a.addressOfX();

    a.setX(50);
    cout<<"x in class testAddress = ";
    a.printX();
    cout<<endl;

    y = 25;
    cout<<"After y = 25, x in class testAddress = ";
    a.printX();
    cout<<endl;

    return 0;
}
```

Output

```
x in class testAddress = 50
After y = 25, x in class testAddress = 25
```

In the preceding program, after the statement:

```
int &y = a.addressOfX();
```

executes, y becomes an alias of the **private** data member x of the object a. Thus, the statement:

```
y = 25;
```

changes the value of x.

Chapter 1 said that **private** data members are not accessible outside the class. However, by returning their addresses, the programmer can manipulate them. One way to resolve this problem is to never provide the user of the class with the addresses of the **private** data members. Sometimes, however, it is necessary to return the address of a **private** data member. How can we prevent the program from directly manipulating the **private** data members? To fix this problem, we use the word **const** before the return type of the function. This way, we can still return the addresses of the **private** data members, but at the same time prevent the programmer from directly manipulating the **private** data members. Let us rewrite the **class testAddress** using this feature.

```
#ifndef H_testAdd
#define H_testAdd

class testAddress
{
public:
    void setX(int);
    void printX() const;
    const int& addressOfX(); //this function returns the
                             //address of the private data
                             //member
private:
    int x;
};

#endif
```

The definition of the function **addressOfX** in the implementation file is:

```
const int& testAddress::addressOfX()
{

    return x;
}
```

The same program now generates a compile-time error.

G

C++ FOR JAVA PROGRAMMERS

This book assumes that you are familiar with the basic elements of C++ such as data types, assignment statements, input/output, control structures, functions and parameter passing, the namespace mechanism, and arrays. However, to help you, this appendix quickly reviews these basic elements of C++. Moreover, if you have taken Java as a first programming language, this appendix helps familiarize you with the basic elements of C++. In addition to describing the basic elements of C++, we also compare the various features of C++ with Java.

For more details about the C++ language, refer to the book, *C++ Programming: From Problem Analysis to Program Design* by the author and listed in the references ([7], Appendix H).

DATA TYPES

C++ data types fall into three categories—simple data types, structured data types, and pointers. Chapter 1 describes the user-defined classes, which fall into the category of structured data types. Chapter 3 describes pointers. This section discusses the simple data types. Moreover, later in this appendix, we briefly discuss arrays, a structured data type, in C++.

C++'s simple data type is similar to Java's primitive data type. There are three categories of simple data—integral, floating-point, and enumeration type.

Like Java, C++'s integral data types have several categories. Some of the integral data types are char, bool, short, int, long, and unsigned int. Table G-1 defines the range of values belonging to some of these data types.

Table G-1 Values and Memory Allocation for Three Simple Data Types

Data Type	Values	Storage (in bytes)
int	−2147483648 to 2147483647	4
bool	true and false	1
char	−128 to 127	1

Use this table only as a guide. Different compilers may allow different ranges of values. Check your compiler's documentation.

The data type int in C++ works the same way as the data type int works in Java.

Notice that the data type char in C++ is a set of 256 values, while the data type char in Java is a set of 65536 values. In addition to dealing with small numbers, the data type char is used to represent characters—that is, letters, digits, and special symbols. Typically, C++ uses the ASCII characters, a set of 128 characters and described in Appendix C, to deal with characters.

The data type bool has only two values: true and false. Also, true and false are called the **logical (Boolean) values**. An expression that evaluates to true or false is called a **logical (Boolean) expression**.

To deal with decimal numbers, C++ provides the floating-point data type. C++ provides three data types to manipulate decimal numbers: float, double, and long double. As in the case of integral data types, the data types float, double, and long double differ in their sets of values. The data types float and double in C++ work the same way as they do in Java.

Arithmetic Operators and Expressions

The five arithmetic operators—+, -, *, /, and %—in C++ work the same way as in Java. Moreover, arithmetic expressions in C++ are formed and evaluated the same as they are in Java. In addition, the increment operator, ++, the decrement operator, --, the compound assignment operators, +=, -=, *=, /=, and %= in C++ work the same way as in Java.

The cast operator in C++ takes the following form:

```
static_cast<dataType> expression
```

You can also use the following C-like cast operator:

```
dataType expression
```

NAMED CONSTANTS, VARIABLES, AND ASSIGNMENT STATEMENTS

Named constants in C++ are declared using the reserved word const. The general syntax of declaring a named constant is:

```
const dataType identifier = value;
```

For example, the following statement declares conversion to be a named constant of the type double and assigns the value 2.54 to it.

```
const double conversion = 2.54;
```

In C++, variables are declared the same way as they are declared in Java, and the syntax of the assignment statement in both languages is the same.

The general syntax for declaring either one variable or multiple variables is:

```
dataType identifier, identifier, . . .;
```

For example, the following statements declare `amountDue` to be a variable of the type `double` and `counter` to be a variable of the type `int`.

```
double amountDue;
int    counter;
```

The syntax of the assignment statement is:

```
variable = expression;
```

In an assignment statement, the value of the `expression` should match the data type of the `variable`. The expression on the right side is evaluated, and its value is assigned to the variable on the left side. For example, suppose that `amountDue` is a variable of the type `double` and `quantity` is a variable of the type `int`. If the value of `quantity` is 20, then the following statement assigns `150.00` to `amountDue`:

```
amountDue = quantity * 7.50;
```

C++ Library: Preprocessor Directives

Only a small number of operations, such as arithmetic and assignment operations, are explicitly defined in C++. Many of the functions and symbols needed to run a C++ program are provided as a collection of libraries. Every library has a name and is referred to as a **header file**. For example, the descriptions of the functions needed to perform input/output (I/O) are contained in the header file `iostream`. Similarly, the descriptions of some very useful mathematical functions, such as power, absolute, and sine, are contained in the header file `cmath`. If you want to use I/O or math functions, you need to tell the computer where to find the necessary code. You use preprocessor directives and the names of the header files to tell the computer the locations of the code provided in the libraries. Preprocessor directives are processed by a program called a **preprocessor**.

Preprocessor directives are commands supplied to the preprocessor that cause the preprocessor to modify the text of a C++ program before it is compiled. All preprocessor commands begin with #. There are no semicolons at the end of preprocessor commands because they are not C++ commands. To use a header file in a C++ program, use the preprocessor directive `include`.

The general syntax to include a system-provided header file in a C++ program is:

```
#include <headerFileName>
```

For example, the following statement includes the header file **iostream** in a C++ program:

```
#include <iostream>
```

Preprocessor directives that include the header files are placed as the first lines of a program so that the identifiers declared in those header files can be used throughout the program. (In C++, identifiers must be declared before they can be used.)

Certain header files are provided as part of C++. Appendix E describes some of the commonly used header files. Individual programmers can also create their own header files. In Chapter 1, you learned how to create your own header files and then include them in a C++ program.

C++ Program

Every C++ program has two parts: preprocessor directives and the program. The preprocessor directives are commands that direct the preprocessor to modify the C++ program before compilation. The program contains statements that accomplish some meaningful results. Taken together, the preprocessor directives and program statements constitute the C++ **source code**. To be useful, this source code must be saved in a file that has the file extension **.cpp**.

When the program is compiled, the compiler generates the object code, which is saved in a file with the file extension **.obj**. When the object code is linked with system resources, the executable code is produced and saved in a file with the file extension **.exe**. The name of the file containing the object code, and the name of the file containing the executable code, are the same as the name of the file containing the source code. For example, if the source code is located in a file named **firstProg.cpp**, the name of the file containing the object code is **firstProg.obj**, and the name of the file containing the executable code is **firstProg.exe**.

The extensions given in the preceding paragraphs—that is, **.cpp**, **.obj**, and **.exe**—are system dependent. To be absolutely sure, check your system's or software development kit's (SDK's) documentation.

A C++ program is a collection of functions and one of the functions is the function **main**. Therefore, every C++ program must have the function **main**. The basic parts of the function **main** are the heading and the body of the function. The heading has the following form:

```
typeOfFunction main(argument list)
```

For example, the statement:

```
int main()
```

means that the function **main** returns a value of the **int** data type, and it has no arguments.

The body of the function must be enclosed between curly braces (**{** and **}**) and contain two types of statements:

- Declaration statements
- Executable statements

Declaration statements are used to declare things such as variables. In C++, variables or identifiers can be declared anywhere in the program, but they must be declared before they can be used. Executable statements perform calculations, manipulate data, accept input, create output, and so on. Some executable statements that you have encountered so far are the assignment, input, and output statements.

The following is an example of a C++ program.

```cpp
#include <iostream>

using namespace std;

int main()
{
    int num1, num2;

    num1 = 10;
    num2 = 2 * num1;

    cout<<"num1 = "<<num1<<", and num2 = "<<num2<<endl;
    return 0;
}
```

The next section discusses input and output (I/O) in detail.

INPUT AND OUTPUT

Inputting data and outputting the results of a program is fundamental to any programming language. Because I/O differs quite significantly in C++ and Java, this section describes I/O in C++ is detail.

Input

Putting data into variables from the standard input device is accomplished via the use of `cin` and the operator `>>`. The syntax of `cin` together with `>>` is:

```
cin>>variable>>variable. . .;
```

This is called an **input (read)** statement. Sometimes this is also called a `cin` statement. In C++, `>>` is called the **stream extraction operator** or simply the **extraction operator**.

The input (or `cin`) statement works as follows. Suppose `miles` is a variable of the data type `double`. The statement:

```
cin>>miles;
```

causes the computer to get a value, from the standard input device, of the data type **double**, and place it in the memory cell named **miles**.

By using more than one variable with **cin**, more than one value can be read at a time. Suppose **feet** and **inch** are variables of the data type **int**. A statement such as:

```
cin>>feet>>inch;
```

gets two integers from the keyboard and places them in the memory locations **feet** and **inch**, respectively.

 The extraction operator >> is defined only for inputting data into variables of simple data types. Therefore, the right-side operand of the extraction operator >> is a variable of the simple data type.

How does the extraction operator >> work? When scanning for the next input, >> skips all the whitespace characters. **Whitespace characters** consist of blanks and certain nonprintable characters, such as tabs and the newline character. Thus, whether you separate the input data by blanks or lines, the extraction operator >> simply finds the next input data in the input stream. For example, suppose that **payRate** and **hoursWorked** are variables of the type **double**. Consider the following input statement:

```
cin>>payRate>>hoursWorked;
```

Whether the input is:

```
15.50 48.30
```

or:

```
15.50   48.30
```

or:

```
15.50
48.30
```

the preceding input statement would store **15.50** in **payRate** and **48.30** in **hoursWorked**. Note that the first input is separated by a blank, the second input is separated by a tab, and the third input is separated by a line.

Now suppose that the input is 2. How does the extraction operator >> distinguish between the character 2 and the number 2? The right-side operand of the extraction operator >> makes this distinction. If the right-side operand is a variable of the type **char**, the input 2 is treated as the character 2 and, in this case, the ASCII value of 2 is stored. If the right-side operand is a variable of the type **int** or **double**, the input 2 is treated as the number 2.

Next, consider the input 25 and the statement:

```
cin>>a;
```

where **a** is a variable of some simple data type. If **a** is of the type **char**, only the single character 2 is stored in **a**. If **a** is of the type **int**, 25 is stored in **a**. If **a** is of the type **double**, the input 25 is converted to the decimal number 25.0. Table G-2 summarizes this discussion by showing the valid input for a variable of the simple data type.

Table G-2 Valid Input for a Variable of the Simple Data Type

Data Type of a	Valid Input for a
char	One printable character except the blank.
int	An integer, possibly preceded by a (+ or −) sign.
double	A decimal number, possibly preceded by a (+ or −) sign. If the actual data input is an integer, the input is converted to a decimal number with the zero decimal part.

When reading data into a **char** variable, after skipping any leading whitespace characters, the extraction operator **>>** finds and stores only the next character; reading stops after a single character. To read data into an **int** or **double** variable, after skipping all the leading whitespace characters and reading the plus or minus sign (if any), the extraction operator **>>** reads the digits of the number, including the decimal point for floating-point variables, and stops when it finds a whitespace character or a character other than a digit.

Input Failure

Many things can go wrong during program execution. A program that is syntactically correct might produce incorrect results. For example, suppose that a part-time employee's paycheck is calculated by using the following formula:

```
wages = payRate * hoursWorked;
```

If you accidentally type a **+** in place of *****, the calculated wages would be incorrect, even though the statement containing the **+** is syntactically correct.

What about an attempt to read invalid data? For example, what would happen if you tried to input a letter into an **int** variable? If the input data did not match the corresponding variables, the program would run into problems. For example, trying to read a letter into an **int** or **double** variable would result in an **input failure**. Consider the following statements:

```
int a, b, c;
double x;
```

If the input is:

```
W 54
```

then the statement:

```
cin>>a>>b;
```

would result in an input failure, because you are trying to input the character `'W'` into the `int` variable a. If the input were:

```
35 67.93 48 78
```

then the input statement:

```
cin>>a>>x>>b;
```

would result in storing 35 in a, 67.93 in x, and 48 in b.

Now consider the following read statement with the previous input (the input with three values):

```
cin>>a>>b>>c;
```

This statement stores 35 in a and 67 in b. The reading stops at . (the decimal point). Because the next variable, c, is of the data type `int`, the computer tries to read . into c, which is an error. The input stream then enters a state called the **fail state**.

What actually happens when the input stream enters the fail state? Once an input stream enters a fail state, all further I/O statements using that stream are ignored. Unfortunately, the program quietly continues to execute with whatever values are stored in the variables and produce incorrect results.

Output

In C++, output on the standard output device is accomplished via the use of `cout` and the operator `<<`. The syntax of `cout` together with `<<` is:

```
cout<<expression or manipulator<<expression or manipulator...;
```

This is called an **output statement**. Sometimes this is also called a `cout` statement. In C++, `<<` is called the **stream insertion operator** or simply the **insertion operator**.

Generating output with the `cout` statement follows two rules:

1. The expression is evaluated, and its value is printed at the current insertion point on the output device. (On the screen, the insertion point is where the cursor is.)

2. A manipulator is used to format the output. The simplest manipulator is `endl` (the last character is the letter `el`), which causes the insertion point to move to the beginning of the next line.

Example G-1 illustrates how `cout` statements work. In a `cout` statement, a string or an expression involving either only one variable or a single value evaluates to itself.

Example G-1

Consider the following statements. The output is shown to the right of each statement.

	Statement	Output
1	`cout<<29/4<<endl;`	7
2	`cout<<"Hello there."<<endl;`	Hello there.
3	`cout<<12<<endl;`	12
4	`cout<<"4 + 7"<<endl;`	4 + 7
5	`cout<<4 + 7<<endl;`	11
6	`cout<<'A'<<endl;`	A
7	`cout<<"4 + 7 = "<<4 + 7<<endl;`	4 + 7 = 11
8	`cout<<2 + 3 * 5<<endl;`	17
9	`cout<<"Hello \nthere. "<<endl;`	Hello there.

setprecision

You use the manipulator **setprecision** to control the output of floating-point numbers. The default output of floating-point numbers is scientific notation. Some software development kits (SDK's) might use a maximum of six decimal places for the default output of floating-point numbers. However, when an employee's paycheck is printed, the desired output is a maximum of two decimal places. To print floating-point output to two decimal places, you use the **setprecision** manipulator to set the precision to **2**.

The general syntax of the **setprecision** manipulator is:

```
setprecision(n)
```

where **n** is the number of decimal places.

You use the **setprecision** manipulator with **cout** and the extraction operator. For example, the statement:

```
cout<<setprecision(2);
```

formats the output of the decimal numbers to two decimal places, until a similar subsequent statement changes the precision. Notice that the number of decimal places, or the precision value, is passed as an argument to **setprecision**.

To use the manipulator **setprecision**, the program must include the header file **iomanip**. Thus, the following include statement is required:

```
#include <iomanip>
```

fixed

To further control the output of floating-point numbers, you can use other manipulators. To output floating-point numbers in a fixed decimal format, you use the manipulator `fixed`. The following statement sets the output of floating-point numbers in a fixed decimal format on the standard output device:

```
cout<<fixed;
```

After the preceding statement executes, all floating-point numbers are displayed in the fixed-decimal format until the manipulator `fixed` is disabled. You can disable the manipulator `fixed` by using the stream member function `unsetf`. For example, to disable the manipulator `fixed` on the standard output device, you use the following statement:

```
cout.unsetf(ios::fixed);
```

After the manipulator `fixed` is disabled, the output of the floating-point numbers return to their default settings. The manipulator `scientific` is used to output floating-point numbers in scientific format.

showpoint

Suppose that the decimal part of a decimal number is zero. In this case, when you instruct the computer to output the decimal number in a fixed decimal format, the output may not show the decimal point and the decimal part. To force the output to show the decimal point and trailing zeros, you use the manipulator `showpoint`. The following statement sets the output of decimal numbers with the decimal point and trailing zeros on the standard output device:

```
cout<<showpoint;
```

Of course, the following statement sets the output of floating-point numbers in a fixed decimal format with the decimal point and trailing zeros on the standard output device:

```
cout<<fixed<<showpoint;
```

setw

The manipulator `setw` is used to output the value of an expression in specific columns. The value of the expression can be either a string or a number. The statement `setw(n)` outputs the value of the next expression in n columns. The output is right-justified. Thus, if you specify the number of columns to be 8, for example, and the output requires only 4 columns, the first four columns are left blank. Furthermore, if the number of columns specified is less than the number of columns required by the output, the output automatically expands to the required number of columns; the output is not truncated. For example, if x is an `int` variable, the following statement outputs the value of x in five columns on the standard output device:

```
cout<<setw(5)<<x<<endl;
```

To use the manipulator `setw`, the program must include the header file `iomanip`. Thus, the following include statement is required:

```
#include <iomanip>
```

Unlike `setprecision`, which controls the output of all floating-point numbers until it is reset, `setw` controls the output of only the next expression.

`left` and `right` Manipulators

Recall that if the number of columns specified by the `setw` manipulator exceeds the number of columns required by the next expression, the output is right-justified. Sometimes you might want the output to be left-justified. To left-justify the output, you use the manipulator `left`.

The syntax to set the manipulator `left` is:

```
ostreamVar<<left;
```

where `ostreamVar` is an output stream variable. For example, the following statement sets the output to be left-justified on the standard output device:

```
cout<<left;
```

You can disable the manipulator `left` by using the stream function `unsetf`. The syntax to disable the manipulator `left` is:

```
ostreamVar.unsetf(ios::left);
```

where `ostreamVar` is an output stream variable. Disabling the manipulator `left` returns the output to the settings of the default output format. For example, the following statement disables the manipulator `left` on the standard output device:

```
cout.unsetf(ios::left);
```

The syntax to set the manipulator `right` is:

```
ostreamVar<<right;
```

where `ostreamVar` is an output stream variable. For example, the following statement sets the output to be right-justified on the standard output device:

```
cout<<right;
```

`flush`

Both the manipulator `endl` and the newline escape sequence \n position the insertion point at the beginning of the next line on the output device. However, the manipulator `endl` also has another use.

When a program sends output to an output device, the output first goes to the buffer in the computer. Whenever the buffer becomes full, the output is sent to the output device. However, as soon as the manipulator `endl` is encountered, the output from the buffer is sent to the output device immediately, even if the buffer is not full. Therefore, the manipulator `endl` positions the insertion point at the beginning of the next line on an output device and helps clear the buffer.

It is quite possible that sometimes you may not see the entire output. This is due to the fact that when the program terminates, the buffer at that time may not be full.

In C++, you can use the manipulator `flush` to clear the buffer, even if the buffer is not full. In contrast to the manipulator `endl`, the manipulator `flush` does not move the insertion point to the beginning of the next line.

The syntax to use the manipulator `flush` is:

```
ostreamVar<<flush;
```

where `ostreamVar` is an output stream variable, such as `cout`.

For example, the following statement sends the output from the buffer to the standard output device:

```
cout<<flush;
```

Consider the following statements in which `num` is an `int` variable:

```
cout<<"Enter an integer: ";          //Line 1
cin>>num;                            //Line 2
cout<<endl;                          //Line 3
```

The statement in Line 1 outputs the following text: `Enter an integer:` . After outputting this line, the insertion point stays positioned after the space after the colon. Recall that the output of the statement in Line 1 first goes to the buffer. If the buffer is not full, this line of text might not be displayed, in which case the user would have no idea of what to do next. You could put the manipulator `endl` at the end of the statement in Line 1. However, by doing so, after printing the line of text, the insertion point is positioned at the beginning of the next line. The user is, thus, prompted to enter the number in the following line, which is sometimes not very appealing. On the other hand, suppose that the statement in Line 1 is replaced by the following statement:

```
cout<<"Enter an integer: "<<flush;    //Line 1
```

In this case, the line of text, `Enter an integer:` , is displayed on the standard output device even if the buffer is not full. Moreover, after outputting the line of text, the insertion point stays positioned after the space after the colon; the user then enters the number after the space after the colon.

File Input/Output

The previous sections discussed how to get input from the keyboard (standard input device) and send output to the screen (standard output device). This section discusses how to obtain data from other input devices, such as a disk (that is, secondary storage), and how to save the output to a disk. C++ allows a program to get data directly from, and save output directly to, secondary storage. A program can use the file I/O and read data from or write data to a file. Formally, a file is defined as follows:

File: An area in secondary storage used to hold information.

The standard I/O header file, `iostream`, contains data types and variables that are used only for input from the standard input device and output to the standard output device. In addition, C++ provides a header file called `fstream`, which is used for file I/O. Among other things, the `fstream` header file contains the definitions of two data types: `ifstream`, which means input file stream and is similar to `istream`; and `ofstream`, which means output file stream and is similar to `ostream`.

The variables `cin` and `cout` are already defined and associated with the standard input/output devices. In addition, `>>` can be used with `cin`; `<<`, and the manipulators described in the preceding section, can be used with `cout`. These same operators are also available for file I/O, but the header file `fstream` does not declare variables to use them. You must declare variables called **file stream objects**, which include `ifstream` variables for input and `ofstream` variables for output. You then use these variables together with `>>` and `<<` for I/O. Remember that C++ does not automatically initialize user-defined variables. Once you declare the `fstream` objects, you must associate these objects with the input/output sources.

File I/O is a five-step process:

1. Include the header file `fstream` in the program.
2. Declare file stream objects.
3. Associate the file stream objects with the input/output sources.
4. Use the file stream objects with `>>`, `<<`, or other input/output functions.
5. Close the files.

We now describe these five steps in detail. A skeleton program then shows how the steps might appear in a program.

Step 1 requires that the header file `fstream` be included in the program. The following statement accomplishes this task:

```
#include <fstream>
```

Step 2 requires you to declare file stream objects. Consider the following statements:

```
ifstream inData;
ofstream outData;
```

The first statement declares `inData` to be an `ifstream` object. The second statement declares `outData` to be an `ofstream` object.

Step 3 requires you to associate the file stream objects with the input/output sources. This step is called **opening the files**. The stream member function **open** is used to open the files. The general syntax for opening a file is:

```
fileStreamVariable.open(sourceName);
```

Here `fileStreamVariable` is a file stream object, and `sourceName` is the name of the input/output file.

Suppose you include the declarations from Step 2 in a program. Further suppose that the input data is stored in a file called **prog.dat** on a floppy disk in drive **A**, and you want to save the output in a file called **prog.out** on a floppy disk in drive **A**. The following statements associate `inData` with **prog.dat** and `outData` with **prog.out**. That is, the file **prog.dat** is opened for inputting data and the file **prog.out** is opened for outputting data.

```
inData.open("a:\\prog.dat");   //open the input file
outData.open("a:\\prog.out");  //open the output file
```

Notice that there are two \'s after **a:**. In C++, \ is the escape character. Therefore, to produce a \ within a string, you need \\. Moreover, if your C++ program and the input file reside in the same directory, then you do not need to include **a:** before the name of the file. Similarly, if you want the output file to be stored in the same directory as the C++ program, you can omit **a:** before the file name.

Step 4 typically works as follows. You use the file stream objects with >>, <<, or other input/output functions. The syntax for using >> or << with file stream objects is exactly the same as the syntax for using `cin` and `cout`. Instead of using `cin` and `cout`, however, you use the file stream object names that were declared. For example, the statement:

```
inData>>payRate;
```

reads the data from the file **prog.dat** and stores it in the variable **payRate**. The statement:

```
outData<<"The paycheck is: $"<<pay<<endl;
```

stores the output—**The paycheck is: $565.78**—in the file **prog.out**. This statement assumes that the pay was calculated as **565.78**.

Once the I/O is complete, Step 5 requires closing the files. Closing a file means that the file stream variables are disassociated from the storage area, and the file stream objects are freed. Once these variables are freed, they can be reused for other file I/O. Moreover, closing an output file ensures that the entire output is sent to the file, that is, the buffer is emptied. You close the files by using the stream function **close**. For example, assuming the program includes the declarations listed in Steps 2 and 3, the statements for closing the files are:

```
inData.close();
outData.close();
```

In skeleton form, a program that uses file I/O is usually of the following form:

```
#include <fstream>

//Add any additional header files that you use

using namespace std;

int main()
{
        //Declare file stream variables such as the following
    ifstream inData;
    ofstream outData;

        //Additional variable declaration

        //Open the files
    inData.open("a:\\prog.dat");   //open the input file
    outData.open("a:\\prog.out"); //open the output file

        //Code for data manipulation

        //Close the files
    inData.close();
    outData.close();

    return 0;
}
```

Step 3 requires the file to be opened for file I/O. Opening a file associates a file stream variable declared in the program with a physical file at the source, such as a disk. In the case of an input file, the file must exist before the **open** statement executes. If the file does not exist, the **open** statement fails and the input stream enters the fail state. An output file does not have to exist before it is opened; if the output file does not exist, the computer prepares an empty file for output. If the designated output file already exists, by default the old contents are erased when the file is opened.

CONTROL STRUCTURES

C++ and Java have the same six relational operators— ==, !=, <, <=, >, and >=, and they work the same way in both languages. The control structures in C++ and Java are the same. For example, the selection control structures are **if**, **if...else**, and **switch**, and the looping control structures are **while**, **for**, and **do...while**. The syntax for these control structures is the same in both languages. However, there are some differences.

In C++, any nonzero value is treated as **true** and the value 0 is treated as **false**. The reserved word **true** is initialized to 1 and **false** is initialized to 0. Logical expressions in C++ evaluate to 0 or 1. On the other hand, logical expressions in Java evaluate to **true** or

false. Moreover, the data type **boolean** in Java cannot be typecasted to a numeric type, and so its values **true** and **false** cannot be typecasted to numeric values.

In C++, the mix-up of the assignment operator and the equality operator in a logical expression can cause serious problems. For example, consider the following **if** statement:

```
if(drivingCode = 5)
...
```

In C++, the expression **drivingCode = 5** returns the value 5. Because 5 is nonzero, the expression evaluates to **true**. So in C++, the expression evaluates to **true**, and the value of the variable **drivingCode** is also changed. On the other hand, in Java, because the value 5 is not a **boolean** value, it cannot be typecasted to **true** or **false**. So the preceding statement in Java results in a compiler error, whereas in C++ it does not cause any syntax error.

NAMESPACES

When a header file, such as **iostream**, is included in a program, the global identifiers in the header file also become global identifiers in the program. Therefore, if a global identifier in a program has the same name as one of the global identifiers in the header file, the compiler generates a syntax error (such as "identifier redefined"). The same problem can occur if a program uses third-party libraries. To overcome this problem, third-party vendors begin their global identifier names with a special symbol. Moreover, compiler vendors begin their global identifier names with an underscore (_). Therefore, to avoid linking errors you should not begin identifier names in your program with an underscore (_).

C++ tries to solve this problem of overlapping global identifier names with the **namespace** mechanism.

The general syntax of the statement **namespace** is:

```
namespace namespaceName
{
     members
}
```

where a member is usually a named constant, variable declaration, function, or another **namespace**. Note that **namespaceName** is a C++ identifier.

In C++, **namespace** is a reserved word.

Example G-2

The statement:

```
namespace globalType
{
     const int n = 10;
     const double rate = 7.50;
```

```
        int count = 0;
        void printResult();
}
```

defines `globalType` to be a `namespace` with four members: named constants `n` and `rate`, the variable `count`, and the function `printResult`.

The scope of a `namespace` member is local to the `namespace`. You can usually access a `namespace` member outside the `namespace` in one of two ways, as described below.

The general syntax for accessing a `namespace` member is:

```
namespaceName::identifier
```

For example, to access the member `rate` of the `namespace globalType`, the following statement is required:

```
globalType::rate
```

To access the member `printResult` (which is a function), the following statement is required:

```
globalType::printResult();
```

In C++, `::` is called the scope resolution operator. Thus, to access a member of a `namespace`, you use `namespaceName`, followed by the scope resolution operator, followed by the member name. That is, you attach the name of `namespaceName` and the scope resolution operator before the member name.

To simplify the accessing of a `namespace` member, C++ provides the use of the statement `using`. The syntax to use the statement `using` is as follows.

(a) To simplify the accessing of all `namespace` members:

```
using namespace namespaceName;
```

(b) To simplify the accessing of a specific `namespace` member:

```
using namespaceName::identifier;
```

For example, the `using` statement:

```
using namespace globalType;
```

simplifies the accessing of all the members of the `namespace globalType`. The statement:

```
using globalType::rate;
```

simplifies the accessing of the member `rate` of the `namespace globalType`.

In C++, using is a reserved word.

You typically put the using statement after the namespace declaration. For the namespace globalType, for example, you usually write the code as follows:

```
namespace globalType
{
    const int n = 10;
    const double rate = 7.50;
    int count = 0;
    void printResult();
}


using namespace globalType;
```

After the using statement, to access a namespace member you do not have to put namespaceName and the scope resolution operator before the namespace member. However, if a namespace member and a global identifier in a program have the same name, to access this namespace member in the program, namespaceName and the scope resolution operator must precede the namespace member. Similarly, if a namespace member and an identifier in a block have the same name, to access this namespace member in the block, namespaceName and the scope resolution operator must precede the namespace member.

Examples G-3 through G-6 help clarify the use of the namespace mechanism.

Example G-3

Consider the following C++ code:

```
#include <iostream>

using namespace std;
.
.
.
int main()
{
    .
    .
    .
}
.
.
.
```

In this example, you can refer to the global identifiers of the header file iostream, such as cin, cout, and endl, without using the prefix std:: before the identifier name. The obvious restriction is that the block (or function) that refers to the global identifier (of the header file iostream) must not contain any identifier with the same name as this global identifier.

Example G-4

Consider the following C++ code:

```cpp
#include <cmath>

int main()
{
    double x = 15.3;
    double y;

    y = std::pow(x, 2);
    .
    .
    .

}
```

This example accesses the function **pow** of the header file **cmath**.

Example G-5

Consider the following C++ code:

```cpp
#include <iostream>
.
.
.
int main()
{
    using namespace std;
    .
    .
    .

}
.
.
.
```

In this example, the function **main** can refer to the global identifiers of the header file **iostream** without using the prefix **std::** before the identifier name. The **using** statement appears inside the function **main**. Therefore, other functions (if any) should use the prefix **std::** before the name of the global identifier of the header file **iostream** unless the function has a similar **using** statement.

Example G-6

Consider the following C++ code:

```
#include <iostream>
using namespace std;                //Line 1

int t;                              //Line 2
double u;                           //Line 3

namespace expNspace
{
    int x;                          //Line 4
    char t;                         //Line 5
    double u;                       //Line 6
    void printResult();             //Line 7
}
using namespace expNspace;

int main()
{
    int one;                        //Line 8
    double t;                       //Line 9
    double three;                   //Line 10

        .
        .
        .

}

void expNspace::printResult() //definition of the function
                              //printResult
{
        .
        .
        .

}
```

In this C++ program,

- To refer to the variable t in Line 2 in **main**, use the scope resolution operator (that is, refer to t as **::t**) because the function **main** has a variable named t (declared in Line 5).

- To refer to the member t (declared in Line 5) of the **namespace expNspace** in main, use the prefix **expNspace::** with t (that is, refer to t as **expNspace::t**) because there is a global variable named t (declared in Line 2) and a variable named t in **main**.

- To refer to the member u (declared in Line 6) of the **namespace expNspace** in main, use the prefix **expNspace::** with u (that is, refer to u as **expNspace::u**) because there is a global variable named u (declared in Line 3).

- You can reference the member `x` (declared in Line 4) of the `namespace exp` in `main` as either `x` or `expNspace::x` because there is no global identifier named `x` and the function `main` does not contain any identifier named `x`.

- The definition of a function that is a member of a `namespace`, such as `printResult`, is usually written outside the `namespace` as in the preceding program. To write the definition of the function `printResult`, the name of the function in the function heading can be either `printResult` or `expNspace::printResult` (because no other global identifier is named `printResult`).

 The identifiers in the system-provided header files such as `iostream`, `cmath`, and `iomanip` are defined in the `namespace std`. For this reason, to simplify the accessing of the identifiers from these header files, we have been using the following statement in the programs that we write:

```
using namespace std;
```

FUNCTIONS AND PARAMETERS

Functions in Java are called methods. C++ has two types of functions—value-returning and `void`.

Value-Returning Functions

The syntax of a value-returning function is:

```
functionType functionName(formal parameter list)
{
      statements
}
```

In this syntax template, `functionType` is the type of value that the function returns. This type is also called the data type of the value-returning function. Moreover, the statements enclosed between the curly braces form the body of the function.

Syntax: Formal Parameter List

The general syntax of the formal parameter list is:

```
dataType identifier, dataType identifier,...
```

Syntax: Function Call

The syntax to call a value-returning function is:

```
functionName(actual parameter list)
```

Syntax: Actual Parameter List

The syntax of the actual parameter list is:

```
expression or variable, expression or variable, ...
```

Thus, to call a value-returning function, you use its name, with the actual parameters (if any) in parentheses.

A function's formal parameter list can be empty. However, if the formal parameter list is empty, the parentheses are still needed.

A value-returning function returns its value via the `return` statement.

`void` Functions

The definition of a `void` function has the following syntax:

```
void functionName(formal parameter list)
{
     statements
}
```

Syntax: Formal Parameter List

The formal parameter list may be empty. If the formal parameter is nonempty, then the formal parameter list has the following syntax:

```
dataType& variable, dataType& variable, ....
```

You must specify both the data type and the variable name in the formal parameter list. The symbol `&` after `dataType` has a special meaning; it is used only for certain formal parameters and is discussed later in this appendix.

Syntax: Function Call

The function call has the following syntax:

```
functionName(actual parameter list);
```

Syntax: Actual Parameter List

The actual parameter list has the following syntax:

```
expression or variable, expression or variable, ...
```

As with value-returning functions, in a function call the number of actual parameters, together with their data types, matches the formal parameters in the order given. Actual and formal parameters have a one-to-one correspondence. A function call causes the body of the called function to execute. (Functions with default parameters are discussed later in this appendix.)

Example G-7

```
void funexp(int a, double b, char c, int& x)
{
    ...
}
```

The function funexp has four parameters.

In general, there are two types of formal parameters: **value parameters** and **reference parameters**.

Value parameter: A formal parameter that receives a copy of the content of the corresponding actual parameter.

Reference parameter: A formal parameter that receives the location (memory address) of the corresponding actual parameter.

When you attach & after the dataType in the formal parameter list of a function, the variable following that dataType becomes a reference parameter.

Example G-8

```
void expfun(int one, int& two, char three, double& four);
```

The function expfun has four parameters:

- one, a value parameter of the type int
- two, a reference parameter of the type int
- three, a value parameter of the type char
- four, a reference parameter of the type double

From the definition of value parameters, it follows that if a formal parameter is a value parameter, the value of the corresponding actual parameter is copied into the formal parameter. That is, the value parameter has its own copy of the data. Therefore, during program execution, the value parameter manipulates the data stored in its own memory space. After copying the data, the value parameter has no connection with the actual parameter.

On the other hand, if a formal parameter is a reference parameter, it receives the address of the corresponding actual parameter. That is, a reference parameter stores the address of the corresponding actual parameter. During program execution to manipulate the data, the address stored in the reference parameter directs it to the memory space of the corresponding actual parameter. In other words, during program execution, the reference parameter manipulates the data stored in the memory space of the corresponding actual parameter. Any changes that a reference parameter makes to its data immediately changes the value of the corresponding actual parameter.

A constant value cannot be passed to a reference parameter.

 In Java, parameters are passed by value only; that is, the formal parameter receives a copy of the actual parameter's data. Therefore, if a formal parameter is a variable of a primitive data type, it cannot pass its value outside the function. On the other hand, suppose that a formal parameter is a reference variable. Then both the formal and actual parameters point to the same object. Because the formal parameter contains the address of the object storing the data, the formal parameter *can* change the value of the actual object. Therefore, in Java, if a formal parameter is a reference variable, it works like a reference parameter in C++.

Reference Parameters and Value-Returning Functions

While describing the syntax of the formal parameter list of a value-returning function, we used only value parameters. You can also use reference parameters in a value-returning function, although this approach is not recommended. By definition, a value-returning function returns a single value; this value is returned via the **return** statement. If a function needs to return more than one value, you should change it to a **void** function and use the appropriate reference parameters to return the values.

Functions with Default Parameters

When a function is called, the number of actual and formal parameters must be the same. C++ relaxes this condition for functions with default parameters. You specify the value of a default parameter when the function name appears for the first time, such as in the prototype. In general, the following rules apply for functions with default parameters:

- If you do not specify the value of a default parameter, the default value is used for that parameter.

- All of the default parameters must be the rightmost parameters of the function.

- Suppose a function has more than one default parameter. In a function call, if a value to a default parameter is not specified, then you must omit all of the arguments to its right.

- Default values can be constants, global variables, or function calls.

- The caller has the option of specifying a value other than the default for any default parameter.

- You cannot assign a constant value as a default value to a reference parameter.

Consider the following function prototype:

```
void funcExp(int x, int y, double t, char z = 'A', int u = 67,
             char v = 'G', double w = 78.34);
```

The function `funcExp` has seven parameters. The parameters `z`, `u`, `v`, and `w` are the default parameters. If no values are specified for `z`, `u`, `v`, and `w` in a call to the function `funcExp`, their default values are used.

Suppose you have the following statements:

```
int a, b;
char ch;
double d;
```

The following function calls are legal:

1. `funcExp(a, b, d);`

2. `funcExp(a, 15, 34.6, 'B', 87, ch);`

3. `funcExp(b, a, 14.56, 'D');`

In statement 1, the default values of `z`, `u`, `v`, and `w` are used. In statement 2, the default value of `z` is replaced by `'B'`, the default value of `u` is replaced by `87`, the default value of `v` is replaced by the value of `ch`, and the default value of `w` is used. In statement 3, the default value of `z` is replaced by `'D'`, and the default values of `u`, `v`, and `w` are used.

The following function calls are illegal:

1. `funcExp(a, 15, 34.6, 46.7);`

2. `funcExp(b, 25, 48.76, 'D', 4567, 78.34);`

In statement 1, because the value of `z` is omitted, all the other default values must also be omitted. In statement 2, because the value of `v` is omitted, the value of `w` should be omitted, too.

The following are illegal function prototypes with default parameters:

1. `void funcOne(int x, double z = 23.45, char ch, int u = 45);`

2. `int funcTwo(int length = 1, int width, int height = 1);`

3. `void funcThree(int x, int& y = 16, double z = 34);`

In statement 1, because the second parameter `z` is a default parameter, all the other parameters after `z` must also be default parameters. In statement 2, because the first parameter is a default parameter, all the parameters must be the default values. In statement 3, a constant value cannot be assigned to `y` because `y` is a reference parameter.

ARRAYS

Like Java, in C++, an **array** is a collection of a fixed number of components wherein all of the components are of the same data type. However, in C++ arrays are not objects and so they need not be instantiated. Next, we describe how one-dimensional arrays work in C++.

A **one-dimensional array** is an array in which the components are arranged in a list form. The general form of declaring a one-dimensional array is:

```
dataType arrayName[intExp];
```

where `intExp` is any expression that evaluates to a positive integer. Also, `intExp` specifies the number of components in the array.

Example G-9

The statement:

```
int num[5];
```

declares an array `num` of 5 components. Each component is of the type `int`. The components are `num[0]`, `num[1]`, `num[2]`, `num[3]`, and `num[4]`.

Accessing Array Components

In C++, array components are accessed just like in Java. The general form (syntax) used for accessing an array component is:

```
arrayName[indexExp]
```

where `indexExp`, called the **index**, is any expression whose value is a non-negative integer. The index value specifies the position of the component in the array. In C++, the array index starts at 0. Consider the following statement:

```
int list[10];
```

This statement declares an array `list` of 10 components. The components are `list[0]`, `list[1]`, ..., `list[9]`. The assignment statement:

```
list[5] = 34;
```

stores 34 in `list[5]`, which is the sixth component of the array `list`. Suppose `i` is an `int` variable. Then the assignment statement:

```
list[3] = 63;
```

is equivalent to the assignment statements:

```
i = 3;
list[i] = 63;
```

If i is 4, then the assignment statement:

```
list[2 * i - 3] = 58;
```

stores 58 in list[5], because 2 * i - 3 evaluates to 5. The index expression is evaluated first, giving the position of the component in the array.

Next, consider the following statements:

```
list[3] = 10;
list[6] = 35;
list[5] = list[3] + list[6];
```

The first statement stores 10 in list[3], the second statement stores 35 in list[6], and the third statement adds the contents of list[3] and list[6] and stores the result in list[5].

Array Index Out of Bounds

Unfortunately, in C++, there is no guard against out-of-bounds indices. Thus, C++ does not check whether the index value is within range—that is, between 0 and arraySize - 1. If the index goes out of bounds and the program tries to access the component specified by the index, then whatever memory location is indicated by the index is accessed. This situation can result in altering or accessing the data of a memory location that you never intended. Consequently, if during execution the index goes out of bounds, several strange things can happen. It is solely the programmer's responsibility to make sure that the index is within bounds.

Arrays as Parameters to Functions

In C++, arrays are passed by reference only. Because arrays are passed by reference only, you do not use the symbol & when declaring an array as a formal parameter. When declaring a one-dimensional array as a formal parameter, the size of the array is usually omitted. If you specify the size of the one-dimensional array when it is declared as a formal parameter, it is ignored by the compiler. In Java, associated with each array is the variable length, which specifies the size of the array. However, no such variable is associated with C++ arrays. To pass the size of the array to a function, we use another parameter as in the following function:

```
void initialize(int list[], int size)
{
    int count;
    for(count = 0; count < size; count++)
        list[count] = 0;
}
```

The first parameter of the function initialize is an int array of any size. When the function initialize is called, the size of the actual array is passed as the second parameter of the function initialize.

When a formal parameter is a reference parameter, then whenever the formal parameter changes, the actual parameter changes as well. However, even though an array is always passed by reference, you can still prevent the function from changing the actual parameter. You do so by using the reserved word **const** in the declaration of the formal parameter. Consider the following function:

```
void example(int x[], const int y[], int sizeX, int sizeY)
{
     ...
}
```

Here the function **example** can modify the array **x**, but not the array **y**. Any attempt to change **y** results in a compile-time error. It is a good programming practice to declare an array to be a constant as a formal parameter if you do not want the function to modify the array.

APPENDIX

H

REFERENCES

1. G. Booch, *Objected-Oriented Analysis and Design*, Second Edition, Addison-Wesley, Reading, MA, 1995.

2. E. Horowitz, S. Sahni, and S. Rajasekaran, *Computer Algorithms C++*, Computer Science Press, New York, NY, 1997.

3. R. Johnsonbaugh, *Discrete Mathematics*, Fifth Edition, Prentice-Hall, Upper Saddle River, NJ, 2001.

4. N. M. Josuttis, *The C++ Standard Library: A Tutorial and Reference*, Addison-Wesley, Reading, MA, 1999.

5. D. E. Knuth, *The Art of Computer Programming*, Vols. 1-3, Addison-Wesley, Reading, MA, 1973, 1969, 1973.

6. S. B. Lippman and J. Lajoie, *C++ Primer*, Third Edition, Addison-Wesley, Reading, MA, 1998.

7. D. S. Malik, *C++ Programming: From Problem Analysis to Program Design*, Course Technology, Boston, MA, 2002.

8. E. M. Reingold and W. J. Hensen, *Data Structures in Pascal*, Little Brown and Company, Boston, MA, 1986.

9. R. Sedgewick, *Algorithms in C*, Third Edition, Addison-Wesley, Reading, MA, Parts 1–4, 1998; Part 5, 2002.

APPENDIX

I

ANSWERS TO SELECTED EXERCISES

Chapter 1

1. a. true; b. false; c. false; d. false; e. false; f. true; g. false; h. false

2.

Precondition: The value of **x** must be nonnegative.

Postcondition: If the value of **x** is nonnegative, the function returns the positive square root of **x**; otherwise, the program terminates.

4. 12

5. a. 43

b. $4n + 3$

c. $O(n)$

7. `#define NDEBUG`

12. a. 6

b. 2

c. 2

13.

a. (i) Constructor in Line 1.

(ii) Constructor in Line 3.

(iii) Constructor in Line 4.

b.
```
CC::CC()
{
    u = 0;
    v = 0;
}
```

c.
```
CC::CC(int x)
{
    u = x;
    v = 0;
}
```

Chapter 2

1. a. true; b. true; c. true; d. false; e. false; f. true; g. true; h. false; i. false; j. true; k. false; l. true; m. false; n. false

4. The `private` members of a class are `private`; they cannot be directly accessed by the member functions of the derived class. The `protected` members of the base class can be directly accessed by the member function of the derived class.

5. a. The statement:

   ```
   class bClass public aClass
   ```

   should be:

   ```
   class bClass: public aClass
   ```

   b. Missing semicolon after `}`.

7.

   a.

   ```
   yClass::yClass()
   {
       a = 0;
       b = 0;
   }
   ```

   b.

   ```
   xClass::xClass()
   {
       z = 0;
   }
   ```

   c.

   ```
   void yClass::two(int u, int v)
   {
       a = u;
       b = v;
   }
   ```

11.

   ```
   In base: x = 7
   In derived: x = 3, y = 8, x + y = 11
   **** 7
   #### 11
   ```

13. Because the left operand of `<<` is a stream object, which is not of the type `mystery`.

14. One.

16.

    a. `friend strange operator+(const strange&, const strange&);`

    b. `friend bool operator==(const strange&, const strange&);`

    c. `friend strange operator++(strange&, int);`

18. In Line 2, the word `friend` before the word `bool` is missing. The correct statement is:

```
friend bool operator<= (mystery, mystery);  //Line 2
```

20. None.

23. Two.

24. Error in Line 4. A template instantiation can be only for either a built-in type or a user-defined type. The word `type` between the angular brackets must be replaced with either a built-in type or a user-defined type.

26. (a) `12`   (b) `Sunny Day`

27. (a) `21`   (b) `OneHow`

28.

```
template<class Type>
void swap(Type &x, Type &y)
{
    Type temp;
    temp = x;
    x = y;
    y = temp;
}
```

Chapter 3

1. a. false; b. false; c. false; d. true; e. true; f. true; g. false; h. false

2. a. valid

    b. valid

    c. invalid; `p` is a pointer variable and `x` is an `int` variable. The value of `x` cannot be assigned to `p`.

    d. valid

    e. valid

    f. invalid; `*p` is an `int` variable and `q` is a pointer variable. The value of `q` cannot be assigned to `*p`.

5. b and c

7. 78 78

8. The statement in Line 5 copies the value of p into q. After this statement executes, both p and q point to the same memory location. The statement in Line 7 deallocates the memory space pointed to by q, which in turn invalidates both p and q. Therefore, the values printed by the statement in Line 8 are unpredictable.

9. 4 4 5 7 10 14 19 25 32 40

12. The statement in Line 7 copies the value of p into q. After this statement executes, both p and q point to the same array. The statement in Line 8 deallocates the memory space, which is an array, pointed to by p, which in turns invalidates q. Therefore, the values printed by the statement in Line 10 are unpredictable.

13.

```
Array p: 5 7 11 17 25
Array q: 25 17 11 7 5
```

16. Classes with pointer data members should include the destructor, overload the assignment operator, and explicitly provide the copy constructor by including it in the class definition and providing its definition.

18.

  a. The statement creates the **arrayListType** object **intList** of size 100. The elements of **intList** are of the type **int**.

  b. The statement creates the **arrayListType** object **stringList** of size 1000. The elements of **stringList** are of the type **string**.

  c. The statement creates the **arrayListType** object **salesList** of size 100. The elements of **salesList** are of the type **double**.

Chapter 4

3. vector<double> doubleList(50);

5. ostream_iterator<int> screen(cout, " ");

6. It produces the following output:

  5 7 9 11 13

7. 0 2 4 6 8

9. 3 7 9

11. 50 75 100 200 95

15. 70 76 34 0 23 5 35 210

Chapter 5

1. a. false; b. false; c. false; d. false; e. true; f. true

3. a. true; b. true; c. false; d. false; e. true

4. a. valid

   b. valid

   c. valid

   d. invalid (B is a pointer, whereas *list is a struct)

   e. valid

   f. invalid (B is pointer, whereas A->link->info is an int);

   g. valid

   h. valid

   i. valid

6. This is an infinite loop, continuously printing 18.

7. a. This is an invalid code. The statement s->info = B; is invalid because B is a pointer and s->info is an int.

   b. This is an invalid code. After the statement s = s->link; executes, s is NULL and so s->info does not exist.

9. 30 42 20 28

10.

   Item to be deleted is not in the list.
   18 38 2 15 45 25

12. intList = {3, 23, 43, 56, 11, 23, 25}

14.

   34 0 45 23 35 50
   46 76 34 0 38 45 23 138

Chapter 6

1. a. true; b. true; c. false; d. false; e. false

4. A function is called directly recursive if it calls itself.

5. A function that calls another function and eventually results in the original function call is said to be indirectly recursive.

6. A recursive function in which the last statement executed is the recursive call is called a tail recursive function.

9. a. It does not produce any output.

b. It does not produce any output.

c. 5 6 7 8 9

d. It does not produce any output.

10. a. 15

b. 6

12. Suppose that `low` specifies the starting index and `high` specifies the ending index in the array. The elements of the array between `low` and `high` are to be reversed.

```
if(low < high)
{
        a. swap(list[low], list[high])
        b. reverse elements between low + 1 and high - 1)
}
```

14. b. C(5,3) = 10; C(9,4) = 126.

Chapter 7

1. x = 3
   y = 9
   7
   13
   4
   7

2. x = 45
   x = 23
   x = 5
   Stack Elements: 10 34 14 5

3. a. 26

b. 45

c. 8

d. 29

4. a. AB+CD++*E-

b. ABC+D*-EF/+

c. AB+CD-/E+F*G-

d. ABCD+*+EF/G*-H+

6. `Winter Spring Summer Fall Cold Warm Hot`

7. `10 20 30 40 50`

Chapter 8

1. a. `queueFront = 50; queueRear = 0.`

   b. `queueFront = 51; queueRear = 99.`

3. a. `queueFront = 25; queueRear = 76.`

   b. `queueFront = 26; queueRear = 75.`

5. `51`

7. `Queue Elements: 5 9 16 4 2`

9. `5 16 5`

10. The function **mystery** reverses the elements of the queue and also doubles the values of the queue elements.

13.

```
template<class Type>
void reverseQueue(queueType<Type> &q, stackType<Type> &s)
{
    Type elem;

    while(!q.isEmptyQueue())
    {
        elem = q.front();
        q.deleteQueue();
        s.push(elem);
    }

    while(!s.isEmptyStack())
    {
        elem = s.top();
        s.pop();
        q.addQueue(elem);
    }
}
```

Chapter 9

1. a. false; b. true; c. false; d. false

2. a. 8; b. 6; c. 1; d. 8

3.

b.

Iteration	first	last	mid	list[mid]	Number of comparisons
1	0	10	5	55	2
2	0	4	2	17	2
3	3	4	3	45	2
4	4	4	4	49	1 (found is true)

The item is found at location 4 and the total number of comparisons is 7.

d.

Iteration	first	last	mid	list[mid]	Number of comparisons
1	0	10	5	55	2
2	6	10	8	92	2
3	9	10	9	98	2
4	10	10	10	110	2
5	11	10	the loop stops		

This is an unsuccessful search. The total number of comparisons is 8.

4.

```
template<class elemType>
class orderedArrayListType: public arrayListType<elemType>
{
public:
    int binarySearch(const elemType& item);
    orderedArrayListType(int n = 100);
};
```

5. There are 30 buckets in the hash table and each bucket can hold 5 items.

10. a. The item with index 15 is inserted at HT[15]; the item with index 101 is inserted at HT[0]; the item with index 116 is inserted at HT[16]; the item with index 0 is inserted at HT[1]; and the item with index 217 is inserted at HT[17].

11. 101

16. The load factor $\alpha = 850 / 1001 \approx .85$.

17. The load factor $\alpha = 500 / 1001 \approx .5$.

   a. $(1/2)\{1 + (1/(1 \ \alpha))\} \approx 1.5$.

   c. $(1 + \alpha /2) = 1.25$.

Chapter 10

1. 3

3. 10, 12, 18, 21, 25, 28, 30, 71, 32, 58, 15

6. a. 36, 38, 32, 16, 40, 28, 48, 80, 64, 95, 54, 100, 58, 65, 55

9. During the first pass, 6 key comparisons are made. After two passes of the heap sort algorithm, the list is:

   85, 72, 82, 47, 65, 50, 76, 30, 20, 60, 28, 25, 45, 17, 35, 14, 94, 100

10.

```
template<class elemType>
class orderedArrayListType: public arrayListType<elemType>
{
public:
    int binarySearch(const elemType& item);
    void insertOrd(const elemType&);

    void selectionSort();
    void insertionSort();
    void quickSort();

    orderedArrayListType(int size = 100);

private:
    void recQuickSort(int first, int last);
    int partition(int first, int last);
    void swap(int first, int second);
    int minLocation(int first, int last);
};
```

Chapter 11

1. a. false; b. true; c. false; d. false

3. L_A = {B, C, D, E}

4. R_A = {F, G}

5. R_B = {E}

6. D C B E A F G

7. A B C D E F G

8. D C E B G F A

9. 80−55−58−70−79

12.

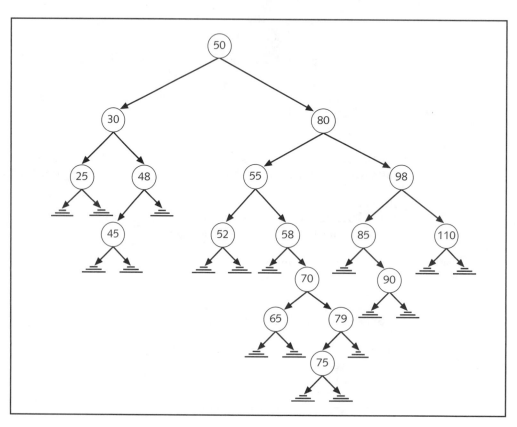

Figure I-1

15.

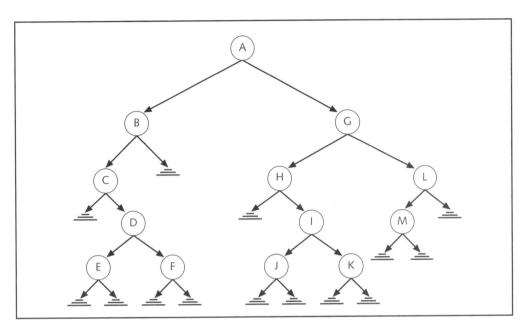

Figure I-2

17. The balance factor of the root node is 0.

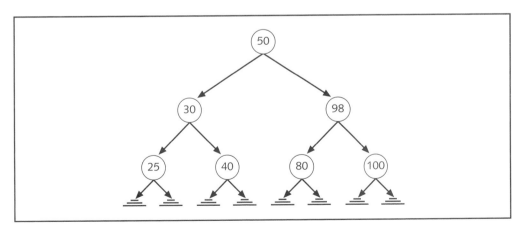

Figure I-3

18. The balance factor of the root node is −1.

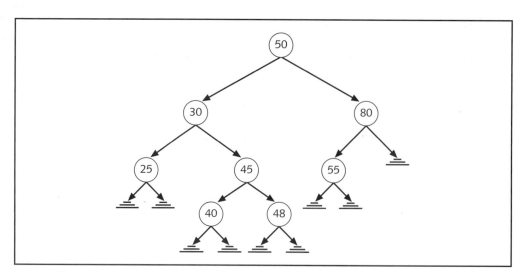

Figure I-4

Chapter 12

2.

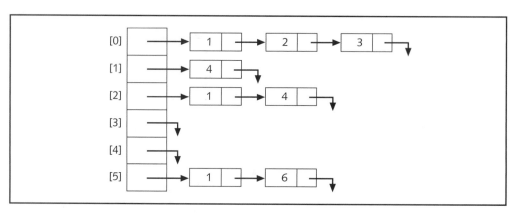

Figure I-5

3. 0 1 4 2 3 5

4. 0 1 2 3 4 5

6.

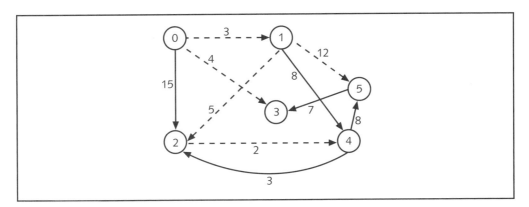

Figure I-6

```
Source Vertex: 0
Shortest Distance from Source to each Vertex
Vertex   Shortest_Distance
  0              0
  1              3
  2              8
  3              4
  4             10
  5             15
```

7.

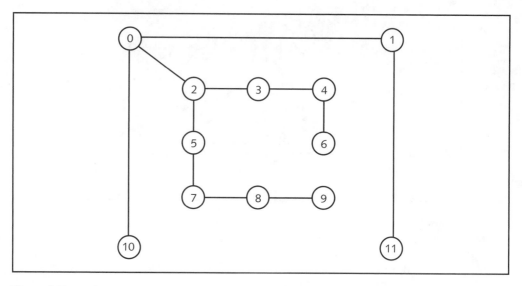

Figure I-7

10. 1, 7, 0, 2, 6, 5, 4, 8, 3, 9

Chapter 13

2. b. cout<<temp.first<<" "<<temp.second<<endl;

3. Duckey Donald

5. a. map<string, string> stateDataMap;

   c. map<string, string>::iterator mapItr;
      cout<<left;
      cout<<"The elements of stateDataMap:"<<endl;
      for(mapItr = stateDataMap.begin();
                  mapItr != stateDataMap.end(); mapItr++)
         cout<<setw(15)<<mapItr->first
             <<setw(15)<<mapItr->second<<endl;
      cout<<endl;

8. A B A K

11. 0

Index